Mozart's Symphonies

Mozart's Symphonies

Context, Performance Practice, Reception

NEAL ZASLAW

CLARENDON PRESS · OXFORD

Oxford University Press, Walton Street, Oxford OX2 6DP

Oxford New York

Athens Auckland Bangkok Bombay
Calcutta Cape Town Dar es Salaam Delhi
Florence Hong Kong Istanbul Karachi
Kuala Lumpur Madras Madrid Melbourne
Mexico City Nairobi Paris Singapore
Taipei Tokyo Toronto

and associated companies in
Berlin Ibadan

Oxford is a trade mark of Oxford University Press

Published in the United States by
Oxford University Press Inc., New York

British Library Cataloguing in Publication Data
Data available

Library of Congress Cataloging in Publication Data
Zaslaw, Neal Alexander, 1939– .
Mozart's Symphonies: context
performance practice, reception/Neal Zaslaw.
Bibliography: Includes index.
1. Mozart, Wolfgang Amadeus, 1756–1791. Symphonies.
Symphony. I. Title.
ML410.M9Z28 1989 785.1'1'0924—dc19
ISBN 0–19–816286–3

3 5 7 9 10 8 6 4 2

Printed in Hong Kong

In Memory Of My Father
Alexander M. Zaslaw (1903–1978)

PREFACE

Mozart's operas and piano concertos have provided the inspiration for many books, but his symphonies have not received comparable attention. For many years the only book about the symphonies in English was a translation of Georges de Saint-Foix's *Les Symphonies de Mozart* (1932), which has been reprinted several times.[1] That such a book, which even for its own time was more fantastic than scholarly and which is now hopelessly outdated in its facts and attitudes, should have been the sole one about Mozart's symphonies in English verges on the scandalous. To be sure, worthwhile English-language studies exist of single symphonies and of small groups of symphonies (mainly the famous last few), but no book has offered the entire panorama of Mozart's very considerable work as a symphonist.

Despite the existence of a virtual industry in Austria and the two Germanies turning out periodicals, articles, pamphlets, books, and scores devoted to Mozart, no book in German has yet dealt with the entire corpus of Mozart's symphonies. For those who read Italian, Della Croce's little book, *Le 75 sinfonie di Mozart*,[2] provided a useful set of programme notes. And more recently two English books with similar information have appeared: Dearling's uneven monograph and Sadie's valuable BBC guide.[3]

The standard life-and-works volumes do of course mention the symphonies, especially the famous last six, but the other fifty-five-odd are mostly given short shrift. Perhaps the best of the chapters devoted to Mozart's symphonies remain those in Einstein's *Mozart: His Character, His Work*[4] (even though in the three and a half decades since Einstein's study was published much new information has emerged and attitudes to eighteenth-century music have undergone a sea-change) and the surveys of Robbins Landon and Larsen.[5]

The present book is on a larger scale than those just mentioned. It attempts to account for every symphony that has ever been associated with the name Wolfgang Amadeus Mozart, that is, to identify each symphony, state what is

---

[1] Saint-Foix. See list of abbreviations.

[2] L. Della Croce, *Le 75 sinfonie di Mozart: Guida e analisi critica* (Turin, 1977). Hereafter cited as *Le 75 sinfonie*.

[3] R. Dearling, *The Music of Wolfgang Amadeus Mozart: The Symphonies* (London, 1982); S. Sadie, *Mozart: Symphonies* (BBC Music Guides) (London, 1986). Hereafter cited as *Symphonies*.

[4] Einstein. See list of abbreviations.

[5] H. C. Robbins Landon, 'Die Symphonien: Ihr geistiger und musikalischer Ursprung und ihre Entwicklung', in P. Schaller and H. Kühner (eds.), *Mozart-Aspekte* (Olten, 1956), 39–62; J. P. Larsen, 'The Symphonies', in H. C. Robbins Landon and D. Mitchell (eds.), *The Mozart Companion: A Symposium by Leading Mozart Scholars* (London, 1956), 156–99.

known about it, and, where there is reason for doubt, examine possible arguments for and against Mozart's authorship. This involves nearly one hundred symphonies. Sometimes the effort of identification and evaluation requires only a few words, and other times many paragraphs or even, exceptionally, most of a chapter.

The fundamental thesis of this book is that Mozart's symphonies, far from being 'art for art's sake', were *Gebrauchsmusik*—music for use, functional music—which, when divorced from its original setting, loses some of its meaning. The book tries, therefore, to place each symphony, in so far as possible, in a musical and cultural context. Limning in a context for Mozart's symphonies requires attempts to answer such questions as how and why the symphonies were written, how they were disseminated, who paid for them, who played them, who listened to them, and what those involved with these activities thought of them. Along the way there is a sustained attempt to discover what role the symphony played in Mozart's creative life and what he in turn may have contributed to the genre as it evolved during his lifetime. This involves the reinterpretation of a number of documents that have been available all along (at least to specialists) but have perhaps been only partially understood or, at least, not understood in this context. Some documents new to the study of Mozart's symphonies are also presented.

The mention of specialists leads to another of the book's goals: to gather, sift, organize, and evaluate a great deal of information about Mozart's symphonies and their context that has, until now, been widely scattered in technical publications, many of them available only in larger libraries and many of them only in German. My debt to those who have toiled in these vineyards before me should be abundantly clear in the footnotes and bibliography.

It is also a goal of the present study to reveal what is known about how Mozart's symphonies and those of his contemporaries were performed. This is, of course, a fashionable subject today, as attempts to play eighteenth-century music in ways approximating how it may have been performed in its own time proliferate in concert-halls and recording studios. I have devoted a chapter to this subject, but in the other chapters too I have endeavoured, whenever possible, to present information that might clarify the nature of the performances documented.

Having discussed this book's goals, I should perhaps state what it does not attempt. Even though incipits and a brief description of each work are included in this book, it is not primarily a book of programme notes. The incipits and descriptions are intended to serve a function similar to that served by the black-and-white reproductions of works of art in art-history books, which, however small and indistinct they may be, convey the works' identities and serve to remind anyone familiar with them of some of their fundamental qualities. The comparable action in a music-history book would be the inclusion of miniature scores, which is obviously not a practical idea. These incipits and brief characterizations, serving as the musical analogues to the art historian's plates, are more important for the obscure works than for the well-known ones, scores, recordings, programme notes, and analyses of which are readily accessible.

This book also does not pretend to be a book of musical analysis, even though from time to time in the descriptions of symphonies or in the use of stylistic features for dating or authentication, analytic ideas do appear. The thoroughgoing analysis of a single symphony can, by itself, fill an entire book, and has in fact more than once done so.[6] Such an approach, multiplied by ninety or so, would be incompatible with the goals of the present publication. So, although any published analysis that improves the understanding, hearing, or performance of music is a laudable venture, this book remains a study in music history.

This is also not a biography of Mozart in the usually understood sense of that term. That is, there is no attempt to cover all of the events of his life, or even all of the most important events. Rather, only those aspects of his life are reported which seem to shed some light on his and other composers' symphonies, or which provide connective tissue necessary to the narrative. That said, it must be added that the structure of the book is more or less chronological, with a variety of small and large excursuses to explore matters germane to the understanding of eighteenth-century symphonies in general and Mozart's in particular. And Mozart's future biographers will find much that is new here in the way of fact and interpretation.

As the reader will quickly discover, Mozart the symphonist does not appear alone on the stage of history. His role is not that of a monologuist, for his remarkable father had an extraordinary influence on the shape of his life and works, and to chronicle the story of the son is automatically to deal with that of the father and with the dialogue between them. That being the case, I have in many passages chosen to refer to them by their first names alone, in order to avoid confusion and clumsy circumlocutions (although in quoting from the writings of others, I have not altered things to conform to this usage). One might have thought that once Wolfgang at the age of twenty-four had made his break with Salzburg, his father would recede into the background in the telling of his story, but that is not the case. And one should have all the more reason to think that after Leopold's death in 1787, his part in the story of Wolfgang's symphonies would definitively end, but he reappears in the last chapter none the less.

Finally, the subtitle of this study, 'Context, Performance Practice, Reception', is meant to indicate that my book is in part a response to Hans Robert Jauss's call for 'a history of art ... based on the historical functions of production, communica-

---

[6] See ch. 11, nn. 153, 167, 175.

tion, and reception'.[7] As my subtitle suggests, I have reorganized Jauss's three categories to fit the historical and artistic materials relevant to music in general and to Mozart's symphonies in particular.

[7] H. R. Jauss, *Toward an Aesthetic of Reception* (Theory and History of Literature, ii) (Minneapolis, 1982), 62. See also R. C. Holub, *Reception Theory: A Critical Introduction* (London, 1984).

ACKNOWLEDGEMENTS

The author of a book of the length and density of this one, written over a period of a decade, inevitably incurs numerous debts. Many of these are acknowledged in footnotes in the course of the work, but others require special mention here. If I have failed to name anyone who helped me, I hope that he or she will believe that the explanation is *lapsus memoriae* rather than lack of gratitude.

From start to finish the editorial and production staff at Oxford University Press has given me gentle encouragement and sound technical advice. My colleagues at Cornell University never failed to urge me on when I lost courage; in particular, I owe much to stimulating discussions over the years with Malcolm Bilson and James Webster. Likewise, Stanley Sadie has been ever ready to debate things Mozartean; from our exchanges I have benefited greatly.

In carrying out my research I made use of the resources of dozens of public and private libraries and archives. Wherever I went, I was received kindly and given appropriate assistance; whenever I wrote for information or photocopies, a helpful reply was not long in arriving. (Such freely offered international co-operation could not necessarily be counted on in the past.) To all the librarians and archivists who made my work possible, I give my sincerest thanks. The Cornell University music librarians, Michael A. Keller at the beginning of my research and, more recently, Lenore Coral, invariably responded vigorously to cries for help; no request was too obscure for them to pursue goodnaturedly and almost always with the desired results.

Two colleagues displayed exceptional generosity. Alan Tyson of All Souls, Oxford, and Cliff Eisen of New York University gave me invaluable data, which they themselves had not yet put into publishable form. Tyson provided information about watermarks, paper types, and dating, which in due course will appear in complete form in a two-volume publication by the Neue Mozart-Ausgabe (Bärenreiter, Kassel). Eisen provided unknown documents from the new documentary biography of Mozart, which he is preparing for publication. Each gave unstintingly of his time, advice, and information. Without their help, this book would have been much the poorer.

When a first draft of most of the book was completed, David Josephson of Brown University read through it, making suggestions on almost every page for improving both form and content. Cliff Eisen read a late draft, and pointed out a number of mistakes and inconsistencies. Such selfless acts can seldom adequately be repaid. Rose Rosengard Subotnik and M. H. Abrams read a late draft of Chapter 13 and reassured me about the use I had made of their work.

The generosity of all these friends and colleagues has made this a better book. Needless to say, however, any errors or other shortcomings that remain are mine and mine alone.

Work on this study was begun while I was involved as musicological adviser and programme-note writer for the complete recordings of Mozart's symphonies by the Academy of Ancient Music led by Jaap Schröder, concertmaster, and Christopher Hogwood, continuo.[1] I learned a great deal about the symphonies from preparing them, participating in rehearsals and recording sessions, and hearing them performed by superior musicians. I owe an inestimable debt to Schröder and Hogwood and to members of the Academy of Ancient Music, who in conversation and by their playing taught me things that I could have learned in no other way. The recordings were made, and the notes for them written, over a period of six years (1977–83), during which my ideas evolved considerably. As the final revision of this book came after the recordings were finished, the reader should assume that, where there are contradictions between the programme notes and the book, they are intentional and the version in the latter contains my newest thoughts on the subject.

Seldom can a student of performance practice have been in a more fortunate position than the one in which I found myself, with first-rate performers in the numbers that I myself had determined, using historical seating plans I had suggested, and playing appropriate instruments in a knowing way. It is as if a historian trying to study, let us say, the Battle of Waterloo were able to restage it to see what the effect of changing the commands, or of adding cavalry here or removing artillery there, would have been on the progress and outcome of the battle. Although I refer only sporadically to these recordings in the course of the book, they served as a laboratory for testing my research and represented the nearest thing I could have hoped for by way of an 'official' performance to be used alongside my text to illustrate it.

Passages in several chapters have been derived from work previously published elsewhere. These include portions of the following chapters: Introduction: [review of R. Dearling, *The Music of Wolfgang Amadeus Mozart: The Symphonies* (London, 1982)], *Music and Letters* (1983), lxiv. 273–4; ch. 4: 'Mozart, Haydn, and the *Sinfonia da chiesa*', *The Journal of Musicology* (1982), v. 95–124; ch. 5: 'Leopold Mozart's List of His Son's Works', in A. Atlas (ed.), *Music in the Classical Period: Essays in Honor of Barry S. Brook* (New York: Pendragon, 1985), 323–58; ch. 6: 'The "Lambach"

[1] London: Decca International—Éditions de L'Oiseau-Lyre, 1979–83 (D167D 3, D168D 3, D169D 3, D170D 3, D171D 4, D172D 4, D173D 3). In addition to these 23 long-playing disks, which are also available on cassettes and compact disks, there is a supplementary disk, likewise available in all three formats (CD 417 234–2).

Symphonies of Wolfgang and Leopold Mozart', in E. Strainchamps, M. R. Maniates, and C. Hatch (eds.), *Music and Civilization: Essays in Honor of Paul Henry Lang* (New York: W. W. Norton, 1984), 15–28; ch. 8: 'Signor Mozart's Symphony in A Minor, K. Anh. 220 = 16a', *Journal of Musicology* (1986), iv. 191–206 (coauthored with Cliff Eisen); ch. 9: 'Mozart's Paris Symphonies', *The Musical Times* (1978), cxix. 753–7, (1979), cxx. 197; ch. 12: 'The Compleat Orchestral Musician', *Early Music* (1979), vii. 46–57, and 'The Orchestral Musician Compleated', (1980), viii. 71–2; 'Mozart's Tempo Conventions', in H. Glahn, S. Sørensen, and P. Ryom (eds.) *International Musicological Society: Report of the Eleventh Congress, Copenhagen 1972* (Copenhagen, 1974), ii. 720–33; 'Toward the Revival of the Classical Orchestra', *Proceedings of the Royal Musical Association* (1976–7), ciii. 158–87; ch. 13: [review of Eugene K. Wolf, *The Symphonies of Johann Stamitz: A Study in the Formation of the Classic Style, With a Thematic Catalogue of the Symphonies and Orchestral Trios* (Utrecht, 1981)], *Journal of Musicology* (1982), i. 362–7; chs. 2–11: 'Mozart and the Symphonic Traditions of his Time', phono-record programme notes for 68 symphonies of Mozart; J. Schröder, concertmaster, C. Hogwood, continuo / Academy of Ancient Music, 24 disks (London: Decca International [L'Oiseau-Lyre], 1979–86). A portion of Chapter 9 is taken from Alan Tyson's 'The Two Slow Movements of Mozart's Paris Symphony K. 297', *The Musical Times* (1981), cxxii. 17–21; and from his 'Mozart's Truthfulness', *The Musical Times* (1978), cxvii. 938. These passages are used here with the permission of the editors or publishers (or, in the case of Alan Tyson, the author) of the books, articles, periodicals, or programme notes in which they originally appeared.

Finally, I should like to thank my wife, Ellen, whose love and moral support provided the *sine qua non* for the completion of this book.

Note concerning the corrected second printing: The correction of mechanical errors in the second printing was materially assisted through the kindness of three reviewers of this book who, in addition to their generous reviews, privately communicated lists of minor errors that they had noticed: Stanley Sadie, Julian Rushton, and Peter Branscombe.

CONTENTS

CONTENTS

LIST OF INCIPITS

LIST OF TABLES

LIST OF PLATES

(between pages 202 and 203)

The publishers would like to thank the following institutions for their kind permission to use the illustrations reproduced in this book. I: Museum Carolino Augusteum, Salzburg; II and III: British Library, London; IV: Municipal Archives, The Hague; V and VI: Zentralbibliothek, Zurich; VIIa and VIIb: Museo Civico di Torino; VIIIa: Spenser Collection, New York Public Library; IX and X: Civica Raccolta Stampe "A. Bertarelli" Castello Sforzesco, Milan; XI: Civici Musei di Venezia, Casa di Goldoni; XII and XIII: Historisches Museum der Stadt Wien; XIV: British Library, London; XV and XVI: Music Library, Cornell University, Ithaca, NY; XVIIa and XVIIb: Spenser Collection, New York Public Library.

LIST OF FIGURES

ABBREVIATIONS

Breitkopf & Härtel Manuscript Catalogue	'Breitkopf—Härtel's / Alter handschriftlicher Catalog von / W. A. Mozart's Original–Compositionen / Abschrift', Vienna, Gesellschaft der Musikfreunde, shelf number 4057/ 38. This is a mid-nineteenth-century copy, made for and annotated by Ludwig von Köchel, of the 'Thematisches Verzeichnis der sämtlichen Werke von W. A. Mozart', an early nineteenth-century manuscript formerly in the archives of Breitkopf & Härtel, Leipzig, but lost or destroyed during the Second World War.
Briefe	W. A. Bauer, O. E. Deutsch, and J. H. Eibl (eds.), *Mozart: Briefe und Aufzeichnungen. Gesamtausgabe*, 7 vols. (Kassel, 1962–75).
Deutsch	O. E. Deutsch, *Mozart: Die Dokumente seiner Lebens* (*Neue Mozart-Ausgabe,* x/34) (Kassel, 1961). English trans. E. Blom, P. Branscombe, and J. Noble as *Mozart: A Documentary Biography* (London, 1965; 2nd edn., 1966). Citations from Deutsch will give the original-language edition first, followed by the English-language edition in brackets, e.g. 474 ($=$ 559).
Einstein	A. Einstein, *Mozart: His Character, His Work* (London, 1946).
GA	*Wolfgang Amadeus Mozarts Werke: Kritisch durchgesehene Gesamtausgabe* (Leipzig, 1877–1910; repr. Ann Arbor, 1947); *Revisionsberichte zu W. A. Mozarts Werken: Kritisch durchgesehene Gesamtausgabe* (Leipzig, 1877–89).
K^1	L. von Köchel, *Chronologisch-thematisches Verzeichnis der Werke W. A. Mozarts* (Leipzig, 1862).
K^2	L. von Köchel, *Chronologisch-thematisches Verzeichnis der Werke W. A. Mozarts*, 2nd edn. by P. von Waldersee (Leipzig, 1905).
K^3	L. von Köchel, *Chronologisch-thematisches Verzeichnis der Werke W. A. Mozarts*, 3rd edn. by A. Einstein (Leipzig, 1937).
K^{3a}	L. von Köchel, *Chronologisch-thematisches Verzeichnis der Werke W. A. Mozarts*, repr. of 3rd edn. with supplement by A. Einstein (Ann Arbor, 1947).
K^6	L. von Köchel, *Chronologisch-thematisches Verzeichnis*

	sämtlicher Tonwerke Wolfgang Amadé Mozarts nebst Angabe der verlorengegangenen, angefangenen, von fremder Hand bearbeiteten, zweifelhaften und unterschobenen Kompositionen, 6th edn. by F. Giegling, A. Weinmann, and G. Sievers (Wiesbaden, 1964).
Letters	E. Anderson (ed.), *The Letters of Mozart and His Family, Chronologically Arranged, Translated, and Edited with an Introduction, Notes and Indices*, 3 vols. (London, 1938); 2nd edn., 2 vols. (London, 1966). Citations from *Letters* give the first edition followed by the second in brackets, e.g. ii. 798–9 (= ii. 540).
The New Grove	S. Sadie (ed.), *The New Grove Dictionary of Music and Musicians*, 20 vols. (London, 1980).
NMA	*Wolfgang Amadeus Mozart: Neue Ausgabe sämtlicher Werke* (Kassel, 1955–).
RISM	*Répertoire international des sources musicales*, Serie A/I, 11 vols. (Kassel, 1971–86).
Saint-Foix	G. de Saint-Foix, *Les Symphonies de Mozart: Étude et analyse* (Paris, 1932), trans. L. Orrey as *The Symphonies of Mozart* (London, 1947). In citations, references to the English translation are given in brackets after the original citation.
The Symphony 1720–1840	B. S. Brook (ed.), *The Symphony 1720–1840: A Comprehensive Collection of Full Scores in Sixty Volumes* (New York, 1979–86).
Wyzewa–Saint-Foix	T. de Wyzewa and G. de Saint-Foix, *Wolfgang Amédée Mozart: Sa vie musicale et son œuvre de l'enfance à la pleine maturité* (Paris, 1912–46), 5 vols.; 2nd edn. 1977, 2 vols., repr. New York, 1980). In citations, references to the second edition are given in brackets after the original citation.

Orchestra statistics given in the form 6–7—6–7—2—3—4 / 0–2—2—0—1 / 2—0—0—1 = 27 are to be read: '6 or 7 first violinists, 6 or 7 second violinists, 2 violists, 3 cellists, 4 double-bass players, 1, 2, or no flautists, 2 oboists, no clarinetists, 1 bassoonist, 2 horn players, no trumpet players, no kettledrummer, 1 keyboard continuo player, equalling a total of 27 members'. (The implication in this instance is that 2 violinists doubled on flutes.) The word 'strings' preceded by an asterisk ('*strings') indicates divided violas.

The equal sign (=) is used for two purposes: the first is to give the Köchel (or 'K.') numbers for one and the same composition as it appears in the first, third, and sixth editions of the Köchel Catalogue, when these differ. The second is to indicate in footnotes the page numbers for cited passages as they appear in the original language and in the English translation, or in the first and second editions, of frequently cited books. The indication *deest*, a form of the Latin verb *desunt*, is used in the formula 'K. *deest*' to indicate works attributed to Mozart but not listed in any edition of the Köchel Catalogue.

The system of numbering Mozart's symphonies from 1 to 41, taken from the old Breitkopf & Härtel editions, has, in general, been avoided in this book, since some of the 41 are not by Mozart, several other genuine symphonies lack numbers in this system, and the superior editions of the *NMA* do not use these obsolete numbers. They can none the less be located in three places in the book: in Appendix B, in the index, and in the list of editions given for each symphony, in which, if a work belongs to 'Serie 8' of the *GA*, then the number that follows is identical with the old numbering system. Thus, for example, the symphony shown in the *GA* as 'Serie 8, No. 41' is the Symphony No. 41, otherwise known as the Symphony in C major, K. 551 ('Jupiter').

I

Salzburg (I): Origins (1756–1764)

In the middle of the eighteenth century the symphony (in the modern sense of the word) was still a new idea, a few decades old. Large numbers of them were written and some published, yet people in many places in Europe, not being near a city, court, cathedral, or monastery, never heard any symphonies. Joseph and Michael Haydn's humble birthplace, Rohrau, was such a place, and these musical young-sters probably had not heard a symphony before going to Vienna to apprentice at Saint Stephen's Cathedral as choirboys. At the other extreme from Rohrau were places renowned for the creation and dissemination of this young art-form. Such symphonic centres—London, Paris, Mannheim, Milan—often had an outstanding orchestra, a flourishing music-publishing industry, a ruler with an intense interest in music, or music-loving patrons in the form either of courtiers and their hangers-on or of a well-to-do middle-class and aristocratic audience. Salzburg fell somewhere between the extremes represented by Rohrau and Mannheim: it was one of a number of lesser cities and minor courts where the symphonic tradition was received from elsewhere and cultivated assiduously.

In seeking to understand something of the formation of a writer of symphonies in the eighteenth century, one must keep in mind the implications of an obvious yet profound difference between our times and earlier ones. Nowadays a musical child can readily hear an extraordinary variety of music from many times and places, through electronic means of sound reproduction and rapid travel. In earlier times the knowledge and taste of a child were formed by the music heard 'live' in his immediate geographical area, much of it of local or regional provenance, written within the lifetimes of his musical mentors or, very occasionally, of their teachers. Thus, an examination of Salzburg's musical life at mid-century cannot fail to clarify the nature of Mozart's symphonic upbringing, even though he was enabled, rather exceptionally, to experience at first hand the music of most of the important centres of Europe during the tours of his youth.

Among documents that bear witness to music-making in Salzburg, one of the most important is the anonymous 'Report on the Present State of the Musical Establishment at the Court of His Serene Highness the Archbishop of Salzburg in the Year 1757', published in a Berlin music magazine.[1] Because of the significance of this 'Report' for understanding the circumstances that fostered more than half of Mozart's symphonies, a complete translation of it is presented in Appendix C. Although published anonymously, the 'Report' was apparently written by Leopold Mozart,[2] who gives himself away by immodestly making his own biography more than twice as long as (and more personal than) any of the others. The cloak of anonymity permitted him this self-indulgence, as well as the possibility of flattering his superiors and criticizing two of his violinist-colleagues. At the time of writing Leopold's prospects were bright: he was able, well placed, and could reasonably hope for promotion to Vizekapellmeister and even to Kapellmeister. His *Violinschule*—recently published—was already receiving favourable critical notice.[3] But despite Leopold's exceptional abilities, he was never to advance beyond the rank of Vizekapellmeister, probably because he virtually abandoned his own career to support his son's. This effort kept him away from Salzburg more than was politic; when the archbishop died, his successor was less sympathetic to Leopold's special situation and unaware of the considerable intellectual, diplomatic, and organizational skills that Leopold might have put at Salzburg's disposal.

The contents of Leopold's 'Report' and its publication in Berlin show him reaching out beyond his provincial surroundings in Augsburg and Salzburg, an aspect of his personality destined to have a lasting influence upon his son's development. Especially telling in this regard is what Leopold wrote about his friend, the singer Meissner (No. 35), whose notice is longer than any other, Leopold's own excepted. What captured Leopold's imagination was the manner in which Meissner had turned musical and entrepreneurial skills into fame and fortune by means of well-planned tours. Leopold, with his interest in languages, literature, music, art, peoples, and customs, would soon discover means to emulate him.

Can the father of any other great man have had a more powerful influence on his education than Leopold Mozart had on his son's? There is no record of Wolfgang's having attended any school. As far can be ascertained, Leopold taught him not only keyboard instruments, violin, harmony, counterpoint, and orchestration, but also the fundamentals of a non-musical education, including languages (Italian, Latin,

---

[1] 'Nachricht von dem gegenwärtigen Zustande der Musik Sr. Hochfürstl. Gnaden des Erzbischoffs zu Salzburg im Jahr 1757', in Friedrich Wilhelm Marpurg (ed.), *Historisch-Kritische Beyträge zur Aufnahme der Musik* (Berlin, 1757), iii. 183–98.

[2] H. Abert, *W. A. Mozart*, 2nd edn. (Leipzig, 1923–4), i. 3; W. Plath, 'Mozart, Leopold', *The New Grove*, xii. 678.

[3] Leopold Mozart, *Versuch einer gründlichen Violinschule* (Augsburg, 1756, repr. 1922; 3rd edn. 1787, repr. 1956). Hereafter cited as *Violinschule*. English trans. by E. Knocker as *A Treatise on the Fundamental Principles of Violin Playing* (Oxford, 2nd edn. 1951). Hereafter cited as *Treatise*. A favourable review from Marpurg, *Historisch-Kritische Beyträge*, (1756) iii. 160–3, is reproduced in Deutsch, 12 (= 10).

French, and English), mathematics, history, grammar, and rhetoric. The extra-ordinary tours on which Leopold took his prodigy were an extension of this education—but that story belongs to later chapters.

Salzburg's political and religious orientation is strikingly revealed by the information that Leopold's 'Report' provides about the origins of the court musicians: there were none from mainly Protestant areas—Scandinavia, England, and northern Germany—or from Catholic regions to the west—France and Iberia. Those Salzburg musicians who were not of local origin came from either central Europe or Italy. Although the musicians from Swabia, Austria, Silesia, Bavaria, Bamberg, Moravia, Bohemia, Carinthia, the Tyrol, Hungary, and the Palatinate total about fifty-six and those from Italy only four, the Italian influence was none the less great. This was because of the church connection to Rome, because there were always Italians in positions of leadership and among the principal singers, and because several of the Salzburgers went to Italy to study or on concert tours.[4]

At the beginning of Wolfgang's life the Salzburg musical establishment was large and apparently well run. Including apprentices and choirboys, Leopold's report chronicled some forty-six instrumentalists and more than fifty singers, leaving aside the organ-builder, the luthier, three organ-blowers, and five vacant positions. On first examination the string section would appear to have consisted of sixteen players (5—5—1-2—2—2), but, since all the choirboys, many woodwind players, four hymn-singers, and twelve or fourteen trumpeters and kettle-drummers also played stringed instruments, this number is deceptive. Further-more, for concerts and perhaps other occasions the court musicians were supplemented by amateur performers, including after his appointment in 1772 the Prince-Archbishop Hieronymus Count Colloredo, who played the violin,[5] Count Czernin, whose 'fiddling' is discussed in Chapter 10, and various courtiers. As some thirty-four of the court musicians (not counting the choirboys) played the violin and viola and seven the cello, the degree of flexibility pos-sible in organizing performances was considerable.

The difficulty of applying these statistics (whether to historical understanding or

[4] Leopold's *Violinschule* drew material from Giuseppe Tartini's unpublished violin treatise without acknowledgement (see P. Petrobelli, 'La scuola di Tartini in Germania e la sua influenza', *Analecta musicologica* (1968), v. 1–17); a report from the 1770s even criticized Leopold for being 'too Tartini-ish' (Ludwig Schubart (ed.), *Christ. Fried. Dan. Schubart's Ideen zu einer Ästhetik der Tonkunst* (Vienna, 1806), 158. Hereafter cited as *Ideen*.) Salzburg's connections with Tartini can also be detected in Leopold's report, for Franz Schwarzmann (No. 11) was in Padua studying with the Italian violinist, and Joseph Lolli (No. 2) is said to have studied with Tartini's pupil Martial Greiner (F. J. Lipowsky, *Baierisches Musik-Lexikon* (Munich, 1811), 187).

The number of musicians at Salzburg from outside the local area made it exceptional for German-speaking courts. See C.-H. Mahling, 'Herkunft und Sozialstatus des höfischen Orchestermusikers im 18. und frühen 19. Jahrhundert in Deutschland', in W. Salmen (ed.), *Der Sozialstatus des Berufsmusikers vom 17. bis 19. Jahrhundert* (Kassel, 1971), 103–36 and esp. 105–7 (= 'The Origin and Social Status of the Court Orchestral Musicians in the 18th and early 19th Century in Germany', *The Social Status of the Professional Musician from the Middle Ages to the 19th Century* (New York, 1983), 219–64 and esp. 224–6).

[5] Leopold Mozart's letter of 24 Sept. 1778. *Briefe*, ii. 485; *Letters*, ii. 920 (= ii. 620).

to modern performances) is further suggested by a letter of Leopold's describing the performance of a Mass by Michael Haydn in the Cathedral in 1777 at which six oboists performed, even though the Court Calendar for that year records only two.[6] Since so many musicians played two, three, or even four instruments, the number of combinations of possible orchestral make-up is too large to permit the list of personnel from Leopold's 'Report' to be of use in deciphering what the day-to-day practice may have been.[7] The annually published roster of the Salzburg orchestra for the period of Mozart's involvement (Tables 1.1, 8.1, and 10.1)[8] may suggest the balance thought proper to orchestral performance in Salzburg, even if it obscures the implications of doubling and possibilities for reinforcements. While for solemn or festive occasions a string section of thirty or forty could have been assembled, for ordinary rounds of music-making the Salzburg musicians undoubtedly adopted the practice of many court musical establishments, which was a system of rotation providing the needed players without everyone's having to play each day. Leopold's 'Report' discusses the rotation in the chapel's leadership and among the accompanists, choir regents, and trumpeters, but not among the string and wind players. For day-to-day performance of concerted music in the Cathedral, surviving sets of parts provide a clue: a complete set normally comprises three organ parts (*organo, organo ripieno, battuta*), two first and two second violin parts, and one part each for bassoon, violone, three trombones, and, occasionally, viola.[9] For concerts at court, larger orchestral forces would have been employed.

Table 1.1 covers a period when significant changes occurred in European orchestras, related to changes in musical style that music historians usually refer to as the transition from 'late baroque' to 'early classical'. The orchestration of the earlier style often involved massed oboes and bassoons (and sometimes horns), either doubling the strings or forming an independent choir that could alternate with the strings. The later style called for pairs of winds (doubled only in exceptionally large orchestras) continuing to perform their original functions, but now sometimes fulfilling a new one: sustaining chords.[10] This development—crucial to the performance of Mozart's early symphonies—may be detected in Table 1.1: the number of oboists changed from three to two (1757–8), and bassoonists from four to three (1761–2).

The conditions under which Austrian church music was performed are clarified

---

[6] Letter of 1 Nov. 1777. *Briefe*, ii. 96; *Letters*, ii. 515 (= i. 352): 'Ferlendis and Sandmayr [the regular oboists] played the oboe solos. The oboist at Lodron's, a certain student, the head wait, and Oberkirchner were the oboists in the orchestra.'

[7] C.-H. Mahling, 'Mozart und die Orchesterpraxis seiner Zeit', *Mozart-Jahrbuch* (1967), 229–43.

[8] E. Hintermaier, 'Die salzburger Hofkapelle von 1700 bis 1806: Organisation und Personal' (Ph.D. diss., University of Salzburg, 1972). The lists of musicians from the annually published Court Calendar are on pp. 540–5.

[9] R. G. Pauly, 'Preface' to Johann Ernst Eberlin, *Te Deum, Dixit Dominus, Magnificat* (Recent Researches in the Music of the Baroque Era, xii) (Madison, 1971), vi.

[10] A third type of wind orchestration is discussed in chs. 11–13.

TABLE 1.1 The Salzburg court orchestra without reinforcements, 1756–1766*

	1756	1757	1758	1759	1760	1761	1762	1763	1764	1765	1766
organ	3	3	3	3	3	2	2	2	2	2	2
concert-master		1	1	1	1	2	1	1	2	2	2
violin	20	20–2	22	20	21	20	20	20	20	19	19
viola†	—	0–2	—	—	—	—	—	—	—	—	
cello	3	3	3	3	2	2	2	2	2	2	2
double bass	2	2	2	2	2	3	3	3	3	2	2
oboe‡	3	3	2	2	2	2	2	2	2	2	2
bassoon	4	4	4	4	4	4	3	3	3	3	3
horn	3	2–3	3	3	3	2	2	2	3	3	3
trumpet	2	2	2	2	2	2	2	2	2	2	2
kettledrummer	1	1	1	1	1	1	1	1	1	1	1
TOTALS	42	43–4	43	41	41	39	38	38	40	39	39

* Tables 1.1, 8.1, and 10.1 place the single trombone player (1757 to 1770), 8 of the 10 trumpet players, and 1 of the 2 kettledrummers among the violins, as presumably they would have been for symphonies.

† The figures for 1757 suggest that when violas were needed two violinists were pressed into service. Michael Haydn, from 1763 one of the organists, played viola in the orchestra. Much Austrian dance and church music of the period is without viola parts.

‡ Double on flute.

Source: The Salzburg *Hofkalendar* as reported in E. Hintermaier, 'Die salzburger Hofkapelle von 1700 bis 1806: Organisation und Personal' (Ph.D. diss., University of Salzburg, 1972), 542–3.

by three engravings, one of a performance of concerted music in the Salzburg Cathedral in 1682, another of a High Mass at Saint Stephen's Cathedral in Vienna in the eighteenth century, and the last of the frontispiece to a polemical pamphlet calling for simplification and desecularization of church music (Plates I–III). In all three engravings one can see the theatrical ambience of Austrian church services, which can be heard in much of the surviving music. In the Salzburg engraving the four 'side-organs' in four balconies filled with musicians are visible, clarifying Leopold's point of reference in his 'Report' when he wrote of the choral singers and their organ as being 'below'.[11]

Other interesting points emerge from the 'Report'. One is Leopold's evident admiration for prolific composition, which he emphasizes in his and Eberlin's outputs. It was an attitude shared by most of his peers. While Leopold knew better than most the difference between competent and incompetent composition, he also knew that, to be useful to an employer and to be guaranteed a steady income, a composer had to write quickly, easily, and to order; for composers were not considered divinely inspired geniuses but skilled craftsmen who could—like good wig-makers, cabinet-makers, jewellers, or portrait-painters—deliver a product when it was wanted. What was admired in a composer was taste and craft, or, as Joseph Haydn put it when expressing to Leopold his admiration for Wolfgang's music: taste and knowledge.[12] In praising productivity Leopold named Scarlatti and Telemann, and one could add Handel, Bach, Vivaldi, Boismortier, Haydn, Hook, and scores of other vastly productive eighteenth-century composers. This attitude to musical productivity is part of what lies behind Leopold's exhortations to Wolfgang not to be lazy and disorganized, to compose more music.[13] It is a matter that will be reconsidered in Chapter 13, in order to see what reasons can be adduced for the fact that in the decade from 1770 to 1779 Wolfgang produced about forty symphonies, but in the decade from 1782 to 1791 only six.

Another aspect of Leopold's 'Report' is his dislike of technical virtuosity, at least when employed for its own sake or as a cover-up for various shortcomings. This attitude is expressed in his remarks about Wenzel Hebelt (No. 8), in correspondence with his son, and in various passages in the *Violinschule*, for instance this passage which, although devoted to performance, presents an aesthetic with implications for composition:

The good performance of a composition according to modern taste is not as easy as many imagine, who believe themselves to be doing well if they embellish and befrill a piece right

---

[11] Leopold's seemingly puzzling statement, that wind instruments were seldom used, is discussed in ch. 4.

[12] Letter of 16 Feb. 1785. *Briefe*, iii. 373; *Letters*, iii. 1321 (= ii. 886): 'I tell you before God, as an honest man, your son is the greatest composer I know either personally or by name; he has taste and moreover, the deepest knowledge of composition.'

[13] Especially in his letters during Wolfgang's tour of 1777–8 to Mannheim and Paris.

foolishly out of their own heads, and who have no sensitiveness whatever for the affect that is to be expressed in the piece. And who are these people? They are mostly those who, hardly at ease with time, get straightway to work on concertos and solos, in order (in their foolish opinion) to force themselves straight into the company of virtuosi. Many succeed so far that they play off with uncommon dexterity the most difficult passages in various concertos or solos which they have practised with great industry. These they know by heart. But should they have to perform only a couple of minuets melodiously according to the instructions of the composer, they are unable to do so; yea, this is to be seen even in their studied concertos. For so long as they play an allegro, all goes well: but when it comes to an adagio, there they betray their great ignorance and bad judgement in every bar of the whole piece. They play without method and without expression: the *piano* and *forte* are not differentiated; the embellishments are in the wrong place, too overloaded, and mostly played in a confused manner; and often the notes are far too bare and one observes that the player knows not what he does. For such people there is rarely any more hope of improvement, for they, more than anyone, are taken up with self-esteem, and he would be in their great disfavour who would candidly attempt to convince them of their errors.[14]

Leopold's ideas were absorbed by Wolfgang, who once wrote to his father that he had enjoyed hearing a difficult violin concerto well performed, then immediately felt constrained to add: 'You know that I am no great lover of difficulties.'[15] This is the aesthetic creed of the galant style: music, if it is to please, must exhibit a certain ease of manner and never bring sweat to the brow; it must charm by a light touch rather than astound either by bravura and pyrotechnics or by rhythmic, harmonic, and contrapuntal complexities, which are said to be 'unnatural'. Leopold wrote to Wolfgang in 1778 urging him to write in an easy style,[16] and the son reflected the father's opinions when he stated concerning a modulation representing Osmin's rage in *Die Entführung aus dem Serail* that it must not be too extreme, because, 'music, even in the most terrible situations, must never offend the ear, but must please the hearer, or in other words must never cease to be music'.[17] Joseph Haydn revealed a similar attitude when, crossing out a chromatic passage in one of his symphonies, he wrote in the margin, 'That was for much too learned ears.'[18] The emphasis on 'ease' should not be taken to mean that Leopold trained Wolfgang to be shallow, although in lesser hands the galant aesthetic often led to that result. Leopold's doctrine was not one of frivolity, for the

---

[14] Ch. xii, para. 2. *Violinschule*, 252–3 (= *Treatise*, 215–16).

[15] Letter of 22 Nov. 1777. *Briefe*, ii. 137–8; *Letters*, ii. 565 (= i. 384). Compare Leopold's letter of 29 Jan. 1778: 'Indeed I am no lover of excessively rapid passages, where you have to produce the notes with the half tone of the violin and, so to speak, only touch the fiddle with the bow and almost play in the air' (*Briefe*, ii. 244; *Letters*, ii. 672 (= i. 455)).

[16] Letter of 13 Aug. 1778. *Briefe*, ii. 444; *Letters*, ii. 888–9 (= ii. 599).

[17] Letter of 26 Sept. 1781. *Briefe*, iii. 162; *Letters*, iii. 1144 (= ii. 769). This passage and the one cited below at n. 20 are discussed in ch. 13.

[18] Symphony No. 42 of 1771. H. C. Robbins Landon, *Haydn: Chronicle and Works* (Bloomington and London, 1978), ii. 279.

full expression of varied affect was accorded the utmost attention. For instance, about the performance of a new serenata, *L'isola dishabitata*, by the Salzburg Kapellmeister Luigi Gatti, Leopold noted: 'Beautiful music—Italian—more for the ears than for the heart, because it often conforms badly with the expression of the words and the true passion.'[19] Hence surface beauty and ease of manner were necessary but not sufficient to guarantee musical success. Needless difficulties were to be avoided and necessary ones concealed beneath a polite surface. Trade secrets were to be kept from those whom they could only confuse or annoy. Wolfgang's formulation of these notions is found in the often-quoted remarks about the piano concertos, K. 413–15:

These concertos are a happy medium between what is too easy and too difficult; they are very brilliant, pleasing to the ear, and natural, without being vapid. There are passages here and there from which connoisseurs alone can derive satisfaction; but these passages are written in such a way that the less learned cannot fail to be pleased, though without knowing why.[20]

Hence the well-trained composer kept in mind both the relatively rare *Kenner* or connoisseur and the more numerous *Liebhaber* or amateur, and knew how to please both at once.

   Although a virtuoso himself, Wolfgang was never attracted to the flamboyant writing found in the instrumental music of the Locatellis and Viottis, Clementis and Dusseks, of the era. Yet ironically, his avoidance of virtuosity for its own sake makes his music harder, not easier, to perform well, for the very reasons implied by Leopold in his *Violinschule*: sheer technique and bravura cannot compensate for a lack of thoughtful, sensitive musicianship.[21] A discussion of technical difficulty is subtler in symphonies than in sonatas, concertos, or arias, for composers of symphonies generally eschewed it, not only because most orchestras of the period could not handle virtuosic writing but perhaps also because the musical idioms suited to single protagonists and crowds were understood to differ.[22] Yet if not every ripieno player was capable of performing a concerto, the good ones had another skill that, according to Leopold and other writers of the time, was just as

---

[19] Diary entry of 17 Jan. 1783. *Briefe*, iii. 251.

[20] Letter of 28 Dec. 1782. *Briefe*, iii. 245–6; *Letters*, iii. 1242 (= ii. 833). These remarks should not be taken to mean that Mozart condescended to the amateur, whom he placed with the connoisseur far above the philistine. See his letter to his wife of 8–9 Oct. 1791 about one Lechleitner who had been to see *Die Zauberflöte* for a second time: 'Though he is no connoisseur, he is at least a true amateur, which [name defaced by Nissen], however, is not—he's a real nonentity, a lover of dining.' *Briefe*, iv. 161; *Letters*, iii. 1441–2 (= ii. 970).

[21] The extraordinary difficulties in certain coloratura arias (for instance 'Popoli di Tessaglia', K. 316 = 300b, 'Martern aller Arten' from *Die Entführung* and the Queen of the Night's arias from *Die Zauberflöte*) are at present impossible to judge, since most modern singers cannot sing them and the dramatic conventions that required them are usually misunderstood by modern directors, singers, and audiences.

[22] Heinrich Christoph Koch, 'Ueber den Charakter der Solo- und Ripienstimmen', *Journal der Tonkunst* (1795), i/2. 143–56.

valuable: the ability to perform accurately orchestral-parts placed in front of them.[23] There is ample evidence (some of it reproduced in Chapter 12) that symphonies were usually performed with one rehearsal, if not read at sight. This too helps to explain why there was little increase in the difficulty of Wolfgang's symphonies during the first two-thirds of his career. Only with the 'Prague' symphony, K. 504, written after Wolfgang had broken with Salzburg's conservative musical establishment and his father's powerful restraining influence, did the level of difficulty noticeably increase and the ideas grow strikingly original.

Avoidance of mindless virtuosity was associated with strength of execution by Leopold, who praised Caspar Cristelli (No. 3) for playing the cello 'manfully' with 'a good tone that is strong and full, yet also pure and calm', and Carl Vogt (No. 7) for being 'a serious player, who knows how to produce a strong, manly tone from the violin'; whereas Wenzel Hebelt (No. 8) compounded his sin of loving technical difficulties with a tone that was 'quite weak and soft'. (To be sure, 'strong' is a relative concept that can be interpreted only in the context of the instruments for which Leopold and Wolfgang composed, played with appropriate techniques and heard in suitable acoustical surroundings.) In the *Violinschule* too Leopold repeatedly stressed the need for strong tone, clearly differentiated loud and soft, and the widest possible range of affect.[24]

Leopold's 'Report' considered oratorios to be 'chamber' music, reflecting a traditional division of music into the categories 'church', 'chamber', and 'theatre'. 'Chamber music' in this sense had nothing to do with modern notions of one instrument or voice to a part. This knowledge is necessary to understanding eighteenth-century writings that refer to 'chamber' symphonies. If it did not involve abandoning well-established terminology, 'chamber music' might properly be rendered as 'concert music'—that is, music performed in a hall or the chambers of a patron, without regard for medium, which could be orchestral or certain types of choral music as well as solo vocal or instrumental 'chamber music' (in the modern sense).

Finally, as a pendant to Leopold's insistence on the fashionable galant style, there was his admiration for those with a command of learned counterpoint—in its correct place of course, which was primarily church music. Much has been made of Wolfgang's encounter in the early 1780s with J. S. Bach's contrapuntal style,[25] but

---

[23] Johann Joachim Quantz, *Versuch einer Anweisung die Flöte traversiere zu spielen* (Berlin, 1752, 3rd edn. 1789, repr. 1953), trans. by E. R. Reilly as *On Playing the Flute* (London, 1966; 2nd edn. New York, 1985), ch. 17; Leopold Mozart, *Violinschule*, 253–4 (= *Treatise*, 216–17); Johann Friedrich Reichardt, *Ueber die Pflichten des Ripien-Violinisten* (Berlin, 1776); Koch, 'Ueber den Charakter der Solo- und Ripienstimme'. In their use of musical metaphors to describe groups of people acting together, the idioms of our language recognize the peculiar nature of the musical tutti or ripieno; such groups of people are said to act 'in unison' or 'in concert', to take 'concerted' action, and to respond 'in chorus'.

[24] Ch. 5, para. 2. *Violinschule*, 101–2 (= *Treatise*, 96–7).

[25] Einstein, 144–56: ch. 9, 'Mozart and Counterpoint'.

sufficient recognition has not always been given to the fact that Wolfgang grew up
surrounded by composers who prided themselves on their command of the *stile
antico*. He studied the church works of his father, and in order to study the church
works of Eberlin and Michael Haydn, father and son copied them out in score.[26]
Wolfgang also had instruction from two Italian contrapuntists, Padre Martini and
the Marquis de Ligniville. In his 'Report' Leopold let his readers know that he
considered his own 'numerous contrapuntal and other church pieces' to be
'especially noteworthy', and a Missa brevis by Leopold long passed as Wolfgang's
work.[27] That Wolfgang's training in counterpoint persisted throughout his
apprenticeship is suggested by surviving canonic, fugal, and other contrapuntal
exercises as well as by the fugal church music that he composed for Salzburg.
Leopold gave Wolfgang a late baroque upbringing, founded on thorough-bass
theory and Fuxian species counterpoint. Wolfgang's mature style was not the result
of his rejection of such traditional categories as church, chamber, and theatre, or
strict and modern styles; rather, it arose from his crossing the boundaries between
them to create hybrid forms and styles.

Beginning a history of symphonies by considering the state of church musicians
may appear odd, for symphonies today are seen as quintessentially secular music.
But the secular–sacred distinction has been drawn differently at various times, and
was certainly not the same in the mid-eighteenth century as it is now construed.
The revolutionary writings of the Enlightenment *philosophes* may have been read
in some sophisticated circles then, but in most of the Continent the medieval order
was still firmly in place. One tenet of that order was a deliberate blurring of the
sacred–secular boundary through the doctrine of the Divine Right of Kings. As the
Prince-Archbishops of Salzburg were both temporal and spiritual leaders, they had
even less reason than other rulers to maintain clear distinctions between the two
realms, and their musicians provided music for cathedral and court alike. Besides
being heard almost daily in concerts at court and at Mass and Vespers in the
Cathedral, the Salzburg musicians played in other venues. At Carnival time
(*Fasching*) they performed in the archiepiscopal theatre and ballroom. They were
active on a freelance basis in private music-making in the homes and gardens of
upper- and middle-class citizens, at Salzburg University, and in out-of-door
serenades in public squares. Music was wanted to celebrate name-days, weddings,
appointments to public office, elevations in rank, visits of dignitaries, festive
holidays, and the ends of school terms. From autumn 1773 when the Mozarts

---

[26] K. Anh. A 1–5 (Eberlin), A 12–15 (M. Haydn), A 71–88 (both composers). See M. H. Schmid, *Mozart und die salzburger Tradition* (Tutzing, 1976), 177–226.
[27] K. 116 = 90a. See W. Senn, 'Mozarts Kirchenmusik und die Literatur', *Mozart-Jahrbuch* (1978–9), 14–18.

moved to the building known as the Dancing-Master's House, they had a large room in which rehearsals, concerts, and balls were from time to time held.[28] They often went to the homes of friends and patrons to participate in private music-making. Symphonies were heard at most such occasions.

Thus far we have discussed only the music-making of Salzburg's educated classes. The activities of popular and folk musicians are harder to trace, having been taken little note of in writings of the period. The Mozart family's extensive correspondence almost never refers to music that they must have heard in the streets, inns, and fairs, at home and in their travels. Yet the influence of such music—whether direct or at second hand through the arrangements of literate musicians—seems unmistakable in certain of Mozart's melodies, in the rustic drones he occasionally affects, and perhaps in the good-humoured high-jinks that, in symphonies at least, are usually reserved for the trios of minuets and rondo-finales. Can such songs as Papageno's strophic 'Ein Mädchen oder Weibchen' be imagined without the influence of popular traditions? 'Popular' is itself an ambiguous term, for it can express music's origin, its destination, or its style. Folk music is a concept as nebulous as popular music, and the two overlap, their boundaries blurred by art music that has entered oral tradition and folk music that has entered popular and art music. For present purposes folk and popular music may be grouped together as music of the type that people play, sing, or hum by memory, without recourse necessarily to written music, and that (we assume) would have been recognized as such by Mozart's contemporaries. This is the tip of an iceberg, the submerged portion of which has yet to receive the study it deserves.[29]

The use of certain tunes in specific pieces has been traced, but uncertainty remains about their significance, about how many other tunes are borrowed from similar sources but remain unrecognized, and about the extent to which 'original' material in the symphonies and elsewhere may be modelled on aspects of folk or

[28] R. Angermüller, 'Der Tanzmeistersaal in Mozarts Wohnhaus, Salzburg, Marktplatz 8', *Mitteilungen der internationale Stiftung Mozarteum* (1981), xxix. 1–13.

[29] H. Simon, 'Mozart und die Bauernmusik', *Das deutsche Volkslied* (1930), xxxii. 61–2; E. F. Schmid, 'Mozart als Meister volkstümlicher Musik', *Zeitschrift für Schwabenland* (1941–2), viii. 100–20; H. Fuhrmann, 'Mozart bei den Vierländer Gemüsebauern: Eine Studie zum Thema "Volksmusik und Kunstmusik"', *Neue Zeitschrift für Musik* (1937), civ. 1016–17; F. O. Souper, 'Mozart and Folk-song', *Monthly Musical Record* (1937), lxvii. 155–7, 180; H. J. Moser, 'Mozart und die Volksmusik', *Die Volksmusik* (1941), vi. 241–3; B. Szabolesi, 'Mozart és a népdal' [Mozart and Folk-song], *Énekszó* (1941), ii. 869–70; A. Bonaccorsi, 'Il folklore nella musica d'arte. Dai segreti di Mozart', *Rassegna musicale delle Edizioni Curci* (1954), ii. 2–3; H. Erdmann, 'Mozart in norddeutscher Resonanz', in E. Schenk (ed.), *Bericht über den internationalen Musikwissenschaft Kongress, Wien, Mozartjahr 1956* (Graz, 1958), 156–69; G. Knepler, 'Mozart á Česká Lidová Hubda' [Mozart and Czech Folk Music], *Hudební rozhledy* (1956), ix. 10–15; E. F. Schmid, 'L'héritage souabe de Mozart', in A. Verchaly (ed.), *Les Influences étrangère dans l'œuvre de Wolfgang Amadeus Mozart* (Paris, 1958), 59–84; W. Wiora, 'Über den Volkston bei Mozart,' *Jahrbuch des österreichischen Volksliedwerkes* (1957), vi. 185–93; T. Helm, 'Ungarische Musik in deutschen Meistern', *Musikalisches Wochenblatt* (Leipzig, 1871), ii. 641–2; D. Bartha, 'Mozart et le folklore musical de l'Europe centrale', in A. Verchaly (ed.), *Les Influences étrangères*, 157–81; K. Reinhard, 'Mozarts Rezeption türkischer Musik', in H. Kühn and P. Nitsche (eds.), *Bericht über den internationalen Musikwissenschaft Kongress Berlin 1974* (Kassel, 1980), 518–23.

popular music without constituting literal borrowing. Identifiable instances of borrowed tunes in Mozart's instrumental music include: the 'Strassburger' tune used in the Finale of the violin concerto K. 216; the folk-songs 'D'Bäuerin hat d'Katz Verlorn' and 'Heissa, hurtig, ich bin Hans und bin ohne Sorge' in the divertimento K. 287 = 271H; 'Eahna achte müassens sein' in the *Galimathias musicum*, K. 32; the Christmas carol 'Joseph, lieber Joseph mein' ('Resonet in laudibus') in the symphony K. 132 and in an early version of the *Galimathias Musicum*; the Tirolian folk-song 'Zu Landshut bei den Musikanten' in the divertimento K. 563; the Lied 'Es fing ein Knab ein Vögelein' as the rondo theme of the violin sonata K. 376; the Czech song 'Hořela lipa, hořela' ('Freu Dich mein Herz, denk' an kein Schmerz') as a theme of the first movement of the piano sonata K. 331; and a number of the melodies that serve as starting-points for sets of variations. Similar ideas appear in some of his symphonies, although their origins usually cannot be traced.[30]

According to Leopold's report, the Salzburg symphonists at the beginning of Wolfgang's career were Adlgasser (No. 16), Cristelli (No. 3), Seidl (No. 5), and Leopold himself (No. 4). They were joined in 1763 by Michael Haydn, after Leopold the most prolific symphonist of the lot and, again after Leopold, probably the local composer who most influenced Wolfgang's symphonic development.[31] Although Leopold did not mention it in his report, Eberlin (No. 1) composed symphonies, for the incipits of a dozen sinfonias, four of which are extant, are preserved in a catalogue of 1768.[32] Four symphonies survive from the hand of Wenzel Hebelt (No. 8),[33] and Domenico Fischetti, Salzburg Court Kapellmeister between 1772 and 1775, composed numerous symphonies.[34] Three symphonies by Johann Georg Scheicher, who studied at Salzburg from 1759 to 1769 and was mentioned—unfavourably—by Leopold Mozart in a letter of 24 October 1785, also survive.[35] In addition, the Mozarts' friend Joseph Fiala, who worked in Salzburg between 1778 and 1785, composed 'Simphonien für grosse Orchester', although probably too late to have had an influence on Wolfgang;[36] the same may also be true of five symphonies by Joseph Hafeneder dating from between *c.*1770 and 1784.[37] Certainly, the production of symphonies in Salzburg was not

---

[30] See the discussions of the symphonies K. 76 = 42a (ch. 5); K. 74 (ch. 7); and K. 75, 114, and 132 (ch. 8).

[31] Wolfgang's symphonic connections to Michael Haydn are discussed in ch. 11.

[32] G. Lang, 'Zur Geschichte und Pflege der Musik in der Benediktiner-Abtei zu Lambach mit einem Katalog zu den Beständen des Musikarchives' (Ph.D. diss., University of Salzburg, 1978), ii. xxi–xxii.

[33] One in the Gesellschaft der Musikfreunde, Vienna; three in the Bibliothek des Bischöflichen Seckauer Ordinariats, Graz (information generously provided by Cliff Eisen).

[34] D. Libby, 'Fischietti, Domenico', *The New Grove*, vi. 615–16.

[35] The symphonies are at Lambach. *Briefe*, vi. 257, and private communication from Cliff Eisen.

[36] Lipowsky, *Baierisches Musik-Lexikon*, 81. Fiala was only two years Mozart's senior. Ten symphonies by him survive; see B. S. Brook (ed.), *The Symphony 1720–1840, Reference Volume* (New York, 1986), 221–2.

[37] Information kindly provided by Cliff Eisen.

inconsiderable: Leopold is credited with approximately seventy, Cristelli with an unknown number (three survive at Lambach), Seidl with 'very many' (according to Leopold), Eberlin with at least the dozen already mentioned, Adlgasser with perhaps ten, and Michael Haydn with about forty-three.[38] Wolfgang wrote thirty-six or so symphonies for his native city. And no doubt there were other works and other composers no longer known.[39]

National, regional, or local 'schools' of symphony-writing were recognized in the eighteenth century and have been discussed since, and we should recognize such distinctions. Discussions of symphonic 'schools', however, are frequently confused by the broad circulation of symphonies and marred by myopic argumentation resulting from overweening nationalism. The 'invention' of the classical symphony, for instance, has been variously claimed for Italy, Austria, Bohemia, and Bavaria.[40] One of the lessons of recent scholarship is that the early symphony was an international art-form. Despite what may seem to us primitive means of communication, music and musicians travelled widely. Instrumental music in particular was widely disseminated, as it was less tied to local requirements than were opera and church music.[41]

What may be heard in a sampling of available Salzburg symphonies by the two Mozarts, Michael Haydn, and Adlgasser seems adequately accounted for by such general categories as 'Italian', 'Austrian', 'Mannheim', etc. Studying these sympho-

---

[38] For Adlgasser's symphonies see W. Rainer, 'Verzeichnis der Werke A. C. Adlgassers', *Mozart-Jahrbuch* (1962–3), 280–91; Hintermaier, *Die salzburger Hofkapelle*, 66–7; W. Rainer (ed.), *A. C. Adlgasser, Drei Sinfonien* (Denkmäler der Tonkunst in Österreich, cxxxi) (Graz, 1980); and M. M. Schneider-Cuvay, W. Rainer, and C. H. Sherman (eds.) *Johann Ernst Eberlin: Three Symphonies; Anton Cajetan Adlgasser: Four Symphonies; Johann Michael Haydn: Five Symphonies* (The Symphony 1720–1840, B/viii) (New York, 1982). Many of Michael Haydn's symphonies have been published by Doblinger, Vienna. About a dozen of Leopold Mozart's symphonies have been published, several under Wolfgang's name; for details see *The New Grove*, xii. 678. See also C. Eisen (ed.), *Leopold Mozart: Three Symphonies* (The Symphony 1720–1840, B/ix) (New York, 1984).

In listing the 'symphonies' of the Salzburg composers, we fall victim to the several meanings of 'symphony' prevalent in the eighteenth century and discussed in chs. 4 and 13. The title 'Sinfonia' can be found at the head of a number of Salzburg works that, from their form and function, most modern writers would be inclined to call 'orchestra trio', 'partita', 'orchestral serenade', 'overture', or 'suite'. Some of these works contain movements suitable to a symphony, but mixed with concerto movements, fugal movements, or movements of the sort found in baroque suites.

[39] Following the Napoleonic invasion and secularization of Salzburg (1803), the various music collections there were mostly destroyed or dispersed. Thus, aside from the symphonies of Wolfgang Mozart and Michael Haydn, which had earlier been sent to Vienna and Esterházà respectively, the Salzburg symphonic tradition now must be reconstructed largely from works that survive elsewhere (W. Rainer (ed.), *A. C. Adlgasser, Drei Sinfonien*, vii; Cliff Eisen, 'The Symphonies of Leopold Mozart and Their Relationship to the Early Symphonies of Wolfgang Mozart' (Ph.D. diss., Cornell University, 1986), *infra*; hereafter cited as 'The Symphonies of Leopold Mozart').

[40] ITALY: F. Torrefranca, 'Le origini della sinfonia', *Rivista musicale italiana* (1913–15), xx. 291–346; xxi. 92–121, 278–312; xxii. 431–2; AUSTRIA: W. Fischer, *Wiener Instrumentalmusik vor und um 1750* (Denkmäler der Tonkunst in Österreich, xxxix) (Vienna, 1912); H. Botstiber, *Geschichte der Ouverture und der freien Orchesterformen* (Leipzig, 1913); G. Adler, *Handbuch der Musikgeschichte*, 2nd edn. (Berlin, 1930); BAVARIA: H. Riemann, *Die Mannheimer Schule* (Denkmäler der Tonkunst in Bayern, iv, xiii, xvi); BOHEMIA: V. Helfert, *Hudba na jaroměřickémku* (Prague, 1924); *idem*, 'Zur Entwicklungsgeschichte der Sonatenform', *Archiv für Musikwissenschaft* (1925), vii. 117–46. See also J. P. Larsen, 'Zur Bedeutung der "Mannheimer Schule"' in H. Hüschen (ed.), *Festschrift Karl Gustav Fellerer zum Sechzigsten Geburtstag* (Regensburg, 1962), 303–9.

[41] H. Rösing, 'Sinn und Nutzen des Versuchs einer weltweiten Erfassung von Quellen zur Musik' in G. Feder, W. Rehm, and M. Ruhnke (eds.), *Quellenforschung in der Musikwissenschaft* (Wolfenbüttel, 1982), 57–66, esp. 63–4.

nies, one does not find them sharing unique features that might be identified with
Salzburg tastes, although there are influences from the west (French dance music),
from the north (Germanic counterpoint, Italian-inspired Mannheim orchestral
devices,[42] touches of *Empfindsamkeit*), from the east (Bohemian and Viennese four-
movement concert symphonies with repeats, brilliant wind-writing), and from the
south (Italianate cantabile melodies, 'orchestral noises', three-movement overture-
symphonies without repeats). Perhaps Salzburg was simply a musical crossroads
without its own symphonic style, or perhaps our ignorance of too many of the
local symphonies prevents us from perceiving specifically local traits and preferences. Judging by the symphonies Wolfgang wrote for his native city, one would
say that tastes there ran to a kind of conventional brilliance in the allegros, leavened
with a gentle lyricism in the andantes, a dash of local colour in the minuets and
trios, and a superficially treated *contredanse*, gavotte, jig, or march in the finale.
Thus it is difficult to say if a Salzburg symphonic 'school' existed in any coherent
social or stylistic sense, in the way we may speak of the Italian, Mannheim, or
Viennese 'schools' of the period, and the way one reasonably refers to a Salzburg
school of sacred music.[43] Undoubtedly the *Kenner und Liebhaber* of Salzburg had
particular musical tastes in symphonies, and undoubtedly too the local composers
strove to satisfy them. It may not have been a handicap for Wolfgang to be born at
a musical crossroads, where his internationalism, catholicity of taste, and universality of style first could flourish.

   The Salzburg symphonies achieved modest distribution by means of manuscript
copies, primarily in Austria and Bavaria, in ecclesiastical establishments and secular
courts. Hardly any were published during their composers' lifetimes. It was
possible, if difficult, to publish music at Salzburg or nearby Augsburg, as Leopold
Mozart did, where there was only one properly constituted music-publisher,
whose output scarcely included symphonies.[44] One might be tempted to suggest
that, had Salzburg been a centre of music-publishing, its symphonies would have
been more widely distributed. But consider Mannheim. Like Salzburg, it was not a
centre for music-publishing, yet the works of its symphonists were distributed
throughout western Europe, partly in manuscript but to a considerable extent
through engraved editions published elsewhere. And what of Italian opera? It
enjoyed international distribution, yet there was little music-publishing in Italy in
the second half of the eighteenth century, and for anything from an Italian opera

---

[42] E. K. Wolf, 'On the Origins of the Mannheim Symphonic Style' in J. W. Hill (ed.), *Studies in Musicology in Honor of Otto E. Albrecht* (Kassel, 1980), 197–239.

[43] M. H. Schmid, *Mozart und die salzburger Tradition*. Schubart, writing in the 1780s, included Salzburg among those musical centres which—unlike Vienna, Berlin, Saxony, and Palatine Bavaria—'never developed their own musical schools' (*Ideen*, 146). See also M. Havlova, 'Der Schulbegriff: Inhalt, Bestimmung und Anwendungsmöglichkeiten in Bezug auf musikgeschichtliche Sachverhalte des 18. Jahrhunderts', *Beiträge zur Musikwissenschaft* (1980), xxii. 209–16.

[44] H. Rheinfurth, *Der Musikverlag Lotter in Augsburg (ca. 1719–1845)* (Tutzing, 1977), esp. 134, 149.

other than overtures or popular arias with reduced accompaniment to be published anywhere in Europe was virtually unheard of. Seeing that Italian opera made its way entirely by manuscript copies and Mannheim symphonies primarily by publication in other cities, we may tentatively conclude that the European music-consuming public and patrons wanted Mannheim symphonies and Italian operas but not Salzburg symphonies, if one may speak of their not wanting something that may have scarcely (if at all) entered their consciousness. Seen another way, while travellers to and from Italy conducted a brisk trade in operatic music, and those to and from Mannheim did so for symphonies, travellers to and from Salzburg (a number of whom can be documented) apparently did nothing comparable. Even Leopold and Wolfgang, with their wide travels and extensive correspondence, did not publish their symphonies, though not for want of trying. The success of the Mannheimers in getting their works published may have had as much to do with the fame of their orchestra as with the inherent merits of their symphonies. The Salzburg orchestra had, as we shall discover, a different reputation.

This, then, is a brief sketch of the musical environment into which Wolfgang was born on 27 January 1756. Leopold realized early that he had on his hands what he later referred to as 'a miracle that God permitted to be born in Salzburg'.[45] Acting with vigour and originality to carry out what he conceived of as a sacred trust, he devoted himself to the education and professional advancement of his son. And so from January 1762, when Wolfgang was just turning six, the Mozart family was frequently on the road, visiting musical centres and courts. These trips were intended to raise money, to spread the fame of the infant prodigy, and to educate him by providing access to the important music and musicians of the era. In the story of Wolfgang's precocious development as a symphonist, Salzburg forms the background and the European tours the foreground.

[45] Letter of 30 July 1768. *Briefe*, i. 271; *Letters*, i. 132 (= i. 89).

2

The Grand Tour (I): London
(1764–1765)

———— ❧ ————

Given the role of symphonies in Salzburg's musical life, the infant Wolfgang undoubtedly heard them performed. Certainly he was not closeted away from public music-making, which would have been contrary to Leopold's policy of educating his son by allowing him to hear a wide range of music. Evidence of Wolfgang's early participation in events that included symphonies is found in the libretto of Eberlin's oratorio *Sigismundus Hungariae rex*, performed in the Great Hall of Salzburg University on 1 and 3 September 1761, which lists the almost six-year-old child among the performers.[1] Wolfgang may also have heard symphonies during a brief visit to Munich early in 1762, although this is speculation. During a short stay in Vienna half a year later he not only heard symphonies but understood something about them, for a letter of 19 May 1763 from there reported, 'We fall into utter amazement on seeing a boy aged six at the keyboard and hearing him . . . accompany at sight symphonies, arias, and recitatives at the great concerts.'[2] Not long afterwards, during the Mozarts' grand tour to Mannheim, Paris, London, and Holland, Wolfgang heard a wide variety of symphonies and became interested in composing them.

Paris, where the Mozart family stayed from 11 November 1763 to 10 April 1764 and from 10 May to 9 July 1766, was a major centre for the performance and publication of symphonies.[3] Although French composers were represented (especially the Franco-Belgian Gossec), the production of symphonies was dominated by foreign composers, notably Germans, Austrians, and Bohemians, some of whom worked in Paris but many of whom merely sent symphonies there to be

---

[1] Deutsch, 15–16 (= 13–14). See also ch. 4, n. 72.

[2] *Augsburgischer Intelligenz-Zettel* (19 May 1763). Deutsch, 22–3 (= 20–1). For the possible meanings of 'symphony' in these passages, see ch. 1, n. 38, the beginning of ch. 4 and nn. 43–4, and the beginning of ch. 13.

[3] B. S. Brook, *La Symphonie française dans la seconde moitié du XVIIIᵉ siècle* (Paris, 1962), esp. chs. 1 and 4. Hereafter cited as *La Symphonie française*.

performed and published.[4] Since Leopold disliked most French music, Wolfgang's models in Paris were a group of German-speaking composers active there: Johann Gottfried Eckard, Leontzi Honauer, Hermann Friedrich Raupach, Christian Hochbrucker, and Johann Schobert. The names of these compatriots appear in Leopold's correspondence and travel diary,[5] and some of their music was given to Wolfgang to rework. In doing so he sometimes changed the genre, as when he fashioned concertos from solo keyboard music by Raupach, Honauer, Schobert, Eckard, and C. P. E. and J. C. Bach (K. 37, 39, 40, 41, 107). Note then that influences on his symphonic style need not have originated solely from symphonies.

Late in April 1764 the Mozarts left Paris and settled in London. By the beginning of August the eight-year-old Wolfgang had to his credit some fifty unpublished keyboard pieces, as well as three collections (Opp. 1–3), published in Paris and London, containing ten accompanied keyboard sonatas. How he came to write his first symphony was recalled some years after his death by his sister Nannerl:

On the fifth of August [we] had to rent a country house in Chelsea, outside the City of London, so that father could recover from a dangerous throat ailment, which brought him almost to death's door. [. . .] Our father lay dangerously ill; we were forbidden to touch the keyboard. And so, in order to occupy himself, Mozart composed his first symphony with all the instruments of the orchestra, especially trumpets and kettledrums. I had to transcribe it as I sat at his side. While he composed and I copied he said to me, 'Remind me to give the horn something worthwhile to do!' [. . .] At last after two months, as father had completely recovered, [we] returned to London.[6]

The earliest symphony listed by Köchel, and number 1 in collected editions of Mozart's symphonies, is the Symphony in E flat, K. 16. The autograph manuscript bears the superscription 'Sinfonia / di / Sig: Wolfgang / Mozart / a london / 1764', possibly in Leopold's hand. But is this the symphony described in Nannerl's account? She mentioned that she copied Wolfgang's first symphony, whereas the score of K. 16 is in Wolfgang's hand with corrections by Leopold.[7] Perhaps after Nannerl had copied a score, Wolfgang so thoroughly revised it that it became illegible, forcing him to make another copy—the one we now have—before continuing his revisions. Or Nannerl may simply have meant she had to copy parts for her brother; other symphonies from this period (K. 19, 19a, 45a) survive as sets

    [4] Ibid. i. 19–20. See also Mozart's letter of 3 Dec. 1777. *Briefe*, ii. 162; *Letters*, ii. 592 (= i. 401); and the publications of the Mannheim composers in *RISM*, Serie A/I.

    [5] *Briefe*, i. 113–45.

    [6] Deutsch, 400, 416 (= 456, 494). Nannerl's anecdote as presented here is a conflation of two different accounts that she wrote, altered from third to first person.

    [7] W. Plath, 'Beiträge zur Mozart-Autographie I: Die Handschrift Leopold Mozarts', *Mozart-Jahrbuch* (1960–1), 82–117; G. Allroggen, 'Mozarts erste Sinfonien', in J. Schläder and R. Quandt (eds.), *Festschrift Heinz Becker zum 60. Geburtstag am 26. Juni 1982* (Laaber, 1982), 392–404; *idem*, 'Mozarts erste Sinfonien', in C.-H. Mahling and S. Wiesmann (eds.), *Gesellschaft für Musikgeschichte: Bericht über den internationalen Musikwissenschaften Kongress Bayreuth 1981* (Kassel, 1982–4), 349; *NMA*, iv/11/1. ix (G. Allroggen).

of parts copied by Leopold and Nannerl. She also mentioned that Wolfgang wrote for trumpets and kettledrums, neither instrument used in K. 16. Of course, many symphonies of the third quarter of the eighteenth century circulated shorn of their trumpet and kettledrum parts, which often were considered optional and sometimes notated separately and absent from the score.[8] Since Mozart's trumpet keys were C, D, and E flat, K. 16 could have included those instruments. As for giving the horn 'something worthwhile to do', Mozart perhaps did that with a passage in the Andante, where the horn plays the motive doh—ray—fah—me, best known from the Finale of the 'Jupiter' symphony, but also found in other works by Mozart and his contemporaries. Yet all this sounds too much like special pleading: the discrepancies between the symphony described in Nannerl's anecdote and the state in which K. 16 survives suggest that the two are most likely not one and the same.[9]

By 'Mozart composed his first symphony with all the instruments of the orchestra', did Nannerl mean 'he wrote his first symphony, which was with all the instruments of the orchestra', or did she mean 'after writing a symphony for another medium, he now wrote his first for all the instruments of the orchestra'?[10] (The original, *'Komponierte Mozart seine erste Symfonie mit allen Instrumenten— vornehmlich mit Trompeten und Pauken'*, has the same ambiguity as the translation.) In either case, clues to the hypothetical, missing 'first' symphony may be found among the pieces in the so-called 'London Notebook', in which Wolfgang wrote some forty-two complete or fragmentary harpsichord pieces (K. 15a–15ss). The first twenty-four pieces are written in pencil, the last eighteen in ink. None of them is dated, but inside the front cover Leopold wrote 'di Wolfgango Mozart / a Londra 1764'.[11] A few of these pieces are written in a quasi-orchestral style and possibly may have been drafts for a symphony. Three pieces singled out for their 'orchestral' style (Table 2.1)[12] cannot have been intended to form a symphony,

   [8] A. Carse, *The Orchestra in the XVIIIth Century* (Cambridge, 1940), 139–40. Mozart's trumpet symphonies that circulated without trumpets include K. 87 = 74a (see ch. 8), 203 = 189b, and 385 (see A. Holschneider, 'Neue Mozartiana in Italien', *Die Musikforschung* (1962), xv. 227–36). Among many examples that might be cited from the symphonies of other composers: Stamitz—Wolf Nos. D-3, D-11, D-15; Joseph Haydn—Hoboken Nos. I: 20, 33, 37, 38, 41, 42, 48, 53, 56, 60, 61, etc.; Dittersdorf—Grave Nos. C-5, C-15, D-17, D-27, E flat-2, E flat-14.

   [9] R. Münster, 'Neue Funde zu Mozarts symphonischem Jugendwerk', *Mitteilungen der internationalen Stiftung Mozarteum* (Feb. 1982), xx. 2–11; Allroggen, 'Mozarts erste Sinfonien'.

   [10] For non-orchestral 'symphonies' that Mozart might have heard in Paris or London in 1763–4, see Porpora's six *Sinfonie da camera a tre stromenti*, Op. 2, published in London in 1736 and Paris *c*.1737; and Schobert's six *Sinfonies*, Opp. 9–10, for harpsichord obbligato, 2 violins, 2 horns, and *basso*, published in Paris *c*.1765 (modern edn., *Das Erbe deutscher Musik*, iv (1960)).

   [11] The ink and pencil sections of the London Notebook seem to be chronological layers, but (contrary to what Wyzewa–Saint-Foix, K[3], and K[6] suggest) the entire manuscript was probably completed by December 1764, when another, now lost notebook—the so-called *Capricci*, K. 32a—was begun. See my discussion of the *Capricci* in 'Leopold Mozart's List of His Son's Works', in A. Atlas (ed.), *Music of the Classic Period: Essays in Honor of Barry S. Brook* (New York, 1985), 323–58, here 349–52.

   [12] G. Schünemann, *Mozart als achtjähriger Komponist* (Leipzig, 1909), vii; review of same by A. Heuss in *Zeitschrift der internationalen Musikgesellschaft* (1908–9) x. 181–2; Wyzewa–Saint-Foix, i. 119.

TABLE 2.1 Keyboard pieces in quasi-orchestral style in the London Notebook

K	Tempo	Metre	Key	Written in
15kk	Allegro	C	E flat	ink
15dd	Andante	C	A flat	ink
15x	Allegro molto	$\frac{2}{4}$	F major	pencil

however, since the sequence of keys is impossible. If, on the other hand, the 'Finale', K. 15x, is eliminated, because it is in the wrong key and among the pencilled pieces, and if the other inked pieces are examined for a suitable finale, two minuets in E flat major, K. 15ee and 15cc, present themselves.

The use of a minuet as a finale may upon first consideration seem peculiar, as many modern descriptions of eighteenth-century symphonies state that the minuet and trio provide an 'optional' movement between the slow movement and the finale. This is true of many symphonies of the period. But numerous others, especially from the 1750s and 1760s, have minuets as finales, and this fits an Italian description of 1772, stating that 'all symphonies that serve as overtures are cast from the same die, and are inevitably made up of a solemn grouping of an allegro, a largo, and a dance'.[13] A symphony finale of the 1760s or 1770s based on a minuet usually consists not of a single dance, but rather of either a minuet and trio (or pair of minuets) or a minuet *en rondeau*. Among three E flat minuets in the inked portion of the Notebook, K. 15cc and 15ee seem slightly more suited to orchestration than does K. 15qq. This speculative reconstruction of a 'symphony' (Example 2.1) is meant to suggest that Mozart may have thought about the genre before he came to write his first, which probably does not survive and which may have been based in some way upon the keyboard pieces of the London Notebook. The use of solo keyboard pieces from Nannerl's Notebook, K. 1a–9b (and other pieces not by Wolfgang), and from the London Notebook, K. 15a–ss, as movements of the accompanied sonatas of Wolfgang's Opp. 1, 2, 3, and 4 (K. 6–15, 26–31) documents a practice comparable to the one hypothesized for his 'first' symphony.

---

[13] Antonio Planelli, *Dell'opera in musica* (Naples, 1772), 135. Several of Sammartini's symphonies have minuet finales, as do some symphonies from Vienna, Mannheim, Paris, and elsewhere. Eight of the symphonies attributed to Leopold Mozart have a minuet and trio as last movement. And, perhaps most important in the present context, no fewer than seven of the symphonies of J. C. Bach and twelve of Abel end with minuets. But although a number of Mozart's later concertos use minuets for their finales, as do some of his early accompanied keyboard sonatas written and published during the period 1764–6, he seems to have preferred jigs, *contredanses*, gavottes, and marches as the basis for his symphony finales. Concerning minuet finales, see also Charles Burney's remark cited below in ch. 4, n. 3.

Ex. 2.1 Symphony No. '0' in E flat major (= London Notebook, K. 15kk–dd–cc–ee)

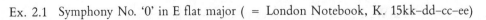

Whichever work Wolfgang's first symphony may have been, once he had written it, his father was quick to exploit this achievement. Having recovered from his illness, Leopold moved his family back to London in late September 1764. Wolfgang and Nannerl resumed their rounds of public and private appearances, while Wolfgang received instruction in singing from the castrato Giovanni Manzuoli. In late November or early December Leopold wrote to Baron von Grimm in Paris that, in order to make up financial losses from the period of his illness, he planned 'to give a subscription concert at each assembly at Mrs Cornelys' in Soho Square'.[14] Mrs Cornelys *née* Theresa Imer, a former opera singer from Venice, had purchased Carlisle House, furbishing it with a lavish ballroom and concert-hall, with 'tea downstairs and ventilation above'. Concerts, balls, suppers, and masquerades quickly made it an important social centre. Wednesday evening subscription concerts were introduced under the direction of Gioacchino Cocchi, who appears in Leopold's travel diary as 'Maestro Cochi', next to the entry 'Madame Cornelys in Soho Square'.[15] The beginning of 1765 saw the first series of the Bach–Abel subscription concerts, held at Carlisle House on 23 and 30 January, 6 February, and 6, 19, and 27 March, directed alternately by Johann Christian Bach and Carl Friedrich Abel. These concerts would bring music and musicians from the Continent, popularizing the sinfonia concertante and giving the first English performances of Haydn's symphonies and of works by the later generation of Mannheim composers.[16] Because visiting virtuosos were important attractions and because the Mozarts were apparently on good terms with Bach and Abel, the Mozarts would most likely have been invited to participate; and Leopold's letter to Grimm may have alluded to the impending Bach–Abel series rather than to the apparently defunct series run by Cocchi or to an undocumented series run by Leopold himself.

From 6 February 1765 notices appeared in London newspapers for a 'Concert of Vocal and Instrumental Music' for the benefit of 'Miss MOZART of Twelve and Master MOZART of Eight Years of Age; Prodigies of Nature'.[17] Two days later Leopold Mozart wrote to his Salzburg friend, patron, and landlord, Lorenz Hagenauer:

On the evening of the 15th we are giving a concert, which will probably bring me in about one hundred and fifty guineas. Whether I shall still make anything after that and, if

[14] Deutsch, 38 (= 37–8). Leopold's letter is lost; this information comes from a letter of 13 Dec. 1764 from Baron von Grimm to a third party. On 17 Apr. 1763, Jérôme Lalande, visiting London, wrote in his diary: 'They have promised to take me to Mme Cornelys' music room, where some lords make a subscription of five guineas for twenty concerts a year, each fortnight in Soho' (H. Monod-Cassidy (ed.), *Journal d'un voyage en Angleterre 1763* (Studies on Voltaire and the Eighteenth Century, clxxxiv) (Oxford, 1980), 45).

[15] *Briefe*, i. 193.

[16] H. Raynor, 'London', *The New Grove*, xi. 193, 202.

[17] *The Public Advertiser* (6 Feb. 1765); Deutsch, 40 (= 40).

so, what, I do not know . . . . Oh, what a lot of things I have to do. The symphonies at the concert will all be by Wolfgang Mozart. I must copy them myself, unless I want to pay one shilling for each sheet. Copying music is a very profitable business here. Our Estlinger would laugh. I send him my compliments.[18]

But this concert, Wolfgang's symphonic début, was postponed until Monday the eighteenth because of a conflict with a performance of Thomas Arne's oratorio *Judith*, which tied up performers upon whose services the Mozarts had counted. A second postponement occurred for unknown reasons. Finally, from 15 February notices again appeared in London newspapers:

HAYMARKET, Little Theatre.

THE CONCERT for the Benefit of Miss and Master MOZART will be certainly performed on Thursday the 21st instant, which will begin exactly at six, which will not hinder the Nobility and Gentry from meeting in other Assemblies on the same Evening.

Tickets to be had of Mr Mozart, at Mr Williamson's in Thrift-street, Soho, and at the said Theatre.

Tickets delivered for the 15th will be admitted.

A Box Ticket admits two into the Gallery.

To prevent Mistakes, the Ladies and Gentlemen are desired to send their Servants to keep Places for the Boxes, and give their Names to the Boxkeepers on Thursday the 21st in the Afternoon.[19]

Notices published on the day of the concert contained the additional sentence, 'All the Overtures [i.e., symphonies] will be from the Composition of these astonishing Composers, who are only eight Years old'.[20] No reviews appeared in the London newspapers other than a laconic note stating: 'One Wolfgang Mozart, a German boy, of about eight years old, is arrived here, who can play upon various sorts of instruments of music, in consort or solo, and can compose music surprizingly; so that he may be reckoned a wonder at his age'.[21] Some weeks later Leopold sent Hagenauer a report of Wolfgang's symphonic début, which, as was often his wont, dealt with financial rather than artistic matters:

My concert, which I intended to give on February 15th, did not take place until the 21st, and on account of the number of entertainments (which really weary one here) was not so

---

[18] Letter of 8 Feb. 1765. *Briefe*, i. 180; *Letters*, i. 78–9 (= i. 54). Concerning the Salzburg copyist Estlinger, see ch. 6. The Viennese music-copying firm of Simon Haschke advertised in the *Wiener Diarium* (1767), No. 10, the rate of 'bögen a 9 kr.' (H. Gericke, *Der wiener Musikalienhandel von 1700 bis 1778* (Graz, 1960), 104). Salzburg was cheaper than Vienna, 4–6 kr. a sheet according to Hübner. But Leopold's letter seems to contradict Hübner about London, citing a rate of 1 shilling per sheet, which may be very approximately converted as 3 groats = 9 kreutzer, or apparently about the same as Vienna.

[19] *The Public Advertiser* (15 Feb. 1765); Deutsch, 41 (= 41).

[20] *The Public Advertiser* (21 Feb. 1765); Deutsch, 42 (= 42). An error made Wolfgang and Nannerl the same age and both composers.

[21] *The London Evening Post* (21–3 Feb. 1765), *Lloyd's Evening Post* (22 Feb. 1765). I owe these citations to Cliff Eisen.

well attended as I had hoped. Nevertheless, I took in about one hundred and thirty guineas. As, however, the expenses connected with it amounted to over twenty-seven guineas, I have not made much more than one hundred guineas.[22]

A curious feature of the advertisement quoted above is that, unlike most others Leopold placed in English and continental newspapers, it does not name a price. The standard price for 'great' concerts (that is, concerts with orchestra) was a half-guinea, as we learn from the concerts the Mozarts participated in and from a visitor to London some years later, who noted in his diary: 'The concerts in London are allowed to be very good, and the English in general prefer them to the music of the opera-house; but as the price of a ticket is half-a-guinea, none but the higher ranks can receive any gratification from them.'[23] From the price of admission and the gross receipts, the size of the audience can be estimated at about 260, some forty fewer than Leopold had hoped for. Even so, in a single evening Leopold's profit was more than his annual salary at the Salzburg court,[24] a circumstance hinting at differences between the vestigial feudal system under which the Mozarts worked at home and the flourishing capitalist system they found in London.

Consider the significance of these financial arrangements to someone in Leopold's position. He lacked independent means. Backing for his family's grand tour came from his landlord and friend Hagenauer, with the intention that through gifts from patrons, concert revenues, and the buying and selling of music and other things, all concerned should turn a profit. There were extraordinary expenses, for not only did the Mozarts have to dress and travel in style if they were to be received at courts, but illnesses were responsible for costly periods without income. The themes of earnings and expenses are woven like the weft and warp through Leopold's correspondence with Hagenauer. If the costs in London were high by Salzburg standards, so was the potential income. Among the many visitors eager to hear the Mozarts' adventures after they returned to Salzburg was Beda Hübner, librarian of St Peter's Abbey, who recorded in his diary:

They never cease to relate how dreadfully expensive everything is in England, and adduced the following in proof thereof: he [Leopold Mozart] heard in England at Court, among other things, some very fine music, perhaps a ballet or an opera; he therefore wished to have this copied there, but asked what they charged for copying per sheet, for which here they ask 4 or at the most 6 *kreuzer*; in England they receive 12 groats, *i.e.* 36 kr.

[22] Letter of 19 Mar. 1765. *Briefe*, i. 180; *Letters*, i. 81 (= 1. 55–6).

[23] Johann Wilhelm von d'Archenholz, *A Picture of England* (London, 1789), ii. 175. The standard half-guinea concert price is mentioned also in Leopold's letter of 28 May 1764 (*Briefe*, i. 151; *Letters*, i. 67 (= i. 47)), and in Deutsch, English edn. only, 238. Some cheaper concerts are mentioned below, however, and the Bach–Abel series of 1765 apparently asked of its subscribers five guineas for six concerts (*The Public Advertiser* (Wednesday, 23 Jan. 1765)). See also n. 14 above.

[24] Leopold's annual salary as Vizekapellmeister in Salzburg was 354 florins, which very approximately equalled 84 guineas, whereas in London he cleared more than 100 guineas for a single concert.

per sheet, and he thereupon gave up the copying, for it would have cost him approximately 100 thalers; indeed he added that, had he sent the whole of this music from England to Salzburg, had it copied at Salzburg, and had it brought from Salzburg to England again, it would not have cost him nearly so much as the copying alone would have cost him in England. He appeared in England exactly as in other countries, appearing with his children on public stages, and at theatres, just as foreign play-actors appear: now if here we pay a 6, 12, or 24 kreutzer piece going to the comedy, in England they pay nothing but guineas, which is a gold coin similar to the Max[imilian] *d'or* or *Carolin* here, so that it is easy to imagine the amount of money this Mr Mozart must have made in England where, moreover, all presents are given purely and solely in ready cash . . . . The journey now accomplished is said to have cost them something near 20,000 florins: I can well believe it; but how much money must he not have collected?[25]

These remarks suggest why the symphonies K. 19, 19a, and 45a come down to us in sets of parts entirely or partially in Leopold's hand, rather than in the hands of professional copyists.

    Further clues to the costs and profits of London concert-giving appear in a letter of Leopold's, reporting on a concert of 5 June 1764:

I have had another shock, that is, the shock of taking in one-hundred guineas in three hours. Fortunately, it is now over . . . . We had a week in which to distribute the 'billets', or rather two or three days only, for before that date there was hardly anyone in London. But although for this kind of concert four to eight weeks are usually necessary for the distribution of the 'billets' (which here they call 'tickets'), to the amazement of everyone there were present more than a couple of hundred persons, including the leading people of all London; not only all the ambassadors, but the principal families in England attended it and everyone was delighted. I cannot say whether I shall have a profit of one-hundred guineas, as I have not yet received the money for thirty-six tickets from Mylord March and for forty tickets from a friend in town and from various others; and the expenses are surprisingly great. Now listen to a few details about the expenses. The hall without lighting and music-stands costs five guineas. Each keyboard instrument, of which I had to have two on account of the concerto for two keyboard instruments, costs half a guinea. The first violin gets three guineas and so on; and all who play the solos and concertos three, four, and five guineas. The ordinary players receive each half a guinea and so forth. But, fortunately for me, all the musicians as well as the hall and everything else only cost me twenty guineas, because most of the performers would not accept anything. Well, God be praised, that is over and we have made something.[26]

    From 11 March a series of notices appeared in London newspapers announcing the Mozarts' final public appearance there. The programme again featured symphonies:

[25] Deutsch, 64 (= 68–9).
[26] Letter of 8 June 1764. *Briefe*, i. 153–4; *Letters*, i. 69–70 (= i. 48).

For the Benefit of Miss MOZART of Thirteen, and Master MOZART of Eight year of Age, Prodigies of Nature.

HICKFORD'S Great Room in Brewer Street, this Day, May 13, will be A CONCERT OF VOCAL and INSTRUMENTAL MUSIC.

With all the OVERTURES of the little Boy's own Composition.

The Vocal Part by Sig. Cremonini; Concerto on the Violin Mr Barthelemon; Solo on the Violoncello, Sig. Cirii; Concerto on the Harpsichord by the little Composer and his Sister, each single and both together, &c.

Tickets at 5s each, to be had of Mr Mozart, at Mr Williamson's, in Thrift-street, Soho.[27]

What determined a lower price for this concert is unclear. The Mozarts had participated in a charity concert on 26 June 1764 for which tickets were also five shillings.[28] Perhaps Leopold, having failed to fill the house at the previous concert or sensing the novelty of his prodigies wearing thin, attempted to attract a larger crowd with a lower price. In any case, this was apparently the last time a symphony by Mozart was heard in London until 18 February 1784 when, at the Concerts of the Nobility in Hanover Square, a 'great and beautiful symphony, varied in all its sections' was performed by an orchestra of 6—6—4—3—4 / 2—2—0—2 / 2, with keyboard continuo.[29]

The programmes of 21 February and 13 May have not been preserved, but programmes from similar occasions show that the Mozarts' concerts usually began and ended with symphonies ('overtures'), which might also end the first half, begin the second half, or both. Between symphonies there would have been performances on the harpsichord or cabinet organ by Wolfgang and Nannerl, together and separately, improvised and prepared. The 'Concerto on the Harpsichord by the little Composer and his Sister' is usually said to be the four-hand sonata, K. 19d, which, however, is not a concerto and does not explain why two harpsichords were needed, as Leopold mentioned in his letter of 5 June 1764. Some of London's favourite virtuosos would have contributed renditions of sonatas, concertos, arias, and operatic scenas, as was the custom at benefit concerts.

Although the make-up of the orchestras for these concerts is not known, there are some clues to consider.[30] Leopold may have called together his musical

---

[27] *The Public Advertiser* (11 Mar., 20 Mar., 9 Apr., 10 May, 13 May 1765); Deutsch, 43–4 (= 43–5).

[28] Deutsch, 37–8 (= 36–7).

[29] Carl Friedrich Cramer, *Magazin der Musik* (Dec. 1784), cols. 225–7. Further concerning performances of Mozart's symphonies in London in the 1780s, see Table 10.2.

[30] One possibly misleading clue is provided by the original sets of parts for the symphonies, K. 19, 19a, and 45a. These have only single parts for each string section, which might lead to the conclusion that there can have been no more than two each of first and second violins. This is probably wrong, however, because in a letter of 1777 discussed in ch. 6, Leopold revealed that it had been his practice while on tour to carry symphonies with single parts only, leaving it to local copyists to create extra parts as needed. Thus, if originally there were doubled string parts for Wolfgang's earliest symphonies, they may

acquaintances with some of their friends to form a 'band', for in his diary are listed sixteen of London's leading instrumentalists, almost all foreigners.[31] But it is more probable that he hired one of the standing theatre orchestras, as, for instance, the cellist Carlo Graziani did for his benefit concert of 17 May 1764 in Hickford's Great Room, at which Wolfgang made a guest appearance.[32]

Statistics are preserved for some London orchestras for a few seasons before and after the period that the Mozarts were there. According to one source, for the 1757–8 and 1760–1 seasons Covent Garden's orchestra contained twenty-one players, while, according to another, in 1760 the same ensemble had nineteen plus the *maestro al cembalo*, although the instrumentation is unknown in all cases.[33] An approximate idea of the balance favoured can perhaps be gleaned from some orchestral rosters of a somewhat later date (Table 2.2). Judging by this evidence, it would probably be close to the mark to imagine an orchestra of about 20 players for the Mozarts' concerts, broken down into perhaps 8 violins, 1 or 2 violas, 1 or 2 cellos, 1 double-bass, 1 or 2 bassoons, and pairs of horns and oboes, the latter able to double on flutes or clarinets if needed. And presiding over a group including many continental instrumentalists must have been the nine-year-old Wolfgang, who had for some years been competent to 'accompany at sight symphonies, arias, and recitatives at the great concerts'. That Wolfgang not only was able to direct his symphonies from the keyboard but did so is confirmed by one of Leopold's newspaper announcements stating that the concert of 13 May would 'chiefly be conducted by his Son'.[34]

Mozart's earliest symphonies reveal how well at the age of nine he had mastered the most up-to-date style of the period. His principal models in London were Johann Christian Bach and Carl Friedrich Abel. (As early in their London visit as 28 May 1764, he had performed at the harpsichord works by Wagenseil, Bach,

---

have been left behind in London, or even deliberately destroyed to prevent their being pirated. A normal set of symphony parts of the period consisted of a single part for each of the string and wind instruments, with *Dubletten* (extra parts, usually one each) for violin I, violin II, and *basso*. *Dubletten* (left behind, as it were) originally belonging to sets of parts in Mozart's possession and containing autograph corrections survive in Frankfurt for K. 110 = 75b, 318, and 319 (W. Plath, 'Mozartiana in Fulda und Frankfurt', *Mozart-Jahrbuch* (1968–70), 333–86).

[31] *Violinists*: Felice de Giardini (leader of the opera orchestra at the King's Theatre), François-Hippolyte Barthélémon (leader of several London ensembles), Giuseppe (Joseph) Agus, Tommaso Mazzinghi (wine merchant and violinist at Marylebone Gardens), Antonin Kammel (a pupil of Tartini's), Mr Noffari; *cellists*: Carlo Graziani (mentioned above), Giovanni-Battista Cirri, John Gordon, Emanuel Sipruntini, Mr Scola, Francesco Zappa, *flautists*: Pietro Grassi Florio, Joseph Tacet, *oboist*: Mr Eiffert (*Briefe*, i. 192–5).

[32] Deutsch, 34–5 (= 33–4).

[33] G. W. Stone, Jr. (ed.), *The London Stage 1660–1800, A Calendar of Plays, Entertainments & Afterpieces Together with Casts, Box-Receipts and Theatrical Diaries of the Period, Part 4: 1747–1776* (Carbondale, 1962), i. cxxvii; R. Fiske, *English Theatre Music in the Eighteenth Century* (London, 1973), 279–85.

[34] *The Public Advertiser* (9 Apr. 1765). Deutsch, 43–4 (= 44).

TABLE 2.2 London orchestras of the 1770s

Orchestra	Date	vn. I	vn. II	va.	vc.	db.	fl.	ob.	cl.	bn.	hn.	tpt.	timp.	cont.	misc.	TOTAL
Drury Lane	1775	4–5	3–4	1–3	2–3	1–2	0–2	0–2	0–2	2	2	1	0	1	0	24
Antient Concerts	1776	8	8	5	4	2	0	4	0	4	4	2	1	1	0	43
Drury Lane	1778–9	4–5	3–4	2–3	2	2	0–2	0–2	0–2	2	2	1	0	2	dbn.	24

Sources: R. Fiske, *English Theatre Music in the Eighteenth Century* (Oxford, 1973); C. B. Hogan (ed.), *The London Stage, 1660–1800*, Part 4 (Carbondale, 1968).

Abel, and Handel for the King and Queen.[35]) Wolfgang copied a score of one of
Abel's symphonies, and more than a century later the existence of this manuscript
(written on the same type of English paper used for the symphony K. 16 and for
God is Our Refuge, K. 20) caused the work to be published in the *GA* as one of his
own early symphonies.[36] In their correspondence the Mozarts showed Bach a
degree of respect that they accorded few other musicians. Yet despite their
association with Abel and Bach, and despite claims to the contrary,[37] there is no
evidence that Wolfgang studied formally with either man.

As much as Mozart may have admired and studied the symphonies of Bach and
Abel, he was doubtless also influenced by other symphonists. London's concert-
and theatre-music was second to none in its quantity and variety. Even the
voracious Leopold became sated by these offerings, complaining (as already
mentioned) of 'the number of entertainments, which really weary one here'.[38] If he
followed his usual custom, Leopold sought every opportunity to expose his son to
music of many kinds, and, as he wrote to Hagenauer, 'What he [Wolfgang] knew
when we left Salzburg is a mere shadow compared with what he knows now. It
exceeds all that one can imagine . . . . in a word, my boy knows in this his eighth
year what one would expect only from a man of forty.'[39]

Each of London's many plays, operas, and oratorios had its overture or sinfonia
(sometimes preceded by a 'first music'), and concerts usually had at least two, an
outpouring of symphonies provided by both imported works and works of local
composers. Composers active in London as symphonists at the time of the Mozarts'
stay included seven mentioned in Leopold's diary (indicated by a cross) and at least
eight others: †Thomas Arne, William Bates, †François-Hippolyte Barthélémon,
William Boyce, †Gioacchino Cocchi, Thomas Erskine Earl of Kelly, †Felice de
Giardini, Tommaso Giordani, William Herschel, Thomas Norris, †Pietro Domenico Paradies, †George Rush, Giuseppe Sammartini, and John Christopher Smith
the Elder.[40] Along with Bach and Abel, this list constitutes as cosmopolitan a

[35] Leopold's letter of 28 May 1764. *Briefe*, i. 151; *Letters*, i. 68 (= i. 47). For thematic similarities between works of Abel or Bach and of Mozart, see Della Croce, *Le 75 sinfonie*, 292–3; and R. Dearling, *The Music of Wolfgang Amadeus Mozart: The Symphonies* (London, 1982), 88.

[36] The Symphony in E flat, K. 18 = Anh. 109¹ = Anh. A 51, published in the *GA*, xx (= Serie 8, No. 3), 23–36. Concerning the paper types, see A. Tyson, 'Mozarts Use of 10-Stave and 12-Stave Paper' in R. Elvers (ed.), *Festschrift Albi Rosenthal* (Tutzing, 1984), 277–89, here 278; and personal communication from A. Tyson.

[37] W. Knape, 'Abel, Vorbild und Lehrer Mozarts' in *Karl Friedrich Abel: Leben und Werk eines frühklassischen Komponisten* (Bremen, 1973), 57–61. J. C. Bach was one of the few musicians about whom only praise appears in the Mozart family's correspondence. When Bach died, Mozart paid him tribute in the Andante of the piano concerto, K. 414 = 385p, and when Abel died Mozart did likewise in the Finale of the violin sonata, K. 526—in each case basing his memorial on a work by the man whom he wished to honour. The model for the piano concerto Andante is Bach's Andante grazioso from his overture for the pasticcio *La calamità de' cuori* (1763); for the violin sonata, the Finale of Abel's violin sonata, Op. 5, No. 5.

[38] See n. 22 above.

[39] Letters of 28 May and 8 June 1764. *Briefe*, i. 151–2, 154; *Letters*, i. 68, 70–1 (= i. 47–9).

[40] This list was established with the aid of the following publications: G. R. Hill, *A Preliminary Checklist of Research on the Classic Symphony and Concerto to the Time of Beethoven (excluding Haydn and Mozart)* (Hackensack, 1970), 11; J. LaRue, 'The

collection of symphonists and symphonic styles as could be found in any European musical centre *c.*1765. At the beginning of his symphonic career, Wolfgang received a nearly ideal introduction to the genre; his earliest symphonies resemble the symphonies of London more than the symphonies of Salzburg discussed in the previous chapter.

Meaningful discussion of whether any of the several lost symphonies, known to Köchel only by their incipits, may have originated during the Mozarts' time in London must assume knowledge of the history of the Köchel Catalogue. A brief history of that venerable publication, with special reference to its handling of symphonies, is therefore presented in Appendix D. In the third edition of the Köchel Catalogue Einstein proposed three lost symphonies for Mozart's stay in London. The first, the A minor symphony K. Anh. 220 = 16a, was placed next to K. 16 in the chronology because, 'The early date of composition is manifestly recognizable, even from the few bars preserved.' K. 16a has recently been rediscovered; investigation shows that it was not connected with London, and it is discussed in Chapter 8.

Ex. 2.2 The lost Symphony in C major, K. Anhang 222 = 19b

The second was the C major symphony, K. Anh. 222 = 19b (Example 2.2), which Einstein put next to K. 19 in K^3 because 'the incipit is under the influence of the kind of symphony-beginning that is typical for J. C. Bach'. Indeed, that kind of beginning was a favourite of Bach's, and he used it, in one guise or another, to start seven symphonies. But if the incipit of K. 19b is to be used to date it, then note that the symphonies of Bach in question post-date Mozart's time in London, and that Mozart himself used the same or similar openings for several later works over a considerable period. This material was common coin—a march-like beginning

English Symphony: Some Additions and Annotations to Charles Cudworth's Published Studies', in C. Hogwood and R. Luckett (eds.), *Music in Eighteenth-Century England: Essays in Memory of Charles Cudworth* (Cambridge, 1983), 213–44; work lists for these composers in *The New Grove* and in *RISM*; B. S. Brook (ed.), *The Symphony and Overture in Great Britain: Twenty Works* (The Symphony 1720–1840, E/i) (New York, 1984). Sammartini had died by the time of the Mozarts' visit to London, but his symphonies, posthumously published, enjoyed a vogue.

that can be found in works by other composers as well (Example 2.3). Hence, even if K. 19b is by Mozart and even if it was influenced by J. C. Bach, it cannot on grounds of its first-movement incipit be dated to 1764–5. On the other hand, documentary evidence presented in the discussion of K. 19 in Chapter 3 suggests that Mozart did write a C major symphony at about the same time as K. 19 and 19a; K. 19b is the only candidate for the honour. And further documentary evidence, discussed in Chapter 6, suggests that K. 19b may be a work by Mozart originating before autumn 1767, possibly, although not necessarily, in London.

Ex. 2.3 Opening ideas similar to that of K. 19b

W. A. Mozart

(See also Ex. 8.11.)

Joseph Toeschi
Symphonies

Symphonies
?Carl Stamitz (Wolf L-20)

?Carl Stamitz (Wolf QS-33)

?Ernst Eichner (Wolf QS-37)

Joseph Schmitt

   Nothing is known about the five other symphony-incipits attributed to Mozart, discussed at the end of Chapter 5,[41] which may include one or more belonging to Mozart's London period. A sketch possibly dating from 1764–5 may give further evidence of his interest in writing symphonies. Eight bars of a C major melody in common time are found in the papers of the nineteenth-century collector Aloys Fuchs, under the rubric 'Mozart's contrapuntal studies with Leopold Mozart'.[42] Although this beginning is listed in K^3 and K^6 as a 'composing sketch for a sonata movement', its style is nearer to that of a first violin part of a symphony (Example 2.4). Whether this sketch has anything to do with the lost C major symphony, K. 19b, cannot be determined until that work re-emerges.

Ex. 2.4 Sketch possibly dating from 1764–5

Symphony in E flat major, K. 16

[Incipits 2.1]

---

[41] K. Anh. 215 = 66c, Anh. 217 = 66d, Anh. 218 = 66e, Anh. C 11.07, and Anh. C 11.08; see Example 5.7.
[42] Staatsbibliothek Preussischer Kulturbesitz, Mus. ms. 15,581. See K^6, remarks for K. 9. W. Plath believes, however, that the papers preserving this melody represent not the child Mozart studying with his father, but the adult Mozart teaching one of his pupils in the mid-1780s ('Beiträge zur Mozart-Autographie I', 112).

Instrumentation: strings, 2 oboes, 2 horns, [bassoon, harpsichord]
Autograph: Jagiellońska Library, Kraków
Principal source: none
Facsimile: *NMA*, iv/11/1, Beilage (complete)
Editions: *GA*, xx. 1–12 (= Serie 8, No. 1); *NMA*, iv/11/1. 3–20

Reasons why the Symphony in E flat, K. 16, may not be the symphony described as his first by his sister (even though it has usually been accepted as such) have already been set forth. If the heading at the top of the first page, 'Sinfonia / di Sig. Wolfgang Mozart a london 1764' is correct, the work must date from after Leopold's illness but before the New Year, that is to say, from October, November, or December of that year. The first page of the manuscript begins tidily, as if intended to be a fair copy, but here and on subsequent pages numerous corrections are entered by Wolfgang and Leopold in larger, cruder hands. The artistic and mechanical struggles in the creation of what is probably Wolfgang's earliest surviving symphony can be examined in the facsimile accompanying the *NMA*, which also offers an edition of the final version in its main volume and will present an edition of the earlier version in its Critical Report. A feature of special interest is that twice in the first movement (but nowhere else in the work) the bass is figured (Example 2.5). This was intended, it would seem, to help the continuo harpsichordist who, with only a basso part to play from, might otherwise have mistaken the changing harmonies over a pedal in the bass. It is unclear why K. 16 should have two chords figured, K. 19a and 22 be figured throughout, and K. 19 and 45a be unfigured.

The first movement opens with a three-bar fanfare in octaves, immediately contrasted by a quieter eight-bar series of suspensions, all of which is repeated. This leads to a brief agitato section, and the first group of ideas is brought to a close on the dominant. At this point the winds fall silent, and the initial idea of the second group is heard, extended by a passage of rising scales in the lower strings accompanied by tremolo in the violins. A brief coda concludes the exposition, which is repeated. The second half of the movement, also repeated, covers the same

Ex. 2.5 Figured-bass passage in the Symphony in E flat major, K. 16, first movement (bars 23–7)

ground as the first, working its way through the dominant and the relative minor to reach the tonic at the beginning of the second group. The movement faithfully captures the early symphonic vocabulary, with its alternations of loud and soft, syncopations, unisons, tremolos, rapid scales, and repeated notes. Only the sing-song melody at bars 37–43 and 99–106 seems to fall flat. Here Wolfgang originally wrote independent parts for first and second violins, but Leopold changed them to play in unison; even so, the melody projects weakly in these passages.

The brevity and lack of development of the Andante—a binary movement in C minor—give it an aphoristic character. Sustained winds, triplets in the upper strings, and duplets in the bass instruments combine effectively to paint a *scena* that would have been at home in an opera of the period, perhaps accompanying a nocturnal rendezvous. Brief as this movement is, however, it wanders a bit. That is, the immature composer had a good idea but perhaps not yet the craft to develop it cogently.

At the beginning of the Presto a new fanfare launches a jig-like finale in the form of a truncated rondo with a diatonic refrain and intervening episodes containing touches of chromaticism in the galant manner. The Köchel Catalogue states—and it has been dutifully repeated elsewhere—that K. 22 was Wolfgang's earliest symphony with a rondo-finale, unaccountably overlooking this movement. From the facsimile, the autograph appears to indicate that—even in the final version?—bars 17 to 61 should be repeated, a repeat omitted in both the *GA* and *NMA*, perhaps because first-time and second-time bars at 61 were left to be worked out by the performers (as in many eighteenth-century pieces). The refrain that follows at bars 62–77 is apparently also to be repeated. Hence, the form of the Finale in at least one version would appear to be: A A B B A [A?] C A coda, with A and the coda in E flat, B and C in B flat.

Writers who, wishing to chronicle Mozart's progress, have taken pains to point out the great differences in length, complexity, and originality between this earliest surviving symphony and his last few, may have missed a crucial point: there is little difference in length, complexity, or originality between K. 16 and the symphonies of Bach's Op. 3 and Abel's Op. 7, which were apparently among Mozart's chief models. The change in Mozart's symphonies over his lifetime must be explained not only by his own artistic and technical development, but by the stylistic evolution of the period.

Symphony in B flat major, K. 17 = Anh. 223a = Anh. C 11.02

[Incipits 2.2]

Instrumentation: strings, 2 oboes, 2 horns, [bassoon, harpsichord]
Autograph: unknown
Principal source: Preussische Staatsbibliothek, West Berlin, Mus. Ms. 15241 (mid-nineteenth century copy of André's lost manuscript made for Otto Jahn)
Facsimile: none
Edition: *GA*, xx. 13–22 (= Serie 8, No. 2)

A symphony once proposed as belonging to Mozart's London period is the Symphony in B flat, formerly K. 17. A set of parts for K. 17 under the name 'Mozart', formerly in the archives of the Lambach Monastery, is lost.[43] In the early nineteenth century the original manuscript score of the work belonged to Johann André, who wrote of it, 'To judge from the musical hand and other details, it

---

[43] The incipit is listed in the 'Catalogus Musicalium et Instrumentorum ad Chorum Lambacensem pertinentium conscriptge MDCCLXIIX 1768', a manuscript at the Lambach Monastery. See G. Lang, 'Zur Geschichte und Pflege der Musik in der Benediktiner-Abtei zu Lambach mit einem Katalog zu den Beständen des Musikarchives' (Ph.D. diss., Salzburg University, 1978), xliv.

appears to have been written during Mozart's tour in the 1760s'.[44] Köchel, perhaps hesitating to contradict André's opinion of the work, assigned it the number 17 in his Catalogue, which made it out to be one of the symphonies that Mozart composed in London in 1764–5. Köchel had examined the score, owned in 1860 by August André, and described it as a 'complete draft score, even nearly completely orchestrated'. On Köchel's authority K. 17 was published in the *GA*, but his remarks in K[1] suggest that he must have had doubts:

The uncommonly large format and better quality of the paper, the neat writing (despite the fact that it is only a draft score), the numerical heading definitely written in an unfamiliar hand, the rather unfamiliar handwriting—all these lead me to believe that the manuscript of Aug. André's under consideration is only a manuscript copy in which Mozart entered a few markings.

Another writer who examined the symphony felt that its style was not that of Mozart's other works of the 1760s, and tentatively assigned the work to the Vienna visit of 1767–8, without however questioning its attribution.[45] Abert accepted this notion, and gave the following reasons for questioning André's and Köchel's dating: (1) the work has four movements rather than three; (2) the first movement dispenses with a contrasting second subject and instead spins forth the opening theme, which is given a full recapitulation; (3) the first movement's march-like character differs from the 'theatrical' (i.e. operatic) character of Mozart's other symphonies of 1764–6; (4) the style of the first movement is not so much that of the 1764–6 symphonies as of Mozart's (and other Austrian composer's) orchestral serenades; (5) the minuet is stylistically reactionary, being developed from a single, principal motive, and having a thematic link to its trio; and (6) the minuet and trio bear the archaic labels 'Minuet I' and 'Minuet II'.[46] Points 2, 5, and 6 might have been cited to question the symphony's authorship and not simply its date. Wyzewa and Saint-Foix apparently accepted the work's genuineness and its assignment to London 1764,[47] but Saint-Foix later wrote of it with great scepticism:

I am strongly tempted, indeed, to pass over in silence a Symphony in B flat (K. 17) . . ., incomplete in its orchestration and containing the four movements of the classical German symphony. With its persistent march rhythm maintained throughout the whole of the first movement, the very short development, its echo effects in the Andante and the Finale, and its archaic and somewhat forced character, I am led to believe that this Symphony in B flat is *perhaps* merely one of Leopold Mozart's compositions—the first minuet in particular has

---

[44] Johann André, 'Thematisches Verzeichnis W. A. Mozartschen Manuskripte, chronologisch geordnet von 1764–1784 . . . abgeschlossen an 6. August 1833'. This manuscript is lost, but a copy made for Otto Jahn is in the British Library, Add. MS 34412.

[45] V. Wilder, *Mozart, l'homme et l'artiste* (Paris, 1880), 28.

[46] H. Abert, *W. A. Mozart*, 2nd edn. (Leipzig, 1923–4), i. 96.

[47] Wyzewa–Saint-Foix, i. 99–100 (= i. 119–22).

the stiffness and poverty of melodic invention that distinguish the Salzburg *Kapellmeister*[48]—that Wolfgang had been made to copy as an exercise. The fact is that, right up to his return to Vienna in 1767, all his boyish symphonies, without exception, will have but three movements and will conform at all points with Johann Christian Bach's idea of the symphony. Now here, all the traits proclaim the school of Leopold Mozart, and we can now ask ourselves if we are not faced with one of his recent compositions offered to his son as an initiation into the symphonic medium. In any case, this Symphony in B flat can scarcely rank as number one in Mozart's symphonic works; as we have seen already, it is unfinished[49]; it is, in fact, an essay in an archaic style that the boy quickly outgrew and to which he never returned.[50]

Reading between the lines, one gets the impression that Saint-Foix believed the symphony to be spurious, but hesitated to contradict Köchel directly, whereas Köchel in turn apparently had hesitated to contradict André. Unfortunately, Saint-Foix did not define what he meant in this context by 'archaic', but in light of the generally melioristic tendencies of his book and his low opinion of Leopold's music, 'archaic' is probably a code-word for 'not very good' rather than a valid assessment of chronology based upon musical style.

In 1932 the manuscript of K. 17 was sold by the Liepmannsohn Antiquariat in Berlin, on which occasion it was reported that the winds were present in only 33 bars of movement 1, 19 bars of movement 2, and 8 bars of the Finale, and that the string parts were missing in Minuet I.[51] When Einstein was preparing K[3] he examined the manuscript, then in the possession of the Hinterberger Antiquariat in Vienna. He altered Köchel's description of the orchestration from 'nearly' to 'fairly' complete. (The score examined by André, Köchel, and Einstein may have been incomplete, but the Lambach parts would not have been, so they were dealing with a defective source rather than an unfinished work.) Einstein responded to Köchel's remarks:

But the manuscript has nothing at all to do with Mozart; at the most a couple of dynamic signs could have been added by him in later years. At least the symphony's first movement is utterly distant from J. C. Bach's symphonic type, which was at that time the only standard one for Mozart. Other 'internal grounds' also testify here against Mozart's authorship. At most Mozart could have added the minuet for purposes of performance, although its orchestration is also not completed.

[48] The belittling of Leopold Mozart as a composer has been responsible for the attribution of a few of his best works to Wolfgang, for scholars who had as an article of faith that Leopold was only a mediocre composer whose style ceased to evolve after the 1750s automatically assigned non-autograph manuscripts by 'Signor Mozart' to Wolfgang if they exhibited a 'modern' style and artistic merit. Further to this point, see ch 6 at n. 26 and the discussion of K. 81 = 73*l*.

[49] As the manuscript of K. 17 is in fact not an autograph, Saint-Foix's argument is weak.

[50] Saint-Foix, 14–15 (= 5–6).

[51] *Versteigerung 62: Musikmanuskripte Wolfgang Amadeus Mozart aus dem Besitz von André Erben, Zweiter und letzten Teil* (Berlin, (1932)), [1]. The *GA*, which reconstructs the missing wind and string parts, does not completely agree with this account of the extent of the lacunae.

To Saint-Foix's hypothesis Einstein replied, 'But a copy does not convey the character of a sketch. And a glance at the manuscript shows that on no account is it an autograph of Wolfgang's; also Leopold is out of the question as its composer.' Einstein misread Abert's suggestion that K. 17 might have come from Vienna in 1767–8 to mean Vienna in the 1780s, and so responded with an astonished exclamation mark. He removed the work from the main chronology and gave it the number K. Anh. 223a, among the works of doubtful provenance. K^6 has taken over Einstein's remarks unchanged, giving K. 17 the designation Anh. C 11.02. Einstein's remarks about the style of this symphony—for instance, that only the minuet is in a style that could be Wolfgang's, that the work cannot have been by Leopold, that 'internal grounds' testify against Wolfgang's authorship—appear to have been based more on musical instincts than on close analysis. It is difficult to know precisely what he may have had in mind.

The purpose in reproducing the remarks of these scholars is to show what is known about K. 17 and to demonstrate how unsatisfactory its treatment has been. Köchel's, Saint-Foix's, and Einstein's statements lack rigour and flout a basic tenet of scholarship: an argument must be either replicable or falsifiable.

Jan LaRue has attempted to ascertain whether Einstein was correct. In a closely reasoned study, he comes to the tentative conclusion, on the basis of certain measurable stylistic features, that the work should not be attributed to Mozart. This is based on the work's 'level of activity', a concept that may be described as the number of 'events' occurring in the melody, rhythm, and harmony in each bar of music. The 'level of activity' is so much lower in K. 17 than in K. 16 and 22 that (LaRue concludes) the work must stem from another composer.[52] He does not raise the question, however, of whether the 'level of activity' in K. 17 might be similar to that in Wolfgang's symphonies of 1767–8 (K. 43, 45, 48), or in some of Leopold's symphonies among which—despite Einstein—most scholars have placed it.[53]

Scores and recordings of K. 17 are available, so the curious may decide for themselves whether what has been written about it is reasonable. To share Einstein's intuitive reaction that the work is not in Mozart's early symphonic style is easy, even if proof that would satisfy the rules of strict scholarship remains elusive. But the weight of the circumstantial and stylistic evidence favours the hypothesis that the work is by Leopold Mozart.[54]

[52] J. LaRue, 'Mozart Authentication by Activity Analysis: A Progress Report', *Mozart-Jahrbuch* (1978–9), 209–14.

[53] Saint-Foix (see n. 50 above); G. Cassaglia, *Il catalogo delle opere di Wolfgang Amadeus Mozart* (Bologna, 1976), 24; W. Plath, 'Mozart, Leopold', *The New Grove*, xii. 678 (= B flat symphony 6); Eisen, 'The Symphonies of Leopold Mozart', 302–3 (= symphony B♭6).

[54] For a convincing demonstration that, in the Lambach Catalogue, 'Mozart' means Leopold whereas Wolfgang is reliably called 'Mozart junior', and that K. 17 is probably by Leopold, see C. Eisen, 'Contributions to a New Mozart Documentary Biography', *Journal of the American Musicological Society* (1986), xxxix. 615–32, here 620–3.

Symphony in F major, K. Anh. 223 = 19a

[Incipits 2.3]

Instrumentation: strings, 2 oboes, 2 horns, [bassoon, harpsichord]
Autograph: unknown
Principal source: parts in Leopold's hand, Bayerische Staatsbibliothek, Munich
Facsimiles: one page in *Forum Musikbibliothek* (February 1981); one page in *NMA*, iv/11/1, xxii
Editions: Bärenreiter, 1981; *NMA*, iv/11/1, 35–48

The existence of this work was long known from the beginning of its first movement, notated on the wrapper of the Symphony in D, K. 19.[55] That it was a completed work and not a fragment had also been known, from its incipit in the Breitkopf & Härtel Manuscript Catalogue, with an indication of instrumentation. K. 19a reappeared at the beginning of February 1981, when press dispatches from Munich reported the discovery of a set of parts in Leopold's hand, found among some private papers.[56]

Leopold entitled the work, 'Sinfonia / in F / à / 2 Violinj / 2 Hautb: / 2 Cornj / Viola / e / Basso / di Wolfgango Mozart / compositore de 9 Añj.' The paper on which Leopold's parts for K. 19a were written is French,[57] but as Wolfgang was in England and Holland during his ninth year, it must have been exported from France. Since Mozart turned nine years old on 27 January 1765, the symphony, if it

---

[55] B. A. Wallner, 'Ein Beitrag zu Mozarts Londoner Sinfonien', *Zeitschrift für Musikwissenschaft* (1929–30), xii. 640–3.
[56] *The New York Times* (14 Feb. 1981), 1, 11.
[57] Private communication from Alan Tyson.

was in fact created in London as suggested by the number K. 19a given it by Einstein in K³, would then have to be placed in February, March, or April of that year, in time for either the concert of 21 February or perhaps one of the Bach–Abel concerts. But Einstein's dating of K. 19a was based upon its link to K. 19, whose dating is also uncertain (see Chapter 3), so K. 19a may possibly belong to the time between the Mozarts' arrival in Holland in September 1765 and Wolfgang's tenth birthday in January 1766.

The first movement opens with a broad melody in the first violins, accompanied by sustained harmonies in the winds, broken chords in the inner voices, and repeated notes in the bass instruments. A brief bit of imitative writing leads to a cadence on the dominant and the introduction of a contrasting second subject. Tremolo in the upper strings accompanying a triadic, striding bass-line leads to a closing subject. The second half of the movement presents the same succession of ideas as the first, and both sections are repeated. As the harmonic movement is from tonic to dominant in the first half and from dominant to tonic in the second, with little that could be described as developmental in the use of themes or harmonies, and as the double return of a recapitulation is absent, the movement is nearer to binary than to sonata form. In this regard the first movements of K. 16 and 19a are alike; in another regard the first movement of K. 19a seems superior: the kind of lapse in the handling of thematic material mentioned above in the discussion of K. 16 is no longer in evidence.

The oboes are silent in the B flat Andante, which, like the first movement, consists of two approximately equal sections, both repeated. The bass-line instruments and horns are assigned supporting roles, and a dialogue between first violins and violas is mediated by the second violins, which join now one, now the other.

Finales in $\frac{3}{8}$, $\frac{6}{8}$, $\frac{9}{8}$, or $\frac{12}{8}$ were common at the time K. 19a was written, and usually took on the character of an Italianate *giga*. Here, however, the rondo refrain has a different sort of rustic character. Many a play and opera on the London stage had a hornpipe, reel, or highland fling danced in it; these 'exotic' touches perhaps tickled the fancy of a nine-year-old composer, who may have tried to capture their spirit in this Finale.

Exactly which symphonies by Wolfgang were performed at the London concerts of 21 February and 11 March 1765, and possibly at some of the Bach–Abel concerts, remains a mystery. The presumably lost 'first' symphony described by Nannerl may have something to do with keyboard pieces in the London Notebook, or with some other work. K. 16b and K. 17 are no longer considered Wolfgang's work, and are listed in K⁶ (Anh. C 11.01 and 11.02) and elsewhere as

Leopold's. The recently rediscovered K. 16a has nothing to do with London. K. 18 is a symphony by Abel that Wolfgang apparently scored and reorchestrated. The possible association of K. 19b with London cannot be assessed unless this work is found, and the same may be said of five other lost symphonies, K. 66c–e and Anhang C 11.07–8. Among extant works, therefore, candidates for the London concerts comprise only three symphonies: K. 16, 19 (although on Dutch paper; see Chapter 3), and 19a (although on French paper).

England was known in the eighteenth century for the enthusiasm with which it received continental musicians and the extravagance with which it rewarded them. Early in the century Mattheson characterized the situation thus: 'He who at the present time wants to make a profit out of music betakes himself to England. The Italians exalt music; the French enliven it; the Germans strive after it; the English pay for it well.'[58] At just the time when the Mozarts were in London, Samuel Sharp suggested that the Italian musician, 'if he be well advised, will certainly set out for England, where talents of every kind are rewarded ten-fold above what they are at Naples.'[59] And at the time of Joseph Haydn's lucrative visits, the situation remained the same: 'Many foreign singers, fiddlers, and dancers are extravagently paid, and, if they are the least frugal, they are enabled to retire to their own country, where they may live in affluence, enriched by English money.'[60]

His correspondence reveals that Leopold Mozart understood this situation and strove successfully to take advantage of it. In the end he was offered a post in England, but chose not to accept because he wished his children to live in a Catholic country.[61] In later years Leopold and Wolfgang may more than once have had occasion to regret that decision. From about 1785 as Wolfgang's fortunes sank ever lower in Vienna he schemed to return to London, whence issued advantageous offers; but he never succeeded in arranging the trip, perhaps because he lacked his father's entrepreneurial skills. Be that as it may, Leopold must have

---

[58] Johann Mattheson, *Das neu-eröffnete Orchestre* (Hamburg, 1713), 211.

[59] Samuel Sharp, *Letters from Italy, Describing the Customs and Manners of that Country, in the Years 1765, and 1766* (London, 1766), 80. In an angry reply to Sharp's perceptions of Italy, Giuseppe Baretti presented another side of the story, however: 'As to the fiddlers and other Italians, who come here to play or to teach music, foolishly attracted by the great renown of English riches, they perform at the Opera and at Madam Cornelys', and trot about from house to house every morning, to give lessons for two guineas a dozen, while the winter lasts: but scarcely one in twenty has found himself twenty pounds the better at the year's end for these past twenty years past' (*An Account of the Manners and Customs of Italy* (London, 1768), i. 149–50).

[60] Friedrich August Wendeborn, *A View of England towards the Close of the Eighteenth Century* (London, 1791), ii. 237, written *c*.1785. I owe this reference to S. McVeigh, 'Felice Giardini: A Violinist in Late Eighteenth-century London', *Music and Letters* (1983), lxiv. 162–72. See further F. C. Petty, 'The Foreign Musician in England', *Italian Opera in London 1760–1800* (Ann Arbor, 1980), 3–17; H. S. Samuel, 'A German Musician comes to London in 1704', *The Musical Times* (1981), cxxii. 591–3.

[61] Letter of 19 Mar. 1765. *Briefe*, i. 180–1; *Letters*, i. 81–2 (= i. 56).

departed England satisfied with the attention given him and his precocious children, the considerable sums of money they had earned, the offer of employment, and the letters of introduction to patrons on the Continent. Perhaps equally valuable, in hindsight, was the fact that his son arrived on the Island the composer of a handful of short harpsichord pieces and left it a year and a quarter later a promising symphonist.

3

The Grand Tour (II): Holland—
France—Switzerland—Bavaria
(1765–1766)

—————————❧—————————

Writing from London, Leopold Mozart informed his correspondents the Hage-nauers, 'We shall not go to Holland, that I can assure everyone', and 'The Dutch Envoy in London several times begged me to visit the Prince of Orange at the Hague, but I let this go in by one ear and out by the other'.[1] Leopold had plans to bring his family home by way of Paris, Milan, and Venice, but then in late July 1765 (as he later wrote), at the beginning of the return journey when they were near Canterbury, something happened to change his mind:

On the very day of our departure the Dutch Envoy drove to our lodgings and was told that we had gone to Canterbury for the races and would then leave England immediately. He turned up at once in Canterbury and implored me at all costs to go to the Hague, as the Princess of Weilburg, sister of the Prince of Orange, was extremely anxious to see this child, about whom she had heard and read so much. In short, he and everybody talked at me so insistently and the proposal was so attractive that I had to decide to come.[2]

This 'proposal'—for the Mozarts to be official guests of the court—resulted in their remaining in Holland from September 1765 to April 1766. The earliest musical results of their detour were concerts in Ghent (5 September), Antwerp (7 or 8 September), The Hague (3 concerts between 12 and 19 September), and Leyden (19 or 20 September). From what is revealed in newspaper announcements, archival documents, and correspondence, none of these concerts involved symphonies, although full details are not known. In any case, the three concerts in the Hague must have met with success, for on 27 September Leopold announced a

---

[1] Letters of 28 May 1764 and 19 September 1765. *Briefe*, i. 147, 201; *Letters*, i. 66, 84 (= i. 46, 58).
[2] Letter of 19 Sept. 1765. *Briefe*, i. 201; *Letters*, i. 85 (= i. 58).

fourth in the *'s-Gravenhaegse Vrijdagse Courant*, and this time there was to be an orchestra:

By permission, Mr MOZART, Kapellmeister to the Prince-Archbishop of Salzburg, will have the honour of giving, on Monday, 30 September 1765, a GRAND CONCERT in the hall of the Oude Doelen at the Hague, at which his son, only 8 [*sic*] years and 8 months old, and his daughter, 14 years of age, will play concertos on the harpsichord. All the overtures will be from the hand of this young composer, who, never having found his like, has had the approbation of the Courts of Vienna, Versailles, and London. Music-lovers may confront him with any music at will, and he will play everything at sight. Tickets cost 3 florins per person, for a gentleman with a lady 5.50 fl. Admission cards will be issued at Mr Mozart's present lodgings, at the corner of Burgwal, just by [the inn called] the City of Paris, as well as at the Oude Doelen.[3]

Thus on 30 September 1765 two or more of Wolfgang's earliest symphonies were performed at the Hague in a hall that may be glimpsed in a drawing made a few years later by the Dutch artist, Johan Daniel de Gijsdaar (Plate IV). This concert too must have been a success for another, also to involve symphonies, was announced from 17 January 1766:

By permission, the children of Mr Mozart, Kapellmeister of the orchestra of the Prince-Archbishop of Salzburg, will have the honour of giving a grand concert on Wednesday, 22 January 1766, at the Oude Doelen at the Hague, at which his little son, 8 years and 11 months of age, and his daughter, aged 14, will play concertos on the harpsichord. All the overtures will be from the hand of this young composer, who, never having found his like, has had the approbation of the Courts of Vienna, Versailles, and London. The price of admission is 3 gulden per person, for a gentleman with a lady 1 ducat. Tickets are issued at Mr Mozart's lodgings at the house of Monsr. Eskes, master watchmaker, on the Hof-Spuy, the Hague, where the Court of Utrecht is situated, and also at the Oude Doelen.[4]

Among the works likely to have been performed at these two concerts was the D major symphony, K. 19.

Symphony in D major, K. 19

[Incipits 3.1]

[3] *'s-Gravenhaegse Vrijdagse Courant* (27 Sept. 1765). Deutsch, 49 (= 49–50). According to Leopold's letter of 12 Dec., Nannerl was unable to play because of illness. Leopold continued to lie about his children's ages in all the announcements quoted in this chapter.

[4] *'s-Gravenhaegse Vrijdagse Courant.* Deutsch, 49 (= 50). This translation and that at n. 22 have been adjusted by comparison with the originals, given in facsimile as plate 15b in W. Lievense, *De Famille Mozart op Bezoek in Nederland* (Hilversum, 1965). Lievense's plate 16 shows the hall of the Oude Doelen as it appears today.

Instrumentation: strings, 2 oboes, 2 horns, [bassoon, harpsichord]

Autograph: unknown

Principal source: parts in Leopold Mozart's hand, Bayerische Staatsbibliothek, Munich (Mus. Ms. Cim. 379i (*olim* 1583))

Facsimile: none

Editions: *GA*, xx. 37–46 (= Serie 8, No. 3); *NMA*, iv/11/1. 21–34

The wrapper that held the original set of parts for K. 19 survives; it is inscribed 'Sinfonia / a 2 Violinj / 2 Hautbois / 2 Corni / Viola / e / Basso / in F [overwritten with] C [crossed out in pencil and added alongside] D'.[5] These notations in Leopold's hand apparently indicate that the wrapper had served first for a Symphony in F (presumably K. 19a) and then for one in C (the missing K. 19b?), before being pressed into service for K. 19. The three symphonies were probably not intended to form an 'opus', since each replaced the one before it. Inside the cover Leopold copied the first fifteen bars of the first violin part of K. 19a. In the absence of other evidence, the sequence F—C—D may be taken to reflect the works' chronology, in which case the F and C major symphonies should receive new Köchel numbers lower than 19. The Dutch paper on which Leopold wrote the parts for K. 19 and the paper of the wrapper, which was manufactured in the Auvergne,[6] provide less useful clues to the date and place of composition of K. 19 than might be expected, for Dutch and French papers were regularly exported to England. None the less, the key sequence on the wrapper (F = K. 19a, C = ?19b, D = 19) will be accepted here as sufficient evidence for tentatively placing K. 19 during the Mozarts' time in Holland.[7]

---

[5] B. A. Wallner, 'Ein Beitrag zu Mozarts Londoner Sinfonien', *Zeitschrift für Musikwissenschaft* (1929–30), xii. 640–3; R. Münster, 'Neue Funde zu Mozarts symphonischem Jugendwerk', *Mitteilungen der internationalen Stiftung Mozarteum* (Feb. 1982), xxx. 2–11.

[6] Personal communication from Alan Tyson.

[7] The wrapper of K. 19, a bifolium of music paper, also has written on it a keyboard version of the symphony's second and third movements, copied (according to W. Plath, 'Beiträge zur Mozart-Autographie', *Mozart-Jahrbuch* (1960–1), 95) in a

The first movement begins with a fanfare of the kind used for signalling by posthorns or military trumpets, which sounds twice and is never heard again. The movement has the bright timbre that sharp keys impart to the strings. Like the first movements of K. 16 and 19a, this one is in binary form, here without repeats. An especially nice touch is the unprepared A sharp with which the second half begins—the kind of quirky chromatic twist much in evidence in Mozart's published sonatas of the period. As in symphonies such unforeseen inflections are connected more with the Hamburg Bach (Emanuel)[8] than with the London Bach (John Christian), it is perhaps worth pointing out that the Kapellmeister at the Hague, Christian Ernst Graaf, was a protégé of Emanuel Bach.

The G major Andante, *sempre p*, possesses a conventional, pastoral serenity, its 'yodelling' melodies and droning accompaniments evoking thoughts of hurdy-gurdies and bagpipes. This movement had its models in certain types of melody originating in Naples and popular in those parts of Europe to which Italian opera had penetrated.[9] An occasional 'yodelling' in the melody of the Finale, a binary movement in jig style with both sections repeated, ties it to the previous movement.

Symphony in B flat major, K. 22

[Incipits 3.2]

'not unfailingly childish hand'. But as the keyboard arrangement incorporates only the viola and *basso* parts, it must be the *secondo* part of a four-hand version; and the 'not unfailingly chidish hand' may be Wolfgang's.

[8] See H. Danuser, 'Das *imprévu* in der Symphonik: Aspekte einer musikalischen Formkategorie in der Zeit von Carl Philipp Emanuel Bach bis Hector Berlioz', *Musiktheorie* (1986), i. 61–81.

[9] W. Fischer, 'Zwei Neapolitanische Melodietypen bei Mozart und Haydn', *Mozart-Jahrbuch* (1960–1), 7–21, esp. 17.

Instrumentation: strings, 2 oboes, 2 horns, [bassoon, harpsichord]
Autograph: lost
Principal source: score in Leopold Mozart's hand, Staatsbibliothek Preussische Kulturbesitz, West Berlin (Mus. Ms. Autogr. W. A. Mozart 22)
Facsimile: none
Editions: *GA*, xx. 47–55 (= Serie 8, No. 5); *NMA*, iv/11/1. 49–62

By the time of the second of the two orchestral concerts at the Hague, Wolfgang had composed this new work. At the top of Leopold's score of K. 22, which is written on the kind of Dutch paper described in the discussion of K. 32 below, is the inscription 'Synfonia / di Wolfg. Mozart à la Haye nel mese December 1765'. A note on the manuscript in Nissen's hand links the work's composition to the installation of William V as Regent of the Netherlands, a suggestion subsequently accepted by a few of Mozart's biographers. But Nissen was surely mistaken, for the installation occurred three months after the date on the symphony manuscript. His reason for connecting K. 22 with the installation was probably a passage in Niemetschek's biography, which reads, 'Early in 1766, for the celebration of the coming-of-age of the Prince of Orange, young Mozart composed several symphonies, variations, and arias';[10] but other works are more probable than K. 22, whose creation is likely to have been for the public concert of 22 January.

The opening movement, binary and without repeats, has no tempo indication, which by eighteenth-century convention is therefore understood to be a generic 'Allegro'. It begins with a tonic pedal in the bass for fourteen bars, in a manner usually asssociated with the Mannheim symphonists but which originated in Italy[11] and which by 1765 could be heard in many parts of western Europe. A contrasting second subject, a dialogue between the first and second violins, is followed by the apparently mandatory theme in the bass instruments accompanied by tremolo in the upper strings. A brief transition section puts the opening idea through the keys of F minor and C minor, returning to the home key shortly after the recapitulation of the second subject, with the rest following essentially as in the exposition.

The G minor Andante, a simple A B A coda, exhibits chromaticism, imitative textures, and occasional stern unisons. Abert even thought that he heard foresha-

---

[10] Franz Niemetschek, *Leben des K. K. Kapellmeisters Wolfgang Gottlieb Mozart nach Originalquellen beschrieben* (Prague, 1798), ed. E. Rychnovsky as *W. A. Mozart's Leben nach Originalquellen beschrieben* (Prague, 1905), 12 (= H. Mautner (trans.), *Life of Mozart* (London, 1956), 22).

[11] E. K. Wolf, 'On the Origins of the Mannheim Symphonic Style' in J. W. Hill (ed.) *Studies in Musicology in Honor of Otto E. Albrecht* (Kassel, 1980), 197–239.

dowings here of the Andante of Mozart's penultimate symphony, K. 550,[12] but such a comparison does injustice to both works, which were composed two decades apart in disparate styles, for varying purposes and different audiences. As if the Andante's intensity of feeling were dangerous in a work intended for polite society, the Finale—a sort of brisk minuet in the form of a rondo, originally marked Allegro moderato—makes amends by leaning in the other direction. Its opening resembles that of the quartet, 'Signore, di fuori son gia i suonatori' in the Finale to the second act of *Le nozze di Figaro* as well as the beginnings of two movements by J. C. Bach (Example 3.1). Indeed, this is a conventional theme-type of the period, the 'theme with turn figures on a triad frame'.[13]

Because this is the first of Mozart's symphonies in B flat, a technical question about the notation of the horns must be raised. (These remarks apply equally to movements with horns in C.) Some but not all of the orchestral horns surviving from the period have crooks enabling them to play in either B flat (or C) basso or B flat (or C) alto—that is to say, so that the sounding pitch is either a ninth (or an octave) below or a second below (or at the unison with) the written pitch. Many B flat and C orchestral horn parts of the 1760s and 1770s do not specify which crook was intended, a circumstance suggesting that there may have been some widely understood convention. This is not merely a technical question but an aesthetic one, for the spacing of the chords in the horns and oboes is radically altered by an octave transposition, and the colour imparted to the orchestra by the mellower, low horns is entirely different from that imparted by the more brilliant, high ones. That Mozart took the spacing of wind chords seriously is shown by not infrequent corrections in his own manuscripts, as well as by the corrections he made to the work of his pupil Thomas Attwood, discussed in Chapter 11.

Prior to the 1960s, recordings and performances of B flat and C orchestral works of the middle and late eighteenth century usually used horns at the lower pitch, which accorded well with post-Romantic notions of orchestral horn timbre and technique. Then, however, in his seminal book on Haydn's symphonies and in his complete edition of those works, H. C. Robbins Landon came out in favour of the high pitch, on the grounds that he was aware that the option existed and liked the brilliant 'clarino' sound it produced.[14] Thus, in the first complete recording of Haydn's symphonies, Antal Dorati used the high-pitched, B flat or C horns because he had players good enough, the sound pleased him, and he could lean on the

[12] H. Abert, *W. A. Mozart* (Leipzig, 1923), i. 95.

[13] J. LaRue, 'Significant and Coincidental Resemblances between Classical Themes', *Journal of the American Musicological Society* (1961), xiv. 224–34.

[14] H. C. Robbins Landon, *The Symphonies of Joseph Haydn* (London, 1955), 340; idem (ed.), *Joseph Haydn: Kritische Ausgabe sämtlicher Symphonien* (Vienna, 1965–8), i. xxi. Landon's opinion about the high horn parts have been widely accepted as fact, for instance in R. Dearling, *Music of Wolfgang Amadeus Mozart: The Symphonies* (London, 1982), 63.

Ex. 3.1 Opening ideas similar to that of K. 22, Finale

J. C. Bach (Terry. p. 288, No. 10)

(p. 292, No. 4)

(p. 306, No. 2)

A. G. Pampani

Le nozze di Figaro, Act I, Scene ix

authority of a distinguished Haydn specialist.[15] Paul Bryan countered with the suggestion that, since Michael Haydn and Mozart sometimes specifically indicated B flat alto and since such parts can be difficult to play, the lack of any indication to the contrary should be understood to mean B flat basso, and taken as the normal practice.[16] Dorati's criteria assume that our intuitive tastes and the eighteenth-century's are compatible, while Bryan's criteria subject eighteenth-century musicians to a test of notational consistency that they are unlikely to pass. That certain horn parts are easy or difficult for modern players is another argument with little validity. The important point is that little historical evidence has been adduced to support the Landon–Dorati high-horn theory.

More interesting is internal evidence in the music itself: the ranges of Mozart's orchestral horn parts. The shorter any instrument is, the fewer upper partials are readily produced on it. Thus a double-bass viol, for example, can produce many more harmonics than a violin, and, indeed, low instruments in general have potentially greater ranges than high ones. Competent eighteenth-century composers knew these acoustical verities, and they called for fewer partials in their high horn parts than in their low ones. This is demonstrated for Mozart in the discussion in Chapter 8 of K. 132, in which a pair of horns in E flat alto uses partials 3 to 9 while a pair in E flat basso uses 3 to 12 (Example 8.7). This comparison is confirmed by other works: horns in B flat basso in *La finta semplice*, K. 51 = 46a, No. 7, reach the twelfth partial, those in B flat alto in No. 20 only the ninth. Horns in the Andante of the symphony K. 130, which must be in B flat basso because Mozart placed them below a pair of horns in F, reach the thirteenth partial; in the symphony K. 319 where the B flat horns are marked by Mozart 'alti', they are restricted to the eleventh. The C alto horns in the other movements of the symphony K. 130 go no higher than the tenth partial, except for one extraordinary soloistic passage in the Trio, where they briefly soar up to the twelfth. The following generalizations may be drawn from these and other horn parts of Mozart's: the first horn seldom goes below the sixth partial except in passages in which the two horns are written in unison; it seldom goes above the tenth or eleventh partial if it is a high-pitched horn, but will do so more often if it is low-pitched. The second horn is written from the third partial upward, and—never written above the first horn—it will seldom exceed the ninth partial except in

[15] Dorati's remarks, made during the Haydn Conference Festival, Washington, 1975, do not appear in the published version (J. P. Larsen, H. Serwer and J. Webster (eds.), *Haydn Studies: Proceedings of the International Haydn Conference, Washington, D. C., 1975* (New York, 1981). Hereafter cited as *Haydn Studies*.)

[16] P. Bryan, 'Haydn's Alto Horns: Their Effect and the Question of Authenticity', *Haydn Studies*, 190–2; *idem*, 'The Horn in the Works of Mozart and Haydn: Some Observations and Comparisons', *The Haydn Yearbook* (1975), ix. 189–255; and a personal communication from Professor Bryan. However S. Gerlach argues that, except for his London works, Haydn's orchestral horns in B flat are *alto* and those in C *basso*, in the absence of indications to the contrary ('Haydns Orchesterpartituren: Fragen der Realisierung des Textes', *Haydn-Studien* (1984), v/3. 169–83, here 180–3).

unison passages and in low-pitched horn parts in which the horns rise briefly above the orchestral texture in high thirds. By these standards (to which there are occasional exceptions), the B flat horns in K. 22 must be basso, as they go right up to the thirteenth and eleventh partials respectively. Although the weight of evidence supports this conclusion, there remains one anomaly: if the horns in K. 22 are pitched in the lower octave, the Andante will begin with a second inversion triad, with the second horn on the fifth of the chord heard below the 'sounding bass' in the violas.[17]

'Symphony' in D major, K. 32, 'Galimathias musicum'

[Incipits 3.3]

[17] This last point was suggested to me by Bertil van Boer. Further concerning the B flat horn problem, see *NMA*, ii/5/12. xxxii–xxxiii and ii/5/2(i). xxi–xxii. Concerning possible interpretations of improperly resolved 6–4 chords caused by the bass-line rising above other parts, see J. Webster, 'The Bass Part in Haydn's Early String Quartets', *The Musical Quarterly* (1977), lxiii. 390–424.

Instrumentation: strings, 2 oboes, 2 horns, [bassoon, harpsichord]
Autograph: Gemeentemuseum, The Hague; Bibliothèque nationale, Paris
Principal source: copyist's score in Donaueschingen
Facsimile: *NMA*, iv/12/1. xxi
Editions: *GA*, xxxix. 107–20 (= Serie 24, No. 12), Critical Report, 6–17; *NMA*, iv/12/1. 3–22, 97–117

On the occasion of the installation of the eighteen-year-old William V, Prince of Orange, as Regent of the Netherlands, the ten-year-old Mozart composed a suite of pieces for small orchestra and obbligato harpsichord, with the title *Galimathias musicum*. The *Galimathias* is a quodlibet, some movements based on tunes known to Wolfgang and his Salzburg compatriots, others on tunes familiar to his Dutch audience. The work survives in two versions: a preliminary draft in which Wolfgang's and Leopold's hands are found intermingled, and a fair copy made by a professional copyist apparently for a performance in Donaueschingen some months later. The draft version is in two sections: the one in the Hague is on upright format paper, the other in Paris on oblong paper. The latter contains four movements and bears the heading in an unknown hand: 'Sinfonia . . . Gallimathias musicum'. (Subsequently another, unknown hand crossed out this heading and substituted the incorrect information that the music belonged to Mozart's opera *Mitridate*.) The 'Sinfonia' manuscript is on a type of Dutch paper similar to that used for the Symphony in B flat, K. 22, and for the arias 'Per pietà, bell' idol mio', K. 78 = 73b, and 'O temerario Arbace—Per quel paterno amplesso', K. 79 = 73d, which (despite erroneously high Köchel numbers) were also composed in Holland in 1766.[18] The Paris–Hague manuscript of K. 32 was unknown to Köchel; von Waldersee gave it the number Anh. 100a in K^2 and published it in the Critical Report of the *GA*. The order of the movements in the Paris and Hague draft version and the Donaueschingen fair copy differs, and movements of the introductory 'sinfonia' (if it was one) have been dispersed in the latter. Wolfgang Plath, who doubts that there ever was to be a sinfonia, bases his edition in the *NMA* on the Donaueschingen version, placing the draft version in an appendix. This is practical, because the draft version is fragmentary whereas the Donaueschingen copy is fully worked out, and also logical, for the Donaueschingen copy, stemming directly

[18] Information kindly communicated by A. Tyson. See also W. Plath, 'Beiträge zur Mozart-Autographie II: Schriftchronologie 1770–1780', *Mozart-Jahrbuch* (1976–7), 131–73, here 139.

from Leopold and Wolfgang, contains a fully authorized version. But as the former dates from before and the latter from after the installation of the Regent, no source survives to reveal what was performed on 11 March 1776 at the court of Orange.

If the four movements of the Paris autograph were intended to form a sort of sinfonia, then it must have been a parody of one, and, indeed, Wyzewa and Saint-Foix dubbed it 'petite symphonie burlesque'.[19] This would have been in keeping with the rest of the work, which, in its quotations of Dutch and German popular songs and other special effects, displays strongly satirical and parodistic elements. The sinfonia movements are on a tiny scale. Without the examples of the Mozart's other symphonies from this period, this extreme brevity might incorrectly have been attributed to the tender age of the composer. Comparison of the 'sinfonia' of K. 32 with his earliest symphonies (K. 16, 19, 19a, 22, 45a) reveals that this so-called sinfonia is an anomaly.

The opening Allegro is merely a few joyful noises—repeated notes, loud chords, rapid scale passages—in short, a brief fanfare. The D minor Andante in binary form is strangely orchestrated, with the melody in the violas. This works well, but it must be some sort of joke, for orchestral music of the period virtually never gives the melody to an inner part. (An intriguing exception in this context, however, is found in Leopold Mozart's *Sinfonia burlesca*, Grove/Eisen G2, which suppresses violins entirely and gives the melodies to the violas.)

In the place where a minuet and trio might be expected (although Mozart's symphonies had not yet had one), a musette is heard in which, over a rustic drone, the Christmas carol, 'Joseph, lieber Joseph mein' (= 'Resonet in laudibus') sounds. The melody is presented in a particular version—not the one usually found in song books of the period, but one known to every denizen of Salzburg because it was played in the appropriate season by a mechanical carillon ('Hornwerk') in the tower of the Hohensalzburg Castle that dominates the city.[20] Wolfgang would return to this tune in 1772, quoting it in the original slow movement of his symphony, K. 132. The musette's contrasting D major trio takes the form of a rustic horn duet, with a bare bass-line as the sole accompaniment. Was this movement deleted from the final version of K. 32 because it was too truly rustic in character? To permit a continuous drone with its concomitant static harmony (or, really, no harmony) was several steps beyond Wolfgang's usual practice, which merely alluded to matters rustic while keeping a safe artistic distance from them.

---

[19] Wyzewa–Saint-Foix, i. 291 (= i. 319).

[20] M. M. Schneider-Cuvay, ' "Josef, lieber Josef mein"—Verarbeitung der Melodie vom 17. bis zum 19. Jahrhundert', in W. Deutsch and H. Dengg (eds.), *Die Volksmusik im Lande Salzburg: 11. Seminar für Volksmusikforschung 1975* (Schriften zur Volksmusik, iv) (Vienna, 1979), 194–8; *idem*, E. Hintermaier and G. Walterskirchen (eds.), *Aufzüge für Trompeten und Pauken—Musikstücke für mechanische Orgelwerke* (Denkmäler der Musik in Salzburg, i) (Munich, 1977), xi–xii. 58.

(Leopold's *Peasants' Wedding*—a piece similar to the *Galimathias*, but intended for a perhaps earthier Salzburg audience—is, on the contrary, filled with rusticisms.)

The Finale offers another happy noise, to close the 'sinfonia' as it began. It is a tiny, two-part form, with more al fresco horn duets at the beginning of the second section. This movement has the character of an entrata or processional march.

Owing to a fortunate accident, a fragment of what may be another symphonic movement survives, on a sheet of music paper inserted into the Divertimento in B flat, K. 186 = 159b of 1772. Apparently needing a bit of paper to finish a movement of K. 186, Mozart had removed this leaf from an earlier manuscript because, aside from the sixteen-bar sketch in E major (Example 3.2), it was blank. The leaf is like paper used in the Symphony in B flat, K. 22, and in the *Galimathias musicum*,[21] so the sketch it contains probably dates from the time in Holland. Einstein, recognizing the earlier character of the inserted leaf, suggested in K^3 that the fragment was intended as an Andante for the Symphony in A minor, K. 16a (then known only by its first movement incipit), but the andantes of Mozart's authentic minor-key symphonies are in the major subdominant (K. 183 = 173dB, 550), not in the dominant. If this fragment was intended as a symphony andante, then a work in B major seems implied, which was not a possibility. Mozart wrote very few movements in E major at any time in his career. The fragment remains an enigma.

The length of the Mozarts' stay in Holland was in part a result of illnesses suffered by Wolfgang and Nannerl, and in part a result of a desire to remain long enough to take advantage of the liberal patronage likely to accompany the prince's installation. But it may also be attributed to favourable reception and success in making money from their concerts. Additional performances occurred in the following cities (an asterisk indicating that an orchestra was involved and symphonies probably performed): Amsterdam (*29 January, 26 February), the court of Orange (*11 March), the Hague (*mid-March), Haarlem (early April), Amsterdam (16 April), and Utrecht (*21 April). The Amsterdam concerts are better documented than the others. Notices for the first of these appeared in the *Amsterdamsche Dingsdagsche Courant* from 21 January. The characteristic announcement on the day before the concert is familiar in most of its contents:

Mr MOZART, Kapellmeister of the orchestra of the Prince-Archbishop of Salzburg, will have the honour of giving, on Wednesday, 29 January 1766, a grand concert in the hall of the Riding-School in Amsterdam, at which his son and his daughter, the one aged 8 years & 11 months, the other aged 14, will perform concertos on the harpsichord. All the overtures will be from the hand of this little composer, who, never having found his like,

---

[21] I am indebted to Alan Tyson for this information.

Ex. 3.2 Reconstruction of an orchestral draft possibly dating from 1766

Mozart's draft contains several mistakes and internal inconsistencies. This reconstruction is based on the assumption that he was hearing it in G sharp minor and B major, but was defeated by certain aspects of musical notation he had yet to master.

was the admiration of the Courts of Vienna, Versailles, and London. Music-lovers may submit pieces of music to him at will, which he will perform entirely at sight. The price per person is two florins. The public is requested to obtain its tickets at Mr Mozart's lodgings at the Golden Lion in the Warmoestraat, or from [the music dealer] J. J. Hummel, on the Vygendam. No money will be received at the entrance to the hall. N.B. They will play with four hands on one harpsichord.[22]

Less than a month later in the same paper one reads that 'the universal contentment & satisfaction given by Mr MOZART's children has induced the lovers of music to desire a second concert, which will be held on Wednesday, 26 February, at the hall of the Riding-School', and later announcements add that 'these two children will not only perform concertos together on different harpsichords, but also on the same with four hands, and at the end the son will play his own caprices, fugues, and other pieces of the most profound music on the organ'.[23] This concert probably did not involve orchestral music, for Leopold would hardly have gone to the expense of hiring an orchestra without mentioning it in his publicity. And, referring to the concert in a letter, he also made no mention of an orchestra or symphonies:

Although during our presence in Amsterdam all public productions were strictly

[22] Deutsch, 49–50 (= 50–1). See note 4.
[23] Ibid. 50–1 (= 52).

forbidden on account of Lent, we were nonetheless allowed to give a concert, specifically because—as the pious and circumspect resolution reads—'the dissemination of the miracle talent serves to praise God'. Nor was anything presented but Wolfgang's own instrumental music.[24]

In 1766 Ash Wednesday fell on 12 February and Easter on 30 March, so the Mozarts' concert of 26 February was indeed a Lenten concert.

Unlike London, which had more than one standing orchestra and a group of what are now called 'free-lance' musicians, Amsterdam had only its Schouwburg Theatre orchestra, which therefore must have been the group employed by the Mozarts for their concert of 29 January 1766. A Prussian visitor some years later informs us that 'the theatre is beautiful, but too small for Amsterdam. It has only fifty-four boxes, and each of them takes only six persons . . . . The orchestra was quite good'.[25] In 1765 the orchestra consisted of 14 musicians,[26] perhaps distributed: 3 first and 2 second violinists, 1 violist, 1 cellist, 1 bass player, 2 oboists (doubling on flute?), 1 bassoonist, 2 horn players, and 1 harpsichordist.

In his travel diary Leopold noted two Amsterdam musicians named Kreusser.[27] Johann Adam Kreusser had been leader of the Schouwburg orchestra since 1752, and his younger brother Georg Anton had from 1759 taken lessons with him while also playing in that ensemble. There is evidence that the latter heard Wolfgang's B flat symphony K. 22 (presumably as a member of the orchestra that performed it), because he paid it the compliment of borrowing the beginning of its first movement for his own B flat symphony, Op. 5, No. 3, published in Amsterdam in 1770.[28] A comparison between the first movements of Mozart's and Kreusser's symphonies (Example 3.3) reveals that they are related for eight and a half bars, after which they diverge, save for the return of the opening passage at the recapitulation. The other movements are entirely unrelated. Leopold and Wolfgang re-encountered Kreusser in Milan in 1770, and—irony of ironies—in 1778 Kreusser's success in obtaining a Kapellmeister's post was held up as an example to Wolfgang, who was failing miserably to achieve the same distinction.[29]

The orchestral situation at the Hague was more complicated than that at Amsterdam. In Leopold's travel diary are listed the names of a number of the Hague musicians:

---

[24] Fragment of a letter from May 1766. *Briefe*, i. 218; not in *Letters*.
[25] Wilhelm Heinse, 'Reise nach Holland, Oct. 1784', *Sämtliche Werke* (Leipzig, 1909), vii. 309–10. The theatre had burnt in 1772 and been rebuilt.
[26] D. Scheurleer, *Het Muziekleven in Nederland in de 18ᵉ Eeuw* (The Hague, 1909), 200.
[27] *Briefe*, i. 217.
[28] B. van Boer pointed out to me the identity of the two incipits.
[29] Letters of 10 Nov. 1770 and 27 Aug. 1778. *Briefe*, i. 403, ii. 453; *Letters*, i. 250 (= i. 170), ii. 897 (= ii. 604). Leopold attributed Kreusser's success to his symphonies, which 'go easily into the ear'.

Ex. 3.3 Georg Anton Kreusser: Symphony in B flat major, Op. 5, No. 3

Christian Ernst Gra(a)f, Court Kapellmeister, composer of symphonies
P. Keller, court musician
W. Keller, violinist, son of the previous
Jan Frederik Weis, court musician
Johann Georg Christoph Schetky, cellist and composer
Johann Christian Fischer, oboe virtuoso and composer
Georg Martin Ulrich, oboist
Giovanni Battista Zingoni, singer, composer of symphonies, Court Kapellmeister
Francesco Pasquale Ricci, maestro and composer of symphonies
Grundlach van Gundelach, double-bass player
Jean Boutmy, harpsichordist, composer, organist to the Portugese ambassador
Spandau, horn player
Major General Wouter Eckhardt, amateur cellist.[30]

This list contains nearly enough instrumentalists to perform one of Wolfgang's early symphonies, but as Kapellmeister Graaf apparently led the Mozarts' public concert of 30 September 1765,[31] and as the Mozarts were official guests of the court, it is more likely that one must reckon with the court orchestra. The court had two

[30] *Briefe*, i. 214–15.
[31] A. Layer, 'Christian Ernst Gra[a]f', *The New Grove*, vii. 610.

regular ensembles, the Chapel of the House of Orange, which, according to rosters of 1766, 1773, and *c.*1781, had ten or eleven members, and the court concert orchestra. During the period 1766–8 the latter consisted of a dozen instrumentalists and three vocalists. Only four musicians (Graaf, Ulrich, Dambach, and Spandau) belonged to both groups. The principal duty of the former group was to provide private music for the royal family, while the latter group gave annual series of public concerts. It seems that members of the Chapel sometimes assisted at the public concerts.[32] Thus, when Mozart's symphonies were publicly performed at the Hague, the orchestra led by Graaf may have been the court concert orchestra supplemented by a few other players from the Chapel, the total numbering a dozen or so, perhaps as small a group as strings 3—3—1—1—1 with pairs of oboes and horns, a bassoon, and a harpsichord. If, on the other hand, all the members of both court ensembles were employed and a few amateur string-players added to reinforce the tuttis, the orchestra might have attained a strength of 23 or 24 members, perhaps strings 5—5—2—3—2, with the rest as before. Figures for the concert and opera orchestra at the Hague for later dates (Table 3.1) tend to support the latter suggestion. These figures and lists of players, extrapolated from archival data, give the range within which may be located the size of the orchestra that gave first or early performances of Mozart's earliest symphonies.

TABLE 3.1 Concert and opera orchestras at The Hague

	vn. I	vn. II	va.	vc.	db.	fl.	ob.	cl.	bn.	hn.	tpt.	kd.	misc.	TOTAL
1775	4	4	2	2	1	0	2	0	2	2	0	0	—	19
1780	5	4	2	2	1	—2—		0	1	2	0	0	serpt.	20

Source: D. Scheurleer, *Het Muziekleven in Nederland in de 18ᵉ Eeuw* (The Hague, 1909).

William V had a strong musical lineage. His mother, Princess Anne of Britain, had been Handel's loyal pupil and patron, and a patron of Jean-Marie Leclair l'aîné. As she gave her son a musical upbringing, it is hardly surprising that there were considerable musical entertainments associated with his installation (as well as fireworks that Leopold characterized as 'astounding'[33]). The orchestra for these entertainments, supplemented for the gala occasion, as surviving archival documents reveal, was the following:

---

[32] M. de Smet, *La Musique à la cour de Guillaume V, prince d'Orange* (Utrecht, 1973), 29–36, 39–42, 53, 56, 70.
[33] *Briefe*, i. 216.

'Musikanten bij de Tafel Musiek'[34]
[8, 10, and 12 March 1766]

Violino 1mo

Violino 1mo

[Christian Ernst] Gra[a]f*†

[W.] Keller jun:†

Groneman [i]

Groneman [ii]

Weber

[Johan Conrad] Spangenberg [also a music dealer]

Viol: 2do

[Jan Frederik] Weiss sen:*†

Weiss jun:†

Schou

Hederich

Steger

Stechway, maj: [viola]*

Halbsmit [viola]*

Stechweg jun: [?viola]

Gretzer [?viola]

Oboe 1

Keller sen: [also flute]*†

Keller minim: +

Oboe 2

Ulrich*†

Klein [also flute]

Hoorn 1

Spandau [sen:]†

Fijnebert

Hoorn 2

Spandau [jun:]

[Buchard] Hummel [also a music dealer]

Fagot

Rhoeling†

Muilman

Contre Bass

[Gundlach van] Gundelach*†

Dampach†

Violoncell:

Mueller*

Gautier

Sch[w]ertzer [Schuetzer]

1 pauker

6 Trompetter.

* Musicians in the regular employ of the court.   † Musicians whose names appear in Leopold's diary.

[34] De Smet, *Guillaume V*, 33–4.

Hence, the orchestra that gave the first performance of K. 32 (and, if Niemetschek was correctly informed, some symphonies) had a make-up of 6—6—3—3—2 / 0–2—2–4—0—2 / 4—(2)—1, or a total of about 36 musicians not counting the continuo player, who was undoubtedly the ten-year-old composer himself.

In Utrecht Leopold requested permission to use the orchestra and hall of the Collegium Musicum Ultrajectinum, a venerable institution dating from 1632, in whose minutes a record of the transaction is found: '18 April [1766]. Monsieur Mozart, Virtuoso, having asked the College for the use of the orchestra and instruments, has been granted this after deliberation according to old usage and custom.'[35] At that time the Collegium consisted of a group of amateurs led by a paid, professional concertmaster. Their repertory included—in addition to such classics as concerti grossi by Corelli, Locatelli, and Geminiani, solo concertos by Vivaldi and Tartini, and overtures by Handel—an up-to-date selection of symphonies by Abel, J. C. Bach, Dittersdorf, Mahaut (the only native composer represented), and Toeschi.[36] Thus the musicians of the Collegium would have been familiar with the style of Wolfgang's early symphonies. On the very day Leopold received permission to use the Collegium orchestra, the customary announcement appeared in the *Utrechtsche Courant*:

Sieur Mozart, Kapellmeister in the service of His Highness the Prince-Archbishop of Salzburg, will have the honour of giving a grand Concert next Monday afternoon, 21 April, in the Music Room of the Vreeburg at Utrecht, at which his little son, aged 9, and his daughter, aged 14, will perform sonatas and concertos on the harpsichord. All the symphonies will be from the hand of this little composer, who has won the admiration of the Courts of Vienna, France, England, and Holland. Price for a gentleman with a lady 3 gulden and for a single person 2 gulden. The tickets are to be had of the aforesaid Mr Mozart, who lodges with Mr Mos in the Plaets-Royal, Utrecht.[37]

Leopold's letters reveal that in Holland he found much to interest him in the architecture, the church organs, the commerce, the customs, and the works of art—especially the paintings of Rubens. Yet in the 1760s Holland was a musical backwater: musical activities were numerous, but there were no major orchestras, no important composers, few well-known virtuosos, and there was hardly any opera; church music was in the doldrums, and a formerly brilliant music-publishing industry in a state of decline. In short, it was no London. The Mozarts apparently arrived with a letter of introduction to the English ambassador at The

[35] Deutsch, 52 (= 54). Facsimile: as in n. 4 above, but plate 37.
[36] J. du Saar, 'Uit de Geschiedenis van het Collegium Musicum Ultrajectinum te Utrecht', *Vlaamsch Jaarboek voor Musiek geschiedenis* (1942), iv. 111–27, and especially 126–7.
[37] Deutsch, 53 (= 54).

Hague, Sir Joseph Yorke, whose name appears twice in Leopold's travel diary.[38] A letter from Yorke to an English friend, written 9 July 1765, a few months before the Mozart's visit, lamented: 'There is nothing here of late of novelty, & this Town is as Empty and as void of novelty as any village in Cumberland'.[39] One can well imagine that the Mozarts, appearing in this cultural vacuum, caused a sensation, which helps to explain the number of concerts they gave and why—even besides the illnesses and the installation of the Regent—they stayed for nine months. Leopold had reason to be satisfied with their time in Holland, yet some years later, when Wolfgang wrote suggesting a trip there in search of patronage, he replied disparagingly:

As for Holland, they have other things now to think of there than music. [. . .] Besides, what will become of your reputation? [Holland and Switzerland] are places for lesser lights, for second-rate composers, for scribblers, for a Schwindel, a Zappa, a Ricci, and the like. Name any one great composer to me who would deign to take such an abject step.[40]

Wolfgang's symphonies available for the performances in Holland were K. 16, 19a, perhaps 19b, 22, and one other; for a recent discovery reveals that Mozart wrote another symphony at The Hague, the Symphony in G, K. 45a, formerly known as the 'Old Lambach' Symphony. K. 45a may have been written for the prince's investiture along with the *Galimathias*, in which case it would have been part of what Leopold referred to in a letter to Hagenauer when he remarked that Wolfgang 'had to compose something for the Prince's concert'.[41]

The five surviving symphonies of the period share common formal patterns (Table 3.2). The kinds of ideas that would be found in most of Mozart's symphonic movements of the late 1760s and early 1770s are already present in these works: the heroic-military contrasted with the lyrical-amorous in first movements, the pastoral-serenata in the second movements, and the dance-popular in the finales. During a Viennese visit of more than a year in 1767–8, Mozart would add to these the courtly and mock-courtly of his minuets and trios.[42]

Wolfgang's symphonies received further performances on the homeward journey. That no performances are recorded from the period when the Mozarts were in Paris and Versailles (about 10 May to 9 July) does not mean that none

[38] *Briefe*, i. 215–16. The Mozarts gave a concert at Yorke's house on 1 October 1765 (British Library, Add MS 35, 367, fo. 347ʳ).

[39] British Library, Stowe MS 261, fos. 103–4.

[40] Letter of 12 Feb. 1778. *Briefe*, ii. 277; *Letters*, ii. 706 (= i. 478). De Smet (*Guillaume V*, 33, and *La Vie du violoniste Jean Malherbe* (Brussels, 1962), 25) errs, therefore, in endorsing the wrong-headed notion of Wyzewa–Saint-Foix that, in going from London to The Hague, the Mozarts had moved from a provincial music centre to a cosmopolitan one.

[41] Letter of 16 May 1766. *Briefe*, i. 219; *Letters*, i. 94 (= 64). The story of K. 45a is related in ch. 6.

[42] Concerning Mozart's earliest symphonies, see further D. Schultz, *Mozarts Jugendsinfonien* (Leipzig, 1900); H. Engel, 'Mozart's Jugendsinfonien' *Deutsche Musikkultur* (1941–2), vi. 51–61; *idem*, 'Über Mozarts Jugendsinfonien', *Mozart-Jahrbuch* (1951), 22–33; Münster, 'Neue Funde zu Mozarts symphonischem Jugendwerk', xx. 2–11.

TABLE 3.2 The morphology of the earliest symphonies

K.	Tempo	Key (if not tonic)	Length	Form
First movements				
(all in common time)				
16	Allegro molto		120 bars	binary, both repeats
19	Allegro		78 bars	binary, no repeats
19a	Allegro assai		93 bars	binary, both repeats
22	Allegro		98 bars	binary, no repeats
45a	Allegro maestoso		84 bars	binary, both repeats
Second movements				
(all in $\frac{2}{4}$)				
16	Andante	relative minor	50 bars	binary, both repeats
19	Andante	subdominant	45 bars	binary, both repeats
19a	Andante	subdominant	60 bars	binary, both repeats
22	Andante	relative minor	57 bars	ABA 'strophic'
45a	Andante	subdominant	84 bars	binary, both repeats
Finales				
(all in $\frac{3}{8}$)				
16	Presto		108 bars	rondo
19	Presto		106 bars	binary, both repeats
19a	Presto		104 bars	rondo
22	Molto allegro		97 bars	rondo
45a	Molto allegro		112 bars	binary, both repeats

occurred. In France in the 1760s, symphonies were, generally speaking, considered a minor genre and seldom mentioned in reviews of public concerts, and most private concerts would not have been reviewed at all. The editor of the *Mercure de France*, for instance, informed his readers that 'In order to avoid useless repetition, we are not in the habit of making mention of the symphonies with which all concerts begin, unless some special circumstances are involved.'[43] That some performances of Wolfgang's symphonies did in fact take place emerges from the newsletter circulated in manuscript to foreign courts by the Mozarts' friend Baron von Grimm who, besides chronicling Wolfgang's extraordinary skills in improvising at the harpsichord and organ, informed his noble subscribers:

This marvellous child is now nine years old. He has hardly grown at all, but he has made prodigious progress in music. He was already a composer and the author of sonatas two years ago . . . . [Now] he has composed symphonies for full orchestra, which have been performed and generally applauded here.[44]

[43] *Mercure de France* (June 1765), 65, n. 1.   [44] Deutsch, 54–5 (= 56–7).

While they were in Paris, the Mozarts were invited to visit Dijon by Louis Joseph de Bourbon, Prince de Condé, the highest ranking member of the provincial parliament (the Burgundian Estates), a largely powerless organization that was just then about to hold its triennial meeting in Dijon. (The Prince perhaps had the idea to use the Mozarts as bread and circus.) Arriving with his family around 12 July for a fortnight, Leopold wasted no time in carrying out the Prince's plan for a public display of the two children. The familiar publicity was distributed ('all the Overtures will be by this young Child'[45]), and on 18 July in the hall of the Hôtel de Ville a public concert took place. An official minute of the occasion survives:

Having been informed that His Serene Highness, My Lord the Prince of Condé, wished to hear a harpsichord concert by the two young children of the Archduke [*sic*] of Salzburg's Kapellmeister—the music of which was composed by one of the said children aged eight [*sic*]—Messrs the Viscount Mayor and aldermen made ready for this gathering the Great Assembly Hall, which was decorated with cut-glass chandeliers and ornate candelabras lit with wax candles, a president's chair of crimson velvet placed on a platform in the middle of the hall for His Said Highness, and risers on all sides for seating the distinguished persons of His retinue. Having arrived at eight o'clock in the evening at the Town Hall, accompanied by Mr de La Tour du Pain, commandant of this province, by the administrative officer, and by several other lords, His Said Highness was received by Messrs the Viscount Mayor, the aldermen, the syndic, the secretary, and the deputies for the syndic's commissioner of police, all dressed in cloaks and cravats in the manner of Pontchartrain; and He was led into the said hall where, being within, His Highness ordered removed the president's chair and platform that had been prepared for Him, and seated Himself on the benches among the ladies. Then refreshments were offered to His Highness—along with assurances [of fealty] inspired by this Prince's goodness—which He accepted, and refreshments were likewise offered to the ladies and lords who accompanied His Highness. And after the concert finished and the Prince arose, He was followed by the entire magistracy and accompanied to His carriage, and when He had ascended into it, everyone retired.[46]

Under the rubric Dijon, Leopold's travel diary lists (in charmingly phonetic French) the names 'Msgr. le Prince de Condé: le Marquis de la Tour rupin commendant de la brovinc et Mdme sa femme, sa fille et son fils. M^r: le Presidente de Brosse. M. Cailleaut acteur Royale du Théâtre Ital. de Paris' and finally 'Les Musiciens'. The names of the Dijon musicians are given, accompanied by a variety of epithets in French, Italian, and English:

[45] Ibid. 55–6 (= 57–8).
[46] E. Fyot, 'Mozart à Dijon', *Mémoires de l'Académie des sciences, arts et belles-lettres de Dijon* (1937), 23–41.

Violinists:	Sotrau	*Très mediocre.*
	Fantini	*Un miserable italien detestable.*
	Paquet	
	Lorenzetti	*Asini tutti.*
	Mauriat	
Viola:	Le Brun	*Un racleur.*
Violoncello [&] Bass:	Du Chargé	
	Amidey	*Miserable.*
Bassoon:	Le Maire	
Hautbois:	Two brothers	*Rotten.*[47]

At this point Leopold's diary breaks off: the pages that once followed are lost, so the names of, and disparaging remarks about, the Dijonnais horn players are lacking. The Dijon orchestra was apparently 3—2—1—1—1 / 0—2—0—1 / [2]—0—0 and continuo, or a total of 14 musicians. Given the intense concentration upon the social and political situation and the poverty of the orchestra, the Mozarts' public concert at Dijon was probably not an artistic triumph. On the other hand, if the orchestra was bad, the harpsichord playing may still have been good, and, with the nobility in town and lacking the amusements of Paris, the Mozarts were doubtless in demand for private performances.

A stay of about three weeks in Lyons at the end of July and beginning of August enabled Wolfgang to be shown off at the Wednesday concert series given by the Académie des Beaux Arts throughout the year except for the fortnight before Easter and the period from the beginning of September to St Martin's day (11 November). At the time of the Mozart's visit, the orchestra numbered twenty. The entire evidence for the event is a newspaper announcement, which—following the usual eighteenth-century custom—emphasized the vocal music and the visiting virtuoso; and a letter from a local businessman, who quite naturally was struck by the aspect of the concert that made it different from others he undoubtedly had attended in Lyons. The announcement in the *Petites affiches* of 13 August reads:

This evening at the Grand Concert will be performed an act from *Hilas* by Mr de Bury, sung by Mrs Charpentier and Mr Lobreau.

Mr J. G. Mozart, a child of nine years, composer and master of music, will perform several pieces for harpsichord alone.

[47] *Briefe*, i. 227; R. Thiblot, 'Le séjour de Mozart à Dijon en 1766', *Mémoires de l'Académie des sciences, arts et belles-lettres de Dijon* (1937), 139–43. From Leopold's listing of a single member of the Théâtre italien of Paris, Eibl (*Briefe*, v. 161–2) incorrectly believed that the entire troupe had come to Dijon to amuse the assembled dignitaries. But at that moment the Théâtre italien was in full swing at home (see C. D. Brenner, *The Théâtre italien, Its Repertory, 1716–1793, with a Historical Introduction* (Berkeley, 1961), 294); furthermore, the names of its orchestral musicians (see the *Almanach des spectacles de Paris . . . pour l'année 1766*, 69, and *. . . pour l'année 1767*, 68) are entirely different from those listed by Leopold in Dijon. Thiblot got this right.

The concert will conclude with the act 'La Danse' from *Les Talents lyriques*, by Mr Rameau.[48]

The letter is dated two days later:

There is here Mr Mozart, Kapellmeister to the Prince of Salzburg, who is touring Europe with his son and his daughter, who are prodigies on the harpsichord .... They gave a concert here in the last few days, at which they played the most difficult pieces, and all the symphonies that were played were of the composition of this little *virtuosus*, and he improvised for a quarter of an hour with the most skilled local master, yielding in nothing to him; in short, he must be seen to be believed, just as the poster announced, and truly I was enchanted by him like everyone else; there were more than 300 persons at this concert at 3 *livres* a head, for they say that he earned nearly 1,000 *livres* that day.[49]

Together, these two documents permit at least a partial reconstruction of the programme of the Lyons concert:

Symphony	W. A. Mozart
Excerpts from *Hylas et Zélie* (1762)	Bernard de Bury
Harpsichord pieces by Mozart alone	
Harpsichord improvisations by Mozart alternating with a	
local master	
'La Danse' from *Les Fêtes d'Hébé* (1739)	Rameau
Symphony	Mozart

There is no evidence for orchestral participation at concerts in Geneva, Lausanne, or Bern.[50] In Zurich, however, where the Mozarts spent a fortnight at the end of September and beginning of October, the minutes of one of the local collegia musica contain the following document:

Insomuch as a few days ago the young Mr Mozart, a nine-year-old virtuoso in composition and at the keyboard, who has won fame at the first courts of Europe and has been marvellously extolled in various papers and journals, together with his fourteen-year-old sister, who also plays the keyboard, and their father, Kapellmeister Mozart of Salzburg, arrived here: the Worshipful Collegium, meeting in the Music Room, permits them, at their request and upon the presentation of good references, to perform publicly on the coming Tuesday the 7th and Thursday the 9th of October in the said Music Room. The Worshipful Collegium moreover deems it proper and incumbent upon them to inform thereof those of Your Excellencies who have upon previous occasions shown yourselves patrons and lovers of Music, and to invite Your Excellencies graciously to honour the

[48] Deutsch, 56 (= 58); L. Vallas, *Un siècle de musique et de théâtre à Lyon, 1688–1789* (Lyons, 1932), 322, 336, 342–3.
[49] Deutsch, 56–7 (= 58–9).
[50] Ibid. 57 (= 59); *Briefe*, i. 230–1; *Letters*, i. 98–9 (= i. 67–7); J. H. Eibl, *Wolfgang Amadeus Mozart: Chronik eines Lebens* (Kassel, 1977), 28–9.

Collegium with your presence, if it so please you. Wherefore the Steward, Mr Meister, is instructed on behalf of our distinguished members to present this written invitation to all highly respected lovers of music with due and seemly deference.

Passed Tuesday 30 September 1766. Present: Guildmaster Werdmüller and other members of the collegium in the Music Room.[51]

Although the contents of the Zurich programmes are unknown, the Mozarts' other concerts suggest what these must have been. That their music pleased the Zurich audience is suggested by a subsequent entry in the Collegium's expense ledger, which reads 'Paid by order to a Salzburger for symphonies and notturni . . . 28 [pounds]'.[52]

Two pictures of this period from Zurich convey something of the ambiance and circumstances of concerts there. One of these (Plate V) shows a concert of the very Collegium Musicum with which the Mozarts collaborated, in their Music Room 'beim Kornhaus'. The orchestra appears to number sixteen, plus two harpsichords. The other picture (Plate VI) shows a concert in a salon with one player per part in the 'orchestra'. This picture, because its title informs us that its keyboard player is performing a harpsichord concerto rather than a continuo part, is especially relevant to the seven pastiche harpsichord concertos Wolfgang had composed not long before his visit to Zurich (K. 37, 39, 40, 41, 107); symphonies too were sometimes performed one on a part.

Arriving at Donaueschingen on 19 October, the Mozarts were well greeted, their way having been prepared by their Salzburg friend Joseph Nicolaus Meissner, who was visiting there, and by their former servant Sebastian Winter, a native of Donaueschingen who now worked for that court. Leopold described their stay in glowing terms:

His Highness the Prince welcomed us with extraordinary graciousness. It was not necessary to announce our arrival, for we were already being eagerly awaited . . . . The Director of Music, Martelli, came at once to welcome us and to invite us to court. Well, we were there for twelve days. On nine days there was music in the evening from five to nine and each time we performed something different. If the season had not been so advanced, we should not have got away. The Prince gave me twenty-four louis d'or and to each of my children a diamond ring. Tears flowed from his eyes when we took leave of him, and truly we all wept at saying good-bye. He begged me to write to him often. Indeed our departure was as sad as our stay had been agreeable.[53]

The discussion of the *Galimathias musicum* above mentioned the presence in the archives at Donaueschingen of a fair copy of that piece, doubtless indicating that

---

[51] Deutsch, 519 (= 60).
[52] Ibid. 65 (= 69). For information about the Zurich collegia, I am indebted to Genette Foster.
[53] Letter of 10 Nov. 1766. *Briefe*, i. 231; *Letters*, i. 99–100 (= i. 68).

the work was performed during one of the nine evenings of music mentioned by Leopold. Since the *Galimathias* called for forces identical to those required for any of Wolfgang's early symphonies, since a letter of Wolfgang's of 1786 mentioned that the court had an orchestra,[54] and since the Mozarts had just presented Wolfgang's symphonies with success in London, the Hague, Amsterdam, Utrecht, Paris, Dijon, Lyons, and Zurich, they undoubtedly did so again in Donaueschingen. The personnel of the Donaueschingen court orchestra at a later date (1790) consisted of two violinists, a violist, a cellist, a double-bass player, and pairs of flautists, oboists, bassoonists, horn players, and clarinettists, the latter doubling on violin. (Perhaps, as happened in other court orchestras of the time, the strings were sometimes reinforced by local amateurs.) The tiny size of this ensemble did not stop its leaders from acquiring a challenging repertory of symphonies during the 1780s.[55]

Two appearances at the Bavarian court in Munich on 9 and 22 November were apparently without benefit of the court musicians.[56] Then the extraordinary journey concluded. The Mozarts reached Salzburg on 29 or 30 November after an absence of three years, five months, and twenty days; and on Sunday, 8 December 1766, a little more than a week after their triumphal return, the St Peter's librarian Hübner wrote in his diary:

About composition, which this boy already understands like an artist, fresh turns of phrase and eulogies would have to be invented anew, for he has already composed very much, and today especially, at High Mass in the Cathedral for a great festivity [the Feast of the Immaculate Conception], a symphony was done which not only found great approbation from all the Court musicians, but also caused great astonishment.[57]

Even diligently tracing the dozen or so public, private, and court concerts in eight or more cities at which Mozart's earliest symphonies were performed has not prepared us to discover that his symphonic début in Salzburg took place not at court, at the University, in a stately home, or in a theatre, but in the Cathedral during High Mass. An adequate explanation for this requires an excursus on the history of the *sinfonia da chiesa*, or 'church symphony'.

[54] Letter of 8 Aug. 1786. *Briefe*, iii. 565; *Letters*, iii. 1337 (= ii. 898).
[55] F. Schnapp, 'Neue Mozart-Funde in Donaueschingen', *Neues Mozart-Jahrbuch* (1942), ii. 211–23.
[56] Deutsch, 65–6 (= 69–70); *Briefe*, i. 231–2, 235; Eibl, *Chronik eines Lebens*, 29.
[57] Deutsch, 66 (= 70).

4

The Sinfonia da Chiesa, and Salzburg (1766–1767)

———————

Although in modern musical life symphonies usually serve as the centre-pieces of orchestral concerts, in concerts of the second half of the eighteenth century, they most often appeared at the beginnings and ends of entertainments at the centres of which were characteristically found vocal and instrumental solos.[1] They also served as overtures and entr'actes to operas, plays, oratorios, and cantatas, and, indeed, the terms 'symphony' and 'overture' were used interchangeably. Although overture (or 'theatre') symphonies and concert (or 'chamber') symphonies are the only types dealt with in recent histories of the early symphony,[2] there was also a third type: the church symphony. As early as 1713 Mattheson wrote on this subject:

Symphony, *Sinfonia* . . . signifies such compositions as are performed solely on instruments . . . . The Italians make use of these symphonies before their operas and other dramatic works, as well as before church pieces; before the former instead of overtures, but before the latter instead of [church] sonatas. Symphonies (especially those belonging to secular pieces) commonly begin with a majestic movement, wherein the top part usually dominates (this is divided into two sections in the same meter, each of which may have its own repeats); and after this conclude with a merry, minuet-like movement (likewise admitting of two or more repeated sections), which in church, however, is never found.[3]

---

[1] Further concerning concert programmes, see N. Zaslaw, 'Toward the Revival of the Classical Orchestra', *Proceedings of the Royal Musical Association* (1976–7), ciii. 158–87, esp. 168–9 and n. 29.

[2] J. LaRue, 'Symphonie. B. Die Entwicklung der Symphonie im 18. Jahrhundert', *Die Musik in Geschichte und Gegenwart* (Kassel, 1965), xii. cols. 1807–10, repr. in *Musikalische Gattungen in Einzeldarstellung, i: Symphonische Musik* (Kassel, 1981), 20–3; L. Hoffmann-Erbrecht, *Die Symphonie* (Cologne, 1967), 5–22; E. Apfel, *Zur Vor- und Frühgeschichte der Symphonie* (Baden-Baden, 1972), 11–42; L. Cuyler, *The Symphony* (New York, 1973), 3–15; U. von Rauchhaupt (ed.), *The Symphony* (London, 1973), 85–109; R. Jacobs, *La Symphonie* (Paris, 1976), 27–51; P. Stedman, *The Symphony* (Englewood Cliffs, 1979), 3–32; J. LaRue, 'Symphony. I. 18th Century', *The New Grove*, xviii. 438–43; L. Hoffmann-Erbrecht, 'Sinfonia', *Dizionario enciclopedico universale della musica e dei musicisti* (Turin, 1984), iv. 291–304.

[3] Charles Burney wrote of the overture to Giovanni Battista Casali's oratorio *Abigail*, 'The two first movements of the overture pleased me very much, the last not at all. It was, as usual, a minuet degenerated into a jigg of the most common cast. This rapidity in the minuets of all modern overtures renders them ungraceful at an opera, but in church they are indecent' (*The Present State of Music in France and Italy* (London, 1771), 363–4). This could be read to mean either that Burney in 1770, unlike Mattheson in 1713, believed slow, dignified minuets might be suitable for use as church music; or that he disapproved of any minuet-like movements in church, and of too fast minuets in opera overtures.

There is otherwise nothing typical or indisputable to report of symphonies, because each [composer] follows his fancy in the matter.[4]

A quarter of a century later Mattheson again attempted to define the symphony:

The *sinfonia* (symphony)

> *da chiesa* (in the church),
> *da camera* (in the chamber),
> *del drama* (in the opera),

is a more moderate-sized genre [than the concerto grosso]. The symphony, although it also requires a suitable instrumentation of both strings and winds, may nevertheless not be so fanciful and luxuriant as the concerto grosso. Irrespective of the fact that symphonies serve to open the *most elegant* musical plays and as introductions to the *most humble*, they have no such voluptuous manner about them. In churches they must be even more moderately contrived than in theatres and halls. Their principal characteristic consists in creating in their brief preface a little sketch of what will follow. And one can easily infer from this that the expression of emotion in such a symphony must be ruled by the same passions that are prominent in the work itself.[5]

Johann Adolf Scheibe referred to Mattheson's second attempt at defining the symphony in his own essay on that subject, from which the following remarks are excerpted:

Ever since Italian opera reached its full maturity, we have been familiar with a genre of instrumental pieces that were performed in front of the theatre curtain in order to prepare the audience in a commodious and ingenious manner. These pieces came to be called 'symphonies'. It was not long before such pieces were introduced here in Germany, and it was here, I might almost say, that they attained fullest perfection . . . .

Symphonies comprise a three-fold genre: to wit, those used for church pieces, those for theatrical and other [secular] vocal pieces, and finally also those intended as purely instrumental works, without connection to any vocal music . . . . Thus we have sacred, theatrical, and chamber symphonies. All symphonies that are to be used with vocal compositions should be in agreement with the vocal compositions of which they form a part. It then follows that both must be composed in the same style. Symphonies not composed with this intention have, as a result, a different character.

Here follows in Scheibe's essay a description of symphonies in the old (i.e., 'baroque') style and those in the new (i.e., 'pre-classical') style, with condemnation of the former and praise of the latter. He then provides the following description of the attributes of symphonies proper for use in church:

---

[4] Johann Mattheson, *Das neu-eröffnete Orchestre* (Hamburg, 1713), 171–2.
[5] Mattheson, *Der vollkommene Capellmeister* (Hamburg, 1739), 234. This passage, a reworking from the same writer's *Kern melodischer Wissenschafft* (Hamburg, 1737), 125, is best understood by consulting both versions.

The symphonies which accompany sacred compositions . . . must be arranged to complement the characteristics of the sacred piece next to be performed; that is, they must prepare the sentiment in which the [following] piece will begin. If the symphony precedes ordinary church music, then it must be very majestic. In that case it must be as though the content of the piece were of such a nature that one had to limit the symphony to conform to it. One should strive in the same symphonies to make the sound full-voiced and expressive. The melody in all its clarity should be at once triumphant, spirited, and moving; it should make the listeners attentive as well as anxious to observe the ensuing production. Symphonies must at one and the same time provide a skillful and ingenious preparation for the coming piece. They can also be embellished with well-devised imitations, for this is in keeping with the attributes of church music. However, the melody must predominate throughout, without the slightest trace of constraint. New and vigourous ideas and phrases must serve constantly to increase the attention. In order to achieve this end, the beginning of such a symphony must always display something new and unknown. One unexpected elaboration must follow after another, but everything must agree exactly with the principal attributes of church music, and more specifically, with the ensuing piece of music, whether it be an ordinary church piece or an oratorio.

With regard to the type and succession of movements, I must still add the following. One does not compose three separate movements, as one usually does for other symphonies, but restricts oneself to one movement or, at the very most, two. The character of these movements is either slow and pathetic at the beginning followed by a faster movement, or a rapid and fiery movement followed by a slower and more sentimental one. The beginning of the [following] vocal piece will determine just how the symphony should commence. There are no hard and fast rules to be given here, because the nature of the words [of the following work] differs too greatly [from work to work], and the composition must therefore be left to the reflection and understanding of the composer. One must observe at least the following, that when two movements are composed, they are not so different that a pause between them is necessary; rather, the end of the first movement must cleverly unite with the beginning of the second movement so as not to appear contrived or artificial, but rather as inevitable.

In such a symphony it is customary to introduce concertante instruments, which can surely produce a good effect when one uses them thoughtfully and circumspectly. The concertante instruments must never clatter or be wild; rather, they must bring forward a concise melody. They must come in unexpectedly and at the appointed moment, never playing alone for long but constantly relieved and accompanied by the remaining instruments.[6]

Mattheson's and Scheibe's definitions of 'symphony' apply to works in earlier styles than even Mozart's earliest symphonies, but as styles changed, definitions

---

[6] Johann Adolf Scheibe, *Der critische Musicus* (Hamburg, 1738–40), 304–10. The quoted passages, from the 65th number dated 24 Nov. 1739, are drawn not from the original periodical, but from Scheibe's revised cumulation, *Critischer Musikus: Neue, vermehrte und verbesserte Auflage* (Leipzig, 1745), 595–602.

remained remarkably constant. For example, Scheibe's remarks about church symphonies were probably known to J. A. P. Schulz, who seemed to echo them (while modifying them) when, more than three decades later, he penned another definition of the symphony:

Symphony.

A piece of instrumental music for many voices that is used in place of the now obsolete overture. The difficulty of performing an overture well and the still greater difficulty of composing a good overture have given rise to the lighter form of the symphony. [This] originally consisted of one or more fugal pieces alternating with dance pieces of various types, which was generally called 'partita'. To be sure, the overture was still used before large pieces of church music and operas, and one made use of partitas only in chamber music. But soon one also became tired of dance pieces without dancing, and finally settled for one or two fugal or non-fugal allegros that alternated with a slower andante or largo. This genre was called 'symphony', and was introduced in chamber music as well as before operas and in church music, where it is still in use today. The instruments that belong to the symphony are violins, violas, and bass instruments; each part is strongly re-enforced [i.e., doubled]. Horns, oboes, and flutes can be used in addition for filling out or strengthening . . . .

   The symphony is excellently suited for the expression of the grand, the festive, and the noble. Its purpose is to prepare the listeners for an important musical work, or in a chamber concert to summon up all the splendor of instrumental music. If it is to satisfy this aim completely and be a closely bound part of the opera or church music that it precedes, then besides being the expression of the grand and festive, it must have an additional quality that puts the listeners in the frame of mind required by the piece to come; and it must distinguish itself through the style of composition that makes it appropriate for the church or the theatre . . . .

   The church symphony distinguishes itself from the rest above all through its serious style of composition. It consists often of only a single movement. It does not tolerate, as does the chamber symphony, extravagance or disorder in the melodic and harmonic progressions, but proceeds in a steady manner, faster or slower, according to the nature of the expression of the church piece [it precedes], and strictly observes the rule[s] of composition. Instead of the magnificent, it often has a quiet nobility as its goal, and best suited for it is a pathetic, well-worked-out fugue.[7]

   [7] Anon., 'Symphonie', in Johann Georg Sulzer, *Allgemeine Theorie der schönen Künste* (Leipzig, 1771–4), ii. 1121–3. The translation is slightly altered from B. Churgin, 'The Symphony as Described by J. A. P. Schulz (1774): A Commentary and Translation', *Current Musicology* (1980), xxix. 7–16. Although Schulz claimed that the old French *ouverture* was more difficult to perform than the new Italian *sinfonia*, Jean-Jacques Rousseau seemed to imply the opposite (*Dictionnaire de musique* (Paris, 1768), 'Ouverture'); see ch. 7 at n. 50.
   It is an unavoidable methodological peculiarity of the present chapter that the theorists cited were north German Protestants while the church symphonies chronicled were composed primarily by south German, Austrian, or north Italian Catholics. A partial exception: Josef Martin Kraus (a Catholic) composed a *Sinfonia per la chiesa* for the Protestant service honouring the opening of the Swedish parliament in 1789.

These definitions fail to answer many questions about the *sinfonia da chiesa*, and, as with many theoretical writings, there is the need to understand the extent to which they deal with everyday practice rather than a kind of idealized proposal of 'how things ought to be'. Nevertheless, they leave no doubt about the existence of the church symphony as a genre, and they suggest that it can be divided into two types, according to function. Those of the first type served as overtures to oratorios, which were non-liturgical and usually performed in halls rather than in churches,[8] or as overtures to sacred cantatas, which were treated like short oratorios in Catholic circles but could be introduced into the liturgy in Lutheran circles. Those of the second type served to introduce 'regular church music' (as Scheibe put it), that is to say, they served to introduce some part of the liturgy. What follows deals with the latter type—symphonies used within the Catholic liturgy—ignoring the use of symphonies as part of concerts in churches (often before or after Vespers) or as part of *Tafelmusik* or concerts in monastic establishments. The inquiry begins with a brief discussion of the history of purely instrumental music in that liturgy.

From early times the organ had added to its original role of accompanying voices the new role of soloist. Organ solos during the Mass were of long standing by the time of the first codification of this practice in Pope Clement VIII's *Caeremoniale episcoporum* (Rome, 1600). Clement permitted the use of the organ on Sundays, except those in Advent and Lent, and on important feast days:

At the solemn Mass the organ is played *alternatim* for the Kyrie eleison and the Gloria in excelsis ... ; likewise at the end of the Epistle and at the Offertory; for the Sanctus, *alternatim*; then more gravely and softly during the Elevation of the Most Holy Sacrament; for the Agnus Dei, *alternatim*, and at the verse before the post-Communion prayer; also at the end of the Mass.[9]

In the mid-seventeenth century the *sonata da chiesa* came to prominence. This new genre may be viewed as the addition of obbligato instruments to the organ in its traditional function of providing preludes, interludes, and postludes. Any church equipped to perform concerted liturgical music would already have had instrumentalists on hand, so no additional expenditures or special arrangements were necessarily implied by the rise of the *sonata da chiesa*. The portions of the Mass usually embellished with 'free' instrumental pieces (that is, pieces not based on plainchant) appear to have been: (1) before the Mass, (2) the Introit, (3) the

---

[8] H. Smither, 'Oratorio and Sacred Opera, 1700–1825: Terminology and Genre Distinction', *Proceedings of the Royal Musical Association* (1979–80), cvi. 88–104.

[9] E. Higginbottom, 'Organ Mass', *The New Grove*, xiii. 780. This passage from the *Caeremoniale episcoporum* deals only with the use of the organ during the Mass, and omits to mention the common pratice of organ preludes and postludes.

Gradual, (4) the Offertory, (5) the Elevation, (6) the Communion, and (7) the Deo Gratias.[10]

At the end of the seventeenth century and beginning of the eighteenth, concerti grossi were sometimes heard in church in place of sonatas. This explains the concertos and sinfonias '*per il santissimo Natale*' of Corelli, Locatelli, Manfredini, Sammartini, Schiassi, Torelli, Valentini, and Werner, which were performed at Christmas Masses. The title of Manfredini's twelve Op. 2 concerti grossi, *Sinfonie da chiesa*, is self-explanatory, and eight of Corelli's Op. 6 concerti grossi are 'da chiesa'—that is, they contain fugal movements and no overtly labelled dances. The trumpet concertos of the Bolognese school were also written for use during the Mass.[11] Mozart wrote a trumpet concerto for this purpose (K. 47c), and his so-called 'Epistle sonatas' are single movements in the form of an organ concerto or a trio sonata with organ continuo. In Austria the *sonata da chiesa* flourished vigourously late into the eighteenth century in an orchestral guise. That is to say, the trio sonatas used in church in Austria were customarily performed by several players to a part.[12]

Works such as Vivaldi's *Sinfonia al Santo Sepolcro* (RV 169) and *Sonata al Santo Sepolcro* (RV 130) belong to the genre known variously as 'concerto for orchestra', 'ripieno concerto', or 'concerto a quattro'. Collections of ripieno concertos were published during the three decades between 1690 and 1720, appearing equally under the rubrics *concerti* and *sinfonie*.[13] Sometimes their churchly functions are acknowledged on title pages—as with Bianchi's *Sei concerti di chiesa*, Op. 2, and Alberti's *Concerti per chiesa e per camera*, Op. 1—and other times not. Such concertos occasionally contain pastoral movements evoked by the Christmas nativity scene, chromatic movements called forth by the Easter sepulchre, or fugal movements in a watered-down *stile antico*. But as these three types of movements also occur in works not specifically designated for church use, there is little to distinguish ripieno concertos entitled *sinfonia da chiesa* or *concerto per chiesa* from their secular counterparts, and works with and without the *da chiesa* or *da camera* in their titles apparently were used interchangeably for sacred and secular purposes.[14]

[10] S. Bonta, 'The Uses of the *Sonata da Chiesa*', *Journal of the American Musicological Society* (1969), xxii. 54–84, and especially Table IV on 72–4; see also R. N. Freeman, 'The Role of Organ Improvisation in Haydn's Church Music' in Larsen, Serwer, and Webster (eds.), *Haydn Studies*, 192–4.

[11] J. Berger, 'Notes on Some 17th-Century Compositions for Trumpets and Strings in Bologna', *The Musical Quarterly* (1951), xxxvii. 354–67; A. Hutchings, *The Baroque Concerto*, 3rd edn. (London, 1978), 64–88.

[12] W. Kirkendale, *Fugue and Fugato in Rococo and Classical Chamber Music* (Durham, NC, 1979), 34–5. Performance in church was a principal forum in which violin virtuosos like Tartini reached their public.

[13] A. Schering, *Geschichte des Instrumentalkonzerts*, 2nd edn. (Leipzig, 1927, repr. 1965), 30–8; E. K. Wolf, 'Important Publications Containing Ripieno Concertos', hand-out for the paper cited in n. 15 below.

[14] Cf. W. S. Newman, *The Sonata in the Baroque Era*, rev. edn. (Chapel Hill, 1966), 34: 'The universally recognized distinction between *sonata da chiesa* and *sonata da camera* . . . throws less light on functions than might be expected, since it is beset by inconsistencies and contradictions from start to finish . . . . The overlapping may occur in both the styles and the titles or inscriptions that are assumed to be appropriate to the two different functions.'

It has recently been convincingly argued that, as an antecedent to the classical symphony, the ripieno concerto was as important as, or perhaps even more important than, the opera-overture sinfonia; and that historians dealing with the emergence of the concert symphony in the mid-eighteenth century have undervalued the conservative ripieno concerto in favour of the more forward-looking opera sinfonia.[15] In any case, it may perhaps have been when the style of the ripieno concertos had begun to show signs of age that the idea arose of using works in a more modern style in church. As we have seen, Scheibe in 1739 favoured the modern style for church symphonies, while still differentiating between them and symphonies intended for the theatre or chamber, and he reported that the popularity of opera sinfonias was such that they could be heard 'even in church'.[16]

More or less well-documented reports of symphonies performed during the Mass in several places in western Europe come down to us from the second half of the eighteenth century and first decades of the nineteenth. As early as 1752 a correspondent of Padre Martini's in Rome answered an enquiry about the instrumental music used in Roman churches by explaining that they used theatre overtures by Perez, Jommelli, Manna, and Galuppi. This correspondent apparently sympathized with the older generation of composers, for he added, 'poor Corelli and Torelli'.[17]

In 1772 Charles Burney reported hearing 'symphonies' by Leopold Hofmann played during Mass at Saint Stephen's Cathedral in Vienna.[18] Symphony manuscripts of Georg Reutter (ii) in the Gesellschaft der Musikfreunde contain annotations indicating that they were intended for performance in Saint Stephen's as well.[19] A third Viennese composer, Carlo d'Ordonez, likewise wrote at least three symphonies to be performed during Mass.[20] A copy of a symphony by Vanhal in Regensburg bears the inscription, 'products die 14ma Aprilis a[nni] 1781 in Templo St. Augustini Ratisbonensi ad S[tum] Sepulcrum'.[21] At Bologna Giacomo Antonio Perti was the author of fifteen *sinfonie avanti la messa*, and Padre Martini's symphonies were apparently played in church too.[22] Martini's disciple and

---

[15] E. K. Wolf, 'The "Ripieno Concerto" (*Concerto a 4*) as the Principal Early Form of the Concert Symphony', paper read at the Annual Meeting of the American Musicological Society, Denver, 7 Nov. 1980. Summary published in *Abstracts of Papers Read at the Forty-Sixth Annual Meeting of the American Musicological Society* (Denver, 1980), 25; idem, *Antecedents of the Symphony: The Ripieno Concerto* (The Symphony 1720–1840, A/i) (New York, 1983), xv–xxix.

[16] Scheibe, *Der critischer Musikus*, 596.

[17] A. Schnoebelen, *Padre Martini's Collection of Letters in the Civico Museo Bibliografico Musicale in Bologna: An Annotated Index* (New York, 1979), 193, No. 1557.

[18] Burney, *The Present State of Music in Germany, the Netherlands, and United Provinces* (London, 1773), i. 322.

[19] Information kindly provided by A. Peter Brown.

[20] A. P. Brown, *Carlo d'Ordonez 1734–1786: A Thematic Catalogue* (Detroit, 1978), 27, 39, 43; idem, 'Ordonez, Carlo d'', *The New Grove*, xiii, 702–3; idem, *Carlo d'Ordonez, Seven Symphonies* (The Symphony 1720–1840, B/iv) (New York, 1979), xii.

[21] G. Haberkamp, *Die Musikhandschriften der Fürst Thurn und Taxis Hofbibliothek Regensburg* (Munich, 1981), 350.

[22] H. Brofsky, 'The Symphonies of Padre Martini', *The Musical Quarterly* (1965), li. 649–73 and esp. 650; A. Schnoebelen, 'Perti, Giacomo Antonio', *The New Grove*, xiv. 555–7; A. Schering, *Geschichte des Instrumentalkonzerts*, 28.

successor at Bologna, Stanislao Mattei, wrote symphonies heard in church there between the 1770s and 1798.[23] Sammartini's symphonies were probably heard in church in Milan.[24] Niccolo Zingarelli's fifty-three one-movement symphonies were written between *c.*1815 and *c.*1835 for use in Neapolitan churches.[25] As we shall see, a symphony by J. Haydn was performed at Mass at the Montserrat Monastery near Barcelona around 1790, just as symphonies by Mozart and Michael Haydn were heard in the Salzburg Cathedral. A symphony by Dittersdorf is found as an instrumental gradual in a Mass attributed to Joseph Haydn (Hob. XXI: C4), and another symphony attributed to Dittersdorf is entitled 'Sinfonia Solennis' in its sole source.[26]

The Berlin man of letters Friedrich Nicolai, in his widely read *Description of a Journey through Germany and Switzerland*, reported attending a Mass at the Bamberg Cathedral in 1781, presided over by the local ruler, Prince Adam Friedrich:

The Mass itself was a low Mass, not a sung Mass . . . . For all that, however, during the Mass music was performed that did not belong to the Mass at all. First the organist preluded in the old-fashioned manner of Tischer or Roberger, on an entirely unremarkable-sounding positive. The court orchestra, which consisted of ten violins, two violas, oboes, horns, violoncellos, two double basses, and one bassoon, then played a symphony rather in the style of Abel—tuneful and beautiful. The performance was quite certainly not excellent but good, however, especially the bass instruments, which were very distinct. Then Madame Fracassini, the Kapellmeister's wife, sang a vigorous bravura aria rather in the style of Traetta. She has a chest register the deep tones of which are not bad, but bear no relationship to the many, more youthful[-sounding] higher tones; her voice over-all is not supple, the passagework not articulated but slurred and unsure; she has no trill. This opera aria was not accompanied by a harpsichord, as it properly should have been, but by a flute stop of the positive. When the aria was over, and the organist had doodled a bit more, there was an all-but-comic symphony, during which the singer read very devoutly in her prayerbook and crossed herself. Next came an Andante that—as we would say in Berlin—'was not much but surely less'; finally, again, a humdrum Allegro. It seemed very odd to me that, especially under such a rigidly religious prince, the divine service was interrupted by operatic music, which does not belong there at all. The greatest part of the onlookers paid attention to neither the opera aria nor the Mass. One part

[23] R. M. Longyear, *Stanislao Mattei, Five Symphonies; Niccolo Zingarelli, Seven Symphonies* (The Symphony 1720–1840, A/viii) (New York, 1980), ix–x. In a list of Mattei's works appended to a posthumous edition of his *Pratica d'accompagnamento sopra bassi numerati* (Turin, *c.*1840?), xxvi, a distinction is made between 'Tre *Sinfonie* a piena orchestra' and 'Trentacinque *Sinfonie* pressoche tutte anteriori al 1800; l'ultima e del 1804', and concerning the latter we are informed, 'Coteste Sinfonie non sono composte che di un solo pezzo, e furono scritte per essere suonate nelle Chiese al momento della messa, chiamato *Offertorio*'.

[24] B. Churgin, *The Symphonies of G. B. Sammartini*, i (Cambridge, Mass., 1968), 11.

[25] Longyear, 'The Symphonies of Niccolo Zingarelli', *Analecta Musicologica* (1979), xix. 288–319; *idem*, 'Zingarelli, Niccolo Antonio', *The New Grove*, xx. 692–4; *idem*, *Mattei, Five Symphonies; Zingarelli, Seven Symphonies*, ix–x.

[26] M. G. Grave, 'Dittersdorf's First-Movement Form as a Measure of his Symphonic Development' (Ph.D. diss., New York University, 1977), 379, 498.

applauded, and (to my surprise) this included common people; one part appeared to stand there entirely stupidly indifferent. The majority knelt to read in prayerbooks, with their lips going, or tugging at rosaries, striking their breasts or crossing themselves, without regard for the Mass and also . . . without their prayers being hindered by the merry music. A footman entered, lightly rattled off a quick 'Ave Maria', and immediately went out the door; and various persons ogled and convulsed their lips into a shape that appeared to be an 'Ave' but not an 'Ave Maria'.[27]

If Nicolai's objectivity is compromised by his Protestant and Enlightenment prejudices against authority in religion, and by a desire to entertain like-minded colleagues back in Berlin, his is none the less the fullest account we have of the context for symphonies during Catholic Mass in south Germany and Austria in Mozart's lifetime. By 'all-but-comic symphony', he may have been referring to an instance of the well-documented use from about 1775 of overtures from *opéras comiques* by Grétry, Gossec, Philidor, and Monsigny in Bavarian and Austrian churches and monasteries.[28]

The repertory at the Cologne Cathedral was rich in symphonies,[29] and as late as 1815 symphonies were performed at Mass there, between the Epistle and Gospel.[30] At Heidelberg a concerto or symphony movement was regularly performed before the Gospel reading, according to a 'Chorverordnung' of 1782.[31] In Fulda in 1800 a visitor heard Wranitzky's 'Coronation' symphony, performed following the Credo of a concerted Mass by Mozart.[32] The symphonies owned by the Schäftlarn monastery were catalogued in 1803 under rubrics parallel to those used to catalogue Mass and Offertory settings: 'Solenne geschriebene Synphonien', 'Solenne geschriebene Pastorell synphonien', and 'Kurzere geschriebene Synphonien'.[33]

---

[27] (Christoph) Friedrich Nicolai, *Beschreibung einer Reise durch Deutschland und die Schweiz, im Jahre 1781. Nebst Bemerkungen über Gelehrsamkeit, Industrie, Religion und Sitten* (Berlin, 1783–96), i. 129. It is interesting that the north German Nicolai expected to hear a harpsichord in the choir-loft, as J. S. Bach had for his Lutheran services in Leipzig; I know of no evidence for this practice in south German and Austrian Catholic church-music of the period.

[28] R. Münster *et al.*, 'Evermodus Groll und die Musikpflege in Schäftlarn im Ausgang des 18. Jahrhunderts', in S. Mitterer (ed.), *1200 Jahre Kloster Schäftlarn 762–1962; Blätter zum Gedächtnis* (Beiträge zur altbayerischen Kirchengeschichte, xxii/3) (Munich, 1962), 132. A dozen symphonies from Austrian monasteries are published with a valuable introduction by R. N. Freeman (ed.), *Austrian Cloister Symphonies* (The Symphony 1720–1840, B/vi) (New York, 1982).

[29] H. Beck, 'Die Musik des liturgischen Gottesdienstes', in K. G. Fellerer (ed.), *Geschichte der katholischen Kirchenmusik*, ii: *Vom Tridentinum bis zur Gegenwart* (Kassel, 1976), 189. The Cologne repertory included symphonies by J. C. Bach, Cambini, Dittersdorf, Filtz, Gossec, Masek, Schmittbauer, Stamitz, Vanhal, and Zimmermann.

[30] Anon., 'Kurze Darstellung des Musikzustandes in Cöln', *Allgemeine musikalische Zeitung* (3 May 1815), Jg. 17, cols. 300–3. The writer of this report objected strongly to the inclusion of 'profane' symphonies in the Mass.

[31] F. Stein, *Zur Geschichte der Musik in Heidelberg* (Heidelberg, 1912), 137–8, 143–4. The repertory of symphonies there included words by (J. C.?) Bach, Bolas[s]i, Cannabich, Dittersdorf, Eichner, Gossec, Holzbauer, Kreusser, Joseph Riepel, Sterkel, Toeschi, and Traetta.

[32] Anon., 'Etwas von dem Musikzustande zu Fulda', *Allgemeine musikalische Zeitung* (16 June 1800), Jg. 2, cols. 729–31.

[33] P. Ruf, 'Die Handschriften des Klosters Schäftlarn', in S. Mitterer (ed.), *1200 Jahre Kloster Schäftlarn 762–1962*, 21–122, here 109–12. Among the 'solenne' symphonies in this list one finds '4 di Heydn. Ex C, D♯ et G minor' and '1 Ouverture di Mozart'. Other composers of 'solenne' symphonies include: Abel, Anfossi, (J. C.) Bach, Bader, Bernardini, Dittersdorf, Gassmann, Gossec, Gra[a]f, Hofmann, Koppauer, Kozeluch, Kurzinger, Lachnith, Malzat, Mysliweczek, Naumann, Piccini,

On feast days, Mass at the court of Koblenz-Ehrenbreitstein apparently required the selection of one each of 'Benediction contrapunct, Messa, Offertorio, Sinfonia'; and 'between the Gloria and Credo, in connection with the Gradual, a symphony was played, and also repeated at the end of the Mass'. Lists of the concerted music performed on two Holy Saturdays have been preserved; they show that the symphony in the Mass was performed between the Confitemini-Laudate Dominum and the Sanctus.[34] Archival records from the monastery at Weyarn transmitting the choices of concerted liturgical works list symphonies by J. Haydn, Hoffmeister, and Mysliveček.[35] The Mass at Trier (Trèves) was frequently embellished by the symphonies of Johann Georg Lang.[36] At the Dresden court chapel, the local composers Cristoforo Babbi, Franz Anton Schubert, Franz Anton Morgenroth, Francesco Morlacchi, and Carl Borromäus von Miltitz wrote single-movement symphonies for large scorings; these served as substitutes for Mass movements on major feast days.[37]

We are better informed about the symphonies of Joseph Haydn than about those of Hoffmeister, Lang, Vanhal, Vogel, *et al*. A passage in Giuseppe Carpani's biography of Haydn, after discussing the orchestral version of Haydn's *The Seven Last Words of Our Saviour on the Cross*, reported:

Some other of Haydn's symphonies were written for the holy days. They were played in the chapel at Eisenstadt, in the chapel of the Imperial court, and in other churches on such sacred feast days. They are written in G major, D major, and C minor. In the midst of the sorrow expressed in them, the characteristically Haydnesque vivacity constantly shines through, and here and there are revealed some hints of the anger with which the author perhaps would take aim at the sinners and the Jews.[38]

Pinder, Pleyel, Pugnani, Rosetti, Schuster, Schwindl, Seyfert, (K.) Stamitz, Storatini, Toeschi, Ullinger, Vanhal, and Zach. The composers of 'solenne pastorell' symphonies: Denni, Hafeneder, Lang, Michl, Storatini, Ullinger, and Zach. The composers of 'kurzere' symphonies: (J. C.) Bach, Beurer, Dittersdorf, Gewey, Ivanschutz, Koppauer, Michl, Sala, Sales, Schwab, Seyfert, Ullinger, and Vanhal.

[34] G. Bereths, *Die Musikpflege am kurtrierischen Hofe zu Koblenz-Ehrenbreitstein* (Mainz, 1964), 179–81, 191, 300–1. The repertory at Koblenz-Ehrenbreitstein is known to have included symphonies by J. Haydn, C. Hergen, J. G. Lang, W. A. Mozart, Nicolai, Pleyel, and J. Schubert.

[35] R. Münster, 'Evermodus Groll', 125, n. 11a; *idem* and R. Machold, *Thematischer Katalog der ehemaligen Klosterkirchen Weyarn, Tegernsee und Benediktbeuern* (Munich, 1971), 18; *idem*, *Thematischer Katalog der Musikhandschriften der Benediktinerinnenabtei Frauenwörth und der Pfarrkirchen Indersdorf, Wasserburg am Inn und Bad Tölz* (Munich, 1975), 118.

[36] S. Davis, 'The Orchestra under Clemens Wenzeslaus: Music at a Late-Eighteenth-Century Court', *Journal of the American Musical Instrument Society* (1975), i. 86–112; *idem*, 'J. G. Lang and the Early Classical Keyboard Concerto', *The Musical Quarterly* (1980), lxvi. 21–52; *idem*, *Johann Georg Lang (1722?–1798): Three Symphonies* (The Symphony 1720–1840, C/i) (New York, 1983), lxiv–lxvii.

[37] H.-G. Ottenberg, *The Symphony in Dresden* (The Symphony 1720–1840, C/x) (New York, 1984), xv. For additional *sinfonie da chiesa* see F. E. Kirby, 'The Germanic Symphony in the Eighteenth Century: Bridge to the Romantic Era', *Journal of Musicological Research* (1984), v. 51–83, esp. 58–9.

[38] Giuseppe Carpani, *Le Haydine, ovvero Lettere sulla vita e le opere del celebre maestro Giuseppe Haydn* (Milan, 1812; 2nd edn., 1823), 111. Of the three of Haydn's biographers who interviewed him in the final years of his life, Griesinger is generally the most reliable, Dies follows closely behind, while Carpani lags at some distance behind the other two (V. Gotwals, 'The Earliest Biographies of Haydn', *The Musical Quarterly* (1959), xlv. 439–59). That is to say, although Carpani saw Haydn

Documentary evidence for the performance of Haydn's symphonies at Masses at the court of Koblenz-Ehrenbreitstein and at the monasteries of Schäftlarn and Weyarn was given above. In a corner of Europe distant from those monasteries, Fernando Sor witnessed the performance of a Haydn symphony during Mass, and left the following first recollection of the Montserrat Monastery near Barcelona, where he arrived around 1790 at the age of twelve to enroll in the Escolanía (choir school):

We were awakened at four o'clock (it was still dark), and we made our way to the church before five o'clock. . . . the Mass was accompanied by a small orchestra consisting of violins, cellos, double basses, bassoons, horns, and oboes, all played by children the oldest of whom cannot have been more than fifteen or sixteen. At the Offertory they played the Introduction and Allegro of one of Haydn's symphonies in D; at the Communion the Andante was done, and at the last Gospel, the Allegro.[39]

There is of course a fundamental difference between Carpani's and Sor's reports: the latter tells us nothing about whether Haydn himself intended some of his symphonies to be used in church, whereas the former implies that that was his intention.

H. C. Robbins Landon has devoted considerable attention to the question of several symphonies, a divertimento, and a baryton trio by Haydn with apparent church connections.[40] A few words may clarify the nature of these sacred connections. The Alleluia melody used in Symphony No. 30 appeared in the liturgy only once during the year, at the end of the Epistle reading of Holy Saturday Mass. (The Alleluia of the Mass was suppressed from Septuagesima Sunday until Good Friday, and replaced by the Tract, except that on the eves of Easter and Pentecost the Alleluia and Tract were both sung.) The reciting tones for the Passion narratives that Haydn quoted in Symphony No. 26 were used on Palm Sunday, Holy Tuesday, Holy Wednesday, and Good Friday for the Gospels

---

between 1796 and 1801, although he interviewed many who knew or had known Haydn, and although his tract is important for the history of early Romantic theories of aesthetics, he cannot be relied upon in matters of detail concerning Haydn's life and music. On the other hand, his account of Haydn also contains some truths, and given the frequency with which symphonies were performed in churches in northern Italy, Austria, and southern Germany, one should not dismiss this passage out of hand. See also R. N. Freeman, 'The Function of Haydn's Instrumental Compositions in the Abbeys', in Larsen, Serwer, and Webster (eds.), *Haydn Studies*, 199–202. For an attempt to identify the symphonies mentioned by Carpani, see N. Zaslaw, 'Mozart, Haydn and the *Sinfonia da chiesa*', *The Journal of Musicology* (1982), v. 95–124, and especially 116–17.

[39] A. Ledhuy and H. Bertini, 'Sor', *Encyclopédie pittoresque de la musique* (Paris, 1835), 154–67, here 156; also reproduced in facsimile in B. Jeffery, *Fernando Sor: Composer and Guitarist* (London, 1977), 117–30. The 'last Gospel' occurs at the end of the Mass; see *The Liber Usualis* (Tournai, 1962), lxxi. The need for music arose from the custom of having a solemn procession to carry the book of Gospel readings from the altar to the pulpit, whence it was read.

[40] *The Symphonies of Joseph Haydn* (London, 1955), 253, 258–9, 286–7, 260, 316, 322, 337, 339, 352, 392, 190–1, 260 n. *Haydn: Chronicle and Works*, 5 vols. (Bloomington and London, 1976–80), i. 273, 290, 292–3, 286, 565, 566, 569–70, 573; ii. 291–5, 297–8, 303, 312, 566. Landon's discussions comprise the symphonies Hob. I: 5, 11, 18, 21, 22, 26, 30, 34, 44, 45, 49, 60, 80; the divertimento II: 23; and the baryton trio XI: 64.

according to the four Evangelists. Finally, the 'Incipit lamentatio', which appears in Symphonies 26 and 80 and in the Divertimento in F major, Hob II: 23, is the chant for the Lamentations of the Prophet Jeremiah, sung on Maundy Thursday, Good Friday, and Holy Saturday. (Mozart—or was it Franz Xaver Süssmayr, who completed this work after Mozart's death?—quoted this melody by way of a joke in the Finale of the horn concerto K. 412, and more seriously in the oratorio, *La Betulia liberata*, No. 15, the Masonic Funeral Music, K. 477, and in the 'Alleluia' of the canon, K. 553.)

Landon coined the term '*sonata da chiesa* symphony' for works beginning with a slow movement. (To be included in Landon's scheme, the first slow movement must be fully fledged and not merely an introduction.) Haydn's early symphonies show great diversity in the arrangement of their movements, and the hypothesis that those beginning with slow movements were in some way more suited to use in church (or at least related in some unstated way to a church tradition) appears questionable. Of the fifteen works that Landon singled out as having church connections, only seven begin with slow movements. Leopold Mozart's *Sonate sei per chiesa e da camera* of 1740 (listed in the Lambach monastery catalogue of 1768 as 'symphonies') are three-movement works cast in a fast—slow—fast format. Wolfgang Mozart's Epistle sonatas are single-movement allegros. The 'church' symphonies of more than two dozen composers chronicled above do not systematically begin with slow movements. Nor do the theoretical writings of Mattheson, Scheibe, and Schulz quoted above lend support to Landon's notion that church symphonies must begin with slow movements: Mattheson does indeed mention the slow-fast pattern, but Scheibe says one or two movements, either slow-fast or fast-slow, and Schulz suggests 'often . . . only a single movement . . . and best suited for it . . . a well-worked-out fugue'.

While Landon's concentration on Holy Week as the destination of Haydn's putative 'church' symphonies would seem logical, given the lamentation titles and chants found in some of them, Carpani's remarks, and the example of *The Seven Last Words*, still there are problems with it. *The Seven Last Words* originated in a Spanish tradition unrelated to liturgical practice in Austria. In most Catholic countries Holy Week called for the banishing of instruments from services (except occasionally the organ) and for the performance of a cappella polyphony and unaccompanied chanting.[41] It was also customary to prohibit opera and other

[41] The twentieth-century, pre-Vatican Council formulation of the prohibitions concerning instrumental music is given in *The Liber Usualis*, cviii–cix. There was a wide variety of local practice in this regard, however, and an archbishop or abbot apparently had considerable leeway in the regulation of the local liturgy. Even in Salzburg, for instance, the Archbishop would not have had direct jurisdiction over the liturgy of establishments run by the Benedictines (the University Church) or the Franciscans (St Peter's Church). See also the reforms of the Salzburg Archbishop discussed below and the diary of the abbot Ignaz Speckle (U. Engelmann (ed.) *Das Tagebuch von Ignaz Speckle, Abt von St. Peter im Schwarzwald: Erste Teil 1795–1802* (Stuttgart, 1966), 114–15, 366). Symphonies by Nicolai and Lang were apparently performed at Mass on Holy Saturday in 1787 and 1790 at the court of Koblenz-Ehrenbreitstein (see n. 34 above).

theatrical performances during the forty days (or in some places, the final fortnight) of Lent. Thus arose the institution of the *concert spirituel*, devoted to instrumental music, oratorios, cantatas, and the like, to provide suitable entertainment during this solemn period. Perhaps Haydn's 'Holy Week' symphonies were written for sacred concerts, which were sometimes held in churches, but would not have been part of the liturgy at Mass or Vespers. Given the prohibitions concerning instrumental music, it is doubtful whether any of these symphonies could have been used in the liturgy during Holy Week.

Contradictions surrounding the works of Haydn discussed above suggest a new hypothesis, namely, that symphonies employing plainsong were not those intended for liturgical use. The theorists are silent concerning the use of cantus firmus in church symphonies. The instrumental pieces used during the Mass, at the seven characteristic moments documented above, were 'free' compositions, that is, without cantus firmus. A cantus firmus would have been redundant in instrumental church music unless that music replaced a chant, a centuries' old practice in the Catholic liturgy (for instance, the Dresden practice mentioned above), but one which would have been most unlikely during Holy Week. Therefore, need for the quotation of plainchant in symphonies would more readily have occurred outside the service when, for programmatic or circumstantial reasons, a composer wished to make reference to sacred matters. Such a hypothesis would also make sense for the Minuet of Mozart's E flat symphony, K. 132, in which the presence of the pseudo-psalm tone and archaic harmonies in the Trio can—in the context of the all-too-worldly dance—have no other intention than ironic or parodistic. Similar intentions undoubtedly prevailed for the 'lamentatione' of the slow movement of Haydn's Symphony in C major, Hob I: 60, 'Il distratto', as all the movements of this symphony were originally intended as entr'actes to a comedy. The role of a *sinfonia da chiesa* was to provide cheerful movements for joyous portions of the service and serious movements for more sombre portions; it was freely composed without cantus firmus, and, therefore, most symphonies could have served. This may explain why, despite attempts by eighteenth-century theorists to maintain distinctions between church, chamber, and theatre symphonies, these categories prove often to have been more sociological than stylistic.

The preceding discussion establishes a context for Mozart's symphonic début in Salzburg on 8 December 1766, when in the cathedral 'a symphony was done which not only found great approbation from all the musicians, but also caused great astonishment'. But it has been suggested that the 'symphony' in question must have been one of the Epistle sonatas;[42] and there are reasons for considering such an

---

[42] H. Klein, 'Unbekannte Mozartiana von 1766/67', *Mozart-Jahrbuch* (1957), 168–85, and esp. 178, n. 15.

interpretation, among them terminological ones. When Charles Burney wrote a retrospective definition of the term 'symphony' in 1804, he included the following eighteenth-century meanings: (1) the instrumental portions of concerted vocal music, (2) any purely instrumental music including sonatas and concertos, (3) the ritornellos of arias, and (4) symphonies proper.[43] As late as 1813, Carpani still used the term 'symphony' in both senses (2) and (3).[44] It is therefore not beyond reason to wonder if the 'symphony' performed in the Salzburg Cathedral may have been an Epistle sonata; yet it almost certainly cannot have been one, for despite their misleadingly low Köchel numbers, even the earliest of them most likely dates from no earlier than 1772.[45]

Another reason for wondering whether Hübner could have meant a symphony in the modern sense arises from a passage in a letter that Mozart wrote to Padre Martini on 4 September 1776, which reads:

Our church music is very different from that of Italy, and what is more, a Mass with all its parts—the Kyrie, the Gloria, the Credo, the Epistle sonata, the Offertory or motet, the Sanctus, and the Agnus Dei—must not last longer than three-quarters of an hour. This applies even to the most solemn Mass said by the Archbishop himself.[46]

The meaning of the purported forty-five-minute time-limit can be somewhat clarified by an examination of Mozart's own church music for Salzburg. If, for instance, one times performances of a Missa brevis, an Epistle sonata, and an Offertory that are all in the same key and possibly intended for one another,[47] one discovers that they amount to around thirty minutes of music. Thus in the

---

[43] Anon., 'Symphony', in Abraham Rees (ed.), *The Cyclopaedia; or, Universal Dictionary of Arts, Sciences, and Literature*, xxxvi (Philadelphia, n.d.), no pagination. The confusion surrounding the meanings of 'symphony' in the eighteenth century creates difficulties in understanding the definitions of Mattheson, Scheibe, and Schulz. It would, for instance, be a legitimate exercise to reread their definitions, substituting the phrase 'any instrumental ensemble piece' for the word 'symphony'. Further concerning Burney's definition, see the beginning of ch. 13.

[44] Carpani, *Le Haydine*, 2nd edn., 100: 'La musica strumentale d'Haydn è formata di sinfonie da camera a più e meno strumenti, e sinfonie da sala a piena orchestra. Le prime sono duetti, terzetti, o trio [sic] che vogliamo chiamarli, quartetti, sestetti, ottavetti, divertimenti. Appartengono a questa classe le sonate a solo di cembalo o pianoforte, quelle a quattro mani, le fantasie, le variazioni, i capricci. Le seconde sono: sinfonie a piena orchestra, concerti per varj strumenti, serenate e marcie.'

[45] H. Dennerlein, 'Zur Problematik von Mozarts Kirchensonaten', *Mozart-Jahrbuch* (1953), 95–111. On the basis of handwriting, W. Plath dates Mozart's earliest Epistle sonatas (K. 67–69 = 41h-k) to 1771–2 ('Beiträge zur Mozart-Autographie II. Schriftchronologie 1770–1780', *Mozart-Jahrbuch* (1976–7), 142, 153). See also A. Tyson, 'Mozart's Use of 10-Stave and 12-Stave Paper' in R. Elvers (ed.), *Festschrift Albi Rosenthal* (Tutzing, 1984), 279. According to M. E. Dounias, (*NMA*, *Kritische Berichte*, vi/6/1. iv) E. Schmid also believed that the work mentioned in Hübner's diary was a symphony and not an Epistle sonata.

[46] *Briefe*, i. 532–3; *Letters*, i. 368 (= i. 266). Except for Wolfgang's signature, this letter is in the hand of Leopold Mozart, who at very least translated and edited it and may be responsible for part or all of its contents.

The rapid Salzburg Mass may be compared to the leisurely Italian approach described in Leopold's letter of 19 May 1770: 'Sunday, the 13th [May], the veiling of a lady was to take place in the convent [at Capua] . . . . We saw the ceremony, which was very magnificent and for which a Kapellmeister with three or four carriages of virtuosos arrived on the evening of the 12th and immediately began the festivities with symphonies and a Salve Regina . . . . The veiling, or rather the Mass, did not take place, however, until noon on Sunday, and the whole affair was over about three o'clock.' *Briefe*, i. 347; *Letters*, i. 198 (= i. 134–5).

[47] D major: K. 194 = 186h, 144 = 124a, 260 = 248a; F major/D minor: K. 192 = 186f, 145 = 124b, 222 = 205a.

remaining fifteen minutes the celebrant and choir would have had to make their way through the Introit, Collect, sonata or symphony (if one were played), Alleluia, Gospel, Preface, Canon, Communion, Post-Communion, and Ite missa est, which would have been possible if everything had been kept moving at a brisk pace. However, either Mozart's letter exaggerated about the time-limit, or the limit did not apply equally to important festivals and to ordinary days, or the Archbishop must have relented, for in 1777 Leopold reported to his son that a Mass by Michael Haydn performed at Salzburg lasted an hour and a quarter.[48] It seems, therefore, that the forty-five-minute limit for Salzburg Masses might be taken with a grain of salt.

While a series of liturgical reforms eventually removed symphonies—and much other music—from Austrian services, the chronology and results of these reforms are difficult to ascertain. The papal encyclical *Annus qui* of 1749 had been tolerant of instrumental music, although it censured pieces of excessive length.[49] Leopold wrote to Mozart from Salzburg on 1 November 1777 that they were to have 'instead of sonatas, the words of the Gradual which the priest is praying',[50] yet Mozart's last Epistle sonata, K. 336 = 336d, is dated 'im Marz 1780'. In February 1783 the Emperor Joseph II promulgated a new 'Gottesdienstordnung' for all of his realm (which excluded Salzburg), limiting instrumental music to Sundays and important feast days. These regulations aroused considerable protest and, as a result, they were softened in 1791 after the Emperor's death to permit more instrumental music.[51] In Salzburg Archbishop Colloredo had anticipated Joseph's 1783 regulations in a pastoral letter of 15 July 1782 banning all instruments other than the organ because 'every good thought is driven out of the hearts of the common people by the miserable fiddling'. This too proved unpopular, and from 1787 it was rescinded for eleven major feast days; it may in any case have applied only to parish churches ('the common people') and not to the Salzburg Cathedral itself,[52] to say nothing of various monastic establishments that did not come under the archbishop's jurisdiction.

The Salzburg reforms also included the introduction of congregational singing of vernacular hymns, whose creation was entrusted primarily to Michael Haydn.

---

[48] Letter of 1 Nov. 1777. *Briefe*, ii. 96; *Letters*, ii. 515–16 (= i. 352). Leopold must have meant that the entire service, including a setting of the Mass ordinary by Haydn, took an hour and a quarter. The widely accepted forty-five-minute limit on Salzburg Masses has also been questioned by W. Senn, 'Beiträge zur Mozartforschung', *Acta Musicologica* (1976), xlviii. 205–27; *idem*, 'Mozarts Kirchenmusik und die Literatur', *Mozart-Jahrbuch* (1978–9), 14–18.

[49] R. G. Pauly, 'The Reforms of Church Music under Joseph II', *The Musical Quarterly* (1957), xliii. 372–82; here 376–7; H. Hollerweger, *Die Reform des Gottesdienstes zur Zeit des Josephismus in Österreich* (Studien zur Pastoralliturgie, i) (Regensburg, 1976).

[50] *Briefe*. ii, 96; *Letters*, ii. 515 (= i. 352).

[51] K. G. Fellerer, 'The Liturgical Basis of Haydn's Masses', *Haydn Studies*, 164–8; W. Pass, 'Josephinism and the Josephian Reforms Concerning Haydn', ibid. 168–71. In their modified form, the regulations remained in force until 1850.

[52] Pauly, 'The Reforms', 378, 381.

An obituary of Haydn related this aspect of the reform to the matter of church symphonies:

With the rapid spread of the ecclesiastical reforms at Salzburg under the wise and unforgettable prince, Archbishop Hieronymus von Colloredo, Haydn was commissioned to write something different, on texts of his own choice, in order to banish the symphonies that had been churned out during the High Mass between the Epistle and Gospel, to the annoyance of pious souls and musical ears.[53]

Can the authors of this obituary really have meant that entire symphonies were performed between the Epistle and Gospel? Perhaps they used 'symphony' in the generic sense demonstrated above, to refer to Epistle sonatas. Still another possibility might be the performance of three-movement symphonies, the first movement as a prelude to the Introit, the second movement as an Epistle sonata, and the Finale as a postlude to the Ite missa est, in the manner observed by Sor at Montserrat. Two symphonies by the Salzburg composer Wenzel Hebelt dating from before 1769 and labelled 'sinfonia solemnis' are in three movements, thus also suggesting the Montserrat procedure.[54]

In this connection it may be relevant to point out that between 1781 or 1782 and 1789 Michael Haydn wrote five three-movement symphonies with fugal finales.[55] Symphonies with fugal finales were rare in the 1780s, and these five were the only ones Haydn wrote. As they came in the wake of the liturgical reforms in Salzburg, we may ask whether (despite the sanctimonious disclaimers of his obituarists) Haydn may not have attempted to preserve the practice of performing symphonies in church by creating especially suitable exemplars.[56]

The most famous symphony with a fugal finale is of course the 'Jupiter' symphony, K. 551. There is no historical evidence to support the idea that the 'Jupiter' symphony was intended by Mozart for performance in church. That this idea would not necessarily have been entirely alien to his contemporaries, however,

---

[53] [Georg Schinn and Franz Josef Otter], *Biographische Skizze von Michael Haydn* (Salzburg, 1808), 18 ff., as quoted in Kirkendale, *Fugue and Fugato*, 37 (= *Fuge und Fugato*, 87).

[54] These symphonies are preserved in the Bibliothek des Bischöflichen Seckauer Ordinariats, Graz. I owe this information to Cliff Eisen.

[55] Perger numbers 19 (28 Sept. 1784), 26 (2 Jan. 1788), 31 (19 Feb. 1788), 33 (26 July 1789), and 43 (undated but perhaps 1781–2). See L. H. Perger, *Michael Haydn: Instrumentalwerke*, i (Denkmäler der Tonkunst in Österreich, Jg. xiv/2 (Vienna, 1907), xxix. ix–xxix; R. G. Pauly and C. H. Sherman, 'Haydn, (Johann) Michael', *The New Grove*, viii. 407–12. Further concerning fugal symphonies, see chs. 11 and 13.

[56] In 1787, it is true, the Archbishop banned instrumental music in the Salzburg liturgy (K. G. Fellerer, 'Mozarts Kirchenmusik und ihre liturgischen Voraussetzungen', *Mozart-Jahrbuch* (1978–9), 24) but, as we have already suggested, this apparently applied only to parish churches. The particular appropriateness of performing a fugue at the end of a Mass is mentioned by Daniel Gottlob Türk, *Von den wichtigsten Pflichten eines Organisten. Ein Beytrag zur Verbesserung der musikalischen Liturgie* (Halle, 1787), 139. Türk, in a section on 'Vorspiel', also remarks, 'Eine Sinfonie, welch vielleicht vor einer komischen Operette die vortrefflichste Würkung that, darf daher auf der Orgel nie gespielt werden; denn die Kirche ist kein Theater' (113). Concerning Mozart playing a fugue at the end of a Mass at Mannheim, see his letter of 13 Nov. 1777. *Briefe*, ii. 120; *Letters*, ii. 544 (= i. 370). Scheibe and Schulz both mentioned the suitability of fugal (or at least contrapuntal) movements in symphonies for church use.

is suggested by the review of a performance of that work in the University Church of Leipzig on 1 September 1828: 'As good a choice as this masterly symphony (which is one of the most appropriate for the church) proved to be, it demonstrated nevertheless (even in a very successful performance) that this genre of music is not appropriate to the church.'[57]

Since the beginning of the twentieth century, church music of the classical period has been 'defrocked'— that is, deemed unsuited for Catholic liturgical use[58]—and much clerical, scholarly and critical commentary has concentrated upon its supposedly worldly (i.e., operatic) character. But Haydn, Mozart, Beethoven, Schubert, and others, must have thought their church music sufficiently spiritual and entirely appropriate, or they would not have composed it as they did. That being the case, it is understandable that many symphonies would also have seemed appropriate. Mozart's symphonies of the 1770s differ little in style from his Epistle sonatas or from the instrumental ritornellos of his sacred vocal music. The Epistle sonatas are especially instructive, as several are so unabashedly in the style of the Italian sinfonia of the day. While secular influences upon sacred music of this era have long been commented on, the reverse influence has not been considered seriously. The new, serious spirit in Austrian symphonies of the 1770s—exemplified by four symphonies that Mozart wrote in 1773 after a visit to Vienna[59]—may be evidence of that influence, and possibly may be related to the use of symphonies in church. Many symphonies of the period were suited to the church, given the rapprochement between the styles of sacred and secular music.

Mozart composed at a time when music was stylistically unified—that is, when many of the same kinds of melodies, harmonies, and rhythms could be (and were) used for serious concert music, operas, light entertainment music, and church music. This helps to explain an aspect of Mozart's music that sorely puzzled many nineteenth-century musicians and that still causes misunderstandings: one finds light-hearted ditties in his serious genres and sublime inventions in his occasional pieces. The transferability of musical idioms explains why Mozart and many of his contemporaries would not necessarily have perceived an aesthetic problem in, for instance, an (early nineteenth-century?) arrangement of the first movement of the 'Linz' symphony, K. 425, as an offertory.[60]

Mozart did not complete much church music during his Viennese years, nor did

[57] Anon., 'Nachrichten . . . . Leipzig. Vom April bis zum 16ten November', *Allgemeine musikalische Zeitung* (19 Nov. 1828), Jg. 30, cols. 787–9

[58] See '*Mediator Dei* of Pope Pius XII on the Sacred Liturgy' and 'The Black List of Disapproved Music' in N. Slonimsky, *Music Since 1900*, 4th edn. (New York, 1971), 1289–91. Pius XII's encyclical was a result of a two-centuries-long struggle in the Catholic Church between conservatives and modernists. The conservatives' efforts to banish concerted music and return to Gregorian chant and a cappella polyphony are referred to as the Cecilian movement (*Caecilianismus*).

[59] K. 182 = 173dA, 183 = 173dB, 201 = 186a, and 202 = 186b. These works are discussed in ch. 8.

[60] The motet *Eja chori resonate*; see K[6], Anh. B, 785.

he compose many symphonies during that period, so it is among the fifty-odd symphonies composed prior to 1780 that any search for possible *sinfonie da chiesa* must take place. The Andante of the Symphony in E flat major, K. 132, makes use of the incipit of a Gregorian melody and quotes the Christmas carol, 'Joseph, lieber Joseph mein'; and the Trio of the Minuet of the same symphony contains psalm-tone-like melodies set to quasi-modal harmonies.[61] Was this intended to render the work suitable for church, or was it parodistic, as suggested above? Does the presence of a Christmas carol mean that the symphony was intended for a Christmas Mass, like the Christmas concertos of Rome? Is the allusion to an Advent hymn in the Minuet and Trio of the Symphony in F major, K. 42a, a clue that the symphony was written for liturgical use? Is the archaic pastoral-siciliano Andante of the Symphony in C, K. 96 = 111b, evidence that it may have been created for a Christmas Mass? Does the mock-pathetic, Miserere-like melody in the Trio of the Minuet of the Symphony in A major, K. 114, connect the work to Holy Week? Is the appearance of the motive doh—ray—fah—me in the symphonies K. 16, Anh. 214 = 45b, 319, and 551 supposed to remind us of 'Credo, credo' (as in the Missa brevis, K. 192 = 186f) or of 'Sanctus, sanctus' (as in the Mass, K. 257)? Is the fugal opening of the jig-like Finale of the Symphony in G major, K. 199 = 161b, intended to remind us of the jig-like finales of dozens of church sonatas, with their token obeisances to the *stile antico?* Should we make anything of the fact that three symphonies discussed in later chapters (K. 84 = 73q, 202 = 186b, 318) begin with the same rhythm Mozart employed for more than a dozen Kyries (♩. ♪ ♩)? Or similarly, what should we say to the fact that two symphonies by Mozart (K. 128, 200 = 189k) begin with the unmistakable double hammerstroke (♩ ♩) that was a characteristic Credo–Sanctus motive? Instrumental church music, Mattheson wrote in 1737, must display 'special solidity, and a well-founded manner of proceeding, so that it does not smack of an undisciplined [opera] overture'.[62] Were any of the above-mentioned features of Mozart's symphonies the results of attempts to 'discipline' them for sacred use; is it a matter of nothing more than common ideas of the period requiring no further explanation; or, indeed, is it a matter of purely secular works alluding to sacred matters?

Schulz, it will be recalled, used the expressions greatness, solemnity, stateliness, and pomp, to describe the effect of the successful symphonies of his time. We may not react precisely the same way to that music, but if Schulz's reactions to symphonies were those of many listeners of the 1760s and 1770s, then we can understand how such music could have been regarded as appropriate to a solemn

---

[61] W. Plath, 'Ein "geistlicher" Sinfoniesatz Mozarts', *Die Musikforschung* (1974), xxvii. 93–5. See the discussion of K. 132 in ch. 8.
[62] *Kern melodischer Wissenschafft*, 19.

Mass. That some symphonies were better suited to a sacred assignment than others was recognized by Schulz's remark that 'in the manner in which it is composed [a symphony] must show whether it befits the church or the theatre'.

Nor should the role played by the manner in which the music was performed be overlooked. Many eminently satisfactory hymns and sacred part-songs and arias were created from pieces whose profane words had been replaced by sacred ones, and the style of performance altered. Such means of 'desecularizing' music were well understood, and discussed in various treatises. Sacred music was to exhibit a certain decorum. This meant, in addition to the possibility of a more conservative style of composition, a more restrained manner of performance. In recent attempts to recreate such performing styles, this has been taken to mean a purer (or so-called 'white') tone with less vibrato and fewer ornaments, combined with generally smoother, more serene modes of articulation and slower tempos. The last not only enhanced the solemnity, but allowed for the resonant acoustic. As Quantz summarized these matters, in church music 'both the execution of the perform-ance, and the tempo, ... must be a little more moderate than in the operatic style'.[63]

Another factor was the continuo instrument. In the 1760s and 1770s in northern Italy, Austria, and southern Germany, the organ was omnipresent in church in both vocal and instrumental music, and—given the church tradition and the evidence presented in Chapter 12 for the use of keyboard continuo in sympho-nies—it is reasonable to conclude that the organ was employed when symphonies were heard in church. Slender testimony supports this supposition. Burney mentioned organ continuo in the Hofmann 'symphonies' he heard at Saint Stephen's. When Haydn received an honorary doctorate at Oxford, he led a performance of a symphony of his in the Sheldonian Theatre from the organ,[64] even though he could easily have requested a harpsichord or fortepiano.

A statement in Leopold Mozart's 'Report' of 1757, that wind instruments were seldom played and the horns never, suggests that soon after he wrote his account, there was a change in performance practices. Plenty of mid-eighteenth-century Austrian concerted church music requires only strings and organ continuo for its performance. Church sonatas in the Salzburg Cathedral archives dating from the

---

[63] Johann Joachim Quantz, *Versuch einer Anweisung die Flöte traversiere zu spielen* (Berlin, 1752), ch. 17, sect. 7, para. 53. See also para. 12: 'A composition for the church requires more majesty and seriousness than one for the theatre, which allows greater freedom. If in a work for the church the composer has inserted some bold and bizarre ideas that are inappropriate to the place, the accompanists, and the violinists in particular, must endeavour to mitigate, subdue, and soften them as much as possible by a modest execution'. The translations are by E. R. Reilly (Quantz, *On Playing the Flute* (London, 1966), 271, 287).

[64] *Morning Herald*, 8 July 1791, as reported in Landon, *Haydn: Chronicle and Works*, iii. 89. Burney (see n. 18) reported that the 'symphonies' of Hofmann that he heard in the cathedral in Vienna were well played except for the sourness of the out-of-tune organ continuo. By 'organ' is meant not the huge cathedral organs but the small organs normally employed for concerted church music; Leopold Mozart made this clear for Salzburg in his 'Report' found in Appendix C.

1730s and 1740s include trumpets and drums and, in one case, oboes.[65] The 1749 papal encyclical *Annus qui* expressly limited church orchestras to strings and organ, although there is evidence that by 1760 or so these regulations were being ignored in some places. The concerted Masses, Vespers, and motets of the principal Salzburg church composers of the second half of the century (the Mozarts, Michael Haydn, Ernst Eberlin, and Joseph Lolli) often require wind instruments, including horns. It has even been suggested that Leopold's Litany in D major for strings and two horns of April 1762, Sieffert *deest*, was the earliest Salzburg church music to break the horn barrier.[66] The introduction of wind instruments into church music sometime between Leopold's report of 1757 and his Litany of 1762 may have opened the way for performance of Mozart's 'astonishing' symphony of 1766 in the Salzburg Cathedral.

The changes in church music discussed in this chapter—the use of galant sinfonias in place of baroque concertos, the application of the modern style of vocal music, the introduction of the full classical orchestra—were presumably behind Schubart's remark upon visiting Salzburg in the mid-1770s that 'the ecclesiastical musical style has begun to deteriorate into the theatrical'.[67] Deteriorate? Mozart knew better. Like Haydn, Beethoven, and so many others, he had been raised on Fux's species counterpoint and taught that the style of church music was supposed to remain stable. But, as he reminded his father, he knew that 'musical taste is continually changing—and what is more . . . this extends even to church music, which ought not to be the case. Hence it is that true church music is to be found only in attics and in a worm-eaten condition.'[68]

To return to Hübner: is it possible to identify the 'symphony' by Mozart that the diarist heard on 8 December 1766? The fact that the auditors were 'astonished' at Mozart's symphony will not help to determine which work it may have been, since their astonishment was undoubtedly due not so much to the music itself as to the age of its composer, then a few weeks short of his eleventh birthday. Doubtless, the symphony of 8 December 1766 should be sought among K. 16, 19, 19a, 22, and 45a,[69] works composed in London and The Hague, and performed in those cities as well as in Amsterdam, Utrecht, Paris, Dijon, Lyons, Zurich, and Donaueschingen.

[65] Information kindly provided by Cliff Eisen.

[66] M. H. Schmid, *Mozart und die salzburger Tradition* (Tutzing, 1976), 257. But see also Eisen, 'The Symphonies of Leopold Mozart', 48, n. 47, which lists other equally early church music by Leopold Mozart with original horn parts, and points out that there is no evidence that these works were composed for the Salzburg Cathedral.

[67] Schubart, *Ideen*, 158; but in the light of a report of the mid-1780s stating that in Salzburg 'the church music is good, tasteful, and entirely suited to sacred subjects' (see ch. 10, n. 12).

[68] Letter of 12 Apr. 1783. *Briefe*, iii. 264; *Letters*, iii. 1259–60 (= ii. 845). In this passage, Mozart was undoubtedly trying to console and flatter his father.

[69] And possibly among the lost works: K. 19b, 66c, 66d, 66e, Anhang C 11.07, and Anhang C 11.08; or among the symphonies without authentic sources: K. 76 = 42a, Anhang 214 = 45b, 81 = 73*l*, 97 = 73m, 95 = 73m, 84 = 73q, Anh. 216 = 74g = Anhang C 11.03, 75, and 96 = 111b.

No unambiguous evidence exists to suggest that Mozart composed symphonies during nine months in Salzburg after the grand tour and before a long stay in Vienna. Yet, besides the performance of a symphony in the Cathedral on 8 December 1766, there were probably others in Salzburg. For example, the Symphony in G major, K. 45a, of 1766 was revised during this period, and the Symphony in D major, K. 73n, possibly may have originated in 1767. Furthermore, two works of the period not initially contributions to Mozart's symphonic *œuvre* may have been used by him as 'chamber' symphonies, and one other symphony, K. 45b, may also date from this period.

Symphony in D major, K. 35, 'Die Schuldigkeit des ersten Gebots'

[Incipits 4.1]

Instrumentation: *strings, 2 oboes, 2 horns, [bassoon, harpsichord]
Autograph: Windsor Castle, England
Principal source: none
Facsimile: *NMA*, i/4/1. xiii–xvi
Editions: *GA*, vi. 1–5 (= Serie 5, No. 1); *NMA*, i/4/1. 1–7

In late 1766 and early 1767 Mozart set Part 1 of a Lenten oratorio, *Die Schuldigkeit des ersten und fürnehmsten Gebots* ('The Obligation of the First and Foremost Commandment'), K. 35. The other parts of this tripartite oratorio, on a libretto by the Salzburg Burgomaster Ignaz Anton Weiser, were set by Michael Haydn and Anton Adlgasser. Mozart's portion received its première in the Knights' Hall of the archiepiscopal palace on 12 March, and a second performance on 2 April; Haydn's portion was performed on 19 March; and Adlgasser's probably on 26 March. According to the libretto for Part 1 of the oratorio, 'The action takes place in a pleasant landscape with a garden and a small wood', and stage directions occur throughout. Nevertheless, this oratorio was probably intended not for stage production but for the theatre of the mind. The protagonists of the allegory are: the Spirit of Christianity (perhaps this should be translated simply as 'Christian', as in Bunyan's *Pilgrim's Progress*), Worldliness, Divine Mercy, Divine Justice, and, later on (in Part II), 'a Lukewarm and afterwards Ardent Christian'. Mozart's setting consists of seven arias and a concluding terzetto, interspersed with recitatives, all prefaced by an orchestral movement headed 'Sinfonia / Allegro'.

Carl Ferdinand Pohl, who in 1864 rediscovered the autograph manuscript of Mozart's portion of *Die Schuldigkeit* in the Royal Library at Windsor Castle, characterized the sinfonia as 'simple and natural in structure'.[70] From the character of its Italianate opening melody in sixths accompanied by a repeated-note bass-line, it could just as well have served to launch an opera as an oratorio. A binary movement with both sections repeated, its opening section rapidly comes to rest on the dominant, and a contrasting 'sigh' motive is introduced, which is then heard in thirds, sixths, and octaves, and in inversion. A brief return of the opening idea leads to a sonorous closing section, with tremolo in the violins and melodic interest transferred to the bass. The second half begins as did the first, but in the dominant. No new ideas are introduced; rather the ideas of the first half are manipulated through several keys and changes of orchestration, before the return of the home key and the opening idea fifteen bars from the end. This one-movement sinfonia is on the same scale as, and in a style similar to, the first movements of the symphonies K. 19, 19a, 22, and 45a, and shows a confidence in the handling of its materials undoubtedly gained in writing those earlier works.

Symphony in D major, K. 38, 'Apollo and Hyacinth'

[Incipits 4.2]

Instrumentation: *strings, 2 oboes, 2 horns, [bassoon, harpsichord]
Autograph: Staatsbibliothek Preussische Kulturbesitz, West Berlin (Mus. Ms. Autogr. W. A. Mozart 38)
Principal source: none
Facsimile: *NMA*, ii/5/1. xxiii–xxv
Editions: *GA*, vi. 1–5 (= Serie 5, No. 2); *NMA*, ii/5/1. 3–10

In Leopold Mozart's 'List' of his son's childhood works[71] is the following entry for the work that now bears the designation K. 38: 'Music to a Latin comedy for Salzburg University, with five singing personae. The original score has 162 pages'. Many years later Nannerl annotated this, 'Written in [Wolfgang's] eleventh year 1767'. The Benedictines who ran Salzburg University had a policy in their schools

---

[70] C. F. Pohl, 'Mozarts erstes dramatisches Werk', *Allgemeine musikalische Zeitung* (1865), iii, cols. 225–33.
[71] See ch. 5 for a discussion of this document.

of mounting didactic plays, operas, and ballets on doctrinal subjects and edifying themes. On 13 May 1767 a three-act spoken tragedy (*Clementia Croesi* by Rufin Widl) was performed by students and teachers in the Great Hall of the University, and Mozart's *Apollo and Hyacinth* was inserted into it, divided into three portions serving as prologue and two entr'actes. Although K. 38 seems to have been well received,[72] no further performances are recorded. Its libretto, in Latin, is in the style of opera librettos of the day. It relates the story found in Ovid and elsewhere of the slaying of the youth Hyacinth, who was metamorphosed into the flower that bears his name.[73]

The work's overture—or 'Entrada' as Mozart labelled it, suggesting that it had a ceremonial or dramatic function at the beginning of the drama—is listed as an independent symphony in the Breitkopf & Härtel Manuscript Catalogue, p. 10, No. 65, one of a set of six early symphonies sent to Breitkopf & Härtel around 1800 by the Salzburg Kapellmeister Luigi Gatti through Nannerl Mozart's good offices. (The possible significance of this set of symphonies is discussed in Chapter 6.) The single-movement work, on the same scale and in the same style as the first movements of Mozart's early symphonies, is in binary form, with only the first section repeated. In the near absence of cantabile melody, there are scales, arpeggios, syncopations, repeated notes, and fanfares—all regular ingredients of the symphonic style of the day and entirely appropriate in a work apparently intended as a processional.

Symphony in B flat major, K. Anh. 214 = 45b

[Incipits 4.3]

[72] Deutsch, 70–1 (= 75–6). Concerning the nature of these Salzburg University performances, usually four to six annually, fully staged, see H. Boberski, *Das Theater der Benediktiner an der alter Universität Salzburg (1617–1778)* (Theatergeschichte Österreiches, vi/1) (Vienna, 1978).
[73] K. 38 is more fully discussed in connection with K. 43 in Chapter 5.

Trio

(18)

Allegro

(144)

Instrumentation: strings, 2 oboes, 2 horns, [bassoon, harpsichord]
Autograph: none
Principal source: Staatsbibliothek Preussischer Kulturbesitz, West Berlin (Mus. Ms.
15305)
Facsimile: none
Edition: *NMA*, iv/11/1. 129–42

K. 45b is one of the ten symphonies known to Köchel solely by first-movement
incipits in the Breitkopf & Härtel Manuscript Catalogue (No. 2). Prior to the
publication of K³ Einstein had located a set of eighteenth-century parts for this
work in the Berlin library. The title-page, on the basso part, reads: 'Synfonie Ex B♭
à 2 Violini, 2 Oboe, 2 Corni, Viola è Basso / Del Sig. Cavaliere Amadeo
Wolfgango Mozart Maestro di concerto di S. A. à Salisburgo'. It is now thought
that these parts, of unknown provenance, date from around 1800.[74] Mozart
received the unpaid post of 'maestro di concerto' to the Salzburg court on 14
November 1769, and earned the right to call himself 'Cavaliere' on 5 July 1770,
when he was decorated by the Pope in Rome with the Order of the Golden Spur.
Einstein felt, on stylistic grounds, that this symphony could not have been written
later than early 1768, so he gave it the number 45b in K³, believing the Berlin
manuscript to be a copy of a pre-1768 work made post-1770. As an indirect
consequence of the Second World War, K. 45b was published twice, once in
Leipzig (Breitkopf & Härtel, ed. Müller von Asow) and once in New York (C. F.
Peters, ed. Einstein). In the latter edition the work is given the subtitle 'Cavaliere'.
This is entirely unjustified as (according to Einstein's own dating of the symphony)

[74] H.-G. Klein, *Wolfgang Amadeus Mozart: Autographe und Abschriften* (Staatsbibliothek Preussischer Kulturbesitz,
Kataloge der Musikabteilung, I/vi) (Berlin, 1982), 272, 467.

Mozart was not yet a Cavaliere in 1767–8, and, in any case, Mozart's name is prefaced by Cavaliere on several symphony autographs.

Since in Chapter 6 dating and attribution solely on stylistic grounds are strongly criticized, the following speculation is ventured with considerable diffidence. K. 45b has much in common with Mozart's symphonies of 1764–6 (K. 16, 19, 19a, 22, 45a, 35, and 38) in the length, format, and style of its movements. The presence of a Minuet and Trio aside, it has less in common with the symphonies he wrote in Vienna in 1768 (K. 43, 45, and 48). It has therefore tentatively been assigned here to the period in Salzburg in 1767, a possibility Einstein left open in considering the beginning of 1768 as the *latest* possible date for the work's composition. Barring the discovery of better documentary evidence, the time and place of creation of K. 45b, and perhaps also its author, remain in doubt.

The first movement is written in a type of sonata form in which the ideas presented in the exposition recur in reverse order in the second part, a mirror technique of which Mozart would later make brilliant use in the first movement of K. 133. While much has been made of the presence in the bass-line of K. 45b of the 'Jupiter' motive doh—ray—fah—me, no one seems to have suggested that it appears too often, sometimes abruptly transposed.

In the E flat Andante, another sonata-form movement, the horns are silent, and the violins, occasionally joined by the oboes, play duets far above the bass-line. A danceable Minuet is contrasted with a Trio in F for strings only. The final Allegro, again in sonata form, concludes the symphony cheerfully if conventionally.

Symphony in D major, K. 95 = 73n

[Incipits 4.4]

Instrumentation: strings, 2 oboes = flutes, 2 trumpets, [bassoon, kettledrums, harpsichord]

Autograph: unknown

Principal source: lost eighteenth-century parts, formerly Breitkopf & Härtel archives, Leipzig

Edition: *GA*, xxxix. 32–41 (= Serie 24, No. 5); *NMA*, iv/11/2. 33–46; reconstructed kettledrum part: R. Dearling, *The Music of Wolfgang Amadeus Mozart: The Symphonies* (London, 1982), 196

This work survived only in an undated, non-autograph manuscript in the Breitkopf & Härtel archives, which is now lost or destroyed. The lack of a proper critical report in the *GA*[75] leaves us in the dark about the nature and possible provenance of the lost manuscript. K. 73n is one of eight symphonies that, although lacking reliable sources, have been accepted as authentic and never seriously enough questioned.[76] In K[3] and K[6] K. 73n has been assigned on unstated grounds to Rome, April 1770; the matter of which symphonies Mozart is likely to have written in Rome is addressed in Chapter 7.

The first movement opens with an idea closely related to that which launches the symphonies K. 97 = 73m and 74, which may explain why Einstein grouped the three together chronologically in K[3]. (If so, this was probably a questionable tactic, given the conventionality of so many symphony incipits of the period.) In sonata form without repeats, the movement is an essay in orchestral 'noises' assembled to create a coherent gestalt, that is, there are no memorable, cantabile melodies, but rather a succession of idiomatic instrumental devices, including repeated notes, scales, fanfares, turns, arpeggios, and abrupt dynamic changes.[77] A sudden halt on a

---

[75] *W. A. Mozart's Werk: Kritisch durchgesehene Gesamtausgabe. Revisionsbericht, Serie VIII*, 'Verzeichnis der benutzen Originalhandschriften' (Leipzig, 1888), no pagination.

[76] The others are: K.76 = 42a, Anh. 214 = 45a, 81 = 73*l*, 97 = 73m, 84 = 73q, 75, and 96 = 111b.

[77] The aesthetic problems posed by such a style of composition are discussed under the Symphony in D, K. 100 = 62a, at the end of ch. 6.

D major chord with added seventh leads directly into the G major Andante, whose opening idea bears a resemblence to a minuet from one of the accompanied keyboard sonatas that Mozart published in Paris in 1764 (Example 4.1).[78] The trumpets and kettledrums drop out and the oboists put aside their instruments to take up flutes, lending the Andante a pastoral hue. Whatever lyricism may have been lacking in the previous movement is more than atoned for in this movement, which is in rounded-binary form with both halves repeated.

The oboes and trumpets return for the Minuet, while the D minor Trio again omits the trumpets and drums, and in its quiet intimacy nicely sets off the return of the Minuet. The final Allegro returns to the sonata form and happy noises of the opening movement, the two movements also being linked by their common opening gesture, a rising triadic figure.

Ex. 4.1 Minuet from the Sonata in G major, K. 9

The first movement of K. 73n exhibits some notable similarities to the first movements of Mozart's earliest symphonies: the organization of its opening paragraph—the grouping and reiteration of two or more contrasting phrases—also occurs only in the certainly genuine symphonies K. 16 and 73 and the questionable K. 45b and 75. Expositions in which the material after the modulation to the dominant is briefer than that before the modulation also occurs only in K. 16, 75b, and 114, and the questionable K. 45b and 73m. A recapitulation shorter than the exposition—most likely to occur in works not having a full recapitulation, as is the case here—is also found only in K. 16 and the questionable 45b. Here, then, is a cluster of stylistic traits uniting the first movement of K. 73n with those of some of Mozart's earliest symphonies, and especially K. 16 and the questionable 45b.[79] The Andante and Finale of K. 73n also fit the patterns established by the known, authentic symphonies of 1764–5: K. 16, 19, 19a, 22, and 45a. The question arises therefore: can K. 73n be the missing symphony (discussed in Chapter 2) that Mozart apparently wrote before K. 16? It even has trumpets to satisfy Nannerl's

---

[78] Wyzewa–Saint-Foix, i. 282 (= i. 311). Roughly the same tune appears in the Kyrie of the Mass in E flat major, K. 139 = 47a, and as the theme of a set of variations in the piano sonata, K. 331 = 300i; it is the German folk-song 'Freu Dich mein Herz, denk' an kein Schmerz' and the Czech folk-song 'Hořela lípa, hořela'.

[79] I am indebted to Christopher Hill for stimulating discussions of these points.

description of Wolfgang's 'first' symphony, although not only does it not 'give the horn something worthwhile to do', but—unlike all of Mozart's authentic symphonies—it lacks horns entirely. A symphony with trumpets instead of, rather than in addition to, horns is a rarity in the 1760s and 1770s. Possibly there may once have been horn parts to K. 73n, which became lost; or possibly these trumpet parts were originally intended for horns.[80] Another stumbling block to the hypothosis that K. 73n may have been the symphony described by Nannerl is the presence of the Minuet and Trio, movements entirely lacking in the symphonies of 1764–5. A possible explanation for their presence, which might rescue this theory, is that on at least one occasion Mozart is known to have added a minuet and trio to a three-movement 'Italian' overture-symphony in order to turn it into a four-movement 'Austrian' concert-symphony,[81] and in K[3], Einstein suggested that the Minuet and Trio of K. 73n may have been a later addition, on the grounds that the other three movements constituted 'a typical "Italian" sinfonia'. On the other hand, perhaps the stylistic similarities between this work and Mozart's earliest symphonies, taken in conjunction with its 'Austrian' minuet, should be interpreted to suggest that the symphony was written in Salzburg in 1767 after the return from the grand tour. In any case, all of this speculation is based on the tricky grounds of style, for having no authentic source for K. 73n, one cannot even be sure of its author, let alone its date.

The personnel of the Salzburg court orchestra in 1767 is shown in Table 8.1. This ensemble (subject to the interpretations and qualifications discussed in Chapter 1) probably performed a number of Mozart's earliest symphonies, works that, despite the tender age of their creator, stand comparison rather well with the compositions of the other Salzburg composers of that period.

[80] Symphonies with trumpets but no horns: Johann Stamitz, Wolf D22 (Swedish manuscript: 'Trompet eu Cornu'), Wolf D25; Dittersdorf, Grave C14, E♭6; Franz Joseph Amman, Symphony in D major, xx/24.

[81] K. 319. See ch. 10.

5

Vienna (I): Orchestra Land (1767–1768)

As the testimony of a well-travelled professional, thoughtfully evaluating music and performances, Charles Burney's reports are especially valuable. The two main theatres in Vienna alternated evenings of activity. Arriving in the Austrian capital on 30 August 1772, Burney learned that the curtain was about to go up at the 'German' Theatre (the Kärntnerthortheater), so he proceeded directly there. He reported:

This theatre [the German theatre] is lofty, having five or six rows of boxes, twenty-four in each row. The height makes it seem short . . . . The orchestra has a numerous band, and the pieces which were played for the overture and act-tunes [to Lessing's *Emilia Galotti*] were very well performed, and had an admirable effect; they were composed by Haydn, Hofman[n], and Vanhall . . . .

The second evening after my arrival, I went to the French theatre, where I saw a German comedy, or rather a farce in five acts . . . . This theatre is not so high as that at which I had been the night before . . . ; here the best players seem to be in the pit . . . . The orchestra here was full as striking as that of the other theatre, and the pieces played were admirable. They seemed so full of invention, that it seemed to be music of some other world, insomuch, that hardly a passage in this was to be traced; and yet all was natural, and equally free from the stiffness of labour, and the pedantry of hard study. Whose music it was I could not learn; but both the composition and performance, gave me exquisite pleasure.[1]

A few years later the report of a Swiss traveller, Johann Kaspar Riesbeck (who was a dilettante, not a professional) concurred with Burney's evaluation of the Viennese orchestras. His remarks, however, went beyond Burney's in attempting to offer an explanation. Following a harsh description of the nobility, whose way of life he found philistine and coarse, he wrote:

[1] Charles Burney, *The Present State of Music in Germany, the Netherlands, and United Provinces* (London, 1773), i. 213–14, 217–20. By 'French' theatre Burney meant the Burgtheater.

Music is the sole [aspect of Viennese life] in which the nobles show taste. Many households have a special group of musicians of their own, and all public musical activities demonstrate that this aspect of art is strongly emphasized. Here one can assemble four or five large orchestras, all of which are incomparable. The number of true virtuosos is small, but as far as orchestral music is concerned, one can hardly hear anything more beautiful in the whole world. I have already heard approximately thirty or forty instruments play together, and they produced a tone so true, so pure, and so distinct that one could believe he heard a single, supernaturally powerful instrument. One stroke [of the bow] animated all the violins and one breath, all the wind instruments. It seemed a miracle, to an Englishman next to whom I sat, that nothing untoward was to be heard in the larger orchestras (I won't say not a clinker), nothing caused by a hasty, early attack, a somewhat too slow release, or a too strong [bow-]grip or too strong breath. The Englishman, though he had just come from Italy, was enchanted by the purity and correctness of the harmony [in Vienna].

There are approximately 400 musicians here who are divided into specific groups and often work together uninterruptedly for many long years. They are accustomed to one another and commonly have strong leadership. They succeed so well through much practice as well as through the industry and cold-bloodedness characteristic of the Germans. On one day of the year in Vienna, these 400 musicians jointly give a concert for the benefit of the widows of musicians. I have been assured that on that occasion all of the 400 instruments play together just as accurately, as articulately, and as in tune as if one heard it from twenty or thirty. This concert is undoubtedly the only one of its type in the world.[2]

Even without such eyewitness accounts, the calibre of the Viennese orchestras might have been guessed by the effect that their playing apparently had on Mozart's music. During and after his visits to Vienna of 1767–8 and 1773 he wrote symphonies of noticeably greater length and seriousness than those he had composed previously. And there is no mistaking the ever-increasing difficulty of the orchestral writing in his piano concertos, operas, and symphonies after he settled permanently in Vienna in 1781. The technical demands of Mozart's orchestral works of the 1780s were the object of complaint in other parts of Europe during his lifetime and into the 1790s,[3] and in much of Italy until well into the nineteenth century his operas were apparently considered nearly impossible to perform because of their orchestral difficulties.[4]

  [2] [Johann Kaspar Riesbeck,] *Briefe eines reisenden Franzosen über Deutschland. An seinen Bruder zu Paris* (Zurich, 1783); modern edn. W. Gerlach (Stuttgart, 1967), 138–40. Riesbeck's final paragraph refers to the annual Lenten and Advent concerts of the Tonkünstler-Societät für Musiker-Witwen und -Waisen, founded in 1772. The number 400 is an exaggeration and, in any case, would have included both choir and orchestra. For Mozart's participation in Tonkünstler-Societät concerts, see ch. 11 and C. F. Pohl, *Denkschrift aus Anlass des hundertjährigen Bestehens der Tonkünstler-Societät* (Vienna, 1871).

  [3] Deutsch, 202–3, 236, 287, 292, 302–3, 310, 334, 335, suppl. 65 (= 228, 270, 328, 333, 345, 353, 380, 381, 386).

  [4] 'Kurze Nachrichten', *Allgemeine musikalische Zeitung* (1801), iii. cols. 497–500, 557–8; H. Stendhal (= M. H. Beyle), 'Mozart en Italie', in *Vie de Rossini* (Paris, 1824), trans. and ed. R. N. Coe (London, 1970), 30–6; anon., 'Introduction of Mozart's Music into Italy', *The Harmonicon* (1824), ii. 14–16.

Recently published archival documents enable us to learn something about the principal Viennese orchestras, which have not received as much attention from music historians as have the orchestras of Mannheim and Paris.[5] In 1773 at the Hofburgtheater (which Burney called the 'French' theatre) the orchestral strings were 6—6—3—3—3, with 1 flute, 1 harpsichord, and pairs of oboes, bassoons, and horns, or a total of 29 instrumentalists. At the Kärntnerthortheater (Burney's 'German' theatre) the strings were 7—7—4—3—3, with pairs of flutes, oboes, bassoons, and horns, and a harpsichord, or a total of 33. In 1775 the numbers of orchestral players were nearly identical to those two years earlier.[6] For the season from April 1776 to March 1777 the strings of the Hofburgtheater were 6–7—6–7—2–3—3—2, while the wind consisted of pairs of oboes and horns. On seven evenings during this season extras were hired, including a harpist, four more horn players, and, for a Singspiel entitled *Der Fuchs in der Falle*, a six-piece wind ensemble, perhaps for a stage band. On certain days concerts were presented instead of plays or operettas, and the archival records for these years show fees paid for the copying of twenty-four symphonies by Franz Aspelmayr, twelve by Dittersdorf, nine by Gassmann, three by Haydn, two by Vanhal, one each by Pugnani and [J. C.?] Bach, and a dozen more.[7]

Mention of Aspelmayr, Gassmann, Vanhal, and the others raises the question of the Viennese school of symphonists. Burney reported that the composers active in Vienna at the time of his visit were Albrechtsberger, Dittersdorf, Gassman, Gluck, Hasse, Haydn, Hofmann, Huber, Kohaut, La Motte, Mysliveček, Salieri, Domenico [rect. Giuseppe] Scarlatti, Stefani, Vanhal, and Venturini. He especially praised the symphonies of Dittersdorf, Haydn, Hofmann, Huber, and Vanhal;[8] and one might add many more German, Bohemian, Italian, and Spanish composers of symphonies active in and around Vienna.[9] The range of styles exhibited by the symphonies of such a large, cosmopolitan group of composers working over several decades is of course great. But their works may be compared in a general way to the works that Mozart had as models in London, and the most striking differences are these: the Viennese symphonists of the late 1760s favoured four rather than three movements, use of winds not only to sustain chords in the tutti passages but also in a concertante vein, and a more contrapuntally conceived texture as a foil to the reigning Italianate homophony.[10]

    [5] See the beginning of ch. 9.
    [6] G. Zechmeister, *Die wiener Theater nächst der Burg und nächst dem Kärntnertor von 1747 bis 1776* (Vienna, 1971), 356–7.
    [7] Ibid. 354, 372.
    [8] Burney, *Germany, the Netherlands, and United Provinces*, i. 364–5.
    [9] G. R. Hill, *A Preliminary Checklist of Research on the Classic Symphony and Concerto to the Time of Beethoven (excluding Haydn and Mozart)* (Hackensack, 1970), 43–6.
    [10] See further G. Adler, 'Die wiener klassische Schule', in *Handbuch der Musikgeschichte*, 2nd edn. (Berlin, 1930), ii. 768–95; J. P. Larsen, 'Some Observations on the Development and Characteristics of Vienna Classical Instrumental Music', *Studia Musicologica* (1967), ix. 115–39; idem, 'The Viennese Classical School: A Challenge to Musicology', *Current Musicology* (1969), ix. 105–12; idem, 'Zur Entstehung des österreichischen Symphonietradition', *Haydn Yearbook* (1978), x. 72–80.

The only evidence of what the twelve-year-old composer made of the symphonies and orchestras of Vienna in 1767–8 is found in the music he wrote: three symphonies, one of them in two versions. But the discussion of his symphonic output of the period begins with a work whose provenance is much less certain.

Symphony in F major, K. 76 = 42a

[Incipits 5.1]

Instrumentation: strings, 2 oboes, 2 bassoons, 2 horns, [harpsichord]
Autograph: unknown
Principal source: lost eighteenth-century parts, formerly Breitkopf & Härtel archives, Leipzig

Facsimiles: none

Editions: *GA*, xxxix. 12–31 (= Serie 24, No. 3 = B&H No. 43); *NMA*, iv/11/1. 63–78

Although attribution of this symphony to Mozart is problematic, its authenticity has until recently not been seriously questioned. Lacking an autograph or other reliable manuscript stemming from the Mozarts or their circle, K. 42a had as its sole source a set of eighteenth-century manuscript parts, sent by Nannerl around 1800 to Breitkopf & Härtel, listed on p. 9 as No. 59 in their Manuscript Catalogue, and now lost. In accepting this work as genuine, Köchel followed Otto Jahn, who had reported that the source for K. 42a in the Breitkopf archives formed part of a collection of twenty symphonies attributed to Mozart. Ten of these were listed in Johann André's catalogue of his collection of Mozartiana. Since André's collection had been purchased from Mozart's widow, its contents could be regarded as reliable, Jahn thought.[11] Two other symphonies of the twenty were versions of the overtures to *Lucio Silla* and *Il sogno di Scipione*. The remaining eight symphonies could (Jahn felt) be adjudged genuine because of the company in which they were found. He dated K. 42a '177?',[12] while Köchel ventured 'perhaps 1769'. On the weighty authority of Jahn and Köchel, K. 42a was published in 1881 in a supplementary fascicle of the *GA*.

Wyzewa and Saint-Foix placed K. 42a in Salzburg between 1 December 1766 and 1 March 1767. They suggested—because of perceived similarities between the first movement of this work and the overture to *Die Schuldigkeit des ersten Gebots*, K. 35, and on the basis of comparisons with Mozart's earliest symphonies—that K. 42a 'was composed before the overture [to K. 35], perhaps around the month of December 1766. It is the great piece that the child wrote, with extreme effort and care, when, returning to Salzburg [from the grand tour], he wished to show his master and his compatriots everything he had learned during his travels.'[13] To call this speculation is too generous; it is sheer fantasy.

Hermann Abert examined Wyzewa's and Saint-Foix's arguments and, while questioning the similarities they had proposed between K. 42a and the overture to K. 35, agreed with them that the work must be earlier than Köchel had thought.[14] Finally, in K[3] Einstein gave as the date of this orphaned work, 'allegedly autumn 1767 in Vienna'. The basis for this judgement was not explained, but a seemingly unrelated remark may reveal his line of reasoning. The Minuet of this symphony,

[11] Predictably, the assumption of the complete reliability of André's holdings has proven incorrect.
[12] O. Jahn, *W. A. Mozart* (Leipzig, 1856–9), i. 701.
[13] Wyzewa–Saint-Foix, i. 178 (= i. 204).
[14] H. Abert, *W. A. Mozart* (Leipzig, 1923), i. 116.

Einstein wrote, 'is of a relatively so much greater maturity than the other three, primitive movements, that we dare to assert that it was composed later'. Einstein pointed out that Viennese symphonies usually had four movements (which they frequently did, even if not so often as he would have had us believe) and that Mozart sometimes added minuets and trios to three-movement symphonies to tailor them for Vienna (as in the case of K. 319); Einstein must therefore have thought that the (hypothetical) addition of a minuet and trio to K. 42a associated it with a visit to the Imperial capital. (Similar reasoning about minuets apparently caused the Symphony in B flat, K. 45b, discussed at the end of the previous chapter, to be assigned to the beginning of 1768 in Vienna.) The clear implication, then, is that the other three movements of K. 42a originated earlier. This rootless symphony has retained Einstein's assignment 'allegedly in autumn 1767 in Vienna' in K^6.

In the absence of sources, further documentary investigation of K. 42a is impossible. That unlike some other symphonies uncertainly attributed to Mozart this one does not have a conflicting attribution to another composer may be merely the fortuitous result of the loss of sources (and the same can be said of the other questionable symphonies, K. 16a, 45b, 73m, and 73n). If K. 42a is to be judged by the company it kept in the Breitkopf archives, as suggested by Jahn and Köchel, then its credentials are weak, for seven of the eight symphonies mentioned by Jahn remain to this day without autographs or other reliable sources.

A noteworthy feature of the first movement is the prominence of the wind, which, in addition to the customary pairs of oboes and horns, includes a pair of obbligato bassoons. Wyzewa and Saint-Foix singled out for mention 'the oboe and bassoon solos, the constant exchanges of melodic ideas between the wind and strings'.[15] In regarding this as a progressive trait, they must have had in mind the innovative concertante wind writing in Mozart's late operas, symphonies, and piano concertos. Perhaps they considered K. 42a a step in that direction. But they failed to notice how very uncharacteristic for Mozart this wind writing was for 1767 or any other period. In Mozart's early symphonies the expositions of first movements typically begin and end tutti, forte, often with semiquaver tremolos in the strings adding to the bustle. In the middle of the exposition, however, more lyrical sections usually appear, corresponding with the arrival on the dominant, at which some or all of the wind fall silent. This procedure strengthens the dynamics by the wind reinforcement of the tuttis, underlines the contrast of character that is one criterion of the style, clearly signals the musical structure to the ear, and gives the wind players breathing space. It was a standard feature of Mozart's orchestration. In the first movement of K. 42a, however, the wind never rest, thereby

---

[15] Wyzewa–Saint-Foix, i. 179 (= i. 205).

giving the movement its uncharacteristically uniform timbre. We of course have no right to deny Mozart an experiment in orchestration. But was this his experiment, or someone else's?

The use of the wind in the classical symphony as outlined above was by no means limited to Mozart. Many symphonies of the period are orchestrated in this manner, and an eyewitness account suggests that Joseph Haydn too subscribed to similar principles. The account comes from the Swedish diplomat Fredrik Samuel Silverstolpe, who paid Haydn a number of visits in 1800. Of one such occasion he wrote:

Once when I called on Haydn, he was looking over the work of a pupil. It was the first Allegro of a symphony, in which genre the young man now submitted his first trial piece. As Haydn cast a glance at the draft and found therein a long period in which the winds rested, he said to the apprentice in a polite yet half-joking tone of voice, 'Rests are harder than anything else to write; you did right to think about what great effect long piano passages can have'. The more he read, the darker his look became. 'I have nothing to criticize about the part-writing', he said. 'It is correct. The proportions are not such as I would wish them, however. See here, a thought that is only half presented: it should not be abandoned so soon. And this phrase is badly connected to the rest. Seek to give a correct balance to the whole, which can't be so difficult because the principal idea is good'. — All this was cordially spoken, and the youth, eager for knowledge, far from appearing hurt, showed Haydn his lively gratitude. I never knew his name; perhaps he is one of those who later on became known.[16]

If for a moment we put ourselves in Haydn's place and look at the first movement of K. 42a as if it had been handed to us by a pupil, we notice not only the uncharacteristic handling of the wind, but another peculiarity as well. The piece begins well, with an original opening idea, although one that is rather uniform in texture, dynamics, and motives compared to the beginnings of Mozart's early symphonies—and even compared to the more characteristic opening of the Finale of K. 42a itself. The first movement continues logically, but at bar 23 something goes wrong with a sequential idea from which the composer cannot seem to extricate himself gracefully. In the recapitulation the problem is exacerbated, because the two bars of tremolo that preceded the sequence in the exposition have been expanded to six limping bars (Example 5.1). Here we have not the half-presented idea that Haydn criticized, but another kind of artistic failure: a phrase used too often and then, in his words, 'badly connected to the rest'. (Mozart may sometimes have had problems of continuity in the first drafts of pieces—see the discussion in Chapter 11 of sketches for the 'Prague' symphony— but such a lapse is rare in his completed symphonies, even in the earliest ones where

---

[16] C.-G. Stellan Mörner, 'Haydniana aus Schweden um 1800', *Haydn-Studien* (1969–70), ii. 27.

the occasional abrupt transition does occur.) Despite weaknesses, the opening movement of K. 42a is attractive and we should like to know who its author was.

As the work comes down to us only under the name 'Mozart', Leopold may be its author. In the absence of documentary evidence such a suggestion is purely speculative, although no more so than the work's attribution to Wolfgang. Although it proves nothing about the authorship of K. 42a, Leopold's description of how he used the wind 'in the modern manner' in an unidentified symphony is certainly closer to what happens in K. 42a than is either Haydn's prescription in his composition lesson or Wolfgang's practice in his undoubtedly genuine early symphonies:

I have ... a symphony for 2 violins, viola, 2 oboes, 2 horns, 2 bassoons, and basso—all obbligato .... In the Adagio the first oboe and first horn have a solo together. It [the symphony] is composed in the newest fashion. It ends with a Minuet, whose Trio is for 2 oboes, 2 horns, 2 bassoons, all solo. Throughout the entire symphony the bassoons play and there are interchanges between the horn and oboe.[17]

The Andante of K. 42a, with its sustained bassoons and mandoline-like pizzicato passages, would have been very much at home as a lover's serenade in a sentimental *opéra comique* of the period, as Della Croce has suggested.[18] For all its considerable charm, however, this movement stumbles too—on a poorly handled sequential passage at bars 33–7.

The particular excellence of the Minuet has already been mentioned. Both sections of the Minuet end with a striking idea, which then becomes the basis of the D minor Trio, where is it reworked almost obsessively. The contour of the trio's principal idea is similar to that of the so-called 'Night-Watchman's Song' quoted by Joseph Haydn in a half-dozen works of the 1760s (Example 5.2).[19] The tune in its many guises was associated with various texts, but most commonly with a Bohemian Advent text later found in both Protestant and Catholic German-language song books:

Der Tag vertreibt die finstere Nacht,
O Brüder, seid munter und wacht,
Dienet Gott, dem Herren.

[The day disperses the dark night,
Oh brothers, be alert and keep watch,
Serve God the Lord.]

[17] Letter of 29 Dec. 1755. *Briefe*, i. 28 (not in *Letters*). For a stylistic argument favouring Leopold Mozart's authorship of K. 42a, see Eisen, 'The Symphonies of Leopold Mozart', 143–53, 187–201.
[18] Della Croce, *Le 75 sinfonie*, 67.
[19] Hob I: 60; II: 17, 21; XI: 35; XII: 19; XVI: 36; XXV: 11, 43.

Ex. 5.1 Symphony in F major, K. 76 = 42a, first movement (bars 61–7)

Ex. 5.2 The Night-Watchman's Song

Dušek, Czech Christmas Mass (eighteenth century)

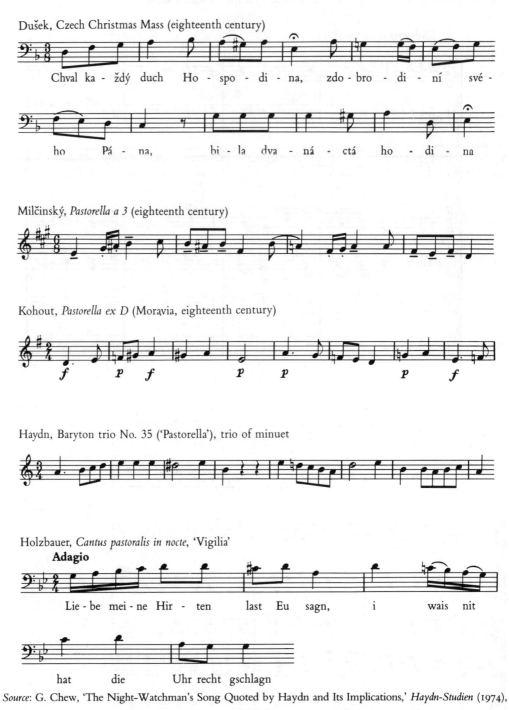

Chval ka - ždý duch Ho - spo - di - na, zdo - bro - di - ní své -

ho Pá - na, bi - la dva - ná - ctá ho - di - na

Milčinský, *Pastorella a 3* (eighteenth century)

Kohout, *Pastorella ex D* (Moravia, eighteenth century)

Haydn, Baryton trio No. 35 ('Pastorella'), trio of minuet

Holzbauer, *Cantus pastoralis in nocte*, 'Vigilia'

Adagio

Lie - be mei - ne Hir - ten last Eu sagn, i wais nit

hat die Uhr recht gschlagn

Source: G. Chew, 'The Night-Watchman's Song Quoted by Haydn and Its Implications,' *Haydn-Studien* (1974), iii. 106–24, here 109–10.

Ex. 5.3 Jean-Philippe Rameau: *Le Temple de la gloire,* first Gavotte (Act III, Scene iii)

The 'exotic' version of this tune, featuring the raised and lowered fourth degree of the scale, appears to have originated in the area of present-day south and south-east Moravia, western Slovakia, and north and east Austria, but both text and melody were apparently known throughout central Europe by the eighteenth century.[20]

The opening idea of the Finale resembles a popular gavotte from Rameau's *Temple de la gloire* (Example 5.3), as Wyzewa and Saint-Foix were the first to point out;[21] but for the rest the two movements are entirely dissimilar. The Finale, with some of the variety of texture lacking in the first movement, develops great momentum, as motives are tossed from section to section until, near the end, the principal motive is briefly entrusted to a high solo horn.

Symphony in F major, K. 43

[Incipits 5.2]

[20] H. C. Robbins Landon, *The Symphonies of Joseph Haydn. Supplement* (London, 1961), 46–7; *idem, Haydn: Chronicle and Works* (Bloomington and London, 1976–80), ii. 280–1; G. Chew, 'The Night-Watchman's Song Quoted by Haydn and Its Implications', *Haydn-Studien* (1974), iii. 106–24,

[21] Wyzewa–Saint-Foix, i. 180 (= i. 206).

Instrumentation: *strings, 2 oboes, 2 horns, [bassoon, continuo]
Autograph: Jagiellońska Library, Kraków
Principal source: none
Facsimile: *Mitteilungen für die Mozart-Gemeinde in Berlin* (Dec. 1905)
Editions: *GA*, xx. 56–68 (= Serie 8, No. 6); *NMA*, iv/11/1. 79–94

With this symphony we escape from the bibliographical swamps of the previous work and find ourselves again on terra firma. The autograph manuscript, a beautifully written fair copy, bears the heading 'Sinfonia di Wolfgango Mozart à Vienne 1767'. Above '1767' was written (apparently in Leopold's hand) 'a olmutz 1767,' but this was subsequently crossed out. The Mozarts visited the North Moravian town of Olomouc (= Olmütz) on only one, unhappy occasion, between approximately 26 October and 23 December 1767. They had fled there from Vienna hoping to avoid an outbreak of smallpox, which, however, both Wolfgang and Nannerl did eventually contract. From the inscriptions on the autograph, Einstein in K[3] concluded that K. 43 must have been either begun in Vienna in the autumn and completed in Olomouc, or begun in Olomouc and completed in Vienna at the end of December, and the editors of K[6] concur. But K. 43 cannot have been completed in Vienna at the end of December 1767, for although the Mozarts did leave Olomouc around 23 December, they reached Vienna only on 10 January of the new year. The reason for the slowness of their journey was this: in the course of fleeing from Vienna they had stopped at Brno (= Brünn), where the Count von Schrattenbach, brother of the Archbishop of Salzburg, had arranged a concert. But Leopold wanted his children even further from Vienna's smallpox epidemic, so he postponed the concert until their return trip. Hence the Mozarts returned to Brno on Christmas Eve and on 30 December gave their concert, which was duly noted in the diary of a local clergyman:

In the evening ... I attended a musical concert in a house in the city known as the 'Taverna', at which a Salzburg boy of eleven years and his sister of fifteen years, accompanied on various instruments by inhabitants of Brno, excited everyone's admiration; but he could not endure the trumpets, because they were incapable of playing completely in tune with one another.[22]

This report of Wolfgang's reaction has the ring of truth to it, for extreme sensitivity to trumpets in his childhood is documented elsewhere.[23] Trumpets aside, however, if Leopold Mozart was anything other than pleased with the local orchestra, he was politic enough to hide the fact, for the leader of the Brno waits reported that 'Mr Mozart, Kapellmeister of Salzburg, was completely satisfied with the orchestra here and would not have believed that my colleagues could accompany so well at the first rehearsal'.[24] If the Brno forces in 1767 were anything like those at nearby Olomouc a decade later, then the strings may have been approximately 2–3—2–3—2–2—1–2, which, with pairs of oboes and horns, a bassoon, and keyboard continuo, would have made an ensemble of 15 to 18, not counting trumpets and drums and leaving out of consideration the possible participation of amateur and apprentice string players in the tuttis.[25]

But what could the trumpets have been playing? As the symphonies composed by Mozart prior to the end of 1767 come down to us, none calls for trumpets. Among his other works with orchestra, only a pastiche keyboard concerto, K. 40, an offertory, K. 34, and a recitative and aria, K. 36 = 33i, require those martial instruments. An offertory certainly would not have been performed at a concert in a hall in a tavern, and, in any case, there is indirect evidence suggesting that the Mozarts had none of these three works with them.[26] The most likely explanation may be that at least one of Wolfgang's earliest symphonies did have trumpet parts, which, as was sometimes the case with him and his contemporaries, were optional and notated separately from the score.[27] This hypothesis is made the more plausible by Nannerl's recollection, discussed in Chapter 2, that Wolfgang's 'first' symphony employed trumpets. K. 43 itself would not have been one of the symphonies with optional trumpets, for Mozart's trumpet keys were C, D, and E flat.

There is one more fact to consider about the genesis of K. 43: the paper on which it was written is of Salzburg origin. Perhaps the symphony was begun prior to departure for Vienna and completed later, but this is not a necessary assumption, as the Mozarts would have carried some music paper with them when travelling.[28]

[22] Deutsch, 72 (= 77).   [23] Ibid. 397 (= 453).   [24] Ibid. 72 (= 77–8).

[25] J. Sehnal, 'Das Musikinventar des Olmützer Bischofs Leopold Egk aus dem Jahre 1760 als Quelle vorklassischer Instrumentalmusik', *Archiv für Musikwissenschaft* (1972), xxix. 285–317, here 311.

[26] N. Zaslaw, 'Leopold Mozart's List of His Son's Works', in A. Atlas (ed.), *Music in the Classic Period: Essays in Honor of Barry S. Brook* (New York, 1985), 323–58, and esp. pp. 353–4.

[27] See n. 8, ch. 2 above.

[28] A. Tyson, 'The Dates of Mozart's Missa brevis KV 258 and Missa longa KV 262 (246a): An Investigation into His "Klein-Querformat" Papers', in W. Rehm (ed.), *Bachiana et alia musicologica: Festschrift Alfred Dürr zum 65. Geburtstag* (Kassel, 1983), 328–39; and *idem*, 'Mozart's Use of 10-Stave and 12-Stave Paper', in R. Elvers (ed.), *Festschrift Albi Rosenthal* (Tutzing, 1984), 277–89.

We may therefore propose the following hypothetical scenario for K. 43: it was drafted in Vienna between 15 September and 23 October 1767 (and perhaps also in Salzburg before 13 September), completed, revised, or recopied in Olomouc after Wolfgang's recovery from smallpox, and it may have received its première on 30 December in Brno. As all of Mozart's unquestionably genuine symphonies datable to before the end of 1767 are in three movements, K. 43 may provisionally be regarded as his earliest four-movement symphony.

The first movement opens with a fanfare identical to one used by J. C. Bach, Johann Stamitz, Toeschi, Dittersdorf, and undoubtedly others to open symphony movements (Example 5.4). Then follows a passage built over a pedal and probably implying a crescendo, the turn to the dominant, the opening fanfare in the bass with tremolo above, a lilting theme (strings alone, piano), and the energetic closing section of the exposition. A concise development section, based on the fanfare in the bass and some new material, leads to the lilting theme, now in the tonic, and then the rest of the exposition by way of recapitulation. The movement thus lacks the 'double return' of opening theme and key found in the first movements of most of Wolfgang's later symphonies.

Listening to an eighteenth-century symphony one sometimes wonders what feelings or dramatic content the composer may have intended to convey. Even if the music itself did not suggest such thoughts (which frequently it does), they would be suggested by those writers of the period who insisted that, in order to succeed, a symphony should tell a story.[29] While some symphonies by Joseph Haydn, Michael Haydn, Leopold Mozart, Dittersdorf, and others are openly programmatic, Wolfgang Mozart's symphonies seem not to have been conceived

Ex. 5.4 Opening ideas similar to that of K. 43

---

[29] Bernard-Germain-Étienne de La Ville sur Illon, comte de Lacépède, *La Poétique de la musique* (Paris, 1785), ii. 329–41. Further concerning programmes in symphonies in Mozart's time, see ch. 13.

Carl von Dittersdorf (Grave G-12)

in this way. None the less, in the present instance it may be possible to learn more than usual about what he had in mind: the Andante of K. 43 is based upon the eighth number of his 'Latin comedy' (we should perhaps call it a 'cantata' or 'serenata') *Apollo et Hyacinthus*, K. 38,[30] the overture of which is discussed at the end of the previous chapter.

The Greek legend of Apollo and Hyacinth as told by Ovid relates that Zephyr and Apollo both loved a youth, Hyacinth, who, however, cared only for Apollo. When out of jealousy Zephyr killed Hyacinth, Apollo gave Hyacinth immortality by turning his blood into the flower that bears his name. This overtly homosexual story was altered for performance by the students of Salzburg University. In the libretto for K. 38 Hyacinth and Zephyr are friends, and Zephyr loves Hyacinth's sister Melia. But Apollo also loves Melia and seeks the friendship of Hyacinth. Zephyr, in a jealous rage, mortally wounds Hyacinth by flinging a discus at him, and then blames Apollo, causing Melia to renounce Apollo. Discovered by his father, Hyacinth reveals in his dying breath that Zephyr, not Apollo, was his murderer. It is here that the duet which became the Andante of K. 43 occurs. The King, having vented his grief and rage at the death of his son, reveals the true story to his daughter, and they sing the following:

OEBALUS: Natus cadit, atque Deus me nolente, nesciente, laesus abit. Regnum sine Numine jam non diu stabit: Numen! Quaeso, flectere, et ad nos revertere.

MELIA: Frater cadit, atque meus te jubente me dolente sponsus abit. Sponsa sine complice quaeso, quid amabit? Noli sponsam plectere, Numen! Ah, regredere!

[OEBALUS: My son is dead, and the god [Apollo], without my wishing it and without my knowledge, has gone away insulted. Without a god's protection my kingdom will not long survive. O god, I beseech thee, be appeased and turn back to us!

MELIA: My brother is dead, and my bridegroom [Apollo], at your command and to my sorrow, has gone away. Whom, I ask, shall a bride without a bridegroom love? Do not punish your bride, O god! Ah, come back![31]]

This supplication has the desired effect: Apollo reappears, turns Zephyr into a wind, transforms Hyacinth's body into a bed of flowers, and agrees to marry Melia.

[30] R. Tenschert, 'Das Duett Nr. 8, aus Mozarts "Apollo et Hyacinthus" und das Andante aus der Sinfonie KV. 43. Vergleichende Studie', *Mozart-Jahrbuch* (1958), 59–65.
[31] Trans. Lionel Salter.

The youthful composer responded not to the sense of anxiety and loss in the words of the duet but rather to the mood of supplication, composing a movement of almost sublime serenity. The duet is in what might be described as a through-composed yet quasi-strophic formal arrangement; the symphony Andante drawn from it is in a simpler binary form. In transforming vocal lines into violin parts, Mozart added many marks of articulation, appoggiaturas, and other ornaments, perhaps to compensate for the loss of the words, perhaps to give the violin section some of the necessary small details that any competent singer of the day would automatically have added. Both versions display the previously mentioned characteristic orchestral colour of Mozart's symphony andantes of this period, here created by a change of key (C major), flutes replacing oboes, first violins muted, second violins and bass instruments pizzicato, and violas, divisi, murmuring in semiquavers.

The Minuet, rather legato compared to others of the period, exploits descending triplet anacruses in the first section, ascending ones in the second. The Trio, in the subdominant, also makes use of triplets, with the wind silent and the articulation more detached. In the second section of the Trio the theme appears in the bass and then, returning to the violins, is interrupted and terminated by an unforeseen touch of chromaticism. The Finale, a binary movement with both halves repeated, is as notable for its careful writing for the strings, including playful dialogues between first and second violins, as for the conservative role assigned the wind, which support the strings and seldom venture out on their own.

Symphony in D major, K. 45 (first version)

Symphony in D major, K. 51 = 46a, 'La finta semplice' (second version)

[Incipits 5.3]

Instrumentation: strings, 2 oboes, 2 horns, 2 trumpets, kettledrums, [bassoon, continuo] (first version); strings, 2 flutes, 2 oboes, 2 bassoons, 2 horns, [continuo] (second version)
Autograph: Staatsbibliothek Preussischer Kulturbesitz, West Berlin (first version) (Mus. Ms. W. A. Mozart 45); Jagiellońska Library, Kraków (second version)
Principal source: none
Editions: *GA*, xx. 69–80 (= Serie 8, No. 7); *NMA*, iv/11/1. 95–114 (first version); *GA*, vii. 1–11 (= Serie 5, No. 4); *NMA*, ii/5/2(i). 5–24 (second version)

The existence of two versions of a single symphony provides an opportunity to learn something about Mozart's working methods. The autograph of K. 45 bears the inscription 'Sinfonia di Sig[no]re Wolfgang Mozart / 1768, 16 Jener'—thus it was completed just a few days after the return to Vienna from the journey to Olomouc and Brno discussed above. It is written on paper of a particularly large, coarse type. The presence of such paper in a Mozart autograph implies purchase in a provincial place (undoubtedly, in this instance, Brno or Olomouc), where large paper of good quality could not be had.[32]

There is no record of the Mozarts' giving a public concert at this time, so we must assume that this symphony was written for a private concert of the sort

[32] Paper information courtesy of Alan Tyson. Even in so important a centre as Prague, Mozart had to make do with poor quality paper; see Tyson's article 'New Light on Mozart's "Prussian" Quartets', *The Musical Times* (1975), cxvi. 126–30, esp. 128–9.

mentioned by Riesbeck and discussed at the beginning of Chapter 11. The Mozarts did have a two-and-a-half-hour audience with Maria Theresa and her son, the recently crowned Emperor Joseph II, only three days after the completion of K. 45. During the audience Wolfgang and Nannerl performed and music was discussed, but as none of the court musicians were present, no orchestral music can have been played.[33] (Joseph suggested that Wolfgang write an opera for Vienna—an action that will figure in this tale of two symphonies.) The earliest documented occasion on which K. 45 could have been heard was near the end of March at a grand Lenten concert which, Leopold reported to his friends in Salzburg, 'was given for us at the house of His Highness Prince von Galitzin, the Russian Ambassador'.[34]

By the time of the Russian ambassador's concert, Leopold had overstayed the leave of absence granted him from his duties at the Salzburg court, and the Archbishop had issued an order stopping his pay until he returned. The reason Leopold had not returned to Salzburg was that—following the Emperor's suggestion—Wolfgang had composed a comic opera, *La finta semplice*, K. 51 = 46a, whose production was repeatedly delayed by intrigues on the part of envious Viennese musicians.[35] Malicious rumours circulated that Wolfgang was a fraud, and that his father did his composing for him. Leopold, a man with an acute sense of honour, felt that he could not leave Vienna before he and his son were vindicated. Yet although he battled valiantly against his opponents, the opera remained unperformed in Vienna.

The overture for the ill-fated *La finta semplice* was a reworking of Wolfgang's most recent symphony, K. 45. And this new version was, in its turn, used as an independent symphony. To turn a concert- or chamber-symphony into an overture-symphony Mozart omitted the Minuet and Trio. He altered the orchestration of the remaining movements, adding pairs of flutes and obbligato bassoons to the original pairs of oboes and horns, while dropping the trumpets and kettledrums. The additional instruments were perhaps to be expected, for the opera house had at its disposal larger orchestral resources than most private concerts would have had, but the omission of the trumpets may at first glance seem surprising, since operas of the period so often call for them, to lend verisimilitude to ceremonial and military scenes. But these are serious operas, and comic operas often dispensed with such accoutrements of the nobility. Mozart also added a considerable number of phrasing and dynamic indications to the reworked symphony, as well as a few changes of rhythm and pitch. (It is unclear whether the

[33] Leopold's letter of 23 Jan, 1768. *Briefe*, i. 253; *Letters*, i. 116–17 (= i. 79–80).

[34] Letter of 30 Mar. 1768. *Briefe*, i. 261; *Letters*, i. 124 (= i. 84).

[35] Complaints of plots against them are found scattered throughout the Mozarts' correspondence, to an extent that might suggest paranoia were it not for such independent, confirmatory evidence of persecutions as found, for instance, in Deutsch, 236, 243–4, 258, 271–2, 291, 325, 437 (= 270, 278, 293, 308, 309, 332, 369–70, 508).

new performance indications in K. 45a represent a spelling out of ideas implicit in K. 45, and conveyed in rehearsal by Mozart, or a rethinking of the piece.) In the Andante he also altered the meter from **C** to **₵**, and the quavers of the melody to dotted quavers and semiquavers. Finally, he added two additional bars of music to the first movement and four to the Finale. In the first movement Mozart repeated a bar at the end of the exposition (44) and the corresponding bar at the end of the recapitulation (93), apparently to create a certain symmetry while lengthening to eleven bars the ten-bar pedals on the dominant and tonic respectively. In the Finale the repeats of both halves were eliminated and changes were made to the ending. Mozart first altered the third bar from the end (104) and replaced the last two bars of K. 45 with two new bars that led directly into the opera's opening chorus and then, when he wanted to use the overture of K. 45a as an autonomous work, he created a concert ending that incorporated the altered bar, the two original bars, the two new bars, and two additional ones—or perhaps Leopold Mozart was responsible for the concert ending, for it appears in the autograph manuscript of *La finta semplice* in his hand.[36]

Ex. 5.5 (a) Leopold Mozart: *Die musikalische Schlittenfahrt*

Intrada

Andante

(b) Del Caro's Hornpipe

[36] R. Angermüller (ed.), *NMA*, ii/5/26. i, viii, xxii–xxiii, 24.

The Finale is based on the kind of idea that, if found in a set of dances, would have been called a *contredanse*, that is, a popular rather than courtly dance. A closely related tune circulated in London around 1800 under the name 'Del Caro's Hornpipe',[37] while another appears in the Intrada of Leopold Mozart's *Musical Sleighride* (Example 5.5). The origins of this vernacular tune-type may be lost in the mists of oral tradition.

Symphony in G major, 'Bastien and Bastienne', K. 50 = 46b

[Incipits 5.4]

Intrada
Allegro

(77)

Instrumentation: strings, 2 oboes, 2 horns, [bassoon, continuo]
Autograph: Jagiellońska Library, Kraków
Principal source: none
Facsimile: *NMA*, ii/5/3. xv–xvi
Editions: *GA*, vi. 1–9 (= Serie 5, No. 3); *NMA*, ii/5/3. 3–5

While struggling unsuccessfully to have *La finta semplice* mounted, Leopold found other occasions to display his son's talent. One of these was the composition of a tiny Singspiel, *Bastien und Bastienne*, K. 50 = 46b, thought to have been performed in the garden of the Viennese physician, Anton Mesmer, inventor or popularizer of the procedure known variously as hypnotism, mesmerism, or animal magnetism. (Many years later—after Mesmer had been run out of Vienna for unethical practices—Mozart and Da Ponte would poke fun at 'animal magnetism' in *Così fan tutte*.) The Singspiel's plot can be briefly summarized. Bastienne, a shepherdess, loves the shepherd Bastien, but he has become interested in a sophisticated lady from the town. Bastienne seeks the assistance of the village magician, Colas, who predicts that Bastien will return to her and advises her to feign indifference. The magician's prediction proves accurate, his advice sound, and soon Bastien is seeking his help in reawakening Bastienne's love. The magician conjures up Bastienne (in a scene that the twelve-year-old composer set with evident relish), and a reconciliation is effected.[38]

---

[37] Del Caro's tune appeared in three London anthologies of the 1790s: *Apollo et Tersichore*, i/6. 47; *L. Lavenu's Musical Journal, or Pocket Companion*, i. 65; *Longman & Broderip's Fifth Selection of the Most Admired Dances, Reels, Minuets & Cotillons with their Proper Figures . . .* , 25.

[38] The libretto of *Bastien und Bastienne* had distinguished forebears. Jean-Jacques Rousseau wrote and composed the operetta *Le Devin du village*, performed in Fontainebleau and Paris in 1752. The following year C. S. Favart and his wife wrote a parody of Rousseau's text as another operetta, *Les Amours de Bastien et Bastienne*, set as a musical pastiche by Guerville de Harny. This in turn was in 1764 translated into German verse for the airs and prose for the dialogues by F. W. Weiskern, and provided with music (now lost) by J. B. Savio. Mozart set Weiskern's version in Vienna in 1768 and later in Salzburg worked on a new version by the court trumpeter and friend of the Mozarts, Johann Andreas Schachtner, who revised the text of some of the airs and rhymed the dialogues for setting as recitatives. See R. Angermüller (ed.), *NMA*, ii/5/3. vii–xiv.

The overture is a one-movement sinfonia, marked 'Intrada', in a style similar to, but on a scale smaller than, the sinfonias that prefaced *Die Schuldigkeit des ersten Gebots*, K. 35, and *Apollo et Hyacinthus*, K. 38. However, whereas there is evidence that the sinfonias of K. 35 and 38 circulated independently as concert pieces, no such evidence exists for K. 46b; yet there is no reason not to regard these three one-movement sinfonias in the same light.

Modern performances of the sinfonia of K. 46b bring involuntary smiles to the faces of audiences, for its opening theme resembles the opening theme of Beethoven's 'Eroica' symphony. It is most improbable that Beethoven knew this work, as in his lifetime it was unpublished and no manuscripts are known to have circulated. Rather, both themes were representatives of a conventional, triadically based type seen elsewhere, for instance, at the beginning of an overture by Koželuk (Example 5.6).[39]

Ex. 5.6 Johann Anton Koželuk: Overture in D major, No. III: 2

Symphony in D major, K. 48

[Incipits 5.5]

[39] The Overture in D major, No. III: 2, in M. Poštolka, *Leopold Koželuk: Života Dílo* (Prague, 1964), 179.

Instrumentation: strings, 2 oboes, 2 horns, [bassoon, continuo]
Autograph: Staatsbibliothek Preussische Kulturbesitz, West Berlin (Mus. Ms.
Autogr. W.A. Mozart 48)
Principal source: none
Facsimile: none
Editions: *GA*, xx. 81–96 (= Serie 8, No. 8); *NMA*, iv/11/1. 143–62

Why, nearly on the eve of his departure from Vienna after a stay of more than a year, did Wolfgang write another symphony? Was there a farewell concert or a private commission? (We know of none.) Was something needed immediately upon his return to Salzburg? (But surely other symphonies written in Vienna could have served?) Were the Mozarts trying to constitute a set of three Viennese symphonies for a patron?[40] (No known manuscript or catalogue groups K. 43, 45, and 48 together.) The autograph manuscript of K. 48 is inscribed 'Sinfonia / di W: Mozart / 1768 / a Vienna / den 13ten dec:'. The very next day Leopold wrote Hagenauer a final letter from Vienna, yet mentioned no forthcoming event that might explain the need for a new symphony. Indeed, he would seem to have been deliberately mysterious about the obligations keeping them in Vienna:

As very much as I wished and hoped to be in Salzburg on His Highness the Archbishop's consecration day [21 December], nonetheless it was impossible, for we could not bring our affairs to a conclusion earlier, even though I endeavoured strenuously to do so. However, we will still set out from here before the Christmas holiday.[41]

As the Mozarts were long overdue at Salzburg and Leopold's pay was being withheld, one might expect that they would have left Vienna immediately after their vindication on 7 December, when, at the consecration of a new church, Wolfgang led performances of his own newly composed Mass, offertory, and trumpet concerto in the presence of the Imperial court and a large audience. Yet something held the Mozarts in Vienna for more than a fortnight longer. That

---

[40] See the discussion in ch. 6 of how Leopold and Wolfgang grouped symphonies.
[41] Letter of 14 Dec. 1768. *Briefe*, i. 285; this passage not in *Letters*.

'something' may have been the unknown occasion for which K. 48 was written, perhaps a farewell concert in the palace of one of the nobility.

Like K. 45, K. 48 is in the festive key of D and calls for trumpets and kettledrums in addition to the usual strings and pairs of oboes and horns. Like both K. 43 and 45, K. 48 is in four movements. Its opening Allegro begins with a striking idea featuring dotted minims alternating forte and piano. In the space of a mere six bars this melody covers a range of two and a half octaves. Wyzewa and Saint-Foix suggested that such wide-ranging melodies were a special feature of Viennese symphonies of the period, which the alert Wolfgang had imitated.[42] This wide-ranging melody is accompanied by nervous quavers in the bass-line soon followed by running semiquavers in the violins which, with an occasional comment from the oboes and one dramatic silence, bring the bustling exposition to its conclusion. The movement, like all four in this symphony, has both sections repeated. Exceptionally for first movements of symphonies from this period in Mozart's life, the development section of K. 48 is nearly as long as its exposition; in the course of its modulations it reviews the ideas already heard. The recapitulation gives them again in full (for the first time in his symphonies), and the movement thus provides a lucid demonstration of the apparently paradoxical description of sonata form as 'a two-part tonal structure, articulated in three main sections'.[43]

The Andante, in G major for strings alone, is a little song in binary form. The peculiar character of the opening idea results from its harmonization in parallel six-three chords and the sing-song quality of its melody, rather like a nursery-rhyme tune. This leads, however, to a second, more Italianate, idea, which, with its larger range and insistent appoggiaturas, conveys a more worldly, perhaps even operatic, ethos.

The Minuet reinstates the wind, although the trumpets and drums drop out for the contrasting G major Trio. Here Mozart perfectly captured the stately pomp that Viennese symphonic minuets of the time provided as a kind of aesthetic stepping-stone between the Apollonian slow movements and the Dionysian finales, which in this case is a jig in a large binary design.

At some time before the Mozarts left Vienna, Leopold drew up a catalogue of his precocious son's musical output, the 'List of everything that this 12-year-old boy has composed since his 7th year, and can be exhibited in the originals'.[44] The

---

[42] Wyzewa–Saint-Foix, i. 223–4 (= i. 273). For other first movements with wide-leaping themes, see K. 74g at the end of ch. 6 and Joseph Haydn's Symphony No. 3.

[43] J. Webster, 'Sonata form', *The New Grove*, xvii. 497.

[44] 'Verzeichniss / alles desjenigen was dieser 12 jährige Knab seit / seinem 7tem Jahre componiert, und in originali / kann aufgezeiget werden'. Later the manuscript came into the possession of Charles Malherbe, who gave it to the library of the Paris Conservatoire, where it is to be found, in the portion of that library now housed in the Music Department of the Bibliothèque nationale (MS 263).

unsigned manuscript, which bears no indication of date or place, was in Nannerl's possession in 1799, when she sent it to Breitkopf & Härtel to assist them in their publication of her brother's *Œuvres complettes*.[45] First published in the appendix to Nissen's biography of Mozart and since republished repeatedly,[46] the 'List' is believed to be connected to Leopold's attempts to arrange for a Viennese production of *La finta semplice*. Leopold, in despair at the intrigues around him and the duplicity of those in charge of the Imperial Theatre, had petitioned the Emperor himself, asking him to order that Wolfgang's opera be produced. Yet even though, according to both Leopold's letter of 30 July 1768 and Nannerl's marginal note on the 'List', the opera was 'written at the command of the Emperor Joseph', the Emperor declined to intercede on the Mozarts' behalf. Among the tactics used by the Mozarts' rivals was the already-mentioned spreading of rumours that the twelve-year-old could compose only with his father's assistance.[47] Leopold most likely drew up the 'List' as a defensive measure against these rumours, appending a copy of it to the unsuccessful petition presented to the Emperor on 21 September 1768.

While the majority of the works on the 'List' are readily identifiable, a number remain problematical, including the works represented by an entry reading: '13 symphonies for 2 violins, 2 oboes, 2 horns, viola, and basso, etc.' Among those who considered the matter, Asow had ventured that twelve of the thirteen were: K. 16, Anhang 220 = 16a, 19, Anhang 223 = 19a, Anhang 222 = 19b, 22, 76 = 42a, 43, 45, Anhang 221 = 45a, Anhang 214 = 45b, and 48; while Müller added K. 16b = Anhang C 11.01 as the thirteenth.[48] This constituted a list of all the symphonies written by Mozart prior to the end of 1768, according to K^3. More recently Eibl stated that the thirteen symphonies must include K. 16, 19, 22, 43, and 45.[49]

An attempt to improve on these identifications begins with the set of six symphonies that Leopold had assembled and was having copied to send to Prince von Fürstenberg in Donaueschingen in October and November 1767.[50] Documentary evidence given in the next chapter suggests that the six were K. 38,

---

[45] Letter of 4 Aug. 1799. *Briefe*, iv. 259; vi. 484–5; not in *Letters*. Concerning the history of the *Œuvres complettes*, see K^6, 915–7.

[46] Editions: Georg Nikolaus Nissen, *Biographie W. A. Mozart . . . . Nach des verfassers Tode hrsg. von Constanze, Wittwe von Nissen, früher Wittwe Mozart* (Leipzig, 1828, repr. Hildesheim, 1964), appendix, 3–5; Jahn, *W. A. Mozart*, 3rd edn. by H. Deiters (Leipzig, 1889–91), ii. 825–30 (and in subsequent edns.); K^3, xxiv–xv (with K^{3a}, 983); K^6, xxv–xxvi; *Wolfgang Amadeus Mozart: Verzeichnis aller meiner Werke*, ed. E. H. Müller von Asow (Wiesbaden, 1956), 2–4; *W. A. Mozart. Gesamtkatalog seiner Werke. 'Köchel-Verzeichnis'* ed. K. F. Müller (Vienna, 1951), 19–21; *Briefe*, i. 287–89; v. 205–7. Facsimiles: *Leopold Mozart. Werkverzeichnis für W. A. Mozart (1768): Ein Beitrag zur Mozartforschung*, ed. K. F. Müller (Salzburg, 1955) (all three pages); Bibliothèque nationale, *Mozart en France* (Paris, 1956), plate viii (p. 1 only); *Briefe*, i. facing 289 (p. 1 only); *NMA*, II/5/3. xviii (p. 3 only); N. Zaslaw, 'Leopold Mozart's List', 355–8 (all three pages).

[47] Similar innuendos by incredulous or malicious Salzburgers had been silenced the previous year when Wolfgang was confined to a room in the archiepiscopal palace with a text to set to music. This resulted in the *Grabmusik*, K. 42 = 35a.

[48] See n. 46 above.

[49] *Briefe*, v. 207.

[50] Ibid. 205–6. See the discussion of this in ch. 6.

16, 45a, 19b, 19, and 19a. Although these six might plausibly be counted among the thirteen in the 'List', the presence of the sinfonia-overture to *Apollo et Hyacinthus*— a work with its own entry in the 'List'— is troublesome. If the sinfonia-overture of K. 38 is, therefore, eliminated, then the overtures to K. 35 and 50 = 46b should probably be passed over for the same reason. And K. 45 should possibly be omitted as well, since Wolfgang revised it as the overture for *La finta semplice*, which also has its own place in the 'List'. K. 16b is now generally thought to be by Leopold.[51] This leaves eleven of the proposed works:

Symphony in E flat major, K. 16
Symphony in A minor, K. Anhang 220 = 16a
Symphony in D major, K. 19
Symphony in F major, K. Anhang 223 = 19a
Symphony in C major, K. Anhang 222 = 19b (lost)
Symphony in B flat major, K. 22
Symphony in F major, K. 76 = 42a
Symphony in F major, K. 43
Symphony in G major, K. Anhang 221 = 45a ('Old Lambach')
Symphony in B flat major, K. Anhang 214 = 45b
Symphony in D major, K. 48

There are problems with several of these works as well. One (K. 19b) survives only as an incipit, making dating and authentication impossible. Three others (K. 16a, 42a, 45b) have neither autographs nor other authentic sources, and were placed chronologically in K[3] and K[6] solely on stylistic grounds.[52] K. 16a in particular is shown in Chapter 8 to be almost certainly not Mozart's. There may also be a problem with including K. 48, whose autograph is dated 13 December 1768: if everything on the 'List' except the three final entries was completed by September, then inclusion of a December symphony would require that '13 symphonies' had been altered from '12 symphonies', of which there is no trace in the manuscript. (It is hard to know what to make of this last point, however, since the document as it comes down to us is apparently a copy preserved by the Mozart family rather than the one presented to the Emperor.) One other symphony from the proposed thirteen (K. 45a) has been claimed as a work of Leopold's, but evidence presented in Chapter 6 establishes it as his son's.

[51] See K[6], 858 (Anhang C 11.01). The work is attributed to Leopold by M. Seiffert (ed.), *Leopold Mozart: ausgewahlte Werke* (Denkmäler der Tonkunst in Bayern, ix/2), xlix, No. 1; E. L. Theiss, *Die Instrumentalwerke Leopold Mozart nebst einer Biographie* (Ph.D. diss., University of Giessen, 1942), abridged in *Neues augsburger Mozartbuch* (Augsburg, 1962), 397–468, No. H.III.1; W. Senn, 'Mozartiana aus Tirol', *Festschrift Wilhelm Fischer* (Innsbruck, 1956), 49–59 and especially 50–51; W. Plath, 'Mozart, Leopold', *The New Grove*, xii. 678, symphony C3; and Eisen, 'The Symphonies of Leopold Mozart', 122–8, 255–6, ?C3. K. Pfannhauser suggested that this symphony might have been the work of the obscure (and unrelated) Philip Kajatan Mozart ('Zu Mozarts Kirchenwerken von 1768', *Mozart-Jahrbuch* (1954), 156), a notion rejected by Senn, Plath, Eisen, and the present writer.

[52] See the discussions of these works in chs. 8, 5, and 4 respectively.

Putting aside our qualms for the moment, omitting K. 16a and 48, and accepting the remaining nine symphonies as the best guess presently possible, let us ask what can be said of the four more needed to make thirteen. Curiously, two other symphonies have been virtually overlooked, the Symphony in D major, K. Anhang C 11.07, and the Symphony in F major, K. Anhang C 11.08. Known only by their incipits in the Breitkopf & Härtel Manuscript Catalogue, where they bear the numbers 60 and 63 respectively, they do not differ in their source situations from K. 19b, 66c, 66d, and 66e, which are also lost symphonies known only by incipits in the Breitkopf & Härtel Manuscript Catalogue. There are no grounds for excluding the first two symphonies from the corpus of authentic works, while including the last four, yet that is what the editors of K^6, following K^3, have done. The dating of the incipits of K. 66c, 66d, and 66e to Salzburg 1769 in K^3 was conjecture on Einstein's part, and should not be taken too seriously. That there is no firm evidence for dating K. 66c, 66d, or 66e clouds matters, for one or more of them may prove to be authentic and earlier than September 1768, and therefore eligible to be among the thirteen symphonies under investigation.[53] Thus, no very satisfactory conclusion is possible about the thirteen symphonies of Leopold's 'List' of September 1768, for at present it is possible neither confidently to omit the symphonies K. 35, 38, 45, 50 = 46b, or 48 from consideration, nor to determine whether any of the symphonies K. 19b, 42a, 45b, 66c, 66d, 66e, Anhang C 11.07, or Anhang C 11.08 should be considered Mozart's work.

Example 5.7 gives the incipits of the six lost symphonies. One reason for presenting them is to show how little stylistic information such incipits convey, so as to suggest the slender grounds on which they have been dated and judged authentic (or not). Another reason is that some of the incipits as they appear in K^6 are incomplete and inaccurate. A final reason is the hope that someone may recognize, and thereby identify, a lost work. This is not as improbable as it may appear, for of ten lost symphonies known only by incipits in K^1 and K^2 (Anhang 214–23), six have since been found, two as recently as 1981 (K. 19a) and 1983 (K. 16a).[54]

One wonders what the Viennese musicians and public can have made of the

---

[53] Yet another symphony attributed to Mozart, not in the Köchel Catalogue, is a two-movement symphony in D major, which survives in the Thurn und Taxis Hofbibliothek in Regensburg. In the eighteenth-century catalogue of this collection the work was attributed simply to 'Mozart', but on the title-page of the manuscript (which was originally anonymous), a later hand has added 'W. A. Mozart'. In fact, it is Johann Adolph Hasse's overture to *Artaserse* (1730) (G. Haberkamp, *Die Musikhandschriften der Fürst Thurn und Taxis Hofbibliothek Regensburg* (Munich, 1981), 95; Eisen, 'The Symphonies of Leopold Mozart', 305).

[54] For these last two works, see chs. 2 and 8 respectively. The identification of K. Anhang C 11.08 presents particular problems because of the extreme brevity of its incipit, which, for example, closely resembles the incipits of the first movements of symphonies by Antonín Vranický (see *The Symphony in Bohemia* (The Symphony 1740–1820, B/xii) (New York, 1984), xlv) and by Simon Le Duc (see Brook, *La Symphonie française*, i. 523). See also Appendix D.

Ex. 5.7 Incipits of Six Lost Symphonies Attributed to Mozart

(a) Symphony in C major, K. Anhang 222 = 19b

Allegro non tanto

(b) Symphony in D major, K. Anhang 215 = 66c

(c) Symphony in B flat major, K. Anhang 217 = 66d

(d) Symphony in B flat major, K. Anhang 218 = 66e

(e) Symphony in D major, K. [Anhang 223 =] Anhang C 11.07

(f) Symphony in F major, K. [Anhang 223 =] Anhang C 11.08

symphonies Mozart composed in his twelfth year, but their opinions on this matter have not been preserved. A note in the minutes of the Collegium Musicum of the City of Memmingen in 1776, however, might capture a reaction similar to what the Viennese had had a few years earlier: 'His Excellency Senator von Heuss from Trunkelsberg submitted [to be performed] a symphony by young Mozard [*sic*], which excited applause and amazement: the former on account of its beautiful composition, the latter because Mozart, when he wrote it, can scarcely have been twelve years old.'[55]

The Mozarts packed up Wolfgang's '13 Synfonien', Leopold's 'List', and the rest of their possessions, and left Vienna around 27 December 1768. An incident that occurred on their journey homeward to Salzburg provides the basis for much of the next chapter.

[55] Deutsch, 521 (= 155).

6

Lambach and Salzburg (1769)

———————⟨❦⟩———————

The Benedictine monastery at Lambach, in Upper Austria near Wels, was a convenient way-station for the Mozart family on their journeys between Salzburg and Vienna. Like many other Bavarian and Austrian monasteries of the time, Lambach provided rooms and meals for travellers, and maintained a musical establishment to ornament its liturgy and to provide entertainment. Amand Schickmayr, a friend of Leopold Mozart's, was at Lambach from 1738 and had become abbot of the monastery in 1746.[1] At the beginning of January 1769 the Mozart family, returning to Salzburg from their stay of more than a year in Vienna, stopped at Lambach. The visit, not mentioned in the family's surviving letters and diaries, is known solely from inscriptions on two musical manuscripts.

The manuscripts in question are sets of parts for two symphonies in G, one inscribed 'Sinfonia / a / 2 Violini / 2 Oboe / 2 Corni / Viola / e / Basso. / Del Sig:^{re} Wolfgango / Mozart. / Dono Authoris / 4ta Jan: $\overline{769}$', and the other bearing a similar inscription but with 'Leopoldo Mozart / Maestro di Capella di S: A: R: / a / Salisburgo' in place of 'Wolfgango Mozart'. For convenience of reference, the symphony at Lambach ascribed to Wolfgang will be referred to as 'K. 45a', that ascribed to Leopold as 'G16'.[2] The two manuscripts, neither of which is an autograph, were discovered in the monastery's archives by Wilhelm Fischer, who in 1923 published K. 45a.[3] Prior to that, however, an entry for K. 45a could be

---

[1] A. Eilenstein, 'Die Beziehungen des Stiftes Lambach zu Salzburg', *Studien und Mitteilungen zur Geschichte des Benediktinerordens* (1923–4) xlii. 196–232; E. Hainisch, *Die Kunstdenkmäler des Gerichtsbezirkes Lambach* (Vienna, 1959); *Briefe*, iii. 291; vi. 158. In the commentary to the last, Eibl claims that Schickmayr and Leopold became friends when both were studying at Salzburg University, but this cannot be correct as Schickmayr received his Ph.D. on 30 Aug. 1735 and Leopold first matriculated on 7 Dec. 1737. They may have become acquainted when Schickmayr revisited Salzburg in January and February 1765, at which time the Archbishop sent his best musicians to serenade Schickmayr, who also attended a performance of an anonymous Italian opera, *L'Adriano in Siria*. During that visit Schickmayr was described by Beda Hübner as an 'excessivus amator musicae' (G. Lang, 'Zur Geschichte und Pflege der Musik in der Benediktiner-Abtei zu Lambach, mit einem Katalog zu den Beständen des Musikarchives' (Ph.D. diss., Salzburg University, 1978), 32–6).

[2] The former is a 'Köchel' number, the latter is from the lists of Leopold Mozart's works by W. Plath, *The New Grove*, xii. 678; Eisen, 'The Symphonies of Leopold Mozart', 294.

[3] W. Fischer, 'Eine wiedergefundene Jugendsymphonie Mozarts', *Mozart-Jahrbuch* (1923), i. 35–68; this article, minus the edition, also in the *Allgemeine Musik-Zeitung* (Charlottenberg, 1923), xl–xli and in G. Croll (ed.), *Wolfgang Amadeus Mozart*

found in the first and second editions of the Köchel Catalogue as Anh. 221, one of
the ten symphonies already discussed, known to Köchel solely by the incipits of
their first movements in the Breitkopf & Härtel Manuscript Catalogue.[4] Köchel's
placing of these works in the portion of his appendix reserved for doubtful works
should not be misconstrued: it reflected nothing more than his admirably cautious
policy of tentatively regarding as suspicious any piece attributed to Mozart whose
style and source situation he was not in a position to evaluate.

In K^3 (1937) Einstein placed the rediscovered Symphony in G, K. Anh. 221, in
the chronology of authentic works according to the date on the Lambach
manuscript. Speculating that the symphony had been written during the Mozarts'
just ended sojourn of more than a year in Vienna, he assigned it the number 45a
representing early 1768. The editors of K^6 accepted Einstein's and Fischer's opinion
of the authenticity of Anh. 221 = 45a, as did Saint-Foix and others who wrote
about Wolfgang's early symphonies.[5] And Einstein's placing of K. 45a in Vienna in
early 1768 was generally accepted too.[6]

Symphony in G major, K. deest, 'New Lambach' [G16]

[Incipits 6.1]

(Darmstadt, 1977), 139–44. Fischer dated this symphony autumn 1767, when Wolfgang was in Salzburg. The Lambach
manuscript of K. 45a remains there (Musikarchiv Sig. 2073), but the manuscript of G16 is now housed in the Stadtarchiv,
Augsburg (MG II 59).

[4] Discussed in ch. 2 and at the end of ch. 5.

[5] Saint-Foix, 27–8 (= 16–17); J. P. Larsen, 'The Symphonies', in H. C. Robbins Landon and D. Mitchell (eds.), *The
Mozart Companion* (London, 1956), 159–61.

[6] The only exception was H. C. Robbins Landon, 'Die Symphonien: Ihr geistiger und musikalischer Ursprung und ihre
Entwicklung', in P. Schaller and H. Kühner (eds.), *Mozart-Aspekte* (Olten, 1956), 43, who held to Fischer's suggestion of
Salzburg 1767 (see n. 3 above).

Instrumentation: strings, 2 oboes, 2 horns, [bassoon, continuo]

Autograph: unknown

Principal source: Staatsarchiv, Augsburg (MG II 59), formerly in the Lambach Monastery

Facsimile: none

Edition: Bärenreiter (Kassel, 1965) ed. A. A. Abert

In 1964 Anna Amalie Abert published a startling hypothesis about the two G major Lambach symphonies. She had come to believe that—like the accidental interchange of infants that underlies the plots of a number of plays and operas—the two symphonies had been mixed up, perhaps by a monkish librarian at Lambach. Abert based her opinion on a stylistic examination of the two, and on comparisons between them and other symphonies thought to have been written by Leopold and Wolfgang at about the same time.

Abert's stylistic comparisons suggested that K. 45a was written in a more archaic style than G16, and her aesthetic evaluations suggested that the former was less well written than the latter. Her hypothesis was supported by reference to the (relative) monothematicism of the first movement of K. 45a, which she considered an archaic trait and therefore likely to have come from the older composer. Certain aspects of the construction of K. 45a—the adding together of many two-bar phrases (*Liedtypus*) and the over-use of sequences—Abert considered to be characteristic of Leopold's works; while the more continuous (*Fortspinnungstypus*) and varied melodic ideas of G16 struck her as akin to Wolfgang's technique. Her doubts about K. 45a had to do, 'above all with the remarkable plainness and monotony of its second and third movements, which immediately catch the eye of the close observer of the symphonies K. 16 to 48'. She then reasoned that, as Leopold was the older, more conservative, and less talented of the two, he must have been the author of K. 45a and Wolfgang of G16. Accordingly, she edited the previously unpublished G16 as a work of Wolfgang's, and it has since been performed, recorded, and discussed as such.[7]

Some relevant documentary evidence, long known but never brought to bear on the question of the authorship of the two Lambach symphonies, is found in the Breitkopf & Härtel Manuscript Catalogue. We may add a few words here about this Catalogue to the description of it given in Chapter 2. It constitutes a conscientious attempt from the early nineteenth century to list the incipits of all known Mozart works, beginning with manuscripts in the Breitkopf archives, and adding works that had been published or that survived elsewhere in manuscript. The source from which Breitkopf & Härtel obtained each work is indicated next to its incipit, in the right-hand margin. The Catalogue is divided into twenty categories: wind music, dances, piano concertos, string quartets, symphonies, operas, and so on. At the end of many categories, pages of empty staves reveal that further entries were anticipated.

The first category, symphonies, contains seventy incipits followed by a few pages of empty staves. Among the symphonies, as in the rest of the Catalogue, the incipits were to have been notated on two staves. Many of the bass-staves are blank, however, and this would seem to be the result of the cataloguer having in front of him a set of parts rather than a score. That is to say, when confronted with sets of parts, he may have copied only the incipits of the first movements of the first violin parts, perhaps intending to go back later to the basso parts but in the event never doing so. The symphonies are arranged neither chronologically, nor by key, nor by number of movements, nor according to size of orchestra required. Their apparently random arrangement suggests that the cataloguer copied the incipits in whatever order the scores or parts happened to be located. Imagine for a moment, therefore, a storeroom in which music has been kept over a period of years in the order in which it was received, and imagine further that the scribe removes the music item by item in order to catalogue it by genre. We see that three principles

---

[7] A. A. Abert, 'Stilistischer Befund und Quellenlage zu Mozarts Lambacher Sinfonie KV Anh. 221/45a', in H. Heussner (ed.), *Festschrift Hans Engel zum siebzigsten Geburtstag* (Kassel, 1964), 43–56; idem, 'Methoden der Mozartforschung', *Mozart-Jahrbuch* (1964), 22–7 (repr. in G. Croll (ed.), *Wolfgang Amadeus Mozart* (Darmstadt, 1977), 385–93); idem, 'Vorwort', *Wolfgang Amadeus Mozart: Sinfonie in G ('Neue Lambacher Sinfonie')* (Kassel, 1965); idem, notes for Archiv Produktion, Period XII, no. 409: *Leopold Mozart, Wolfgang Amadeus Mozart, 4 Sinfonien* (Hamburg, 1967): Camerata Accademia des Salzburger Mozarteums, B. Paumgartner. Another recording: L'Oiseau-Lyre DSLO D173D 3 (London, 1982): The Academy of Ancient Music, J. Schroeder/C. Hogwood. See further: G. Allroggen, 'Mozarts Lambacher Sinfonie', in T. Kohlhase and U. Scherliess (eds.), *Festschrift Georg von Dadelsen zum 60. Geburtstag* (Stuttgart, 1978), 7–19; N. Zaslaw, 'The "Lambach" Symphonies of Wolfgang and Leopold Mozart', in E. Strainchamps, M. R. Maniates, and C. Hatch (eds.), *Music and Civilization: Essays in Honor of Paul Henry Lang* (New York, 1984), 15–28.

might apply: (1) more recently acquired items would be catalogued first while earlier acquisitions would be catalogued later; (2) items that came in at the same time might well have remained together and would therefore (if they were of the same genre) be catalogued together; and (3) items discovered or acquired after the initial cataloguing was completed would be added at the ends of appropriate categories, using blank staves left for the purpose. Examining the list of seventy symphonies for some confirmation of this imagined scenario, we notice early in the list—implying (according to our hypothesis) a relatively recent acquisition— numbers 16, 17, and 18, whose incipits reveal them to be Mozart's final trilogy of symphonies, K. 543, 550, and 551 respectively. These three works must have formed some kind of unit in the Breitkopf archives.

The unit in question is the 'opus'. Title pages, catalogues, and advertisements of the second half of the eighteenth century customarily list symphonies as being either 'périodique' or 'en œuvre', meaning (respectively) symphonies issued singly (that is, periodically, from time to time, or in a series) and those issued at once in a group as an 'opus'. Symphonies issued 'en œuvre' usually numbered six, but sometimes three, twelve, or another number. Dozens of publications of symphonies were in sixes or twelves. Joseph Haydn produced not only his famous twice six London symphonies, but some earlier groups of three or six.[8] Wolfgang and Leopold were well aware of these conventions—which applied both to manuscripts and to prints—and they sometimes assembled symphonies that way. Two sets of six and one of four of Leopold's own symphonies appeared in the Breitkopf Thematic Catalogue in 1762 and 1766,[9] although whether at his instigation is uncertain. He organized nine of his son's symphonies 'en œuvre' in the mid-1770s, possibly with an eye toward a presentation or a publication that never materialized.[10] Leopold also assembled three of Wolfgang's orchestral serenades 'en œuvre' with the intriguing title, *3 / Serenate cio e gran Synfonie*.[11] In 1784 Wolfgang selected three recent symphonies, which he planned to publish dedicated to the Prince von Fürstenberg.[12] Other groups of six were perhaps assembled as well. When, for instance, in 1810 the Leipzig publisher Ambrosius Kühnel wrote to Mozart's Prague acquaintance and biographer Franz Xaver Niemetschek seeking

[8] H. C. Robbins Landon (ed.), *Joseph Haydn: Collected Correspondence and London Notebooks* (London, 1959), 42–3, 68–9, 89 (hereafter cited as *Collected Correspondence and London Notebooks*). Haydn began this practice only after 1780, when he renegotiated his contract with Prince Esterhazy so that the Prince no longer had exclusive rights to his music, freeing him to sell or publish it as he wished.

[9] B. S. Brook (ed.), *The Breitkopf Thematic Catalogues* (New York, 1968), cols. 22, 214.

[10] K. 162, 181 = 162b, 182 = 173dA, 183 = 173dB, 184 = 161a, 199 = 161b, 200 = 189k, 201 = 186a, 202 = 186b. See the facsimile of Leopold's title page in *NMA*, iv/11/4. xiv.

[11] K. 203 = 189b, 204 = 213a, 250 = 248b. See K⁶, p. 213, and [F. Rochlitz,] 'Drey Bände Original-Handschriften W. A. Mozart's', *Allgemeine musikalische Zeitung* (9 Nov. 1831), xxxiii/45, cols. 733–7.

[12] *Briefe*, iii. 319, and vi. 704, but in light of vii. 574. The symphonies were K. 319 and 385 (published by Artaria without dedication) and a third (which never appeared and may have been K. 338 or 425).

unknown works to publish, Niemetschek replied that, in addition to certain familiar symphonies, he knew of 'six small symphonies ... a few of which are uncommonly beautiful'.[13] And there was Leopold's exhortation to Wolfgang in 1777 (in a letter cited more fully below) to give 'six good symphonies' to be copied at once, in order to have them ready for presentation to a patron. But it is another collection of six symphonies that forms the object of the present investigation.

Early in the 1767–8 visit to Vienna, Leopold wrote to his Salzburg friend Maria Theresia Hagenauer, 'I left Mr Estlinger certain symphonies to copy, which I hope are now ready. These are the symphonies that I have to send to Donaueschingen. By the next post I shall send you a letter for the Prince, which should be enclosed with the symphonies and sent off by the mail coach.'[14] A lost reply must have informed Leopold that the symphonies were ready, for less than a month later he wrote to Maria Theresia's husband Lorenz, 'The six symphonies, which Estlinger has copied, should be rolled up well and given to the mail coach with the address: *A son Altesse S[erenissi]me Le Prince de Fürstemberg etc: à Donaueschingen*. I shall write a letter to the Prince from here.'[15] It has been proposed that the six symphonies copied in Salzburg in the autumn of 1767 were by Leopold Mozart.[16] This seems unlikely because it overlooks the extent to which, during the grand tour, Leopold had given up the advancement of his own career in order to devote himself to promoting his son's. For instance, those announcements that survive for orchestral concerts from the homeward-bound portion of the grand tour of 1765–6 invariably include a statement to the effect that 'all the symphonies will be of this little boy's own composition'. The discussion at the end of Chapter 3 about the October 1766 visit to Donaueschingen concludes that Wolfgang's symphonies were performed there. Taken together, all this suggests that the copying of symphonies in October and November 1767 was in compliance with a request from Prince von Fürstenberg to own some of Wolfgang's symphonies.

Emily Anderson opined that the symphonies copied for Donaueschingen were indeed by Wolfgang and may have been six from among K. 16, 16a, 16b (= Anh. C 11.01), 19, 19a, 19b, 22, and 76 (= 42a),[17] which is a list of the earliest symphonies as found in K³. Here the Breitkopf & Härtel Manuscript Catalogue provides a possible clue.

As already noted, whoever copied that Catalogue left space to add incipits at the

---

[13] R. Angermüller and S. Dahms-Schneider, 'Neue Brieffunde zu Mozart', *Mozart-Jahrbuch* (1968–70), 211–41, here 235.

[14] Letter of 14 Oct. 1767. *Briefe*, i. 241; *Letters*, i. 108–9 (= i. 74).

[15] Letter of 10 Nov. 1767. *Briefe*, v. 179; *Letters*, i. 114 (= i. 77). In fact, Leopold (and later on Wolfgang) did correspond with the Prince, and this connection was strengthened by the presence there of the Mozarts' former manservant, Sebastian Winter, a native of Donaueschingen who served at the court from 1764. As discussed at the end of ch. 3, the Mozarts had visited Donaueschingen in October 1766.

[16] *Briefe*, v. 176. See also Eisen, 'The Symphonies of Leopold Mozart', 183, n. 12, where the possibility is raised that the six symphonies might be by both father and son, or by someone else entirely.

[17] *Letters*, i. 199, n. 1 (= i. 74, n. 5).

TABLE 6.1 The 'Gatti' symphonies

B&H	Key	K¹	K³	K⁶	Year	Source (comment)
65	D	38	38	38	1767	autograph score (overture, *Apollo & Hyacinth*)
66	E flat	16	16	16	1764	autograph score ('first' symphony)
67	G	A221	45a	45a	1765	The Hague parts in Leopold's & Nannerl's hands; Lambach parts in Estlinger's hand ('Old Lambach' symphony)
68	C	A222	19b	19b	?1765	lost (incipit only)
69	D	19	19	19	1765	parts in Leopold's hand
70	F	A223	19a	19a	1765	parts in Leopold's hand

A = Anhang.

end of many of the categories of works, including the symphonies. Examining the list of symphony incipits, one sees that after sixty incipits had been entered, two further groups of symphonies were added: a group of four whose source is given as 'Westphal',[18] and a group of six whose source is shown as 'Gatti'.[19] The contents of the 'Gatti' group—all six apparently scores rather than parts—are shown in Table 6.1. It is my hypothesis that the 'Gatti' manuscript of six symphonies in the Breitkopf & Härtel archives was a copy of the set of six symphonies that Estlinger copied and Leopold Mozart had sent to Donaueschingen at the end of 1767. If this is correct, it has important implications.

For present purposes the most important implication of the hypothesis is, of course, that the 'Old Lambach' symphony, K. 45a, must be by Wolfgang and the 'New Lambach' symphony, G16, by Leopold. And not only do these original attributions hold, but K. 45a—as it was left behind in Salzburg to be copied—must be assigned an earlier date. The earlier date is confirmed by a fact (known to A. A. Abert but not to Einstein) that the Lambach copies of both K. 45a and G16 were the work of a Salzburg copyist, who has proven to be the very Joseph Richard Estlinger whom Leopold had commissioned to copy the six symphonies for Donaueschingen.[20] The Salzburg origin of the two Lambach manuscripts suggests that they were completed prior to the Mozarts' departure from Salzburg in

[18] These symphonies are discussed in ch. 8 in connection with K. 16a.
[19] 'Gatti' refers to Luigi Gatti (1740–1817), Hofkapellmeister in Salzburg from about 1782. Between 1801 and 1804 he first helped and then hindered Nannerl Mozart in her attempts to locate unknown pieces of her brother's in Salzburg to send to Breitkopf & Härtel for the publication of the so-called *Œuvres complettes* (see *Briefe*, v. 223; and especially Eisen, 'The Symphonies of Leopold Mozart', 143–53).
[20] Estlinger's hand was partly established by E. Hintermaier. Estlinger is also Lang's 'Schreiber 20' (Lang, *Zur Geschichte und Pflege*, ii. cii and facsimiles on clv–cviii). For a more nearly complete accounting of the Mozarts' friend and most important copyist, see Eisen, 'The Symphonies of Leopold Mozart', 19–27, 76–81.

October 1767, for the correspondence between the Mozarts and the Hagenauers contains not the slightest hint of a request for the copying of any works other than the six symphonies left behind specifically for that purpose. Furthermore, advice that Leopold sent to Wolfgang some years later, when the son was in Munich and the father at home in Salzburg, contains revealing details of the Mozarts' manner of dealing with symphonies and copyists while on tour, and suggests how improbable it would have been for a symphony composed in Vienna to have been sent to Salzburg to be copied (even though copying was cheaper in the latter city):

You should try to find a copyist, and ... you should do this wherever you stay for any length of time .... Then ... have in readiness copies of symphonies and divertimenti to present to a Prince or some other patron [*Liebhaber*]. The copying should be arranged so that the copyist writes out at your lodgings in your presence at least the *violino primo* or some other principal part [i.e., to prevent theft]. The rest he can copy out at home. It is absolutely essential that you should have something ready for Prince Taxis, and you should therefore quickly give the oboe-, horn-, and viola-parts of six good symphonies at once to one or (to speed up matters) to several copyists. You would thus be in a position to present the symphonies in fair copy to the Prince and still have the fair-copy duplicated violin and bass [parts] to be used on other such occasions ... to which you would only have to add the [parts for] oboes, horns and viola .... Basta! Wherever you are, you must look about immediately for a copyist, or else you will lose a great deal! Otherwise, of what use to you will be all the music which you have taken away? You really cannot wait until some patron has them copied; and, now that I come to think of it, he would thank you for allowing him to do so and would not pay you a farthing. It is far too laborious to have your compositions copied from the score, and a thousand mistakes will creep in unless the copyist works the whole time under your supervision. But he could come *for a few mornings*, when you happen to be in, copy out *the principal parts* and then write out the remainder at his house. That is absolutely necessary.[21]

A few weeks later when Wolfgang had reached Mannheim, his father again broached the subject of the symphonies Wolfgang had taken with him:

I am not going to say anything more about having your works copied, which you ought to have arranged during your long visits to Munich and Augsburg, as the farther you travel the more expensive does copying become. You will remember, however, that I was very much against your taking so many symphonies with you. I just picked out a good number of them, but I naturally thought that you would leave some of them behind. Yet instead of putting several aside, you added to them others, and thus made such an enormous pile that you could not pack any of your church music. If I had been healthy and not so ill that I could hardly speak, I should have let you take with you not more than

---

[21] Letter of 15 Oct. 1777. *Briefe*, ii. 58–9; *Letters*, ii. 465–6 (= i. 319–20).

about four or six symphonies with the parts doubled for concert use, and all the others in single parts or scores.[22]

As these two passages form part of the harangues that the nervous father addressed to his son, exhorting him to conduct his tour in the same manner as the earlier tours that the father himself had conducted, they support the inference that on the earlier tours it was Leopold's practice to bring four to six symphonies in the form of scores with doubled parts, ready for immediate use, and some others in score or single parts, which could quickly be put into performable or saleable form by local copyists.[23]

If the hypothesis is correct that symphonies 65 to 70 in the Breitkopf & Härtel Manuscript Catalogue are the same works as the six symphonies copied by Estlinger at the end of 1767, then K. 45a must once have existed in several copies: the one left behind in Salzburg for Estlinger to copy, the copy he made to send to Donaueschingen, and the set of parts (also in Estlinger's hand) taken to Vienna and then presented to the Lambach monastery. Leopold was able to make this gift because he knew that, having reached the end of their tour, they no longer needed symphonies held in readiness for unexpected opportunities for performances and patronage. Furthermore, since K. 45a should be dated before the departure for Vienna (11 September 1767), then another apparent enigma vanishes. For in accepting Vienna as the place of creation of K. 45a, commentators were made uncomfortable by the fact that it was in the three-movement Italian sinfonia format of the earliest symphonies written in London and Holland (K. 16, 19, 19a, and 22), rather than the four-movement 'concert' symphony format favoured in Vienna and employed by Wolfgang in the three symphonies (K. 43, 45, and 48) that can confidently be assigned to the 1767–8 sojourn there.

To return to Abert's arguments: her stylistic observations are acute, and in the absence of documentary evidence we should perhaps be inclined to accept her conclusions. But are her music-analytical methods fine enough to make decisions about attribution? Consider for instance that Abert found that the stringing together of two-bar phrases in K. 45a was atypical of Wolfgang, yet according to Ludwig Finscher, 'the technique of many minor composers of the 1760s and 1770s—including Mozart—was to place two-bar, four-bar, and eight-bar sections in a row, sometimes adding a bar, or changing the order of sections'.[24] Besides, as the more 'spun-forth' style of G16 was a late baroque trait and the more segmented style of K. 45a a galant trait, this distinction, far from supporting Abert's new

---

[22] Letter of 11 Dec. 1777. *Briefe*, ii. 182–3; *Letters*, ii. 616 (= i. 417).
[23] Concerning *Dubletten* see ch. 2, n. 30.
[24] In Larsen, Serwer, and Webster (eds.), *Haydn Studies*, 103.

attributions, contradicts them. To this we may add four additional points, which tend further to weaken Abert's attempted attributions.

1. The earlier we think K. 45a was composed, the less we should be surprised at finding the apprentice-composer writing in an 'archaic' style. In particular, Abert's comparisons of K. 45a and G16 with K. 43 and 48 are weakened by an earlier dating of K. 45a, for if the latter was composed in 1766 or the first part of 1767, then its 'immature' style in comparison with works from the end of 1767 and the end of 1768 is not surprising. This was, after all, a period during which Wolfgang's musical knowledge and craft were growing by leaps and bounds.

2. Wolfgang himself claimed to be able to write in any style,[25] and even if his remark may have been written either to please his father or tongue in cheek, its veracity is in some measure borne out by his life's work and, in particular, by the fluent manner in which he assimilated musical styles and ideas during his tours.

3. Although Leopold belonged to an older generation and may not have had his son's originality, he was none the less an able, well-informed musician. He too had made the tours and heard the latest musical styles of western Europe. In the 1760s, he was a thoroughly up-to-date composer, while Wolfgang had yet to find his distinctive 'voice'. It is thus not difficult to believe that during that period father and son may have written symphonies in which the father's style was in some aspects more modern than the son's. And is it not reasonable to suppose that some of Leopold's mature works may have been better made than some of his son's childhood works, in the genesis of which he so often took part as teacher, adviser, editor, and copyist?[26]

Further objections to Abert's proposal along similar lines have been summarized by Gerda Lang:

[According to Wilhelm Fischer] 'hardly any doubt exists about Wolfgang's authorship' of K. 45a . . . . To the analyses and reflections of the two scholars [Fischer and A. A. Abert] may be added that neither Leopold nor the eleven- or twelve-year-old Wolfgang could really produce an unmistakeable personal style or standard of

---

[25] Letter of 7 Feb. 1778. *Briefe*, ii. 265; *Letters*, ii. 692 (= i. 468).

[26] Two scholars earlier voiced concern about the assumption that youthful works by Wolfgang were always more ably composed than his father's mature works. See E. Ripin's remarks in The John F. Kennedy Center for the Performing Arts / American Musicological Society, *A Mozart Festival-Conference* [Washington, DC, 1974], p. [5]; and W. Plath, 'Zur Echtheitsfrage bei Mozart', *Mozart-Jahrbuch* (1971–2), 19–36 and especially 24 (concerning K. 81 = 731). This point is more fully developed in Eisen, 'The Symphonies of Leopold Mozart'.

In his article Plath also expresses scepticism about Abert's general hypothesis, interchanging Leopold and Wolfgang as authors of K. 45a and G16. J. P. Larsen also expressed this doubt (see n. 30 below). T. E. Warner, on the contrary, 'completed some analysis on melodic frequencies and melodic plateaus, but with mixed, inconclusive result. K. 45a certainly resembles some of Wolfgang's work, and could possibly be by Wolfgang tho[ough] perhaps not at his best' (same reference as Ripin above).

quality, and in the father's and the son's works of this period these are seldom are found. Given these considerations, a satisfactory clarification of this question on a style-critical basis is hardly possible. A noteworthy argument [was] mentioned [to me] in conversation by Manfred H. Schmid, . . . who is not willing to credit the experienced fiddler Leopold with 'such unviolinistic manœuvres' as occur in the second violin part of K. 45a. Bernhard Paumgartner too . . . showed himself to be unconvinced by Abert's theory, both in private conversation and in the contents of his concert programmes.[27]

4. Finally, we must ask ourselves, how plausible is it that the names on the manuscripts of the two symphonies were interchanged? After all, the titles and the inscriptions 'Del Sig:^re Wolfgango [or 'Leopoldo'] Mozart' on the manuscripts of K. 45a and G16 were written by a Salzburg copyist who was a personal friend of the Mozarts. Only the final phrase on each manuscript, 'Dono Authoris 4ta Jan. 769' are in a different hand, perhaps that of one of the Lambach monks. Can one really believe that these two manuscripts were accepted from a Salzburg copyist who knew the Mozarts well, carried around by them for more than a year, used for performances, and presented to the Lambach monastery, without the usually punctilious Leopold having corrected these supposedly incorrect attributions? And the title-pages must have been connected to the same music to which they are still attached, as in the eighteenth-century manuscript catalogue of the music at Lambach, the incipit of K. 45a is listed as 'Mozard. junior', the incipit of G16 as 'Mozard. senior'.[28]

The difficulties of assigning authorship to unauthenticated works written at about the same time in similar styles are very great, although there have recently been some promising attempts in the study of the mid-eighteenth-century symphony.[29] In the present instance, however, the objective reader could hardly be blamed for wondering whether, in the balance, the uncertainties of Abert's stylistic analyses may constitute no greater weakness than my proposed identification between symphonies 65 to 70 of the Breitkopf & Härtel Manuscript Catalogue and the six symphonies copied in 1767 for Donaueschingen. But the Salzburg origins of the two Lambach symphony manuscripts and of their inscriptions constitutes evidence of a different order. Two leading experts in music of the classical period

[27] Lang, *Zur Geschichte und Pflege*, i. 38–9.

[28] For convincing evidence for the accuracy of the Lambach Catalogue's attributions to Leopold as 'Mozard' or 'Mozard. senior' and to Wolfgang as 'Mozart. junior', see C. Eisen, 'Contributions to a New Mozart Documentary Biography', *Journal of the American Musicological Society* (1986), xxxix. 615–32, here 620–2.

[29] See J. LaRue, 'Mozart Authentication by Activity Analysis', *Mozart-Jahrbuch* (1971–2), 40–9; E. K. Wolf, 'Authenticity and Stylistic Evidence in the Early Symphony: A Conflict in Attribution between Richter and Stamitz', in E. H. Clinksdale and C. Brook (eds.), *A Musical Offering: Essays in Honor of Martin Bernstein* (New York, 1977), 275–94; S. Fruehwald, 'A Method for Determining Authenticity by Style', *The Journal of Musicological Research* (1985), v. 297–317.

have laid down a precept in this matter which, while perhaps distressing for what it implies about the primitive state of our stylistic understanding, probably represents the better part of wisdom: when in matters of attribution stylistic and documentary evidence conflict, the documentary evidence must nearly always be given precedence.[30]

The text of Chapter 6 to this point was, in its essentials, written in the autumn of 1981. In February 1982 new evidence was published confirming the correctness of arguments in favour of Wolfgang's authorship of, and an earlier date for, K. 45a. The Munich Staatsbibliothek had acquired the recently discovered, original set of parts for K. 45a. They comprise first and second violin parts apparently in the hand of a professional copyist, a basso part in Nannerl's hand, and the other parts in Leopold's hand. (This division of copying duties may bespeak haste or the desire to save on copying expenses, but it also confirms that Leopold's instructions to Wolfgang in his letter of 15 October 1777 represented their practice while on tour.) The title-page of the rediscovered manuscript, also in Leopold's hand, reads: 'Sinfonia / à 2 Violini / 2 Hautbois / 2 Corni / Viola / et / Basso / di Wolfgango / Mozart di Salisburgo / à la Haye 1766'.[31] K. 45a therefore forms a pendant to the Symphony in B flat, K. 22, also composed at the Hague, where—as demonstrated in Chapter 3—the reception granted the Mozarts appears to have been enthusiastic. K. 45a may have been written (along with the *Galimathias*) for the investiture of Prince William, in which case it would have been part of what Leopold referred to in a letter to Hagenauer when he said that Wolfgang 'had to compose something for the Prince's concert', an occasion for which Niemetschek thought Wolfgang had composed 'several symphonies'.[32]

---

[30] H. C. Robbins Landon, 'Problems of Authenticity in 18th-Century Music', in D. G. Hughes (ed.), *Instrumental Music: A Conference at Isham Memorial Library, May 4, 1957* (Cambridge, Mass., 1959), 31–56; Larsen, Serwer, and Webster (eds.), *Haydn Studies*, 74–5; J. P. Larsen, 'Über die Möglichkeiten einer musikalischen Echtheitsbestimmung für Werke aus der Zeit Mozarts und Haydns', *Mozart-Jahrbuch* (1971–2), 7–18, reprinted with the title 'Über Echtheitsprobleme in der Musik der Klassik' in *Die Musikforschung* (1972), xxv. 4–16. Larsen, like Plath, expresses doubt about Abert's hypothesis.

[31] R. Münster, 'Neue Funde zu Mozarts symphonischem Jugendwerk', *Mitteilungen der internationalen Stiftung Mozarteum*, (Feb. 1982), xxx. 2–11.

[32] For details of the Mozarts' activities at the court of Orange, see ch. 3. Concerning the implications of the confusion between K. 45a and G16 for a proper evaluation of Leopold as a composer and for a clearer understanding of the connections between his works and the early works of his son, see in general Eisen, 'The Symphonies of Leopold Mozart'.

Symphony in G major, K. Anh. 221 = 45a, 'Old Lambach'

[Incipits 6.2]

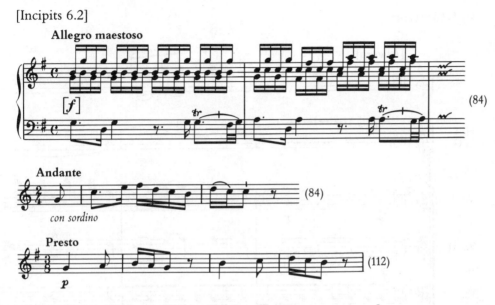

Instrumentation: strings, 2 oboes, 2 horns, [bassoon, continuo]
Autograph: unknown
Principal source: Staatsbibliothek, Munich (first version); Lambach Monastery (second version)
Facsimile: *NMA*, iv/11/1. xxiii (title-page and one page of *basso* part, first version)
Editions: *Mozart-Jahrbuch* (1923) ed. W. Fischer (second version); *NMA*, iv/11/1. 189–204 (first version), 115–28 (second version)

It remains to add on the subject of K. 45a that between the copying of the original set of parts in The Hague in 1766 and the copying of the Lambach parts by Estlinger in Salzburg in 1767, the work underwent a careful revision. The two versions are very much the same work: no bars of music have been added or deleted and no new ideas introduced. Rather, hundreds of details large and small have been altered. An example may serve to indicate the nature of these changes (Example 6.1). The corrections occur mostly in the inner parts, while the first violin and 'basso' parts remain comparatively untouched. Thus what Leopold once referred to as 'il filo'[33]—'the thread'— of the piece was adjudged sound. A similar instance in Wolfgang's corrections to a symphonic movement by Thomas Attwood is discussed in Chapter 11.

---

[33] Letter of 13 Aug. 1778. *Briefe*, ii. 444; *Letters*, ii. 889 (= ii. 599).

Ex. 6.1 Symphony in G major, K. Anhang 221 = 45a (bars 49–58)

(a) 1766 version

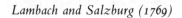

(b) 1767 version

The first movement of K. 45a is one of only two of Mozart's more-than-sixty symphonies (cf. K. 185 = 167a, Chapter 8) that begin with the melody in the bass, a texture he otherwise reserved for near the ends of expositions and of recapitulations. In a number of his early symphonies the incipits of the first and final movements are related in melodic contour. In K. 45a something else occurs: the second or lyrical subjects of the first and third movements are the ones that are connected (Example 6.2). (A related procedure is found in the piano concerto, K. 414 = 385p, in which the first theme of the opening Allegro reappears transformed as the second theme of the Andante.) The Finale of K. 45a is so much of a piece with the finales of K. 16, 19, 19a and 22 that all may be said to belong to the same general conception and, keys aside, to be virtually interchangeable. As for the Andante, the revised version is the first of Wolfgang's symphonic andantes to use an orchestral texture that would be his favourite for a number of years: in these movements (the andantes of K. 43, 100 = 62a, 75, 130, 183 = 173dB, 201 = 186a, 203 = 189b, 200 = 189k) the wind are either silent or reduced, the violins are muted, and the cellos and basses play pizzicato.

Ex. 6.2 Symphony in G major, K. Anhang 221 = 45a, second subjects

(a) First movement (bars 23–6)

(b) Third movement (bars 17–24)

Here, as in the case of K. 45 vs. K. 51 = 45a (ch. 5), a potential danger exists in having two versions of the same piece: the temptation falsely to interpret one in terms of the other. That is, it is often difficult and sometimes impossible to decide which if any of the large number of indications of dynamics and phrasing added to the second version were inherent in the piece to begin with (and conveyed during rehearsal) and which constituted rethinkings. Both versions are valid, both were used by the Mozarts in public concerts, and neither is the definitive one. It is best therefore to avoid conflating them except in instances in which comparison can clarify faulty notation or copying errors.

As Wolfgang would scarcely have revised his symphony merely as an academic exercise, he probably had occasion to perform the second version of K. 45a in Salzburg between the return from the grand tour in December 1766 and the departure for Vienna in October 1767, and the results of the Salzburg performance (or performances) must have encouraged Leopold to take the work on tour to Vienna.

Having returned (by way of Lambach) to Salzburg on 5 January 1769 from the stay of more than a year in Vienna, Wolfgang busied himself with composing works useful in Salzburg. These included several large-scale church works, a *licenza*, three serenades, and an extraordinary number of ballroom minuets. It is uncertain whether he created any new symphonies during this period aside from one drawn from a serenade.

Symphony in D major, K. 100 = 62a

[Incipits 6.3]

Instrumentation: strings, 2 oboes, 2 horns, trumpets, [bassoon, continuo]

Autograph: Staatsbibliothek Preussische Kulturbesitz, West Berlin (Mus. Ms. W. A. Mozart 100) (serenade)

Principal source: set of parts, formerly Breitkopf & Härtel archives, now lost (symphony)

Facsimile: none

Editions: *GA*, xxiii. 33–56 (= Serie 9, No. 1) ; *NMA*, iv/12/1. 67–94.

The undated autograph manuscript of the serenade, written on Salzburg paper,[34] is among the large group of sources that was in Berlin until the Second World War and is now in Kraków. The work is lacking in Leopold's December 1768 'List' of his son's works but is mentioned by Wolfgang in a letter of 4 August 1770,[35] providing *termini a quo* and *ad quem* for its creation. Furthermore, since orchestral serenades were a Salzburg genre not used (as far as we know) during the Mozarts' tours, and since Wolfgang and Leopold left Salzburg for Italy on 13 December 1769, the *terminus ad quem* may confidently be advanced to some time prior to that date.

The greater length of the movements and larger number of repeats in Wolfgang's serenades, compared to his symphonies of the same period, is an objective measurement. The impression that the symphonies of the 1770s are often more conventional and more conservative than the serenades written contemporaneously falls into a more subjective realm. Yet such a difference between the two genres makes sense in light of the uses to which they were put. Salzburg serenades were usually written either for such private celebrations as weddings, birthdays, or

---

[34] Information kindly provided by Alan Tyson.
[35] *Briefe*, i. 378; *Letters*, i. 226–7 (= i. 154).

name-days, investitures, and promotions, or for the public celebration of the end of the summer term at the university. As such, a serenade constituted the main musical event of the day. Symphonies, on the contrary, were used in a church, theatre, or hall to frame or punctuate an event in which other music or activities were the principal attractions. As such, a symphony constituted a formality. These factors may explain the otherwise unexpected observation that a number of Mozart's symphonies from the decade 1769–79, which by their scope and originality most closely conform to modern expectations of good classical symphony composition (anachronistic expectations, founded on Mozart's and Haydn's late symphonies and all of Beethoven's and Schubert's), are those drawn from the supposedly light-hearted orchestral serenades, rather than the symphonies proper.

Extracting a symphony from an orchestral serenade was an entirely logical procedure, which Michael Haydn followed too.[36] Given that the occasions for serenades and for symphonies were different, and that serenades were made up of symphony, dance, and concerto movements intermixed and prefaced by a march, the constituent parts of one work could later effectively serve other purposes. In the present instance, the layout of the movements is:

    1. Marche. Maestoso (K. 62)[37]
*2. Allegro. Serenata.
    3. Andante†
    4. Menuetto†
    5. Allegro†
*6. Menuetto
*7. Andante
*8. Menuetto
*9. Allegro

* symphonic movements
† movements of a sinfonia concertante for oboe and horn

This is the first of Wolfgang's six or seven orchestral serenades, all of which reckon with symphony versions.[38] For four of these (K. 204 = 213a, 250 = 248b, 320, and

---

[36] At least four of Haydn's early Salzburg symphonies, Perger Nos. 9 (movements 1–3), 9 (4), 38 (1–4), and 52 (1–3), and one later one, Perger No. 37, were drawn from serenades. Of Leopold Mozart's 'more than thirty grand serenades, in which solos for various instruments are introduced' (see Appendix C), only one survives, but the fact that that one was the source from which he extracted his trumpet concerto, suggests that in all likelihood he too dismembered his orchestral serenades into their constituent genres.

[37] The marches of orchestral serenades are usually in separate manuscripts and bear independent Köchel numbers. Wolfgang's letter of 4 August 1770 cites K. 100 = 62b by the incipit of its March rather than of its opening Allegro. This March, long thought to be lost and known only from Wolfgang's letter, recently turned up in a score of *Mitridate, rè di Ponto*, K. 87 = 74a, in which Wolfgang apparently reused it (*NMA*, II/5/4. xiii, xxiv, 8).

[38] The others are: K. 185 = 167a, 203 = 189b, 204 = 213a, and 250 = 248b (discussed in ch. 8); K. 320 (ch. 9); and K. 385 (ch. 11).

the present work) there are (or were) sets of orchestral parts of the symphony
versions at least partly in Leopold's or Wolfgang's hand, demonstrating that they
themselves were responsible for the transformations from serenade to symphony;
these passed from Mozart's estate to André in 1799. In a fifth case (K. 203 = 189b)
only a copyist's manuscript of the symphony version survives, but (by analogy
with the other four) this may be presumed to derive from an original coming from
the Mozarts or their immediate circle. For the sixth serenade no symphony
manuscript survives, but a listing of the work (K. 185 = 167a) as a symphony in
the Breitkopf & Härtel Manuscript Catalogue suggests that one once existed.
Finally, K. 385 is a special case, discussed in Chapter 11.

    The symphony version of K. 62a was undoubtedly made in Salzburg, perhaps
with an eye to the Mozarts' first Italian journey, discussed in the next chapter.
Concerning its first movement Günter Hausswald has written of 'the echoes of a
festive, boisterous opera overture on the Italian model'. Characteristics of this style
are, he continues, thematic materials built on broken triads and fanfare-like ideas, as
well as 'a true *al fresco* style worked into a large-scale over-all structure'. The
melodies are 'essentially conventional and traditional in scope' and 'limited to
repeated broken chords; to rigidly maintained chains of scales; to instrumentally
idiomatic, free figuration; to punctuating chords. Only two subsidiary ideas reveal
an individual profile.'[39] Lurking behind Hausswald's description of the movement
one senses regret at what he apparently considered to be a lack of originality and of
cantabile melody. But the eighteenth century was more interested in suitability
than in originality, and the lack of singable melody places the movement in the
category of abstract art, a category with which aestheticians of both the eighteenth
and the twentieth centuries have had difficulties. In the former period Leopold
Mozart referred to symphonies by Stamitz in such an 'abstract' vein as 'nothing but
noise',[40] and the writer Lacépède tried to cope with the problem by requiring that
symphonies contain 'a kind of drama'.[41] In our century Schultz dismissed such
movements as 'purely decorative',[42] which remark, like Hausswald's, hints at a
perceived 'lack of meaning'.

    Descriptions and explanations of musical form have always been based on either
mathematical or linguistic models. Linguistic analogies, beloved of musical analysts
of both eighteenth and twentieth centuries, speak of music's phrases, sentences,
periods, and paragraphs, and of its rhetoric. In the face of works like the first
movement of K. 62a, however, a linguistic analogy might lead one into the absurd

    [39] G. Hausswald, *Mozarts Serenaden*, 2nd edn. (Kassel, 1975), 109.
    [40] Letter of 29 June 1778. *Briefe*, ii. 386; *Letters*, ii. 823 (= ii. 556). See also E. K. Wolf, *The Symphonies of Johann Stamitz*
(Utrecht, 1981), 134, n. 36.
    [41] Bernand-Germain-Étienne de La Ville sur Illon, comte de Lacépède, *La Poétique de la musique* (Paris, 1785), ii. 329–41.
    [42] D. Schultz, *Mozarts Jugendsinfonien* (Leipzig, 1900), 11.

position of having to imagine meaningful prose composed primarily of conjunctions, prepositions, and articles. Here is an aspect of musical creativity in which practice has thus far outstripped the ability of theory to explain it. (This eighteenth-century aesthetic dilemma may profitably be compared with the difficulties surrounding the acceptance of non-representational painting in the twentieth century.)

Undoubtedly composers continued to compose such movements, and audiences to enjoy them, despite the complaints of theoreticians, as the style offered its particular rewards. Freed of the need to present a cantabile melody with simplified accompaniment, or to return to the counterpoint of the strict style, composers could exploit timbral, dynamic, and registrational effects, could (in other words) experiment with texture and harmony in ways that were difficult in the other styles. Or was the motivation less exalted: the creation of a grand *frisson*, quickly apprehended and just as quickly forgotten? Which of these two (by no means mutually exclusive) explanations applied doubtless depended on the composer, the piece, and the circumstances for which it was written.

The Minuet that follows is also based upon fanfares and scales. Its opening idea seems to announce tongue in cheek (as Machaut had a circular creation of his proclaim), 'Ma fin est mon commencement'. The Trio, in G major and for strings alone with divided violas, offers us a chamber-music intimacy that contrasts with the pomp of the minuet.

The striking change of tone evident from the first note of the Andante is due to a combination of factors—factors (as mentioned above) many of which figure in a number of Wolfgang's subsequent symphony andantes and were heard for the first time in the revised version of K. 45a: the horns, trumpets, and kettledrums drop out; the violins are muted; the cellos and basses play pizzicato; the key changes (here to the dominant; more often to the subdominant); and the oboists put down their instruments and take up flutes. This pastoral movement is dominated by the timbre of the flutes, whether they are sustaining slowly-changing harmonies or adding melodic fillips.

A second minuet and trio, an almost mandatory part of a serenade, is unusual although not unheard of in a symphony.[43] The second Minuet in K. 62a exhibits less pomp than the first, but even more scales. The scherzo-like Trio, again for strings alone but now in D minor, makes much of jocular grace-notes and a slapstick comedy of high vs. low and loud vs. soft.

The Finale, a jig in the form of a rondo, brings the festivities to a suitably lively conclusion. Its principal theme, which occurs no fewer than fourteen times, bears a passing resemblance to the popular German round *Am Abend*, the first line of

---

[43] Brook, *La Symphonie française*, i. 469.

which is 'O wie wohl ist mir am Abend' and which in English-speaking countries is known by the words 'O how lovely is the evening'.[44] On the other hand, it also resembles a hunting call entitled 'Le vol-ce-l'est'.[45] These three tunes and Mozarts' Finale tune (Example 6.3) are probably not directly related, but rather have common ancestors in the same tune family.

Ex. 6.3 Symphony in D major, K. 100 = 62a. Tunes similar to the beginning of the Finale

(a) 'O wie wohl ist mir am Abend' ('Oh, how lovely is the evening')

(b) Le vol-ce-l'est

[44] D. de Charms and P. F. Breed, *Songs in Collections: An Index* (Detroit, 1966), 84.
[45] *Dictionnaire de toutes les espèces de chasses* (Paris, An 3 (1794–5) (Encyclopédie méthodique, lxiv), Plate 3, Figure 5) which reports, 'One sounds this fanfare when one again sees the hunted stag', and p. 438, which states, 'VOL-CE L'EST, the term people use when one sees again the fauve beast that is going to flee, which one knows when it spreads all its legs.'

Symphony in B flat major, K. Anh. 216 = 74g = Anh. C 11.03

[Incipits 6.4]

Instrumentation: strings, 2 oboes, 2 horns, [bassoon, continuo]
Autograph: lost
Principal source: set of parts of unknown provenance, formerly in Berlin, now lost (possibly in the Jagiellońska Library, Kraków)
Facsimile: none
Edition: Breitkopf & Härtel, 1910 (= *GA*, Serie 24, No. 63); *NMA*, x/29, in preparation

The story of this symphony is nearly as peculiar as that of the 'Lambach' symphonies. K. 74g is another one of the ten symphonies known to Köchel only by its incipit in the Breitkopf & Härtel Manuscript Catalogue; he assigned it the number Anh. 216. In the first decade of the twentieth century a set of parts for K.

74g was discovered in the Berlin library, and the work was published by Breitkopf & Härtel in 1910. This set of parts is not now to be found in the music libraries of West or East Berlin,[46] so, if it has survived, it may be found in the Kraków library, where the remainder of the pre-Second World War Berlin collections is now located. According to a list of the contents of the *GA*, the 1910 edition of K. 74g formed the final fascicle of the supplementary volumes, as 'Serie 24, No. 63'.[47] And indeed, like other scores published by Breitkopf & Härtel as offprints from the *GA*, the copy of K. 74g available to me has at the top of the first page 'Mozarts Werke' and at the bottom 'Stich und Druck von Breitkopf & Härtel in Leipzig', 'W. A. M. [K.] Anh. IV. 216' and (in English) 'Copyright 1910, by Breitkopf & Härtel, New York'. However, also at the top is the incomplete indication 'Serie 24 No.   ', perhaps suggesting some confusion about the work's status. Copies of the *GA* examined by me lack the fascicle containing K. 74g, and this must also have been true of the copy used as the basis for the slightly revised reprint edition issued in Ann Arbor after the Second World War, for K. 74g is not included in it. As this somewhat mysterious 1910 edition is the only one K. 74g has ever had, copies are difficult to locate and the work has sunk into obscurity.

When it was published, K. 74g was reviewed by Alfred Heuss, who offered a few *ex cathedra* pronouncements on its worth, while not questioning its genuineness:

A newly discovered symphony of Mozart's ... does not enlarge our store of knowledge about the symphonies of his youth. It belongs with a few others in the period of the Italian journey of 1770–1 and bears unmistakably the characteristics of the period. Furthermore, the previously-known symphonies [of Mozart's] from this time are somewhat more significant [than K. 74g].[48]

Einstein, faithfully following Wyzewa and Saint-Foix, who apparently also heard in this work sounds that Wolfgang absorbed during his travels in Italy in 1770, assigned it the number 74g in K^3, which represents the early summer of 1771 when the fifteen-year-old composer spent a little over four months in Salzburg between his first and second trips to Italy.[49] If K. 74g is by Wolfgang, it may or may not date from 1770 or 1771; and we take note below of a similarity of its first movement to that of the Viennese symphony K. 48 of late 1768. K. 74g has divided violas throughout, a trait sometimes considered an archaic form of orchestration

[46] H.-G. Klein, *Wolfgang Amadeus Mozart: Autographe und Abschriften* (Berlin, 1982), (Staatsbibliothek Preussischer Kulturbesitz, Kataloge der Musikabteilung, I/vi) *infra*; G. Allroggen, 'Zur Frage der Echtheit der Sinfonie KV Anh. 216 = 74g', *Analecta musicologica* (1978), xviii. 237–45, repr. in G. Croll (ed.), *Wolfgang Amadeus Mozart* (Darmstadt, 1977), 462–73; *idem*, *NMA*, iv/11/2. ix.

[47] K^6, 933.

[48] *Zeitschrift der internationalen Musikgesellschaft*, (1909–10), xi. 364.

[49] Wyzewa–Saint-Foix, i. 374 (= i. 409–12). These arguments and this dating of K. 74g are also accepted by Della Croce, *Le 75 sinfonie*, 111–13.

peculiar at this date to Salzburg (said to be descended from the practices of Lully through his disciple, the Salzburg Kapellmeister Georg Muffat), and therefore regarded as a reliable clue to Salzburg origins in Wolfgang's music. But Wolfgang's Viennese symphonies of 1768 also used divided violas, divided violas have sometimes been considered a trait of Mannheim orchestration,[50] and the Chiari engraving of the 1780s discussed in Chapter 7 (Plate IX) shows divided violas in Italy, a practice still mentioned by Galeazzi in 1791.[51] Divided violas cannot be used as proof of Salzburg origins. Yet the work may be of Salzburg origin, and Wolfgang or Leopold may have written it.

Although Heuss, Wyzewa and Saint-Foix, and Einstein had expressed no doubts about the authenticity of K. 74g, the editors of K^6 relegated it to the appendix of doubtful and spurious works as Anh. C 11.03, offering as their explanation only that 'on internal grounds' the symphony could 'hardly be genuine'. This does not give the sceptic much to argue against.

Mindful of the dangers of attempting dating and authentication solely on the basis of style, we may pursue another line of reasoning.[52] The circumstances of K. 74g are similar on the one hand to those of the several other symphonies known to Köchel only by their incipits and subsequently rediscovered in non-authoritative copies, and on the other hand to those of the group of symphonies accepted by Köchel as authentic although known to him only through non-authoritative sources. The subsequent fate of the symphonies known to Köchel only as incipits may be briefly summarized here: in two cases (K. 19a and 45a) authoritative sources reappeared confirming Wolfgang's authorship. In a third case (K. Anh. 291 = C 11.06) a lost symphony re-emerged in an authentic copy, proving that it was actually Leopold's work. Three further cases involved the rediscovery of symphonies in non-authentic sources (K. 16a, 45b, 74g). Six others are still lost: K. 19b, 66c, 66d, 66e, and the two overlooked by Köchel (K^6 Anh. C 11.07 and 11.08). Köchel placed seven symphonies known only by non-authoritative manuscript copies among the authentic works (K. 76 = 42a, 81 = 73*l*, 97 = 73m, 95 = 73n, 84 = 73q, 75, and 96 = 111b). The important point is this: the reasons for accepting or rejecting the last-named six symphonies, as well as the subsequently re-emerged 45b, are the same as those for accepting or rejecting K. 74g. While the style of many of these works may be close enough to Wolfgang's not to exclude his authorship out of hand, their provenance remains unclear. By any standard of logical consistency, therefore, either all seven of these symphonies must join K. 74g

[50] A. L. Ringer, 'The Chasse: Historical and Analytical Bibliography of a Musical Genre' (Ph.D. diss., Columbia University, 1955), 258–315.

[51] Francesco Galeazzi, *Elementi teorico-pratici di musica con un saggio sopra l'arte di suonare il violino* (Rome, 1791–6), i. 215.

[52] I derive this argument from G. Allroggen, 'Zur Frage der Echtheit' (see n. 46 above).

among the doubtful works, or K. 74g must be included among the possibly authentic ones.

Despite this clear line of reasoning from G. Allroggen, who is editor of the early symphonies for the *NMA*, the leaders of that edition have decided to place K. 74g in volume x/29, which is reserved for works of doubtful authenticity, while keeping the other questionable symphonies—hallowed and unquestioned by the monuments of Mozart scholarship—in the main volumes. Thus the canon of Mozart's symphonies as transmitted in the *GA* and the Köchel Catalogue may, apparently, not be toyed with lightly.

The listing of K. 74g in the Breitkopf & Härtel Manuscript Catalogue indicates that the symphony calls for two flutes and two horns, whereas the 'Berlin' parts that constituted the work's only known source had oboes rather than flutes. This apparent contradiction may have arisen because there were originally flutes in the Andante and oboes in the other movements, following a practice found in eight of Wolfgang's other symphonies and in a few other of his orchestral works.[53] Of course, the reverse is also a possibility: flutes in the outer movements replaced by oboes in the Andante, as in the A major symphony, K. 114. A letter of Leopold's referring to Wolfgang's early symphonies as calling for 'two oboes or transverse flutes'[54] suggests that (especially given that the two instruments were handled by the same players in most orchestras of the period) there may have been some flexibility in the matter.

The first movement of K. 74g opens with dotted minims in the first violins and wind, accompanied by tremolo semiquavers in the lower strings. This melody ranges over an octave and a sixth in its first six bars. The texture and the wide ranging melody (which, as mentioned in connection with the discussion of K. 48 in Chapter 5, Wyzewa and Saint-Foix claimed was a characteristically Viennese trait), the alternation of forte and piano, and the triple meter—all are reminiscent of the opening of the D major symphony, K. 48. After the cadence on the dominant, a contrasting idea—a staccato theme, also wide ranging—answering back and forth between first violins and bass instruments, leads at bars 42–7 to an unusual restatement of the opening idea. Then follows an energetic closing section of considerable length. A rather serene development section of only twenty bars is based on new material forming another dialogue between the first violins and bass instruments. A literal recapitulation with the retransition nicely recomposed is concluded by a four-bar codetta. There are no repeated sections.

The Andante, a binary design in the subdominant, is cast from a mould very similar to that used to create the andantes of a number of other of Wolfgang's

---

[53] Symphonies: K. 43, 100 = 62a, 73, 95 = 73m, 110 = 75b, 133, 185 = 167a, 182 = 173dA, 204 = 213a, 250 = 248b; other works with orchestra: K. 35, 50 = 46b, 103 = 61d, 61h, 118 = 74c, 127, 135, 203 = 189b, 196, 208, 216, 238, 243, 320.
[54] Letter of 7 Feb. 1772. *Briefe*, i. 456; *Letters*, i. 306 (= i. 209).

symphonies of the early 1770s, except that it does not have the muted violins and pizzicato cellos and basses. After a buoyant Minuet, the Trio for strings alone sounds four-square and rhythmically repetitious. The Finale is in sonata form with both sections repeated. As in the first movement, the opening idea reappears after the modulation to the dominant. A well-made development section, based entirely on an idea from the exposition and featuring a false reprise, leads to a literal recapitulation.

The personnel of the Salzburg court orchestra in 1769 shown in Table 8.1. This ensemble (subject to the interpretations and qualifications discussed in Chapter 1) undoubtedly performed a number of Wolfgang's works of the period, perhaps including the symphonies K. 100 = 62a and K. 74g. But Leopold's and Wolfgang's sights were already turned elsewhere, to the land that was the birthplace and fount of opera, symphonies, and much else—the land of music to the south of them.

7

Italy: Fons et Origo (1769–1773)

———————— ✤ ————————

Mozart's youth in Salzburg was punctuated by three journeys to Italy lasting from 12 December 1769 to 28 March 1771, 13 August to 15 December 1771, and 24 October 1772 to 13 March 1773. Thus from just before his fourteenth birthday until shortly after his seventeenth, he spent a total of about twenty-two months in the land where the terminology and much else of modern music had originated. (Sonata, cantata, concerto, opera, oratorio, and sinfonia were, after all, not just Italian terms, but Italian inventions.) Mozart and his father followed a well-trodden path, for generations of German composers had served apprenticeships in Italy, among them Schütz, Muffat, Handel, J. C. Bach, Hasse, and Gluck. The nature and import of the German musical pilgrimages of the mid-eighteenth century were perceptively discussed in an essay by Nicolas Étienne Framery entitled 'Some Reflections upon Modern Music':

While the French and Italians were disputing which of them possessed music, the Germans learned it, going to Italy for that purpose. Before the Germans had the advantage of having any great men themselves, they had that of sensing the merit of their neighbours. The German artists filled the public conservatories of Naples; people of quality sent their sons to the most famous masters .... They had all the raw materials required of great musicians; they lacked only the discipline to organize those materials, and they had no trouble acquiring that ....

The Italians have for a long time divided their music into two genres: church music and theatre music. In the first they bring together all the forces of harmony, the most striking chord progressions—in a word, the effect; and that is what they seek to combine with melody, which they never abandon. Here it is that one finds such well-worked-out double and triple fugues, those pieces for two choirs or for double orchestra—in fact, the most elaborate things that the art of music is capable of producing. The theatrical genre rejects absolutely all of these *tours de force*. Here the Italians employ nothing learned; everything devolves upon the melody ....

It is quite simple on this basis to teach composition to young people: one makes them work only on church music; one shows them matters of labour before showing them matters of taste. Upon leaving the schools, the Italian pupils remain in their own country. Those who intend their talents to be employed in the theatre learn its procedures and genres: in frequent examples they see what they must remember and what they must forget. The Germans, on the contrary, return to their country. They have carefully preserved their prodigious accumulation of [musical] science. They have tested the very fortunate use of wind instruments of which their nation makes much use, and they have known how to draw the most from them. If they wished to work for the theatre, they had only scores for models. Score-reading is not as seductive as live theatre . . . . They have realized that all expression does not suit vocal melody; that there are a thousand nuances which the orchestra is much more fit to render [than the voice]. They have tried, they have succeeded, and have raised themselves far above their masters, who now rush to imitate them. Here is what formed the likes of Hasse, [J. C.] Bach, Gluck, and Holzbauer. Let the Italians bring out symphonies of their best masters, and let them compare them with those of Stamitz, Toeschi, and Van Malder! Is not Mr. Gossec himself—the only one among us French who can walk alongside these great men in the symphonic genre—a student of the German school?[1]

A second French author, writing at the same time as Framery, had further observations about the nature of Germanic symphonies. Asserting that the unity of good music arose from avoiding too great a profusion of ideas and instead developing a principal motive (grounds on which a number of eighteenth-century commentators preferred Haydn's symphonies to Mozart's), he explained one aspect of the success of Germanic symphonies:

The German symphonists . . . are less interested in finding simple motives than in producing beautiful effects by the harmony that they draw from the great number of instruments that they use, and from the manner in which they work them successively. Their symphonies are a kind of concerto in which the instruments shine, each in its turn, provoking and responding, arguing and making up. It is a lively and sustained conversation. However, throughout all these contrasts, you always recognize (and above all in the good works) a motive that serves as the foundation of the entire edifice. Each part, it is true, occupies itself with the motive in turn. One such passage is intended for the hunting horn, another such for the oboe; it is a period that is divided among the sections of the orchestra—a canvas on which each instrument paints a small detail.[2]

Apparently, France (whose indigenous instrumental music had been transformed almost beyond recognition by an invasion of foreign music, performers, and composers; whose capital city was a major centre for the performance and publication of symphonies) provided excellent 'neutral' territory from which to

---

[1] Nicolas Étienne Framery, 'Quelques réflexions sur la musique moderne', *Journal de musique historique, théorique, et pratique* (May 1770), i. 3–18, here 14–17.

[2] François-Jean Chastellux, *Sur l'union de la poésie et de la musique* (The Hague and Paris, 1765), as quoted in the *Journal de musique* (Aug. 1770), i/8. 3–32.

observe the beginnings of the shift of hegemony in instrumental music from Italian- to German-speaking regions. Or, at least, the remarks of Framery and Chastellux are among the first to document this shift. One could hardly ask for clearer contemporary statements of the matrix of cultural forces in which Mozart's symphonic development took place in the 1770s.

The significance of the Italian journeys to the formation of Mozart's style was recognized as early as January 1792, when a German eulogist wrote, 'Unquestionably these trips of the immortal Mozart had a great influence on the development of his taste ... for in addition to an intense fullness of ideas, which prevails in his compositions, these travels particularly manifest themselves in the pairing of his serious native muse with Italian grace.'[3] This brief explanation of the principal ingredients of Mozart's style is, *mutatis mutandis*, that given two decades earlier by Framery for the rise of the Germanic symphony in general.

The letters that Wolfgang and Leopold wrote home during their Italian journeys (for now Wolfgang's mother and sister remained in Salzburg) reveal that they needed symphonies for public and private music-making, that they brought some with them from Salzburg, and that Wolfgang composed others while on the peninsula. Leaving Salzburg for their first Italian voyage on 12 December 1769, the Mozarts gave concerts in Innsbruck (17 December) and Roverto (Christmas Day) but, as far as can be ascertained, without an orchestra. The first orchestral concert, which took place in Verona on Friday, 5 January 1770, in the Teatrino of the Accademia Filarmonica, is probably typical of others during their Italian tours. Leopold described the occasion in a letter to his wife:

In all my life I have never seen anything more beautiful of its kind .... It is not a theatre, but a hall built with boxes like an opera house. Where the stage ought to be, there is a raised platform for the orchestra and behind the orchestra another gallery built with boxes for the audience. The crowds, the general shouting, clapping, noisy enthusiasm and cries of 'Bravo!' and, in a word, the admiration displayed by the listeners, I cannot adequately describe to you.[4]

A newspaper account confirms the enthusiasm of Wolfgang's reception, mentioning 'a most beautiful introductory symphony of his own composition, which deserved all its applause'.[5]

A similar programme, given in Mantua at the Teatro Scientifico on 16 January 1770 to acclaim apparently equal to that received in Verona, confirms the

---

[3] 'Biographische Nachricht', *Musikalische Korrespondenz der teutschen Filarmonischen Gesellschaft* (4 Jan. 1792), 2.

[4] Letter of 26 Jan. 1770. *Briefe*, i. 306; *Letters*, i. 158 (= i. 108). For two contemporary representations of the Veronese Teatrino, see O. E. Deutsch, *Mozart and His World in Contemporary Pictures* (NMA, X/32) (Kassel, 1961), 90; *The New Grove*, xix. 675.

[5] *Gazzetta di Mantova* (12 Jan. 1770). Deutsch, 95 (= 105).

characteristic function then assigned symphonies—they provided a 'frame' for an event:

1. First and second movements of a symphony by Wolfgang
2. Harpsichord concerto played at sight by Wolfgang
3. Aria sung by the tenor Francesco Antonio Baldassare Uttini
4. Harpsichord sonata played at sight and ornamented by Wolfgang, and then repeated in a different key
5. Violin concerto by a local virtuoso
6. Aria improvised by Wolfgang upon a poem handed him on the spot, sung by him to his own harpsichord accompaniment
7. Two-movement harpsichord sonata improvised by Wolfgang on two themes given him on the spot by the concertmaster; at the end the two themes were 'elegantly' combined
8. Aria sung by the soprano Angiola Galliani
9. Oboe concerto by a local virtuoso
10. Harpsichord fugue improvised by Wolfgang on a theme given him on the spot
11. 'Sinfonia concertata con tutte le parti' accompanied by Wolfgang on the harpsichord from a first violin part handed him on the spot
12. Duet by two professional musicians
13. Trio 'by a famous composer' in which Wolfgang performed at sight the first violin part, ornamenting it
14. Finale of the opening symphony.[6]

As for his opinion of the Mantuan musicians, Wolfgang wrote in a postscript to a letter of his father's, 'The orchestra was not bad.'[7] The only drawback to this otherwise brilliant event was explained by Leopold to his wife:

Neither this concert in Mantua nor the one in Verona was given for money, for everybody goes in free; in Verona this privilege belongs only to the nobles who alone keep up these concerts; but in Mantua the nobles, the military class, and the eminent citizens may all attend them, as they are subsidised by Her Majesty the Empress. You will easily understand that we shall not become rich in Italy.[8]

Wolfgang and Leopold participated in two further gala concerts with orchestra, one at Count Firman's palace in Milan on 12 March, the other at the palace of Count Pallavicini in Bologna on 26 March. The programme of the former occasion included a recitative and three arias by Wolfgang; that of the latter is unknown.[9] There were also concerts in Milan (23 February, 12 March), Florence (2

---

[6] Deutsch, 96–7 (= 106–7). For a contemporary picture of the Mantuan Teatro Scientifico, see Deutsch, *Mozart and His World in Contemporary Pictures*, 95.

[7] Letter of 26 Jan. 1770. *Briefe*, i. 310; *Letters*, i. 162 (= i. 110).

[8] Letter of 26 Jan. 1770. *Briefe*, i. 307; *Letters*, i. 159 (= i. 108).

[9] Deutsch, 100–1 (= 111–12). Leopold's letter of 13 Mar. 1770. *Briefe*, i. 320; *Letters*, i. 173 (= i. 118). For full details see A. Ostoja, *Mozart e l'Italia* (Bologna, 1955), 29.

April), and Naples (28 May), details of which are lacking.[10] Symphonies played at Verona, Mantua, Bologna, Milan, Florence, and Naples apparently were brought from Salzburg, following Leopold's policy to have ready while on tour 'four or six symphonies with the parts doubled for concert use'.[11] Likely candidates include K. 62a, the three Viennese symphonies (K. 43, 45, and 48), the revised version of K. 45a, and (if it is genuine and has been correctly placed chronologically) K. 74g.

The first hint of symphonies composed in Italy appears in a letter of Wolfgang's to his sister, written from Rome on 25 April 1770: 'When I have finished this letter, I shall finish a symphony of mine which I have begun . . . . A symphony has been given to the copyist—who is father, for we do not wish to give it out to be copied, as it would be stolen.'[12] On 4 August in another letter to his sister, now from Bologna, he remarked, 'In the meantime I have already composed four Italian symphonies'.[13] These two letters suggest that one symphony was completed just before 25 April, a second one shortly thereafter, and two more prior to 4 August— or did Mozart refer to two Roman and four Bolognese symphonies, so one must reckon with six in all? Köchel, at any rate, interpreted the letters to refer to four symphonies, so he assigned four stylistically plausible, poorly documented symphonies to Italy in 1770 as K. 95, 96, 97, and 98. The last of these (= K^6 Anh. C 11.04)—now believed to be Leopold's work, although it was also attributed in the eighteenth-century to '[Michael?] Haydn'—is discussed in Chapter 11. The remaining three were removed from 1770 by Einstein in K^3, but his redatings do not prove entirely satisfactory: K. 95 = 73n has been assigned an earlier date in Chapter 4 (on admittedly shaky stylistic grounds) while K. 96 = 111b possibly belongs to 1775, as explained below; hence, only the redating of K. 97 = 73m bears up under scrutiny.

All four of these works lack authentic sources, as do two of an additional three symphonies that exist only in sets of non-autograph parts with indications of Italian provenance (K. 83 = 73*l* and 84 = 73q). Two other symphonies sometimes claimed for the Italian journeys, both without autographs or other authentic sources, have been assigned respectively to Chapters 6 (K. Anh. 216 = 74g = Anh. C 11.03) and 8 (K. 75). Problems of authenticity are severe among all these symphonies: two have attributions to both Leopold and Wolfgang in various sources (K. 81 = 73*l* and 84 = 73q). Lack of reliable sources for these works and for K. 97 = 73m and 95 = 73n makes resolution of the confusion difficult. Three

---

[10] Deutsch, 100–11 (= 110–22). Leopold's letters of 27 Feb., 3 Apr., and 29 May 1770. *Briefe*, i. 316–17, 330–2, 353–5; *Letters*, i. 169–70, 183–5, 206–7 (= i. 115–16, 124–5, 140).

[11] See above, ch. 6, at n. 22.

[12] Letter of 26 Jan. 1770. *Briefe*, i. 342; *Letters*, i. 194 (= i. 131). G. Allroggen (*NMA*, iv/11/2. xi) believes that the completed symphony being copied by Leopold on 25 Apr. 1770 was K. 81 = 73*l*, concerning which see below.

[13] *Briefe*, i. 377; *Letters*, i. 226 (= i. 153).

additional symphonies, which (it is arbitrarily suggested in K^3 and K^6) Mozart may have written in Salzburg in 1769 on the eve of his departure for Italy, are even more problematic, for they do not have even non-authentic sources and are known only from incipits in the Breitkopf & Härtel Manuscript Catalogue (K. 66c, 66d, 66e). Finally, there are seven symphonies firmly authenticated by autograph manuscripts: K. 73, 74, 87 = 74a, 118 = 74c, 120 = 111a, 112, and 135.

Most of Wolfgang's symphonies believed to originate in Italy are in D major. A clue to why this is so may be contained in a cryptic remark to his father about the 'Haffner' symphony, K. 385: 'I have composed my symphony in D major, because you prefer that key.'[14] D major is a brilliant, 'easy' key for string players, which, unlike the other 'easy' violin keys (G and A major), was also one of the trumpet keys, permitting the addition of those instruments whenever they were to be had. Mozart's D major symphonies of the 1770s seem more conventional in character than several he wrote in other keys. And D major may have been regarded as a brash, impersonal, 'public' key. Thus William Jackson could write of J. C. Bach, 'It is an odd circumstance that his symphonies in the vulgar key of D two sharps are superior to his others',[15] while various theoretical writers characterized the key as 'enlivening, heroic, impudent' (Vogler, 1779), 'triumph, rejoicing, war-cries, marches' (Schubart, 1784), 'pompous, noisy' (Knecht, 1792), and 'cheerful, gay, tumultuous, festive' (Galeazzi, 1796).[16] That D major need not be conventional and that Mozart had hardly exhausted its symphonic possibilities would be brilliantly demonstrated some years later by the 'Haffner' and 'Prague' symphonies. For the 1770s, however, D major was a conservative choice, which must have suited the formal functions of Mozart's Italian symphonies. Perhaps his mysterious statement to his father about the key of the 'Haffner' symphony should be troped as follows: 'I have composed my [thoroughly modern] symphony in [the conventional key of] D major, because you [and the other fuddy-duddies of Salzburg] prefer that key.'

Mozart's expression 'Italian symphonies' in his letter of 4 August 1770 has been taken to mean three-movement symphonies, that is to say, symphonies without the minuet and trio characteristic of the so-called Viennese symphony of the period. Hence it has sometimes been asserted, concerning those of Mozart's symphonies thought to originate in Italy which have minuets, that the minuets must have been added later to transform an Italian sinfonia into an Austrian concert symphony, on the model of K. 319.

Some light may be shed on this matter by Wolfgang's remarks to his sister from Italy:

[14] Letter of 27 July 1782. *Briefe*, iii. 215; *Letters*, iii. 1207 (= ii. 810).
[15] 'William Jackson of Exeter [1730–1803], Musician, An Autobiography', *The Leisure Hour* (1882), xxxi. 273–8, 360–2, 433–6, 504–6, 569–71, 620–5, 718–20; here 277. I owe this item to Cliff Eisen.
[16] R. Steblin, *A History of Key Characteristics in the Eighteenth and Early Nineteenth Centuries* (Ann Arbor, 1983), Table 7.2.

I shall soon send you a minuet which Mr [Carlo de] Picque danced in the theatre and which everyone danced to afterwards at the *feste di ballo* in Milan—solely in order that you may see how slowly people dance here. The minuet itself is very beautiful. It comes, of course, from Vienna and was most certainly composed by [Florian Johann] Deller or [Joseph] Starzer. It has plenty of notes. Why? Because it is a stage minuet which is danced slowly. The minuets in Milan, in fact Italian minuets generally, have plenty of notes, are played slowly and have many bars, *e.g.*, the first part has sixteen, the second twenty or twenty-four.

I like [Michael] Haydn's six minuets [sent from Salzburg] . . . . We have often had to perform them for the Countess [Pallavincini]. We should like to be able to introduce the German taste in minuets into Italy, where they last nearly as long as a whole symphony.[17]

While these remarks concern theatre and ballroom minuets, Wolfgang may also have had symphonies in mind as part of his plan 'to introduce German taste in minuets into Italy'. There is no evidence against this suggestion, and the testimony of his four-movement 'Italian' symphony, K. 112, in its favour. By 'Italian symphonies', then, Wolfgang may simply have meant symphonies written in and for Italy, without reference to the presence or absence of minuets.[18]

A minuet written by Wolfgang in Italy in 1770 does survive: the Minuet in A, K. 61gI, discussed in Chapter 8 in connection with the Symphony in A, K. 114. Although this curious piece calls for strings and two oboes, thus lacking the pair of horns normal in symphony minuets, it does require violas, which are usually absent from ballroom minuets. The work in any case does not fail to observe the concision that Mozart wished to promulgate in Italy (Example 8.3). It is likely to have nothing to do with Mozart's symphonies and something to do with the various minuets mentioned in the family's letters between 24 March and 22 September 1770, which were being sent between Italy and Salzburg.

It would help to establish a context for Wolfgang's 'Italian' symphonies if one knew what symphonies he heard during his visits, but the voluminous correspondence he and his father sent back to Salzburg is silent on this matter. The sole symphony mentioned is not by an Italian at all, but by the Bohemian Mysliveček.

Ex. 7.1 Joseph Mysliveček: Symphony in C major (overture to *Demofoonte*)

[Allegro]

---

[17] Letters of 24 Mar. and 22 Sept. 1770. *Briefe*, i. 323, 392; *Letters*, i. 178–9, 238–9 (= ii. 121, 162).
[18] E. F. Schmid, 'Zur Entstehungszeit von Mozarts italienischen Sinfonien', *Mozart-Jahrbuch* (1958), 71–7, here 72.

TABLE 7.1 Operas attended by Leopold and Wolfgang Mozart in Italy

Date	Place	Composer	Title, genre (première)	Librettist
23 Jan. 1770	Verona	Pietro Guglielmi	*Ruggiero*, opera seria (Venice, 1769)	C. Mazzolà
10 Jan. 1770	Verona	J. A. Hasse	*Demetrio*, opera seria (Venice, 1732, 1747)	Metastasio
20 Jan. 1770	Cremona	J. A. Hasse	*La clemenza di Tito*, opera seria (Pesaro, 1735; Naples, 1759)	Metastasio
2 Feb. 1770	Milan	Nicola Piccinni	*Cesare in Egitto*, opera seria (Milan, 1770)	G. F. Bussani
30 May 1770	Naples	Niccolò Jommelli	*Armida abbandonata*, opera seria (Naples, 1770)	F. S. de Rogati
12 Feb. 1771	Venice	Antonio Boroni	*Le contadine furlane*, dramma giocoso (Venice, 1771)	Chiari
16 Oct. 1771 26 Oct. 1771	Milan	J. A. Hasse	*Ruggiero*, opera seria (Milan, 1771)	Metastasio
30 Jan. 1773	Milan	Giovanni Paisiello	*Sismano nel Mongol*, dramma per musica (Milan, 1773)	G. de Gamerra

This work, the overture to Mysliveček's *Demofoonte*, Leopold and Wolfgang liked
so well that they planned to obtain a copy to bring home with them (Example
7.1).[19] The only other Italian symphonies that Wolfgang can be shown to have
heard are the overtures to the operas that they attended, three of which, however,
prove to be the work of his compatriot Hasse (Table 7.1).

The prominence of Hasse's works raises the question whether his music could
have served as a Germanizing artistic filter interposed between Mozart and Italian
musical ideas, the way the music of Bach and Abel to some extent stood for
'English' music and the music of Raupach, Honauer, and Eckard, for 'French'. But
the answer to this question seems to be no, for even a superficial examination of
two dozen sinfonias by Hasse, Piccinni, Jommelli, and Paisiello which are to hand,
suggests otherwise.[20] By the 1770s Hasse's sinfonias were quite old-fashioned, and
Mozart's own were much closer in idiom to the more modern Italian works that he
heard. Besides such general stylistic impressions, there is clear evidence that Mozart
knew and admired a symphony by Paisiello, for he took over one movement and
arranged it as the third movement, Andante grazioso, of his Divertimento in E flat
major, K. 166 = 159d.[21]

Symphony in D major, K. Anh. 215 = 66c

[Incipits 7.1]

Instrumentation: strings, 2 oboes, 2 bassoons, 2 horns, [continuo]
Autograph manuscript: none
Principal source: none

---

[19] The incipit of Mysliveček's symphony is known because Wolfgang gave it in a postscript to Leopold's letter of 22 Dec.
1770. *Briefe*, i. 411; *Letters*, i. 258–9 (= i. 176).

[20] Sinfonias examined: Hasse—*Alcide al bivio, Arminio, Don Tabarrano, Euristeo, Larinda e Vanesio, ovvero L'artigiano
gentiluomo, Ruggiero*, Sinfonia à 5 in G major, *Siroe, rè in Persia, La serva sealtra, Il trionfo di Clelia*; Jommelli—*Armida,
Demofoonte, Fetonte, L'Olimpiade, l'Uccellatrice*; Paisiello—*Il barbiere di Siviglia, Il duello comico, La Frascatana, Il marchese
Tulipano, Nina, ovvero La pazza per amore, Pirro*, Sinfonia in tre tempi, *Socrate immaginario*; Piccinni—*Atys, La buona figliuola,
Catone in Utica, Diane et Endimion, Didon, Iphigénie en Tauride, La molinarella, Roland*, Sinfonia in D major.

[21] R. Angermüller discovered that this movement had appeared in Noverre's ballet *Annette et Lubin* of 1778 (*W. A.
Mozarts musikalische Umwelt in Paris (1778): Eine Dokumentation* (Munich, 1982), lix–lx), but its true origin in Paisiello's
symphony was revealed in a letter to the editor from A. M. Stoneham (*The Musical Times* (1984), cxxv, 75). Paisiello's
symphony is dated 1772 (*NMA*, vii/17/1. ix-x (F. Giegling)). Both Paisiello's Andante and the Parisian reduction of it are
published in the *NMA*, Kritische Bericht, VII/17/1. a/46–54.

Symphony in B flat major, K. Anh. 217 = 66d

[Incipits 7.2]

Instrumentation: strings, 2 flutes, 2 horns, [bassoon, continuo]
Autograph manuscript: none
Principal source: none

Symphony in B flat major, K. Anh. 218 = 66e

[Incipits 7.3]

Instrumentation: strings, 2 flutes, 2 oboes, 2 bassoons, 2 horns, [continuo]
Autograph manuscript: none
Principal source: none

The very nature of the Köchel Catalogue engenders speculative behaviour on the part of otherwise cautious scholars, for, as the Catalogue is chronological, a work cannot be entered into it without an attempt at dating that work. This encourages guesswork. Einstein's explanation for inserting these three incipits into the chronology of the Köchel Catalogue just at the end of the time in Salzburg in 1769 offers a case in point:

It is pure, but perhaps not unfounded, speculation of mine that the symphonies K. Anh. 215 = 66c, Anh. 217 = 66d, and Anh. 218 = 66e were written with a view to the forthcoming Italian trip. On 16 January Mozart performed three symphonies in Mantua including a 'Sinfonia concertata con tutte le parti'. He would scarcely have reused the symphonies from the grand tour [of 1765–6] for that purpose, but would have written new ones . . . .
    From its orchestration [K. 66e] could be the 'Sinfonia concertata con tutte le parti' that was performed in the Mantuan concert of 16 January 1770.

The editors of K[6] take over this muddle virtually unchanged and without comment. As shown above, however, the 'Sinfonia concertata con tutte le parti' was not by Mozart. And these three symphonies, K. 66c–e, may not be by him either. The opening of K. 66c does, it is true, have the same rhythmic *Gestalt* as the opening of *Eine kleine Nachtmusik*, K. 525, and is not unlike that of the less exalted Symphony in D major, K. 84 = 73q, another work of unclear provenance. The incipit of K. 66d reveals the three *premiers coups d'archet* that open hundreds of eighteenth-century orchestral pieces, including a number of Mozart's. K. 66e's incipit has a more individual character not unrelated to the opening of the perfectly genuine Symphony in G major, K. 110 = 75b, of 1771; and similar too to a D major symphony falsely attributed to Joseph Haydn (Hob. I: D19). The point of these comparisons is to suggest that symphony incipits were conventional almost by definition and that, in the absence of other information, such incipits provide poor materials for dating and authentication. By themselves most symphony incipits of the mid-eighteenth century will not permit precise chronological, geographical, or authorial placement of the works that they represent.

Symphony in C major, K. 73 = 75a = 73

[Incipits 7.4]

Instrumentation: strings, 2 oboes = flutes, 2 horns, 2 trumpets, kettledrums, [bassoon, harpsichord]
Autograph: Jagiellońska Library, Kraków
Principal source: none
Facsimile: none
Editions: *GA*, xx. 97–109 (= Serie VIII, No. 9); *NMA*, iv/11/i. 163–86

The autograph manuscript of K. 73 bears only the inscription 'Sinfonie' in Wolfgang's hand. The date '1769' was added in another hand, perhaps Leopold's, perhaps Johann Anton André's. Köchel accepted that date, and the editors of K^6 have reverted to it, thus calling into question Alfred Einstein's attempt in K^3 to redate the work to the summer of 1771.[22] Because a sketch for the Minuet of this symphony is found in the autograph of a series of minuets (K. 103 = 61d) that K^3 and K^6 claim Wolfgang wrote for Carnival 1769, it might seem logical to propose that the symphony was completed around the same time, in which case even the Köchel number 73 would be too high. But the dating of the minuets themselves rests on vague stylistic grounds and should only with great caution be used as a basis for dating the symphony. From Wolfgang's writing, Plath assigns the manuscript of the minuets, K. 103 = 61d, to early summer 1772,[23] while Alan Tyson reports that its paper is a type that Wolfgang is known to have used between December 1771 and March 1772.[24] Again on the basis of writing, the manuscript of the symphony was originally dated 'probably not before early summer 1772' by Plath,[25] but more recently—after examining the autograph in Kraków—he has reverted to Köchel's estimate of late 1769 or early 1770.[26] Tyson reports that the paper of K. 73 is a Salzburg type that cannot be closely dated.[27]

The evidence connecting K. 73 with Italy is also ambiguous: there is a single leaf that began its existence as an attempt by Leopold to copy out a 'basso' part for this symphony. For unknown reasons, he abandoned his effort after only twelve bars, and Wolfgang later used the mostly empty sheet of music-paper to work out a

[22] Because of Einstein's redating of K. 73, based upon Wyzewa–Saint-Foix's opinion (i. 379 (= i. 415)) that the work was composed in May or June 1771, this symphony will occasionally be found designated as K. 75a. As Einstein believed—despite the evidence of K. 112 to the contrary—that Wolfgang's 'Italian' symphonies could not have minuets unless these had been added after the return to Austria, he would automatically have avoided dating K. 73 to a time when Wolfgang was in Italy.
[23] W. Plath, 'Beiträge zur Mozart-Autographie II: Schriftchronologie 1770–1780', *Mozart-Jahrbuch* (1976–7), 131–73, here 161–2.
[24] Personal communication from Alan Tyson.
[25] Plath, 'Schriftchronologie', 161–2.
[26] *NMA*, iv/11/1. xiii.
[27] Personal communication from Alan Tyson.

puzzle canon from the second volume of Padre Martini's *Storia della musica*, a book that came into the Mozarts' possession in Bologna in early October 1770.[28] But this date is only a *terminus a quo*; Wolfgang continued to work sporadically on Martini's puzzle canons for a few years. In sum, even with its autograph, the 'basso' fragment, and the other version of the Minuet available for examination, K. 73 has so far resisted efforts firmly to date it.

Schultz wrote of the first movement of K. 73 that its 'principal theme departs from the overture-type. It is a hybrid form in which a first phrase, built of chordal figurations in the Italian style, gives way to a cantabile phrase in a manner unknown to the theatre symphony. In other respects the movement still bears a pronounced overture character.'[29] Likewise indicative of the movement's hybrid nature is that fact that, even though the symphony as a whole is a four-movement concert symphony along Germanic lines rather than a three-movement Italianate overture-symphony, the first movement lacks the repeats usually found in the former genre. This is Mozart's first C major symphony: it has the trumpets and a bit of the pomp of his last symphony, also in this key, but little of its seriousness or originality.

The Andante, a subdominant binary movement with both halves repeated, is treated similarly to the andantes of a number of Wolfgang's symphonies of the period: the horns, trumpets, and kettledrums drop out and the oboists, taking up their flutes, soar above the treble staff, colouring the movement from beginning to end. Larsen singles out this movement from Wolfgang's symphonies of the period 'for its fine cantabile'.[30]

Wyzewa and Saint-Foix find the stately Minuet Haydnesque (Joseph, not Michael), and especially the Trio, which is for strings alone,[31] even though both are more four-square than the older master's best minuets. The violas, by their simple doubling of the bass-line in the Minuet, reveal the movement's ballroom origin. (Other symphony minuets that exist also in versions for the ballroom and likewise lack independent viola parts are found in K. 112 and 320.) Given the probable

Ex. 7.2 Symphony in C major, K. 73 = 75a = 73. Rebarring of the Finale

[28] Letter of 6 Oct. 1770. *Briefe*, i. 394; *Letters*, i. 241 (= i. 164).

[29] D. Schultz, *Mozarts Jugendsinfonien* (Leipzig, 1900), 14.

[30] J. P. Larsen, 'The Symphonies', in H. C. Robbins Landon and D. Mitchell (eds.), *The Mozart Companion* 3rd edn. (New York, 1969), 156–99, here 165.

[31] Wyzewa–Saint-Foix, i. 379–81 (= i. 415–16).

ballroom origin of this Minuet, and if the dating of the dance to 1772 is correct, then the symphony may have been written in Salzburg in the summer of 1772, in time for the Mozarts' third and final Italian journey.

The Finale is a gavotte (or *contredanse*) *en rondeau*. Although the movement is marked Allegro molto $\frac{2}{4}$, its rondo theme is based on an underlying moderate-tempo $\frac{2}{2}$ gavotte, which can be sensed by beating time once in a bar, starting with an upbeat (Example 7.2). The Finale is 176 bars long, but Wolfgang wrote out only eight passages totalling 72 bars. These he numbered one to twenty in such a way that an alert copyist could piece together the whole movement. Over the first eight bars, for instance, he wrote '1 2 5 6 8 9 16 17', signifying the four pairs of appearances of the movement's refrain. This method, which saved time, paper, and ink, suggests how clearly Wolfgang must have had the movement's straightforward structure (A B A C A D A) in mind as he came to write it down. The whole projects an impression of deliberate naïveté, from the nursery-rhyme character of the refrain to the comically sing-song quality of the D section in C minor.

Symphony in D major, K. 81 = 73l

[Incipits 7.5]

Instrumentation: strings, 2 oboes, 2 horns, [bassoon, continuo]
Autograph: lost
Principal source: Gesellschaft der Musikfreunde, Vienna (XIII 20026, *olim* Q 18464)
Facsimiles: none
Editions: *GA*, xxxix. 22–31 (= Serie 24, No. 4); *NMA*, iv/11/ii. 3–14

The set of manuscript parts of K. 73*l* in the Gesellschaft der Musikfreunde is inscribed 'Del Sig[no]re Cavaliere Wolfgango Amadeo Mozart' and 'in Roma, 25. April 1770',[32] but in a fascicle of the Breitkopf Thematic Catalogue published in 1775 the work is listed as Leopold's, paired with the Symphony in G major, K. Anh. C 11.09[33] (Example 7.3), a work widely accepted as Leopold's although also ascribed to Wolfgang.[34] Despite its questionable pedigree, K. 73*l* has generally been accepted as being by Wolfgang, perhaps because of its high quality and the previously discussed tendency to underrate Leopold as a composer. Leopold's symphonies have just received their first serious study, and those available in modern editions and recordings are not necessarily representative, being dominated by his 'novelty' works ('Sleighride', 'Peasant Wedding', 'Toy', 'Pastoral'). One 'serious' symphony that is available in a good edition and recordings is the so-called 'New Lambach' symphony, a work that bears comparison to Wolfgang's early symphonies.[35] Lacking a chronology of Leopold's works with which to trace his development as a symphonist, one has little idea of his capabilities at a given date.

The editor of Mozart's earliest symphonies for the *NMA* originally believed that K. 73*l* was one of the symphonies referred to in Wolfgang's letter of 25 April 1770, but subsequently he decided in favour of Leopold as its author. Most recently, however, he appeared to be suspending judgement in the matter of attribution.[36] Supporting Leopold's authorship is an assertion in his letter of 12 February 1781 to Breitkopf & Son that of Wolfgang's work they had seen only a few accompanied sonatas.[37] If Leopold's remark was accurate, then the attribution to him of K. 73*l* in the Breitkopf Catalogue is correct. The most that can be inferred from the evidence to hand is that there is a strong possibility that this symphony is by Leopold, not Wolfgang. With some hesitation, Leopold's principal proponent has accepted K. 81 = 73*l* as Leopold's.[38]

The first movement opens with an upwardly arpeggiated D major chord, an idea that is inverted for the opening of the Finale. It continues as a compactly organized sonata form, without repeats and with a literal recapitulation. The tiny 'development' section of twelve bars hardly deserves the name, and could more aptly be called a transition. The G major Andante, a serene binary movement with

---

[32] These parts, of unknown eighteenth-century provenance, were a gift of Aloÿs Fuchs in 1843.

[33] B. S. Brook (ed.), *The Breitkopf Thematic Catalogue* (New York, 1966), 563.

[34] This work is Seiffert 3.28 = Theiss D27 = New Grove G8 = Eisen ?G8. See esp. Eisen, 'The Symphonies of Leopold Mozart', 288.

[35] See ch. 6 and Eisen, 'The Symphonies of Leopold Mozart', 294–5.

[36] Allroggen, 'Mozarts Lambacher Sinfonie', 17–19; *NMA*, iv/11/2. x–xi.

[37] Letter of 12 Feb. 1781. *Briefe*, iii. 92–3; *Letters*, ii. 1054 (= ii. 710). The text of this letter is corrupt in *Briefe*; for the correct text see R. Schaal, 'Ein angeblich verschollener Brief von Leopold Mozart', *Acta Mozartiana* (1979), xxvi. 50–1.

[38] Eisen, 'The Symphonies of Leopold Mozart', 267–8. But W. Plath, 'Mozart, Leopold', *The New Grove*, xii. 678, labels the work 'probably by W. A. Mozart'.

Ex. 7.3 Leopold Mozart: Symphony in G major, K. Anhang 293 = Anhang C 11.09

both sections repeated, features a dialogue between the first and second violins, the conversation soon broadening to include the oboes. The Finale—cast in the kind of binary arrangement described in Chapter 2 for the first movement of K. 19a—is a 'chasse' or 'caccia', that is, a kind of a jig filled with hunting-horn calls. This 'hunt', however, would seem to be one contemplated from the comfort of the drawing room, far from the mud, commotion, and gore of the real thing. Hunting symphonies, all but one in D, were written by Leopold Mozart (G9, D23 [lost]), Gossec (1774), C. Stamitz (1775), Rosetti (1781–2), Wranitzky (?), J. Haydn (No. 73, 177?), Hoffmeister (1791), and others. At a remove of two centuries it is difficult to understand the great popularity of the 'chasse' finale, with its predictable clichés but generally lacking the witty twists with which Mozart would later pepper the finales of his horn concertos. Certainly, hunts organized in the French manner were popular at many courts that aspired to the splendour of Versailles; and from 1766, when Philidor's popular *Tom Jones* included a hunting scene, the 'chasse' moved from purely instrumental music into *opéra comique*, thus intensifying the fashion for these simple fanfares.[39]

[39] A. L. Ringer, 'The Chasse: Historical and Analytical Bibliography of a Musical Genre' (Ph.D. diss., Columbia University, 1955), 259 ff.

Symphony in D major, K. 97 = 73m

[Incipits 7.6]

Instrumentation: strings, 2 oboes, 2 horns, 2 trumpets, kettledrums, [bassoon, continuo]
Autograph: lost
Principal source: *GA*
Facsimiles: none
Edition: *GA*, xxxix. 52–62 (= Serie 24, No. 7); *NMA*, iv/11/2. 15–32

This work is listed in the Breitkopf & Härtel Manuscript Catalogue (p. 7, No. 46) with an annotation that seems to mean that the Leipzig firm had two manuscripts, one from its own archives and another provided by Mozart's sister. Although neither survives, presumably one or both served as the basis for the *GA*. But because no proper critical report was issued for that edition of K. 73m, nothing is known of the work's possible provenance. In K^3 K. 73m was assigned, on unstated grounds (but see the proposed explanation at the beginning of this chapter), to Rome, April 1770. This assignment has been accepted by the editors of K^6. And grounds (other than stylistic guesswork) may exist for both the proposed date and the genuineness of this symphony. In Chapter 6 the grouping of chronologically related symphonies in the Breitkopf & Härtel Manuscript Catalogue was posited. One possible grouping comprises the symphonies numbered 46, 47, and 48 in that Catalogue, which prove to be K. 97 = 73m, 73, and 84 = 73q respectively. If this link proposed between K. 73m and the indisputably authentic K. 73 should prove valid, then the case for the genuineness of the former work would be strengthened.

The first movement of K. 73m, an Italian overture in style and spirit, is in sonata form with no repeated sections. A brief development section touches on G major, E minor, and B minor, before re-establishing the home key. The Andante, a binary movement in G major with both sections repeated, exhibits an attractive kind of mock-naïveté. The twenty-four-bar Minuet certainly satisfies Wolfgang's preference (documented above) for brevity, with its sixteen-bar G major Trio omitting the wind.

Ex. 7.4 Symphony in D major, K. 97 = 73m, Finale (bars 40–57)

The Finale is a jig-like movement in sonata form, with a brief but well-wrought development section. Its 'short' metre can only have been intended to speed along the Presto tempo, as the movement's phrase structure and placement of dissonance and consonance would work perfectly in $\frac{6}{8}$. In bars 40–55 and 138–53 the Finale contains an uncanny adumbration of a passage in the first movement of Beethoven's seventh symphony, not just the shape and rhythm of the theme but the way in which it is immediately repeated with a turn to the minor (Example 7.4). Since Beethoven is unlikely to have known K. 73n, for no manuscript copies seem to have circulated and the symphony was first published only in 1881 in the *GA*, one can merely speculate about coincidence or a common model.

Symphony in D major, K. 84 = 73q

[Incipits 7.7]

Instrumentation: *strings, 2 oboes, 2 horns, [bassoon, continuo]
Autograph: lost
Principal source: Gesellschaft der Musikfreunde, Vienna (XIII 20027, *olim* Q 18465)
Facsimiles: none
Editions: *GA*, xx. 121–34 (= Serie 8, No. 11); *NMA*, iv/11/2. 47–66

This symphony survives in early manuscripts in Vienna (attributed to Wolfgang), in Berlin and Prague (attributed to Leopold, the former merely a nineteenth-century copy of the latter), and twice more in Prague (attributed to Dittersdorf and 'Sig:^re Mozart' respectively).[40] The Breitkopf & Härtel Manuscript Catalogue included K. 73q (p. 8, No. 48), but, even though Breitkopf had obtained the work from Nannerl Mozart, a marginal annotation in the Catalogue expressed doubt as to its authenticity. A comparison of the results of two stylistic analyses of the work's first movement with analyses of unquestionably genuine symphony first movements of the period by the three composers in question has suggested that Wolfgang is the most likely of the three to have been the composer K. 73q,[41] but the work's status remains uncertain.

[40] G. Allroggen, 'Zur Frage der Echtheit der Sinfonie KV Anh. 216 = 74g', *Analecta musicologica* (1978), xviii. 237–45, repr. in G. Croll (ed.), *Wolfgang Amadeus Mozart* (Darmstadt, 1977), 462–73; H.-G. Klein, *Wolfgang Amadeus Mozart: Autographe und Abschriften* (Berlin, 1982), 260; Eisen, 'The Symphonies of Leopold Mozart', 313–14.
[41] J. LaRue, 'Mozart or Dittersdorf—KV 84/73q', *Mozart-Jahrbuch* (1971–2), 40–9; S. Davis in J. LaRue (ed.), *A Mozart Festival-Conference: Summary Report of the Sessions on Authenticity and Performance Problems* (Washington, 1974), unpaginated.

The Vienna manuscript bears two inscriptions of the sort found on many of Wolfgang's autographs and on some authentic copies of the period: 'In Milano, il Carnovale 1770 / Overtura' and 'Del Sig[no]re Cavaliere Wolfgango Amadeo Mozart a Bologna, nel mese di Luglio, 1770'. These apparently contradictory bits of information may be resolved in the following manner: in the year 1770 Carnival lasted from 6 January until 27 February, and the Mozarts were in Milan from 23 January to 15 March, and in Bologna from 20 July to 13 October. If, therefore, the inscriptions are to be trusted, this symphony may have been drafted in Milan in January or February and revised in Bologna in July. K. 73m, 73, and 73q are grouped together in the Breitkopf & Härtel Manuscript Catalogue as Nos 46, 47, and 48 respectively; they may have formed an 'opus'.

Ex. 7.5 Opera buffa style

(a) Symphony in D major, K. 84 = 73q, Finale (bars 24–32)

(b) Gioacchino Rossini: Figaro's prattling from *Il barbiere di Siviglia* (Act I, Scene ii)

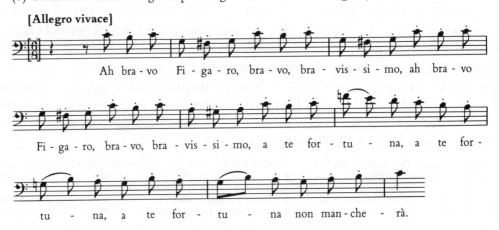

The opening Allegro exhibits a fully-fledged sonata form with—as suggested by the indication 'overtura' on the Viennese source—no repeated sections. There are, well differentiated, an opening group of ideas, a second group, a closing group, a transitional 'development' section of eleven bars, and a full recapitulation. The Andante has a Gluck-ish ambience and, like the first movement, is in sonata form but without development section. The Finale opens with a fanfare borrowed from the first movement; the idea is then withheld during the rest of the exposition, development, and recapitulation, to serve as a coda at the end. The fanfare aside, most of the movement has a constant flow of triplets, which turns it into a kind of jig. By its kinship to Figaro's prattling in Rossini's *Barber of Seville*, one passage in particular reveals the opera buffa inspiration behind this movement (Example 7.5).

Symphony in G major, K. 74

[Incipits 7.8]

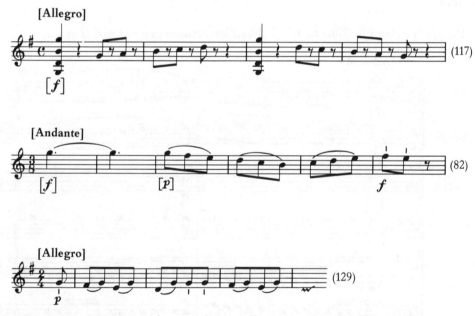

Instrumentation: strings, 2 oboes, 2 horns, [bassoon, continuo]
Autograph: Jagiellońska Library, Kraków
Principal source: none
Facsimile: *NMA*, iv/11/2. xvii
Editions: *GA*, xx. 110–20 (= Serie 8, No. 10); *NMA*, iv/11/2. 67–82

The autograph of K. 74 bears neither date nor title, although at the end of the last movement Mozart expressed his gratitude (or perhaps relief?) at its completion by writing 'Finis Laus Deo'. At the beginning someone else wrote 'Ouverture (zur Oper Mitridate)', but this inscription was subsequently crossed out. Although Mozart would not have composed an opera overture more than a half-year in advance of the première, he might have thought of reusing a symphony as an overture, as he did in Vienna in 1768 when the symphony K. 45 became the overture to *La finta semplice*. However, as Mozart's opera sinfonias of the period are in the 'public' trumpet keys of C, D, or E flat (with the sole exception of the G major sinfonia for *Bastien und Bastienne*, which was intended for a small-scale private performance) and most use pairs of both oboes and flutes, the inscription must be an error.

Unable in the early 1970s to examine the autograph of K. 74, Plath had to content himself with echoing the Köchel Catalogue's 'probably 1770 in Milan'.[42] Alan Tyson, more fortunate a few years later, discovered that K. 74 is written on the same rare type of paper that Wolfgang used for the aria 'Se ardire, e speranza', K. 82 = 730, composed in Rome in April 1770.[43] This places the work reasonably securely.

Ex. 7.6 Symphony in G major, K. 74. Transition between first and second movements

⁴² W. Plath, 'Schriftchronologie', 138.   ⁴³ Personal communication from Alan Tyson.

[Andante]

K. 74 is written in Italian overture style, that is, the first movement is in sonata form without repeats and, after a complete recapitulation, an altered codetta flows into the second movement not only without a halt but even without a new tempo indication or double barline. At this juncture the quavers in the oboes continue on unperturbed, as the metre shifts from common time to $\frac{3}{8}$ and the key from G major to C major (Example 7.6). The Finale is marked simply 'Rondeau', whose spelling gives a hint of the character of its refrain, which is that of a French *contredanse*. Noteworthy in this movement is an 'exotic' episode in G minor (Example 7.7), which is perhaps the earliest manifestation of Wolfgang's interest in 'Turkish' music—an interest also exhibited in portions of the ballet music for *Lucio Silla*, K. Anh. 109 = 135a, the violin concerto, K. 219, the piano sonata, K. 331 = 300i, *The Abduction from the Seraglio*, K. 384, the aria, 'Ich möchte wohl den Kaiser sein', K. 539, and the *contredanse* 'La bataille', K. 535. These pieces have little to do with true Turkish music, but draw on a style found occasionally in the music of Michael and Joseph Haydn, Leopold and Wolfgang Mozart, Dittersdorf, Gluck, and other Austrian composers of the period. The apparent origin of their 'Turkish' music is found in the indigenous music of Christian-ruled regions bordering the Ottoman Empire, where the Hungarian peasants and gypsies imitated or parodied the music of their Muslim neighbours. In parts of Hungary the peasants referred to this style of music as 'Törökös', which means the same thing as Wolfgang's 'alla turca', that is, 'in the Turkish manner'. 'Exotic' elements include: a leaping melody, a harmonically static bass with drum-like reiterated notes, odd chromatic touches in the melody, a minor key, a march tempo in $\frac{2}{4}$, and swirling ornamentation in the form of grace notes, trills, and turns.[44]

A remarkable aspect of the Mozart family's voluminous correspondence is its almost exclusive concentration on people and their creations. Did they never peer out the windows of their carriage or of the buildings in which they stayed? Did they fail to look about themselves when they went out walking? It is as if in their view of the world nature hardly existed or was little worthy of comment. But in

Ex. 7.7 Symphony in G major, K. 74, minor section of the Finale (bars 49–56)

[44] D. Bartha, 'Mozart et le folklore musical de l'Europe centrale', in A. Verchaly (ed.), *Les Influences étrangères dans l'œuvre de W. A. Mozart* (Paris, 1958), 157–81. For a different explanation of Mozart's Turkish music, see K. Reinhard, 'Mozarts Rezeption türkisher Musik', in H. Kühn and P. Nitsche (eds.), *Bericht über den internationalen musikwissenschaftlichen Kongress, Berlin 1974* (Kassel, 1980), 518–23.

Rome in the spring of 1770 the fourteen-year-old Mozart perhaps did notice something, for in the first movement of K. 74 at bars 17–22 and the parallel passage in the recapitulation (bars 77–82) there occurs what appears to be the call of the *cinciallegra* or titmouse.[45]

Symphony in D major, K. 87 = 74a, 'Mitridate, rè di Ponto'

[Incipits 7.9]

Instrumentation: strings, 2 flutes, 2 oboes, 2 horns, [2 bassoons, 2 trumpets, kettledrums, continuo]
Autograph: lost
Principal source: Lisbon, Biblioteca Ajdua (for the opera); Donaueschingen (for the symphony)
Facsimile: none
Editions: *GA*, viii. 1–8 (= Serie 5, No. 5); *NMA*, ii/5/4. 5–15; trumpet parts in *NMA*, ii/5/4, Kritische Bericht, 171–3

Mitridate, rè di Ponto, K. 87 = 74a, was begun in Milan at the end of July 1770. Mozart composed the recitatives first, then turned to the arias, and probably wrote the overture last. The opera had its first general rehearsal on 17 December and its première on 26 December, to general approbation. As was then the custom and required by his *scrittura* (the official commission), Wolfgang presided over the first three performances at the first harpsichord—dressed in a new 'suit of scarlet,

---

[45] Della Croce, *Le 75 sinfonie*, 294.

trimmed with gold braid and lined with sky-blue satin'. The Milan orchestra over which he presided had strings 14 − 14 − 6 − 2 − 6 and wind 0 − 2 − 2 − 4 − 0 − 2 / 4 − 2 − [1], plus two harpsichords.[46]

The overture to *Mitridate* circulated widely in the eighteenth century as an autonomous symphony, judging by eighteenth-century sets of parts found in Donaueschingen, Český Krumlov, Zurich, Milan, Vienna, and Graz, and a listing among the symphonies in the Breitkopf & Härtel Manuscript Catalogue (p. 8, No. 50). The autograph of the opera is lost, and all that survives in Mozart's hand are sketches for a few numbers. In the extant sources for the opera, the orchestra employed in the overture calls for strings with pairs of flutes, oboes, and horns. Examination of the rest of the opera reveals, however, that the orchestra also included pairs of trumpets and bassoons—instruments that would hardly have been silent during the festive overture.[47] Performers of this overture (whether as an independent concert work or prefacing the opera) should, therefore, pay special attention to a set of eighteenth-century manuscript parts for the overture in Donaueschingen, which provide for bassoons doubling the bass-line throughout and trumpets and kettledrums in the first and last movements. Or rather, they once provided for kettledrums, for that part has been lost, so modern performers will have to invent one.[48] Because, as discussed in Chapters 2 and 6, Donaueschingen was a court to which Mozart and his father had ties, these parts may have authentic origins.

In a definition of 'symphony' contemporaneous with *Mitridate*, J. A. P. Schulz stated the widely-held theory of the functions of the overture-symphony:

The symphony is excellently suited to the expression of the grand, the festive, and the noble. Its purpose is to prepare the listener for an important musical work . . . . If it is to satisfy this purpose completely and be a closely bound part of the opera . . . that it precedes, then, besides being an expression of the grand and the festive, it must have an additional quality that puts the listeners in the frame of mind required by the piece to come.[49]

According to this theory, then, a brief synopsis of the plot of *Mitridate* should serve to indicate the intended 'expression' of the symphony, K. 74a.

The libretto was the work of Vittorio Amedeo Cigna-Santi, freely adapted from Racine's *Mithridate*. Mithridates VI Eupator (111–63 BC) had conquered Cappadocia and other provinces beyond the Bosphorus as far as the Crimea. In the third

---

[46] The story of the composition, rehearsals, intrigues, and performances of *Mitridate* is found in a series of letters from Leopold to his wife between 20 Oct. 1770 and 12 Jan. 1771. *Briefe*, i. 397–416; *Letters*, i. 244–65 (= i. 166–80). For the orchestral forces, see n. 47 and Table 7.2 below.

[47] Leopold reported the presence of trumpets and bassoons in the Milan orchestra in his letter of 15 Dec. 1770. *Briefe*, i. 408; *Letters*, i. 256 (= i. 174).

[48] A kettledrum part may easily be improvised by an experienced player from the second trumpet part.

[49] See ch. 4, n. 7.

Mithridatian War, however, he was defeated by the Romans under Sulla and Pompey and fled to his kingdom of Pontus by the Bosphorus where, believing himself to have been betrayed by his sons and wife, he killed himself by falling on his sword, opening the way for a happy ending—at least for the other characters. But not a trace of this story can be detected in Mozart's brilliant D major overture, which neither sets the scene psychologically nor provides a foretaste of the opera's music, rather serving as a neutral, festive curtain-raiser. As such, it could without compunction be detached from the opera which gave it birth and turned into a concert symphony, as Mozart would do with all of his overture-sinfonias prior to the overture to *Idomeneo*, K. 366 (1781).

Thus, at this stage of his career, Mozart did not subscribe to the 'modern' theory of the overture, put forth by Schultz, Gluck, Algarotti, and other eighteenth-century writers, as programmatic or psychological preparation for the drama. Rather, he held to the older Italian idea of the functioning of opera sinfonias, as explained by Rousseau:

The Italians . . . begin by a striking, lively movement in duple or common time; then they offer *sotto voce* an andante in which they aim at displaying all the ornaments of beautiful melody; and they conclude with a brilliant allegro, generally in triple time.

The reason they give for this arrangement is that in a large audience, where the spectators make a great deal of noise, it is necessary first to bring them to silence and capture their attention by means of a glittering, striking beginning. The Italians say that the *grave* section of our *ouvertures* is neither heard nor listened to by anyone; and that our *premier coup d'archet*—of which we boast with such great emphasis, even though it is less noisy than, and confounded with, the tuning of instruments that precedes it—is more suitable for preparing the audience for boredom than for alertness. They add that, once the spectator is made attentive by less noise, his interest should be engaged by an agreeable and flattering melody, which disposes him to the tenderness with which he is to be inspired [during the opera]; and lastly, to conclude the overture with a movement of a different character which, contrasting with the beginning of the drama, marks by its loud ending the silence that the actor, on his entrance to the stage, requires of the spectator.[50]

Perhaps the most striking aspect of the sinfonia to *Mitridate* is its concision. The three movements—the opening Allegro with its well-etched contrast between the flamboyant and the lyrical, the Andante with its unmistakable timbre of high flutes in octaves with the low violins, and the driven jig-finale with its crescendo opening and irregular phrase lengths—together take less than six minutes to perform, or about a third of the time required for a concert symphony like K. 112 (also written for Italy). But the sinfonia's brevity did not hinder Mozart from creating a fully satisfying musical landscape, limned with a sure hand.

[50] Jean-Jacques Rousseau, 'Ouverture', *Dictionnaire de musique* (Paris, 1768), 356–8.

Symphony in D minor, K. 118 = 74c, 'La Betulia liberata'

[Incipits 7.10]

Instrumentation: strings, 2 oboes, 2 bassoons, 4 horns, 2 trumpets, [kettledrums?, continuo]

Autograph: Staatsbibliothek Preussische Kulturbesitz, West Berlin (Mus. Ms. W. A. Mozart 118)

Principal source: none

Facsimiles: *NMA*, i/4/2. xii

Editions: *GA*, v. 1–9 (= Serie 4, No. 4); *NMA*, i/4/2. 5–13

Homeward bound from their first Italian tour, Wolfgang and Leopold spent a single day (13 March 1771) in Padua. They had hoped merely to be tourists there (or so Leopold claimed), but word of their presence got out immediately and Wolfgang had to perform at two noble homes.[51] As a result, he was commissioned by a 'local' nobleman, Don Giuseppe Ximenes, Prince of Aragon, to set Metastasio's oratorio text of 1734, *La Betulia liberata*. The work was apparently completed in Salzburg by the summer of 1771; it is written on Salzburg paper.[52] In a letter of 19 July to an Italian patron, Leopold reported his plan to leave the manuscript in Padua on the way south to Milan in August, in order to permit the

[51] Letter of 14 Mar. 1771. *Briefe*, i. 425; *Letters*, i. 273 (= i. 185).   [52] Personal communication from Alan Tyson.

oratorio to be copied, and on the return journey to visit the town in order to attend the dress rehearsal and performance.[53] For unknown reasons these plans fell through; the Mozarts did not revisit Padua going south or north, and the Paduans performed another setting of the same libretto, probably by the local composer Giuseppe Calegari. There is, furthermore, no evidence that Wolfgang's oratorio was performed in Padua or Salzburg at a later date, nor can vague reports of performances in Munich in 1775 or in Vienna in 1786 be substantiated. Hence, this major work of Wolfgang's youth may have remained unperformed during his lifetime.[54]

The Symphony in D minor, K. 118 = 74c, intended to serve *La Betulia liberata* as overture, is an extraordinary work, which deserves to be better known. Aspects of the G minor symphony, K. 183 = 173dB, that have fascinated commentators (as discussed in the next chapter) are already present in this work of two years earlier. The marvellous sounds in the efflorescence of minor-key symphonies of the early 1770s by Mozart, J. C. Bach, Dittersdorf, J. Haydn, Vanhal, and Ordonez, were not entirely new: opera houses required such tempestuous effects to portray the storms of nature and of human emotion. As suggested in Chapter 2, Mozart was familiar with this style some years before he composed K. 74c, for in the London Notebook of 1764 he wrote a G minor keyboard piece in a quasi-orchestral vein, K. 15p, which has some of the tempestuous character that has erroneously been claimed as an innovation of the 1770s.

Metastasio's story is drawn from the Apocrypha. Its central figure is Judith who, when the Jewish city of Betulia was under siege by the Assyrians and nearing surrender, left the city and sought out the enemy commander, Holofernes. While pretending to seduce him, she managed to behead her disarmed foe. Their leader dead, the Assyrians withdrew and Betulia was spared. This provides as stormy a subject as anyone could wish for, and in his overture Mozart rose fully to the occasion.

The 'Overtura', as it is labelled in Mozart's hand, consists of three sections in common time, $\frac{3}{4}$ and $\frac{2}{4}$ respectively, without any indications of tempo. These sections, which are connected by incomplete cadences, are usually interpreted by editors and performers as a weighty Allegro, a flowing but poignant Andante (highly chromatic, touching on F major/minor but beginning and ending in D minor), and a fiery Presto. This is by analogy with other Italianate sinfonias that have this structure, including Mozart's K. 181 = 162b, another continuously played work the movements of which are marked Allegro spiritoso, Andantino grazioso, and Presto assai.

---

[53] *Briefe*, i. 428; not in *Letters*.   [54] See L. Tagliaferro's foreword to *NMA*, i/4/2. vii–xi.

It may be no coincidence that this work is in the same key as the overture to Gluck's *Alceste* (1767) and shares with it a rising-third motive. The Mozarts were familiar with Gluck's opera, which figured in their correspondence as early as 1768.[55]

Symphony in C major, K. 96 = 111b

[Incipits 7.11]

Instrumentation: strings, 2 oboes, 2 horns, 2 trumpets, kettledrums, [bassoon, continuo]

Autograph: none

Principal source: lost set of parts, formerly Breitkopf & Härtel archives, Leipzig

Facsimile: none

Editions: *GA*, xx. 42–51 (= Serie 24, No. 6); *NMA*, iv/11/2. 133–50

---

[55] Leopold's letter of 30 Jan. 1768. *Briefe*, i. 258; *Letters*, i. 122 (= i. 83).

This symphony confronts us with another sourceless, rootless composition once found in a now lost set of manuscript parts in the Breitkopf & Härtel archives. The work's assignment in K^3 and K^6 to Milan at the end of October or beginning of November 1771 is arbitrary, as the editors of K^6 admit. A possible reason for placing it in Salzburg four or five years later is suggested below.

With a bright tantivy, of a sort that opens many an eighteenth-century work,[56] the first movement is off and running. And run it does, with tremolo and scales, through a concise ternary form to a rather predictable conclusion. The Andante is in the parallel minor, whereas Wolfgang's other major-key symphonies of the period most often have their andantes in the subdominant. (Among certainly authentic early symphonies, only K. 16, 22, 43, 62a, and 74a fail to adhere to this generalization: the first two have andantes in the relative minor, the others, in the dominant.) The present movement is a siciliano in an archaic style that recalls such works as the Pastoral Symphony and 'How beautiful are the feet' in Handel's *Messiah*, and certain slow movements in violin sonatas of Locatelli, Tartini, Nardini, and Vivaldi. This is an exceptionally profound slow movement for a symphony of *c.*1770–1; the stylistic disparity between its 'baroque' intensity and the conventional, galant modernity of the movements surrounding it is puzzling.

The case for the genuineness of K. 111b may be strengthened by a link between its Andante and the aria 'Intendo, amico rio' from the serenata *Il rè pastore*, K. 208, of April 1775. ('Intendo, amico rio' is discussed at the end of the next chapter in connection with the Symphony in C major, K. 102 = 213c, which is made up of the overture to *Il rè pastore*, an instrumental version of the selfsame aria, and a newly composed Finale.) The Andante of K. 111b is based on a minor-key version of the aria's ritornello,[57] which suggests that it may have originated in Salzburg near in time to the creation of *Il rè pastore*, April 1775. Furthermore, the C minor movement's exceptional character suggests that it may have been written for a special purpose. This may have been performance at a concert or Mass for Christmas 1774 or 1775, since (as discussed in Chapter 4) pastoral or siciliano movements were a common feature of 'Christmas' concertos, intended to evoke thoughts of the shepherds visiting the manger in Bethlehem. In the absence of further material evidence, such speculations are the best that can be ventured. (If these speculations prove grounded, then this discussion belongs in Chapter 8.)

Following the singular Andante of K. 111b, the Minuet and Finale return to the galant extroversion and conventionality of the first movement, although the Trio (in the subdominant) has a few tricks up its sleeve. The Finale, fashioned from a

---

[56] Compare, for example, the incipit of J. C. Bach's D major symphony given in C. S. Terry, *John Christian Bach* (London, 1929), 2nd edn. by H. C. Robbins Landon (London, 1965), 272–3.
[57] H. Engel, 'Über Mozarts Jugendsinfonien', *Mozart-Jahrbuch* (1951), 28.

kind of quick-step march that is based on the opening materials of the first movement, is in sonata form with both halves repeated, rather than the rondo form of Wolfgang's early symphony finales.

Symphony in D major, K. 111 + 120 = 111a, 'Ascanio in Alba'

[Incipits 7.12]

Instrumentation: strings, 2 flutes, 2 oboes, 2 horns, 2 trumpets, kettledrums, [bassoon, continuo]
Autograph: Staatsbibliothek Preussische Kulturbesitz, West Berlin (Mus. Ms. Autogr. W. A. Mozart 111 (serenata), 120 (symphony finale))
Principal source: none
Facsimile: *NMA*, ii/5/5. xvi
Editions: *GA*, vii. 1–10 (= Serie 5, No. 6) + xxxix. 69–72 (= Serie 24, No. 9); *NMA*, iv/11/2. 115–32

This symphony also began its life as an overture, in this case to the 'theatrical serenata' *Ascanio in Alba*, K. 111, written for the celebrations surrounding the wedding of the Austrian Archduke Ferdinand and the Princess Maria Ricciarda Beatrice of Modena. Mozart began work on it in late August 1771, completing it by 23 September. Its first performance in Milan on 17 October was a success, apparently eclipsing a new opera by the veteran J. A. Hasse, which was also part of the festivities.[58] That the great choreographer Noverre created the ballets in *Ascanio* doubtless added to its éclat.

In this instance Mozart went against his usual custom and composed the overture first, because he had decided to integrate the end of his overture into the beginning of the serenata. Thus, following the opening Allegro, the Andante served as a ballet, to be danced by 'the Graces'. The libretto sets the scene that the Andante was to accompany:

A spacious area, intended for a solemn pastoral setting, bordered by a circle of very tall and leafy oaks which, gracefully distributed all around, cast a very cool and holy shade. Between the trees are grassy mounds, formed by Nature but adapted by human skill to provide seats where the shepherds can sit with graceful informality. In the middle is a rustic altar on which may be seen a relief depicting the fabulous beast from whom, according to legend, the City of Alba derived its name. A delicious, smiling countryside—dotted with cottages and encircled by pleasant, not-too-distant hills from which issue abundant and limpid streams—is visible through the spaces between the trees. The horizon is bounded by very blue mountains, which merge into a most pure and serene sky.[59]

For a Finale, the overture had an Allegro in $\frac{3}{4}$ with choruses of spirits and graces singing and dancing, thus anticipating (in a most diminutive way) Beethoven's innovation in his Ninth Symphony.[60] Leopold Mozart described the effect as follows:

The Andante of the symphony is danced by eleven women, that is, eight genii and three graces, or eight graces and three goddesses. The last Allegro of the symphony, a chorus of thirty-two voices, eight sopranos, eight contraltos, eight tenors, and eight basses, is danced by sixteen persons at the same time, eight women and eight men.[61]

When Mozart decided to turn the overture into a concert symphony, he kept the first two movements unchanged, replacing the choral Finale with a brief *giga* in the form A B A coda. On the basis of Mozart's writing, the autograph of the new Finale has been dated 'probably the end of October or beginning of November 1771 in Milan'.[62] This is confirmed by the Finale's paper, the main type used by Wolfgang during the second Italian journey, which is also found in *Ascanio in Alba* (completed September 1771), the Symphony in F major, K. 112 (dated 2 November 1771), and the Divertimento in E flat, K. 113 (dated November 1771).[63]

---

[58] Leopold Mozart's letters of 19 and 26 Oct. 1771. *Briefe*, i. 444–5; *Letters*, i. 296–7 (= i. 202–3).

[59] *NMA*, ii/5/5. 14. This Andante has two reprises during the course of the serenata, so Wolfgang apparently invested it with some special significance.

[60] Two-movement overture-sinfonias (allegro-andante), for which an opera's opening chorus or aria-ritornello did double duty as finale, were not uncommon.

[61] Letter of 13 Sept. 1771. *Briefe*, i. 436; *Letters*, i. 287 (= i. 196).

[62] Plath, 'Schriftchronologie', 141.

[63] Personal communication from Alan Tyson.

Symphony in F major, K. 112

[Incipits 7.13]

Instrumentation: strings, 2 oboes, 2 horns, [bassoon, continuo]
Autograph: Pierpont Morgan Library-Heinemann Foundation, New York
Principal source: none
Facsimiles: *NMA*, iv/11/2. xx–xxi
Editions: *GA*, xx. 149–60 (= Serie 8, No. 13); *NMA*, iv/11/2. 151–64

The autograph manuscript is a clearly-written fair copy inscribed 'Sinfonia / del Sig[no]re Cavaliere Amadeo / Wolfgango Mozart / à Milano 2 di Novemb. / 1771' (the first word in Wolfgang's hand, the remainder in Leopold's). It probably had its first performance at an orchestral concert ('*eine starke Musik*') that Leopold and Wolfgang gave in Milan on 22 or 23 November at the residence of Albert Michael von Mayr, who was keeper of the privy purse to Archduke Ferdinand, governor of Lombardy and son of Empress Maria Theresa.[64]

That K. 112 was conceived as a concert piece and not an overture can be seen in the first, second, and fourth movements, in which all sections but the coda of the Finale are repeated. Whereas the three previous works (K. 74a, 74c, 111a) require five to seven minutes to perform, K. 112 takes about fifteen. From the beautifully proportioned sonata form of the first movement, through the careful part-writing of the B flat Andante (for strings alone) to the characteristic jig-like rondo-finale, a spirit of confidence and solid workmanship seems to emanate from this symphony, a spirit perhaps garnered from the success of *Ascanio* the previous month.

The first movement was originally marked 'Molto Allegro', but Wolfgang or Leopold crossed out the 'Molto', probably to avoid pre-empting that greater degree of velocity from the Finale. The opening of the Andante is a type of idea found in J. Stamitz's orchestra trio, Op. 1, No. 1, Jommelli's overture to *Ifigenia in Aulide*, and Gluck's overture to *L'innocenza giustificata*.[65] The Minuet shows sign of other origins, however. In that movement the violas, instead of having an independent part to play, as is customary in Mozart's symphonic minuets, double the bass-line. Given that his ballroom dances are without viola parts, this feature of the Minuet of K. 112 may mean either that it had fulfilled another function before being pressed into service in this symphony, or that, with this sonority, Mozart wished to evoke memories of the ballroom in his listeners. In the Trio (for strings alone), however, the violas do carry an independent voice. That the Minuet probably existed before the rest of the symphony is suggested by the fact that it (but not the Trio or any of the rest of the symphony) is copied into Wolfgang's autograph manuscript in Leopold's hand.[66] In addition, the Trio contains a tiny lesson in composition, for what Mozart first wrote (Example 7.8) was symmetrical and banal, but then, with a few light touches, he added a significant if unobtrusive dose of artistry.

Ex. 7.8 First version of the Trio of K. 112

---

[64] Leopold Mozart's letter of 23–4 Nov. 1771. *Briefe*, i. 451; *Letters*, i. 302 (= i. 266). *Letters* incorrectly renders 'eine starke Musik' merely as 'music'.

[65] Stamitz, Andante of the Orchestra Trio C-1 (E. K. Wolf, *The Symphonies of Johann Stamitz* (Utrecht, 1981), 377); Jommelli, Andante of the overture to *Ifigenia in Aulide* (Rome, 1751) (H. S. Livingston, 'The Italian Overture from A. Scarlatti to Mozart' (Ph.D. diss., University of North Carolina, 1952), 130); Gluck, Andante of the overture to *L'Innocenza giustificata* (ed. A. Einstein, Denkmäler der Tonkunst in Österreich (Graz, 1960), xliv/82. 7–8).

[66] Plath, 'Schriftchronologie', 136.

Symphony in D major, K. 135, 'Lucio Silla'

[Incipits 7.14]

Instrumentation: strings, 2 oboes, 2 horns, 2 trumpets, kettledrums, [bassoon, continuo]
Autograph: Jagiellońska Library, Kraków
Principal source: none
Facsimile: *NMA*, ii/5/7/i. xliv
Editions: *GA*, ix. 1–12 (Serie 5, No. 8); *NMA*, ii/5/7/i. 5–14

In 1771 Wolfgang was granted the *scrittura* for the first opera of the Milanese Carnival season of 1773. By October 1772 the libretto of Giovanni da Gamerra's *Lucio Silla* had reached him in Salzburg. As he could not begin composing arias until he had heard the principal singers so as to reckon with their strengths and weaknesses, Wolfgang began by thinking about those numbers that did not tax the soloists: the recitatives, choruses, and overture. On 24 October he and Leopold left for Milan, where they arrived ten days later. By 14 November Leopold could report to his wife that only one of the principal singers had yet shown up: 'Meanwhile, Wolfgang has got much amusement from composing the choruses, of which there are three, and from altering and partly rewriting the few recitatives which he composed in Salzburg . . . . He has now written all the recitatives and the overture.'[67] *Lucio Silla*, K. 135, was a success and received twenty-six performances between its première on Boxing Day 1772 and 25 January 1773. Upon his return to

Salzburg, Wolfgang was unable to have his opera performed, for Salzburg had no opera house, but he did extract certain arias to use as concert pieces[68] and the three-movement overture circulated as a concert symphony, as its presence among the symphonies in the Breitkopf & Härtel Manuscript Catalogue (p. 1, No. 4) reveals.

Like the plots of most serious operas of the period, that of *Lucio Silla* concerns the conflict between love (or personal inclination) and honour (or duty to dynasty and country). The Roman Emperor Silla loves Giunia who, however, loves the senator Cecilio. When, under the influence of assorted bad and good advice, Silla unsuccessfully tries sweet talk, banishment, imprisonment, and threats of death to gain his end, but fails, he comes to his senses, removes all obstacles to Guinia's marrying his rival, and abdicates, to the cheers of the Roman people.

The sinfonia, again a neutral 'curtain-raiser', opens in the frequently noted festive, Italianate vein with a binary movement nearly as long as the two other movements combined. The Andante in A major is dominated by cantabile melody in the treble, avoiding the more elaborate part-writing of several of the symphony andantes written for Salzburg. This gives way to a second Molto allegro, a kind of jig in which running semiquavers throughout much of the movement create the impression of a *moto perpetuo*.

Symphony in C minor, K. deest

[Incipits 7.15]

---

[68] For the arias, see K[6], 163–4.

Instrumentation: *strings, 2 oboes, 2 bassoons, 2 horns
Autograph: Upsala University (Imh. Caps. 26) (Kraus)
Principal source: manuscript parts, Conservatorio Giuseppe Verdi, Milan (Noseda M.41.3)
Facsimile: none
Editions: Wiesbaden: Breitkopf & Härtel, 1956 (ed. Walter Lebermann); Stockholm: Monumenta Musicæ Svecicæ, ii, 1960 (ed. R. Engländer)

There is one more symphony connected with both the name Mozart and the city Milan. In 1971 the Bibliothèque nationale in Paris catalogued under the number Vma. ms. 251 a gift from the estate of the distinguished Mozart scholar Georges de Saint-Foix, a 130-page manuscript orchestral score whose title page reads: 'Sinfonia / in / Do-Minore / del M[aestr]o / Mozart / [ornamental device] / (da manoscritto nella Bibl. del R° Conservatorio Verdi in Milano—Italia) / PARTITURA'. Inquiries to the library of the Conservatorio Giuseppe Verdi reveal that the source from which the Paris score was copied is in fact there. It proves to be an apparently late eighteenth-century single set of manuscript parts, with nineteenth-century *Dubletten* and score. The title-page, attached to the bass part, reads: 'Sinfonia in C minor / à / 2. violini / 2. Oboe / 2. Corni / 2. Fagotti / 2. Viole / Violoncello / e / Basso / Del Sig[no]re Wolfgango Mozart'. The last two words, however, are written over an erasure, which seems originally to have read 'Giuseppe Mozart'.[69]

Although this is a strikingly romantic symphony, its orchestration is extremely conservative, in both the small size of the wind contingent and the handling of the bassoons which, when they play, double the cellos except for two brief duets in the Andante and one passage in the Finale where they double the violas. The basses sometimes drop out leaving the cellos alone, but it is rare for the two sections to sustain independent parts. This old-fashioned orchestration seems somewhat at odds with the more modern style of the music, which in certain passages seems to anticipate the symphonies of von Weber (1786–1826) and Spohr (1784–1859), although not of Beethoven.

Investigation reveals this symphony to be the work of Mozart's exact contemporary, the German-Swedish composer Joseph Martin Kraus (1756–92), so the Milanese title-page did once read 'Giuseppe . . .', but not 'Mozart'. Published twice and recorded four times in recent decades,[70] this impressive work of 1783—so admired by Joseph Haydn—shows that in the 1780s Kraus, like Haydn and like Mozart, was interested in deepening the content of the symphony, but that, unlike

[69] Letter of 6 Mar. 1984 from Prof. A. Z. Laterza, librarian of the Conservatorio di musica "Giuseppe Verdi".
[70] B. H. van Boer, Jr., 'Joseph Martin Kraus', in B. S. Brook (ed.), *The Symphony 1720–1840 . . . Reference Volume* (New York, 1986), 338 (No. 140).

those better-known composers, he may have lacked some of the orchestrational skills needed to project the genre's new conception. The attempts of the 1780s to increase the import of symphonies, and the bewilderment with which these attempts were met in some circles, are discussed in Chapter 13.

The best Italian orchestras in the early 1770s were those of Turin, Milan, and Naples. Pictures of performances by the orchestras of Turin and Naples along with seating diagrams of both (Plates VII, VIII, and XV) show the typical disposition of such groups in the pit: the players sat facing one another in long rows, half toward the audience and half toward the stage. How such orchestras rearranged themselves when performing concerts rather than operas was described by Galeazzi:

The best placement for good effect is to arrange the players in the middle of the hall with the audience all around them; but the visual impression is more satisfying if you arrange them to one side, against one of the walls of the drawing-room (supposing a rectangular-shaped area), because the audience thus enjoys the entire orchestra from the front. The violins are then placed in two rows, one opposite the other so that the firsts are looking at the seconds . . . . With regard to the bass-line instruments, if there are only two, place them near the harpsichord (if there is one) in such a way that the violoncello remains near the leader of the first violins and the double-bass on the opposite side, and between them the maestro or harpsichordist; but if there are more bass-line instruments, and if they are played by good professional musicians, place them at the foot—that is, at the other extremity—of the orchestra; otherwise [if they are not played by good professional musicians] you should place them as near to the firsts as you possibly can. The violas are always best near the second violins, with whom they must often unite in thirds, in sixths, etc., and the oboes are best alongside the firsts. The brass can then be placed not far from the leader. In this disposition all the heads of sections—namely, the leader, the principal second violin, the principal cello, the maestro, the singers, etc.—are neighbours, by which means perfect ensemble cannot but result.[71]

This description is similar to the disposition of the orchestra on the Chiari 'secular' title-page discussed below (Plate IX), except that, according to Galeazzi, both oboes would be on the left, both violas on the right, and the horns and trumpets moved to the back behind the maestro and singers. A bassoon or bassoons, if included in Galeazzi's orchestra, would presumably join the other bass-line instruments at the back on the side nearest the oboes.

The forces of the large Italian orchestras are shown in Table 7.2. Employment of two harpsichords was usual in Italian opera houses in all parts of Europe during most of the eighteenth century. They were the remnants of what had been, in

---

[71] Francesco Galeazzi, *Elementi teorico-pratici di musica con un saggio sopra l'arte di suonare il violino* (Rome, 1791–6), i. 216. Forces of the strength of the Milan orchestra of 1770–1 (Table 7.2) seated according to Galeazzi's description can be heard in the Academy of Ancient Music's recordings of the symphonies K. 97 = 73m, 95 = 73n, 111 + 120 = 111a, and 96 = 111b.

TABLE 7.2 Large Italian orchestras

	vn. I	vn. II	va.	vc.	db.	fl.	ob.	cl.	bn.	hn.	tpt.	timp.	cemb.	TOTAL
Milan 1770–1	14	14	6	2	6	0–2	2–4	0	2	4	2	1	2	63
Milan 1771–2	12	12	6	2	6	0–2	2–4	0	2	4	2	1	2	53
Naples 1773	16	16	4	3	4	0	4	0	0?	0	4	0?	2	53
Naples 1786	15	14	4	2	8	2	2	2	2	2	2	1	1	58
Naples 1796	13	12	4	2	6	0–2	2	2	4	4	0–2	0–1	2	51–7
Turin 1774	15	13	5	{ 10	}	{ 6	}		4	4	2	1	2	62
Turin 1780–1	14	12	4	3	6	0	4	2	3	4	2	1	2	57
Turin 1789–90	11	11	6	2	8	0	5	2	3	{ 6	}	1	(2)	59
Turin 1790–1	{ 23	}	7	5	7	{ 5	}	2	3	4	2	1	2	61

seventeenth- and early eighteenth-century opera, a larger corps of continuo instruments sometimes including harpsichords, portative organs, theorboes, and harps. Reasons for maintaining two harpsichords may have included: (1) the acoustical necessity of providing continuo chords audible at both ends of the long narrow orchestra pits;[72] (2) the notion that the second harpsichord would be manned by an assistant or apprentice, who could be counted on to carry on playing when the maestro at the first harpsichord had to leave off to give a cue, conduct with his hands, or audibly beat time on his instrument;[73] (3) the division of orchestras into ripieno and solo groups, each of which may have required its own continuo support;[74] and (4) the possibility that in recitative in dialogue, the two characters could each have had independent continuo accompaniment, so that the back and forth on the stage would be matched in the pit.[75]

The great strength of the violins and double-basses and the relative weakness of the violas and cellos in large Italian orchestras created a sound distinct from that favoured north of the Alps. The predominance of the double-basses in the 16′ register over the cellos in the 8′ register creates an organ-like sonority that makes the acoustic of a theatre or hall resemble that of a cathedral. The timbre is more archaic, tending toward the 'baroque' ideal of polarization of treble and bass, and away from the 'classical' and 'romantic' ideals of more equal distribution of parts. A strong contingent of bassoons in the 8′ register compensates for the small number of cellos, imparting to the bass-line a characteristic edge that gives it great clarity. A German musician of the period accurately described the effect of such Italian orchestral balance: 'I noticed that the Italians man their orchestras with more bass instruments than is commonly done with us, and I always found the results of it very good—also, the other parts were thereby made more prominent rather than covered'.[76]

---

[72] Galeazzi mentions the acoustical problem of the long, narrow pit, but not in connection with the continuo instruments (*Elementi*, i. 213–27).

[73] See: (1) a caricature by Pierleoni (not Pierluigi) Ghezzi (British Museum, Department of Prints and Drawings), reproduced on the cover of J. Rosselli, *The Opera Industry in Italy from Cimarosa to Verdi: The Role of the Impresario* (Cambridge, 1985), of the composer Nicola Bonifacio Logroscino (1698–?1766) playing continuo for one of his operas in Rome; Ghezzi's inscription reports that the evening on which he took his picture the ensemble was so shaky that Logroscino had to beat time against the side of his harpsichord, as the drawing clearly shows; (2) a 1754 description of opera performances in Italy reporting that, when things went badly, Jommelli and other maestros had been seen to bang so hard on their harpsichords that three or four days' work was required to restore them to working order (de Rochemont, *Réflexions d'un patriote sur l'opéra françois, et sur l'opéra italien, qui présentent le parallele du goût des deux nations dans les beaux arts* (Lausanne, 1754), 54–5 n.).

[74] As in the concerto grosso tradition, which apparently originated in the overtures of Roman oratorios (O. Jander, 'Concerto grosso Instrumentation in Rome in the 1660's and 1670's', *Journal of the American Musicological Society* (1968), xxi. 168–80).

[75] I know of no eighteenth-century source for this idea, but compare the way in which Monteverdi uses the continuo instruments in *Orfeo* and a description of a similar practice in his letter of 21 Nov. 1615, in D. de' Paoli (ed.), *Claudio Monteverdi: Lettere, dediche e prefazioni* (Rome, 1973), 79–81 (= D. Stevens (ed.), *The Letters of Claudio Monteverdi* (London, 1980), 107–8).

[76] Georg von Unold, 'Einige Bermerkungen über die Stellung der Orchester und Einrichtung der Musiksäle', *Allgemeine musikalische Zeitung* (23 Aug. 1802), iv/48, cols. 783–4 n.

For smaller Italian orchestras, a semicircular arrangement of the players was sometimes employed in churches and halls.[77] A passe-partout title-page engraving showing this sort of orchestral layout (Plate IX) was used by the music-publisher Giovanni Chiari of Florence, a city where the Mozarts gave a concert on 2 April 1770.[78] An orchestra is shown either on a stage with sets representing a formal garden or in an actual garden with topiary trees. As many eighteenth-century writings recommend the separation of the first and second violins on the left and right (see Chapter 12), the orchestra portrayed in Chiari's engraving may be interpreted as follows: at the left, from front to back, are 2 horns, 4 first violins, the first oboe, and the first viola; at the right 2 trumpets (showing plainly why Mozart designated them 'trombe lunghe' in his scores), 4 second violins, the second oboe, and the second viola. In the centre at the back is the *maestro al cembalo* surrounded by a cello, a double-bass, and two singers. Another man, near the centre of the semicircle, seems to be directing, while fashionably attired ladies and gentlemen stroll, chat or listen, a dog barks, and a man sweeps up.[79] The layout of the orchestra in the Chiari engraving emphasizes a feature of the orchestration of some of Mozart's 'Italian' symphonies: the first oboe often doubles the violin at the unison or the first viola at the octave, while the second oboe bears the same relationship to the second violin and the second viola (Example 7.8). The two oboes are seldom called upon to play duets unaccompanied by their stringed neighbours.

A second passe-partout title-page, also from Chiari, shows a performance of music in a church (Plate X). Again, fashionably dressed ladies and gentlemen stroll about or stop to listen, a dog barks, and a woman with an arm of absurd length guides a child. The orchestra in a balcony has in the upper tier left trumpets and drums, right oboes and horns; in the lower tier left a choir of nine men, centre, the organ, the maestro beating the tactus, and a cello and violone (or two cellos?), and right, six violins and violas. As Chapter 3 demonstrates, concerted church music of the sort portrayed here regularly included—in addition to settings of the Mass ordinary, motets, and sacred arias—church sonatas, concertos, or symphonies.

The Mozarts gave 'a fine concert' in a Venetian *palazzo* on 5 March 1771.[80] The

---

[77] Galeazzi too mentions the semicircular arrangement (*Elementi*, i. 216–20), which has been used successfully by several modern, conductorless chamber orchestras.

[78] Such title-pages were used as covers for music manuscripts copied on demand, and on Chiari's title-pages space was provided for the copyist to insert the author, title, and incipit. This engraving dates from the 1780s, if one may judge by the style of the women's dresses, for in the 1770s the bows at the back would have been larger whereas by the 1790s they had vanished entirely (information kindly provided by Professor Esther Dotson of the Department of Art History, Cornell University).

[79] Forces placed according to Chiari's engraving may be heard in the Academy of Ancient Music's recordings of K. 81 = 73*l*, 84 = 73q, 74, 87 = 74a, and 112; of these only K. 87 = 74a calls for trumpets.

[80] Leopold Mozart's letter of 6 Mar. 1771. *Briefe*, i. 422; *Letters*, i. 271 (= i. 184).

Ex. 7.9 'Italian' doubling of oboes with violins or violas, Symphony in F major, K. 112

(a) First movement (bars 24–30)

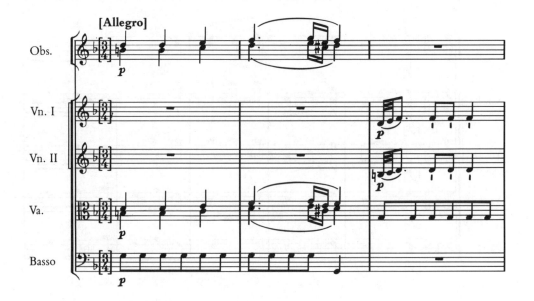

(b) Finale (bars 1–16)

sole description of the event is incomplete, mentioning only Wolfgang's prowess at improvising fugues on subjects given him on the spot.[81] Some idea of the ambience of such a concert may be conveyed by an anonymous oil-painting attributed to 'the school of Longhi', perhaps dating from the 1760s, which shows a concert in a Venetian *palazzo* (Plate XI).[82] As in the Chiari engravings, the social setting is emphasized. Judging from their exaggeratedly rendered gestures, the elegantly dressed people in the room are conversing.[83] As two children and a dog frolic, a servant enters with a tray of refreshments. In the balcony, plainly dressed, lower-class people listen too. The orchestra, at a long table, has pairs of horns and oboes, four violins (or is it two violins and two violas?) and, at the far end, either two cellos or a cello and a violone flanking the maestro at the harpischord. (In his

---

[81] 'Aus Italien vom 7. März', *Staats- und gelehrte Zeitung des hamburgischen unpartheyischen Correspondenten* (27 Mar. 1771). See C. Eisen, 'Contributions to a New Mozart Documentary Biography', *Journal of the American Musicological Society* (1986), xxxix. 615–32, here 624–5.

[82] Casa Carlo Goldoni, Venice. The proposed dating, on the basis of fashions, is by E. Dotson (see n. 78 above).

[83] Like many eighteenth-century representations of music-making in social situations, these three Italian pictures show people talking and walking about while the music is played. This has led modern commentators to suppose that the music was not listened to attentively, which doubtless was the case under some circumstances; yet letters, diaries, and other accounts of musical salons and academies often reported serious listening followed by sometimes heated discussion of the music's merit. An explanation for this apparent contradiction may arise from the plight of an artist called upon to portray such an event: he had to capture in a single rendering both the musical and the social aspects of the occasion. One way of doing that would have been to engage in a bit of poetic licence, telescoping into a single image two activities that had occurred seriatim. Barbara Russano Hanning, to whom I am indebted for this interpretation, is preparing a study of this misunderstood aspect of musical iconography.

rendering the artist has reversed the harpsichord left to right.) As no singers are visible, this may be a concert of instrumental music.

Of the many small Italian orchestras encountered by Wolfgang and Leopold, their correspondence mentions only two, at Mantua and Cremona in January 1770. Wolfgang, then just a week shy of his fourteenth birthday, reported to his mother and sister: 'The opera at Mantua was charming. They played *Demetrio* .... The orchestra was not bad. At Cremona the orchestra is good, and the first violin is called Spagnoletto.'[84] The 'not bad' Mantuan orchestra had 2 maestros, 5 soloists, and 11 ripienists,[85] while the 'good' Cremonese orchestra had a few more players: strings 5—5—2—1—3, pairs of oboes and horns, and a harpsichord.[86]

Little is known about the specific uses to which Wolfgang's symphonies were put during his second and third trips to Italy. Presumably there were private and public concerts of the sort better documented from the first trip. It was the Mozarts' custom, wherever possible, partially to finance their tours by giving concerts in each city they visited. Undoubtedly something of the sort was attempted in the second and third journeys in Italy, although details are generally lacking. To Leopold's report cited above about unpaid concerts in Verona and Mantua, one can add his remarks from Milan, that 'it is not so easy to give a public concert here, and it is scarcely any use attempting to do so without special patronage, while even then one is sometimes swindled out of one's profits'.[87] The fullest account that survives of further Italian concerts is Leopold's brief description of a series of private Advent concerts in which he and Wolfgang participated in Milan in December 1772:

On the evenings of the 21st, 22nd, and 23rd great parties took place in Count Firmian's house at which all the nobles were present. On each day they went on from five o'clock in the evening until eleven o'clock with continuous vocal and instrumental music. We were among those invited and Wolfgang performed each evening.[88]

Symphonies formed an integral part of such music-making, but which ones may have been heard on given occasions can seldom be ascertained, for the identity and even the presence of symphonies were aspects of these events that attracted little comment.

---

[84] Letter of 26 Jan. 1770. *Briefe*, i. 310; *Letters*, i. 162 (= i. 100).

[85] E. Schenk, 'Mozart in Mantua', *Studien zur Musikwissenschaft* (1955), xxii. 1–20, here 7. The distribution of forces was 3—3—2—1—2 / 0—2—0—1 / 2—0—0 plus the two maestros *al cembalo* (O. E. Deutsch, *Mozart und seine Welt in zeitgenössischen Bildern/Mozart and His World in Contemporary Pictures* (NMA, x/32) (Kassel, 1969), 97.

[86] *Briefe*, v. 613..

[87] Letter of 14 Nov. 1772. *Briefe*, i. 460; *Letters*, i. 315 (= i. 222).

[88] Letter of 26 Dec. 1772. *Briefe*, i. 470; *Letters*, i. 324 (= i. 222).

PLATE I. The interior of Salzburg Cathedral during a Solemn High Mass, 1682

PLATE II. The interior of Saint Stephen's Cathedral, Vienna during a Solemn High Mass,
8 November 1712

PLATE III. Frontispiece of *Bildergalerie Katholischer Missbrauche*

PLATE IV. Johan Daniel de Gijsdaar: interior of the 'Oode Doelen', The Hague

PLATE V. Concert of the Collegium Musicum 'beim Kornhaus', Zurich

PLATE VI. Collegium Musicum Concert, Zurich

PLATE VII*a*. The Turin orchestra in the pit of the Teatro Regio, 1740

PLATE VII*b*. The Turin orchestra in the pit of the Teatro Regio, 1740 (detail)

PLATE VIIIa. The Naples orchestra, 1747

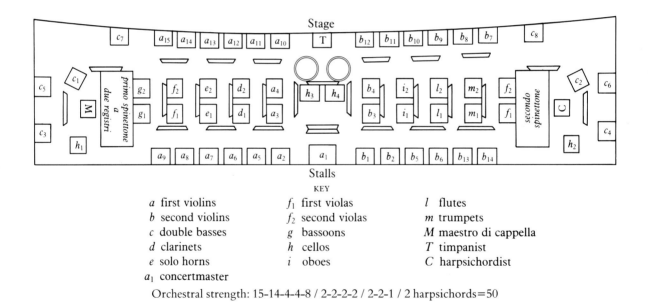

KEY

a first violins	*f*₁ first violas	*l* flutes
b second violins	*f*₂ second violas	*m* trumpets
c double basses	*g* bassoons	*M* maestro di cappella
d clarinets	*h* cellos	*T* timpanist
e solo horns	*i* oboes	*C* harpsichordist
*a*₁ concertmaster		

Orchestral strength: 15-14-4-4-8 / 2-2-2-2 / 2-2-1 / 2 harpsichords=50

PLATE VIIIb. Seating plan of the Naples orchestra, 1786

PLATE IX. A secular concert, Florence

PLATE X. A sacred concert, Florence

PLATE XI. Concert in a Venetian palazzo, mid-eighteenth century

PLATE XII. Music in the Graben on the eve of the Feast of Saint Anne, Vienna, 1805

PLATE XIII. Private concert, Vienna *c.*1785

Mozart's celebrated Symphony

"THE JUPITER,"

newly adapted for the Piano Forte, with accompaniments

— for a —

Flute, Violin and Violoncello,

by Muzio Clementi.

Nº 6.

Ent. Sta. Hall

London, Published by Clementi & Comp.ᵗ 26 Cheapside

Price 8ˢ

PLATE XIV. Title-page of earliest edition of K. 551 with the designation 'Jupiter', *c.* 1822

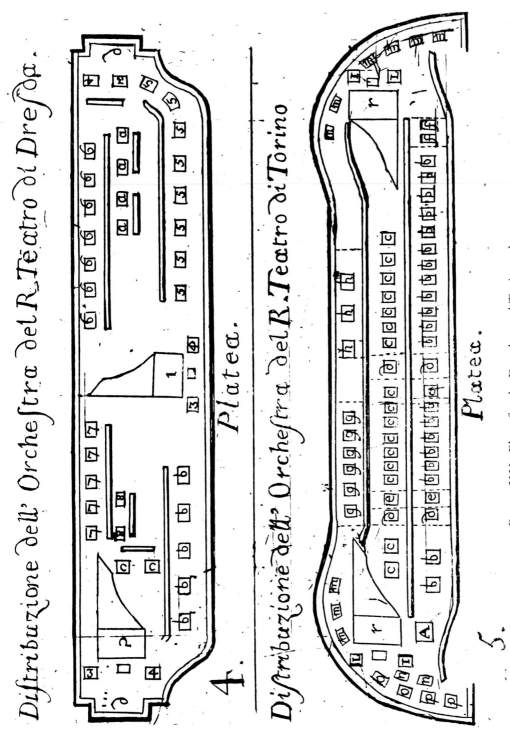

PLATE XV. Plans for the Dresden and Turin orchestras

DRESDEN (*upper*): *1* first harpsichord [J. A. Hasse]; *2* second harpsichord; *3* violoncellos; *4* contrabasses; *5* first violins; *6* second violins, with backs turned toward the stage; *7* oboes [also with backs toward the stage]; *8* flutes [ditto]; *a* violas [ditto]; *b* bassoons; *c* hunting horns; *d* a platform on each side for the trumpets and timpani.

TURIN (*lower*): A the director of the orchestra [Gaetano Pugnani], more elevated than the others; *b* first violins; *c* second violins; *d* oboes; *e* clarinets; *f* hunting horns; *g* violas; *h* bassoons; *l* first violoncellos; *L* first contrabasses; *m* basses, that is, violoncellos and contrabasses; *n* other hunting horns; *o* timpanum; *p* trumpets; *q* first violinist for the ballets; *r* harpsichords.

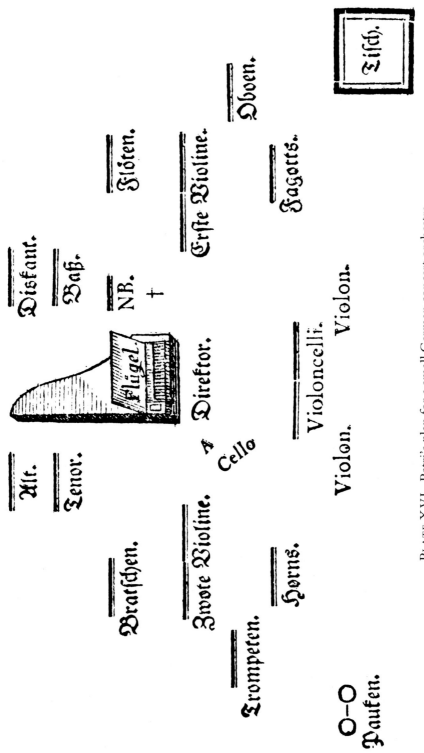

PLATE XVI. Petri's plan for a small German concert orchestra

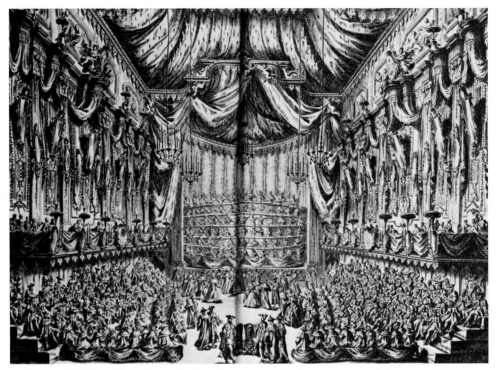

PLATE XVIIa. Characteristic tiered arrangement for concert and dance orchestras

PLATE XVIIb. Detail of tiered arrangement

8

Salzburg (II): Limbo (1770–1777)

Sometime between 1772 and 1777 the musician and writer Christian Friedrich Daniel Schubart visited Salzburg and reported:

For several centuries this archbishopric has served the cause of music well. They have a musical endowment there that amounts to 50,000 florins annually, and is spent entirely in the support of a group of musicians. The musical establishment in their cathedral is one of the best manned in all the German-speaking lands. Their organ is among the most excellent that exist: what a pity that it is not given life by the hand of a Bach! . . . .

Their [Vize]kapellmeister Mozart (the father) has placed the musical establishment on a splendid footing. He himself is known as an esteemed composer and author. His style is somewhat old-fashioned, but well founded and full of contrapuntal understanding. His church music is of greater value than his chamber music. Through his treatise on violin playing, which is written in very good German and intelligently organized, he has earned great honour . . . .

His son has become even more famous than the father. He is one of the most precocious musical minds, for as early as his eleventh year he composed an opera that was well received by all the connoisseurs. This son is also one of the best of our keyboard players. He plays with magical dexterity, and sightreads so accurately that his equal in this regard is scarcely to be found.

The choirs in Salzburg are excellently organized, but in recent times the ecclesiastical musical style has begun to deteriorate into the theatrical—an epidemic that has already infected more than one church! The Salzburgers are especially distinguished in wind instruments. One finds there the most admirable trumpet- and horn-players, but players of the organ and other keyboard instruments are rare. The Salzburgers' spirit is exceedingly inclined to low humour. Their folk songs are so comical and burlesque that one cannot listen to them without side-splitting laughter. The Punch-and-Judy spirit shines through everywhere, and the melodies are mostly excellent and inimitably beautiful.[1]

A far less enthusiastic account of the musical scene in Salzburg from about the

---

[1] Schubart (ed.), *Ideen*, 157–8, but see also 121 and 280.

same time was published by Charles Burney. Although Burney travelled as far east as Vienna, he could not visit Salzburg; in order to remedy that defect in his survey of musical centres, he solicited a letter from an Englishman resident in Salzburg, the gist of which he published anonymously in his travel memoirs. The original letter, dated 20 September 1772, reveals Burney's correspondent to have been the diplomat Louis de Visme, whose name does not appear in the Mozart family's correspondence or diaries. De Visme's letter reads:

The archbishop and sovereign of Saltzburg [*sic*] is very magnificent in his support of music, having usually near a hundred performers, vocal and instrumental, in his service. The prince is himself a dilettante, and a good performer on the violin; he has lately been at great pains to reform his band, which has been accused of being more remarkable for coarseness and noise, than delicacy and high-finishing. Signor Fischietti, author of several comic operas, is at present the director of this band.

The Mozart family were all at Saltzburg last summer; the father has long been in the service of the court, and the son is now one of the band . . . . I went to his father's house to hear him and his sister play duets on the same harpsichord . . . and . . . if I may judge of the music which I heard of his composition, in the orchestra, he is one further instance of early fruit being more extraordinary than excellent.[2]

De Visme's evaluation suggests that even this early in his career, Mozart encountered those who preferred orchestral music simpler and even more conventional than his own. Burney's correspondent's opinion of Salzburg's orchestra was similar to Mozart's own jaundiced view, presented *in extenso* at the beginning of Chapter 10.

The official roster of the Salzburg court orchestra for the period of Mozart's journeys to Italy up to his second trip to Paris (Table 8.1) shows that ensemble's make-up to have consisted of 2–3 organists, 9 violinists, 1 cellist, 3 double-bass players, 2 bassoonists, 3 oboists, 2–3 horn players, 10 trumpeters, and 2 kettledrummers.[3] Even a casual examination of this list suggests that something is missing, however, for Mozart's Salzburg works of this period often include parts for flutes, as well as divided viola parts and, occasionally, 4 horns. This in turn suggests that the arrangements revealed in Chapter 1 were still in force in the 1770s: many of the approximately 37 musicians of Table 8.1 played more than one instrument (especially, violinists the viola, trumpeters and drummers stringed instruments, and oboists the flute) and there were others who could be—and were—called upon to

    [2] Charles Burney, *The Present State of Music in Germany, the Netherlands, and United Provinces* (London, 1773), ii. 322–3. A photocopy of de Visme's letter is in the Burney Project, McGill University, Montreal. See also C. B. Oldman, 'Dr Burney and Mozart', *Mozart-Jahrbuch* (1962–3), 75–81, and *Mozart-Jahrbuch* (1964), 109–10; *idem*, 'Charles Burney and Louis de Visme', *The Music Review* (1966), xxvii. 93–7.
    [3] From the annually published *Salzburger Hofkalender*, as reported in E. Hintermaier, 'Die salzburger Hofkapelle von 1700 bis 1806: Organisation und Personal' (Ph.D. diss., University of Salzburg, 1972), 543–4.

TABLE 8.1 The Salzburg court orchestra without reinforcements, 1767–1777

	1767	1768	1769	1770	1771	1772	1773	1774	1775	1776	1777
organists	2	2	2	2	2	2	2	2	3	3	3
concert-masters	2	2	2	3	3	4	3	2	2	2	2
violinists*	19	19	19	19	19	19	19	17	17	17	18
violists†	—	—	—	—	—	—	—	—	1	1	1
cellists	2	2	1	1	1	1	1	1	1	—	1
bass players	2	2	2	3	3	3	3	4	3	3	3
oboists‡	2	2	2	2	2	2	2	2	2	2	2
bassoonists	2	2	2	2	2	2	2	2	2	2	2
horn players	3	3	3	3	2	2	2	3	3	3	3
trumpet players	2	2	2	2	2	2	2	2	2	2	2
kettledrummer	1	1	1	1	1	1	1	1	1	1	1
TOTALS	37	37	36	38	37	38	37	36	37	36	38

* These figures place the single trombone player (to 1770, after which the position was vacant), 8 of the 10 trumpet players, and 1 of the 2 kettledrummers among the violins, as presumably they would have been for symphonies.
† Drawn from the violinists as needed.
‡ Double on flutes.
For the possibilities for doubling and additional players, see Chapter 1.

Source: The Salzburg *Hofkalendar* as reported in E. Hintermaier, 'Die salzburger Hofkapelle von 1700 bis 1806: Organisation und Personal' (Ph.D. diss., University of Salzburg, 1972), 543.

supplement the orchestra, including members of the choir who also played instruments, the town waits, and amateur performers. Thus whereas for ordinary music-making the orchestra may, at an educated guess, have consisted of strings approximately 9—9—2—1—3 and pairs of oboes, bassoons, horns, and trumpets with kettledrums, on important occasions it would have been reinforced.

In the early 1770s Mozart produced symphonies at an almost frenzied pace, for during the six-year span 1770–5 he created more than thirty. In the following eight years the frenzy subsided, however, and only nine symphonies are recorded; and in the remaining nine years of his life, only four. Mozart's reduced production of symphonies after 1775 but prior to his move to Vienna was undoubtedly at least in part because of the disillusionment with Salzburg. If in the early 1770s he was determined to try to make his way by means of a steady outpouring of symphonies, by the second half of the 1770s he was turning his thoughts to employment elsewhere and so perhaps was less interested in impressing his compatriots; he must often have fallen back on his stock of older works when symphonies were called for. (The low production of symphonies in the Viennese years probably had entirely different grounds, which are explored in Chapter 11.)

None of the symphonies Mozart composed during this period were published in his lifetime, although they are usually equal to, and often better than, hundreds of symphonies that did issue from the presses. This might appear the result of a deliberate policy, for in 1778 his father wrote to him, 'I have not given any of your symphonies to be copied, because I knew in advance that when you were older and had more insight, you would be glad that no-one had got hold of them, though at the time you composed them you were quite pleased with them. One gradually becomes more and more fastidious.'[4] But these remarks of Leopold's can only seem hypocritical in light of a letter that he had written six years earlier to the Leipzig music-publisher J. G. I. Breitkopf: 'Should you wish to print any of my son's compositions . . . you have only to state what you consider most suitable. He could let you have [compositions in various genres including] symphonies for two violins, viola, two horns, two oboes or transverse flutes, and *basso*.'[5] And again, three years later: 'As I decided some time ago to have some of my son's compositions printed, I should like you to let me know as soon as possible whether you would like to publish some of them, that is, symphonies [and various other works].'[6] And in a third and final attempt to interest Breitkopf in Wolfgang's

    [4] Letter of 24 Sept. 1778. *Briefe*, ii. 485; *Letters*, ii. 919 (= ii. 619). Leopold's prediction that Wolfgang would eventually renounce his earlier works may have been correct; at least Nannerl wrote in 1799, 'I know well that, the stronger my brother grew in composition, the less he could tolerate his older works' (*Briefe*, iv. 259; not in *Letters*).
    [5] Letter of 7 Feb. 1772. *Briefe*, i. 456; *Letters*, i. 306 (= i. 209). Concerning this correspondence, see N. Zaslaw, 'The Relationship between Breitkopf and the Mozarts', in B. S. Brook (ed.), *Breitkopf Studien* (New York and Leipzig, in preparation).
    [6] Letter of 6 Oct. 1775. *Briefe*, 527; *Letters*, i. 384 (= i. 265).

works, Leopold wrote, 'I have been wishing for a long time that you would print some of my son's compositions . . . . You might try what you can do with a couple of symphonies [and works in other genres].'[7]

Leopold's proposals show an uncharacteristic lapse of understanding, for, as Breitkopf pointed out in his reply,[8] symphonies were published in parts, which normally were engraved, whereas printing by movable music-type, the sole technology used by Breitkopf at that time, was suited only to keyboard pieces, songs, and other small-scale genres commonly published in score. Breitkopf sometimes did 'publish' symphonies in manuscript parts, however, and perhaps this is what Leopold had in mind in making his proposal. To what extent, if any, Wolfgang's early symphonies found in the early nineteenth-century Breitkopf & Härtel Manuscript Catalogue were there as the result of his father's correspondence with Breitkopf is not clear; none of Wolfgang's symphonies were listed for sale in Breitkopf's published thematic catalogues prior to 1785, and even then, the pair of symphonies listed by Breitkopf in 1785 were published not by him but by Artaria in Vienna for whom he was acting as agent. Leopold's relations with Breitkopf deserve further investigation.

Symphony in F major, K. 75

[Incipits 8.1]

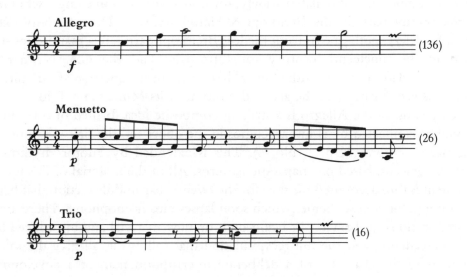

---

[7] Letter of 12 Feb. 1781. *Briefe*, iii. 92–3; *Letters*, ii. 1054 (= ii. 710). For an improved text of this letter, see R. Schaal, 'Ein angeblich verschollener Brief von Leopold Mozart', *Acta Mozartiana* (1979), xxvi. 50–1.

[8] Schall, 'Ein angeblich verschollener Brief', 51.

Instrumentation: strings, 2 oboes, 2 horns, [bassoon, continuo]
Autograph: lost
Principal source: set of parts, formerly in Breitkopf & Härtel archives, Leipzig; now lost
Facsimile: none
Editions: *GA*, xxxix. 1–11 (= Serie 24, No. 2); *NMA*, iv/11/2. 83–96

No autograph or other authentic manuscript of this symphony is known. On unstated grounds, Köchel assigned K. 75 to the period between 28 March and 13 August 1771, which Wolfgang spent in Salzburg between his first and second trips to Italy; this dating was accepted by Wyzewa and Saint-Foix, Abert, K³, and K⁶. The work cannot have circulated widely, for it survived only in a single set of now lost manuscript parts in the Breitkopf & Härtel archives. Thus the only extant sources for K. 75, both drawn from the lost Breitkopf parts, are a manuscript score copied in the nineteenth century for Otto Jahn and the *GA*. Neither the symphony's date nor its authenticity has ever been questioned, despite its mysterious provenance and the atypical position of its Minuet and Trio.

The opening of the Allegro is a striking composite idea formed of turns in the first violins connected by rising arpeggios in the oboes (cf. the first movement of J. C. Bach's sinfonia, Op. 3, No. 6). This is extended by 'motor rhythms' of Vivaldian descent, based on anapaestic patterns. All of the material of this ternary movement is thus accounted for save for the twenty-bar middle section that begins with a fugato on a new theme, which soon lapses into homophony. There are no repeated sections. Its brevity, its being built on new material and introduced by a deceptive cadence, and the full recapitulation that follows it, all give the middle section more the character of a deliberate interruption than of a development section.

The Minuet is atypical in two regards: it occupies the second rather than the third position in the four-movement scheme, which was not Wolfgang's usual practice,[9] and it has many slurs. Symphonic minuets, tracing their descent from French ballroom and stage dances, are usually in the detached, rhythmic style of such dance music, rather than in the legato, cantabile style associated with Italian vocal music and with instrumental music modelled after it. This Minuet leans in the cantabile direction, however. The Trio, for strings alone, thematically related to the opening of the first movement, seems more chamber than symphonic music.

Like several of Wolfgang's other symphony andantes of this period, the Andantino is in $\frac{2}{4}$ in the subdominant with violins muted and horns silent, although the pizzicato texture frequently connected with this style is absent. The movement's character is that of an Italian cantabile aria, worked into a rounded-binary movement with both sections repeated. The two sections 'rhyme', that is, they end with the same material. The delicate way in which the ideas at the end of the second section are ornamented adds a fine touch to the movement's conclusion.

The Köchel Catalogue gratuitously labels the finale 'rondeau', which it most assuredly is not. Rather, the movement is in rounded binary form, influenced by a rudimentary sonata-form aesthetic, with both sections repeated. Wyzewa and Saint-Foix believed that the opening theme exhibits the character of a French dance, while Abert thought that it is based upon a German folk dance,[10] but in neither case is an example offered for comparison. This otherwise quite ordinary idea is made memorable by a special feature: an unexpected pause, which turns what the ear expects will be a eight-bar phrase into one of nine bars. (The nature of the pause will be familiar to those who recall Brahms's Hungarian Dance No. 6 in D flat.) Possible national influences aside, there can at least be agreement on the high spirits and dance-inspired nature of the Finale.

Symphony in G major, K. 110 = 75b

[Incipits 8.2]

[9] See, however, the discussion of K. 385 in ch. 11. Leopold Mozart frequently composed four-movement symphonies with a minuet and trio in second place; Wolfgang's string quintets, K. 464, 499, 515, and 516 share that configuration of movements.

[10] Wyzewa–Saint-Foix, i. 387 (= i. 414); H. Abert, *W. A. Mozart* (Leipzig, 1919–21), i. 343.

Menuetto

Trio

Allegro

Instrumentation: strings, 2 oboes = flutes, 2 bassoons, 2 horns, [continuo]
Autograph: Jagiellońska Library, Kraków
Principal source: incomplete set of parts of Salzburg origin from Mozart's estate, Stadt- und Bezirksbibliothek, Leipzig
Facsimiles: *NMA*, iv/11/2. xviii–xix
Editions: *GA*, xx. 135–48 (= Serie 8, No. 12); *NMA*, iv/11/2. 97–114

Wolfgang headed the autograph manuscript of this work, 'Sinfonia / del Sgr. Cavaliere Amadeo / Wolfg. Mozart in Salisburgo / nel Luglio 1771'. As mentioned in the discussions of the symphonies K. 45b (Chapter 4) and 73q (Chapter 6), the title 'Cavaliere' refers to the Cross of the Golden Spur, or Knighthood of the Golden Order, which the Pope conferred upon the fourteen-year-old prodigy in Rome in July 1770. A year later plans were already well advanced for a second trip to Italy, and this symphony was doubtless intended for (undocumented) concerts in Salzburg that summer and (documented) concerts during his second Italian journey, in Milan (22 or 23 November) and Brixen (11 and 12 December).[11]

A work has usually received a new Köchel number only after evidence emerged suggesting a changed date of origin. In the present instance, however, the date has always been known, and the change in the Köchel listing occurred because revisions in K[3] to Köchel's original chronology for 1771 were so extensive (many works having been found to be in the wrong order, in the wrong year, or spurious)

---

[11] Deutsch, 121–4 (= 135–8); J. H. Eibl, *Wolfgang Amadeus Mozart: Chronik eines Leben* (Kassel, 1977), 46–7.

that an almost entirely new chronology had to be worked out. When the dust settled, it was no longer possible to use the number 110 for this symphony, and so it acquired the new number 75b without its date changing from July 1771.

It is difficult to regard this symphony as having been born of the same creative impulses that spawned K. 75 and 75a. It is worked out on a grander scale and apparently with more care. The care is manifested in all movements in the more contrapuntal conception of the inner parts and, especially, of the bass-line. The opening Allegro tends toward the monothematic, a tendency that has been noted in the symphonies K. 75, 114, and 134. That is, the opening idea reappears, somewhat transformed, in the dominant as a 'second subject' and again in its original guise in the closing section of the exposition. The development section is based on an imitatively treated descending scale, followed by striding quavers in the bass, an idea previously heard in the closing section of the exposition. The recapitulation is not literal: the retransition is extended in a developmental way. The monothematicism and the introduction of developmental aspects in the recapitulation are relatively unusual for Wolfgang but common for Joseph Haydn, whose influence has been suggested, without much supporting evidence, in many discussions of Wolfgang's early symphonies. It is not unreasonable to suspect that he had encountered some of Haydn's symphonies, given their widespread distribution, the Mozarts' journeys to Vienna, and the presence of Michael Haydn at Salzburg. Copies of Joseph Haydn's symphonies Hob. I: 27 (by about 1770), I: 31 (by about 1776–8), I: 37 (date unsure) and I: 60 (in 1775) can be demonstrated to have reached Salzburg by the dates indicated.[12]

The second movement of K. 110 bears no tempo indication, although it is without question an andante or andantino. The oboes are replaced by flutes, the horns fall silent, and a pair of bassoons, previously and subsequently tacitly subsumed along with the cellos, double-basses, and harpsichord under the rubric 'basso', suddenly blossoms forth with obbligato parts.[13] If the movement had been given a title, it might have been 'romanza'. The romance (to give the word its English and French form) was originally a strophic poem telling a galant love story set in olden times, which in mid-eighteenth-century Paris began to be set to folk-like melodies for use in salons and stage works. This style of music was transferred to purely instrumental pieces, and the violinist Pierre Gaviniès (1728–1800) and organist Claude Balbastre (1727–99) were each well known in Paris for performing celebrated romances of their own composition. The romance was first used in a symphony by Gossec around 1761 in Paris, and in 1773 Dittersdorf tried it in a

[12] Eisen, 'The Symphonies of Leopold Mozart', 251–4, documents the presence of these and other works of Joseph Haydn in Salzburg in the 1770s.

[13] Bassoons are treated in the same fashion in Michael Haydn's Symphony in B flat, Perger No. 51, probably from the 1770s.

symphony in Vienna.[14] According to Galeazzi, the character of the romance is 'simplicity', and it 'must be written without artifice or a too elaborate melody— tender and expressive'.[15] Mozart took the mock-naïf musical style of the romance in the 'simple' key of C major and worked it into a sonata-form movement with two repeated sections. Many of the movement's two-bar phrases are immediately repeated, creating a kind of musical construction that the French called 'couplets', and which may be rendered in performance by echos, or perhaps even by a division of the orchestra into solo and ripieno groups (although no such instructions are found in the score). The carefully wrought inner parts in Mozart's movement reveals the German craftsman hidden beneath the French finery, while a touch of harmonic colour is provided by the major chord on the flatted sixth degree, which sounds twice near the end of each section.

The Minuet is canonic, a device found in a number of Joseph Haydn's symphony minuets of this period,[16] and one to which Mozart would occasionally return, for instance, in the F major symphony, K. 130, the C minor wind serenade, K. 388, and the G minor symphony, K. 550. This application of learned canonic devices to the insouciant ballroom minuet may be considered an attempt to render the dance more 'symphonic'. The aggressively striding Minuet is set off by the more sedate E minor Trio for strings alone. The Köchel Catalogue claims that the da capo of the Minuet is fully written out in the autograph, which is incorrect and would have been peculiar for Mozart, who customarily used every workable abbreviation when writing down his compositions. The source of this error seems to be the edition of K. 75b in the *GA*, in which the da capo is for some reason printed in full.

Ex. 8.1 Symphony in G major, K. 110 = 75b, rebarring of the Finale

Like the Finale of K. 73, the present Finale is a $\frac{2}{4}$ Allegro in which one can sense the moderate-tempo $\frac{2}{2}$ gavotte or *contredanse* underlying the theme by beating time half as often (Example 8.1). This rondo has a G minor middle section, itself binary in structure, which is exotic in character (Example 8.2); the origins and associations of such exoticism are explored in connection with K. 74 in the previous chapter.

[14] R. Hickman, 'Romance', *The New Grove*, xvi. 125.

[15] Francesco Galeazzi, *Elementi teorico-pratici di musica con un saggio sopra l'arte di suonare il violino* (Rome, 1791–6), ii. 286. Galeazzi also says that the romance is a rondo, which is certainly not true for Mozart, judging by his best-known examples, in the piano concerto, K. 466, and *Eine kleine Nachtmusik*, K. 525.

[16] e.g., Hob. I: 44.

Ex. 8.2 Symphony in G major, K. 110 = 75b, minor section of Finale (bars 49–58)

Symphony in A major, K. 114

[Incipits 8.3]

Instrumentation: *strings, 2 flutes/oboes, 2 horns, [bassoon, continuo]
Autograph: Jagiellońska Library, Kraków
Principal source: none
Facsimile: *NMA*, iv/11/2. xxii
Editions: *GA*, xx. 161–74 (= Serie 8, No. 14); *NMA*, iv/11/2. 165–82

This, the first of a series of eight symphonies written for Salzburg in the period of less than a year between the Mozarts' second and third Italian trips, marks the onset of Mozart's symphony frenzy. Undoubtedly practical motives lay behind this outpouring of symphonies. The Italian trips had not proven lucrative, and a portion of Leopold's salary had been withheld during his absence. The time had come for him and his son to dig in their heels at home, in order to re-establish their usefulness there and to pay off their debts. Wolfgang and Leopold returned from Italy on 15 December 1771, and next day the Archbishop Sigismund Christoph von Schrattenbach died. The autograph manuscript of K. 114 is dated a fortnight later. Symphonies may have been needed for the period of mourning, for muted Carnival festivities, for Lent, and for the installation of the new Archbishop in March. In addition, Wolfgang sought a promotion, for his title of concertmaster had been honorary. Having proven his mettle, the sixteen-year-old was decreed a regularly paid member of the court orchestra on 9 August 1772 by the Archbishop, at the modest annual salary of 150 florins.[17]

It has been suggested that in this symphony Wolfgang declared himself for the 'Viennese' or 'Austrian' symphonic style, while still keeping key Italian elements.[18] (Such observations are the more difficult to evaluate because the 'Austrian' symphonic style itself contained a rich admixture of Italian elements.) In this context, 'Austrian' apparently refers to the greater length, more extensive use of winds, more contrapuntal texture, four-movement format, and greater use of non-cantabile thematic materials. Schultz thought the first theme to be 'Viennese' in style,[19] but in fact, with its mid-bar syncopation, it is closer to the style of J. C. Bach than to that of Vienna. (Not only were Bach's symphonies known to Wolfgang from London, but they were widely performed in Germany and Austria in the 1770s.[20]) Larsen considers K. 114 'one of the most inspired [symphonies] of the period. One could point out many beauties in this work, such as [in the first movement] the developmental transition, the second subject with its hint of quartet style, and the short, but delicately wrought development with elegant wind and string dialogue.'[21] Even the gentle opening bars, which forgo loud chords or fanfares and begin piano, suggest something new. The relatively high-pitched horns in A were probably responsible for suggesting to Mozart that flutes be used in place of oboes; once the decision was made on technical grounds, however, it seems to have coloured the whole symphony.

The first movement exhibits that 'fullness of ideas' noted as a hallmark of Mozart's style in an obituary of 1792 and even during his lifetime. The Emperor Joseph II has been mocked by modern admirers of Mozart's music for having told him that the music of *Die Entführung aus dem Serail* was 'too full of notes', but the Emperor was not alone in this perception, for published reviews of Mozart's operas hinted at the same 'problem': there was more variety and complexity than many of

---

[17] Deutsch, 127 (= 142).

[18] Wyzewa–Saint-Foix, i. 419–21 (= i. 459–61); Della Croce, *Le 75 sinfonie*, 127–9.

[19] D. Schultz, *Mozarts Jugendsinfonien* (Leipzig, 1900), 17.

[20] Note, for instance, how often in ch. 4 Bach's name is found in the lists of symphonies owned by ecclesiastical establishments of central Europe.

[21] J. P. Larsen, 'The Symphonies', in H. C. Robbins Landon and D. Mitchell (eds.), *The Mozart Companion* (London, 1956), 166–8. Mozart's frequently extravagant use of ideas is usually contrasted with the symphonic procedures of Joseph Haydn, which were to base a movement more nearly on the development of a single motive (*idem*, 'The Viennese Classical School: A Challenge to Musicology', *Current Musicology* (1969), ix. 105–12, here 110). These two ways of composing may be referred to as deduction (Mozart: working from the general to the particular) and induction (Haydn: working from the particular to the general).

Mozart's contemporaries wanted in music.[22] That current perceptions find the music of many of Mozart's contemporaries too empty of notes should not be permitted to obscure how things stood then. The variety of the first movement of K. 114 is described by Larsen as 'the dominant tendency' to present 'a whole series of fine cantabile themes: symphonic development results from their interplay and contrast'.[23] The sole conservative trait of this strikingly modern movement is the handling of the winds in the development section, more in a concerto-grosso style than in a symphonic style.

In a number of symphonies Mozart required that the oboists take up flutes in the andantes; here the reverse is the case, oboes replacing flutes and the horns dropping out. Schultz considered this movement the highpoint of Mozart's symphonic andantes to this date.[24] It is in sonata form with both sections repeated. The violas, which had already had a divisi passage in the development section of the first movement, here form an important series of duets, often doubling the oboes at the octave below or engaging in dialogue with them. The development section, written in continuous quavers, gives the somewhat curious impression of baroque *Fortspinnung* intercalated between the more characteristic periodic style of the exposition and recapitulation.

Ex. 8.3 Minuet in A major, K. 61gI

---

[22] This point is examined in ch. 13.   [23] Larsen, 'The Symphonies', 166.

[24] Schultz, *Mozarts Jugendsinfonien*, 21–2.

The editors of the *NMA* and of the *Mozart-Handbuch* claim that an unpublished A major Minuet, K. 61gI (Example 8.3), was originally intended for this symphony, but according to Mozart's writing in the work's autograph it probably dates from as early as 1770, and the paper on which he wrote it is almost certainly a type he used in Italy that very year.[25] Furthermore, the work is scored for flutes and strings, and lacks the horns called for by K. 114. That K. 61gI may have had some sort of symphonic connections, though, is suggested by the fact that, unlike Mozart's ballroom minuets, it does call for violas. And the absence of horns suggests that K. 61gI was conceived as the trio of a symphony minuet.

When Einstein examined the autograph manuscript of K. 114 prior to 1936, he found there another fully-scored Minuet, without Trio, that Mozart had crossed out (as he reported in K^3). The opening theme of the rejected movement is a reworking of the theme of the Andante. This seemingly perfect Minuet is published for the first time as an appendix to *NMA*, iv/11/2. 199.

The Minuet Mozart finally provided is a particularly stately one, spiced with some well-placed secondary-dominant chords near the end of each section. Its Trio, in A minor, is in a mock-pathetic vein. The pathos is provided by the repeated-note melody on the fifth degree of the scale rising the semitone to the flatted sixth; this melodic shape would have been familiar to Mozart from such plainchant settings as that for the somber Holy Week text 'Miserere mei Deus'. The mocking comes from the second violins, which, with their triplets and trills, gad about as if making variations on a comic-opera tune. It is suggested in Chapter 4 that the intention behind the juxtaposition of high and low styles was ironic or parodistic.

The Finale begins with a brief tucket and a response, once repeated. Then something strange happens. Instead of developing the tucket or introducing a proper first theme, as would normally be expected, Mozart has the orchestra play, twice in a conspicuous manner, the harmony-primer chord-progression I—IV— V—I. This is apparently an allusion to the 'bergamasca', a kind of dance or song in which a melody is composed or improvised over many repetitions of these four chords. In German-speaking countries a text commonly sung to the tune most often associated with the bergamasca was 'Kraut und Rüben', which runs this way:

> Kraut und Rüben haben mich vertrieben,
> Hätt meine Mutter Fleisch gekocht,
> So wär ich länger blieben.
>
> [Cabbages and turnips drove me away.
> Had my mother cooked some meat,
> Then I'd have stayed longer.[26]]

[25] Information kindly communicated by Alan Tyson.

[26] German text as given by R. Kirkpatrick (ed.) in *J. S. Bach: Keyboard Practice, Consisting of an Aria with Thirty Variations* (New York, 1938).

J. S. Bach quoted the 'Kraut und Rüben' tune in the quodlibet at the end of his *Goldberg Variations*. Mozart did not quote the tune, but the presence of his little joke in the Finale supports the suggestion that this symphony may have been composed with Carnival in mind. The rest of the movement, in sonata form with both sections repeated, is also in high, if more conventionally symphonic, spirits.

The mockery of the Trio of the Minuet and the 'bergamasca' at the beginnings of the Finale's exposition and recapitulation bring to mind the remarks of a German visitor to Salzburg in the mid-1770s, surely describing Carnival: 'Here everyone breathes the spirit of fun and mirth. People smoke, dance, make music, make love, and indulge in riotous revelry, and I have yet to see another place where one can with so little money enjoy so much sensuousness'.[27]

Symphony in G major, K. 124

[Incipits 8.4]

[27] [Johann Kaspar Riesbeck,] *Briefe eines reisenden Franzosen über Deutschland: An seinen Bruder zu Paris*, 2nd edn. (Zurich, 1784), 159; mod. edn. (Stuttgart, 1967), 80.

Instrumentation: strings, 2 oboes, 2 horns, [bassoon, continuo]
Autograph: Jagiellońska Library, Kraków
Principal source: none
Facsimile: *NMA*, iv/11/2. xxiii
Editions: *GA*, xx. 175–86 (= Serie 8, No. 15); *NMA*, iv/11/2. 183–96

Carnival ends on *Mardi gras* (Shrove Tuesday) and with the next day, Ash Wednesday, the forty days of Lent begin; in 1772 these days fell on 3 and 4 February respectively. Mozart wrote at the top of the autograph manuscript of K. 124, 'Sinfonia / del Sig^r. Cavaliere Wolfgango Amadeo Mozart Salisburgo 21 Febrario 1772'. Hence the work may have been intended either for a Lenten *concert spirituel* or for the new Archbishop, who took office on 29 April. The Archbishop was an amateur violinist who liked to join his orchestra in performance of symphonies, standing next to the concertmaster,[28] perhaps for maximum professional guidance or perhaps to be seen symbolically at the orchestra's centre of power. It will be recalled that, half a year after the Archibishop had been installed, de Visme could write to Dr Burney that the new ruler 'has lately been at great pains to reform his band, which has been accused of being more remarkable for coarseness and noise, than delicacy and high-finishing'.

The first movement of K. 124 has a character quite different from that of the previous symphony. Its angular opening theme is of a more abrupt sort than the genial theme of K. 114, although, curiously, the two themes outline the same scale degrees: doh—soh—me—ray—soh—fah—me. For the rest, the first movement of K. 124 is more compact, less inclined to a 'fullness of ideas' than that of K. 114. An attractive touch is the metric ambiguity of the second subject, which for an instant leaves the listener unsure of whether he is hearing $\frac{3}{4}$ or $\frac{6}{8}$ (Example 8.4). A fermata on a diminished chord allows listeners and performers alike to catch one last breath before plunging with great momentum toward the final cadence of the exposition. The development section begins calmly, but a false reprise in E minor soon introduces some of the agitated effects often associated with symphonic development. The recapitulation is literal, with a four-bar codetta added. Both main sections are repeated.

The C major Andante, a binary movement with both halves repeated, is notable for its concertante writing for horns and oboes. The Minuet and Trio (for strings only) illustrate Kirnberger's description of minuets as being 'ruled by *galant* agreeableness united with calm dignity. There is hardly another dance where so much elegance, noble decorum, and such a highly pleasing manner are to be met.'[29]

---

[28] See Abert, *Mozart*, i. 323; Leopold's letter of 24 Sept. 1778 (*Briefe*, ii. 485; *Letters*, ii. 920 (= ii. 620)).

[29] [Johann Philipp Kirnberger], 'Menuet', in Johann Georg Sulzer, *Allgemeine Theorie der schönen Künste* (Leipzig, 1771–4); 2nd edn. (Leipzig, 1792–4), ii. 388–9.

Ex. 8.4 Symphony in G major, K. 124, first movement (bars 13-20)

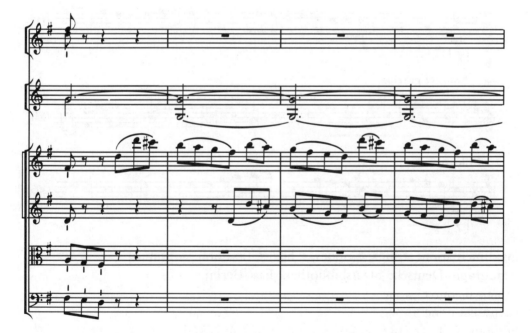

The rondo-finale begins with the same tucket as did the Finale of the previous symphony, but here it is not instantly repeated, and the movement continues in an apparently straightforward manner. The joke—and it surely is one—comes in the coda, where the melody suddenly evaporates, leaving only some chords, syncopations, tremolos, an oom-pah bass, and a fanfare or two. The effect is rather like the music-hall's 'vamp til ready', but instead of serving as introduction, here it serves as conclusion.

The autograph manuscripts of the symphonies K. 129 and 130 are in the West Berlin library, while K. 128 is in East Berlin. Each of these three manuscripts and that of the *Regina coeli*, K. 127, also in West Berlin, is inscribed 'nel mese di maggio 1772 à Salisburgo', an exceptional output for a single month even for the prolific sixteen-year-old Mozart. Was this fire lit under him by a desire to attract the favourable notice of the newly installed Archbishop? Perhaps, too, Mozart was girding his loins for the third (and final) trip to Italy from October 1772 to March 1773, which would require new symphonies.

Symphony in C major, K. 128

[Incipits 8.5]

Instrumentation: strings, 2 oboes, 2 horns, [bassoon, continuo]
Autograph: Deutsche Staatsbibliothek, East Berlin
Principal source: none
Facsimile: none
Editions: *GA*, xx. 187–99 (= Serie 8, No. 16); *NMA*, iv/11/3. 1–14

That the opening movement of the first of these works is marked not simply 'allegro' but also 'maestoso' suggests something broader in tempo than the typical first movement of this period of Mozart's symphonic production. It is notated in $\frac{3}{4}$, but, as the rhythm of the first half of the exposition comprises entirely quaver triplets, the listener at first takes it for $\frac{9}{8}$. The second theme, a memorably leaping melody, first reveals the true underlying metre. After a touch of the second theme in the minor, an energetic bass-line figure ushers in the closing section. The exposition is repeated but the rest is not. The development section is announced by the sudden appearance of an E flat chord, which proves to be a herald of D minor. Then follow in rapid succession hints of E minor, A minor, G major, F major, and again G major, the dominant needed to establish the recapitulation. The development takes only thirty-one bars during which the thematic material is almost entirely scales, yet it is so tightly and logically constructed that one has the impression of having traversed great tonal distances. The recapitulation is not literal, containing a number of telling developmental touches.

Just as the previous Allegro was maestoso, so the Andante is grazioso, which has equally the result of slowing the movement's tempo and deepening its affect. The movement, for strings only, is in sonata form with both sections repeated. A chamber-music texture involves the players in dialogue, most often between the first and second violins or the upper and lower strings.

The Finale is a jig in the form of an oddly proportioned rondo: A A B A B A C A coda, in which the B section is roughly five times the length of the A section. When the end of the Finale is nearly reached and Mozart seems already to have shown his hand, he kicks up his heels with a series of hunting-horn calls. This is all the more unexpected as the wind writing in the rest of the symphony is conservative.

Symphony in G major, K. 129

[Incipits 8.6]

Instrumentation: *strings, 2 oboes, 2 horns, [bassoon, continuo]
Autograph: Staatsbibliothek Preussische Kulturbesitz, West Berlin (Mus. Ms. Autogr. W. A. Mozart 129)
Principal source: none
Facsimile: none
Editions: *GA*, xx. 199–214 (= Serie 8, No. 17); *NMA*, iv/11/3. 15–30

The autograph manuscript of K. 129 has the usual sort of heading that Wolfgang, with or without the help of his father, put on his works during this period: 'Sinfonia / del Sgr: Cavaliere Amadeo Wolfgango / Mozart nel mese di Maggio 1772 / à Salisburgo'. Such inscriptions have been, and generally must be, taken at face value, for they are often the only information about the provenance of Wolfgang's instrumental works, which usually do not leave behind additional clues, the way operas and other occasional works do. The studies (often referred to in the course of this book) of the evolution of Wolfgang's writing and of the paper types used in his music manuscripts have confirmed the reliability of most of the dates on the manuscripts. The same studies show that K. 129 was begun, put aside and then resumed at a later time.[30] This in turn could suggest either that the symphony was begun in May 1772 and completed at a later date, or that it was begun earlier and completed on that date. The latter suggestion is most likely the correct one, for the headings on Wolfgang's many manuscripts of his Salzburg period, so often completed with Leopold's assistance, seem to represent the tidying-up or finalizing of the manuscripts, rather than their beginnings; in the absence of evidence to the contrary, Wolfgang's and Leopold's datings should be taken to indicate times of completion—which still leaves open the possibility that, if a manuscript contains revisions, these may have occurred either before or after the date of 'completion'.

The first movement of K. 129 begins with a great chord reinforced by quadruple-stops in the violins. There follows an odd little tune, based on the so-called Lombardic rhythm or Scotch snap, which rhythm is heard again as part of the second subject and as the most important motive of the development section. A tremolo passage over a pedal with a crescendo leads into the closing section of the

---

[30] W. Plath, 'Beiträge zur Mozart-Autographie II: Schriftchronologie 1770–1780', *Mozart-Jahrbuch* (1976–7), 145, 147–8; A. Tyson, 'The Mozart Fragments in the Mozarteum, Salzburg', *Journal of the American Musicological Society* (1981), xxxiv. 505 n.; Eisen, 'The Symphonies of Leopold Mozart', 49.

exposition, in which the first and second violins engage in witty repartee. Both sections of this sonata-form movement are repeated. A temperamental development section alternates brief moments of lyricism with forte outbursts of the Lombardic rhythm; the recapitulation is literal.

The C major Andante begins like a serene song with the strings playing alone. The oboes and horns join and the song is repeated. For the rest of the exposition no other striking ideas are introduced, but Mozart spins a magical web of melodic fragments. The 'development' section is a concise eight-bar fugato, leading to a literal recapitulation. Again both halves are repeated.

The Finale begins with a hunting-horn flourish virtually identical to one Mozart was to use in 1773 played by horns as the trio of a minuet (K. 205 = 173b), and again years later to begin his piano sonata, K. 576. This, then, may have been the kind of symphony which Burney denigrated for having its Finale based on 'a minuet degenerated into a jigg'. Although the movement consists of two repeated sections with the sonata-form modulatory scheme, at the moment the tonic returns, the opening theme is merely hinted at and no true recapitulation occurs. The movement is thus perhaps best considered in rounded-binary rather than sonata form. The function of jig-finales like the present one is analogous to that which Mozart later ascribed to an act finale of *Die Entführung aus dem Serail*, which 'must go very fast—and the ending must make a truly great racket . . . the more noise the better—the shorter the better—so that the audience doesn't grow cold before the time comes to applaud.'[31]

Symphony in F major, K. 130

[Incipits 8.7]

[31] Letter of 26 Sept. 1781. *Briefe*, iii. 163; *Letters*, iii. 1145–6 (= ii. 770).

Instrumentation: *strings, 2 flutes, 4 horns, [bassoon, continuo]
Autograph: Staatsbibliothek Preussische Kulturbesitz, West Berlin (Mus. Ms. Autogr. W. A. Mozart 130)
Principal source: none
Facsimile: *NMA*, iv/11/3. xii–xiii; see also K⁶, p. 154
Editions: *GA*, xx. 215–32 (= Serie 8, No. 18); *NMA*, iv/11/3. 31–51

Mozart inscribed the autograph of this work simply 'Sinfonia', to which his father added 'del Sgr: Cavaliere Amadeo Wolfg: Mozart / à Salisburgo nel Maggio 1772'. Several commentators, following Saint-Foix, have regarded K. 130 as the first of Mozart's 'great' symphonies,[32] and, it must be agreed, the piece does contain inspired ideas, beautifully worked out. In addition to its fine ideas, this symphony also has a distinctive timbre, arising from the key, which is unusual for Mozart's symphonies; from flutes in place of, and occupying a higher tessitura than, oboes; and from the two pairs of horns in C alto and F (or F and B flat basso in the Andantino grazioso).

Mozart had begun the first movement with the customary single pair of horns in F in mind, and continued that way through the Andantino. By the time he reached the Minuet, however, he decided to add another pair of horns, found in this movement and the Finale, and he subsequently went back and wrote parts for the additional horns on blank staves between systems in the first and second movements. Mozart's change of mind may have been motivated by the return to Salzburg from a European tour of the horn virtuoso Ignaz Leutgeb, for whom he was later to write his horn quintet and horn concertos.[33] This symphony is the first of only five symphonies (K. 118 = 74c, 130, 132, 183, 318) and one Divertimento (K. 131) in which Mozart called for four rather than the customary two horns, although in its original conception, K. 550 too was to have four horns. (In the four

---

[32] Saint-Foix, 51 (= 34).
[33] P. R. Bryan, 'The Horn in the Works of Mozart and Haydn: Some Observations and Comparisons', *The Haydn Yearbook* (1975), ix. 189–255, here 194–5.

works of 1772 that use four horns, Mozart made a distinction between the three orchestral works, in which the horns use only open notes, and the one-on-a-part divertimento, in which the horns are also required to play stopped tones.)

At the beginning of the Finale of K. 130, the flutes, doubling the violins, twice rush down the scale to middle C, a note usually lacking on eighteenth-century flutes. (Middle Cs also occur in the solo part of the flute and harp concerto, K. 299 = 297c, however.) Were the Salzburg wind players trying out experimental instruments, or was this a little joke at their expense? Or did Homer nod? Probably none of the above. In this sort of *colla parte* orchestration, the copyist who created the orchestral parts, or the wind players themselves, were expected to alter the flute part to render it playable, by putting the C up an octave or by substituting another chord tone (here G, not E, so as to avoid doubling the third of the chord in the bass). Neither edition of K. 130 takes note of this problem.

The first movement, in sonata form with the first section repeated, begins quietly without fanfare. The opening motive, also heard at the end of the exposition, in the development section, and at the beginning and end of the recapitulation, prominently features the short-long rhythm mentioned in connection with the first movement of the previous symphony—a rhythm associated not only with Lombardy and Scotland but also with Hungarian folk music, some of which Mozart may have have encountered in his travels or heard from Michael Haydn, who had worked in Hungary before moving to Salzburg.

Mozart's first attempt at an Andante, abandoned after only eight bars (Example 8.5), has a more complex, less conventional texture than that of the beginning of the completed Andante. Could the cancellation have been the result of Leopold's looking over Wolfgang's shoulder and urging him (as he once did in a letter) to write something 'only short—easy—popular'?[34] Be that as it may, the completed Andantino grazioso is a placid movement in binary form, whose opening idea features three-bar phrases rather than the usual even-numbered ones. Once again the violins are muted, the cellos and basses pizzicato; as in other andantes that feature this orchestration, the violas are without mutes, perhaps confirming a puzzling feature of so many of the orchestras of the period: the tiny number of violas. The metre is $\frac{3}{8}$ rather than the customary $\frac{2}{4}$. Joseph Haydn first wrote symphonic andantes in $\frac{3}{8}$ in four symphonies from the years 1770–2. Could Mozart have known and imitated any of them in K. 130, or was the timing mere coincidence?

The Minuet is wittily constructed around a canon between the bass-line and the violins in octaves, with the violas adding a rustic drone wobbling back and forth

---

[34] Letter of 13 Aug. 1778. *Briefe*, ii. 444; *Letters*, ii. 888 (= ii. 599).

Ex. 8.5 Symphony in F major, K. 130, Andante, false start

Ex. 8.6 Symphony in F major, K. 130, Trio, original bars 13–23

between C and B natural, in good-natured contradiction of the F major harmonies.[35] The Trio offers a bit of musical slapstick: quasi-modal harmonies and stratospherically high horn writing. (Such high passages are not uncommon in the symphonies of some other Austrians, e.g. Joseph Haydn's, Vanhal's, and Leopold Mozart's, but exceptional in Wolfgang's.) Wyzewa and Saint-Foix called this Trio (along with that of K. 132) 'daring and bizarre',[36] which it is. Here was something special for the recently returned Leutgeb, and a bit of Punch and Judy into the bargain. Lest the gay exterior of this movement deceive, however, note that Mozart crossed out and rewrote a ten-bar passage in the Trio (Example 8.6) on the way to achieving the unassuming perfection of his final results.

The Finale, marked Molto allegro in pencil, probably in Leopold's hand, balances the first movement in length and substance, and, like it, is in sonata form; it thus departs from the short, dance-like finales of the Italian symphonists and of many of Wolfgang's own earlier symphonies, imparting new substance to a formerly lightweight design. The movement is filled with rushing scales, sudden changes of dynamic, tremolos, and other joyous sounds much in favour in symphonies of the period. Although Leopold once referred to such writing in the symphonies of Stamitz as 'nothing but noise',[37] Wolfgang understood how to make brilliant use of the style.

Symphony in E flat major, K. 132

[Incipits 8.8]

---

[35] Canonic minuets are discussed above in conjunction with K. 110 = 75b.
[36] Wyzewa–Saint-Foix, i. 456 (= i. 493).   [37] Letter of 29 June 1778. *Briefe*, ii. 386; *Letters*, ii. 823 (= ii. 556).

Instrumentation: *strings, 2 oboes, 4 horns, [bassoon, continuo]
Autograph: Staatsbibliothek Preussische Kulturbesitz, West Berlin (Mus. Ms. Autogr. W. A. Mozart 132)
Principal source: none
Facsimile: none
Editions: *GA*, xx. 233–51 (= Serie 8, No. 18); *NMA*, iv/11/3. 52–77

Leopold's hand is in evidence in the autograph manuscript of this symphony too. Besides adding to Wolfgang's heading 'Sinfonia' the information 'del Sgr: Cavaliere Amadeo Wolfgango Mozart / nel Luglio 1772 à Salisburgo', he also provided the tempo indications for the first, second, and fourth movements. In failing to write the tempos, Wolfgang must have thought that the conventional character and function of these movements would identify their tempos—hence the usefulness of the eighteenth-century concept 'tempo ordinario'—and perhaps he expected that he or his father would in any case be directing the orchestra. Leopold was more of a stickler for detail than his son and already had posterity in mind, for the saving of letters, keeping of diaries, and labelling of scores was not mere compulsiveness on his part but doubtless was also calculated to form the foundation for a planned but never executed biography of his son.[38]

The notation of the horns presents a problem. Mozart marked the pairs of horns '2 Corni in E la fa alti / 2 Corni in E la fa bassi', that is, 'two horns in high E flat,

---

[38] Letter of 10 Nov. 1767. *Briefe*, i. 247; *Letters*, i. 113 (= i. 77).

two horns in low E flat', but the horns that survive from the period—the type called *Inventionshorn*—generally have crooks enabling them to play at most pitch levels between low B flat and high B flat or, sometimes, high C, never higher.[39] What could Mozart have had in mind? Three possible solutions present themselves: (1) a low E flat crook combined with the dying baroque clarino technique, enabling the part to be played an octave higher than written; (2) an experimental instrument, which has not survived, pitched in high E flat, perhaps brought back to Salzburg by Leutgeb from his European tour; or (3) the shortest regular crook (usually high B flat, occasionally high C) in conjunction with the elimination of the usual tuning bit between the mouthpiece and the body of the horn, thus inserting the mouthpiece further up the horn than was the regular practice. This last procedure can be discovered by experimentation with some late eighteenth-century horns to yield an instrument pitched in high E flat.

Between the first and third alternatives a comparison may be made: the first will yield the thin, brilliant 'clarino' sound that characterizes a valveless brass instrument on its higher partials, whereas the third gives a fatter, more bugle-like sound by employing the lower partials. The first method may be said to give a characteristically eighteenth-century sound, the third method a sound generally associated with a later period. If this were correct, then Mozart's horn nomenclature, which is usually understood to indicate simultaneously the nature of the transposition and the name of the crook, would here indicate only the former. But perhaps it is not correct, for an examination of the partials used by each of the four horns in K. 132 reveals a striking difference between his handling of horns 1 and 2 and of horns 3 and 4 (Example 8.7). Horns 1 and 2 are not written above the ninth partial, whereas horns 3 and 4 use the tenth and 3 uses the eleventh and twelfth as well. Since shorter instruments have fewer available partials, this suggests that horns of two lengths were employed. Furthermore, if the notation were octave-transposing for a longer instrument rather than at pitch for a shorter one, additional pitches would have been available, some of which Mozart could have used. That is to say, the octave above partials 3, 4, 5, 6, 8, and 9 would yield partials 6, 8, 10, 12, 16, and 18, but also 7, 9, 14, and 15 (Example 8.14c). The absence of any of this last set of pitches seems to confirm the use of short instruments for horns 1 and 2. Hence, of the three methods proposed for rendering the first and second horn parts, either the second or third is correct, while the first may be ruled out.[40]

The triadic figure with trill, which opens the first movement of K. 132, serves as the beginning of two other compositions in the same key: the probably spurious

---

[39] R. Morley-Pegge/F. Hawkins, R. Merewether, 'Horn', in S. Sadie (ed.), *The New Grove Dictionary of Musical Instruments* (London, 1984), ii. 232–47, here 241–4.

[40] In recording this symphony the Academy of Ancient Music made two takes, one with the first method, one with the third. Although the former created a brilliant effect, it sounded technically insecure, so the version issued was the latter.

Ex. 8.7 Symphony in E flat major, K. 132, horn partials employed

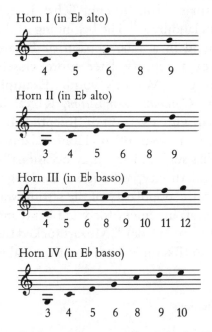

Sinfonia concertante for winds, K. Anh. C 14.01, and the thoroughly authentic piano concerto, K. 482. Although the movement's orchestration is conservative (i.e., the winds are used as a choir rather than as soloists), few symphony movements of the 1770s show better Mozart's extraordinary ear for orchestral sonorities. Indeed, the movement seems to be as much about orchestral sonorities as about themes or modulations.

Two complete slow movements survive for this symphony: an Andante in $\frac{3}{8}$ found in the expected position between the first movement and the Minuet, and a substitute movement, an Andantino grazioso in $\frac{2}{4}$, added in the manuscript after the Finale. In both one pair of horns is tacet and the other pair inserts B flat crooks (presumably B flat alto). The $\frac{3}{8}$ movement is based in part upon borrowed materials. Its opening melody reproduces the incipit of a Gregorian Credo (Example 8.8). (The reader is referred to Chapter 4 for a discussion of the probable

Ex. 8.8 Plainsong: 'Credo in unum Deum'

Cre - do   in   u - num   De - um

Source: *Missale Romanum* (Antwerp, 1716), 238.

significance of such a quotation in a symphony.) Later in the movement there appears a variant of a popular German Christmas carol, 'Joseph, lieber Joseph mein', also known with the Latin text 'Resonet in laudibus'.[41] The beginning of the carol in a commonly disseminated form is found in a 1599 version of Erhard Bodenschatz (Example 8.9a), but a version of a century later more closely resembles the tune as it was known in Salzburg in Mozart's youth (Example 8.9b).[42] As mentioned in the discussion of the *Galimathias musicum*, K. 32, in Chapter 3, the residents of Salzburg were familiar with a version of 'Joseph, lieber Joseph mein' played by the mechanical carillon in a tower of the Hohensalzburg Castle each Christmas season. That instrument has survived and may occasionally still be faintly heard above the noises of the modern city, although it no longer plays the tune in question. Fortunately, however, the popularity of the setting was such that it survives elsewhere, in an anonymous arrangement for wind band and in a keyboard version by Johann Ernst Eberlin (Example 8.9c).[43] Mozart tucked the quotation into the second-violin part in bars 37–56 (Example 8.9d) and the parallel passage at bars 128–47.

Ex. 8.9 'Joseph, lieber Joseph mein' = 'Resonet in laudibus'

(a) Erhard Bodenschatz, 1599

(b) Philip Rättich, 'De Nativitate Domini', 1697

[41] W. Plath, 'Ein "geistlicher" Sinfoniesatz Mozarts', *Die Musikforschung* (1974), xxvii. 93–5.

[42] Erhard Bodenschatz, *Das schöne und geistreiche Magnificat der hochgelobten Jungfrauen Mariae, wie es in der christlichen Kirchen zu singen breuchlichen, samt dem Benedicamus, &c., auf die zwölff modos musicales in ihrer natürlichen Ordnung unterschiedlich mit vier Stimmen gesetzt* (Leipzig, 1599). Example 8.9b is from M. M. Schneider-Cuvay (n. 43 below).

[43] M. M. Schneider-Cuvay, 'Josef, lieber Josef mein': Verarbeitung der Melodie vom 17. bis zum 19. Jahrhundert', in W. Deutsch and H. Dengg (eds.), *Die Volksmusik im Lande Salzburg. 11. Seminar für Volksmusikforschung 1975* (Schriften zur Volksmusik, iv) (Vienna, 1979), 194–8; idem, E. Hintermaier, and Gerhard Walterskirchen (eds.), *Aufzüge für Trompeten und Pauken—Musikstücke für mechanische Orgelwerke* (Denkmäler der Musik in Salzburg, i) (Munich and Salzburg, 1977), xi–xii. 58.

Bring - get Schall - me - yen und Pfei - fen mit Euch. Lau - ffet nach

Beth - le-hemb in den Stall; Gri - tet das Kin - de - lein

al - le zu mall. Me - ßi - am, Me - ßi - am.

(c) Johann Ernst Eberlin: 'Für den Christmonat: Das Wiegenlied'

Tempo di Menueto [*sic*]

(d) Mozart: Symphony in E flat major, K. 132. Second movement, violin II (bars 37–56)

[Andante]

Although unaware of the presence of musical quotations, Einstein found Mozart's first Andante 'full of personal spiritual unrest and rebellion' and even 'expressionistic', and Della Croce, so 'personal' as to require replacement.[44] Besides its other eccentricities, the movement was too long, as may be seen by comparing it with the andantes of the seven other symphonies written around the same time, which in performance average roughly five and three quarter minutes, whereas K. 132's first Andante lasts about nine and a half minutes. This exceptional movement must have had some local significance, an allusion to Salzburg affairs or a private joke, but whatever that may have been is lost to us. Perhaps its very specificity led to its being replaced by an all-purpose, 'abstract' movement, containing (as far as anyone knows) no quotations. This new, more conventional movement features a cantilena, shared between violins and oboes and maintaining a dialogue with the rest of the orchestra.

The Minuet begins with a canonic exchange between the first and second violins. This tune is soon imitated by the bass instruments and then heard in one voice or another throughout the piece, once after a humorously timed pause just before the return of the opening theme in the middle of the second section. The Trio, for strings only, was (along with that of K. 130) called 'daring and bizarre' by Wyzewa and Saint-Foix, while Abert too noted a 'tendency toward eccentricity'.[45] It appears to be based upon a melody in the style of a psalm tone, set in a parody of the texture of the *stile antico* of a post-Renaissance motet. A brief outburst of ballroom jollity at the beginning of the second section is the only intrusion of the secular world into the mock-sanctity of the psalmody. Was this Mozart's commentary on the curious mix of secular and sacred at the court of the Prince-

[44] Einstein, 222; Della Croce, *Le 75 sinfonie*, 145.
[45] Abert, *Mozart*, i. 206; Wyzewa–Saint-Foix, i. 456 (= i. 493).

Archbishops of Salzburg? As with the $\frac{3}{8}$ Andante, to which this Trio is linked in spirit, the intentions behind the programmatic elements may never be redis-covered. If Mozart had programmes for his symphonies, he preferred to keep them secret, unlike his father, Michael Haydn, Dittersdorf, and some others. An exception, such as his *Musical Joke*, K. 522, perhaps only proves the rule. In this regard, Mozart apparently would have agreed with a contemporary who admon-ished composers that 'The musician should always attempt to convey feelings rather than depict their actual causes. He should present the state of mind and body after contemplation of a certain matter, rather than try to depict that matter or event itself.'[46]

The Finale, a substantial movement in the form of a gavotte or *contredanse en rondeau*, is as French as Mozart's symphonic music ever becomes. The rondo resounds with a kind of mock naïveté of which, one imagines, members of the French nobility who enjoyed playing at shepherds and shepherdesses would have approved. Mozart had harsh things to say about most French music of his time, exasperatedly calling it 'trash' and 'wretched',[47] and he was loath to admit any indebtedness to it. Yet in 1778 he wrote of a group of his symphonies that 'most of them are not in the Parisian taste',[48] implying, of course, that some of them were in that taste.

Symphony in D major, K. 133

[46] Johann Jacob Engel, *Über die musikalische Malerey* (Berlin, 1780), 25. A manifestation of the opposite philosophy is a work entitled *Musical Sleigh-Ride* (not Leopold's work by the same name, which it antedates), which exists in an eighteenth-century manuscript in the Thurn und Taxis Library, Regensburg, with the designation 'Sinfonia' and a spurious attribution to Wolfgang. This other 'Musical Sleighride' is the work of one Johann Georg Wassmuth (d. 1766). See E. Valentin, 'Musikalische Schlittenfahrt, ein Wolfgang Amadeus Mozart zugesprochenes Gegenstück zu Leopold Mozarts Werke', *Zeitschrift des historischen Vereins für Schwaben* (1942–3), lv–lvi. 440 ff; and H. C. Robbins Landon, 'Two Orchestral Works Wrongly Attributed to Mozart', *The Music Review* (1956), xvii. 29–34.

[47] Letter of 5 Apr. 1778. *Briefe*, ii. 332; *Letters*, ii. 770 (= ii. 522).

[48] Letter of 11 Sept. 1778. *Briefe*, ii. 476; *Letters*, ii. 913 (= ii. 615). Concerning Mozart's ideas of French tastes in symphonies, see ch. 9.

Instrumentation: *strings, 1 flute/2 oboes, 2 horns, 2 trumpets, [bassoons, kettle-drums, continuo]

Autograph: Staatsbibliothek Preussischer Kulturbesitz, West Berlin (Mus. Ms. Autogr. W. A. Mozart 133)

Principal source: none

Facsimile: none

Editions: *GA*, xx. 252–70 (= Serie 8, No. 20); *NMA*, iv/11/3. 78–101; reconstructed kettledrum part: R. Dearling, *The Music of Wolfgang Amadeus Mozart: The Symphonies* (London, 1982), 197

The autograph bears the characteristic inscription 'Sinfonia / del Sgr: Cavaliere Amadeo Wolfgango / Mozart. nel Luglio 1772 à Salisburgo'. The first movement opens with three tutti chords, after which a rising sequential theme with trills follows in the strings. (The theme of this rising sequence is related to the opening idea from a sonata of J. C. Bach's, which Mozart used as the basis of the first movement of his pastiche piano concerto, K. 107/3.) Flourishes from the trumpets (and kettledrums, if these are added), as well as from the other winds, define this as a festive work, and there is much dialogue between the winds and strings throughout the movement. A contrasting lyrical section of the exposition features the 'Lombardic' rhythm noted in several other of Mozart's symphonies of this period. Both halves are repeated. A well-worked-out development section returns to the tonic key without presenting the opening theme. That theme Mozart saves for the end, where it is heard in the strings and then, in a grand apotheosis, heard again doubled by the trumpets. This handling of sonata form thus creates a kind of mirror form, which works especially well here because the closing theme of the exposition is derived from (and both precedes and follows) the primary theme, imparting to the movement striking unity despite an apparent variety of themes.

At bars 160–1, where the opening theme returns, Mozart has written (and all editions reproduce) something for the second oboe that looks logical on paper and sounds reasonable heard in the mind or tried at the piano. In orchestral performance, however, the passage sounds not like the elision that Mozart apparently conceived here, but like the entrance of a hapless oboist two beats too late (Example 8.10c). Such rushing scales are a tutti gesture in evidence in other Mozart symphonies of the period, used to articulate formal subsections (Examples 8.10a-b). The staggering of the second oboe in K. 133 renders a clear-cut, characteristic gesture a muddle; it can be emended by having the second oboe play in unison with the first. As this error—if it is one—can hardly be a slip of the pen, it must be considered a rare instance of failed artistic judgement on Mozart's part.

Exceptionally, the binary Andante is in the dominant instead of the subdominant. It is scored for strings (once again violins muted and the bass instruments pizzicato), with the addition of a solitary 'flauto traverso obligato'. Do not fall into the anachronism of imagining the poor flautist sitting disconsolately during the other three movements with nothing to play; instead recall the habits of the Salzburg musicians—which in this regard were no different from the habits of court musicians all over western Europe at the time—and imagine a player of another instrument (probably the oboe) picking up his flute for this movement. The translucent timbre of the orchestra, with the flute doubling the first violins at the octave above and occasionally venturing forth as a soloist, is handled with felicity. Did Mozart know the similar writing for solo flute found in the Andante of Joseph Haydn's Symphony in C major, Hob. I: 30, of 1765?

The Minuet is short, simple, and fast, something Mozart favoured at this time judging by his complaint, discussed in Chapter 7, about Italian minuets that 'generally have plenty of notes, are played slowly and are many bars long'. The Trio, for strings accompanied by the oboes, once again provided an opportunity for him to shake a few tricks from his sleeve, in this case syncopations, suspensions, and other contrapuntal devices, or an ironic negation of the homophonic texture normally found in dance music.

The Finale is an enormous jig in sonata form that, once begun, continues virtually without rest to its breathless conclusion. This movement bears no tempo indication, and none would have been needed, as jig-finales were common and everyone knew how they went. In addition, the finales of symphonies were usually faster than their first movements (which in the case of K. 133 also lacks its tempo indication), an effect commonly achieved either by means of a shorter or more rapid metre (most often, $\mathbb{C}$ $\frac{2}{4}$, $\frac{3}{8}$, $\frac{6}{8}$, $\frac{9}{8}$, or $\frac{12}{8}$ replacing $\mathbf{C}$ or $\frac{3}{4}$) or by a more rapid

Ex. 8.10 Formal articulation by upwardly rushing scales

(a) Symphony in G major, K. 129, first movement (bars 83–7)

(b) Symphony in E flat major, K. 132, first movement (bars 24–9)

(c) Symphony in D major, K. 133, first movement (bars 159–62)

tempo indication (allegro molto or presto replacing allegro, allegro ma non troppo or allegro moderato), or by both of these means. Thus the first and last movements of this symphony should bear the generic, editorial tempo indications '[Allegro]' and '[Allegro molto]' respectively.

Symphony in A major, K. 134

[Incipits 8.10]

Instrumentation: *strings, 2 flutes, 2 horns, [bassoon, continuo]
Autograph: Staatsbibliothek Preussische Kulturbesitz, West Berlin (Mus. Ms. Autogr. W. A. Mozart 134)
Principal source: none
Facsimile: none
Editions: *GA*, xx. 271–88 (= Serie 8, No. 21); *NMA*, iv/11/3. 102–22

With their customary division of labour, Wolfgang headed the autograph manuscript of K. 134 'Sinfonia' and his father added 'del Sgr. Caval: Amadeo Wolfg: Mozart. / in Salisburgo nel Agosto 1772'. Since the symphonies K. 128, 129, 130, 132, 133, and 134 are dated May (three works), July (two works) and August 1772 respectively, there must have been a pressing need for new symphonies. It may have been the Mozarts' intention to form an 'opus' of six, although as the works' manuscripts come down to us, they consist of two separate works (K. 128, 129) and then the four others bound together in the nineteenth century.

Even though the orchestra for K. 134 is at its smallest, Saint-Foix finds the result 'astonishingly imaginative and poetic', and Stanley Sadie considers it to be 'among Mozart's most closely argued'.[49] The first movement eschews the more usual march-like, common-time opening in favour of one in $\frac{3}{4}$. For Mozart, this is an exceptionally monothematic movement. The opening idea is heard repeatedly in the tuttis of the exposition and recapitulation and in the development section as well.[50] Perhaps the approach to monothematicism is the reason that Mozart felt the need, rather unusually for him during this period, to add an eighteen-bar coda in which, after a brief allusion to the principal theme, a few triadic flourishes assure even an inattentive listener that the close has been reached.

The Andante is once again in $\frac{2}{4}$ and in the subdominant. It opens with a melody that Mozart may have been inspired to write by Gluck's aria 'Che farò senza Euridice?' from *Orfeo*.[51] On the other hand, this is a melodic type much in use at the time, which may have much broader origins than a specific aria by Gluck. The movement's cantabile beginning is spun out into a sonata-form movement of considerable subtlety, its texture carefully worked out, with an elaborate second violin part and divided violas.

The Minuet has a brusque quality audible in a number of Mozart's and Joseph Haydn's symphonic minuets. The previously dubbed 'Punch-and-Judy tendency' appears again in the Trio, with its virtually melodyless first section and (in the second section) chords tossed antiphonally between winds and violins, pizzicato, over a drone in the violas, arriving at a peculiarly chromatic passage to prepare the return of the opening 'non-melody'.

The Finale begins with a bourrée, which is subjected to full development in sonata form with coda. One might expect a dance turned into a symphonic finale

[49] Saint-Foix, 52–3 (= 35); S. Sadie, *The New Grove Mozart* (New York, 1982), 26.

[50] Compare the first movements of the symphonies K. 75, 110 = 75b, and 114.

[51] The Mozarts arrived in Vienna on 6 Oct. 1762, the day after the première of Gluck's celebrated and controversial opera, and on 10 Oct. Leopold attended a performance of it. For the Viennese reception of *Orfeo*, see H. C. Robbins Landon, *Haydn: The Early Years 1732–1765* (Haydn: Chronicle and Works, i), 379–80. Joseph Haydn used the 'Che farò' theme in an early baryton trio (ibid. 542); echoes of it can be heard in the Andante of Mozart's bassoon concerto, K. 191 = 186e, and it seems still to have been resounding in his mind in 1786 when he wrote the Countess's cavatina 'Porgi amor' in *Le nozze di Figaro*. See also below, at n. 109.

to be in the 'lighter' form of a rondo rather than sonata form; but apparently this was not seen by Mozart as an aesthetic problem of disparity between form and content, and his penultimate symphony, K. 550, observes the same procedure. The spirit of the dance continually peers through the 'serious' symphonic façade.

Symphony in D major, K. 126 + 161/163 = 141a, 'Il sogno di Scipione'

[Incipits 8.11]

Instrumentation: *strings, 2 flutes, 2 oboes, 2 horns, 2 trumpets, kettledrums, [bassoons, continuo]

Autograph: Staatsbibliothek Preussische Kulturbesitz, West Berlin (serenata and third movement of the symphony) (Mus. Ms. Autogr. W. A. Mozart 126)

Principal source: Staatsbibliothek Preussische Kulturbesitz, West Berlin (symphony) (Mus. Ms. 15268)

Facsimile: none

Editions: *GA*, ix. 1–9 (= Serie 5, No. 7); *GA*, xl. 73–9 (= Serie 28, No. 10); *NMA*, iv/11/3. 123–40

Until recently it was believed that Mozart's setting of Metastasio's 'serenata drammatica' *Il sogno di Scipione*, K. 126, was composed for ceremonies connected with the installation of the new Archbishop of Salzburg, and performed in early May 1772. This was logical enough, as on the autograph could be seen the date 1772, apparently in Leopold's hand, and the name 'Girolamo' (i.e., Hieronymus) appears in the text. It now emerges, however, that 'Giralamo' was written over an erasure, which can be deciphered as 'Sigismondo', the name of the previous Archbishop, who died on 16 December 1771. Hence, this occasional cantata must date from between April and August of 1771, when the Mozarts were in Salzburg between Italian sojourns, and it was probably revived in 1772 with the necessary change of name.[52]

The overture of K. 126 consisted of an Allegro moderato and an Andante; Mozart later added a Finale, to make an autonomous symphony. This explains the complex of K. numbers: K. 126 is the entire serenata in all editions of the Köchel Catalogue; K. 161 was the three-movement symphony as found in a set of manuscript parts owned by Breitkopf & Härtel; K. 163 redundantly represented just the Finale as found in Mozart's autograph. The last two are reunited in recent editions of the Catalogue under the number 141a. On the basis of the writing in the autograph manuscript of the Finale, Wolfgang Plath believes it to date from the summer of either 1773 or 1774, when Mozart was in Salzburg,[53] and Alan Tyson reports that the paper on which it is written is a type used by Mozart mostly between May and October 1772, although a few bits of it also turn up in *Il rè pastore* (1774–5) and *La finta giardiniera* (1775).[54] The symphony version thus cannot be more precisely dated than 1772–4.

Metastasio's 'azione teatrale' of 1735, *Il sogno di Scipione*, although based on Cicero's *Somnium Scipioris* with personæ and incidents from Roman history, offers much philosophy and little 'azione', featuring among its cast of characters the allegorical figures of Constancy and Fortune. Instead of trying to create some kind of music of the spheres, Mozart responded to the libretto's abstractions with an all-purpose sinfonia that would have been at home in any church, chamber, or theatre of the period, regardless of the occasion.

The first movement opens *unisono*, a device that Mozart would later mock as a mannerism of Mannheim symphonies.[55] The exposition continues in the most brilliant Italian-overture style, with the requisite lyrical interlude. The development section jumps into B minor, leaving behind it the tremolo of the exposition, and—in a reversal of the common pattern—deals with newly introduced, calmer material. After twenty bars of the recapitulation, it is interrupted by new developments, which abbreviate the section and lead it to the Andante, a movement of pastoral serenity. The three movements of K. 141a, linked by incomplete cadences, are played without a break, the Finale even beginning on a dominant seventh rather than a tonic chord, an unusual gesture that may also be heard at the beginning of the Finale of Schubert's second symphony. (In Schubert's

---

[52] J.-H. Leder, *NMA*, ii/5/6. vii–ix; Plath, 'Schriftchronologie', 153.   [53] Plath, 'Schriftchronologie', 150.
[54] Personal communication.   [55] Letter of 20 Nov. 1777. *Briefe*, ii. 135; *Letters*, ii. 556 (= i. 378).

case, however, the dominant seventh is just a transition heard once, whereas in K. 141a it is integral to the movement's opening idea and, as such, is repeated.) The Finale, whose Presto indication is written in pencil by an unknown hand (perhaps Leopold's), is a kind of *menuet en rondeau* under a strong sonata-form influence.

The autograph manuscripts of a group of nine symphonies written after Mozart returned from his third and last trip to Italy are bound together in the so-called 'Cranz volume 3'. This refers to August Cranz, a music-publisher in Hamburg and later Leipzig, whose ownership of a number of Mozart's autographs was announced in an article in 1831.[56] The contents of Cranz's three volumes of Mozart's autographs are as follows:

I

Serenade in D major, K. 185 = 167a (? August 1773)
March in D major, K. 189 = 167b (? 1773)

II

Concertone in C major, K. 190 = 186E (31 May 1774)
Serenade in D major, K. 203 = 189b (? August 1774)
Serenade in D major, K. 204 = 213a (5 August 1775)
Serenade in D major, K. 250 = 248b (? July 1776)

III

Symphony in C major, K. 162 (?19 or 29 April 1773)
Symphony in D major, K. 181 = 162b (19 May 1773)
Symphony in B flat major, K. 182 = 173dA (3 October 1773)
Symphony in B flat major, K. 183 = 173dB (5 October 1773)
Symphony in E flat major, K. 184 = 161a (30 March 1773)
Symphony in G major, K. 199 = 161b (?10 or 16 April 1773)
Symphony in C major, K. 200 = 189k (?17 or 12 November 1774)
Symphony in A major, K. 201 = 186a (6 April 1774)
Symphony in D major, K. 202 = 186b (5 May 1774)

The three volumes were put together by Leopold. Before volume I came into Cranz's hands, it belonged to Franz Schubert's friend Leopold von Sonnleithner. In 1964 K[6] reported that it was in private possession in central Europe, its owner

---

[56] *Allgemeine musikalische Zeitung* (1831), xxxiii. cols. 733–7.

unknown; since then, however, the March, K. 167b, has come into the possession of the West Berlin library, while the autograph of the Serenade, K. 185 = 167a, has been dismembered and scattered by some vandal or vandals. Volume II went from Cranz's possession to private ownership in Vienna and is now in a private collection in Switzerland. Like volume I, volume III, with its nine symphonies, passed from Leopold von Sonnleithner to Cranz, and it too was thought to be in private hands in Vienna. But on 22 May 1987, when volume III was auctioned at Sotheby's London for $4.34 million, its anonymous owner was said to be Swiss. The nine symphonies were bought by an anonymous collector and have been placed on permanent deposit in the Pierpont Morgan Library, in New York.[57]

Prior to the arrival of the three volumes in Cranz's or Sonnleithner's hands, someone attempted to obliterate the dates provided for each work by Leopold. As a result Sonnleithner could only with great difficulty decipher the year (sometimes), the month (frequently) and the day (very often). This explains the many queries before the dates, for Köchel relied on Sonnleithner's decipherments, and Einstein was unable to re-examine the manuscripts while preparing K[3]. It was possibly Mozart himself in the 1780s who attempted to obscure the dates, in hopes of passing off early works as late ones, for publication or sale to patrons, as, for instance, in his brazen attempt to do just that to the Prince of Donaueschingen in 1786, documented in Chapter 11. Or the dates may have been effaced in the 1790s by Mozart's widow or one of her helpers, Nissen or the Abbé Stadler, in order to sell the manuscripts as late works. That this ploy was in the long run unlikely to succeed is seen from the fact that, when four of the symphonies (K. 162, 173dB, 161b, 186b) were published in 1799 by the Hamburg firm of Günther & Böhme, a reviewer saw immediately that these were not to be compared with Mozart's or Joseph Haydn's symphonies from the 1780s and (in Haydn's case) 1790s.[58]

Symphony in E flat major, K. 184 = 166a = 161a

[Incipits 8.12]

[57] K[6], 186–7; H.-G. Klein, *Wolfgang Amadeus Mozart: Autographe und Abschriften* (R. Elvers (ed.), Staatsbibliothek Preussischer Kulturbesitz, Kataloge der Musikabteilung, I/vi) (Berlin, 1982), 52 ; Sotheby's, *Wolfgang Amadeus Mozart: Autograph Manuscript of Nine Symphonies* (London, 1987). The last contains bibliographical descriptions of the manuscripts of all nine symphonies and facsimiles from K. 162, 181 = 162b, 199 = 161b, 182 = 173dA, and 201 = 186a, as well as of Leopold Mozart's title-page for the entire volume. Private communications from Alan Tyson and from The Morgan Library.

[58] '*Quatre Simphonies pour l'Orchestre, comp. par Wolfgang Amad. Mozart. Œuv. 64. Hambourg chez Günther et Böhme. (Preis à 1 Rthlr.)*', *Allgemeine musikalische Zeitung* (1799), i, cols. 494–6. This review is reproduced and discussed in ch. 13 at n. 28.

Instrumentation: *strings, 2 flute, 2 oboes, 2 bassoons, 2 horns, 2 trumpets, [kettledrums, continuo]
Autograph: Pierpont Morgan Library, New York
Principal source: none
Facsimile: *Mozart-Jahrbuch* (1960–1), between pp. 112 and 113
Editions: *GA*, xxi. 58–78 (= Serie 8, No. 26); *NMA*, iv/11/4. 15–36

The first two pages of the 'autograph' manuscript of K. 161a were written by Leopold, the remainder of the first movement by the Salzburg copyist Felix Hofstätter, and the other movements by Wolfgang. Recent examination by the *NMA* editors of the heavily defaced date confirms that it probably reads '30 March 1773' following the usual inscription 'Del Sigr: Cavaliere Amadeo Mozart'. This was about a month after the seventeen-year-old composer and his father returned from their third and last Italian journey.

Every commentator has remarked on the dramatic character of this work, for instance, Saint-Foix in his typically extravagant diction: 'The violence of the first movement followed by the infinite despair of the Andante (in the minor), and the ardent and joyous rhythms of the finale mark this symphony as something quite apart; romantic exaltation here reaches its climax.'[59] In addition, the work seems filled with familiar ideas. The intense opening gesture of the Molto presto later served Mozart as a model for the more relaxed openings of two other E flat pieces: the Sinfonia concertante, K. 364, and the Serenade for winds, K. 375 (Example 8.11). The C minor Andante, replete with sighing appoggiaturas and other effects borrowed from tragic Italian arias, is the first in a series of powerful minor-key andantes, discussed in Chapter 10 in connection with a D major symphony, K. 320. The theme of the jig-like Finale of K. 161a resembles that of the rondo-finale of the horn concerto, K. 495, again in E flat. Thus, Mozart had in mind a group of ideas

[59] Saint-Foix, 60 (= 40).

associated with E flat major and C minor, which reappeared in various guises over a period of years. Throughout all three movements of K. 161a concertante writing for the winds is especially prominent for this period.

The jig-finale makes no attempt to maintain the high drama of the two previous movements. That Mozart thought of its function as relaxing the tension generated earlier appears in the reversal of the tempo indications of the first and third movements from his usual practice.

Two clues about the possible origins of this exceptionally serious symphony: its three movements are played without a break, in the manner associated with many Italian overture-sinfonias, and the orchestration calls for pairs of flutes and oboes to play simultaneously. Mozart's practice in his orchestral serenades and earlier symphonies was to use either oboes or flutes, not both, and in his last symphonies to use a pair of oboes plus a single flute. The few early symphonies requiring pairs of flutes and oboes played simultaneously originated as overtures to theatrical works: *Die Schuldigkeit des ersten Gebots*, K. 35; *La finta semplice*, K. 51 = 46a; *Mitridate, rè di Ponto*, K. 87 = 74a; *Ascanio in Alba*, K. 120 = 111 + 111a; and *Il sogno di Scipione*, K. 126 + 161/163 = 141a. Especially telling in this regard is the overture to *La finta semplice*, which began life as the concert symphony, K. 45, and then had a pair of flutes added to it for the theatre.[60] Hence, K. 161a (unless it once existed in an earlier version without flutes) was likely intended from the start to serve in the

Ex. 8.11 Opening ideas similar to that of K. 184 = 161a

(a) Sinfonia concertante in E flat major, K. 364 = 320d, first movement

(b) Serenade for winds in E flat major, K. 375, first movement

(See also Exx. 2.2 and 2.3.)

---

[60] Exceptions to the rule that two flutes plus two oboes means a symphony for the theatre: two symphonies drawn from orchestral serenades (K. 320 and 385) and the 'Paris' symphony (K. 297 = 300a), which was written for a particular ensemble working within traditions outside Mozart's south-German—Austrian—north-Italian orbit.

theatre as an overture, a function that would not then have precluded (nor should it now preclude) its use in concerts.

Appropriately, therefore, K. 161a was pressed into service during the 1780s, apparently with Mozart's consent, by the travelling theatrical troupe of Johann Böhm as the overture to *Lanassa* by the Berlin playwright Karl Martin Plümicke. A German adaptation of Antoine-Marin Lemierre's *La Veuve du Malabar*, *Lanassa* concerns the plight of a Hindu widow who, unable to reconcile herself to her husband's death, eventually flings herself on to a funeral pyre. Böhm's production of *Lanassa* not only employed K. 161a as an overture, but was decked out with the not-inconsiderable incidental music Mozart had composed for *Thamos, King of Egypt* (K. 345), to which new texts had been set. This may be why one sometimes reads the probably erroneous statement that K. 161a was originally intended as an overture for *Thamos* itself.[61]

Symphony in G major, K. 199 = 162a = 161b

[Incipits 8.13]

Instrumentation: *strings, 2 flutes, 2 horns, [bassoon, continuo]
Autograph: Pierpont Morgan Library, New York
Principal source: none
Facsimile: none
Editions: *GA*, xxi. 79–94 (= Serie 8, No. 27); *NMA*, iv/11/4. 37–56

---

[61] A Frankfurt manuscript, probably from the late 1780s, of the *Thamos* incidental music with the *Lanassa* texts uses the first movement of K. 161a alone (without trumpets) as an overture (W. Plath, 'Mozartiana in Fulda und Frankfurt. (Neues zu Heinrich Henkel und seinem Nachlass)', *Mozart-Jahrbuch* (1968–70), 333–86, here 366). Johann Böhm's connections with Salzburg and with the Mozarts are discussed in ch. 10.

The date on the autograph is, once again, defaced and difficult to decipher with confidence; the paper is a type used by Mozart between about March 1773 and May 1775.[62] The first movement of K. 161b is a small-scale, finely proportioned sonata-form movement exuding high spirits. As in the first movement of K. 124, an attractive hemiola pattern is hinted at (Example 8.12).

In the D major Andantino grazioso the upper strings are muted, the lower ones play mostly pizzicato, and the flutes, previously limited to reinforcing the tuttis, come into their own, offering up the kind of air sung beneath the balconies of young Mediterranean women in many an eighteenth-century opera. With its mild parallel sixths and thirds and flowing triplets, the movement offers only a touch of chromaticism occasioned by augmented-sixth chords toward the end of each of its two repeated sections to hint that the world might contain any darkness.

Ex. 8.12 Symphony in G major, K. 199 = 162a = 161b, first movement (bars 44–51)

---

[62] A. Tyson, 'The Dates of Mozart's Missa brevis KV 258 and Missa longa KV 263 (264a): An Investigation into His "Klein-Querformat" Papers', *Bachiana et alia Musicologica: Festschrift Alfred Dürr zum 65. Geburtstag* (Kassel, 1983), 328–39, here 334.

The Finale begins with some contrapuntal gestures, which coexist uneasily with the galant ideas in the rest of the movement. Saint-Foix describes the effect as 'a sort of fugato that soon takes on a waltz rhythm'.[63] The subject of the fugato, G—C—F sharp—G, is derived from the opening theme of the first movement. Mozart would later comment wryly on this sort of quasi-contrapuntal writing in the Finale of his *Musical Joke,* K. 522. The short-windedness of the opening is somewhat redeemed by a more extended version of the same material that occurs at the recapitulation, where it serves both as main theme and as retransition. As discussed in connection with the Symphony in B flat, K. 319, in Chapter 10, such suggested rather than actual counterpoint was an essential element of symphonic style of the period. Counterpoint aside, the movement jogs as nice a jig as could be wanted *circa* 1773 to bring a symphony to a jolly conclusion.

Symphony in C major, K. 162

[Incipits 8.14]

Instrumentation: *strings, 2 oboes, 2 horns, 2 trumpets, [bassoon, kettledrums, continuo]
Autograph: Pierpont Morgan Library, New York
Principal source: none
Facsimile: *NMA,* iv/11/4. xv
Editions: *GA,* xxi. 1–12 (= Serie 8, No. 22); *NMA,* iv/11/4. 1–14; reconstructed kettledrum part: R. Dearling, *The Music of Wolfgang Amadeus Mozart: The Symphonies* (London, 1982), 199

---

[63] Saint-Foix, 69 (= 47).

The Symphony in C major, K. 162, calls for a pair of 'long trumpets' ('trombe lunghe'—see Plates IX and X) in addition to the usual strings and pairs of oboes and horns. If kettledrum parts once existed, they have been lost. Once again the date on the autograph has been tampered with, but perhaps reads 19 or 29 April 1773; this date is contradicted neither by the form of Mozart's writing nor by the paper employed, a type used by Mozart in Salzburg between about March 1773 and May 1775.[64]

The opening gestures of the first movement establish the festive character of the entire work, by an alternation of tutti outbursts *tremolando* with a quiet staccato motive. Where the brief development section leads back to C major, these first twelve bars are absent, reserved for the end where they serve as closing section. This is thus a mirror-form movement of the sort discussed above in connection with the first movement of K. 133. The Andantino grazioso in F major temporarily retires the trumpets and hews to the customary pastoral spirit of such movements. The prominently featured concertante writing for the oboes and horns brings this movement close in style to a number of andantes in Mozart's orchestral serenades of the period. The jig-like Finale—which brings back the trumpets with a vengeance, opening with a transformation of the fanfare that, in the bass instruments, began the first movement—is worked out in a concise sonata form.

Symphony in D major, K. 181 = 162b

[Incipits 8.15]

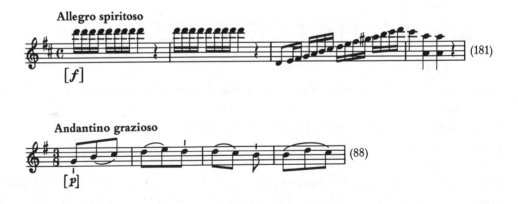

⁶⁴ Plath, 'Schriftchronologie', 152; Tyson, 'The Dates of Mozart's Missa brevis KV 258 and Missa longa KV 263 (264a)', 334.

Instrumentation: *strings, 2 oboes, 2 horns, 2 trumpets, [bassoon, kettledrums, continuo]
Autograph: Pierpont Morgan Library, New York
Principal source: set of parts from Mozart's estate (lost; see below)
Facsimile: none
Editions: *GA*, xx. 13–26 (= Serie 8, No. 23); *NMA*, iv/11/4. 57–74; reconstructed kettledrum part: R. Dearling, *The Music of Wolfgang Amadeus Mozart: The Symphonies* (London, 1982), 199

This symphony and K. 162 open with similar flourishes. The present first movement, with the unusual tempo indication Allegro spiritoso, is (like several other symphony movements already encountered) an essay in the use of orchestral 'noises' to form a coherent and satisfying whole. That is, there are few memorable melodies, but rather there is a succession of timbral devices, including repeated notes, fanfares, arpeggios, sudden fortes and pianos, scales, syncopations, dotted rhythms, and so on. The aesthetic problems raised by such works are discussed in Chapter 6 in connection with the Symphony in D, K. 100 = 62a.

The G major Andantino grazioso follows the first movement without pause. The trumpets again fall silent, and the movement in some sense compensates for the previous lack of beautiful melody, offering an oboe solo in the style of a siciliano. This leads, again without break, straight into a rondo in the style of a *contredanse* or march, to which Saint-Foix correctly applied the eighteenth-century appellation 'quick step'.[65]

This symphony must have enjoyed some success in the eighteenth century, as early sets of parts are found in Brno, Frankfurt, and Regensburg. The parts in Brno and Frankfurt have condensed the two viola parts into one and omitted the trumpets, those in Regensburg specify a choice between two oboes and two flutes. André owned a set of parts that came from Mozart's estate and had been used by him.[66] The subtitle 'Overture' in the Köchel Catalogue and elsewhere is unjustified: the autograph is headed 'Sinfonia'.

---

[65] Saint-Foix, 64 (= 43).

[66] Plath, 'Mozartiana in Fulda und Frankfurt', 360; G. Haberkamp, *Die Musikhandschriften der Fürst Thurn und Taxis Hofbibliothek Regensburg* (Munich, 1981), 163. K⁶ incorrectly claims that Berlin Mus. Ms. 15250 is from Mozart's estate (see Klein, *Autographe und Abschriften*, 262–3).

Symphony in D major, K. 185 = 167a

[Incipits 8.16]

Instrumentation: *strings, 2 oboes/flutes, 2 horns, 2 trumpets, [kettledrums, bassoon, continuo]
Autograph: disrupted in various locations
Principal source: set of parts, formerly in the Breitkopf & Härtel archives, Leipzig (lost)
Facsimile: *NMA*, iv/12/2. xxi
Editions: *GA*, xxiii. 61–8 (= Serie 9, No. 5); *NMA*, iv/12/2. 76–85, 100–19

The so-called Cranz volume 1, containing an orchestral serenade and its introductory march, has recently been dismembered and scattered. Alan Tyson reports that the date on the serenade autograph might be deciphered as 'nell' Agosto 1773', as reported in K³ and K⁶, but that it has been so heavily defaced that no secure reading is possible. If that date were correct, then the serenade was written in Vienna, where the Mozarts were in August 1773; but this is itself suspicious since Wolfgang's orchestral serenades appear to have been a Salzburg genre, and the paper of the autograph is a type Mozart used in Salzburg between approximately March 1773 and May 1775.[67] True, the Serenade autograph was annotated (in an unknown hand) 'Serenata / del Sgr. Cavaliere Amadeo Wolfgango / Mozart accademico di Bologna e di / Verona à Vienna', but this may have been added later, for the inscription in Leopold's hand on the accompanying march, although otherwise identical, omits the last two words. A Berlin manuscript of the work is dated 'August 1775',[68] which was the date read from the autograph by Sonnleithner in 1862.[69]

A possible explanation is the following: before Leopold and Wolfgang left Salzburg for Vienna on 17 July 1773, Wolfgang had apparently agreed to provide a *Finalmusik* for the graduation from Salzburg University of the family's friend Judas Thaddäus von Antretter in August. Traces of this commission appear in Leopold's correspondence, where he ends a letter of 21 July to his wife with, 'I must close, so there is still time to write a couple of lines to the young Mr von Antretter, and to send the beginning of the *Finalmusik*.' By his next letter three weeks later news of a successful performance had already reached Vienna and Leopold wrote, 'We are delighted that the *Finalmusik* went off well. Wolfgang will thank Mr Meissner later; meanwhile we send him our greetings.'[70] This correspondence suggests a work started in Salzburg before 17 July and brought to Vienna along with enough

---

[67] Tyson, 'The Dates of Mozart's Missa brevis KV 258 and Missa longa KV 263 (264a)', 334. It must be admitted, however, that in 1785 Gyrowetz did offer the Viennese publisher Artaria 'two grand serenades for full orchestra in the manner of a symphony' (see his letter fully quoted in ch. 11).

[68] Klein, *Autographe und Abschriften*, 275, 281.

[69] L. von Sonnleithner, [review of K¹], *Recensionen und Mittheilungen über Theater, Musik und Bildende Kunst* (1862), viii/38. 612–16, here 614.

[70] *Briefe*, i. 485, 486; *Letters*, i. 342, 344 (= 1. 236, 237).

Salzburg paper to complete it. The most likely work is K. 167a–b, which (if this identification is correct) received its first performance on Wednesday, 4 August, under the direction of the Mozarts' old friend Joseph Meissner.[71]

Wolfgang and his father turned all of his other orchestral serenades into symphonies, and there is no obvious reason why K. 185 = 167a would not have received the same treatment, although a set of parts that would have revealed the symphonic version of this work has not survived. That it once existed is confirmed by the Breitkopf & Härtel Manuscript Catalogue, p. 2, No. 6, where the incipit of the Allegro assai of K. 167a is listed as the first movement of a 'Sinfonia / a 2. Viol. 2 Oboi / 2 Cor: 2. Clari / Viola et Basso', whereas on p. 73 an incipit for movement three is found as the first movement of a 'Conc: p. Violin / 2 Viol. 2 Ob: / 2 Corni Viola e / Basso'. Thus, as with the other orchestral serenades, the components of K. 167a were 'recycled' as self-sufficient works.

The interpenetration of the F major concerto and D major symphonic movements are shown below, with the movements suggested for the symphony starred:

Serenade movements	Genres
March (K. 189 = 167b)	march
*Allegro assai	symphony
Andante	violin concerto
Allegro	violin concerto
Menuetto–Trio	dance
*Andante grazioso	symphony
*Menuetto–2 Trios	dance/violin concerto
*Adagio–Allegro assai	symphony

The starred movements, like the comparable movements of Mozart's other Salzburg serenades (and unlike those of his symphonies of the same period), are expansive and their orchestration exceptionally concertante. The Adagio and Allegro indications in the Finale are in Leopold's hand.

The Mozarts visited Vienna from the middle of July until the end of September 1773; the autograph manuscript of the B flat symphony, K. 182 = 173dA, is dated 3 October 1773, of the G minor symphony, K. 183 = 173dB, 5 October 1773, of the A major symphony, K. 201 = 186a, 6 April 1774, and of the D major symphony, K. 202 = 186b, 5 May 1774. These four symphonies are preserved in

---

[71] The Divertimento in D major, K. 205 = 173a = 167A, for violin, viola, double-bass, bassoon, and 2 horns, was apparently also commissioned by the Andretter family, for the mother rather than the son. It seems highly unlikely, however, that this was the work referred to in the Viennese correspondence, for a one-on-a-part divertimento would not have been called a 'Finalmusik', by which term the Mozarts usually designated what are now called orchestral serenades (although this is a tricky point since 'Finalmusik' signifies in the first instance a social function and only by association a musical genre).

the Cranz volume 3 and, as in all the manuscripts in that collection, the dates have been tampered with. Three of the four symphonies are longer and more serious than most of Wolfgang's previous symphonies, and commentators suggest that, in some way, this may have been a result of the Viennese visit. Particular occasions for which these four works may have been composed are unknown.

Symphony in B flat major, K. 182 = 166c = 173dA

[Incipits 8.17]

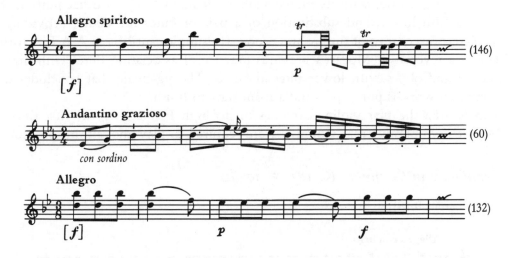

Instrumentation: *strings, 2 oboes = flutes, 2 horns, [bassoons, continuo]
Autograph: Pierpont Morgan Library, New York
Principal source: set of parts from Mozart's estate, Staatsbibliothek Preussische Kulturbesitz, West Berlin (Mus. Ms. 15271)
Facsimile: iv/11/4. xvi
Editions: *GA*, xxi. 27–38 (= Serie 8, No. 24); *NMA*, iv/11/4. 75–86

The autograph manuscript of K. 173dA bears the inscription 'Sinfonia / del Sigr. Cavaliere / Wolfgango Amadeo Mozart il 3 d'ottobre / a Salisburgo 1773', with the date strongly crossed out. This symphony has been undervalued by modern commentators and conductors, yet Mozart must have thought well of it, for a decade after he composed it, he wrote from Vienna to his father in Salzburg requesting that it be sent (along with other works) for use in his concerts in the Austrian capital.[72] What Leopold sent Wolfgang on that occasion was probably the

---

[72] Letter of 4 Jan. 1783. *Briefe*, iii. 248 and facsimile facing 225; *Letters*, iii. 1244–5 and facsimile facing 1242 (= ii. 835 and facsimile facing 838).

set of parts by Salzburg copyists found in West Berlin, with corrections in Wolfgang's hand and a title page in Leopold's reading 'Sinfonia del Sgr. Cavaliere Amadeo Wolfgango Mozart, Accademico di Bologna e di Verona'.[73] These parts were sold by Mozart's widow to Johann André in 1799. K. 173dA enjoyed some circulation, as other eighteenth-century sets of parts for it are found in the libraries at Modena and Frankfurt.[74]

Although the opening movement is nearly as dependent on orchestral 'noises' for its content as the first movement of K. 162b, a few melodies of note emerge including one in which the 'Lombardic' rhythm again features prominently. The Andantino grazioso, with its muted violins, change of key to E flat putting the horns a fifth lower, and substitution of a pair of flutes for oboes, providing a characteristic contrast of timbre and mood, is a simple cantilena in A A B A form. This is a reversal of Mozart's previous practice of associating flutes with higher pitched and oboes with lower pitched horns. The jig-finale that concludes this Dionysian work is pure opera buffa from start to finish.

In K. 182 the first violin part goes up to high F, marking the first time in Mozart's symphonies that violinists were required to play above third position.

Symphony in G minor, K. 183 = 173dB

[Incipits 8.18]

---

[73] Klein, *Autographe und Abschriften*, 265–6 (Mus. Ms. 15271).

[74] Plath, 'Mozartiana in Fulda und Frankfurt', 362; A. Holschneider, 'Neue Mozartiana in Italien', *Die Musikforschung* (1962), xv. 227–36, here 229.

Instrumentation: *strings, 2 oboes, 2 bassoons, 4 horns, [continuo]
Autograph: Pierpont Morgan Library, New York
Principal source: a set of parts from Mozart's estate, in the possession of C. A. André, Frankfurt, 1860, now lost
Facsimile: iv/11/4. xvii
Editions: *GA*, xxi. 39–57 (= Serie 8, No. 25); London: Eulenburg, 1959 (ed. H. E. Redlich); iv/11/4. 87–106

Debussy once wrote of Beethoven's Ninth Symphony that it 'has long been surrounded by a haze of adjectives. Together with the Mona Lisa's smile—which for some strange reason has always been labelled "mysterious"—it is the master-piece about which the most stupid comments have been made. It's a wonder it hasn't been submerged entirely beneath the mass of words it has excited.'[75] On a more modest scale, the same might be said of the verbiage surrounding Mozart's two G minor symphonies—the famous one, K. 550, and the so-called 'Little' G minor, K. 183 = 173dB. The majority of eighteenth-century symphonies are in major keys and appear to convey the optimism of 'the grand, the festive, and the noble' mentioned by Schulz, rather than the darker, more pessimistic or more passionate feelings of the few minor works. The adjectival excesses result from a melioristic view of music history, which regards Mozart's minor-key symphonies as adumbrations, forerunners, of the monumental symphonic masterpieces of the Romantic era. Adherents to this school of thought assure us that K. 173dB is pre- or proto-Romantic, that it is the result of 'the romantic crisis in Austrian music around 1770', and that it is a manifestation of the cultural trend which has been dubbed 'Sturm und Drang', after Klinger's play of that name.[76] The 'haze of

---

[75] C. Debussy, *Monsieur Croche et autres écrits*, ed. F. Lesure (Paris, 1971), 36; trans. R. L. Smith as *Debussy on Music* (New York, 1977), 29.
[76] H. C. Robbins Landon, 'La Crise romantique dans la musique autrichienne vers 1770: Quelques précurseurs inconnus de la Symphonie en sol mineur (KV 183) de Mozart', in A. Verchaly (ed.), *Les Influences étrangères dans l'œuvre de W. A. Mozart* (Paris, 1958), 27–47; B. S. Brook, 'Sturm und Drang and the Romantic Period in Music', *Studies in Romanticism* (1970), ix. 269–84; M. Rudolf, 'Storm and Stress in Music', *Bach, the Quarterly Journal of the Riemenschneider Bach Institute* (1972), iii. 3-11; iv. 8–16.

adjectives' can be at least partially dissipated by attempting to view K. 173dB (and other minor-key works of the period) looking forward from the first two-thirds of the eighteenth century, rather than backwards from the nineteenth.

Much of the music made by the generation between J. S. Bach and Wolfgang Mozart was lighter, shorter, and simpler—moving away from the seriousness, complexity, and monumentality of some of the music of the previous generation. This lightening of spirit is nicely captured by the difference between Andreas Werckmeister's late seventeenth-century definition of music as 'a gift of God, to be used only in His honour'[77] and Charles Burney's mid-eighteenth-century statement that music is 'an innocent luxury, unnecessary, indeed, to our existence, but a great improvement and gratification of the sense of hearing'.[78]

The 'romantic crisis' theory is based upon the intriguing observation that, whereas the symphonies of the late 1750s and early 1760s largely avoided the minor keys, in the late 1760s and early 1770s there was a notable production of such works by (besides Mozart) J. C. Bach, Dittersdorf, J. Haydn, Vanhal, and Ordonez. Landon points out that in contrast to most symphonies of the previous decade these works have in common more frequent use of counterpoint, themes incorporating wide leaps, greater use of syncopations, more extended finales, and more frequent occurrence of unison passages. (As seen in Chapter 4, virtually all of these traits were, only a few years later, considered by J. A. P. Schulz to be the normal attributes of any concert symphony and not just those in minor keys.) Unfortunately for this theory, not a single word occurs in the correspondence, diaries, or periodicals of the period suggesting a 'romantic crisis'. And as each of the composers mentioned wrote only one, two, or at the most three such symphonies, such 'crisis' as it was must have been rapidly overcome.

As for 'Sturm und Drang', of the key literary works of that movement, Goethe's novel *The Sorrows of the Young Werther* dates from 1774 and Klinger's play from 1776, while the works in the visual arts usually considered representative of 'storm and stress'[79] date from even later. Hence we are being asked to imagine that the prescient Austrian musicians participated in a cultural movement that had yet to come into existence. To dub the generation that included Bach's sons, Leopold Mozart, and Gluck (as well as Vanhal, Ordonez, and Dittersdorf) as 'forerunners' is fallacious. These talented composers did not rise from their beds each morning in order to 'forerun'; they composed music that was thoroughly modern and that appealed to them and their contemporaries. At first they must have been enchanted by the light, galant style they had helped to create. Later perhaps the novelty of

[77] Andreas Werckmeister, *Der edlen Music-Kunst, Würde, Gebrauch und Missbrauch* (Frankfurt, 1691), preface.

[78] Charles Burney, *A General History of Music* (London, 1776), i. xiii.

[79] By H. Füssli, F. Müller, J. A. Carstens, F. Kobell, J. C. Reinhart, W. Tischbein, and others.

these sounds and forms began to pall, and the musicians sought to reintroduce certain serious elements of the older style while continuing other aspects of the new style. This stylistic evolution was hardly a 'crisis', therefore, but rather, as Larsen has pointed out, 'the breakthrough of the Classical style—the final synthesis'.[80] This synthesis occurred in major- as well as minor-key works, but it was the sombre chromaticisms and stormy character of the latter that appealed to romantic critics, and it is those works that continue to call forth a 'haze of adjectives'.

As mentioned in connection with the Symphony in D minor, K. 74c, the sounds of the minor-key symphonies of the early 1770s were not entirely new ones. These tempestuous effects had been invented in the opera houses to portray nature's storms as well as storms of human emotion. A thorough investigation of opere serie of the 1760s might reveal the musical sources of the so-called 'Sturm und Drang' symphonies of the 1770s.

Both the opening Allegro con brio and the closing Allegro of K. 173dB display, in addition to their often-mentioned stormy character, large-scale sonata form with both halves repeated plus a coda. The special sound of the symphony's outer movements is partly a result of four horns in place of the usual two, which imparts a certain solidity to the work's texture. Putting the two pairs of horns in different keys (G and B flat) gave Mozart a wider palette of pitches to exploit in writing his horn parts, enabling him to allow those primarily diatonic instruments to participate in some of the work's chromaticism. The first movement, which has recently acquired notoriety in the sound-track of the film *Amadeus*, exhibits the 'urgent tone of the repeated syncopated notes . . . the dramatic falling diminished seventh and the repeated thrusting phrases that follow. The increased force of the musical thinking is seen in the strong sense of harmonic direction, the taking up of melodic figuration by the bass instruments, and the echo sections, which are no longer merely decorative but add intensity'.[81]

The Andante in E flat major is also in sonata form with both halves repeated, but without coda. Here storminess gives way to other passions, portrayed by the appoggiaturas of longing and sadness. These are tossed back and forth between the muted violins and the obbligato bassoons, and also heard in the violas, cellos, and basses. (The obbligato bassoons appear only in the Andante and the Trio, the movements in which one pair of horns is silent. In the other movements they should double the bass-line.) An especially fine moment occurs eight bars into the recapitulation where, in a passage not present in the exposition, a rising sequence of sighs touches in rapid succession upon F, G, and C minor, and then A flat, E flat, and B flat major. Mozart had originally begun the Andante differently (Example

[80] J. P. Larsen, 'The Viennese Classical School: A Challenge to Musicology', *Current Musicology* (1969), ix. 105–12.
[81] S. Sadie, *The New Grove Mozart* (New York, 1983), 40.

Ex. 8.13 Symphony in G minor, K. 183 = 173dB, Andante, false start

8.13), but when he had progressed only two bars he must have decided that something was amiss (the halting quality of the repeated E flats?), and he started again with the same initial three-note motive carried through in a more convincing manner.

The Minuet's stern unisons and chromaticism contradict received ideas about the polite social graces of that dance, illustrating Kirnberger's remark that 'because minuets of this type are really not for dancing, composers have departed from the original conception'.[82] The four-bar phrases and rounded binary form are traditional, but the movement's demeanour is no longer that of the ballroom. This disparity between what is expected of a minuet and what Mozart wrote is emphasized in the G major Trio, written for *Harmonie*—that is, for the favourite Austrian wind-band consisting of pairs of oboes, horns and bassoons. Such groups (sometimes joined by a pair of clarinets or of English horns and occasionally reinforced by a contrabass viol, contrabassoon, trombone, or serpent) were much employed in and around Vienna to provide music for banquets, out-of-doors social occasions, evening serenades, and the like. Wind players provided Burney with dinner music during his stay at the Viennese *Gasthof* 'At the Sign of the Golden Ox',[83] and a decade later Wolfgang wrote a wind serenade, K. 375, and then was pleasantly surprised by a sextet of itinerant musicians playing it under his window on his name-day.[84] This Trio offers a breath of fresh air and relaxation, as it were, placing in sharp relief the sterner Minuet that flanks it.

That the first movement of K. 173dB is marked Allegro con brio and the last only Allegro may appear to contradict the principle that the tempos of last movements are generally faster than those of first movements. Here, however, the first movement includes semiquavers and important rhythmic, harmonic, or melodic events on all four crochets of the bar, whereas the most rapid notes in the Finale are quavers and important events tend to occur only twice per bar.[85]

[82] [Kirnberger], 'Menuet' (see n. 29 above).
[83] Burney, *Germany, the Netherlands, and United Provinces*, i. 330. Concerning the Viennese wind band, see *NMA*, vii/17/2. viii–ix (D. N. Leeson and N. Zaslaw).
[84] Letter of 3 Nov. 1781. *Briefe*, iii. 171–2; *Letters*, iii. 1155–6 (= ii. 776).
[85] See Mozart's letter of 20 Feb. 1784, which makes a similar point about the Adagio of a flute concerto composed and performed by one Johann Philipp Freyhold, which threw the accompanying musicians into confusion because, although it was notated in common time, Freyhold performed it *alla breve* (*Briefe*, iii. 301; *Letters*, iii. 1293 (= ii. 867)).

Landon has sugggested that this extraordinary work may have been modelled on, or inspired by, Joseph Haydn's equally extraordinary Symphony No. 39 of the late 1760s, which is also in G minor with four horns.[86] For a discussion of what music of Haydn's the Mozarts may have known in the 1770s, see above under K. 110.

Wolfgang asked Leopold to send him K. 173dB in his letter of 4 January 1783, but the set of parts he received, which passed from his widow to J. André (who listed it in as No. 279 of his 1841 catalogue) to C. A. André (who had it in 1860), has been lost. Other eighteenth-century sets of parts survive in Graz and Frankfurt. The copyist of the Frankfurt parts reduced the two viola parts to one, and the four horn parts to two, in an attempt to accommodate the work to the resources of an orchestra smaller than Salzburg's.[87]

Symphony in A minor, K. Anh. 220 = 16a

[Incipits 8.19]

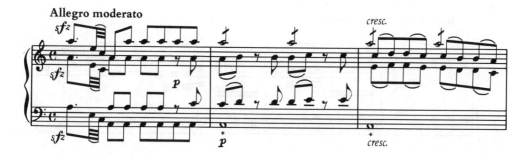

(133)

* The bass line in bars 2-3 of the first movement should probably continue as quavers:

[86] H. C. Robbins Landon, *Haydn: Chronicle and Works*, ii. 286, 390 ff.; iii. 506.
[87] Plath, 'Mozartiana in Fulda und Frankfurt', 362.

Andantino

(64)

Rondo. Allegro moderato

(133)

Instrumentation: strings, 2 oboes, 2 bassoons, 2 horns, [continuo]

Autograph: none

Principal source: eighteenth-century parts, formerly in the library of the Odense Byorkester, Denmark, now in the Odense University library

Facsimiles: *W. A. Mozart: Symphony K16a, 'Odense'* (Odense, 1984), 4, 20; J. P. Larsen and K. Wedin (eds.), *Die Sinfonie KV 16a "del Sigr. Mozart"* (Odense, 1987), cover

Editions: Bärenreiter, 1985 (ed. W. Plath); *NMA*, x/29, in preparation

Early in 1982 the municipal orchestra of Odense, Denmark, was preparing to move to new quarters. As part of the effort the orchestra's archivist-librarian, Gunnar Thygesen, re-examined a bundle of old music, which had been transferred to the orchestra in 1943 from the basement of the town hall, where it had lain for more than a century. In the bundle—which included symphonies by Gyrowetz, Joseph Haydn, Pleyel, Wranitzky, and Mozart—Thygesen found a set of parts for the lost A minor symphony listed in recent editions of the Köchel Catalogue as 16a. This collection of eighteenth-century music had belonged to the Odense Music Club (or collegium musicum), which, in the 1790s at the height of its activities, purchased an impressive repertory and, during the season, gave weekly concerts at Overgabe, a stately home.

The official announcement of the discovery in February 1983 was followed by a silence of about a year and a half, while it was determined who controlled the rights to the foundling symphony. During this 'blackout' musicians and scholars were unable to examine K. 16a, except for senior Danish musicologist Jens Peter Larsen, who had been called in to authenticate it. Agreement among the concerned parties reached, the work's première by the Odense Symphony Orchestra under its conductor Tamas Vetö took place on 9 December 1984. A colourful, Chagall-like painting by local artist Carl-Henning Pedersen entitled 'Mozart Odense Symphony' provided the cover for a handsome booklet as well as for a recording, which was simultaneously available in fifteen countries.[88] On the day following the première a conference was held so that experts could discuss the 'find'.[89] Coverage in the press, radio, and television included special television productions seen in western Europe and North America. Soon thereafter, K. 16a was published.[90]

With the excitement of the discovery, première, and publicity dying away, a more objective appraisal of the work may be possible, which will involve answering several questions: (1) How did this lost symphony come to be listed in the Köchel Catalogue? (2) What can be deduced about the provenance of the Odense manuscript? (3) Can the odds that a symphony like K. 16a is correctly

[88] Unicorn Kanchana DKP 9039.

[89] The proceedings are published as J. P. Larsen and K. Wedin (eds.), *Die Sinfonie KV 16a "del Sigr. Mozart": Bericht über das Symposium in Odense anlässlich der Erstaufführung des wiedergefundenen Werkes Dezember 1984* (Odense, 1987). The individual contributions to this volume will be found in the bibliography under the names of the following authors: G. Allroggen, E. Badura-Skoda, M. Flothuis, J. P. Larsen, W. Plath, S. Reventlow, A. Tyson, and K. Wedin.

[90] In 'The Mozart Miracle', an English-language production from Channel Four, London, and the Arts and Entertainment Network in the United States, the histories of Odense, of Mozart's youthful tours, and of the discovery of K. 16a were told; interviews with Larsen, Thygesen, Alan Tyson, Jan LaRue, Kamma Wedin (music librarian of Odense University) and others presented; and the première itself seen and heard. Information in this discussion of K. 16a whose source is not otherwise identified has been drawn from: the television broadcast; a radio interview with Alan Tyson, 'Music Now', BBC World Service, 22–3 Dec. 1984; a private discussion with Dr Tyson; a BBC news interview with Stanley Sadie, 9 Dec. 1984; the Odense booklet and accompanying press release; the recording cited in n. 88; and a description and critique of the Odense manuscript privately circulated by Jens Peter Larsen.

attributed be estimated? (4) What can be said about the work's musical style? (5) Might not *Leopold* Mozart be the symphony's author? (6) How should a work like K. 16a be listed in a new edition of the Köchel Catalogue?

The way in which a dozen lost symphonies listed in the Breitkopf & Härtel Manuscript Catalogue have been dealt with in the various editions of the Köchel Catalogue is discussed in Appendix D. In K^3 Einstein had some documentary evidence for dating three of the dozen; he was forced to date the other nine symphonies solely on stylistic grounds—a risky venture for an entire symphony, let alone for an incipit of a few bars of a violin part. He proposed that K. 16a came from Mozart's visit to London in 1764–5, placing it next to K. 16 in the chronology solely because 'the early date of composition is manifestly recognizable, even from the few bars preserved'. The question is: now that all of K. 16a is available and not just an incipit, can we do better than this?

    The title-page of the Odense manuscript of K. 16a (affixed to a basso part) is transcribed as Table 8.2. This set of parts originally consisted of nine in one or two hands, to which were added the usual *Dubletten* (two violins and basso) copied in two other hands. (Two additional violin parts once existed, their listing now crossed out on the title-page.) None of the hands belongs to Salzburg copyists

TABLE 8.2 Symphony in A minor, K. Anhang 220 = 16a: Diplomatic transcription of the title-page of the Odense manuscript

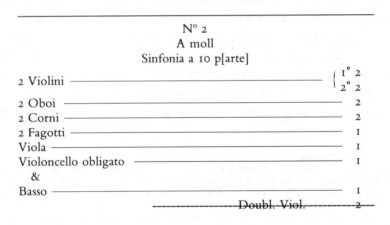

N° 2
A moll
Sinfonia a 10 p[arte]

2 Violini	1° 2 / 2° 2
2 Oboi	2
2 Corni	2
2 Fagotti	1
Viola	1
Violoncello obligato	1
&	
Basso	1
~~Doubl. Viol.~~	~~2~~

12 Part[e]

del
Sig^r Mozart
[ornamental device]
[incipit: 3 bars of violin 1]

associated with the Mozarts or their circle. A note on the title-page of the manuscript of 16a suggests that it was acquired by the Odense Music Club in 1793; but it was probably not newly copied then, for its watermark reads 'FIN DE / M. IOHANNO[T] / DANNON[AY] / 1779', with a countermark containing a cross, the monogram 'IHS' (for Jesus) and a flaming heart, all contained within a circle. *Dubletten* in the hand of a second copyist are on paper with the watermark 'HONIG', which is probably Dutch in origin although it was often forged. (The other 'Westphal' Mozart symphony manuscript extant in Odense (K. 203 = 189b) has this reversed: the principal copyist is the same as in the manuscript of K. 16a, but he appears on 'HONIG' paper while *Dubletten* in another hand are on 'IOHANNOT' paper.)[91]

Numbers added at the top and bottom of the title-page represent various hands cataloguing the symphony at one time or another: '46', '269', '19', and '7 A$\flat$', the last the indication by which the symphony was entered in the Club's ledger on a page dated 1797 (see n. 96 below).

A possible clue to the geographical origin of the manuscript (or at least of one of its copyists): one of the basso parts is labelled 'Passo'. Failure to distinguish between *p* and *b* is a characteristic of the German dialects spoken south of the so-called 'Benrath Line',[92] where, for example, one sometimes finds in documents Pach for Bach, Bixis for Pixis, Bachelbel for Pachelbel, and so on.

In the Breitkopf & Härtel Manuscript Catalogue, K. 16a is one of several works whose source is given as 'Westphal', that is, the Hamburg music dealer Johann Christoph Westphal.[93] And it had been suggested that Westphal was the source of the Odense copy of K. 16a, although no direct evidence was adduced to show that this was the case. It now seems probable that the Odense Music Club did obtain its copy of K. 16a from Westphal, for not only do vouchers show that the Club had

---

[91] This information about the copyists and watermarks of the Odense manuscript of K. 16a is from Larsen's private communication, Tyson's remarks during the television broadcast, and a private communication from him. The hands of the copyists associated with the Mozarts are fully explicated in Eisen, 'The Symphonies of Leopold Mozart'.

Annonay is a paper-making town about forty miles south of Lyons. See H. Gachet, 'Vieilles papeteries françaises: Les Papeteries d'Annonay. 1. Les Papeteries Johannot', *Courrier graphique* (1949), xiv/41. 27–34. If the distribution of Johannot's paper was similar to that of his Annonay rivals Vidalon and the Montgolfier brothers, then most of his paper was sold to Brittany and the regions of Orléans and Paris, and especially Paris; sales to other parts of France and foreign countries were rare (M.-H. Reynaud, *Les Moulins à papier d'Annonay à l'ère pré-industrielle: Les Montgolfier et Vidalon* (Lyons, 1981), 196–9). The date 1779, of course, constitutes only a *terminus a quo* for the copying of K. 16a.

[92] The Benrath Line 'begins in the West at Aachen [Aix-la-Chapelle], arches up above Cologne to the town of Benrath [on the Rhine], then—after dipping briefly to the south—runs east by northeast just below Düsseldorf, Kassel, Magdeburg, and Frankfurt an der Oder until it reaches Slavic linguistic territory' (J. T. Waterman, *A History of the German Language*, rev. edn. (Seattle, 1976), p. 54).

[93] 'Westphal' should not be confused with Johann Jakob Heinrich Westphal (Schwerin, 1756–1825), whose collection of C. P. E. Bach manuscripts, acquired by François Joseph Fétis, is now in Brussels. See M. Terry, 'C. P. E. Bach and J. J. H. Westphal: A Clarification', *Journal of the American Musicological Society* (1969), xxii. 106–15. Nor is it likely that Breitkopf & Härtel obtained their 'Westphal' manuscripts from Johann Christoph Westphal's son (Hamburg 1773–1828), who had the same name. After J. C. Westphal senior's death in 1797, Westphal junior did not carry on his father's business; the firm was dissolved, and the remaining stock auctioned off (Ernst Ludwig Gerber, *Neues historisch-biographisches Lexikon der Tonkünstler* (Leipzig, 1814), part 4, col. 559).

dealings with him,[94] but a recently-discovered document reveals that Westphal advertised K. 16a in the mid-1780s along with other Mozart symphonies.[95]

A register of the Odense Music Club's library drawn up in 1797 lists nine Mozart 'symphonies', including the overture to *Die Zauberflöte* (Table 8.3, col. 1).[96] Printed editions are identified there by opus number (and, in one instance, place of publication); manuscript copies, by number and key. All of the symphonies listed in the register were advertised by Westphal during the period 1785–94 (Table 8.3, cols. 1 and 2). The printed editions can be identified: two symphonies drawn from orchestral serenades, K. 320 ('Posthorn') and 250 = 248b, both published by André in 1792 as opp. 22 and 25, respectively; K. 425 ('Linz'), published by André in 1793 as op. 34; and the overture to *La clemenza di Tito*, published by André in 1795 as op. 49.[97]

Two of the manuscript copies can be identified with certainty: the symphony '7' in A minor is K. 16a, and the 'Sinfonie a 11. D dur No. 1' is K. 203 = 189b, for the title-page of the copy of this work still extant in Odense carries both notations: 'N: 1' and 'a 11. pp:'. The identities of the other manuscript copies, which can only be guessed at by comparing the Club's register with the rather fuller information given in the Westphal catalogues, are not so easily determined, partly because both register and catalogues are non-thematic, partly because it would be naïve to assume that the catalogues are free of typographical errors.[98] Moreover, various eighteenth-century manuscript copies of a single symphony often differ with regard to both scoring and the number of parts for identical scorings.[99]

[94] The earliest document to show that the Odense Music Club had dealings with Westphal is a voucher of November 1791 for symphonies by Mozart, Pleyel, Dittersdorf, and Wranitzky, among other works. I am indebted to Kamma Wedin of the Odense Universitetsbibliotek for a copy of this voucher, photocopies of the title-pages of the Mozart symphonies still extant in Odense, and a copy of the paper she read at the Odense symposium prior to its publication.

[95] *1786 Julius. / Verzeichniss / einiger neuen Werke, welche / in der musicalischen Niederlage / bey / Johann Christoph Westphal & Comp. / in Hamburg angekommen sind*, 12: 'Geschriebene Musicalien . . . Sinfonien . . . Mozart, 1 ditto [= Sinfonie] a 10. A moll. N[eu].' Copies of Westphal's catalogues are extant in Brussels, Bibliothèque royale, Fonds Fétis 5205; Vienna, Gesellschaft der Musikfreunde, Sign. 205/3 and Sign. 559/8. Both runs are incomplete. I owe the information about Westphal's catalogues to Cliff Eisen.

[96] A facsimile of this page from the Club register is published in the Odense booklet (see p. 266 above) and in K. Wedin, 'The Discovery of the Copy of K. 16a and the Orchestral Music by Mozart owned by the Odense Club', in J. P. Larsen and K. Wedin (eds.), *Die Sinfonie KV16a*, 9–24.

[97] Wolfgang Matthäus, *Johann André Musikverlag zu Offenbach am Main: Verlagsgeschichte und Bibliographie 1772–1800* (Tutzing, 1973), 235, 248, 290 (see also below, Table 11.2). 'Opus 49 Berlin' may be the overture to *La clemenza di Tito*, published as Op. 49 not by Hummel in Berlin but by André in Offenbach, 1795. There is, apparently, no known Hummel edition of a Mozart 'Opus 49' or of the overture to *Tito*. Could the notation 'Berlin' in the Odense Music Club register opposite 'Opus 49' be a mistake for 'Offenbach,' or could the copy sold by Westphal have been obtained not from André, but from Hummel in Berlin, who would have pasted his own label over André's imprint?

[98] Gerber (see n. 93 above) describes Westphal's 1782 catalogue as 'voll Fehler'.

[99] K. 250 = 248b, a symphony owned by the Odense Club in an engraved edition, is a case in point. The authentic set of parts in Berlin, manuscript copies in Florence and Prague, and André's edition all consist of twelve parts (vn. I, vn. II, va., vc., ob. I, ob. II, bn., hn. I, hn. II, tpt. I, tpt. II, and timp.). An early nineteenth-century manuscript in Göttweig has fourteen parts (va. I and II, bn. I and II), while a copy in the Nationalbibliothek, Vienna, probably from the late eighteenth century, has thirteen parts (va. I and II but bassoons together), as do copies in the Sächsischen Landesbibliothek, Dresden (but one viola part and two for bassoons) and the Landeskonservatorium, Graz (with 'viole' instead of 'viola'). A number of Mozart's symphonies survive in various sources with and without timpani parts.

TABLE 8.3 Dissemination of music attributed to 'Mozart' in the Westphal catalogues and advertisements

Odense 1797	Westphal	Traeg/Lausch	Breitkopf/Westphal	Work
N: 1 D♯	1785 Sinfonie a 11. D dur No. 1	Feb./Mar. 1785		K. 203 = 189b (symphony)
—	Sinfonie a 13. D dur No. 2	3 Sinfonien	23. Westphal No. 2	K. 320 (symphony)
—	Sinfonie a 14. D dur No. 3			*
—	1785 (July) Sinfonie a 6. D dur No. 4	—	61. Westphal No. 4	K. Ash. C 11.06
N: 7 A♭	1786 (July) Sinfonie a 10. A moll	Apr. 1785	62. Westphal	K. 16a
—	Sinfonie a 14. C dur	2 Neue Sinfonie in C und D		†
—	Sinfonie a 13. D dur No. 4			*
—	Divertimento a 6. F dur	Aug./Sept. 1785 Cassazio [à 6] in F		K. 247
—	6 Quatuor	—		K. 387, 421, 428, 458, 464, 465 ('Haydn')
—	Quatuor G moll	Mar. 1785 Quartetto		K. 478
—	Trio Es dur	Sept. 1785 Trio		?K. 481 (trio = K^6 Anh. B, pp. 788–9)
N: 5 D♯	1787 (Mar.) Sinfonie a 13. D dur No. 5	—	63. Westphal	*
—	1793 (Mar.) Sinfonie a 9. F dur	—		K. Anh. C 11.08
N: 4 C♯	1793 (Mar.) Sinfonie a 15. C dur No. 4	—		?K. 551
Zauberflöte	1793 (Mar.)	—		K. 620 (overture)
Opus 25	1793 (July)	—		K. 250 = 248b (symphony)
Opus 34	1794 (Feb.)	—		K. 425
Opus 22	1794 (Sept.)	—		K. 320 (symphony)
Opus 49	1795 (Sept.)	—		K. 621 (overture)

* Probably one of the following symphonies: K.204 = 213a, 250 = 248b, 385.
† Probably one of the following symphonies: K.200 = 173e = 189k, 338, 425.

One may nevertheless hazard some guesses as to which other Mozart symphonies were once owned by the Odense Music Club. The symphony '4' in C major is almost certainly the 'Jupiter', K. 551, the only one of Mozart's C major trumpet and kettledrums symphonies likely to have circulated in as many as 15 parts (and it is probably no accident that this symphony was first advertised by Westphal only sometime later than his other Mozart symphonies, in March 1793, the same year the work was first published by André). Candidates for the symphony *à 13* include K. 204 = 213a (if it had kettledrums), K. 250 = 248b (unlikely since the Club owned an engraved edition), and K. 385 (published by Artaria in the version without flutes and clarinets and which might, therefore, have circulated in only thirteen parts). And the Club owned a printed edition of K. 425. Even if each of the symphonies once owned by the Odense Music Club cannot be identified with certainty, it is probable, given the exact correspondences between the Club's register and Westphal's catalogues (extending even to distinctively identified manuscript copies) that all of them were purchased from Westphal.

Westphal's advertisements of printed editions show that he had good connections with publishers in Berlin and Amsterdam, Leipzig, Offenbach, London, Paris, and Vienna. He may also have had similarly good connections with the two principal Viennese dealers in musical manuscripts, Traeg and Lausch. Significant parallels between Traeg's and Lausch's 1785 advertisements for manuscript copies of Mozart's works and Westphal's catalogues for 1785 and 1786 suggest that this was probably the case (Table 8.3, cols. 2 and 3). If these correspondences are more than coincidental, then K. 203 = 189b and 320 must have been among the three Mozart symphonies offered for sale in Vienna on 16 February 1785, for it is fairly certain from a comparison of Westphal's catalogues with the Breitkopf & Härtel Manuscript Catalogue (Table 8.3, cols. 2 and 4) that K. 203 = 189b and 320 were among the three symphonies offered by Westphal in his 1785 catalogue. In fact, all three of the works advertised by Traeg are likely to have been D major symphonies; Deutsch's suggestion that he offered for sale K. 319, 338, and 385 is therefore untenable.[100]

The other Mozart symphonies advertised by Westphal in 1785, 1786, and 1787 (a symphony *à 6* in D, 'No. 4'; K. 16a; and a symphony *à 9* including obbligato bassoon) were not offered for sale in Vienna at this time, and they seem, therefore, to have a different provenance. The comparison of Westphal's catalogues with the Breitkopf & Härtel Manuscript Catalogue suggests that these three works may be

---

[100] Deutsch, 217 (= 237). For Traeg, see A. Weinmann, *Johann Traeg: Die Musikalienverzeichnisse von 1799 und 1804* (Beiträge zur Geschichte des alt-wiener Musikverlages, ii/17) (Vienna, 1973); idem, *Die Anzeigen des Kopiaturbetriebes Johann Traeg in der wiener Zeitung zwischen 1782 und 1805* (Weiner Archivstudien, vi) (Vienna, 1981); for Laurenz Lausch, see idem, *Wiener Musikverlag 'am Rande'* (Beiträge zur Geschichte des alt-wiener Musikverlages, ii/13) (Vienna, 1970), p. 39.

uniquely 'Westphal' symphonies, that is, works not available from other dealers at the time.[101]

Numbers 61 to 64 in the Breitkopf & Härtel Manuscript Catalogue form a group of four symphonies acquired by Breitkopf from Westphal. But the last of these, the unquestionably authentic K. 318 of 1779, is in odd company, for the remaining three are the A minor symphony under discussion, the doubtful symphony K. Anh. C 11.08 (known only by its incipit in the Breitkopf & Härtel Manuscript Catalogue), and the spurious symphony K. Anh. C 11.06, a work in D major *à 6* by Leopold Mozart.[102]

The doubtful symphony K. Anh. C 11.08 was advertised by Westphal in 1787 as 'I [Sinfonie] à 9, mit obl. Fagott, F dur', which can describe no other symphony attributed to Mozart.[103] K. Anh. C 11.06, listed in the Breitkopf & Härtel Manuscript Catalogue as 'Westphal No. 4', must be the symphony offered in Westphal's catalogue of July 1785 as 'Mozart, 1 dito [= Sinfonie] 6 D No. 4'.[104]

Hence, it seems almost certain that, in addition to authentic symphonies of Mozart obtained from Vienna, Westphal also handled a group of works, including at least one spurious symphony, obtained from somewhere else. K. 16a formed part of the latter group.

The best hypothesis, then, is that the Odense Music Club purchased nine 'Mozart' symphonies from Westphal, including K. 16a. The material handled by Westphal came from various sources, some more reliable than others. Since the provenance of K. 16a, Anh. C 11.06, and C 11.08 was probably not Vienna, and since the group includes a demonstrably spurious symphony, we must tentatively regard the provenance of all three works with suspicion. The sudden appearance in 1786 of an otherwise unknown Mozart symphony (K. 16a) in what is probably a non-authentic source is highly problematic.

One should not quit this discussion without pointing out a problem with the hypothesis that Westphal was the source of the Odense copy. When firms like Westphal, Breitkopf, Lausch, or Traeg advertised music in manuscript, they presumably had master copies from which other copies were made on demand; in Westphal's case this practice is documented by a letter of March 1789 from the firm

---

[101] Both K. 185 = 167a and 202 = 186b could be symphonies *à 11*, if they circulated with kettledrum parts; K. 181 = 162b, although not scored for kettledrum in the autograph (or in authentic parts from Mozart's estate), is none the less listed in the Breitkopf & Härtel Manuscript Catalogue as having them. See also Table 11.3.

[102] In addition, the Breitkopf & Härtel Manuscript Catalogue lists the following as having been obtained from Westphal: K. 207, 368, 375 (arr. string quintet), 423, 499, 505, 521, 537, 546, and 588/14 and 588/25. For a possible source of some of Westphal's offerings, see the discussion in ch. 11 of Mozart's 1789 visit to Berlin.

[103] This, incidentally, supplies some information about the scoring of K. Anhang C 11.08, which is otherwise unknown.

[104] The only extant copy (partly authentic) of Leopold Mozart's symphony (Universitätsbibliothek, Augsburg (Fürstlich Oettingen-Wallerstein'sche Bibliothek 4° 536)) probably dates from no later than 1751. A lost copy with expended instrumentation is listed in the Sigmaringen catalogue of 1766, p. 91: 'Mozart. *Synfonia* in D / a. 2. VV. 2. Corn. / 2. Clarinj. Tymp. / Viola. et Basso.' See Eisen, 'The Symphonies of Leopold Mozart', 265.

to J. H. Westphal in Schwerin.[105] Why, then, would a copy of a symphony acquired in the 1790s from a Hamburg firm have had a French watermark dated 1779? Until other 'Westphal' copies are identified and evaluated, this question is likely to go unanswered.

Anyone who has never studied sources of eighteenth-century symphonies might well be surprised by the extent of the conflicting attributions. In Jan LaRue's Union Thematic Catalogue of Eighteenth-Century Symphonies, which contains the incipits of more than 16,000 symphonies drawn from all known prints and manuscripts, 7 per cent of symphonies are attributed to two or more composers.[106] But if one wishes to estimate the chances that a given work was misattributed, 7 per cent is too low, because, by that way of reckoning, works surviving in only a single source are not candidates for misattribution.[107]

Since some misattributed works may survive in (for instance) ten correctly labelled sources and one incorrectly labelled, but others just the reverse, the 7 per cent figure, which refers to *works* rather than to *sources*, does not permit an estimate of the chances of any given source's having a correct attribution. A tabulation of attributions of symphonies to some composers for whom detailed catalogues exist (Table 8.4) suggests a higher percentage of misattributed *works* at least for well-known composers, but this still does not provide an estimate of the percentage of misattributed *sources*. A meaningful estimate of the likelihood that the Odense manuscript is correctly attributed would require knowledge of the percentage of non-authentic copies of symphonies that are incorrectly attributed. But even without that information we can see that misattributions are fairly common and that it would be no very surprising thing if future research revealed the Odense manuscript to be incorrectly ascribed.

The Symphony in A minor, K. 16a, is in three movements: an Allegro moderato in common time and sonata form without repeats; an A major Andantino in $\frac{2}{4}$ in sonatina form with both sections repeated; and a rondo-finale in $\frac{2}{4}$, also Allegro moderato. The first movement is in the so-called 'Sturm und Drang' style of the late 1760s and early 1770s,[108] the Andantino in the pastoral vein of many of

---

[105] M. Terry, 'C. P. E. Bach and J. J. H. Westphal', 111.

[106] J. LaRue, 'Symphony' *The New Grove*, xviii. 439, and in the Odense television interview. The Union Catalogue is an unpublished card file housed at New York University, an index to which has been published as *A Catalogue of 18th-Century Symphonies, Volume I: Thematic Identifier* (Bloomington, 1988).

[107] K. 16a is precisely such a work, surviving in a single source only. Although the Odense manuscript of K. 16a, the Breitkopf & Härtel Manuscript Catalogue, and Westphal's advertisement all attribute K. 16a to 'Mozart', these are not three independent sources but rather three manifestations of the proliferation of a single source once owned by Westphal. Yet Robert Dearling, in the sleeve notes to Unicorn-Kanchana DKP 9039, declares in favour of its assignment to W. A. Mozart, on the grounds of lack of conflicting attribution in his own 'thematic finder (a card index of some 45,000 eighteenth-century works filed in thematic order)'.

[108] See n. 76 above.

TABLE 8.4 Attribution of symphonies to eight composers*

Composer	Genuine		Questionable		Spurious		Total	Source
	No.	%	No.	%	No.	%	No.	
J. C. Bach	55	83	11	17%			66	Terry-Landon
Boccherini	28	90	2	6	1	4	31	Gérard
Dittersdorf	114	56	36	18	52	26	202	Grave
Gossec	34	92	3	8%			37	Brook
J. Haydn	106	40	1	0	159	60	266	Hoboken
L. Mozart	48	71	20	29	0	0	68	Eisen
W. A. Mozart	57	58	16	16	25	26	98	K^6-Zaslaw
J. Stamitz	56	47	31	26	31	26	118	Wolf
AVERAGE %		67		14		19		

* These precise-looking figures must be taken as mere approximations, since the criteria for the categories 'genuine', 'questionable', and 'spurious' vary from catalogue to catalogue, and symphonies shift status as new evidence emerges.

Mozart's symphony andantes of the period,[109] and the Finale occasionally in the style then called 'alla Turca'.[110] Thus, in its general style and morphology the work is similar to several of Mozart's early symphonies. Working at a more detailed level, Larsen has pointed to some melodic and formal similarities between K. 16a and Mozart's symphonies K. 45a (1766), 43, 45, 48 (1767–8), and 134 (1772). His conclusion: if K. 16a is by Wolfgang Mozart, it was most likely composed in the late 1760s or early 1770s, at a time when interest in minor keys and stormy affect in symphonies was strong.

But there are also some features of K. 16a that make it quite unlike Mozart's other early symphonies:

¶The exposition of the first movement ends in F instead of C, that is, in the submediant instead of the relative major, which is the invariable procedure in Mozart's minor-key sonata-form movements that modulate to a major key—for instance, in his three authentic minor-key symphonies K. 118 = 74c, 183 = 173dB, and 550.

¶The motivic contents of the first movement are derived from the opening three bars, a parsimony of means that Joseph Haydn usually favoured, whereas Mozart liked stringing together a variety of ideas.[111]

¶All three movements of K. 16a are in A major or minor; Mozart always preferred a new tonal centre for his symphony andantes.

¶Both first and last movements of K. 16a are Allegro moderato; Mozart's pattern is for the finale to be faster than the first movement, often Allegro molto, Molto allegro, or Presto, except when both movements are simply the generic 'Allegro', in which case a 'shorter' metre—$\frac{2}{4}$, $\frac{3}{8}$, $\frac{6}{8}$, or $\frac{12}{8}$—makes the finale faster than the common time or $\frac{3}{4}$ first movement.[112] K. 16a has the correct sequence of metres (₵ to $\frac{2}{4}$), but in Mozart's early symphonies Allegro moderato is uncommon and used only for first movements, never for finales.[113]

¶The cellos and double basses of K. 16a are divisi in the first and third movements.[114] There are brief passages in K.19 and 73, but Mozart first system-

---

[109] This connection is particularly clear in the Andantes of the symphonies K. 120 = 111a and 102 = 213c, drawn from pastorale numbers in Mozart's early operas.

As Daniel Heartz kindly points out (personal communication), Frantisek Xaver Dušek's lost Concertino for harpsichord, flute, violin, cello, and basso begins with more or less the same melody (for two bars) as the Andante of K. 16a, and is in the same key (Supplement IX (1774) of the Breitkopf Thematic Catalogue (= B. S. Brook (ed.), *The Breitkopf Thematic Catalogue* (New York, 1966), col. 5521)). See the discussion of this theme-type in connection with K. 134, at n. 51 above.

[110] Cf. the minor section of the rondo-finale of the symphony K. 74. The nature of the 'Turkish' music is discussed by D. Bartha, 'Mozart et le folklore musical de l'Europe centrale,' in A. Verchaly (ed.), *Les Influences étrangères dans l'œuvre de W. A. Mozart* (Paris, 1958), 157–81; and K. Reinhard, 'Mozarts Rezeption türkischer Musik', in H. Kühn and P. Nitsche (eds.), *Bericht über den internationalen Musikwissenschaft Kongress Berlin 1974* (Kassel, 1980), 518–23.

[111] J. P. Larsen, 'The Viennese Classical School: A Challenge to Musicology', *Current Musicology* (1969), ix, 105–12, esp. 110. Also *Studia Musicologica* (1967), ix, 115 ff.

[112] See the discussion of tempo in ch. 12.

[113] e.g., K. 114, 141a.

[114] Movement I, bars 19–20, 92–4; III, 24–8, 32–40, 48–62, 64–80, 88–92, 102–5, 112–20.

atically used bass-line divisi in a symphony only in 1779 (K. 318); he continued to use it thereafter, although not to the extent found in K. 16a. In K. 16a the double-basses rest in the kind of passage where Mozart often had the so-called *bassetto*, a texture in which all regular bass-line instruments rest and violas provide the sounding bass.

¶The 'violoncello obbligato' on the title-page of K. 16a would have been alien to Mozart, who to the end of his life used the designation 'Basso' for the lowest line of his symphonies.[115]

¶K. 16a uses some indications not part of Mozart's symphonic notation—'mancando' and 'smorzando' in the Andantino—and the rarely used *ff* in the outer movements.[116]

¶The horn writing of K. 16a is conservative in the number of different pitches, rhythms, and spacings employed. The first of these can be seen in Example 8.14a, which compares the horn pitches used in K. 16a with those in two of Mozart's very early symphonies, in his earliest minor-key symphony, and in his earliest A major symphony. The idiomatic 'horn fifth' sonorities (Example 8.14b), which Mozart used regularly in his symphonies, are entirely absent from K. 16a, because the instruments' fifth and eleventh partials are systematically avoided.

Ex. 8.14 Writing for valveless horns

(a) Pitches used in one doubtful and four genuine symphonies

Symphony in A minor, K. Anh. 220 = 16a

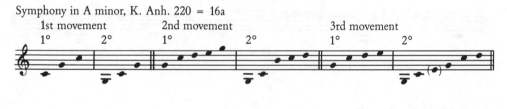

Symphony in F major, K. Anh. 223 = 19a (England or Holland, 1765)

[115] For Mozart's bass-line terminology, see J. Webster, 'The Scoring of Mozart's Chamber Music for Strings', in A. Atlas (ed.), *Music in the Classic Period: Essays in Honor of Barry S. Brook* (New York, 1985), 259–96.

[116] Exceptionally, however, *ff* does occur in the (fully authentic) version of K. 45a from The Hague (1766), first movement, bar 57, concertmaster's part only; in the first movement of K. 22 from the previous year, concertmaster's part only, bar 14; in K. 134, first movement, bars 167 ff.; and in K. 203, Andante, bar 32.

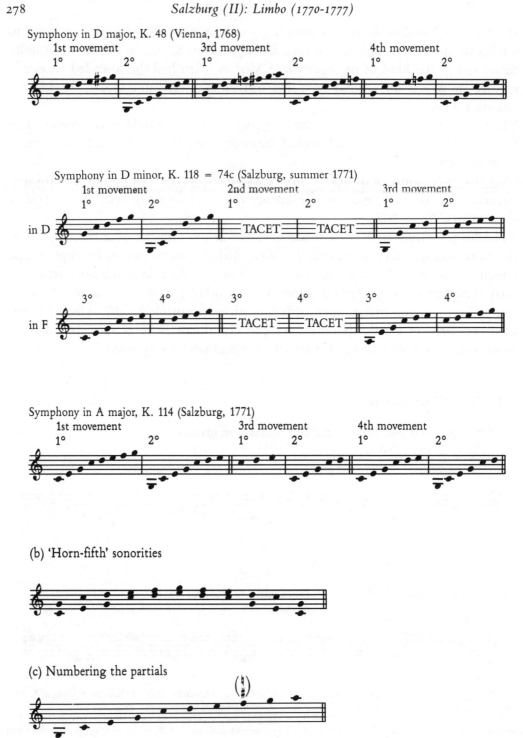

Symphony in D major, K. 48 (Vienna, 1768)

Symphony in D minor, K. 118 = 74c (Salzburg, summer 1771)

Symphony in A major, K. 114 (Salzburg, 1771)

(b) 'Horn-fifth' sonorities

(c) Numbering the partials

At this point any reader unfamiliar with the hidden assumptions of Mozart scholarship could be forgiven if he feels inclined to cry out: 'Why shouldn't the "Signor Mozart" of K. 16a have been Leopold, who was a prolific composer of symphonies?' A reasonable question, to be sure, but one that flies in the face of well-established prejudices. (It also flies in the face of a form of mania called *Entdeckungsfreude*—the joy of discovery; news of the discovery of a lost symphony by *Leopold* Mozart will not, after all, appear on the front page—or any other page—of *The New York Times*.[117])

Most writings about Mozart *père* take it as given that he was a poor composer, that his style never 'developed' beyond that of the 1740s and 1750s, and that he stopped composing to devote himself to his son's education and career. This is not the place for a detailed refutation of these long-held prejudices, which have in any case finally begun to be questioned,[118] but perhaps they may be addressed briefly. Leopold Mozart went on extended tours of Europe with his son and, along with him, learned the latest styles. His music, like that of many skilled, second-rank composers, is inconsistent in quality, but his best works have genuine artistic merit, are well made, and several, attributed to his son, fooled the experts for many years. For instance, his symphony, incorrectly claimed for Wolfgang as the 'Neue Lambach' symphony, probably dates from the 1760s and is in a 'modern' style.[119] The idea that Leopold stopped composing perhaps derives from two documents: the first is a remark in a letter of 4 September 1776 to Padre Martini, written by Leopold but signed by Wolfgang, that Leopold 'no longer puts his whole heart into his work, but has taken up literature, which was always a favorite study of his'.[120] This letter does not state that Leopold had stopped composing and would never compose again, but rather that, because of poor treatment by his employer, he was devoting less time to his work; in general, the remark represented news from the interval since the Mozarts had last communicated with Martini in January 1771, and in particular, since the installation of the new Archbishop of Salzburg in April 1772. The second document is a reminiscence of Mozart's sister Marianne von Berchtold ('Nannerl'), who in 1792 wrote of their father that 'he entirely gave up his violin-instruction and his composing so as to devote all the time remaining

---

[117] *The New York Times* (14 Feb. 1981): rediscovery of K. Anh. 223 = 19a; ibid. (5 Feb. 1983): rediscovery of K. Anh. 220 = 16a.

[118] W. Plath, 'Zur Echtheitsfrage bei Mozart', *Mozart-Jahrbuch* (1971–2), 19–36; *idem*, 'Mozart, Leopold', *The New Grove*, xii. 676–7; E. Ripin in The John F. Kennedy Center for the Performing Arts—American Musicological Society, *A Mozart Festival-Conference* (Washington, DC, 1974), [5]; G. Allroggen, 'Zur Frage der Echtheit der Sinfonie KV Anh. 216 = 74g', in F. Lippmann (ed.), *Colloquium 'Mozart und Italien' (Rom 1974)* = *Analecta musicologica* (1978), xviii, 237–45, repr. in G. Croll (ed.), *Wolfgang Amadeus Mozart* (Darmstadt, 1977), 462–73; C. Eisen, 'Introduction', *Leopold Mozart: Three Symphonies* (The Symphony: 1720–1840, B/vii) (New York, 1984), lxxviii; and especially *idem*, 'The Symphonies of Leopold Mozart' and summarized in *idem*, 'The Symphonies of Leopold Mozart: their Chronology, Style, and Importance for the Study of Mozart's Early Symphonies', *Mozart-Jahrbuch* (1987–8), 181–93.

[119] This symphony is published and recorded under Wolfgang's name: see ch. 6, n. 7.

[120] *Briefe*, i. 532; *Letters*, i. 386 (= i. 266).

to him after his princely duties to the education of his children'.[121] But it can be shown that this statement is not literally true: there were at least some pupils and at least some compositions during and after the time Leopold was educating his children.

K. 16a fits Leopold's style of the 1760s no better than it fits his son's. Some of the objections—the lack of melodic and motivic variety, the tempo indication Allegro moderato for the Finale,[122] the divisi cellos and double-basses, and the conservative writing for the horns—are the same. Moreover, the relative weight of the first and second groups in the opening movement, the elision of the exposition and development, the omission of repeat signs, and the opening of the development with material from the second group, are all foreign to his style. The last movement of K. 16a, a rondo with variations, has no parallel in Leopold's symphonies.[123] And not one of the symphonies attributed to him is in a minor key.

Some features of K. 16a do have parallels in Leopold Mozart's earlier works: the dynamic signs $f\!f$ and pp (though never *mancando* or *smorzando*) occur in authentic sets of parts to three symphonies (Eisen *D9, *D11, and *G7), while slow movements and trios of minuets in the tonic major or minor can be found in three others (*D6, *D9, and *G5). Lack of tonal variety is, in any case, not uncommon in mid-century symphonies such as these, and hardly constitutes a distinguishing characteristic.

Since the Odense manuscript attributes K. 16a simply to 'Signor Mozart', one should not entirely overlook a third Signor Mozart composing in the 1770s: the unrelated and obscure Philip Kajatan.[124]

As has been suggested more than once in the course of this study, the way in which works of uncertain provenance are dealt with in K^6 is unsatisfactory. Questionable and doubtful symphonies, for instance, are found in the main chronology as well as in Appendix C 11, where they are mixed indiscriminately with spurious symphonies. The editors of any new edition of the Köchel Catalogue should take greater pains to clarify the status of every problematic work. As for K. 16a, it belongs in an appendix reserved for doubtful works, for although the specialists mentioned in this essay are nearly unanimous in their scepticism about Mozart's authorship of K.

---

[121] Deutsch, 398 (= 454).

[122] I owe the stylistic information about Leopold Mozart's symphonies to Cliff Eisen. (Eisen's numbering system for Leopold's symphonies prefixes an asterisk for unquestionably genuine works, nothing for probably genuine works, and a question mark for works of uncertain authenticity.) Exceptionally among authentic symphonies by Leopold Mozart, the $\frac{3}{8}$ Finale of Seiffert 3/18 = *New Grove* F1 = Eisen *F1, a 'Sinfonia di [*sic*] Camera' for two violas, two cellos, bassoon, and violone, is marked Allegro moderato.

[123] The last movement of K. Anh. C 11.09 is also a curious rondo, but the work is questionable as a 'Mozart' symphony— either Leopold or Wolfgang—and cannot be used here as evidence in a stylistic investigation.

[124] For Philip Kajatan (or 'Gajatan') Mozart, see K. Pfannhauser, 'Zu Mozarts Kirchenmusiken von 1768', *Mozart-Jahrbuch* (1954), 150–76, here 155–6.

16a,[125] and strong circumstantial and stylistic evidence suggests that it is spurious, that cannot yet be proven.

It would be lovely to be able to conclude by announcing the composer of the Symphony in A minor, K. 16a, but this is not yet possible. Perhaps it will be only a matter of time until an authentic source for the work is discovered, solving the mystery.[126] In the meanwhile, however, the best that can be stated is that K. 16a most likely has nothing to do with Wolfgang or Leopold Mozart. It is discussed at such length in order to debunk claims recently made for it in the press and electronic media by musicians and scholars who ought to know better. It is placed in this chapter to associate it with the discussion of minor-key symphonies evoked by Wolfgang's G minor symphony, K. 183 = 173dB.

Whatever the dangers of succumbing to *Entdeckungsfreude* may be, grounds for cautiously continuing to search for lost symphonies by Wolfgang do exist. The thirteen symphonies of Leopold's 'List', discussed at the end of Chapter 5, have still not been satisfactorily identified. The six incipits, K. 19b, 66c–e, Anh. C 11.07, and Anh. C 11.08 (Example 5.7) await the kind of rebirth granted K. 16a in Odense. The basis for the 1789 Leipzig anecdote about a C major symphony with a $\frac{6}{8}$ finale containing hemiola cross-rhythms (see Chapter 11) has not been determined. And, finally, there is Mozart's wife Constanze's claim after his death that 'one original symphony by Mozart . . . is said to be in the possession of Mr Stoll, choirmaster at Baden, not far from Vienna. The Grand Duke of Tuscany [Ferdinand III] . . . is said to possess two symphonies by Mozart that are quite unknown.'[127]

Symphony in A major, K. 201 = 186a

[Incipits 8.20]

---

[125] In addition to those already mentioned, the television broadcast as seen in Britain contained extremely sceptical interviews with Wolfgang Rehm and Wolfgang Plath, leaders of the *Neue Mozart-Ausgabe*, which were cut in the American broadcast.

[126] In the absence of further evidence, stylistic intuitions on the part of specialists may provide preliminary guidance about which haystacks to search in for this particular needle. Daniel Heartz finds the type of rondo of the Finale of K. 16a typically French; this suggests the possibility of a French composer, or a German working in France or at one of the French-influenced German courts, for instance Berlin. I am reminded of the music of two composers I think of as more talented for dramatic music than for abstract instrumental music: Georg Benda and Josef Martin Kraus. Stanley Sadie finds K. 16a a characteristic north German symphony. These guesses are reported here with all due hesitation, in hope of encouraging further discussion and investigation.

[127] Letter of 31 May 1800. *Briefe*, iv. 355; *Letters*, iii. 1477.

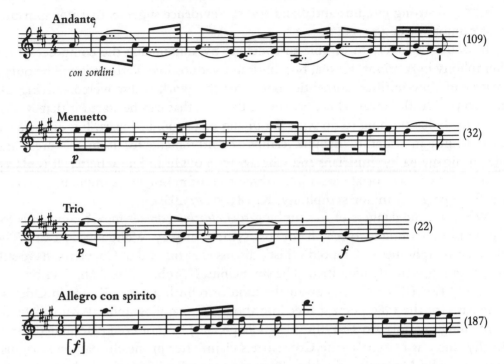

Instrumentation: strings, 2 oboes, 2 horns, [bassoon, continuo]
Autograph: Pierpont Morgan Library, New York
Principal source: manuscript parts with autograph corrections from Mozart's estate, lost? (owned by C. A. André in April 1860)
Facsimile: *NMA*, iv/11/5. xi
Editions: *GA*, xxi. 117–40 (= Serie 8, No. 29); *NMA*, iv/11/5. 1–25

  Much of what was stated about K. 183 = 173dB could be repeated about this work, including (despite its major key) the agitated and serious character of the first and last movements, the use of sonata form in three of the four movements, the strongly contrasted character of the Andante (in this case perhaps noble serenity rather than longing), the symphonic rather than dance quality of the minuet, and the basing of the opening of the Finale on a transformation of the opening of the first movement. The thoroughgoing excellence of this symphony has long been recognized; it and K. 183 = 173dB are the earliest of Mozart's symphonies in the repertories of major orchestras.

  The first movement begins piano, without the more usual loud chords or fanfare. The opening theme consists of an octave drop (which reappears at the beginning of the Finale) and a group of forward-moving quavers leading to a second octave drop, and so on in a rising sequence, the whole then repeated an octave higher, tutti, and in canon between the violins and the lower strings. Several subjects of contrasted character appear in the dominant, leading to a closing section with repeated notes and arpeggios. The compact development section, bustling with scalewise passages, repeated notes, modulations and syncopations, leads to a literal recapitulation. Both sections are repeated, and the movement is brought to its jubilant close by a coda based upon the opening idea heard in canon.

The Andante and Minuet have in common the prominent use of dotted and double-dotted rhythms, characteristic of marches and of the slow sections of French *ouvertures* and considered to convey stateliness, nobility, and even godliness.[128] The Andante, another with muted strings, is perhaps the most eloquent of the several that Mozart wrote in this vein. The energy of the outer movements spills over into the Minuet, which seems presided over more by the spirit of Mars than by that of Terpsichore.

Despite its fully-worked-out sonata form, including a development section that Einstein described as 'the richest and most dramatic Mozart had written up to this time',[129] the Finale has the character of a *chasse*, with its mandatory repeated notes and other hunting-horn calls. At the ends of the exposition, development, recapitulation, and coda, Mozart gave the violins a rapid ascending scale: clear aural signposts to articulate the movement's formal structure. In this symphony Mozart seems to have achieved a successful equilibrium between the lyrical elements and the abstract, instrumental ones.

Erich Leinsdorf has raised a question about notational inconsistencies found in the autograph of K. 201:

The bass note in bar 36 [Example 8.15a] must be moved from the third to the fourth quarter. The correct version occurs 100 bars later [Example 8.15b]. It may be asked how we can be sure that bar 36 is in error and not bar 142. The answer is that if the bass note is played on the third quarter, the resulting interval is a tritone, a most unlikely occurrence even in Mozart's most daring moments. On encountering a Mozart symphony in which only one detail amid an otherwise identical pattern of recapitulation is different, it is not only permissible but mandatory to make the necessary adjustment.[130]

But this can be argued other ways. Given the well-documented situation that symphonies were usually performed with but a single rehearsal (see Chapter 12), most of the small and not-so-small differences between expositions and recapitula-

---

[128] U. Kirkendale, 'The King of Heaven and the King of France', unpubl. paper, abstract in *Abstracts of Papers Read at the Thirty-fifth Annual Meetings of the American Musicological Society, Saint Louis, Missouri, December 27–29, 1967* (n.p., n.d.), 27–8.

[129] Einstein, 224.

[130] E. Leinsdorf, *The Composer's Advocate: A Radical Orthodoxy for Musicians* (New Haven, 1981), 15–16.

Ex. 8.15 Symphony in A major, K. 201 = 186a, first movement

(a) Bars 3–7

(b) Bars 139–43

tions must have been performed just that way. (This refers not to true errors of omission or commission, but to alternative ways of performing a passage.) Eighteenth-century musicians and audiences must have tolerated, and perhaps even appreciated, a greater degree of variation in such matters than we do. So the argument really comes down to a determination of whether or not a tritone with the bass is an 'error' and to how far scholarly or so-called *Urtext* editions—editions of record, not interpretive editions—should go in ironing out irregularities that may please some and displease others. Inestimable harm has been done, for instance, by editors following textbook rules, who systematically removed probably intentional cross-relations in, for instance, the music of Purcell and Marais. The editors of the *GA* and of the *NMA* were right to keep Mozart's original notation, although they might have pointed out the discrepancy by means of a footnote, and Leinsdorf is right in his capacity as an interpretive artist to reject one of the readings according to his taste and judgement. But he is wrong to suggest that there exist fixed 'rules' by which questionable pitches or rhythms can be emended in editions.

Symphony in D major, K. 202 = 186b

[Incipits 8.21]

Instrumentation: strings, 2 oboes, 2 horns, 2 trumpets, [bassoon, kettledrums, continuo]

Autograph: Pierpont Morgan Library, New York

Principal source: none

Facsimile: none

Editions: *GA*, xxi. 141–56 (= Serie 8, No. 30); *NMA*, iv/11/5. 26–43; reconstructed kettledrum part: R. Dearling, *The Music of Wolfgang Amadeus Mozart: The Symphonies* (London, 1982), 201

The first and last movements begin with a melody constructed around the descending tonic triad D—A—F sharp—D. The first movement is in a tightly-knit sonata form, featuring manipulations of a common-coin trill figure that occurs unobtrusively on D in the fourth bar, with more emphasis on E some nineteen bars later, then eleven bars after that with considerable force on A as an interruption of a lyrical theme, and finally invades the texture toward the end of the exposition, like a hive of musical bumblebees trying to sing polyphony.

The Andantino con moto, in A major, is in a diminutive sonata form and scored for strings alone. The apparent simplicity of its cantabile melodies belies the care that Mozart must have taken to make all four voices active and interesting. The Minuet and Trio exude a ballroom spirit, but comparison with sixteen minuets, K. 176, which Mozart wrote for the Carnival of 1774, reveals some differences: the ballroom minuets are shorter and more homophonic, and always omit violas. The simpler textures and more four-square phrase structures of K. 176 were apparently designed to be easily perceptible in a noisy social setting, whereas the more elaborate symphony minuet was meant to have closer attention paid to it by both performers and listeners. How much minuets were still regarded as current ballroom dances in the 1770s and 1780s and how much simply a relic of a former age is not clear. Writing from the centre of the tradition that spawned and sustained the minuet, one musician had the following observations, which provide a context for understanding its changing status:

The metre of the minuet is always in triple time, with a moderate tempo. The minuet must proceed four by four, eight by eight, in such fashion that the metre is in agreement with the four *temps* that dancers make in each *pas de minuet*. Thus the phrases must be straightforward, so that the dancers are unsure neither of the metre nor of the *repos* that ends each repeated section. One should, as much as possible, avoid using many notes. The more simply the beats are indicated, the easier the metre is to follow. Nowadays people hardly dance the minuet any longer, for the same reason that the fox [in Aesop's fable] gave for refusing to eat the grapes.[131]

The writer remarks that at French balls, a couple of minuets would be played to please grandma and grandpa, after which the evening consisted of *contredanses* for the young folks. As Mozart continued to compose ballroom minuets to the last year of his life, however, they may still have been popular in Vienna. The significance of the old-fashioned minuet (however fast its tempo or however many harmonic or rhythmic complexities it may have acquired) in the context of the 'modern' symphony has yet to be adequately accounted for.[132]

---

[131] J. J. O. de Meude-Monpas, *Dictionnaire de musique* (Paris, 1787), 94.

[132] See the discussion of the symphony minuet in connection with the 'Prague' symphony, K. 504, in ch. 11; J. Gmeiner, *Menuett und Scherzo: Ein Beitrag zur Entwicklungsgeschichte und Soziologie des Tanzsatzes in der wiener Klassik* (Wiener Veröffentlichungen zur Musikwissenschaft, xv) (Tutzing, 1978).

The Finale, like the first movement in sonata form with both sections repeated and a coda, displays a bold mixture of serious and not-so-serious ideas. The opening fanfare in dotted rhythms is in the spirit of a 'quick step'. This march-like opening is contrasted, however, with patches of lyricism; and if the development section, with its diminished chords and abrupt pauses, causes us momentarily to be quite serious, then the way in which the coda simply evaporates rather than offering a 'proper' ending reminds us that the composer was, after all, an eighteen-year-old with a well-developed sense of humour.

Saint-Foix, Einstein, and other commentators have detected a retrenchment in this symphony, a return to the sheer entertainment and *galanterie* of earlier works after the greater seriousness of K. 173dB and 186a.[133] Whether this is a cause for regret or pleasure depends upon one's aesthetic; for Saint-Foix and Einstein it was the former. But why should a festive work in D with trumpets be 'serious', and what anachronistic (i.e., romantic) overvaluation of 'seriousness' is implied? Who knows what gala occasion in Salzburg may have required just such spirited music as this?

Symphony in D major, K. 203 = 189b

[Incipits 8.22]

[133] Saint-Foix, 73–5 (= 50–1); Einstein, 224–5.

Instrumentation: *strings, 2 oboes, bassoon, 2 horns, 2 trumpets, [kettledrums, continuo]

Autograph: private possession, Switzerland (the serenade)

Principal source: eighteenth-century manuscript parts, of Viennese origin, Biblioteca Estense, Modena (the symphony) (Mus. E. 158)

Facsimile: *NMA*, iv/12/3. xv

Editions: *GA*, xxiii. 97–103, 118–32 (= Serie 9, No. 6); *NMA*, iv/12/3. 7–15, 37–54

Another symphony extracted from an orchestral serenade, K. 203 is listed as a symphony in the Breitkopf & Härtel Manuscript Catalogue, p. 4, No. 24, and found in Modena as a 'Sinfonia in D / à 2. Violini / 2. oboe / 2. Corni / Viola / e Basso / Del Sig.^re Wolffg. Amadeo Mozart'—that is, without parts for bassoon or trumpets.[134] The relationship between the D major symphonic movements and B flat violin-concerto movements is as follows (an asterisk indicates movements in the symphony version):

Serenade movements	Genres
Marcia (K. 237 = 189)	march
*Andante maestoso–Allegro assai	symphony
(Andante)	violin concerto
Menuetto	violin concerto
(Allegro)	violin concerto

[134] Holschneider, 'Neue Mozartiana in Italien', 229–30. Another eighteenth-century set of parts to the symphony version is found in Odense, Denmark.

*Menuetto	dance
*(Andante)	symphony
*Menuetto	dance/symphony
*Prestissimo	symphony

The serenade from which the present symphony was drawn is one of three in the second Cranz volume, which Leopold gathered together with the suggestive title-page: '3 / Serenate cio e gran Sinfonie', a further example of the generic meaning of 'symphony' in the eighteenth century.[135] The August date on the serenade autograph suggests that, like several of the other serenades, it was written as a 'Finalmusik' for the closing ceremonies at Salzburg University. The identification of K. 203 as a *Finalmusik* would seem to be confirmed by a letter of Leopold's describing a concert given at the Salzburg court by the oboist Fiala on 21 November 1778, for which 'the first symphony was a *Finalmusik*-symphony of yours, [the one] with oboe solo in the Andante and Trio'.[136]

The first movement's stately seven-bar introduction prepares the energetic Allegro assai, a sonata-form movement with both sections repeated, containing a couple of attractively lyrical themes contrasting with the general bustle of the rest of the movement, and a stormy, contrapuntally conceived development section. In the Andante, also in sonata form, the violins are again muted, with a cantabile melody in the firsts supported by whirring demisemiquavers in the seconds. A solo oboe makes a plaintive appearance in each half of the movement as well as in the coda. The pastoral tranquillity is broken only by three fortissimo unison outbursts in the development section, each serving to announce the sudden arrival at a new key.

The Minuet sparkles with pomp and circumstance (though hardly of the Elgarian variety) while the Trio, in which the solo oboe reappears, is as simple as the Minuet is pompous. The repeated use of the rhythm ♫ ♩ ♩ in the Minuet gives it the character of a polonaise. The concertante treatment of the solo oboe in the Andante and Minuet is the only feature of this symphony that reveals its serenade origins.

The Prestissimo, again in sonata form with both halves repeated and a coda, goes by so rapidly that one can hardly believe that, counting repeats, it is some 538 bars long. The marvellously timed gestures in the exposition and recapitulation, where the orchestra lands on and holds a chromatically altered note, are reminiscent of some of the quirkier moments in C. P. E. Bach's symphonies, although the rest of the movement would appear to be under the more southerly influence of opera buffa.

---

[135] For meanings of the word 'symphony', see ch. 13 at n. 6.
[136] Letter of 23 Nov. 1778. *Briefe*, ii. 514; this passage not in *Letters*.

Symphony in C major, K. 200 = 173e = 189k

[Incipits 8.23]

Instrumentation: *strings, 2 oboes, 2 horns, 2 trumpets, kettledrums, [bassoons, continuo]

Autograph: Pierpont Morgan Library, New York (without kettledrums); autograph drum part, auctioned by Leo Liepmannsohn's on 12 October 1929, now lost

Principal source: a set of parts from Mozart's estate was in C. A. André's possession in 1860 (now lost); it had a bassoon part but none for kettledrums (for which the lost autograph mentioned above presumably served)

Facsimile: *NMA*, iv/11/4. xviii

Editions: *GA*, xxi. 95–116 (= Serie 8, No. 28); *NMA*, iv/11/4. 107–29; reconstructed drum part: R. Dearling, *The Music of Wolfgang Amadeus Mozart: The Symphonies* (London, 1982), 200

The autograph of K. 189k is apparently dated 17 November 1774, although because (as on all the Cranz volume title-pages) the date has been tampered with, the day can also be read as 12 November or the year as 1773. The paper used by Mozart was a type that appears in works of his dated between about March 1773 and May 1775.[137] If the date 17 (or 12) November 1774 is correct, then K. 189k brings to an end the great outpouring of symphonies composed for Salzburg in the early 1770s. After this he was not to write another symphony proper until he arrived in Paris in 1778. (The four symphonies between that date and the 'Paris' symphony are reworkings of serenades and opera overtures.)

The autograph manuscript of K. 189k contains no kettledrum part, and an autograph drum part that once belonged to C. A. André has been lost since it was sold at auction in 1929.[138] The hypothetical drum parts provided by Landon and Dearling are, however, unnecessary as what may be a copy of the original one can be rescued from an early set of parts in Modena.[139] A set of parts from Mozart's estate with corrections in his hand, bought by Johann André from Constanze and owned by C. A. André in 1860, is unfortunately also lost;[140] it contained a bassoon part but none for drums, for which the lost autograph part must have served.

Several commentators have heard echoes of other music in this piece. Abert pointed to the similarity between the first movement and that of the B flat symphony, K. 173dA.[141] Wyzewa and Saint-Foix heard Joseph Haydn's influence in the first movement. They judged the opening idea of the Andante to be in the style of a German popular song, and they considered the Minuet 'like a first draft of the minuet from the "Jupiter" symphony'.[142] (The present writer, however, finds the opening of the Minuet closer to that of the Minuet of Haydn's 'Farewell' symphony, No. 45.) Hocquard is reminded of *Die Zauberflöte*, finding in the Finale what he calls 'the Monostatos motive'.[143] This game of 'find the tune' and 'name the influence' is difficult to resist and, as several studies have been devoted largely to it, one should try to understand what may lie behind it. Composers of the period were not as interested in originality *per se* as were those of a later period. As more attention was paid to craft and less to inspiration, great works could be based upon common materials. This may be compared to the attitude of a skilled cabinet-maker commissioned to build a fine table: his choice of materials and shape need

---

[137] Tyson, 'The Dates of Mozart's Missa brevis KV 258 and Missa longa KV 262 (246a)', 335.

[138] Leo Liepmannssohn Antiquariat Catalogue No. 55 (12 Oct. 1929), item No. 6 = No. 275 in Johann André's *Thematisches Verzeichnis derjenigen Originalhandschriften von W. A. Mozart* (Offenbach, 1841).

[139] H. C. Robbins Landon, 'Die Symphonien: Ihr geistiger und musikalischer Ursprung und ihre Entwicklung', in P. Schaller and H. Kühner (eds.), *Mozart-Aspekte* (Olten, 1956), 39 ff., here 50, 61; R. Dearling, *The Music of Wolfgang Amadeus Mozart: The Symphonies* (London, 1982), 200; Holschneider, 'Neue Mozartiana in Italien', 229.

[140] K⁶, 218.

[141] Abert, *Mozart*, i. 382.

[142] Wyzewa–Saint-Foix, ii. 98–100 (= i. 670–4).

[143] J.-V. Hocquard, *La Pensée de Mozart* (Paris, 1958), 329.

not be novel for the table to be beautiful to look at and well functioning, provided he knows how to choose wood and work with it.

Symphony in D major, K. 196 + 121 = 207a, 'La finta giardiniera'

[Incipits 8.24]

Instrumentation: *strings, 2 oboes, 2 horns, [bassoon, continuo]

Autograph: Jagiellońska Library, Kraków (contains Acts 2 and 3 only, hence not the overture); Staatsbibliothek Preussische Kulturbesitz, West Berlin (symphony Finale) (Mus. Ms. Autogr. W. A. Mozart 121)

Principal source: score copied from the autograph, formerly in the Royal Library, Munich, now lost

Facsimile: *NMA*, ii/8/6/i. xxiii

Editions: *GA*, ix. 1–7 (= Serie 5, No. 9) (movements 1 and 2) + xxv. 42–7 (= Serie 24, No. 10) (movement 3); *NMA*, ii/5/8/i. 5–11 (movements 1 and 2), iv/11/ 5. 44–56 (all 3 movements)

A trip to Munich from 6 December 1774 to 7 March 1775, to attend the rehearsals and performances of *La finta giardiniera*, did not lead Mozart to write symphonies, the way an earlier trip to Vienna had done. This is surprising, given the opportunities for concerts which must have existed in Munich during Carnival, given the excellence of the Munich orchestra, and given that on 16 November 1775, directly across the Hannibalplatz from the Mozarts' house, the Archbishop of

Salzburg opened a new theatre, the existence of which must have created a demand for music to grace the plays presented there.[144] It may be an indication of a profound disillusionment with Salzburg that Mozart failed to respond to these opportunities, especially the last of them.

This new Italian comic opera, 'The pretended gardener-girl', K. 196, was performed on 13 Janaury 1775 and had a favourable reception. Later on the work was given in a number of German-speaking cities as a *Singspiel*, *Die Gärtnerin aus Liebe* (or sometimes *Das verstellte Gärtner-Mädchen*), with the recitatives as spoken dialogue. As befitted its function, the first movement of the overture is shorter and less serious than first movements of other symphonies Mozart had recently written. The brief Andantino grazioso in A major is for strings alone. At some other time, in a separate manuscript, Mozart wrote a light-weight but brilliant Finale, K. 121 = 207a. On the basis of the writing in the autograph of this Finale the date of spring 1775 has been suggested,[145] but the paper proves a Milanese type from the third Italian journey, used mainly between November 1772 and early 1773.[146] Was the paper left over from Italy, or did Mozart have an older movement around that he decided to press into service when a finale for the *Finta giardiniera* overture was needed? It is also puzzling not to find larger forces in the overture-symphony, since various numbers in the opera make use of two bassoons, third and fourth horns, two trumpets, and drums. Yet the parts for flutes, clarinets, trumpets, and drums found in a Dresden manuscript (Öls 85) are probably not Mozart's, for the Finale autograph calls for only the same limited forces as do the first two movements.

Mozart's overture-symphony is neither programmatic nor even pyschological in nature. But as it was his practice to write the overture of an opera after he had familiarized himself with the story and composed most of the music, a brief summary of the opera's intrigues may serve to suggest why the symphony's first movement is so gay and its second so galant. The Marchesa Violante, slighted by Count Belfiore whom she loves, disguises herself and her valet as gardeners and the two seek employment at the Podesta's palace. The Podesta is charmed by Violante, and the Podesta's maid by the valet. Meanwhile, Count Belfiore is about to marry the Podesta's niece who is, in turn, being pursued by Ramiro. All appears lost, but the plot receives the necessary twists and Violante and the Count, the valet and the maid, and Ramiro and the niece are joined together in pairs by mutual love, leaving only the Podesta alone.

[144] E. Hintermaier, 'Das fürsterzbischöfliche Hoftheater zu Salzburg (1775–1803)', *Österreiche Musik Zeitschrift* (1975), vii. 351–63. After the opening of this theatre, the so-called 'Ballhaus', a series of theatrical troupes visited Salzburg annually. Prior to 1775 such theatre as there was in Salzburg was usually performed in the Archbishop's palace (the Residenz), the Trinkstube (an inn or tavern), or in the Great Hall of the University. The Mozarts' regular attendance at theatre productions in the Ballhaus in the second half of the 1770s is chronicled in the surviving pages of Nannerl's diary, published in *Briefe*.

[145] Plath, 'Schriftchronologie', 164.

[146] Personal communication from Alan Tyson.

Symphony in D major, K. 204 = 213a

[Incipits 8.25]

Instrumentation: *strings, 2 oboes/flutes, bassoon, 2 horns, 2 trumpets, [kettle-drums, continuo]

Autograph: private possession, Switzerland (serenade)

Principal source: manuscript parts from Mozart's estate, Staatsbibliothek Preussische Kulturbesitz, West Berlin (symphony) (Mus. Ms. 15333/4)

Facsimile: *NMA*, iv/11/7. xii–xiii

Editions: *GA*, xxiii. 133–9, 156–76 (= Serie 9, No. 7); *NMA*, iv/11/7. 89–131; reconstructed kettledrum part: R. Dearling, *The Music of Wolfgang Amadeus Mozart: The Symphonies* (London, 1982), 202

This is another symphony drawn from an orchestral serenade, comprising movements 2, 6, 7, and 8 of the larger work:

Serenade movements	Genre
Marcia (K. 215 = 213b)	march
*Allegro assai	symphony
Andante moderato	violin concerto (A major)
Allegro	violin concerto (A major)
Menuetto & Trio	dance
*(Andante)	symphony
*Menuetto & Trio	dance/symphony
*Andantino grazioso—Allegro	symphony

As the autograph manuscript of the serenade is inscribed 'li 5 d'agosto 1775', it too is believed to have been written to provide a musical finale for the end of the summer term at Salzburg University. This would appear to be confirmed by Mozart's letter of 2 October 1777, which mentions 'die Finalmusik mit den Rondeau auf lezt [*sic*]'; this is almost certainly K. 204 = 213a and not, as usually claimed, K. 251.[147] In 1783 Wolfgang wrote to his father asking to be sent the symphony version of K. 213a for his Lenten performances in Vienna.[148] The set of orchestral parts that Leopold sent in response to this request has corrections in Wolfgang's hand and was in his possession at the time of his death.[149] Early sets of parts for the symphony version also survive in Prague (three sets of parts from three different collections) and Berlin.[150]

The first movement begins with the three tutti chords that launch hundreds or perhaps thousands of eighteenth-century works, and were believed to have been the invention of Lully who, it was claimed, wanted to show off the good ensemble of his orchestra from the very first chords. This was the famous *premier coup d'archet*. Writing from Paris in 1778, Mozart made fun of this notion in a letter to his father: 'What a fuss these oxen here make of this trick! The devil take me if I can see any difference! They all begin together, just as they do in other places.'[151] Entertaining his father at the expense of the French (who were at that moment not

[147] *Briefe*, ii. 29; *Letters*, i. 422 (= i. 289). The identification of K. 251 as the work referred to in this letter is found in K⁶, the *NMA*, *Briefe*, and elsewhere. For the correction, see R. Leavis, 'Mozart's Divertimentos for Mixed Consort', *The Musical Times* (1980), cxxi. 372–3.

[148] Letter of 4 Jan. 1783. *Briefe*, iii. 248 and facsimile facing 225; *Letters*, iii. 1244–5 and facsimile facing 1242 (= ii. 835 and facsimile facing 838).

[149] These parts, now in West Berlin (Mus. ms. 15333/4), were purchased from Mozart's widow by J. André, who listed them as No. 274 on p. 76 of his *Thematisches Verzeichnis derjenigen Originalhandschriften von W. A. Mozart* (Offenbach, 1841). Klein, *Autographe und Abschriften*, 283–4.

[150] K⁶, p. 239; M. Svobodová, 'Das "Denkmal Wolfgang Amadeus Mozarts" in der prager Universitätsbibliothek', *Mozart-Jahrbuch* (1967), 353–86, here 360.

[151] Letter of 12 June 1778. *Briefe*, ii. 378–9; *Letters*, 818 (= ii. 553).

treating him particularly well), Mozart probably did not know the extent to
which, in the late seventeenth and early eighteenth centuries, French orchestral
discipline, along with the newly invented French 'baroque' woodwind instruments
and a repertory of French *ouvertures* and dance music, formed the basis of secular
music-making in German and Austrian court orchestras. That everyone began
together in the same way in 1778 is not proof that that had been the case a century
earlier.

The Andante shows its serenade origins in the concertante writing for a flute, an
oboe, a bassoon, and a pair of horns. The solo flute also reappears in the trio of the
Minuet. The Finale has an idiosyncratic structure, alternating between an Andantino grazioso in $\frac{2}{4}$ and an Allegro in $\frac{3}{8}$, with each appearing four times. This
interesting experiment was repeated by Wolfgang only two months later in the
finale of his violin concerto, K. 218, in which an Andante grazioso in $\frac{2}{4}$ and an
Allegro ma non troppo in $\frac{6}{8}$ alternate five times. The Finale of the violin concerto is
marked 'rondeau', which provides a clue to the interpretation of the Finale of K.
213a: it is an original sort of rondo.

Symphony in C major, K. 208 + 102 = 213c, 'Il rè pastore'

[Incipits 8.26]

Instrumentation: *strings, 2 oboes, 2 horns, 2 trumpets, [bassoon, continuo]
Autograph: Jagiellońska Library, Kraków (opera); Staatsbibliothek Preussische
Kulturbesitz, West Berlin (symphony finale) (Mus. Ms. Autogr. W. A. Mozart
102)
Principal source: Breitkopf & Härtel Manuscript Catalogue, p. 5, No. 30 (sym-
phony version; lost)

Facsimile: *NMA*, ii/5/9. xix; iv/11/5. xiv

Editions: *GA*, xi. 1–6 (= Serie 5, No. 10) + xxxix. 60–8 (= Serie 24, No. 8); *NMA*, ii/5/9. 5–20 (movements 1 and 2 (= first aria) after opera autograph); iv/11/5. 139–54 (movements 1 and 3 and a fragment of 2); reconstructed kettledrum part: R. Dearling, *The Music of Wolfgang Amadeus Mozart: The Symphonies* (London, 1982), 203

The Symphony in C major, K. 213c, is derived from the overture to Mozart's serenata *Il rè pastore* ('The shepherd king'), K. 208, a famous libretto by Metastasio set by an extraordinary number of composers including Gluck, Uttini, Sarti, Agricola, Hasse, Piccini, Galuppi, Jommelli, Giardini, and many others. The work, which Mozart composed in the space of about six weeks before its première in Salzburg on 23 April 1775, had been commissioned to celebrate the visit to Salzburg by the Archduke Maximilian, youngest son of the Austrian Empress Maria Theresa. As Salzburg lacked a proper opera house, this work was cast as a serenata and given in concert form; the Archduke's travel diary therefore, speaks only of attending a 'cantata'.[152]

The story concerns the conflicts between love and duty in a foundling prince who, having been raised a shepherd, is reluctant to give up rustic pleasures for the burdens of the throne. Mozart's one-movement 'overtura' to the opera has the same opening gesture as the previous symphony, but there follows in this case a movement more concise and Italianate. In the concert symphony version this leads directly into an Andantino that Mozart manufactured from the first aria of the opera. This he accomplished by substituting a solo oboe for the shepherd king Aminta (sung by a castrato) and by writing eight new bars that lead, again without halt, into an entirely new finale. The aria of which the middle movement of the symphony is a barely altered arrangement finds Aminta on the banks of a stream with shepherd's pipes in hand (the orchestration features a pair of flutes), wondering what fate holds for him and his shepherdess:

> Intendo, amico rio,
> Quel basso mormorio,
> Tu chiedi in tua favella;
> Il nostro ben dov'è?
>
> [I understand, O friendly brook,
> Your low murmuring;
> You are asking in your way
> Where our beloved is.]

---

[152] The Salzburg counsellor Joachim Ferdinand von Schiedenhofen, who attended the dress rehearsal and the performance, also called it a serenata in his diary. Deutsch, 136–7 (= 151–2).

The newly created Finale, a rondo in the style of a country dance, is written on a type of paper that Mozart used in K. 243 (March 1776) and in the entr'actes to K. 345 (undatable), so the symphony was probably created around 1776.[153] Mozart eventually rejected this type of light, dance-like finale and chose a more contrapuntally and developmentally conceived type in which sonata form replaced rondo. The new type of finale, instead of simply being (so to speak) the last dance of the evening, contained some of the work's most important artistic content and provided a weighty counterbalance to its first movement. Perhaps, therefore, Mozart was commenting privately to himself about what he had abandoned when, in 1787, with the 'Haffner', 'Linz', and 'Prague' symphonies behind him, he used a theme with a strong resemblance to the theme of the Finale of K. 213c in his satirical *Musical Joke*, K. 522 (Example 8.16).

K. 213c is none the less an ably constructed work in the style of the 1770s. Mozart took it with him to Paris in 1777–8, using it to close a concert at the house of the Mannheim composer and concertmaster Christian Cannabich on 13 February 1778. The rest of the programme on that occasion consisted of an opening symphony by Cannabich; Mozart's piano concerto in B flat, K. 238, played by Cannabich's daughter Rosa, then studying with Mozart; the oboe

Ex. 8.16 *Ein musikalischer Spass*, K. 522, first movement, closing subject (bars 78–82)

---

[153] Private communication from Alan Tyson. Hence the date of August 1775 for K. 213c given in K[6] and accepted by Plath, 'Schriftchronologie', 164, is probably too early.

concerto in C major, K. 314; two arias from *Lucio Silla*, K. 135, sung by Mozart's current love and future sister-in-law, Aloysia Weber; the piano concerto in D, K. 175, performed by Mozart, along with half an hour of his extemporization at the fortepiano.[154] Mozart greatly admired Cannabich's prestige and success as leader of the famous Mannheim orchestra, but Leopold called him a *Synfonischmierer*. Still, Leopold owned some of Cannabich's symphonies in the 1760s, so perhaps his calling him a 'symphony scribbler' was a burst of defensiveness or professional jealousy.[155]

Symphony in D major, K. 250 = 248b, 'Haffner Serenade'

[Incipits 8.27]

---

[154] Letter of 24 Mar. 1778. *Briefe*, ii. 326–7; *Letters*, ii. 762 (= ii. 571).

[155] Letter of 6 Apr. 1778. *Briefe*, ii. 336; *Letters*, ii. 775 (= ii. 525). Letter of 17 Feb. 1770. *Briefe*, i. 316; this passage not in *Letters*.

Menuetto galante

[*f*]   *p*   (50)

[Trio]

sempre **p**   (34)

Andante

(216)

Menuetto

f   (30)

Trio I

p   (24)

Trio II

f   (24)

Adagio

p   (16)

Allegro assai

p   (459)

Instrumentation: *strings, 2 oboes/flutes, 2 bassoons, 2 horns, 2 trumpets, kettle-drums, [continuo]
Autograph: private possession, Switzerland (serenade)
Principal source: parts from Mozart's estate with entries by him and by Leopold, Staatsbibliothek Preussische Kulturbesitz, West Berlin (symphony) (Mus. Ms. Autogr. W. A. Mozart 250)
Facsimile: *NMA*, iv/11/7. xiv–xv
Editions: *GA*, xxiii. 193–219, 251–92 (= Serie 9, No. 9); *NMA*, iv/11/7. 31–88

The Haffners and Mozarts were friends of long standing, and when Maria Elisabeth ('Lisl') Haffner (1753–84) was to marry, the twenty-year-old Wolfgang was asked for some suitable music. The serenade that resulted received its first performance at an eve-of-the-wedding party, and the Salzburg court councillor von Schiedenhofen who was present entered in his diary: '21 July 1776: After dinner I went to the bridal music that young Mr Haffner ordered to be put on for his sister Liz. It was by Mozart, and done at their summer house in Loreto Street.'[156]

At some later date Wolfgang or Leopold ordered a copyist to extract a set of orchestra parts containing only the symphonic movements, as follows:

Serenade movements	Genres
Marcia—Maestoso (K. 249)	march
*Allegro maestoso—Allegro molto	symphony
Andante	violin concerto in G major
Menuetto & Trio	violin concerto in G major/dance
Rondeau	violin concerto in G major
*Menuetto galante & Trio	dance
*Andante	symphony
*Menuetto and two Trios	symphony/dance
*Adagio—Allegro assai	symphony

To this Leopold added a part for kettledrums (lacking in the serenade score) and Wolfgang looked through the parts and entered a few corrections and clarifications. At yet a later date, these corrected parts were used by another copyist as the basis for *Dubletten*. The resulting set of sixteen orchestral parts was in Mozart's possession at his death, later passing into the possession of Johann André. This set of parts was copied on paper identical to that found in the Finale of the symphony, K. 213c, in the entr'actes for *Thamos*, K. 345 = 336a and in the Litany, K. 243;[157] only the last of these is firmly dated: March 1776. Possibly the symphony was created to

<hr/>

[156] Deutsch, 141 (= 157).   [157] See n. 153 above.

satisfy a commission of December 1776 to send a 'symphony and other pieces' in return for twenty ducats to Count Prokop Adalbert Czernin in Prague.[158] An investigation of the early copies of the symphony in Brno, Prague, and Kremsier, to see if they may have had something to do with Czernin's purchase, may some day clarify this matter.

On 24 September 1779 an entry in Nannerl's diary in Wolfgang's hand mentions a performance in Salzburg 'at 9:00 p.m. in the Kollegienplatz [or Universitätsplatz] on the street in front of Mr Dehl's house, an evening serenade [Nachtmusik]: the march from my last *Finalmusik* [K. 335 = 320a], [the Swabian folksong] "Lustig sind die Schwobemedle", and the Haffner music'. This last probably refers to the entire serenade, K. 250 = 248b, but six months later, on 18 March 1780, Wolfgang again entered details of a concert programme in his sister's diary, and the first item on it is clearly designated 'A symphony (namely the Haffner music)'.[159]

The opening Allegro maestoso is little more than an extended fanfare moving from tonic to dominant, spread over thirty-five bars and decorated with orchestral figuration. The Allegro molto begins *unisono,* a texture that recurs several times during the movement to good dramatic effect. The movement is on a large scale for a symphony movement of the 1770s, with an unusually extended and chromatic development section based on material from the Allegro maestoso introduction. Changes wrought to the serenade to create the symphony (aside from added kettledrums) include omission of the repeat of the exposition and the addition of a fanfare by oboes, horns, and trumpets at the end, where originally there was a grand pause.

Menuetto galante is an unusual designation, perhaps best rendered 'fashionable minuet'. Its trio is not without its touches of pathos. Mozart rewrote this trio for the symphony version, changing a broken-chord triplet accompaniment in the second violins (like the first movement of Beethoven's 'Moonlight' sonata) to repeated notes, and adding oboes and bassoons to the original strings.

The Andante, taken over unchanged from the serenade, reveals its origins by its sprawling dimensions. The movement is of a particularly original formal design, perhaps best described as an elaborate rondo influenced by the double theme-and-variations format—a formal arrangement favoured by Joseph Haydn for a number of his symphony andantes, but rare with Mozart.

Two or three minuets, and minuets with two or three trios, were common in Salzburg orchestral serenades but uncommon (although not unheard of) in symphonies. Certain late eighteenth- and early nineteenth-century manuscripts of this symphony have the 'superfluous' movements excised, suggesting the rise of a concept of the symphony more rigid than that to which Mozart himself might

[158] Deutsch, 141 (= 158).   [159] *Briefe,* ii. 554, iii. 3. The latter programme is discussed in ch. 10.

have subscribed in the 1770s. In a bit of rustic drone near the end of the Minuet's second section, Mozart hints at the sound of the hurdy-gurdy or bagpipes, with some rusticatedly 'wrong' notes, rather like some in his father's 'Toy Symphony' of many years earlier or in his own *Musical Joke* of several years later. A pair of flutes replaces the oboes in the second minuet and its two trios, while the first trio features a flute and bassoon duet and the second gives the entire wind band a chance to shine.

The Finale opens with a sixteen-bar Adagio of great beauty, leading into a large-scale jig movement in sonata form with both repeats and a coda. Some of this music is similar in character to the Finale of Joseph Haydn's Symphony No. 8—a movement entitled 'La Tempesta'.

Saint-Foix comments upon 'the abnormal length of the movements, their variety, their brilliance' and Della Croce, with justification, calls the work 'one of the richest, most solid and most elaborate symphonies' that Mozart had thus far composed.[160] The symphony enjoyed wide distribution, manuscript copies of it of the late eighteenth and early nineteenth centuries surviving in Vienna, Salzburg, Berlin, and Frankfurt, in addition to the Czech copies already discussed. While the symphony was published by André in 1792 (see Table 11. 2), the serenade from which the symphony was drawn remained unknown.

Symphony in C major, K. Anh. C 11.15

[Incipits 8.28]

---

[160] Saint-Foix, 82–3 (= 57–8); Della Croce, *Le 75 sinfonie*, 192.

Trio

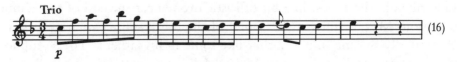

(16)

Allegro moderato

(94)

Instrumentation: strings, 2 oboes, 1 bassoon, 2 horns, [continuo]

Autograph: none

Principal source: set of eighteenth-century parts, Národní Muzeum (National Museum), Prague (II E 163)

Facsimile: none

Editions: none

The sole source for this symphony once formed part of the Waldstein music collection in the Mnichovo Hradiště Castle in northern Bohemia. (This is the same Waldstein family as that of the dedicatee of Beethoven's piano sonata, Op. 53. The Waldsteins were also Mozart's patrons; three members of the family are found in the list of subscribers to his 1784 Lenten concerts, which is discussed at the beginning of Chapter 11.) Along with about 55 other music manuscripts from the Waldstein collection (including symphonies by Mysliveček, Leopold Hofmann, Dušek; many in the hand of the same copyist), the manuscript of K. Anh. C 11.15 later came into the possession of a local schoolteacher, Roman Nejedlý (1844–1920), who in turn bequeathed it to the Národní Muzeum.[161] The title-page of its cover reads: 'Sinfonia in C / à / 2 Violini / 2 Oboe / 2 Corni / Fagotti / Viola / Violone è Violoncello / Del Sig.: Mozart'. At the upper right is an old shelf number (I. g.), at the upper and lower left the present shelf number (II. E. 163.), and at the bottom centre the stamp of the Národní Muzeum. Also, oddly placed, near the middle of the right edge of the page and immediately after '2 Violini' is written, in darker ink, 'Andante'.

The parts themselves, however, do not entirely agree with what is stated on the cover's title-page. There is only one bassoon part, labelled 'fagotto obligl:'; Mozart's obbligato symphonic bassoon parts come in pairs. A cello part is lacking, there being one for violone only, which, however, plays in every bar of every movement (thereby forgoing Mozart's practice of employing the *bassetto* texture)

---

[161] Letter of 16 Feb. 1982 from Dr Milada Rutová of the Národní Muzeum, Prague.

and seems to convey an all-purpose bass-line intended for both cellos and double-basses. Then the 'C' in 'Sinfonia in C' shows signs of having been written over an erasure, as does, possibly, the name 'Mozart'; and the mysterious 'Andante' and 'Del Sig^r: Mozart' appear to be written in a different hand from and in darker ink than the rest (as well as can be judged from a photocopy). 'Mozart' has been written in the upper right-hand corner of the title-page of each of the parts, in the same hand as 'Mozart' on the cover but a different hand from the one that copied the parts and the remainder of the cover's title-page. Nejedlý's signature is found in the lower right-hand corner of the title-page of the 'violino primo' part. The title-page, therefore, was probably originally written for some other set of parts, then taken over and altered for its present purpose.

The opening Allegro is a sonata-form movement, with both sections repeated. The ideas do not sound particularly like those in other early Mozart symphonies, and the handling of the orchestra is equally uncharacteristic: there are endless repeated notes, measured tremolo, and frequent use of double stops (or perhaps divisi?). The treble and bass are competently written, but the inner voices are weak. The Andante, in which the horns rest, is a set of variations on a not un-Mozartean theme. But the variations themselves are banal and mechanical, and, unlike the several beautiful variation andantes in Joseph Haydn's symphonies, this one is unsymphonic and lacking in development. Mozart did not favour variation-form for his symphonic andantes, using it only once, and in an idiosyncratic manner, in the Andante of the Serenade (and Symphony) in D major, K. 250 = 248b, where neither its texture nor its working out resembles the Prague movement. (Mozart did use this sort of variations in keyboard and chamber music—for instance, in the opening Andantino of the flute quartet in C major, K. 298, which, despite its misleadingly low Köchel number, probably dates from no earlier than 1786.) Although no shorter than some of Mozart's earliest minuets and trios, the Prague Minuet and Trio are plainer and cruder. The Finale is the weakest movement of the four, a feeble rondo based on a puerile theme; unlike Mozart's rondos, it shows traces of sonata-form influence neither in its modulatory pattern nor in its deployment of thematic material.

There are no compelling source or musical reasons to believe that K. Anh. C 11.15 came from the pen of Wolfgang Mozart; the editors of K^6 were fully justified in placing it in the appendix of their catalogue. Likewise, Eisen sees no reason to consider it a work of Leopold Mozart's, and places it among the questionable symphonies.[162]

---

[162] Eisen, 'The Symphonies of Leopold Mozart', 165, 318–19.

9

Mannheim and Paris: Frustration (1777–1778)

On 23 September 1777 Mozart and his mother left Salzburg for Mannheim, in the hope of finding him a position there or at some other court. Although he was twenty-one years old, his father did not trust his judgement sufficiently to permit him to undertake the journey on his own. As the Mozarts' finances were strained, Leopold had to stay at home to continue his salary, and sent his wife. She proved unable to handle her impulsive, headstrong son, and the trip was a disaster, for Mozart not only failed to obtain a post, but he composed relatively little, ran his father into considerable debt, and his mother succumbed to illness.

The first important stop was Munich (24 September–11 October) where, even though Mozart had caused a sensation there during visits in 1762, 1763, 1766, and 1775, he was told—after some evasiveness on the part of the authorities—that there would be no position for him. He participated in a private concert with orchestra on 4 October, but symphonies were not performed.[1] The next important stop was Leopold's native city, Augsburg, where they visited Leopold's brother's family, remaining for a fortnight (11–26 October) even though, with no court, there was little possibility of a suitable position. Mozart gave two concerts while in Augsburg, with the Protestant Collegium Musicum. The first was on the 16th, apparently without a rehearsal, and Mozart reported, 'I had brought a symphony too, which was performed and in which I played the fiddle. But the Augsburg orchestra is enough to give one a fit . . . . I [also] played a concerto which, save for the accompaniment, went very well. At the end I played a sonata as well.'[2] For the second concert on the 22nd, notices appeared in the local paper promising an opening symphony 'with the proper instruments' and a closing symphony.[3] On the 19th two symphonies were rehearsed at the house of Johann Andreas Stein, the

---

[1] Letter of 6 Oct. 1777. *Briefe*, ii. 40–1; *Letters*, i. 437–8 (= i. 299–300).
[2] Letter of 16 Oct. 1777. *Briefe*, ii. 65–6; *Letters*, ii. 476 (= i. 326).
[3] *Augsburgische Staats- und gelehrten Zeitung* (22 Oct. 1777); Deutsch, 149 (= 166–7).

distinguished builder of organs, harpsichords, and fortepianos, although Mozart's report of the concert mentions a symphony only in passing:

Now what does Papa think that we played immediately after the [opening] symphony? Why, the concerto for three keyboard instruments [K. 242] . . . . Then I gave a solo, my last sonata in D [K. 284] . . . and after my Concerto in B flat [K. 238] . . . I then played another solo, quite in the style of the organ, a fugue in C minor and then all of a sudden a magnificent sonata in C major, out of my head, and a rondo to finish up with. There was a regular din of applause.[4]

This concert undoubtedly also included another symphony, since two had been rehearsed and the newspaper announcement mentioned a closing symphony. The only account of the concert stated merely that Mozart 'displayed all of his powers'.[5] In the afternoon of the same day as the Collegium rehearsal, Mozart and his uncle had lunch at the Holy Cross Monastery, where Mozart joined in the *Tafelmusik* by leading one of his symphonies and appearing as soloist in a violin concerto by Vanhall. He reported that, 'In spite of their poor fiddling, I prefer the monastery players to the Augsburg orchestra.'[6]

Mozart and his mother arrived at Mannheim on 30 October 1777 and remained until 14 March 1778. Mozart had appeared there in 1763 as an infant prodigy. Now he found himself regarded primarily as a keyboard virtuoso, and had surprisingly little opportunity to show what he could do as a composer. He was to visit Mannheim again at the end of 1778 and in 1790, yet there is no evidence that a symphony of his was ever performed by the orchestra that was, until the Elector moved to Munich in 1780, the most famous in Europe. Leopold had reported in a letter of 19 July 1763 from Mannheim that 'the orchestra is without contradiction the best in Germany'[7] and in a letter of 20 November 1777 he twice stressed the orchestra's excellence.[8] After Mozart had left Mannheim without being offered a post or even appropriate compensation for the teaching and performing he had done while there, however, Leopold wrote in a different vein: 'To tell the truth, I never liked the Mannheim compositions. The orchestra there is good—and very powerful—but the interpretation is not in that true and delicate style which moves the hearer.'[9] But Mozart would gladly have traded Salzburg's orchestra for

[4] Letter of 23 Oct. 1777. *Briefe*, ii. 82, 84; *Letters*, ii. 494, 497–8 (= i. 338, 340).

[5] Paul von Stetten, *Kunst-, Gewerb- und Handwerks-Geschichte der Reichs-Stadt Augsburg* (Augsburg, 1779); Deutsch, 165–6 (= 186). Reprinted in the *Musikalische Korrespondenz der teutschen Filarmonischen Gesellschaft* (23 Mar. 1791), No. 12, cols. 89–90.

[6] Letter of 23 Oct. *Briefe*, ii. 82; *Letters*, ii. 494 (= i. 338).

[7] *Briefe*, i. 79; *Letters*, i. 35 (= i. 25).

[8] Ibid. ii. 131, 134; i. 35 (= i. 25).

[9] Letter of 6 Apr. 1778. *Briefe*, ii. 336; *Letters*, ii. 775 (= ii. 525). Apparently one could also have too much nuance in an orchestra; at least, Schubart criticized Rosetti's leadership of the Oettingen-Wallerstein orchestra because he 'sometimes carried his observances of the most delicate gradations of tone to the bounds of pedantry' (*Ideen*, 169).

Mannheim's, as he made clear in a letter of 9 July 1778 quoted at the beginning of Chapter 10, for not only was the latter a finer group, but its musicians were better paid and treated with greater respect. The membership of this famous ensemble has been well documented,[10] but such information is of limited value without knowledge of the system of rotation that determined how many players were required to appear for various occasions. Mozart provided some information in a description that he sent his father:

Now I must tell you about the musical establishment here. On Saturday, All Saints' Day, I was at High Mass in the [Electoral] chapel. The orchestra is very good and strong. There are ten or eleven violins on either side, four violas, two oboes, two flutes, and two clarinets, two horns, four violoncellos, four bassoons, and four double basses, also trumpets and drums. They can produce fine music, but I should not care to have one of my masses performed here. Why? On account of their shortness? No, everything must be short here too. Because a different style of sacred composition is required? Not at all. But because, as things are at present, you must write principally for the instruments, as you cannot imagine anything worse than the voices here. Six sopranos, six altos, six tenors, and six basses against twenty violins and twelve bass-instruments is just like zero to one .... The reason for this state of affairs is that the Italians are now in very bad odour here. They have only two castrati, who are already old and will just be allowed to die off. The soprano would actually prefer to sing alto, as he can no longer take the high notes. The few boys they have are miserable. The tenors and basses are like our funeral singers.[11]

Despite continual rounds of music-making in Mannheim during the period that Mozart was there, the only documented performance of one of his symphonies was a private concert in the home of the Mannheim composer and Kapellmeister Christian Cannabich. There Mozart's Symphony in C, K. 102 = 213c, was performed on 13 February 1780, as described at the end of the previous chapter. A second concert at Cannabich's on 12 March 1780 may also have included one of Mozart's symphonies but, if so, he failed to mention it in his account of the occasion.[12]

Mozart and his mother left Mannheim on 14 March, arriving on 23 March in the French capital, which was then an international centre for the creation, performance, and dissemination of symphonies.[13] By common report, the best Parisian orchestra in 1778 was not that of the well-established Concert spirituel, but rather that of the newer Concert des amateurs, founded in 1769 by the Franco-Belgian

---

[10] R. Würtz, *Verzeichnis und Ikonographie der kurpfälzischen Hofmusiker zu Mannheim nebst darstellendem Theaterpersonal, 1723–1803* (Quellenkataloge zur Musikgeschichte, viii) (Wilhelmshaven, 1975).

[11] Letter of 4 Nov. 1777. *Briefe*, ii. 101; *Letters*, ii. 521–2 (= i. 355–6).

[12] Letter of 24 Mar. 1778. *Briefe*, ii. 326–7; *Letters*, ii. 762 (= ii. 571).

[13] This is fully documented in Brook, *La Symphonie française*.

composer François Gossec.[14] The Concert des amateurs flourished until January 1781, when one of its principal patrons withdrew, abruptly ending the series, to the regret of everyone involved. Performances were held at the Hôtel de Soubise two or three times a week during the autumn and spring. In order to have the best possible way of presenting his symphonies to the Parisian public, therefore, Mozart should logically have approached the organizers of the Concert des amateurs. (The musical director in 1778 was the violinist and composer Joseph Boulogne, Chevalier de Saint-Georges.) And he may have had some such plan in mind, for in a letter of 3 December 1777 he reported hearing from musicians in the Mannheim orchestra (who would have been in a position to know, since several of them had visited Paris and had symphonies published and performed there) that both the Concert spirituel and the Concert des amateurs paid the handsome sum of five Louis d'or for a new symphony.[15] In the event, however, Mozart was introduced to Joseph Legros, director of the Concert spirituel, and it was for that organization that he composed a symphony.

Symphony in D major, K. 297 = 300a

[Incipits 9.1]

---

[14] Elements of a history of the Concert des amateurs, which has yet to be written, are found in: anon., 'Dissolution de la société musicale, connue à Paris sous le nom de Concert des amateurs', *Almanach musical* (1782), 67–8; M. Brenet, *Les Concerts sous l'Ancien régime* (Paris, 1900, repr. New York, 1969), 301–2, 357–64; Brook, *La Symphonie française*, i. 672; R. J. Macdonald, 'François-Joseph Gossec and French Instrumental Music in the Second Half of the Eighteenth Century' (Ph.D. diss., University of Michigan, 1968), 401–14; R. Angermüller, 'Mozarts pariser Umwelt (1778)', *Mozart-Jahrbuch* (1978/79), 122–32, esp. 127.

[15] Letter of 3 Dec. 1777. *Briefe*, ii. 162; *Letters*, ii. 592 (= i. 401).

Instrumentation: *strings, 2 flutes, 2 oboes, 2 clarinets, 2 bassoons, 2 horns, 2 trumpets, kettledrums

Autograph: Staatsbibliothek Preussische Kulturbesitz, West Berlin (Mus. Ms. Autogr. W. A. Mozart 297)

Principal sources: partially autograph score, Mozarteum, Salzburg; sketch, Einsiedeln Monastery, Switzerland; autograph trumpet part probably from late 1786, sold at auction by Leo Liepmannsohn, Catalogue 55 (12 October 1929), and again by Sotheby (21 November 1978); Sieber edition (discussed below)

Facsimiles: first six pages of Mozarteum partial autograph (Lucerne, 1949); three pages of Berlin 'autograph': *NMA*, iv/11/5. xii–xiii; the Einsiedeln sketch (see n. 49)

Editions: *GA*, xxi. 157–96 (= Serie 8, No. 31); London: Eulenberg, 1956 (ed. H. F. Redlich); *NMA*, iv/11/5. 57–103 (autograph version, complete), 106–27 (first edition version, first movement)

Mozart's letters document the history of this work. He must have completed it—at least in his head if not on paper—by 12 June 1778, on which date he wrote to his father reporting that earlier in the day he had played it through at the keyboard for the singer Anton Raaff and Count Sickingen, minister of the Palatinate, after lunch at the latter's house.[16] The symphony had its première at the Concert spirituel on Corpus Christi (18 June) after only one rehearsal—the usual practice—on the previous day. Mozart reported:

I was very nervous at the rehearsal, for never in my life have I heard a worse performance; you cannot imagine how they twice bumbled and scraped through it. I was really in a terrible state and would gladly have rehearsed it again, but as there is always so much to rehearse there was no time left. So I had to go to bed with an anxious heart and in a discontented and angry frame of mind. Next day I had decided not to go to the concert at all; but in the evening, the weather being fine, I at last made up my mind to go, determined that if [my symphony] went as badly as it had at the rehearsal I would certainly go up to the orchestra, take the violin from the hands of Lahoussaye, the first violinist, and lead myself! I prayed to God that it might go well, for it is all to His greater honour and glory; and *Ecce*, the symphony began . . . . Right in the middle of the first Allegro was a passage that I knew they would like; the whole audience was thrilled by it and there was a tremendous burst of applause; but as I knew when I wrote it what kind of an effect it would produce, I repeated it again at the end—when there were shouts of 'Da capo'. The Andante also found favour, but particularly the last Allegro because, having observed that here all final as well as first allegros begin with all the instruments playing together and generally *unisono*, I began mine with the two violin[-section]s only, piano for the first eight bars—followed instantly by a forte; the audience, as I expected, said 'Shh!' at the soft

---

[16] *Briefe*, ii. 378–9; *Letters*, ii. 817–18 (= ii. 552–3).

beginning, and then, as soon as they heard the *forte* that followed, immediately began to clap their hands. I was so happy that as soon as the symphony was over I went off to the Palais royal where I had a large ice, said the rosary as I had vowed to do—and went home.[17]

In a perceptive commentary on this letter, Nikolaus Harnoncourt remarks on differences between Mozart's audiences and ours: the 1778 audience required new music and expressed its appreciation and understanding not only after each movement but—exceptionally—during a movement. Harnoncourt also suggests that the passage in the first movement of K. 297, which so pleased the members of the Parisian audience that they burst into applause, may be bars 65–73 (Example 9.1a), recurring at 220–7, where a staccato melody in the violins and violas supported above by sustaining wind and below by cellos and basses pizzicato creates a brilliant effect.[18]

Ex. 9.1 Symphony in D major, K. 297 = 300a, first movement

(a) bars 65–73

[17] Letter of 3 July 1778. *Briefe*, ii. 388–9; *Letters*, ii. 825–6 (= ii. 557–8).
[18] N. Harnoncourt, 'Gedanken eines Orchestermusikers zu einem Brief von W. A. Mozart', *Musik als Klangrede* (Salzburg, 1982), 264–8.

(b) bars 84–92

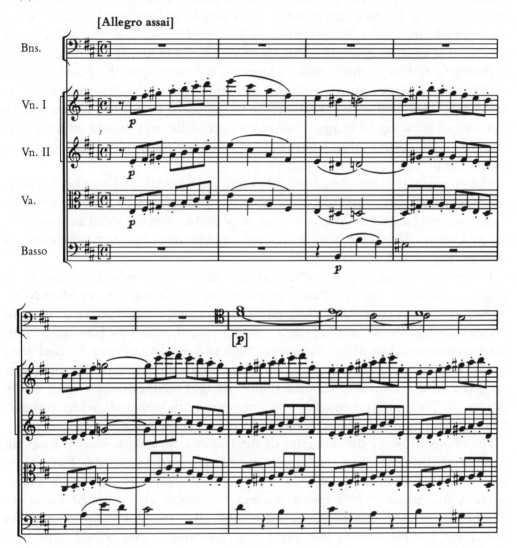

On the other hand, Stanley Sadie has proposed a different identification for the passage that Mozart 'knew they would like'. The passage in question (Example 9.1b) occurs in the exposition at bars 84–92, then in the recapitulation at bars 238–50, and finally in the coda at 257–69.[19] This suggestion prompts a re-examination of the place in Mozart's letter given above in Emily Anderson's translation as: '. . . as I knew when I wrote it what kind of an effect it would

---

[19] Sadie, *Symphonies*, 55–6.

produce, I repeated it again at the end'. The German ('weil ich aber wuste, wie ich sie schriebe, was das für einen Effect machen würde, so brachte ich sie auf die lezt noch einmahl an') could also be translated, 'because I knew, however, as I wrote it, what kind of an effect it would make, therefore I brought it in again one more time at the end'. Although this is still ambiguous, it leaves open the possibility that Mozart took for granted in writing to his father that in the first movements of symphonies ideas will automatically come twice, in the exposition and recapitulation, so that bringing 'it in again one more time at the end' would imply a third appearance. If correct, this interpretation favours Sadie's identification of the sensational passage over Harnoncourt's.

The success of the new symphony is to some extent confirmed by a brief review, which remarked that 'This artist, who from the tenderest age had made a name for himself among harpsichordists, can today be placed among the ablest composers',[20] and by Legros's decision to publish it as, presumably, one of the best symphonies in his repertory.

The programme of 18 June 1778, as gleaned from the periodicals listed in Table 9.1, was as follows: Mozart's 'Paris' symphony, an Italian aria sung by Mme Saint-Huberti, a bassoon concerto performed by Destouches, a motet for two voices by Gossec sung by Chéron and Legros, a cello sonata performed by Jannson, a violin concerto performed by Mlle Deschamps, 'Non so d'onde viene' by J. C. Bach sung by Raaff, by special request an Italian aria by Gluck sung by Mme Saint-Huberti, and *Suzanne*, a new oratorio by Bambini.[21] Mozart mentions not a word of this other music (he must have heard at least some of it at the rehearsal), which certainly made up in quantity anything it may have lacked in quality.

The composition of the orchestra of the Concert spirituel is known from the membership lists published annually in the *Almanach des spectacles de Paris*. These lists, or summaries of them, have been republished several times, but not always correctly interpreted.[22] In a recent attempt to provide an annotated list of the membership of the orchestra that performed Mozart's symphony, for instance, the assumption has been made that the list of performers who would have been

---

[20] *Courrier de l'Europe* (London), 26 June 1778; Deutsch, 158 (= 176). The only other Parisian reaction to Mozart's symphonies was to performances at the Concert spirituel on 23 May and 3 June 1779. On the former occasion a symphony of his, although 'perhaps as learned and as majestic' as one by J. F. X. Sterkel, 'did not excite the same interest'. On the latter, the *Mercure de France* found 'in the first two movements, great richness of ideas, and motives followed through. As regards the third, in which all the science of counterpoint shines forth, the author obtained the suffrages of lovers of the kind of music that interests the mind without touching the heart' (Deutsch, 165 (= 185)).

[21] A concert-by-concert listing of the programmes of the Concert spirituel assembled by A. Bloch-Michel is found in C. Pierre, *Histoire du Concert spirituel 1725–1790* (Paris, 1975), 227–370. The contents of Table 9.1 were, however, arrived at independently and, for Mozart's symphonies, are more complete than Bloch-Michel's listings.

[22] E. Borrel, 'L'Orchestre du Concert spirituel et celui de l'Opéra de Paris, de 1751 à 1800 d'après "Les Spectacles de Paris"', *Mélanges d'histoire et d'esthétique musicales offerts à P. M. Masson* (Paris, 1955), ii. 9–15; Brook, *La Symphonie française*; Pierre, *L'Histoire du Concert spirituel*; R. Angermüller, 'Wer spielte die Uraufführung von Mozarts "Pariser Symphonie" KV 297?', *Mitteilungen der internationalen Stiftung Mozarteum* (Aug. 1978), xxvi/3–4. 12–20.

TABLE 9.1 Performances of Mozart's symphonies at the Concert spirituel according to announcements in Parisian periodicals

Concert	Announcement	Journal (date)
18 June 1778	'une nouvelle symphonie'	AA (18 June), CE (26 June), JP (16 & 18 June)
15 Aug. 1778	'une symphonie'	AA (13 Aug.), JP (12 & 15 Aug.)
8 Sept. 1778	'une nouvelle symphonie'	AA (7 Sept.), JP (4–8 Sept.)
28 Mar. 1779*	'une symphonie'	JP (27 & 28 Mar.)
23 May 1779	'une symphonie'	AA (21 & 23 May), JP (21 & 23 May), MF (5 June)
3 June 1779	'une symphonie'	AA (3 June), JP (3 June), MF (15 June)
23 Mar. 1780	'une nouvelle symphonie'†	AA (23 Mar.), JP (23 Mar.), MF (1 Apr., p. 39)
14 May 1780	'une symphonie'	AA (13 & 14 May), AM (1781, p. 107), JP (13 & 14 May)
8 Apr. 1780	'une symphonie'	AM (1782, p. 107), JP (8 Apr.)
27 Mar. 1782	'une symphonie'	AA (27 Mar.), AM (1783, p. 175), JP (27 Mar.)
17 Apr. 1783	'une symphonie'	AA (17 Apr.), JP (17 Apr.)
22 Mar. 1785	'une symphonie'	AA (22 Mar.), JP (22 & 24 Mar.)
25 Mar. 1786	'une symphonie'	AA (22 & 25 Mar.), JP (23 & 25 Mar.)
10 Apr. 1786	'une symphonie'	AA (10 Apr.), JP (10 & 11 Apr.)
3 Apr. 1789	'une symphonie'	AA (2 & 3 Apr.), JP (2 & 3 Apr.)

AA = *Annonces, affiches et avis divers*
AM = *Almanach musical*
CE = *Courrier de l'Europe*
JP = *Journal de Paris*
MF = *Mercure de France*

* The performance incorrectly claimed for 18 Mar. 1779 by K⁶, p. 318, is presumably a misprint for this date.

† AA only; JP reads simply 'une symphonie'; MF merely includes Mozart in a list of symphonists whose works were heard.

available for a concert on 18 June 1778 is that published in the 1778 volume of the *Almanach*.[23] Almanacs, however, were published at the end of the year prior to their date, in order to be available for the New Year. As the annual seasons seem generally to have ended in February or March (as if still on the 'Old Style' calendar), and changes in the membership or leadership of the orchestra were effected in the spring of each year, the membership of the orchestra in June 1778 will be found in the almanac for 1779, probably published in December 1778.

In the years prior to Mozart's stay in Paris, the Concert spirituel was in a state of flux, which was reflected in notices in the press:

September 1762: They have made some advantageous changes in the disposition of the orchestra, dividing equally the first and second violins on each side, which enables the harmony much better to reach the ears of each listener, in whatever part of the hall he is placed.[24]

October 1762: By the means of placing Mr Gaviniès at the head of the first violins and Mr Capron at the head of the seconds, they have (as it is done in Italy) dispensed with beating time with a baton in all the instrumental music; an advantage that no doubt has its price and that is much less marvellous to true musicians than to demi-savants of this art, blindly idolatrous of all that is foreign to our national practice.[25]

March 1771: ... the poor disposition of the orchestra ... hinders performance. The first and second violins neither see nor hear each other; consequently they are liable to lack good ensemble. The flutes and oboes are buried among the bass instruments and lose their effect; the horns are no better placed, and the miserable organ, which is in the midst of the violas, divides and destroys all the harmony .... One would furthermore wish, for the improvement of this concert series, more precision in the rehearsals. Several of them are needed, and for pieces of any consequence they must be undertaken with great care, in order to attain that delightful ensemble without which music is unworthy of the name.[26]

April 1773: The new directors of the Concert spirituel, Messrs Gaviniès, Gossec, and Leduc ... [caused to be] performed in a superior manner a symphony for full orchestra ... by a numerous orchestra directed by Messrs Gaviniès and Leduc, excellent violinists who were at the head of the first and second violins respectively. The section leaders, closer together and more prone to hear one another, were able to put more precision and better ensemble into the performances.[27]

April 1773: We noticed that the orchestra was raised higher than on the previous Thursday, rendering the effect of the instruments more salient. The orchestra's disposition was also better.[28]

[23] *[Almanach des] Spectacles de Paris ... pour l'année 1778* (Paris, [1777]) (title varies). The reference is to Angermüller (see n. 22 above).
[24] *Mercure de France*, 177–80.
[25] Ibid. 184.
[26] Anon., 'Concert spirituel', *Journal de musique*, ii. 206–19, here 208–9.
[27] *Mercure de France*, i. 169–70.
[28] Ibid. ii. 164–5.

12 April 1773: The Concert spirituel has a much greater following since the new arrangement .... They have nearly Italianized it, and people agree that, as far as the instrumental portions are concerned, it is at present the best regulated concert in all of Europe.[29]

30 June 1773: It is with great pleasure that we announce a revolution of interest to lovers of good music. Until now the Concert spirituel has been the object of jesting among true connoisseurs .... The new directors ... have undertaken to rescue it from this sort of endorsement, and their efforts have succeeded. [...] By their integrity they knew how to win the confidence and constant application of the musicians. Under their command, everything became easy; rehearsals are carried out with diligence and zeal. The directors have changed the orchestra's disposition and augmented the number of musicians. Although there was insufficient time before the fortnight prior to Easter to collect as great a number of good pieces of music as might have been hoped for, it would have been difficult to add to the precision, the ensemble, and the intelligence of the performance.[30]

22 March 1777: We cannot conceal the fact that one of the greatest obstacles to the progress of music in France has been the lack of intelligence in performance. The instrumental part in particular, offering nothing to the spirit [i.e., having no words], demands effects so much the more conspicuously, and these different effects depend entirely on the manner in which the instrumental part is performed.

Mr Legros took a course that proves how important this matter is to him: he knew that the number of instruments must be relative to the size of the hall and that most often one produced greater effects with a less large number of performers. Consequently, he reduced the number of performers in both the orchestra and the choir. Thus the first symphony [by Gossec] that was played last Wednesday absolutely amazed the audience.[31]

25 March 1777: Not for a long time have we heard a Concert spirituel as brilliant as that of the day before yesterday. Mr Lahoussaye's taste and intelligence were remarked by the audience. This able musician spent fifteen years in Italy and seven in London. The first symphony [by Gossec, from the repertory of the Concert des amateurs] produced the greatest effect. We especially admired a crescendo that produced an entirely new impression.[32]

April 1777: The public noted the fine execution and superior intelligence of Mr Lahoussaye, concertmaster, who is entirely worthy to lead the orchestra over which he presides.[33]

8 April 1777: In general the Concert spirituel, which had gradually improved during the last few years, has taken on an absolutely new face since Mr Legros has been presiding there, as much by the excellence of the music and the virtuosos in all genres that he

[29] Louis Petit de Bachaumont, *Mémoires secrets pour servir à l'histoire de la république des lettres en France* (London, 1780–9), xxiv. 260.

[30] *Journal de musique,* i. 75–6.

[31] *Journal de Paris,* 2–3.

[32] Ibid. 3.

[33] *Mercure de France,* 160.

collected together there as by great skill in the performances. He decreased the number of performers in the orchestra and the choir, and with fewer instruments and voices he produced more of an effect.[34]

These reforms at the Concert spirituel were occasioned in the first instance by the fact that the orchestra had been founded to perform a repertory of French music in the style of Delalande, whose motets, and their imitations, were mainstays of the series' repertory. Only gradually did the Concert spirituel come to perform less French and more Italian and German, less archaic and more modern, music, to which new tasks it was at first ill suited. The crises were undoubtedly exacerbated, and the reforms motivated, by invidious comparisons with the Concert des amateurs, whose orchestra was from the start designed to perform 'modern' music. The reform of March 1777 involved both a change of management, with Gaviniès, Leduc, and Gossec resigning as directors and Legros replacing them, and a change in the membership of the orchestra. The composition of the orchestra that, according to the *Almanach* for 1779, gave the première of K. 297 is given in Table 9.2. Of course, all fifty-seven players may not have been present on 18 June 1778: some may have been ill, others on leave, or taking turns in some kind of system of rotation, although, unlike German and Austrian court orchestras with daily services, the orchestra of the Concert spirituel played only a handful or two of concerts a year, and most members were probably present for most of these occasions.

Certain aspects of this orchestra deserve comment: one is the large number of bassoons, a feature of several orchestras of the period, which gives the bass-line a characteristic 'etched' sound quite different from that of a modern orchestra's bass-line. Because the upper woodwind players were doublehanded, the orchestra could play French motets, ouvertures, and suites of dances with three first and three second oboes, or it could play works with 'modern' orchestration (like Mozart's symphony) with pairs of flutes, oboes, and clarinets. Another noteworthy feature is the apparent absence of a keyboard continuo player. The orchestra's roster included an organist up to the 1772–3 season, after which no keyboard player is listed. Among the directors in the 1770s and 1780s, however, there were always one or more persons qualified to play keyboard continuo; works containing recitative continued to appear on the programmes, and someone must therefore have been available to play continuo even if a newer practice may have eliminated the continuo instrument for many, most, or even all other types of music.

Nothing is known about the orchestra's seating plan, beyond what is revealed in passing by the series of reforms documented above: the first and second violins

---

[34] Bachaumont, *Mémoires secrets*, x. 94–5.

TABLE 9.2 The orchestra of the Concert spirituel, 1776–1791

season*	vn. I	vn. II	va.	vc.	db.	fl.	ob.	cl.	bn.	hn.	tpt.	timp.	TOTAL
1776–7	10	10	4	10	4	2	2	2	4	2	2	1	53
1777–8	10†	10†	6	8†	6		6		4		5	1	56–9
1778–9	11	10	5	8†	5		7		4		5	1	56–7
1779–80	10	9	5	8†	4		6		3		5	1	51–2
1780–1	9	9‡	4	8	4		6		4		4	1	49–52
1781–2	10	10	5	8	4		6		4		5	1	56
1782–3	10	10	4	8	4		6		4		5	1	52
1783–4	10	10	4	9	4		6		4		6	1	54
1784–5	11	12	4	10	4		6		4		6	1	58
1785–6	11	10	4	10	4		6		4		6	1	56
1786–7	11	12	4†	10	4		6		4		6	1	58–9
1787–8	10	10	5	10	4		6		4		6	1	56
1788–9	11	10	5	10	4		6		4		6	1	57
1789–91	10	8	4	10	4		7		3	5	5	1§	54

(From 1777–8 the fl., ob. and cl. columns are joined by a brace to a single figure, as are the hn. and tpt. columns.)

* The date of each almanac is the latter of the two years given in this column. For example, the statistics from the almanac 'pour l'année 1785' appear under '1784–5.'
† Plus one supernumerary.
‡ Plus three supernumeraries.
§ Plus one trombone.

Source: Almanach des spectacles de Paris [title varies] *pour l'année* . . . . .

were on the left and right, each led by a distinguished virtuoso; there was no baton conductor; some (or all?) of the instruments were on risers. As the reform of the orchestra was at least partly in response to the success of the Concert des amateurs, and as Gossec, who was brought in to carry out that reform, had been for many years director of the rival group, the description of a seating arrangement by a Parisian violinist-composer involved with the Concert des amateurs is relevant:

The orchestra's disposition counts for much, and one must observe the following rules, namely: put the second violins opposite and not alongside the firsts; place the bass instruments as near as possible to the first violins, for in harmony the bass is the essential part of the chords; finally, bring together the wind instruments—such as the oboes, flutes, horns, etc.—and finish it off with the violas.

Of all the orchestras, the best composed and the best arranged was, without doubt, that of the Concert de l'Hôtel de Soubise, otherwise called the Concert des amateurs. However, they had the bass instruments separated too much from the first violins, and I recall that, when I performed solos there, I took care, on the example of the famous violinist Lamotte, to ask the celebrated [cellist] Duport or Jannson to draw near me, so that I could indicate and strictly mark the tempo that the orchestra had to follow. For the delay of the sound caused by distance must necessarily disturb the musical ensemble and, as the bass is the foundation of a concert, it must then be close to the melody.

Hence, put the first and second violins alongside the bass instruments; then the ensemble will be perfect.[35]

An attempt at a hypothetical reconstruction of the seating arrangement described by Meude-Monpas is presented as Figure 9.1; the sound of the fifty-seven-member Concert spirituel orchestra of June 1778 placed according to this reconstruction may be heard on the Academy of Ancient Music's recordings of both versions of K. 297 = 300a.

After the performance of his symphony, Mozart had a falling out with Legros, because of the latter's failure to perform the Sinfonia concertante, K. Anhang 9 = 297B. Then one day the two men had a chance encounter:

I spoke to Piccinni at the Concert spirituel . . . . I told you already that my symphony at the Concert spirituel was a tremendous success . . . . For next Lent I have to compose a French oratorio, which is to be performed at the Concert spirituel. Monsieur Legros, the director, is amazingly taken with me. You must know that, although I used to be with him every day, I have not been near him since Easter; I felt so indignant at his not having performed my sinfonia concertante. I often went to the same house to visit Monsieur Raaff and each

---

[35] J. J. O. de Meude-Monpas, *Dictionnaire de musique* (Paris, 1787), 132–3. The size of the famous orchestra of the Concert des amateurs is unknown, but its successor, the orchestra of the Société Olympique, which commissioned Joseph Haydn's symphonies Nos. 82–7 and 90–2, had the following forces in the mid-1780s: 14—14—7—10—4 / 3—2—2—2 / 4—2—1 = 65, of which 66 per cent were professionals, 18 per cent amateurs, and 16 per cent not identified (J.-L. Quoy-Bodin, 'L'Orchestre de la Société Olympique en 1786', *Revue de musicologie* (1981), lxx. 95–106).

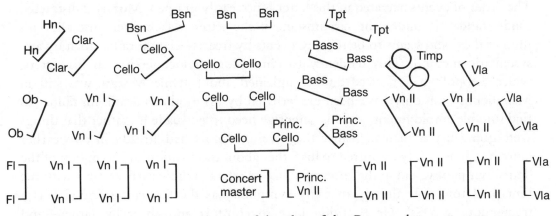

FIG. 9.1 Reconstruction of the plan of the Concert des amateurs

time I had to pass his rooms. His servant and maids often saw me and I always sent him my compliments. It is really a pity that he did not perform it, as it would have made a great hit—but now he no longer has an opportunity of doing so, for [now that the Mannheim wind players have returned home] where could four such players be found to perform it? One day, when I went to call on Raaff, I was told that he was out but would certainly be home very soon and I therefore waited. M. Legros came into the room and said: 'It is really quite wonderful to have the pleasure of seeing you again.' 'Yes, I have a great deal to do.' 'I hope you will stay to lunch with us today?' 'I am very sorry, but I am already engaged.' 'M. Mozart, we really must spend a day together again soon.' 'That will give me much pleasure.' A long pause; at length, 'A propos. Will you not write a grand symphony for me for Corpus Christi?' 'Why not?' 'Can I then rely on this?' 'Oh yes, if I may rely with certainty on its being performed, and that it will not have the same fate as my sinfonia concertante.' Then the dance began. He excused himself as well as he could but did not find much to say. In short, the symphony was highly approved of—and Legros is so pleased with it that he says it is his very best symphony. But the Andante has not had the good fortune to satisfy him; he says that it has too many modulations and that it is too long. He derives this opinion, however, from the fact that the audience forgot to clap their hands as loudly and as long as they did at the end of the first and last movements. For indeed the Andante has won the greatest approval from me, from all connoisseurs, music-lovers, and the majority of those who have heard it. It is just the reverse of what Legros says—for it is quite simple and short. But in order to satisfy him (and, as he maintains, several others) I have composed another Andante. Each is good in its own way—for each has a different character. But the new one pleases me even more .... On 15 August, the Feast of the Assumption, my symphony is to be performed for the second time—with the new Andante.[36]

[36] Letter of 9 July 1778. *Briefe*, ii. 397–8; *Letters*, ii. 836–7 (= ii. 564–5).

The order of events narrated in this letter is not easily grasped. Mozart is distracted (understandably, under the circumstances: the letter was written just after his mother died) and seems to be relating events by free association rather than by any systematic method. This tendency to chronological incoherence in his letters, which Leopold had noticed and complained about while Mozart was still in Mannheim,[37] can only have been exacerbated by his mother's death, his failure to find suitable employment, and his defensive need to persuade his father that things were going better than in reality they were. Mozart had already in two earlier letters (12 June, 3 July) reported to his father about the creation and reception of the 'Paris' symphony, and in the letter of 9 July he refers to those earlier letters with the remark 'I told you already that my symphony at the Concert spirituel was a tremendous success'. He is trying here to comfort and cheer his father—and perhaps himself—with optimistic (and largely unrealistic) plans for the future. He hopes for a commission to set a French libretto for the Paris Opéra. He says that he has been asked to compose a French oratorio for the Concert spirituel for Lent of 1779. He remarks of Legros that 'although I used to be with him every day, I have not been near him since Easter' (i.e. since 19 April), because 'I felt so indignant at his not having performed my sinfonia concertante'. His boycott of Legros was carried out even though 'I often went to the same house to visit Monsieur Raaff and each time I had to pass [Legros's] rooms.' It is at this point in his narrative that Mozart recounts the commissioning of a symphony. In the past, scholars have taken this to be a retrospective account of the commissioning of K. 297; but that must be wrong, for close examination of the letter's chronology reveals that something is seriously amiss. Mozart's boycott of Legros cannot have dated from as early as 19 April, since in his letter of 1 May he reported that 'the day before yesterday' he had been at Legros's place discussing the Sinfonia concertante, which was the subject of their falling out. And he was, of course, 'near' Legros on 17–18 June, the days on which K. 297 was rehearsed and performed at the Concert spirituel. Hence, Mozart's letter must mean that he had not been 'near' Legros 'since 18 June', rather than 'since Easter'. As the conversation reported in the letter of 9 July must have taken place during the period in which Mozart was boycotting Legros, it apparently took place between 18 June and 9 July (but enough before 9 July for Mozart to have composed a second Andante for K. 297); and the symphony in question therefore cannot be K. 297, which was already in existence and had been performed. (The matter of the second Paris symphony implied by Legros's commission is discussed below.)

---

[37] Letter of 13 Nov. 1777. *Briefe*, ii. 114–15; *Letters*, ii. 535–6 (= i. 365).

Another Andante for the Symphony in D major, K. 297 = 300a

[Incipits 9.2]

(58)

sempre **p** *sotto voce*

Instrumentation: strings, 1 flute, 1 oboe, 1 bassoon, 2 horns

Autograph: lost

Principal source: *Du Repertoire Du Concert Spirituel / Simphonie / A Deux Violons Alto et Basse / Deux Hautbois Deux Cors / 2 Clarinette[s] [2] Flutes 2 Bassons / [2] trompette[s] et timballe adlibitum* (Paris: Sieber) = *RISM* M 5508.

Editions: London: Eulenberg, 1956 (ed. H. F. Redlich); Vienna: Doblinger, 1956 (ed. E. H. Mueller von Asow); *NMA*, iv/11/5. 128–32

The portion of Mozart's letter of 9 July suggesting the creation of a second Andante for K. 297 is confirmed by the sources: the Berlin and Salzburg 'autographs' contain one Andante while the Parisian first edition has an entirely different one.[38] There seems to be general agreement today as to which was the original Andante and which the movement written to replace it, and K[6] treats the matter as if it were beyond doubt: 'The Andantino is the middle movement of the original version; the middle movement (Andante) that was played on a later occasion in Paris is found only in the first edition.' By the 'Andantino' the editors of Köchel mean the movement in $\frac{6}{8}$ consisting of ninety-eight bars (called 'Andantino' in a draft but 'Andante' in the final score); the movement found in the first edition is in $\frac{3}{4}$ and consists of fifty-eight bars. To avoid confusion, I shall refer to them by their time signatures. The view stated in K[6] that the $\frac{3}{4}$ movement is the later of the two has been held by several reputable Mozart scholars in recent years: for instance, by Hermann Beck, Otto Erich Deutsch, J. H. Eibl[39] and also Alfred

[38] The following discussion of the two andantes, written by Alan Tyson, appears here with his kind permission. With editing and emendation to adjust it to its new context, I have taken it over from his 'The Two Slow Movements of Mozart's Paris Symphony K. 297', *The Musical Times* (Jan. 1981), cxxii. 17–21; from his letter to the editor on 'Mozart's Truthfulness', *The Musical Times* (Nov. 1978), cxviii. 938; and from personal correspondence. The *Musical Times* article also appears, slightly revised, in A. Tyson, *Mozart: Studies of the Autograph Scores* (Cambridge, Mass., 1987), 106–13. For a collation of the Berlin 'autograph', see H.-G. Klein, *Wolfgang Amadeus Mozart: Autographe und Abschriften* (Berlin, 1982), 65–6. Whereas the middle movements of K. 297 found in the Sieber print and the Berlin 'autograph' are entirely different, the first and last movements are merely different versions of the same music. (The first movement differs sufficiently that the *NMA* included a separate edition of it; the differences in the two versions of the last movement are difficult to gauge, since the 'autograph' is not one.) All three editions listed above of the Sieber Andante (and the *NMA*'s edition of Sieber's first movement) were based on sets of parts lacking their bassoon parts. The 'missing' bassoon parts are reproduced here as Appendix F, from a complete set of parts owned, and generously made available, by Alan Tyson.

[39] H. Beck, 'Zur Entstehungsgeschichte von Mozarts D-dur Sinfonie KV 297', *Mozart-Jahrbuch* (1955), 95–112; *idem*, foreword to *NMA*, iv/11/5; Deutsch, 160 (= 178); *Briefe*, v. 537.

Einstein in K^{3a}; it was perhaps first voiced by Georges de Saint-Foix in 1936.[40] On the other hand, in K^3 Einstein originally thought that the two movements were the other way round, following the opinion found in the first two editions of the Köchel Catalogue, an opinion also held by E. H. Müller von Asow and Hans F. Redlich.[41]

So, although two entirely different Andantes for K. 297 exist, there has been some confusion about which is the earlier one and which the later. It looks as though the proponents of the view that the $\frac{6}{8}$ movement preceded that in $\frac{3}{4}$ have relied on two considerations. Firstly, if Legros found the earlier movement too long, is not its replacement, designed to please him, likely to have been shorter? The $\frac{6}{8}$ movement, as we have already said, has ninety-eight bars, whereas the $\frac{3}{4}$ movement has only fifty-eight. But the latter's first section is marked to be repeated, bringing it up to eighty-four bars; thus in performance there is little to choose between them. In a recent recording of the two movements in which the repeats are observed, the $\frac{6}{8}$ movement lasts about 5′ 55″ and the $\frac{3}{4}$ movement about 4′ 30″.[42] Such 'data' are not without value, even though one can never be sure that the tempos chosen for any modern performance are comparable to those that Mozart would have experienced in Paris. Besides, perceptions of musical length are always somewhat subjective, and Legros may have used 'too long' as a euphemism for 'boring'. In Mozart's mind, in any case, the $\frac{3}{4}$ movement felt faster than the $\frac{6}{8}$, as a sketch of the former (discussed below) is marked Andante con moto whereas the draft version of the latter reads Andantino (for the meaning of which, see Chapter 12).

Difficult as deciding the matter of length may be, it is even harder to evaluate Legros's reported complaint that the Andante played on 18 June contained 'too much modulation'. Neither the $\frac{3}{4}$ nor the $\frac{6}{8}$ movement exhibits striking modulations, in the modern sense of that term. But Mozart and his father probably did not use the verb *modulieren* to refer to harmonic motion to new keys, for which they would most likely have employed *ausweichen*. Rather, for them *modulieren* meant 'to change ideas'. If this is what Legros complained about, then he was only the earliest of a number of Mozart's contemporaries who (as documented in Chapter 13) found his music too rich, too full of ideas.

Secondly, the version of the symphony that Mozart left with Legros must have

[40] Saint-Foix, 95 (= 67); also Wyzewa–Saint-Foix, iii. 79–83 (= ii. 84–85).
[41] E. H. Müller von Asow, 'Die Urfassung von Mozarts "Erster" Pariser Symphonie / La Version initiale de la "première" symphonie parisienne', *Grand Festival Mozart en commémoration du 150ᵉ anniversaire de la mort de W. A. Mozart* (Paris, 30 Nov.–7 Dec. 1941); idem (ed.), 'Vorwort', *W. A. Mozart, Andante der Urfassung der 1. Pariser Symphonie (K. V. 297)* (Vienna, [1956]); H. F. Redlich (ed.), 'Preface', *Edition Eulenburg, Symphony, D major (Paris) by Wolfgang Amadeus Mozart, Köchel No. 297 (Two Versions of 2nd Movement)* (London, [1956]).
[42] Jaap Schröder and Christopher Hogwood, The Academy of Ancient Music, in *Wolfgang Amadeus Mozart: The Symphonies*, vi (London: L'Oiseau-Lyre D172D 4).

been the one with the $\frac{3}{4}$ movement, since that is what is found in the first edition, published under the rubric 'Du Répertoire du Concert Spirituel'. But the question of what Mozart did and did not leave with Legros needs further consideration. Legros may have had sets of parts for both versions, but chose to publish the one with the $\frac{3}{4}$ movement. In any case, in a letter of 3 October 1778 on his homeward journey, Mozart wrote to his father from Nancy in a vein that seems designed to prepare Leopold for the meagre harvest of works resulting from the Paris sojourn:

I am not bringing you many new compositions, for I haven't composed very much . . . so I shall bring no finished work with me except my sonatas—for Legros purchased from me the two overtures [i.e., symphonies] and the sinfonia concertante. He thinks that he alone has them, but that is not true; they are still fresh in my mind, and as soon as I get home I shall write them down again.[43]

Despite Mozart's remarks, one of the things that he clearly did not leave in Paris with Legros was a collection of papers that amounted to a complete score of the symphony, K. 297. This composite manuscript, which formed the basis of André's edition of 1800 and is today in West Berlin, bears the heading 'Sinfonia à 10 instrumenti. / di Wolfgango Amadeo Mozart' to which Nissen added 'und seine Handschrift' and André 'Paris, Juny 1778'. The manuscript was in Mozart's possession at his death, was catalogued for his widow by Nissen and sold to André, who passed it on to his son Anton, who in turn brought it to Philadelphia when he emigrated to the United States but in 1873 sold it to the Prussian Library. This is the manuscript often referred to as 'the autograph', but as not all of it is in Mozart's hand, it is perhaps better considered as four separate but related sources, since it consists of the following:

1. Autograph score of the first movement. On sixteen-stave upright-format paper. The paper, as one might expect, was made in France; its watermark consists of a crowned shield enclosing a bunch of grapes, and the words 'FIN DE / M [fleur-de-lis] IOHANNOT / DANNONAY / 1777'. The score includes a substantial number of deleted and rewritten passages.

2. Autograph draft of the $\frac{6}{8}$ movement, marked 'Andantino'. On sixteen-stave upright-format paper with the same watermark as (1). There are a great many crossed-out bars, but the movement is in fact complete, so that draft can be called the 'first autograph score' of the movement. Among the deleted passages is an episode in E minor following bar 48, with a long flute solo, and (after an eight-bar return of the opening theme) an episode in C, with an oboe solo; this breaks off after seven bars (see the *NMA*, iv/11/5. 137–8).

3. Autograph score of the $\frac{6}{8}$ movement in its final form, marked 'Andante'. On upright-format paper; the staves have been drawn singly and vary between sixteen and twenty on each page. The paper is of Swiss origin; its watermark reads: 'NIC: HEISLER'. The text in

---

[43] *Briefe*, ii. 492; *Letters*, ii. 924 (= ii. 622).

general follows (2), but in writing out the movement again Mozart incorporated a number of small improvements.[44]

4. Score of the Finale, in the hand of a copyist. On sixteen-stave upright-format paper with the same watermark as (1).

There is general agreement that (1) represents the original score of the first movement; indeed, its numerous deleted passages and alterations scarcely permit any other interpretation. And paper with an identical watermark is found in several of the autograph scores that Mozart is known to have written in Paris, the paper being ruled either with sixteen staves, as here in (1), (2), (4), the Gavotte, K. 300, and the fragment known as 'La Chasse', K. Anhang 103 = 299d; or with fourteen staves, as in the D major Violin Sonata, K. 306 = 300l and the A minor Piano Sonata, K. 310 = 300d. The presumption is that this paper was bought by Mozart in Paris, and that anything written on it will have been composed in Paris or in the weeks following his departure from there.[45]

But a score written on paper from Basel—as is the case with (3), the finished version of the $\frac{6}{8}$ movement—must be viewed rather differently. Mozart would not have bought this paper, which was made by the Basel firm of Heisler (or Heusler, as it is better known)[46] in Paris. Swiss paper travelled down the Rhine, in much the same way as Dutch paper travelled up the Rhine, and the young Beethoven used both[47]—some of it made by Heusler—in his earliest compositions written in Bonn in the 1780s and the beginning of the 1790s. Thus is it possible that Mozart acquired the paper for writing out the final version of the $\frac{6}{8}$ movement in Strasburg, which he reached on about 14 October 1778, eighteen days after leaving Paris, and where he stayed until 3 November.[48] Or he may even have waited until he reached Mannheim on 6 November, where he was to remain for over a month.

An additional source was first described in 1965.[49] It is a sketchleaf of Mozart's discovered in the music library of the monastery at Einsiedeln in Switzerland. One side of the leaf includes the melodic line of the $\frac{3}{4}$ movement, here marked 'Andante con moto'. Although the size and character of its writing identifies it as a 'sketch', it

---

[44] See n. 55 below.

[45] Two exceptions are the March, K. 408, No. 1 = 383e (probably dating from Mozart's early Vienna years), and the Masonic song *Gesellenreise*, K. 468 (entered by Mozart in his catalogue of his works under the date 26 Mar. 1785). The presumption is that these tiny works (which occupy three leaves and one leaf respectively) were written on blank leaves taken from an older manuscript by the always impecunious composer.

[46] See W. F. Tschudin, *The Ancient Paper-mills of Basle and Their Marks* (Hilversum, 1958).

[47] For instance, in the autographs of the 1785 piano quartets, WoO 36, the 1783 organ fugue, WoO 31, the four-hand *Variations on a Theme of Count Waldstein*, WoO 36, and the piano part, in the hand of a copyist, of the very early E flat piano concerto, WoO 4.

[48] At the time Strasburg was, from the point of view of tariffs, a special enclave even within Alsace. French paper would have been very expensive there, since French export duties and probably internal tariffs *en route* had to be paid on it. There was a large trade between Strasburg and Basel, not only by river but also by road. See F. L. Ford, *Strasbourg in Transition 1648–1789* (Cambridge, Mass., 1958), 132, 147.

[49] Ernst Hess, 'Ein neu entdecktes Skizzenblatt Mozarts', *Mozart-Jahrbuch* (1964), 185–202.

is neatly written, is furnished with slurs, staccato marks, and dynamic signs, and has repeat marks after the first twenty-six bars. This 53-bar sketch differs rather little in concept from the finished form of the movement, which contains 58 bars: the first two bars differ somewhat; in place of bars 37–40 the sketch has two bars of dominant preparation; bars 50–3 are not present in the sketch; and bar 58 appears as two bars.

Below this extended draft of the $\frac{3}{4}$ movement there are a couple of short sketches for what are apparently dances; however, the other side of the sketchleaf brings a surprise, for it contains a sketch for bars 136–42 of the Finale of the 'Paris' symphony. This passage too is not yet in its final form. The natural inference is that while Mozart's work on the Finale of the symphony had still some way to go, the $\frac{3}{4}$ movement was almost ready. That would put the date of the sketchleaf's contents to a time before 12 June, the day on which he informed his father of the symphony's completion. Noverre's ballet-pantomime *Les Petits riens*, to which Mozart contributed some music (K. Anhang 10 = 299b), was performed for the first time in Paris on 11 June, and that commission may account for the presence of the dance sketches on the leaf.[50]

Today the sketchleaf measures 182 × 202 mm. and has eleven staves on each side. But it has been cut; for careful examination indicates that it was originally a sixteen-stave upright-format leaf, identical with the paper of K. 297's first-movement autograph and other sources described above. The watermark can just be made out: '[DA]NNONAY / 1777'.[51]

There is yet another document that must be taken into account, however. That is a copyist's score of the symphony, now in the Mozarteum in Salzburg. Hitherto its prime claim to scholarly attention has been the fact that on the first six pages the wind parts (but not the string parts) were written in by Mozart.[52] But what is equally relevant to the present discussion is that it is written on the upright-format paper made by Johannot of Annonay already referred to, though this time it is of the fourteen-stave and not the sixteen-stave variety. And although the Salzburg score is not complete, it includes the whole of the first movement and the first six bars of the $\frac{6}{8}$ movement—not in its draft form but in its final form. Does that mean that the $\frac{6}{8}$ movement was composed and ready to be copied—indeed, was copied to the extent of six bars—before the time Mozart left Paris?

An examination of the Salzburg score reveals that it consists of two gatherings each of six bifolia, making twenty-four leaves in all, undoubtedly bought in Paris.

---

[50] Another (less likely) possibility is that Mozart wrote the side of the sketchleaf containing the draft of the Finale early on, leaving the other side empty. Later, working on the $\frac{3}{4}$ replacement Andante, he needed paper for a sketch and found this leaf with one side still blank.

[51] Watermark established with the kind assistance of Pater Lukas Helg of Kloster Einsiedeln.

[52] W. A. Mozart, *Symphonie parisienne: Fragment* (Lucerne, 1949).

But they were not all used at the same time, while Mozart was still in Paris, for five pages at the end are still unused today, and there are not two hands in the score, but three: Mozart's and those of two copyists whose work was quite separate both in time and place. The hand of the first copyist is familiar to us, as he copied the Finale of the symphony in the Berlin 'autograph', number 4 in our enumeration of the Berlin source. In the Salzburg score he wrote the string parts from the beginning of the symphony down to the end of p. 33—i.e. to bar 231 of the first movement. It is likely that this was copied before Mozart began to write in the score, and it is certain that it was copied in Paris during his residence there, for these string parts were copied from the autograph score of the first movement (1) at a time before he made a number of small changes in it—mainly ones of altering triplet quavers to semiquavers.[53] And we know that these changes, visible as alterations in the autograph, were made while Mozart was still in Paris, because they are found in the first edition of the symphony, which was based on material (probably a set of parts) that he left with Legros prior to his departure from the French capital.

Thus we can speak of a 'Paris' copyist. But it should not be assumed that the rest of the score, although on French paper, was written in Paris. From p. 34 (bar 232 of the first movement) another copyist takes over, who not only completes the string parts of the first movement but who also copies the wind parts that Mozart had stopped writing in at the end of p. 6 (bar 40 of the first movement). This second copyist also wrote out the first six bars of the $\frac{6}{8}$ movement on p. 43, and then stopped; as has already been said, the last five pages of the score were left blank.

Unlike the first copyist, this second has a 'Viennese' hand. His work is known from other Mozart scores, mainly from the Viennese years—for example, a score of the late String Quintet, K. 593—but is not found among the 'authentic' sources, the scores emanating from Mozart's immediate circle. There is no particular reason to suppose that he was close to Mozart, and some of his scores may even have been copied after Mozart's death.[54] The matter need not be pursued further here: what is relevant is that there is no reason for supposing the six bars of the $\frac{6}{8}$ movement in the Salzburg score to have been copied before the 1780s (at the earliest), or to have been copied in Paris. They have no bearing on the time and place at which the $\frac{6}{8}$ movement was composed.

Let us therefore return to the sketchleaf and the Berlin scores. As has already been pointed out, the natural inference from the former is that the $\frac{3}{4}$ movement was more or less finished by the time at which the Finale was still being worked out, and thus was part of the symphony performed on 12 June 1778. And the natural inference from the Basel paper used for (3) of the latter, the revised version of the $\frac{6}{8}$

---

[53] For instance, violins I and II in bars 82, 93–8, 101–2, 178–85, and elsewhere. In bars 53 and 207 the violin's fourth and eighth notes were originally crotchets, not quavers. See also Beck's Critical Report to the *NMA*, iv/11/5.

[54] The information about this second copyist was generously provided by Wolfgang Plath.

movement, is that this revision was carried out in Strasburg (where Mozart gave an orchestral concert on 24 October and seemingly another one on 31 October), or possibly in Mannheim—in all events, after Mozart had left Paris behind him forever.

But there is nothing in this to prevent the further conclusion that the $\frac{6}{8}$ movement was first written in Paris. It would seem to be the version represented by (2) of the Berlin scores that was played when the 'Paris' Symphony was performed for the second time on 15 August. Later, apparently while in Strasburg (or Mannheim), Mozart felt that there were at least some small ways in which it could be improved, and accordingly produced the revised version of the movement, (3) of the Berlin scores.[55]

The difficulty, of course, is to reconcile this apparently straightforward state of affairs with the statements in Mozart's letters to his father. If Mozart left Paris with autograph scores of the first two movements of the Paris Symphony and a copyist's score of the Finale, why should he have written to his father from Nancy implying that he had been unable to bring any orchestral music with him—that it had all been left with Legros—though he hoped when back home to write it all down from memory? Here we must enter the realm of conjecture. For most of the information about Mozart's activities in Paris we are dependent on a single source: his letters to his father. Mozart's biographers have sometimes taken these invaluable documents as purely factual accounts, without inquiring into his motivations and, dare we say it, his tendency to distort the truth. Some of his letters appear to strain the bounds of truth in order to be entertaining. Others adopt a defensive tone which he employed to fend off his father's frequent and sometimes justified complaints of disorganization and indolence. Circumstances and events were often given an unjustifiably favourable interpretation by Wolfgang, in the hope of avoiding paternal criticism. Leopold was aware of these less than attractive traits and, catching his son in a lie or inconsistency, would scold him roundly. We have already noted, for instance, that Wolfgang claimed to have left all copies of K. 297 in Paris, whereas he must have had with him both the Berlin and Salzburg manuscripts. In fact, there is a lot of evidence that is hard to match with what Mozart says in his letters; his lack of veracity when writing to his father is still not sufficiently taken into account by biographers.

It has been suggested above that Legros commissioned a second symphony and, as Mozart in his letter of 3 October mentioned two symphonies, the question of the identity of the second of these must be considered. Unlike the detailed comments

---

[55] The most easily recognizable feature of the first version is that bars 73–4 are in the major and bar 75–6 in the minor. Mozart reversed this in the later version, which is the one normally heard today, although orchestras occasionally use editions based on the *GA* (1880), which followed the first version.

accorded the first Paris symphony in Mozart's letters, his comments devoted to the second are sketchy, besides the remark of 3 October consisting of only one other: 'I have made quite a name for myself by my two symphonies, the second of which was performed on the 8th [September].'[56] The second symphony cannot have been the other symphony commissioned by Legros, according to Mozart's already quoted letter of 9 July, for Corpus Christi meant 3 June 1779, and Mozart never fulfilled commissions so far in advance of their deadlines. Two avenues of investigation suggest themselves: the programmes of the Concert spirituel, and the known publications of Mozart's symphonies in Paris.

The programmes of the Concert spirituel may be mostly reconstructed from notices that appeared in the press. Those which involved symphonies by Mozart are summarized in Table 9.1. This chronicle confirms the dates cited in Mozart's letters: the première of K. 297 on 18 June 1778, its repetition on 15 August, and the performance of another symphony on 8 September. As we have seen, Mozart claimed to have left two 'ouverturen' behind in Paris for publication: the publisher Sieber and the entrepreneur Legros opened a subscription list for several symphonies in the *Annonces, affiches et avis divers* of 20 February 1779, and included in their list of offerings were two symphonies by Mozart.[57] Can these be identified?

Several symphonies were published in Paris under Mozart's name in the years following his visit there. One of these is the first edition of K. 297, which (as stated above) bears the legend 'Du Répertoire du Concert Spirituel' on its title-page.[58] The second, also published by Sieber, is the Symphony in D, K. 385, the 'Haffner' symphony, and this edition bears the identical legend on its title-page, as well as the indication, '2me Symphonie'.[59] The 'Haffner' symphony may with complete confidence be ruled out as a candidate for the second Paris symphony of 1778, however, since its creation in Vienna in 1782, and its transformation in 1783 into the commonly-known version, is fully documented in Mozart's letters of the period, as presented in Chapter 11. These two editions are supposed by K^6 to have been published in 1788, but there are reasons to believe that this is wrong. First of all, as mentioned above Sieber advertised two symphonies as early as 1779. Secondly, Sieber's edition of K. 297 first appeared without plate number and later bore the number 73 and subsequently 773, while his edition of K. 385 was assigned the number 1025. Sieber's plate numbers cannot always be used to date the publications on which they appear: the numbers below 1,000 seem to be in random

[56] Letter of 11 Sept. 1778. *Briefe*, ii. 473; *Letters*, ii. 909 (= ii. 613).

[57] G. de Saint-Foix, 'Les Éditions françaises de Mozart (1765–1801)', *Mélanges de musicologie offerts à Lionel de La Laurencie* (Paris, 1933), 247–58; C. Johansson, *French Music Publishers' Catalogues of the Second Half of the Eighteenth Century* (Stockholm, 1955), ii. 150; Bibliothèque nationale, *Mozart en France* (Paris, 1956), 34, 70.

[58] *RISM* M 5508.

[59] *RISM* M 5523.

order. However, he did start assigning numbers to unnumbered publications around 1783, and numbers above 1,000 stay fairly close to chronological order, beginning *c*.1790. Hence the first state of Sieber's edition of K. 297 (without plate number) probably dates from before *c*.1783, the state bearing the number 73 from after that date, that bearing 773 from later still, and the Haffner edition from 1789.[60] It seems that Sieber's call in 1779 for subscribers may have failed, for not only can no surviving copy of his edition of Mozart's K. 297 be dated that early, but the other symphonies offered at the same time—by Cannabich and Sterkel— appear also not to have been issued then.[61]

Symphony in B flat major, K. 311a = Anh. C 11.05

[Incipits 9.3]

Instrumentation: strings, 2 flutes, 2 oboes, 2 clarinets, 2 bassoons, 2 horns, 2 trumpets, kettledrums
Autograph: none
Principal source: *Ouverture | A Grand Orchestre | par | Mozart | . . . A Paris | A l'Imprimerie du Conservatoire = RISM M 5646*
Facsimile: none
Edition: Braunschweig: Litolff, 1937 (ed. A. Sandberger)

When this symphony, published in Paris between 1802 and 1806, was rediscovered, it was thought to be the 'missing' second Paris symphony, and, as such, appeared in K[3] as 311a. It consists of two movements in a third-rate imitation of a French operetta overture, rather than a first-rate work in three movements in the style of Mozart's symphonies and overtures of the 1770s. It must be one of the

[60] F. Lesure and A. Devriès, *Dictionnaire des éditeurs de musique française* (Geneva, 1979), i. 141–5; F. Lesure (ed.), *Catalogue de la musique imprimée avant 1800 conservée dans les bibliothèques publiques de Paris* (Paris, 1981), 454.
[61] Letter of 10 Dec. 1980 from A. Tyson. See also *RISM*, Serie A/I, under Cannabich, Mozart, and Sterkel.

many forgeries committed in Mozart's name as his posthumous fame grew. The piece has now been relegated to its rightful place in the appendix of K^6.[62]

The fourth symphony published in Paris, another in D, is the symphony drawn from the orchestral serenade, K. 320, discussed in Chapter 10. This edition, published by Imbault, says nothing on its title-page about 'Du Répertoire du Concert Spirituel';[63] it can have nothing to do with Mozart's Paris visit of 1778, as the serenade from which the symphony was drawn was composed in Salzburg in August 1779.

How any of the Parisian publications of Mozart's symphonies may link up with performances at the Concert spirituel is a bit of a mystery. From reading several years' concert announcements one soon learns that the description of a work as 'nouvelle' signified its first performance at the Concert spirituel and not necessarily its world première. Besides the première of K. 297 and the unidentified symphony of 9 September 1778, another 'new' symphony by Mozart was apparently heard on 23 March 1780, which, again, cannot have been the 'Haffner' symphony. And the designation 'new' may in this instance have been an error, for it appeared only in the notice in the *Annonces, affiches et avis divers* and not in those in the *Journal de Paris* or the *Mercure de France*. The Paris edition of the 'Haffner' symphony may be labelled 'Du Répertoire du Concert Spirituel', but no further 'new' symphonies appear on our list. None the less, its Parisian première may have been on 25 March 1786, since the rapidity with which the next date followed suggests the repetition of a novelty by popular request, a not uncommon occurrence at the Concert spirituel.

The Parisian edition of the 'Haffner' symphony may have been pirated from the edition published in Vienna by Artaria in 1785. On the other hand, Mozart corresponded with the publisher Sieber and the entrepreneur Legros in 1782–3,[64] and, as seems not to have been remarked previously, he held an official position as 'Compositeur' to the Concert spirituel from 1778 to 1783. This we learn from the

---

[62] Although this symphony was published in 1937, the Second World War intervened and a recording of it was issued only in 1952 (Lyrichord LL 32); since then the tide of critical opinion has turned against it. Those in favour: Saint-Foix, 98–105 (= 70–5); Wyzewa–Saint-Foix, iii. 105–8 (= ii. 111–14); A. Sandberger in the edition just cited; H. C. Robbins Landon in the sleeve notes for the recording just cited; B. Paumgartner, 'Mozart à Paris', *Revue d'Autriche* (1918), i/8. 183–6; *idem, Mozart* (Berlin, 1927), 472; R. Tenschert, 'Mozarts Ouverture in B-dur (KV Anh. I, No. 8)' *Zeitschrift für Musikwissenschaft* (1929), xii. 187–91; and M. L. P[ereyra], 'A propos de l'Ouverture en si bémol de Mozart', *Revue de musicologie* (May–Aug. 1937), NS 62–3/xxi. 55. Those opposed: E. Hess, 'Zur Frage der Echtheit der Ouvertüre in B-dur, KV Anh. 8 (311a)', *Schweizer Musikzeitung* (1956), xcvi. 66–72; *idem*, 'Über einige zweifelhafte Werke Mozarts', *Mozart-Jahrbuch* (1956), 100–29; *idem*, 'Remarques sur l'authenticité de l'ouverture de W. A. Mozart', in A. Verchaly (ed.), *Les Influences étrangères dans l'œuvres de W. A. Mozart* (Paris, 1958), 227–35; Della Croce, *Le 75 sinfonie*, 198–203; K^6; and the *NMA*.

[63] *RISM* M 5656.

[64] Letter of before 17 Aug. 1782 to Legros (lost). *Briefe*, iii. 220. Letter of 26 Apr. 1783 to Jean Georges Sieber. *Briefe*, iii. 266; *Letters*, 1261–2 (= ii. 846). That there could be rapid communication between Vienna and Paris is suggested by the case of Mozart's 'Haydn' quartets, published by Artaria in September 1785 (*Wiener Zeitung* (17 Sept. 1785), lxxv. 2191; Deutsch, 221–2 (= 252)) and by December advertised in Paris by Le Duc (*Journal de Paris* (31 Dec. 1785), 1516; citation courtesy of Cliff Eisen).

'État des personnes qui composent le Concert spirituel' in the *Almanach des spectacles*, in which Mozart is listed in that capacity in the volumes for 1779, 1780, 1782, and 1783.[65] Hence, when the 'Haffner' symphony was put into its final form in 1783, Mozart still had an official connection with the Concert spirituel.

To return to the matter of the identity of the symphony performed on 8 September 1778, it is worth noting that the major works that Mozart composed in Paris, and even projects that he never brought to fruition, are discussed in his correspondence. The putative 'second Paris symphony', on the contrary, received only casual mention, as if in passing. The reason for this must be that it was not a new work. The letter of 11 September does not specifically state that the symphony performed three days earlier was a new one, although that is the clear implication, intended, one suspects, to deceive Leopold, just as it has misled musicologists in our time. Wolfgang was undoubtedly trying to appease his father, who had bombarded him with complaints about how badly he had fared financially on his journey, and how little music he had produced.

We know that Mozart brought symphonies from Salzburg with him, for they are documented in several letters prior to his arrival in Paris,[66] and on the eve of his departure from the French capital, when he was trying to sell quickly a number of pieces to publishers in order to raise cash for his homeward journey, he wrote, 'As for the symphonies, most of them are not in the Parisian taste',[67] in order to explain to his father why they could not all be sold. And what did Mozart and his father think the Parisian taste in symphonies to be? According to Leopold: 'To judge by the Stamitz symphonies that have been engraved in Paris, the Parisians must be fond of noisy symphonies. All is noise, the remainder a mish-mash, with here and there a good idea awkwardly introduced in the wrong place.'[68] And Wolfgang wrote of his 'Paris' symphony, 'I have been careful not to neglect the *premier coup d'archet*—and that is quite enough. What a fuss the oxen here make of this trick! The devil take me if I can see any difference. They all begin together too, just as in other places. It is really a joke.'[69] If we add to orchestral 'noises' and the *premier coup d'archet* Mozart's remark that 'here all final as well as first Allegros begin with all

[65] The position of 'Compositeur', listed from 1778 to 1784 and held by eight or ten composers at a time, included (besides Mozart) Alessandri, Bonesi, Cambini, Cannabich, Deshayes, Floquet, Gossec, Haydn, Le Froid de Méreaux, Rey, Richter, Rigel, Sterkel, and Vogel. From 1785 the position of 'Compositeur' no longer figures in the rosters of the Concert spirituel published in the *Almanach des spectacles*.

[66] See especially Leopold's letters of 15 Oct. and 11 Dec. 1777 discussed in ch. 6 at nn. 21 and 22.

[67] Letter of 11 Sept. 1778. *Briefe*, ii. 476; *Letters*, ii. 913 (= ii. 615).

[68] Letter of 29 June 1778. *Briefe*, ii. 386; *Letters*, ii. 823 (= ii. 556). Leopold's criticism of Stamitz's symphonies may be compared with Burney's of Mannheim symphonies in general: 'The symphonies of Man[n]heim, excellent as they are, have been observed, by persons of refined taste, to be *manierées*, and tiresome to such as continue there any time, being almost all of one craft, from the writers of them giving too much into imitation' (*The Present State of Music in Germany, the Netherlands, and the United Provinces* (London, 1771), 220 n.).

[69] Letter of 12 June 1778. *Briefe*, ii. 378–9; *Letters*, ii. 818 (= ii. 553).

the instruments playing together and generally *unisono*', we have a summary of the Mozarts' impression of Parisian taste in symphonies *circa* 1778. To this we might add a preference for the major mode and for three rather than four movements.[70] Mozart's K. 297 fits this composite description, with the exception (which he himself noted) of the way in which the Finale begins—and one other feature: repetition. Mozart's 'Paris' symphony, quite exceptionally for one of his concert symphonies of the late 1770s, has no repeated sections, but it does have an extraordinary number of phrases that are immediately repeated, more than any other symphony of his. K. 297 shares this characteristic with another D major symphony, written for Paris by the Mannheim composer Toeschi; Mozart, fresh from Mannheim, may have used Toeschi's 'Paris' symphony (which had been successful) as a model.[71] Possibly Toeschi and Mozart after him were thinking of the characteristic construction in 'couplets' found in so many French chaconnes and passacailles.

In any case, the symphony performed at the Concert spirituel on 8 September 1778 must have been one of the symphonies that Mozart had brought with him, for there is no trace of a 'missing' Paris symphony,[72] and if he believed that most of the symphonies he had with him were 'not in the Parisian taste', then he must also have believed that at least one of them was in that taste. If we give him the benefit of the doubt and allow that there was some truth in his claim that he had no copies with him of the two symphonies he had sold to Legros, then perhaps even if the claim was untrue of K. 297 (could his papers have been in such disarray that he himself did not know he still had the score, or was he ashamed of the messy state of his manuscript and planning to hide the work from Leopold until he could create a fair copy?), it may have been true for another work he had left behind, which unfortunately remains unidentified.

---

[70] Brook, *La Symphonie française*, i. 280–2, 287. For speculation on which of his earlier symphonies Mozart may have had performed at the Concert spirituel on 8 Sept. 1778, see N. Zaslaw, 'Mozart's Paris Symphonies', *The Musical Times* (1978), cxix. 753–7; (1979), cxx. 197.

[71] R. Münster, 'Die Sinfonien Toeschis: Ein Beitrag zur Geschichte der Mannheimer Sinfonie' (Ph.D. diss., University of Munich, 1956), p. 65, n. 2; *idem*, 'Mannheimer Musiker', *Musica* (1961), xv. 113–17; *idem*, 'Toeschi', *The New Grove*, xix. 24–5. Toeschi's symphony is Riemann D–11 = Münster 44.

[72] Cf. the letter of 12 Mar. 1783 in which Mozart wrote in the singular of 'my symphony for the Concert spirituel' (*Briefe*, iii. 259; *Letters*, iii. 1254 (= ii. 842)), and his sister's reminiscences (spring 1792), also in the singular: 'In Paris he composed a symphony for the Concert spirituel' (Deutsch, 404 (= 461)).

IO

Salzburg III: Serfdom (1779–1780)

Mozart's letters between 1775 and 1781 are filled with contumelies against his native city. His bitter harangues are difficult to evaluate objectively, arising as they do out of such emotional subjects as his father's lack of promotion, his own poor pay, the Archbishop's policy of treating his musicians as servants rather than professionals (let alone geniuses), and the censorship and factionalism at court. Leopold Mozart, resigned to his plight after years of fruitless struggle, continued to hope for a better position for Wolfgang, who wanted desperately to be done with Salzburg. Wolfgang's defensive contempt for Salzburg can be understood: a childhood and youth spent as the darling of various courts, opera houses, and cities had prepared him badly for the realities of provincial Salzburg. Amid the torrent of his invective one can glean clues to the nature of his specifically musical discontents:

9 July 1778: One of my chief reasons for detesting Salzburg [is] those coarse, slovenly, dissolute court musicians. Why, no honest man, of good breeding, could possibly live with them! Indeed, instead of wanting to associate with them, he would feel ashamed of them. It is probably for this very reason that musicians are neither popular nor respected among us. Ah, if only the orchestra were organised as it is at Mannheim. Indeed, I would like you to see the discipline which prevails there and the authority which Cannabich wields. There everything is done seriously. Cannabich, who is the best director I have ever seen, is both beloved and feared by his subordinates. Moreover he is respected by the whole town and so are his soldiers. But certainly they behave quite differently from ours. They have good manners, are well dressed, and do not go to pubs and swill. This can never be the case in Salzburg, unless the Prince will trust you or me and give us full authority as far as the musical establishment is concerned—otherwise it's no good. In Salzburg everyone—or rather no-one—bothers about the musical establishment. If I were to undertake it, I should have to have complete freedom of action. The Chief Steward should have nothing to say to me in musical matters, or on any point relating to music. For a courtier can't do the work of a Kapellmeister, but a Kapellmeister can well be a courtier![1]

---

[1] *Briefe*, ii. 395; *Letters*, ii. 832–3 (= ii. 562).

7 August 1778: Salzburg is no place for my talent. In the first place, professional musicians there are not held in much consideration; and, secondly, one hears nothing, there is no theatre [not strictly true], no opera; and even if they really wanted one, who is there to sing? For the last five or six years the Salzburg orchestra has always been rich in what is useless and superfluous, but very poor in what is necessary, and absolutely destitute of what is indispensable; and such is the case at the present moment.[2]

11 September 1778: To tell you my real feelings, the only thing that disgusts me about Salzburg is the impossibility of mixing freely with the people, and the low estimation in which the court musicians are held there—and—that the Archbishop has no confidence in the experience of intelligent people who have seen the world .... If the Archbishop would only trust me, I should soon make his orchestra famous; of this there can be no doubt.[3]

3 December 1778: Ah, if only we too had clarinets [as they do in Mannheim]! You cannot imagine the glorious effect of a symphony with flutes, oboes and clarinets. I shall have much that is new to tell the Archbishop at my first audience, and perhaps a few suggestions to make as well. Ah, how much finer and better our orchestra might be, if only the Archbishop desired it. Probably the chief reason why it is not better is because there are far too many performances. I have no objection to the chamber music, only to the concerts on a larger scale.[4]

26 May 1781: In Salzburg—for me at least—there is not a farthing's worth of entertainment. I refuse to associate with a good many people there—and most of the others do not think me good enough. Besides, there is no stimulus for my talent! When I play or when any of my compositions are performed, it is just as if the audience were all tables and chairs. If at least there were a theatre there worthy of the name.[5]

It may have been true that the people of Salzburg were, as Schubart put it in the 1770s, 'exceedingly inclined to low humour',[6] but there is an inescapable irony in Mozart's complaints to this effect for, despite his superior education and haughty attitude, he was very much of the same persuasion. Many of his letters are filled with Salzburg dialect expressions, local puns, coarse jokes, and foul language. And his constant complaining obscures the fact (documented in the Mozarts' correspondence) that they had dear friends and loyal supporters in their native city.

An important factor was Leopold's snobbery, for he had taught his son to be socially ambitious and to avoid unnecessary contact with the lower classes, including even most rank-and-file musicians. Hence his displeasure at Wolfgang's choice of wife and his delight at arranging for Nannerl to marry into a higher social class. The son attempted to please the father when he wrote that he refused 'to associate with a good many people', but he was also expressing the anguished predicament of a young man raised as a bourgeois in the midst of the vestigial feudalism of Salzburg—where the middle class was small and powerless—when he

[2] Ibid. 439; 882 (= 594).   [3] Ibid. 473; 909 (= 612).   [4] Ibid. 517; 948 (= 368).
[5] Ibid. iii. 121; iii. 1095 (= ii. 736).   [6] Schubart, *Ideen*, 158. For the whole passage, see ch. 8, n. 1.

added, 'and most of the others do not think me good enough'. The Mozarts'
profound disillusionment arose from the painful contrast between the treatment
accorded them by the Archbishop and the way in which they were greeted
elsewhere: during their extensive travels, because they dressed well, spoke well, and
came well introduced, they were usually treated with respect and sometimes
handsomely remunerated by the upper classes of dozens of European courts and
cities.

Although the Archbishop may deserve the anger of generations of Mozart
worshippers, there is another side to the story. It cannot be denied, for instance,
that Leopold was passed over time and again for the position of Kapellmeister, a
position for which he was fully qualified; he died still Vizekapellmeister. But he
had been away on tour a good deal of the time, and his best energies had gone into
raising his son, not into serving the court and working toward advancement at
home. In Wolfgang's case it is instructive to note that none of the Viennese nobility
who so admired his playing and compositions offered him a permanent post after
he settled there, perhaps because he could be difficult, haughty, defensive,
mercurial, and painfully conscious of his unusual gifts. In short, he may have lacked
the personality to make a good courtier or the maturity to serve as administrative
head of a musical establishment. (The comparison with Joseph Haydn, a reliable
administrator and loyal subject, is instructive.)

Leopold's letters from Salzburg reveal that the local orchestra was going
through a difficult period; for a time in 1778 there were many vacancies and no
Kapellmeister.[7] Confirmation of the difficulties reported by Leopold is found in the
remark of Charles Burney's correspondent de Visme that the orchestra was 'more
remarkable for coarseness and noise, than delicacy and high-finishing'.[8] The
membership of the orchestra as listed in the annual court calendars of this period—
without the reinforcement of musicians from the cathedral, from the town waits,
or from the amateur performers at court—is shown in Table 10.1.[9] These figures
suggest that without reinforcement the orchestra that probably gave the first
performances of symphonies K. 318, 319, 320, and 338, and early performances of
K. 300a, 385, and 425, had a membership (when trumpets and drums were called
for) of about 10–11—10–11—2—2—4 / 0–2—2–4—0—2–3 / 2–2—1, and
keyboard continuo as required. When trumpets and kettledrums were not needed,
three more fiddles were available. The 'concerts on a larger scale'—that is, the
court's orchestral concerts, which Wolfgang thought too frequent and under-
rehearsed—were briefly described in letters of Leopold's written late in 1778:

---

[7] Letter of 11 June 1778. *Briefe*, ii. 372–3; *Letters*, ii. 809–10 (= ii. 547–8).

[8] See ch. 8, n. 2.

[9] E. Hintermaier, 'Die salzburger Hofkapelle von 1700 bis 1806: Organisation und Personal' (Ph.D. diss., University of Salzburg, 1972), 540–5.

TABLE 10.1 The Salzburg court orchestra without reinforcements, 1778–1784

	1778	1779	1780	1781	1782	1783	1784
organists	2	2	3	3	2	3	3
concert-masters	1	1	1	1	1	1	1
violinists*	15	20	20	20	21	21	20
violists†	1	2	2	2	1	1	1
cellists	1	2	2	2	2	2	2
bass players	4	4	4	4	4	4	4
oboists‡	3	5	5	5	5	5	3
bassoonists	2	3	3	3	2	2	2
horn players	2	2	2	2	2	2	2
trumpet players	2	2	2	2	2	2	2
kettledrummer	1	1	1	1	1	1	1
TOTALS	34	44	45	45	43	44	41

* The violinists include 1 kettledrummer and all but two trumpet players.
† Additional violists drawn from the violinists as needed.
‡ Double on flutes.
For the possibilities for doubling and additional players, see Chapter 1.

Source: The Salzburg *Hofkalendar* as reported in E. Hintermaier, 'Die salzburger Hofkapelle von 1700 bis 1806: Organisation und Personal' (Ph.D. diss., University of Salzburg, 1972), 544.

Yesterday I was for the first time [this season] the director of the great concert at court. At present the music ends at around a quarter past eight. Yesterday it began around seven o'clock and, as I left, a quarter past eight struck—thus an hour and a quarter. Generally only four pieces are done: a symphony, an aria, a symphony or concerto, then an aria and with this, 'Addio!'[10]

And again, a week later: '. . . as the [court] concert is so short at present and consists of only four items, believe me that to play is an amusement, for one doesn't know what to do with oneself in the evenings.'[11]

The reports of outsiders, who were in a position to be more impartial about the Salzburg orchestra than the Mozarts, provide a context for evaluating the situation. To the positive statement of Schubart and the equally negative one of Burney's correspondent de Visme (see the beginning of Chapter 8) can be added a third opinion, which would appear to confirm the Mozarts' and de Visme's point of view, and a fourth, which would appear to confirm Schubart's. The former was recorded by Friedrich Siegmund von Boeklin, who visited Salzburg in the mid-1780s:

[10] Letter of 17 Sept. 1778. *Briefe*, ii. 482; this passage not in *Letters*.
[11] Letter of 24 Sept. 1778. *Briefe*, ii. 485; *Letters*, ii. 920 (= ii. 620).

While in this pretty and lively town the church music is good, tasteful, and entirely suited to sacred subjects, and several fine wind players are also to be heard here, the concert orchestra on the other hand is by no means particularly brilliant; although there are nevertheless a few excellent and well-known musicians to be found, who in sonatas and concert pieces mitigate these shadows by their charming playing; and indeed, shed a light over their weak accompanists which to a visitor often conveys a most favourable impression of the whole.[12]

The fourth outsider was Wolfgang's friend Michael Kelly, who, on his return to London from Vienna with a British party that included Thomas Attwood, Anna and Stephen Storace and their mother, visited Leopold in Salzburg. On the evening of 26 February 1787 Anna Storace sang for the Archbishop of Salzburg at a court concert, and Kelly, who was present, recalled (many years later in his ghost-written memoirs), 'The music was chiefly instrumental, admirably performed; the band numerous and excellent.'[13]

Then there were some Salzburg performances run by the Mozarts. When a friend or patron commissioned Wolfgang to write an orchestral serenade to celebrate some occasion, the Mozarts presumably gathered and rehearsed the performers themselves, and apparently achieved the discipline and quality lacking at court. The artistic control and sympathetic audiences (along with the different functions assigned serenades and symphonies[14]) may explain why the symphonic movements of Mozart's orchestral serenades of the 1770s are generally longer and more elaborate, difficult, and unconventional than comparable movements of his symphonies written then. It follows, then, that the symphonies drawn from serenades are among the finest of the period.

Although the Mozarts were engaged in frequent public and private music-making during all their years in their native city, one usually learns of it only when members of the family were travelling, so that letters were exchanged. A good example is provided in a letter of Leopold's from Salzburg in 1778, to Wolfgang in Paris:

Count Czernin is not content with fiddling at court, and as he would like to do some leading, he has collected an amateur orchestra which is to meet in Count Lodron's hall every Sunday after three o'clock. Count Sigmund Lodron came to invite Nannerl (as an amateur) to play the keyboard and to ask me [as a professional] to keep the second violins in order. A week ago today, on the fifth [of April], we had our first performance. There was Count Czernin, first violin, then Baron Babbius, Sigmund Lodron, young Weinrother, Kolb, Kolb's student from Nonnberg, and a couple of young students whom I did not know. The second violins were myself, Sigmund Robinig, Cusetti, Count

[12] Deutsch, 382 (= 336).   [13] Ibid. 252, 459 (= 286, 535).
[14] See the discussion of K. 62a at the end of ch. 6.

Altham, Cajetan Andretter, a student, and Ceccarelli *la coda dei secondi*. The two violas were the two ex-Jesuits, Bullinger and Wishofer; the two oboes were Weiser, the lackey, and a certain Schulze's son, who acted in the Linz play. Two apprentice waits played the horns. The double basses were Cassel and Count Wolfegg, with Ranftl doing duty occasionally. The cellos were the new young canons, Counts Zeill and Spaur, Court Councillor Mölk, Sigmund Andretter, and Ranftl. Nannerl accompanied all the symphonies and she also accompanied Ceccarelli, who sang an aria *per l'apertura della accademia di dilettanti*. After the symphony Count Czernin played a beautifully written concerto by Sirmen *alla* Brunetti, and *dopo una altra sinfonia* Count Altham played a horrible trio, no-one being able to say whether it was scraped or fiddled — whether it was in ¾ or common time, or perhaps even in some newly invented and hitherto unknown metre. Nannerl was to have played a concerto, but as the Countess wouldn't let them have her good harpsichord (which is solely *casus reservatus pro summo Pontifice*), and only the Egedacher one with gilt legs was there, she didn't perform. In the end the two Lodron girls had to play. It had never been suggested beforehand that they should do so. But since I have been teaching them they are always quite well able to perform. So on this occasion too they both did me credit.[15]

Even if this concert should not necessarily be taken as wholly typical, Leopold's wry account of it reveals some characteristic aspects of such occasions. The audiences and patrons for whom he and Wolfgang performed and composed included many persons with musical training, who were therefore often both connoisseurs and amateurs. A common feature of such concerts, in much of Europe at this time, was leadership by a handful of professionals with the ranks filled by amateurs, and, like most concerts of the period, this one mixed vocal and instrumental music, orchestral music and solos. The ubiquitous symphonies (or movements from them) were present too. The orchestra on this occasion had strings 8—7—2—4—5—2–3, with pairs of oboes and horns, and the faithful Nannerl—who was hardly an amateur—playing continuo. These were full forces for the period.

Further evidence of Salzburg concerts is found in Nannerl's diary, in which Wolfgang sometimes made entries. (He also teased her about it, calling her 'the living chronicle of Salzburg'.[16]) An entry for March 1780 in Wolfgang's hand transmits, through an obfuscating haze of spoonerisms and other puns, the programme of a 'second concert'[17] that may have been given by the Mozarts in the

---

[15] Letter of 12 Apr. 1778. *Briefe*, ii. 338–9; *Letters*, ii. 777–8 (= ii. 526–7). This Count Czernin was the son of the Count Czernin whose payment for a symphony and other works to be sent to Prague is discussed in ch. 8 in connection with the Symphony in D major, K. 250 = 248b.

[16] Letter of 4 July 1781. *Briefe*, iii. 138; *Letters*, iii. 1117 (= ii. 751).

[17] *Briefe*, iii. 3. There is no record of the first of these two Lenten concerts, as the pages from Nannerl's diary for the period 17 Dec. 1779 to 17 Mar. 1780 are missing.

so-called dancing-master's room in their home.[18] As it is difficult to translate such word-play, this document is given twice: in a punning translation that attempts to capture some of the spirit of the original, and as if it were a modern concert programme. But first it will help the reader to meet the cast of characters:

¶Madame Schmitt, soprano, a member of Johann Böhm's visiting theatrical troupe, who sang first romantic lead in operettas and acted second lead in plays.

¶Marianne Böhm née Jacobs, soprano, wife of the director of the troupe, who acted young maids in plays and sang character roles in operetta.

¶Zimmerl (= Kammerl; both words mean 'small room'), baritone, first lead in operetta and second in plays.

¶Kerscher (= Weichsler; a 'Weichsel' is a sour-tasting type of 'Kirsche', which is a cherry), sang older men, fathers, and servants.

¶Joseph Fiala, friend of the Mozarts, oboist, flautist, and composer, Salzburg court musician 1778–85; also active in Wallerstein, Vienna, Saint Petersburg, Prague, Regensburg, Munich, Donaueschingen; mentioned in Chapter 1.

¶Johann Georg Murschhauser, romantic lead in plays, tenor in bravura arias in operetta.

¶Francesco Ceccarelli, castrato, friend of the Mozarts, Salzburg court musician 1778–88.[19]

A free translation of Mozart's punning diary entry:

On [Saturday] the 18th [of March 1780] the second schmoncert—

1st: a symphony (namely, the Haffner music).

2nd: an Italian Wop aria trilled by Madame Schmitt.

3rd: a three-voice trio by Mr Salieri, sung by Madame Böhm, Mr Kammerl, and Mr Weichsler.

4th: a Fiala on a concerto, composed and performed by Mr Violoncello.

5th: an aria by Mr Grétry with one oboe and harp solo, sung by Mr Fiala, the oboe by Madame Böhm, and the Murchhausner by Madame Harp.

6th: the aria with trumpets, kettledrums, flutes, oboe[s], violas, bassoons, and bass-instruments, by *me*.

7th: the first finale from Anfossi's *Persequita incognitata*.

8th: after loud begging by Ceccarelli, we allowed him to sing a little round-dance.

9th: to close we performed the entire City of Milan *N.B.*: with strumpets and metaldrums.

Reduced to the format of a modern programme, with the puns deconstructed, the Mozarts' concert might look as follows:

---

[18] See ch. 1, n. 28.
[19] Based on *Briefe*, vi. 3–5; vii. 693. See also ch. 8 at n. 159.

A Lenten Concert

At the Dancing Master's House in the Hannibalplatz
Passion Saturday * 18 March 1780

Programme[20]

Symphony in D major, K. 250	W. A. Mozart
An Italian aria	[unknown]
Mme Schmitt, soprano	
A Trio	Antonio Salieri
Mme Böhm, Mr Zimmerl, Mr Kerscher	
Concerto for violoncello	Joseph Fiala
Mr Fiala, violoncello	
'Du dieu d'amour en bravant la puissance' from	
L'amitié à l'épreuve	A. E. M. Grétry
Mme Böhm, soprano, Mr Fiala, oboe, Mr Murschhauser, harp	
'Dentro il mio petto' from *La finta giardiniera*, K. 196	Mozart
Mr Murschhauser, tenor	
'Dove vado, tremo tutta' from	
L'incognita perseguitata	Pasquale Anfossi
four sopranos, tenor, and two basses	
'Ombre felice—Io ti lascio', K. 255	Mozart
Signor Ceccarelli, castrato	
'The entire city of Milan with trumpets and kettledrums'	[Mozart?]

Items on this programme of particular interest for a study of Mozart's symphonies are the first and last. Numerous concerts in which Mozart participated confirm a general practice of the time: on a long programme complete symphonies began and ended the event, whereas on a short programme the finale of the opening symphony might be saved for the conclusion. But what symphony or symphonic movement of Mozart's could have had the sobriquet 'The City of Milan'? A search for tunes current in the eighteenth century and having titles or texts associated with Milan yielded a number of items, but none proved related either to the Finale of K. 250 or to any of the following symphonies that have either firm or putative Milanese connections:

---

[20] I am grateful to Elizabeth Bartlet for suggesting the probable identity of the aria by Grétry and to Mary Hunter for identifying the ensemble by Anfossi.

1. Symphony in D, K. 84 = 73q (?Carnival [January] 1770)
2. Symphony in D, K. 87 = 74a (July–December 1770)
3. Symphony in D, K. 96 = 111b (?December 1770)
4. Symphony in D, K. 120 = 111a (August–October 1771)
5. Symphony in F, K. 98 = Anhang C 11.04 (?November 1771)
6. Symphony in F, K. 112 (2 November 1771)
7. Symphony in D, K. 161 + 163 = 141a (?end of 1772?)
8. Symphony in D, K. 135 (November–December 1773)

The authenticity of the first, third, and fifth of these works is doubtful. The sixth cannot have had trumpets, which were generally available only in C, D, and E flat. The seventh is dated 'presumably the end of 1772 in Milan' by K[6], but on the basis of Wolfgang's writing it has been dated to Salzburg in the summer of 1773 or 1774, while the paper is a type used by him mostly in the period May to October 1772.[21] The remaining three symphonies are in D and do have, or can have had, trumpets. Any of the three, then, could be considered candidates for 'the entire City of Milan with trumpets and kettledrums', although the possible nature of the connection to Milan is unclear, and one may be forgiven for wondering why Mozart would have been performing works from several years before when he had in his portfolio a number of impressive, more recent symphonies, for instance the 'Paris' symphony and the three splendid works discussed next. 'The entire city of Milan, with trumpets and kettledrums' remains an enigma.

Symphony in G major, K. 318

[Incipits 10.1]

---

[21] See the discussions of these symphonies in ch. 7.

Instrumentation: *strings, 2 flutes, 2 oboes, 2 bassoons, 4 horns, 2 trumpets, [kettledrums]

Autograph: New York Public Library

Principal source: Salzburg parts with Viennese *Dubletten*, from Mozart's estate, Stadt- und Universitätsbibliothek, Frankfurt, Mus. Ms. 208

Facsimile: *NMA*, iv/11/6. xiii

Editions: *GA*, xxi. 197–212 (= Serie 8, No. 32); *NMA*, iv/11/6. 3–22

This was the first symphony Mozart composed after his unfortunate trip to Paris. Because its format bears a resemblance to some Parisian opéra comique overtures by Grétry, biographers have exerted themselves trying to guess for which stage work this 'overture' may have been intended. Hermann Deiters suggested that K. 318 was intended for *Thamos, König von Aegypten*, K. 345 = 336a,[22] while Einstein thought that it was for the untitled and never completed Singspiel now known as *Zaïde*, K. 334 = 336b.[23] But this symphony, dated 26 April 1779, was composed too late for the first version of *Thamos* (1773) and almost certainly too early for *Zaïde* (1779–80) or the second version of *Thamos* (?winter 1779–80). Furthermore, when in the 1780s the incidental music to *Thamos* was reused with new words as incidental music to a Viennese play, not K. 318 but the E flat symphony, K. 184 = 161a, was the overture.[24] Finally, the one-movement da capo form for sinfonias was not the invention of Grétry and other composers of opéra comique, but had been taken over by them from Italian models; Mozart had previously composed such a work in the D minor symphony written as the overture for his oratorio *La Betulia liberata*, K. 118 = 74c, discussed in Chapter 7.

The *NMA* as well as all editions of the Köchel Catalogue give K. 318 the subtitle 'Ouvertüre', and the widely circulated Breitkopf & Härtel edition dubs the work 'Overture in Italian Style'. However justified these labels may seem, there is no authority for them. They were apparently intended to make a distinction between concert symphonies and theatre overtures—a distinction that in Mozart's time was largely observed in the breach, as his own practices reveal. He gave the score no title at all, simply writing 'di Wolfgango Amadeo Mozart mpr. d. 26 April 79'. Certainly he approved the work's use in the theatre (as he probably would have done with most of his symphonies): in 1785 he provided it (along with two new vocal numbers, K. 479 and 480) as the overture for a Viennese production of Bianchi's opera buffa, *La villanella rapita*, which was how the symphony was published and known in the nineteenth century. That pasticcio was performed in Paris in 1789, in London in 1790, and in Berlin in 1793; these performances

---

[22] O. Jahn, *W. A. Mozart*, 3rd edn. by H. Deiters (Leipzig, 1889–91), i. 591.   [23] K³; Einstein, 228.

[24] W. Plath, 'Mozartiana in Fulda und Frankfurt', *Mozart-Jahrbuch* (1968–70), 366.

contained some vocal music by Mozart but may not have made use of K. 318 as overture.[25]

The autograph score calls for pairs of flutes, oboes, and bassoons, with four horns and strings. A set of parts of Salzburg origin with *Dubletten* of Viennese origin and corrections in Mozart's hand contains no parts for trumpets and kettledrums.[26] Mozart did write trumpet parts, however, on two separate leaves now kept with the autograph. These parts are on paper of a type that Mozart used mostly in 1782 and 1783.[27] He must therefore have performed K. 318 at his Viennese concerts around that time.

K. 318 is Mozart's only G major symphony for which trumpet parts exist. The technical means of writing for trumpets in a G major work, at a time when trumpets in G were not available, was generally known: one used trumpets in D, which gave enough of the necessary notes of G major and closely related keys to enable the construction of functional parts. For example, Joseph Haydn employed this technique in his G major symphonies, Hob. I: 54 (trumpets added in 1790s), 88, 92, 94, and 100, as did Michael Haydn in a G major *Domine Deus*, and Beethoven later did the same in the Finale of his fourth piano concerto in G major of 1805–6.[28] Mozart would use the technique again in the Andante of the 'Linz' symphony, K. 425, calling for trumpets in C for a movement in F major; he likewise added trumpets to his Missa brevis in F major, K. 192 = 186f of 1774 at some later date.

While no autograph kettledrum part for K. 318 survives, a part of unknown provenance for drums in G and D is found in some early scores and sets of parts.[29] In 1822 a correspondent in the *Allgemeine musikalische Zeitung* believed of K. 318

---

[25] PARIS: *Mercure de France* (26 June 1789), 184; *L'Année littéraire* (1789), xxxvi/5. 115–18; LONDON: *The World* (1 Mar. 1790); *The Times* (1 Mar. 1790); *The Public Advertiser* (1 Mar. 1790) (Deutsch, 320 (= 364)); *The Gazetteer and New Daily Advertiser* (2 Mar. 1790); BERLIN: *Annalen des Theaters* (1793), xiii. 16–17. I owe these references to Cliff Eisen. K. 318 was published as *OUVERTURE / pour l'Opéra / la Villanella rapita* ... (Leipzig: A. Kühnel, Bureau de Musique, (1826–7)), plate no. 1872 = RISM M 5511. The assertion in K⁶ that this edition was based on a score published in Paris during Mozart's lifetime is an error; the Parisian publication contains not Mozart's K. 318 but an overture for *La villanella rapita* by Jacopo Gotifredo Ferrari. See *RISM*, B/II (*Recueils imprimés, XVIIIᵉ siècle*) under *La villanella rapita*; *RISM*, A/I, vol. iii (*Einzeldrucke vor 1800*) under F329–33; and F. Lesure (ed.), *Catalogue de la musique imprimée avant 1800 conservée dans les bibliothèques publiques de Paris* (Paris, 1981), 202, under J. G. Ferrari.

[26] W. Plath, 'Mozartiana in Fulda und Frankfurt', 360. The Frankfurt sources reported on by Plath were discovered by Eugene Wolf.

[27] Information kindly provided by Alan Tyson.

[28] This practice is related to, but should not be confused with, that of pitching two brass instruments (or two pairs of brass instruments) in separate keys in order to increase the number of different pitches available, as Wolfgang did in the G minor symphony, K. 173d (horns in G and B flat); as Leopold did in the second version of his Mass in C, Seiffert 4/1, and his Litany in C, *Denkmäler der Tonkunst in Bayern*, ix/2. 188 ff. (horns in G, trumpets in C); and as Michael Haydn did in his *Lauda Sion*, c.1795 (horns in G, trumpets in C) and his *Domine Deus* (horns in G, trumpets in D). See M. H. Schmid, *Mozart und die salzburger Tradition* (Tutzing, 1976), 257.

[29] Concerning the unidiomatic qualities of the drum parts, which are reproduced in both the *GA* and the *NMA* (in the latter in small notes), see N. Del Mar, *Orchestral Variations: Confusions and Error in the Orchestral Repertoire* (London, 1981), 142–4. Del Mar also presents a useful critique of the many differences among editions of K. 318 published by the *GA*, the *NMA*, Breitkopf & Härtel, and Ricordi. For most of the discrepant readings he cites, the *NMA* version is preferable.

that it 'may have been pieced together from some little-known early symphonies of Mozart's, and the instrumentation at least belongs to a more recent era and immediately reveals the literary fraud'.[30] One modern scholar concurs, concluding that not only the drums but even the trumpets do not belong to the work's 'genuine' orchestration;[31] given the existence of autograph parts for the trumpets, this last assertion makes little sense, although one can with justice speak of a Salzburg version without trumpets and a Viennese version with them.

There is also a nineteenth-century manuscript score of K. 318 in Prague containing parts for two clarinets at the end, whose title-page has been reported to read: '2 clarinets in A as supplement by Wolf. Amad: Mozart'.[32] And Mozart in fact sometimes did add clarinet parts to works lacking them for performances in Vienna or other places where (unlike in Salzburg) those instruments were available.[33] The reported wording of the Prague title-page would seem to suggest that the copyist thought the clarinet parts to be genuine, but, as an examination of the manuscript shows that the work's title, the list of instruments, and the composer's name are written in large characters, whereas the phrase '2 Clarinetten in A: als später Zusatz' is in much smaller characters, it must be read: 'Symphony in G major . . . (with 2 clarinets in A as later supplement) by W. A. Mozart', the attribution not necessarily applying to the parenthetical information. This interpretation is not contradicted by the clarinet parts themselves, which are labelled '*Anhang:* mit später zugesetzten Instrumenten' without mention of Mozart's name. These parts prove to be simply the oboe parts transposed, and perhaps intended to substitute for them.

K. 318 enjoyed considerable popularity, for early sets of manuscript parts survive in Brno, Prague, Augsburg, and Frankfurt. The Frankfurt parts, from Mozart's estate, have already been mentioned. But the edition in score reported by K[6] as published in Paris near the end of Mozart's lifetime is a bibliographical error and never existed.[34]

The work's opening Allegro spiritoso is a sonata-form movement in which, for the first time in Mozart's symphonies, the *basso* of baroque tradition is in several passages resolved into independent parts for bassoon, cello, and double bass,

[30] [Review of concert in the Theater an der Wien, Vienna], *Allgemeine musikalische Zeitung* (July 1822), xxiv, cols. 464–5. As evidence for his patchwork theory, the anonymous reviewer described the Andante section as 'a long, old-fashioned Tempo di Menuetto', contrasting this with two 'modern' crescendos, one in the dominant, the other in the tonic, found in the opening and closing allegros at bars 49–57 and 236–44. The reviewer (incorrectly) believed that such crescendos were not part of the symphonic style at the time K. 318 was composed.

[31] Schmid, *Mozart und die salzburger Tradition*, 257, n. 20.

[32] M. Svobodova, 'Das "Denkmal Wolfgang Amadeus Mozarts" in der prager Universitätsbibliothek', *Mozart-Jahrbuch* (1967), 353–86, here 361.

[33] He added clarinets to the second versions of K. 365 = 316a (concerto for two pianos), 375 (wind serenade), 385, and 550 (symphonies).

[34] See n. 25 above.

creating novel timbral effects. (Could this have been part of what struck the correspondent of the *Allgemeine musikalische Zeitung* as too modern to have been written by Mozart?) At the point in the movement where the recapitulation might be expected, the Allegro breaks off at a grand pause and a G major Andante, organized in the form of a rondo A B A' C A" B', is heard. After ninety-eight bars this too breaks off, leading without pause to a Tempo primo which, after a few bars of transition, presents a literal recapitulation not from the beginning but from six bars before the return of the so-called 'second subject', telescoping the exposition's 109 bars to 67. The 'missing' opening of the recapitulation finally sounds at the end, functioning as a brilliant coda. The resulting shape is an asymmetrical arch- or mirror-form, which, if the opening group of ideas is A, the second group of ideas B, and the Andante C, has the design A B C B' A'.

Symphony in B flat major, K. 319

[Incipits 10.2]

Instrumentation: strings, 2 oboes, 2 bassoons, 2 horns, [continuo]
Autograph: Jagiellońska Library, Kraków
Principal sources: five Salzburg parts (vn. I, vn. II, violone) in Estlinger's and Hofstätter's hands, Graz; complete set of parts sent from Vienna by Mozart, Donaueschingen
Facsimile: *NMA*, iv/11/6. xiv
Editions: *GA*, xxi. 213–38 (= Serie 8, No. 33); *NMA*, iv/11/6. 23–58

The autograph is headed 'di Wolfgango Amadeo Mozart mpr. Salisburgo li 9 di giuglio 1779'. The pages from Nannerl's diary covering the period between 16 June and 14 September of that year are missing, and no other document gives us a clue to Mozart's reason for having written this symphony. If intended for something other than the usual round of church, court, or private concerts, K. 319 was probably for Johann Heinrich Böhm's theatrical troupe, a few members of which figured in Mozart's comical concert programme discussed above. Böhm's troupe, which had in its repertory at least two of Mozart's works (*Thamos* and the Italian opera buffa *La finta giardiniera* transformed into a Singspiel as *Die verstellte Gärtnerin*), was first in Salzburg from late April to early June 1779, at which time the Mozarts became acquainted with him and a number of his leading players. The company of nearly fifty actors, dancers, and singers returned to Salzburg in early September and stayed until the beginning of Lent 1780. K. 319 thus may have been written in anticipation of their return.[35]

This symphony originally had only three movements, but sometime after he moved to Vienna Mozart added a Minuet and Trio. The added movement is inserted into the autograph on paper of a type that he used mainly from June to the end of 1785 but also in one or two scores of the previous year.[36] Like the previous symphony, this one enjoyed considerable circulation, with early sets of parts found in Salzburg, Schwerin, the Reichersberg Monastery in Upper Austria, Bozen, Prague, Modena, Frankfurt, and Donaueschingen.[37] Four authentic violin parts, two copied by the Mozarts' friend and principal Salzburg copyist Estlinger and two by the piratical Felix Hofstätter, and a violone part, are found in Graz.[38]

The story of the Donaueschingen parts is revealing. K. 319 was among twelve works that in 1786 Mozart offered as his 'latest' works to Prince von Fürstenberg of

[35] Further concerning Böhm, his troupe, and their repertory, see H. G. Fellmann, *Die böhmschen Theatertruppe und ihre Zeit* (Leipzig, 1928) and H. F. Deininger, 'Die deutsche Schauspielergesellschaft unter der Direktion von Johann Heinrich Böhm, einem Freunde der Familie Mozart, in Augsburg in den Jahren 1779 und 1780', *Augsburger Mozartbuch* (*Zeitschrift des historischen Vereins für Schwaben* (1942–3), lv–lvi), 299–397; G. Rech, 'Böhm und Schikaneder: Zwei salzburger Theaterimpressarios der Mozartzeit', *Festschrift Walter Senn zum 70. Geburtstag* (Munich and Salzburg, 1975), 188–95; E. Hintermaier, 'Das fürsterzbischöfliche Hoftheater zu Salzburg (1775–1803)', *Österreichische Musik Zeitschrift* (1975), xxx. 351–63.
[36] Information kindly provided by Alan Tyson.
[37] K⁶, p. 341.
[38] Eisen, 'The Symphonies of Leopold Mozart', 80. For Mozart's accusation against Hofstätter, see ch. 11.

Donaueschingen. When that happened, K. 319, represented to the Prince as new, was seven years old and had already been published. Although the deception was immediately uncovered, the Prince, in an apparent display of *noblesse oblige*, purchased three symphonies (K. 319, 338, 425) and three piano concertos (K. 451, 459, 488).[39]

The publication of K. 319 had come about in the following way: in 1784 Mozart planned to publish a set of three symphonies with the Viennese firm of Artaria, dedicated to the Prince von Fürstenberg. The next year two symphonies were published (K. 319, 385), but without any dedication.[40] Aside from K. 300a (and possibly another symphony), published in Paris in 1779 or perhaps a few years later, these were the only symphonies of Mozart's in print in the 1780s. The non-appearance of the third of the Artaria symphonies reminds one that Leopold and Wolfgang earlier, and Wolfgang alone later, had little success getting his symphonies published. It may be that they were too complex or too subtle to fulfil the conditions usually imposed on symphonies, which had to make a good effect played by orchestras that included amateurs and doublers with a single rehearsal or sometimes none. That Leopold was fully aware of this problem emerges from his letters. Speaking of the matter generally, he wrote to his son:

If you have not got pupils, well then compose something more . . . . But let it be something short, easy, and popular . . . . Do you imagine that you would be doing work unworthy of you? If so, you are very much mistaken. Did [J. C.] Bach, when he was in London, ever publish anything but such-like trifles? What is slight can still be great, if it is written in a natural, flowing and easy style—and at the same time bears the marks of sound composition. Such works are more difficult to compose than all those harmonic progressions, which the majority of people cannot fathom, or pieces which have pleasing melodies, but which are difficult to perform. Did Bach lower himself by such work? Not at all. Good composition, sound construction, *il filo*—these distinguish the master from the bungler—even in trifles. If I were you, I should compose in advance something of that kind and then move Heaven and Earth to get a commission for an opera. You must try to sell a work or two to some engraver or other. You must have money in order to live. And if your pupils are in the country, what other way is there for you to make money? You really must do something![41]

[39] Letters of 8 Aug. and 30 Sept. 1786. *Briefe*, iii. 565–7, 589–91; *Letters*, iii. 1337–41 (= ii. 897–901).

[40] Mozart planned to publish three, not six symphonies. Editions of his letter of 9 June 1784 that read 'three of the six symphonies' are the result of a misreading of the autograph. See *Briefe*, iii. 319; vi. 183, 704; and especially vii. 574. K. 319 was issued as Op. 7, No. 2 (plate No. 54), and K. 385 as Op. 7, No. 1 (plate No. 55). The former also bears the handwritten indication 'No. 8' on the title-page and the latter, 'No. 9'. These manuscript notations refer to Artaria's series *Grandes symphonies périodiques à plusieurs instruments*, to which Mozart's two symphonies belonged. The three sets of numbers—opus, plate, and series—are garbled in K⁶ and *RISM* M 5512. See A. Weinmann, *Vollständiges Verlagsverzeichnis Artaria & Comp.* (Vienna, 1952), 16.

[41] Letter of 13 Aug. 1778. *Briefe*, ii. 444; *Letters*, ii. 888–9 (= ii. 599).

The principle enunciated by Leopold in this letter, applied to symphonies, is behind his explanation of how it was that Georg Anton Kreusser, whom the Mozarts had known in Amsterdam in 1766 and Milan in 1770 (and who, as Chapter 3 demonstrates, borrowed something from one of Wolfgang's earliest symphonies), gained a good post when Wolfgang was failing to do the same:

Kreusser went [to Mainz] at the right time, that is, just after Jacobi, the concertmaster, had died. His easy symphonies, which are pleasant to listen to, were a success, so that he was immediately appointed concertmaster. At present he is working hard to fit himself for the post of Kapellmeister.[42]

This sort of thing must have been difficult for Leopold and Wolfgang to take, for they were keenly aware of Wolfgang's superiority to Kreusser and, as Leopold wrote to Breitkopf in one of a series of fruitless letters attempting to interest him in his son's symphonies and other works, he saw 'many works engraved and printed which really arouse my pity'.[43]

One of the most successful symphony composers at the time of Leopold's despairing remarks was Joseph Haydn, yet even he, whose symphonies were found in virtually every corner of Europe and in parts of the New World as well, had to keep in mind ease and difficulty when his symphonies were to be disseminated outside Eisenstadt and Esterháza, as his letter of 15 July 1783 proffering his Symphonies 76–8 to the Parisian publisher Boyer suggests:

Last year I composed three beautiful, splendid, and by no means over-lengthy symphonies, scored for 2 violins, viola, *basso*, 2 horns, 2 oboes, 1 flute, and 1 [rect. 2] bassoon[s]—but they are all very easy, and without too much *concertante* . . . . I assure you that these three symphonies will have a huge sale.[44]

That Haydn calculated correctly is suggested not only by the extremely wide circulation of his symphonies but also by a remark of Schubart's from the mid-1780s that Haydn's symphonies 'are rightly beloved throughout all Europe, because they are composed in the true symphonic style, *easily practicable*, often written with rushing passion and with entirely original humour'.[45]

The publication of a symphony of course greatly increased its dissemination. It may, for instance, have been the publication of two symphonies in Paris in the

[42] Letter of 27 Aug. 1778. *Briefe*, ii. 452–3; *Letters*, ii. 897 (ii. 604).

[43] Letter of 12 Feb. 1781. *Briefe*, iii. 92–3; *Letters*, ii. 1054 (= ii. 710); R. Schaal, 'Ein angeblich verschollener Brief von Leopold Mozart', *Acta Mozartiana* (1979), xxvi. 50–1.

[44] The text of this letter is flawed as published in D. Bartha (ed.), *Joseph Haydn: Gesammelte Briefe und Aufzeichnungen* (Kassel, 1965), 130 (hereafter cited as *Haydn: Briefe*), and as translated in H. C. Robbins Landon (ed.), *Joseph Haydn: Collected Correspondence and London Notebooks* (London, 1959), 42–3. For the corrected text, see H. C. Robbins Landon, *Haydn: Chronicle and Works*, ii. 476–7.

[45] *Ideen*, 277 (emphasis added).

years following their announcement in 1779 that led in 1784 to the first documented performances of Mozart's symphonies in London since 1765. The Concerts of the Nobility of 18 February and 28 April began with symphonies of Mozart's, the first of which impressed one listener as 'a great and beautiful symphony, varied in all its movements' and the second as 'very brilliant'.[46]

The Artaria editions of Mozart's symphonies had greater distribution than the Parisian editions.[47] K. 319 and 385 were listed for sale in the Breitkopf Thematic Catalogue for 1785.[48] On 6 March 1786, Anton von Weber, the father of Carl Maria and a cousin of Mozart's wife, wrote to Artaria requesting 'all the symphonies, quartets, and keyboard pieces of Mozart [and] no less, the newest three symphonies of our immortal Father Haydn'.[49] Not later than 1788 Mozart's engraved symphonies were for sale in Prague at the establishment of Karl Helmer, an instrument maker, performer, and music seller of that city.[50]

A sudden show of interest in Mozart's symphonies in London from December 1787 may have been related to a new consignment of music received from the Continent by the music publishers Longman & Broderip.[51] On 12 December at the Anacreontic Society, 'An overture of Mozart was first introduced, the effect of which was sensibly felt. Mr [Johann Baptist] Cramer, jun.[,] again distinguished himself upon the harpsichord, which did honour to Mozart the composer; we know not on which to bestow the greatest praise.'[52] On 1 January 1788 both Artaria symphonies were advertised for sale by Longman & Broderip.[53] A few days later an 'Overture' by 'Mr Mozart' was heard at a benefit concert for Wilhelm Cramer at Haberdashers' Hall in Maiden Lane, Wood Street.[54] Then a few weeks after that a 'New Overture' by Mozart was performed at the Professional Concerts, Hanover Square.[55] (A 'review' of the concert did not deal with specific works, remarking only that 'the selections were particularly happy, and marked by the best judgement'.[56] The orchestra for these concerts was 6—6—4—3—3 / 2—2—0—2 / 2—0—0, and fortepiano continuo.[57]) Finally, an 'overture' by Mozart

[46] C. F. Cramer (ed.), 'Nachrichten von dem grossen Concerte unter der Oberdirection des Lord Abington in London', *Magazin der Musik* (Dec. 1784), ii/1. 225–34, here 226, 231. I owe this item and those cited in nn. 50–8 below to the research of Cliff Eisen, whose collection of new documents to supplement Deutsch is in preparation.

[47] Judged not only by the advertisements cited in nn. 48, 50, and 51, but by the number of surviving copies listed in *RISM*.

[48] B. S. Brook (ed.), *The Breitkopf Thematic Catalogue* (New York, 1968), col. 846; K⁶, 341.

[49] R. Hilmar, *Der Musikverlag Artaria & Comp.* (Tutzing, 1977), 25

[50] Joseph Anton Stephan, Ritter von Riegger, *Materialien zur alten und neuen Statistik von Böhmen* (Leipzig and Prague, 1788), 162.

[51] *The Universal Daily Register* (1 Dec. 1787). *The Universal Daily Register* became *The Times* on 1 Jan. 1788.

[52] *The Universal Daily Register* (14 Dec. 1787).

[53] *The Times* (1 Jan. 1788).

[54] Ibid. 9 Jan. 1788.

[55] Ibid. 11 Feb. 1788.

[56] Ibid. 13 Feb. 1788.

[57] Ibid. 31 Jan. 1788.

TABLE 10.2 Performances of Mozart's symphonies in London, 1784–1791

Date	Concert	Source(s)	Comments
18 Feb. 1784	Professional Hanover Square	MdM, GNDA, MCLA, MHDA, MPDA, PA	'eine grosse und in allen Theilen abwechselnde schöne Simphonie' (MdM); orchestra: 6—6—4—3—2 / 2—2—0—2 / 2—0—0—harpsichord (MCLA, MHDA)
3 Mar. 1784	Professional Hanover Square	GNDA, MCLA, MHDA, MPDA, PA	—
28 Apr. 1784	Professional Hanover Square	PA, MHDA, MdM	'pleased us by many brilliant Passages, not wandering from the Line of either Taste or Judgment' (PA); 'sehr brillant' (MdM)
5 May 1784	Professional Hanover Square	PA, MHDA	—
2 Mar. 1786	Salomon Hanover Square	MCLA, MHDA, MPDA	orchestra (30 Jan. 1787): 6—6—4—3—3 / 2—2—0—2 / 2—0—0—harpsichord (PA)
22 Feb. 1787	Mme Mara Hanover Square	PA	—
7 Nov. 1787	Anacreontic Crown & Anchor	DUR	*first symphony 'was well received and had great merit'; second symphony 'very inferior to the first'
12 Dec. 1787	Anacreontic Crown & Anchor	DUR	'the effect . . . was sensibly felt. Mr. [J. B.] Cramer, jun. again distinguished himself upon the harpsichord, which did honour to Mozart the composer; we know not on which to bestow the greatest praise'
9 Jan. 1788	benefit Wilhelm Cramer Haberdashers'	T	—
11 Feb. 1788	Professional Hanover Square	MCLA, MPDA, PA, T	*'the selections were . . . particularly happy and marked by the best judgment' (T); orchestra: 6—6—4—3—3 / 2—2—0—2/2—0—0—pianoforte (T, MPDA, MCLA)
25 Feb. 1788	Professional Hanover Square	MPDA	*

Date	Place / Series	Sources	Notes
11 Mar. 1788	benefit Salomon Hanover Square	T	'the selection … was such as might be expected from [Salomon's] judgment and taste'
[13 Mar. 1788]	benefit Miss Abrams Hanover Square	T	announced but probably never took place
24 Mar. 1788	Professional Hanover Square	MPDA	—
31 Mar. 1788	Professional Hanover Square	MPDA	—
14 Apr. 1788	Professional Hanover Square	MPDA	—
2 Feb. 1789	Professional Hanover Square	MPDA, W	—
[27 Feb. 1790]	*La villanella rapita* King's Theatre Haymarket	T, W, MH, GNDA, PA	impossible to know if K. 318 served as overture; 'all of the music of the opera deserving celebrity is by Mozart' (MH)
13 Feb. 1791	Pleyel Professional Hanover	unknown	Pohl, ii. 185–6
18 Mar. 1791	Salomon Hanover Square	PA	orchestra (18 Mar. 1793): 6–8–6–8–4–3–4 / 2–2— 0–2 / 2–2–2–1 [pianoforte] (BMz)
27 May 1791	Salomon Hanover Square	GNDA, MCLA, MPDA PA, T, W	—
13 Feb. 1792	Professional Hanover Square	GNDA, MCLA, MH, PA T, W	—

* 'New' symphony.

BMz	*Berlinische musikalische Zeitung*
DUR	*Daily Universal Register* (*The Times*)
GNDA	*Gazetteer and New Daily Advertiser*
MCLA	*Morning Chronicle and London Advertiser*
MdM	*Magazin der Musik*, ed. C. F. Cramer (Hamburg)
MH	*Morning Herald*
MHDA	*Morning Herald and Daily Advertiser*
MPDA	*Morning Post or Daily Advertiser*
PA	*The Public Advertiser*
Pohl	C. F. Pohl, *Mozart und Haydn in London* (Vienna, 1867, repr. New York, 1970)
T	*The Times*
W	*The World*

When this book was in the press, an important article appeared which contains fuller information than is found in this table: S. McVeigh, 'The Professional Concert and Rival Subscription Series in London, 1783–1793', *The Research Chronicle of the Royal Musical Association* (1989), xxii. 1–135.

was heard on 11 March of the same year at Johann Peter Salomon's benefit concert in the Hanover Square Rooms.[58]

K. 319 and 385, then, must be at least part of what Charles Burney referred to when, in a review of 1791, he defended modern music against the opinions expressed in a tract by William Jackson, organist of Exeter Cathedral, who believed that music had been steadily deteriorating since Handel's death. Jackson's view of the state of music in 1791 was that,

The old CONCERTO is now lost, and the modern full-pieces are either in the form of OVERTURES or SYMPHONIES. The overture of the Italian opera never pretends to much; that of English opera always endeavours to have an air somewhere, and the endeavour *alone* makes it acceptable .... [L]ater composers, to be grand and original, have poured forth such floods of nonsense, under the sublime idea of *being inspired*, that the present SYMPHONY bears the same relation to good music, as the ravings of a bedlamite do to sober sense.[59]

To this the infuriated Burney responded,

Richter's eternal repetitions, and Abel's timidity, are praised [by Jackson], for they are no more .... Now, might not the ingenious writer as well have said, at once, that the authors of these *floods of nonsense* are HAYDN, VANHALL, PLEYEL, and MOZART, and the admirers of them tasteless idiots, as leave us to guess who he means?[60]

By 1791 when Burney wrote this, Mozart's British friends Anna and Stephen Storace, Thomas Attwood, and Michael Kelly had been in London for some time, arranging for the performance and publication of some of his music and attempting to arrange a visit by him.[61] Given the activities of Mozart's London-based friends, and the European dissemination of symphonies in manuscript, Burney may have been referring to more of Mozart's symphonies than the handful in print. That unpublished symphonies by Mozart reached London is shown by the publication there *c.*1790 of an arrangement of the symphony version of K. 320.[62]

All three of the original movements of K. 319 are in sonata form, share thematic resemblances, and begin their development sections with new ideas rather than with manipulations of previously presented ones. In the development section of the first movement the four-note motto doh—ray—fah—me sounds at bars 143–6 and

[58] Ibid. 11 Mar. 1788. A review says simply, 'The selection of Tuesday evening was such as might be expected from his [Salomon's] judgment and taste' (ibid., 13 Mar. 1788). Another performance of a Mozart symphony announced in *The Times* of 11 Mar. for two days later probably never took place.

[59] William Jackson, *Observations on the State of Music in London* (London, 1791).

[60] [Charles Burney], 'Art[icle] XVIII', *The Monthly Review* (Oct. 1791) vi. 196–202, here 198.

[61] Further concerning Mozart's British friends as a conduit for his works in London, see the discussion of the 'Prague' symphony in ch. 12.

[62] The two London editions of *c.*1790 of a piano-trio version of K. 320 are found in K⁶, Anh. B, p. 777 (Zu 320) = *RISM* M 5662–3. The André edition of the piano-trio version (Offenbach, 1792) = *RISM* M 5653.

151–4, and again, altered, in the Andante at bars 44–7, and the Minuet (9–12) and Trio (1–4).[63] The Andante is in the form A B A′ B′ A coda, with the A′ section written in imitative texture, first in the strings in the dominant, then in the winds in the tonic.

The Finale begins as if it were simply one more brisk jig; but the jig's triplets alternate with a march's duplets (and in four passages the two overlap), the wind writing is more prominent than earlier, and the development section offers an example of that kind of pseudo-counterpoint which, while never exceeding two real voices, creates the illusion of many-layered polyphony. This way of handling counterpoint has important implications for the technique of symphony composition in the eighteenth century. It may also be connected to Mozart's methods of sketching and of writing out his music—indeed, to his conception of that music. Among the rather few sketches that survive, some are on a single line, but many occupy two lines on which are found the *Hauptstimme* (principal melody) and the *basso seguente* (lowest sounding part). From those scores that Mozart began as fair copies and then abandoned, and from scores in which he changed ink or quill while writing, one sees that those two structural voices were written first, and the others filled in later.[64] A report suggesting that Joseph Haydn employed and taught a similar way of composing symphonies comes from his pupil, the composer and pianist Frederick Kalkbrenner, who wrote concerning imitation: 'The best are the imitations in two parts, which were the only ones that Haydn used, even in his symphonies for full orchestra. He said that imitations of more than two parts "befuddle the ear".'[65]

Symphony in D major, K. 320

[Incipits 10.3]

[63] M. Flothuis, 'Eine zweite "Jupiter-Symphonie"?', *Mitteilungen der internationalen Stiftung Mozarteum* (1983), xxxi. 18–20.

[64] E. Hertzmann, 'Mozart's Creative Process', *The Musical Quarterly* (1957), xliii. 187–200; repr. in P. H. Lang (ed.), *The Creative World of Mozart* (New York, 1963), 17–30.

[65] Frederick Kalkbrenner, *Traité d'harmonie du pianiste* (Paris, 1849), 8; see H. Walter, 'Kalkbrenners Lehrjahr und sein Unterricht bei Haydn', *Haydn-Studien* (1982), v. 23–41. I am grateful to James Webster for calling Kalkbrenner's remark to my attention.

Instrumentation: *strings, 2 oboes, 2 bassoons, 2 horns, 2 trumpets, kettledrums,
[continuo]
Autograph: Deutsche Staatsbibliothek, East Berlin (serenade)
Principal source: manuscript parts of Viennese origin with corrections in Mozart's
hand, Bibliothek des Steiermärkischen Landeskonservatoriums, Graz (symphony)
(Ms. 40572 (*olim* Lannoy 56))
Facsimile: *NMA*, iv/11/7. xvi–xvii
Editions: *GA*, xxiii. 325–43, 372–8, 383–98 (= Serie 9, No. 11); *NMA*, iv/11/7.
89–131

   The autograph of the serenade from which this symphony was taken is inscribed
'di Wolfgango Amadeo Mozart mpr. / Salisburgo li 3 d'Augusto 1779'. Mozart's
Prague acquaintance Niemetschek claimed that it was written for Archbishop
Colloredo's name-day,[66] which was 30 September, but Mozart, who seldom
composed so far in advance of a deadline, called the work *Finalmusik*,[67] the term
used for a serenade presented by students of Salzburg University's Faculty of
Philosophy at the end of the Academic year, first to the Prince-Archbishop at his
summer residence, Mirabell, and then to their professors in the square in front of
the University. The term ended in early August, and the serenade was presented on
a Wednesday because Thursdays were school holidays.[68]
   Mozart created the symphony version by omitting the serenade's two marches,
its two movements for concertante winds, and both of its minuets with their trios.
(The posthorn that gives the serenade its nickname is sounded in one of the trios.)
The separability of the constituent genres of the serenade are demonstrated with
exceptional clarity in the case of K. 320. First, a Salzburg manuscript contains the
minuets and trios from K. 320, along with another minuet and trio (not in the

---

[66] Franz Niemetschek, letter of 27 May 1799 to Breitkopf & Härtel (see K⁶, p. 343).
[67] Letter of 29 Mar. 1783. *Briefe*, iii. 261; *Letters*, iii. 1257 (= ii. 843).
[68] Deutsch, 139 (= 154).

Köchel Catalogue).[69] These three minuets and trios have no viola parts, as was normal for dance music. Then, the marches to almost all the serenades come in separate manuscripts (and therefore have separate Köchel listings); the two marches intended for K. 320 are no exception in this regard. Finally, the concertante movements also exist in a separate manuscript, and Mozart gave a performance of this two-movement Sinfonia concertante in a Viennese concert of 23 March 1783.[70] Thus we have:

Serenade movements	Genres
Marcia (K. 335 = 320a/1)	march
*Adagio maestoso—Allegro con spirito	symphony
Menuetto—Trio	dance
Concertante: Andante grazioso	sinfonia concertante
Rondeau: Allegro ma non troppo	sinfonia concertante
*Andantino	symphony
Menuetto—Trio I–II	dance
*Finale: Presto	symphony
Marcia: Maestoso assai (K. 335 = 320a/2)	march

A set of parts of the symphony version, preserved at Graz, is of Viennese origin and has corrections in Mozart's hand. Other eighteenth-century sets of parts for the symphony survive in Regensburg, Berlin, Salzburg, Modena, and Vienna, and the work was published by Johann André in 1791. A year earlier an arrangement of the three symphony movements plus one of the minuets was published in London.[71] Thus, as with other examples of this almost exclusively Salzburgian genre, the serenade was generally unknown while the symphony drawn from it received modest distribution.

An unusual feature of the first movement deserves comment. At the recapitulation the material of the opening Adagio reappears in a slightly recomposed form without tempo change, which Mozart accomplished by doubling the note values so that a semibreve in allegro equals a crotchet in adagio (Example 10.1). This procedure may have implications for Mozart's notation of tempo, which are discussed in Chapter 12.

The D minor Andantino is in the 'tragic' vein of the minor-key andantes of the Sinfonia concertante, K. 364 = 320d, the piano concerto, K. 271, and the symphony, K. 184 = 161a. In these movements one can hear Mozart straining at

---

[69] R. Angermüller, 'M. Haydniana und Mozartiana: Ein erster Bericht', *Acta Mozartiana* (1981), xxix. 49–66, here 66.

[70] *Briefe*, vi. 137, and Deutsch (English verson 213), mistakenly claim that this sinfonia concertante comprised only the third movement of K. 320, but André, who owned the manuscript, reported that it contained movements three and four (Jahn, *Mozart*, ii. 351). This is confirmed by the manuscript itself, Salzburg parts with Viennese *Dubletten*, now in Frankfurt (Plath, 'Mozartiana in Fulda und Frankfurt', 360).

[71] See n. 62 above.

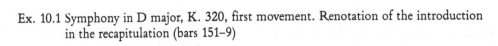

Ex. 10.1 Symphony in D major, K. 320, first movement. Renotation of the introduction in the recapitulation (bars 151–9)

the boundaries of polite entertainment music of the 1770s. Johann André, in his published catalogue of Mozart's works, called the Andantino of K. 320 'in the form of an entr'acte', perhaps reacting to its overtly dramatic character (its *form* is a confidently handled sonata form with both halves repeated). Commentators have attempted to link such movements to tragic moments in Mozart's life, but one must be careful not to deny an artist his art. The movements are not personal but theatrical; they successfully strike tragic poses. We can perhaps imagine Mozart pouring his own joys and sorrows into a song or keyboard fantasia intended for private use in a small circle of intimates. But to Leopold, Wolfgang, and their contemporaries, the notion of expressing intensely personal sentiments in an 'official', public, ceremonial genre like the symphony or orchestral serenade would have made little sense. Even when in the following decade the symphony became a more profound genre and no longer simply 'a mere formality', what it expressed may be understood as the general aspirations of groups of people, rather than the introspection of a single individual. The 'public' nature of the work is perhaps affirmed by the fanfare that opens the Finale, which is similar to one which Wolfgang had used to begin the F major symphony, K. 43, a decade earlier. The blaze of trumpets and drums, the tremolo, large scale sonata form of the movement show Mozart moving away from dance-inspired finales to something more elaborate, more symphonic.

Symphony in C major, K. 338

[Incipits 10.4]

Instrumentation: *strings, 2 oboes, 2 bassoons, 2 horns, trumpets, kettledrums, [continuo]

Autograph: Bibliothèque nationale, Paris (leaves 1–18) (Malherbe Collection, Ms. 227); Jagiellońska Library, Kraków (leaves 19–28)

Principal source: parts with corrections in Mozart's hand, Donaueschingen

Facsimile: *NMA*, iv/11/6. xv–xvii

Editions: *GA*, xxi. 239–74 (= Serie 8, No. 34); *NMA*, iv/11/6. 59–112

This, the last symphony Mozart wrote in (although not the last he wrote for) Salzburg, is inscribed 'Sinfonia di Wolfgango Amadeo Mozart mpr. li 29 Agosto, Salsbourg 1780'. Nannerl's diary reports that her brother played at court on 2, 3, and 4 September;[72] one of those dates probably was the première of K. 338. By then Mozart knew that he was to leave for Munich in a few weeks to oversee the preparation of *Idomeneo*, so this symphony could have served both as farewell to Salzburg and introduction to Munich during Carnival. No Munich performance is in fact recorded, however, but K. 338 was performed by Mozart in Vienna in the early 1780s, and in 1786 he sold a set of parts with corrections in his own hand to the Prince von Fürstenberg, still found in the archives at Donaueschingen.[73] Other early sets of parts survive at Salzburg, Berlin, Vienna, and Prague, but the work was not published before 1797.[74]

The first movement of K. 338—originally headed 'Allegro', to which Mozart added 'vivace'—is in sonata form without repeats. The opening fanfare is the prototype for the nearly identical gestures that begin the overtures of *Così fan tutte* and *La clemenza di Tito*; but here, by inserting echoes and extensions of the material that follows, Mozart has created an entirely different shape and character.

The first movement was originally followed by a minuet, or least Mozart began one, but it has been torn from the autograph, leaving only the first fourteen bars, which are on the back of the last page of the first movement (Example 10.2). A number of four-movement symphonies by other composers of the period place the minuet second instead of third, but as Mozart's practice was the latter pattern, this fragmentary minuet is an enigma.[75] The notion promulgated by Einstein in K³ that the C major symphonic Minuet, K. 409 = 383f (Example 10.3), was written to be added to K. 338 is improbable.[76] K. 383f is too long to fit the proportions of K. 338, and calls for a pair of flutes not found in it. The editors of K⁶ suggest that Mozart

[72] *Briefe*, iii. 9.

[73] F. Schnapp, 'Neue Mozart-Funde in Donaueschingen', *Neues Mozart-Jahrbuch* (1942), ii. 211–23.

[74] See Table 11.2 below, and K⁶, p. 359.

[75] See the discussions of the minuets of the symphonies K. 73 and 112, ch. 7, and of the lack of a minuet in the 'Prague' symphony, ch. 11.

[76] Einstein, 299.

Ex. 10.2 Symphony in C major, K. 338, Minuet fragment

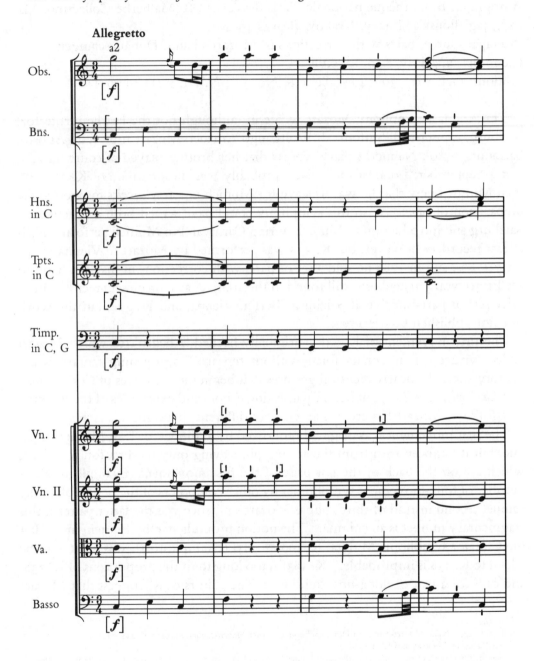

Ex. 10.3 Minuet in C major, K. 409 = 383f

could have added flutes to the first and last movements of K. 338, as he did to the Viennese version of K. 385; but there is not a shred of evidence to suggest that he actually did so. From its large scoring, length, relative complexity of texture, and the presence of violas, K. 383f must have been intended as a concert piece and not as dance music.[77]

In the autograph Mozart labelled the middle movement of K. 338 'Andante di molto', but he must have found that it was performed more slowly than he wished, for in the concertmaster's part that he sent to Donaueschingen he added 'più tosto allegretto'. This indication offers a clue to Mozart's tempo indications, discussed in Chapter 12. The Finale, another large jig in sonata form with both sections repeated, gives a special concertante role to the oboes, yet this is still not the kind of elaborate writing for wind that would be a hallmark of Mozart's Viennese orchestration of the 1780s. After K. 338, Mozart abandoned the commonplace jig-finale forever.[78]

Mozart was to write one more symphony for the musicians of Salzburg with whom he had such ambivalent relations: the 'Haffner' symphony, K. 385. By the time he composed it, however, he was permanently installed in Vienna, far from his father, the Archbishop, the 'coarse, slovenly, dissolute court musicians', and the other citizens of Salzburg with whom he found it 'impossible to mix freely'. But, as is suggested in Chapter 11, he was probably thinking about all of them as he composed K. 385.

[77] The paper on which K. 383f is written, the same type found in the trumpet parts for K. 318, was mostly used by Mozart in 1782 and 1783 (Alan Tyson).

[78] Landon (*Haydn: Chronicle and Work*, ii. 275–6) suggests that Mozart modelled K. 338 on Joseph Haydn's C major symphony, Hob. I: 56 of 1774. To my ears the resemblances between the two works seem of a common-coin sort, and there is no evidence that Haydn's symphony was known in Salzburg. Mozart must, however, have known another C major symphony of his, Hob. I: 60, which served as the overture and entr'actes for the play *Der Zerstreute*, performed in Salzburg in Jan. 1776. See R. Angermüller, 'Haydns "Der Zerstreute" [= "Il distratto"] in Salzburg', *Haydn-Studien* (1978), iv. 85–93.

II

Vienna (II): Independence
(1780–1791)

Perhaps the most important turning-point in Mozart's life came at the age of twenty-five, when he already had to his credit a corpus of music that many a lesser talent would gladly have accepted as the fruits of a lifetime. He decided to break with his father and Salzburg, and to remain in Vienna as a free-lance teacher, performer, and composer—a decision that had far-reaching effects on his music and, hence, on the evolution of the Viennese classical style as a whole. Evidence of his disaffection toward Salzburg is presented at the beginning of the previous chapter: the Archbishop was stingy and unappreciative, Leopold was continually looking over his son's shoulder and passing judgement, musical life was circumscribed and taste conservative in Salzburg, and Wolfgang's opportunities to show what he could do in his favourite genres—piano concerto and opera—were few. Vienna, on the contrary, Mozart described to his father as 'keyboard land';[1] he might equally have called it 'orchestra land' or even, as his admirer Johann Friedrich Schink put it, 'the land of the blessed, the land of music'.[2] In this 'land of music' symphonies naturally played their role.

Eyewitness accounts cited at the beginning of Chapter 5 suggest that Vienna had a brilliant orchestral tradition, even though the Imperial Court Orchestra was in a period of severe decline and there was no single orchestra of international repute, comparable, for example, to the Mannheim orchestra before its dismantling in 1779, the opera orchestras of Milan and Turin, or the Parisian orchestra of the Concert des amateurs between 1769 and 1781. That the level of orchestral performance remained as high at the time of Mozart's mature operas, piano concertos, and symphonies as it was reported to be by Burney in 1772 and by Riesbeck c.1780 is suggested by a letter from a British visitor in 1787, who wrote

---

[1] Letter of 2 June 1781. *Briefe*, iii. 125; *Letters*, iii. 1099 (= ii. 739).
[2] Johann Friedrich Schink, *Litterarische Fragmente* (Graz, 1785), ii. 288; in Deutsch, 206 (= 233).

home to a friend, 'I wish you could hear a German symphony. God! what fire & spirit & with what accuracy they execute them. Oh that I had been here in Lent when they say they are *surfeited* with Music . . . .'[3]

If Vienna at the beginning of the 1780s lacked the kind of flourishing music-publishing industry found in Paris and London,[4] the Imperial capital on the Danube offered other advantages to music making. It was the economic, political, and cultural centre of an empire that encompassed not just Austria and Hungary, but substantial portions of present-day Czechoslovakia, northern Italy, Germany, Yugoslavia, Poland, Russia, and Romania. Many noble families from those regions maintained homes in Vienna, where they lived during the 'season', and a surprising number of the members of these families were musically literate, demanding a steady supply of music. Thus, even in the absence of a major orchestra or major music-publisher, Vienna in the last quarter of the eighteenth century could boast a musical life of sufficient vigour to explain why Gluck, Haydn, Mozart, and Beethoven—none of whom was a native—preferred it to all other cities.

Mozart's decision to stay in Vienna in 1781 may have arisen in the first instance from an accident (his firing for insubordination by the Archbishop of Salzburg) and from his romantic interest in the two Weber daughters, but he was probably also acting on long-held plans to escape from Salzburg and gain his freedom at the earliest opportunity. Having spent almost three months in the Imperial capital when he was six, more than a year there when he was twelve, and two months when he was seventeen, Mozart was keenly aware of Vienna's musical possibilities. At six Mozart was still three years away from writing his first symphony, but by 1767–8 he had several to his name, and wrote a few more while in Vienna (see Chapter 5). He may have composed one during his brief stay in 1773 (on 18 August he participated in an orchestral concert in Dr Franz Anton Mesmer's garden), but in any case he was apparently inspired by what he heard to write several upon his return to Salzburg (see Chapter 8). After settling permanently in the Imperial capital he wrote his most famous essays in the genre: the 'Haffner', the 'Prague', the 'Linz', the Symphony in E flat, K. 543, the 'Great' G minor Symphony, and the 'Jupiter'. Thus, however much the formation of Mozart's symphonic style owed to the Italian sinfonia, to the 'English' symphonies of J. C. Bach and C. F. Abel, to the brilliant orchestral writing of Mannheim composers, and to local Salzburg traditions, it was also indebted to a Viennese (or, perhaps more accurately, Austrian) influence, culminating in the final flowering of symphonic masterpieces.

[3] Letter of 27 July 1787 from Thomas Brand in Vienna to Robert Wharton (Durham University Library, uncatalogued); kindly communicated by Cliff Eisen.

[4] The history of the rise of music publishing in Vienna has been written almost single-handedly by Alexander Weinmann; see bibliography. Also, R. Hilmar, *Der Musikverlag Artaria & Comp.: Geschichte und Probleme der Druckproduktion* (Tutzing, 1977).

Yet the nature and extent of this influence on Mozart's symphonies must be qualified. The 'Haffner' symphony was written for Salzburg, the 'Linz' and 'Prague' for the cities whose names they bear, and the final trilogy possibly for an unrealized trip to England. The first three of these six great symphonies certainly, and the last three most likely, were also pressed into use for Viennese concerts; it seems, however, that Mozart, who constantly wrote new piano concertos for his own use, often was content, when in need of symphonies, to perform old works or those of other composers.[5]

The theatre orchestras of Vienna required a constant supply of symphonies to serve as overtures, entr'actes, and afterpieces to operas, operettas, and plays. High Mass in Saint Stephen's Cathedral, and perhaps in some of the other large churches of the City, was sometimes embellished with symphonies, as Chapter 4 demonstrates. During Lent, Advent, and other festivals of the liturgical calendar, stage works were replaced by oratorios or concerts ('academies'), calling for further symphonies. There were no concert halls as such; public concerts took place in theatres, palace salons, and the great rooms of taverns or other commercial buildings. The nobility and court held private concerts, which also often needed symphonies.[6] Finally, another of Vienna's charms was its informal outdoor music—music of a sort that leaves few traces in the form of newspaper announcements, posters, or programmes. A description published in December 1793 suggests that this too was a venue in which symphonies were heard:

During the summer months, if the weather is fine, one comes across serenades performed in the streets almost daily and at all hours, sometimes at one o'clock and even later. One is to a certain degree constrained to hold the serenades very late, because the clatter of the carriages that continually roll to and fro from the dinner parties—even in the remoter streets—does not cease until then. These serenades, however, do not consist of one singer with the simple accompaniment of a guitar, mandora, or another instrument, as in Italy or Spain, for here one offers serenades neither to waft one's sighs into the air nor to declare one's love, for which there are a thousand more comfortable opportunities; rather, these night musics consist of trios [and] quartets (mostly from operas) of several vocal parts, of wind instruments, frequently [even] of an entire orchestra; and the grandest symphonies are performed. Such music especially abounds on the eves of the better known saints' days, particularly on the eve of the feast of Saint Anne [July 26—see Plate XII]. It is just these nocturnal concerts that show very clearly the universality and greatness of the love of

---

[5] Thus, for instance, we find him writing to his father on 4 Jan. 1783, asking to be sent four of his symphonies from 1773–7 for his concerts in Vienna. *Briefe*, iii. 248; *Letters*, iii. 1244–5 (= ii. 835). See below for Mozart's use of symphonies by Gyrowetz, Michael Haydn, and, possibly, Joseph Haydn.

[6] In general, see E. Hanslick, *Geschichte des Konzertwesens in Wien* (Vienna, 1869); O. Biba, 'Grundzüge des Konzertwesens in Wien zu Mozarts Zeit', *Mozart-Jahrbuch* (1978–9), 132–43; M. S. Morrow, 'Concert Life in Vienna 1780–1810' (Ph.D. diss., Indiana University, 1984); *idem*, 'Mozart and Viennese Concert Life', *The Musical Times* (1985), cxxvi. 453–4.

music, since, no matter how late at night they take place—at hours when, usually, everyone is hurrying home—one nevertheless soon discovers people at their open windows, and within a few minutes the musicians are surrounded by an applauding crowd of listeners (often, as in the theatre, demanding that a piece be repeated) who rarely depart until the serenade has come to an end, and then troupes of them often accompany [the musicians] to yet other neighbourhoods of the city.[7]

The variety of occasions on which symphonies were performed combined with a desire for novelty (familiar in present-day popular music if not usually associated with symphonies, which in the eighteenth century, however, were a sort of popular music) go a long way towards explaining the steady demand for symphonies in Vienna in the 1780s.

Besides the small groups that frequently performed at private concerts and the good-sized orchestras used in theatres and elsewhere, there was the occasional huge group gathered together for a special event. In the last category a concert of 1781 is often mentioned at which a symphony of Mozart's was performed by an orchestra whose strings were 20—20—10—8—10, and the wind all doubled except for the bassoons, which were tripled. This exceptionally large orchestra was a traditional part of the annual Lenten benefit concerts given by the 'Society of Musicians' to aid the widows and orphans of musicians.[8] It was natural that on those occasions a large number of performers would wish to be seen supporting the worthy cause. The announcement of the 1781 concert reads:

NOTICE

Tomorrow, Thursday, 3 April 1781, will be held

in the Imperial Playhouse next to the Kärntnertor

FOR THE BENEFIT OF

the newly established Society of Musicians

A GRAND MUSICAL CONCERT,

which will commence with

a Symphony composed by Mr Wolfgang Amadi [*sic*] Mozart, Knight, in actual service of His Serene Highness the Archbishop of Salzburg.

---

[7] Anon., 'Ueber den Stand der Musik in Wien. Erster Brief', *Wiener Theater Almanach für das Jahr 1794* (Vienna, [1793]), 173–4. See also Mozart's letter of 3 Nov. 1781, in which he describes being serenaded in the courtyard of the house where he then lived by a wind sextet playing K. 375. *Briefe*, iii. 171–2; *Letters*, iii. 1155–6 (= ii. 776).

[8] Mozart's letters of 24 Mar., 4 Apr., and 11 Apr. 1781. *Briefe*, iii. 99, 101, 106; *Letters*, iii. 1066–7, 1070, 1076 (= ii. 718, 720, 724); C. F. Pohl, *Denkschrift aus Anlass des Hundertjährigen Bestehens der Tonkünstler-Societät, im Jahre 1862 reorganisirt als 'Haydn', Witwen- und Waisen-Versorgungs-Verein der Tonkünstler in Wien* (Vienna, 1871). When, in his letter of 24 March, Mozart speaks of an 'orchestra' 180 strong, he is employing a well-documented eighteenth-century usage by which 'orchestra' means 'total performing forces, instrumental as well as vocal'. Hence, since his letter of 11 April identifies the orchestra (in the modern sense) as having 85 to 90 members, the choir may have contained approximately 90 voices.

Mr Mozart, Knight, will then be heard on the pianoforte all by himself.
He was already here himself as a boy aged seven, and even then earned the general applause of the public, partly in the matter of composition and partly in that of art altogether, as well as for his especial skill and delicacy of touch . . . .
To begin at 6:30.[9]

Mozart reported to his father that 'the symphony went *magnifique* and had all possible success'.[10] Much has been written about this event, suggesting that if Mozart was so pleased, then this must have been the sort of orchestra he would have preferred but usually could not muster.[11] In evaluating Mozart's words, however, one must reckon with the defensiveness in letters to his father, with his striving to be entertaining and to make his affairs sound more brilliant than they were, and with the fact that, even if Mozart honestly thought that the symphony had gone magnificently and with all possible success, he was still not necessarily expressing his opinion about the kind of orchestra with which he would have preferred to work regularly. Like his contemporaries, he must have recognized that in enlarging an orchestra one traded clarity, flexibility, and intimacy for power and brilliance.[12] The orchestras upon which Mozart's training and taste were formed and for which he most often composed, in Vienna and elsewhere, were usually of middling size, rather than tiny private groups or the occasional mammoth ensemble. (The exception was the small but accomplished Prague orchestra, with which Mozart developed a special relationship.) He was a practical musician who wrote for the customary performing conditions of his day, and we should not foist upon him and his music practices derived from exceptional circumstances that with hindsight may appear to prefigure later trends.

While Vienna was not a centre of music-publishing, the 1780s saw the first serious expansion of the industry. The leading firm was Artaria & Cie. which, because of its origin as a publisher of maps and 'views', already employed engravers, although the quality of their musical work was the cause of annoyance

[9] Deutsch, 173 (= 195).
[10] Letter of 11 Apr. 1781. *Briefe*, iii. 106; *Letters*, iii. 1076 (= ii. 724). Based on another passage in this letter, it has often been said that this concert received two rehearsals: 'Have I been to Bonno's place? Why, we rehearsed my symphony there for the second time.' As it is unlikely that Kapellmeister Bonno had a room in his house large enough to accommodate an orchestra of 85 or 90, Mozart's remark would appear to mean that there had been two so-called 'quartet rehearsals' (i.e., by the first chair players only), before the usual single general rehearsal was held in the theatre.
[11] For instance, C. Rosen, *The Classical Style: Haydn, Mozart, Beethoven* (New York, 1972), 143; W. Blok, 'Mozart: The Symphonies', *Musick, a Quarterly Journal Published by the Vancouver Society for Early Music* (Winter 1981–2), iii. 24–8; W. Hildesheimer, *Mozart* (New York, 1982), 233–4.
[12] Evidence that Mozart's contemporaries were fully aware of the potential problems of large orchestras and often preferred smaller ones is presented in ch. 12. On the other hand, there was also a tradition of so-called 'monster' concerts, traceable in the eighteenth century to performances led by Corelli in Rome around the turn of the century (see G. Dixon, 'The Origins of the Roman "Colossal Baroque"', *Proceedings of the Royal Musical Association* (1980), cvi. 115–28). For 'monster' concerts of Mozart's time, see D. J. Koury, *Orchestral Performance Practices in the Nineteenth Century: Size, Proportions, and Seating* (Ann Arbor, 1986), 26–8.

for Haydn[13] and for Mozart, who wrote to the Parisian publisher Sieber in 1783 that he was 'not very well pleased ... with the engraving' in Vienna.[14] Almost all of what was published of Mozart's by Artaria (and by Koželuch, Hoffmeister, and Torricella, the only other Viennese publishers to offer several of his works during his lifetime) was small-scale music for modest domestic use; only two symphonies appeared, K. 319 and 385, both in 1785.

The dissemination of Mozart's symphonies in the 1780s was mostly by manuscript copies, and the principal conduit for those copies was the Viennese copying house of Johann Traeg. Traeg offered a number of Mozart's works during his lifetime and later presumably received others from Mozart's widow Constanze. He advertised his wares in the *Wiener Zeitung* from 1782, listing a symphony by Mozart for the first time in 1784. Finally, in 1799 Traeg issued a cumulative printed catalogue of his holdings. His business must have extended well beyond Vienna, for copies of his are found in libraries and archives in several parts of the former Austrian Empire, and Johann Nikolaus Forkel, working in Göttingen but publishing in Leipzig, noted about Mozart at the end of 1788, 'Since 1784 various symphonies ... have become publicly known',[15] referring apparently to Traeg's offerings from 1784, as well as Artaria's two prints of 1785, and, much less probably, to the Paris editions.

Those portions of Traeg's advertisements and 1799 catalogue that concern Mozart's symphonies are summarized in Table 11.1.[16] Some interesting points emerge from this table. It has always been known that after 1784 Mozart composed only four symphonies. That no new symphonies were announced by Traeg between 1785 and 1792 must mean that Mozart had also lost interest even in selling his still unavailable, earlier symphonies. When Leopold died in 1787, Nannerl packed up almost all of Wolfgang's compositions still in the family's home in Salzburg and sent them to him, and these, together with works Leopold had sent him piecemeal and those Wolfgang may have brought back from his visit to Salzburg in 1783, were in his possession at his death. That so many of the symphonies of the 1770s exist in the form of Salzburg originals with Viennese *Dubletten*, often with corrections in Mozart's hand, suggests that he found use for the earlier works in his concerts of the 1780s. Perhaps their less imposing content meant that they could provide a lively framework for concerts without overshadowing the piano concertos and arias. If so, this would weaken the force of

---

[13] See Haydn's letters to Artaria of 20 Mar. and 8 Apr. 1783. D. Bartha (ed.), *Haydn: Briefe*, 126–8; (=Landon (ed.), *Haydn: Collected Correspondence and London Notebooks*, 40–1).

[14] Letter of 26 Apr. 1783. *Briefe*, iii. 266; *Letters*, iii. 1261 (= ii. 846). This may have been written to flatter Sieber, whose edition of the six violin sonatas K. 301–6 is itself full of errors.

[15] Deutsch, 291 (= 332).

[16] A. Weinmann, *Johann Traeg: Die Musikalienverzeichnisse von 1799 und 1804* (Beiträge zur Geschichte des alt-wiener Musikverlages, ii/17) (Vienna, 1973); idem, *Die Anzeigen des Kopiaturbetriebes Johann Traeg in der wiener Zeitung zwischen 1782 und 1805* (Wiener Archivstudien, vi) (Vienna, 1981).

TABLE 11.1 Johann Traeg's advertisements of Mozart's symphonies

Weiner Zeitung Date	No.	Page	Text	Weinmann Page
27 Oct. 1784	86	2241	'symphonies'	18
16 Feb. 1785	14	370	'3 symphonies'	19
30 Apr. 1785	35	1022–3	'2 new symphonies in C and D'*	20
14 Sept. 1785	74	2165	'various new symphonies'	21
21 Apr. 1792	32	1084	'14 symphonies, handwritten'*	32
11 Aug. 1792	64	2229	'15 symphonies'	34
24 Oct. 1792	85	2892	'1 grand symphony in C.... This symphony is one of his last works and is among his masterpieces, in manuscript' [K. 551]	35
18 May 1793	40	1462	'New music.... 1 symphony in D—1 ditto in C'	38
29 June 1793	52	1919	[repeat of previous announcement]	38
18 Dec. 1793	101	3635	'1 grand symphony in G minor (this is one of the last and most beautiful symphonies of this master) [K. 550].—1 ditto in D'	42
19 Feb. 1794	151	515–16	'1 symphony in G minor, his last [K. 550]—1 symphony in D'	43
29 Oct. 1794	87	3116–17	'1 [grand symphony] in Bb. 6 Fl. 40 Kr.' [?K. 319]	47
13 Dec. 1794	100	3560	'1 grand symphony in D. 9 Fl.'	48
20 Feb. 1796	15	465	'1 symphony, Op. 45. 2 Fl. 24 Kr.' [?K. 550: see Table 11.2]	55

*7 Kreutzer per Bogen.

Source: A. Weinmann, *Die Anzeigen des Kopiaturbetriebes Johann Traeg in der wiener Zeitung zwischen 1782 und 1805* (Wiener Archivstudien, vi) (Vienna, 1981).

Nannerl's assertion, after her brother's death, that '. . . I know full well that, the more accomplished he became in composition, the less he could suffer his early works.'[17]

Along with Mozart's autographs, the Salzburg–Vienna sets of parts became the object of intense cataloguing, correspondence, and attempts at publication or sale for more than a decade after his death.[18] Evidence of Constanze's attempts to raise money from her husband's works can be detected in Table 11.1, in the appearance of fourteen and then fifteen symphonies in Traeg's advertisements of 1792, followed by several others during the next few years. Tentative identification of many of Mozart's symphonies in Traeg's 1799 catalogue (Table 11.3) is possible because, taken together, key, instrumentation, price, and (in four cases) opus number reveal a great deal. Opus numbers refer to symphonies published by Johann André of Offenbach in the 1790s (Table 11.2).[19] Some of Traeg's indications of instrumentation appear to include inconsistencies and errors; in each such instance discrepancies between his listed instrumentation and that of the proposed symphony is signalled by underlining the instrument(s) in question. That a D major symphony might have circulated without its trumpet and kettledrum parts (Traeg's No. 282) was a common condition of eighteenth-century musical life. The accidental inclusion of oboes in the listing for K. 543 is also understandable, because symphonies without oboes are rare, K. 543 being the only such symphony Mozart wrote, and the cataloguer tended to write each entry with reference to the previous one. The absence of bassoons in the putative listing of K. 319 is interesting, for the work must have circulated without those instruments, and was so indicated in K^1, K^2, and K^3, an error first corrected only in 1947 in K^{3a}. That Traeg and his copyists regarded most of these symphonies as having divided violas reveals an aspect of Mozart's orchestration and performance practice sometimes misrepresented in historical writings and editions.

The use of price as an aid to identifying symphonies is possible because, like any such firm, Traeg would have charged for a piece according to the amount of copying it required. The currency was 1 Florin (or Gulden) = 60 Kreutzer. In his advertisements of symphonies in 1785 and 1792 he charged 7 Kreutzer for each *Bogen*, the term for a large sheet of paper, which in music manuscripts was usually folded once to make two folios (or leaves) or four pages (or sides). Naturally, the more bars of music and the larger the orchestration, the more *Bögen* required. In order to make use of prices in identifying symphonies, an arbitrary index of the

[17] *Briefe*, iv. 259; not in *Letters*. Compare this to Leopold's remarks about not giving Wolfgang's early symphonies to be copied (see ch. 8, n. 4).

[18] This activity is documented in the correspondence of Mozart's widow, sister, and others in *Briefe*, iv. 204–524; *Letters*, iii. 1459–1513 (only in 1st edn.).

[19] W. Matthäus, *Johann André Musikverlag zu Offenbach am Main: Verlagsgeschichte und Bibliographie* (Tutzing, 1973). Constanze's earliest preserved correspondence with André dates from 1795 (*Briefe*, iv. 205; not in *Letters*).

Table 11.2 Johann André's early editions of Mozart's symphonies

Opus	Plate No.	K.	RISM	Year published
22	520	320	M 5653	1792
25	521	250	M 5648	1792
34	594	425	M 5524	1793
38	622	551	M 5573	1793
45	685	550	M 5562	1794
57	1063	338	M 5514	1797
58	1103	543	M 5543	1797

Source: W. Matthäus, *Johann André Musikverlag zu Offenbach am Main: Verlagsgeschichte und Bibliographie* (Tutzing, 1972).

'size' of each symphony has been estimated by multiplying the number of bars in a movement by the number of instrumental parts to be copied for that movement, totalling these figures for the movements of each symphony, dividing the result by one thousand, and rounding off to the nearest whole number. Table 11.3 shows the correlation between 'size' and price of these symphonies as established by their proposed identities.

An advertisement by Traeg in 1784 is enlightening about the kind of music environment in which Mozart worked. It reads:

Notice for the Music-Lover

Johann Traeg, on the first floor of the Pilate House by Saint Peter's, has the honour of certifying to the highly esteemed public that, encouraged by the success thus far granted him, he has drawn up a plan that will be most welcome to music-lovers, by means of which they will be enabled at little cost to entertain themselves with the best pieces by the greatest masters. There are many families of this very city that amuse themselves with large or small musical gatherings. Many of them do not wish to be overloaded with sheet-music, or at very least wish to have an introductory hearing of the things that they have a mind to buy. Inasmuch as I now possess a fine stock, which I endeavour daily to enlarge further, of the best and newest music of all types, I therefore offer to hire out weekly either three symphonies or six quintets, six quartets, six trios, etc. for a quarterly payment in advance of three florin. If anyone wishes to give concerts twice a week and, accordingly, requires six symphonies or twelve other pieces for that purpose, he likewise can subscribe in that fashion and pay quarterly only five florin. However, because I must strive to serve everyone fairly, no-one should have misgivings at returning the pieces received directly the following day. Because of my broad acquaintanceship with the best local musicians, I can also provide skilled musicians for large and small concerts at a very reasonable price. In order best to be able to execute these commissions, I request that people place their orders at my establishment any time before midday.[20]

[20] *Wiener Zeitung* (16–25 Feb. 1784), 395–6, as given in Weinmann, *Die Anzeigen des Kopiaturbetriebes Johann Traeg*, 16–17.

TABLE 11.3 Mozart's symphonies in Traeg's 1799 catalogue, pp. 17–18

Cat.	Symph.	Op.	Key	[K.]	Orchestration†	['Size']	Price (fl./kr.)
272	1	—	D	[?135]	*0–2–0–0 / 2–2–2–0	[3]	2/30
273	2	—	G	[318]	2–2–0–2 / 4–2–1	[4]	3/30
274	3	—	B♭	[?173dA]	*0–2–0–0 / 2–0–0–0	[3]	2/30
275	4	—	A	[186a]	0–2–0–0 / 2–0–0–0	[4]	3/30
276	5	—	C	[?162]	*0–2–0–0 / 2–2–1	[3]	3/30
277	6	—	D	[?213a]	1–2–0–1 / 2–2–1	[8–9]	4/—
278	7	22	D	[320]	*0–2–0–2 / 2–2–1	[10]	5/—
279	8	—	C	[338]	*0–2–0–2 / 2–2–1	[9]	3/—
280	9	25	D	[248b]	*0–2–0–2 / 2–2–1	[14]	4/24
281	10	—	B♭	[?319]	0–2–0–2 / 2–0–0–0	[7–9]	4/—
282	11	—	D	[?189b or ?186b or ?162b]	0–2–0–2 / 2–0–0–0	[—]	4/—
283	12	34	C	[425]	*0–2–0–2 / 2–2–1	[12]	4/—
284	13	—	D	[?385 or 300a]	*0–2–2–2 / 2–2–1	[11]	5/—
285	14	—	D	[504]	2–2–0–2 / 2–2–1	[12]	6/—
286	15	38	C	[551]	*1–2–0–2 / 2–2–1	[14]	6/—
287	16	[45]	E♭	[543]	*1–2–2–2 / 2–2–1	[12]	6/—
288	17	—	g	[550]	*1–2–0–1 / 2–0–0–0	[8]	5/—
289	18	—	F	[?112]	0–2–0–0 / 2–0–0–0	[2]	2/—
500	19	—	D	[?207a]	0–2–0–0 / 2–0–0–0	[3]	3/30

*violas divisi.

† Figures underlined differ in some way from the orchestration of the proposed symphony as it appears in Mozart's autograph manuscript.

Some notion of the ambience of the private concerts for which Traeg's music-rental scheme catered, and at which Mozart so often performed in the early and mid-1780s, may be gleaned from a small engraving of *c*.1785 (Plate XIII).

As for public music-making, in the 1770s the only regular public concerts in Vienna had been those given in the Hofburgtheater on certain evenings on which no theatrical productions were scheduled. A great boom occurred in the early and mid-1780s, until war, recession, and the deaths of Joseph II and Leopold II began a decline that reached its nadir in the Napoleonic wars. There is some indication that Mozart's frenetic activity in both public and private arenas may have been not only a symptom of the boom but one of its causes. As documented in his letters to his father, during the Lenten concert season Mozart played somewhere different every evening for many weeks running, during which time he also continued to give private lessons and to add compositions to the catalogue of his works. When Leopold visited Wolfgang in Lent 1785, he wrote to Nannerl about her brother's concerts:

16 February: On the same evening [Friday, 11 February] we drove to his first subscription concert, at which a great many members of the aristocracy were present. [. . .] [For the rest of this passage, see below.] On Saturday evening Mr Joseph Haydn and the two Barons Tinti came to see us and the new quartets were performed, or rather, the three new ones . . . . On Sunday the Italian singer, Madame Laschi, who is leaving for Italy, gave a concert in the theatre, at which she sang two arias. A cello concerto was performed, a tenor and a bass each sang an aria and your brother played a glorious concerto [?K. 456] . . . . When your brother left the platform the Emperor waved his hat and called out 'Bravo, Mozart!' And when he came on to play, there was a great deal of clapping. We were not at the theatre yesterday, for every day there is a concert . . . . Yesterday, the 15th, there was again a recital in the theatre given by a girl who sings charmingly. Your brother played his new grand concerto in D minor [K. 466] most magnificently. [. . .] This evening there is another one in the theatre, at which your brother is again playing a concerto.[21]

21 February: . . . this evening your brother is performing at a grand concert at Count Zichy's . . . but your sister-in-law and Marchand have gone to the concert at Mr von Ployer's . . . . As usual, it will probably be one o'clock before we get to bed . . . . On Friday, the 18th . . . we drove to your brother's second concert at the Mehlgrube at seven o'clock. This concert too was a splendid success. Heinrich [Marchand] played a violin concerto. [. . .] The two concerts which Mr Le Brun and his wife are giving in the theatre are on Wednesday, the 23rd, and Monday, the 28th. All the boxes for the first concert were sold out on the 18th. These people are going to make an enormous amount of money.[22]

12 March: Your brother made 559 gulden at his concert, which we never expected, as he is giving six subscription concerts at the Mehlgrube to over 150 people, each of whom pays a

---

[21] *Briefe*, iii. 372–3; *Letters*, iii. 1320–2 (= ii. 885–7).   [22] Ibid. 374–5; 1323–4 (= 887–8).

souverain d'or for the six . . . . We never get to bed before one o'clock and I never get up before nine. We lunch at two or half past . . . . Every day there are concerts; and the whole time is given up to teaching, music, composing and so forth. I feel rather out of it. If only the concerts were over! It is impossible for me to describe the rush and bustle. Since my arrival your brother's fortepiano has been taken at least a dozen times to the theatre or to some other house . . . . It is taken to the Mehlgrube every Friday and has also been taken to Count Zichy's and to Prince Kaunitz's.[23]

Leopold was not exaggerating the extent of his son's activities, for the number of Wolfgang's concerts that can be documented in the busy concert seasons to the end of 1785, before either he withdrew or the public tired of him or the war and a depressed economy put a damper on high living in Vienna, staggers the imagination.[24] The majority of these concerts included one or two of Mozart's piano concertos; hence orchestral forces were present and one or more symphonies were probably usually heard too.

The amount of music Mozart composed, the number of lessons he gave, and the number of concerts he performed suggest extraordinary, almost supernatural fluency and energy, and no little entrepreneurial skill. For three Lenten concerts in the hall in Trattner's casino in 1784, for instance, Mozart rounded up 174 subscribers, each of whom paid 6 florin.[25] The list of subscribers he sent to his father reveals the nature of his audiences, at least for such subscription concerts: 50 per cent from the high nobility, 42 per cent from the lesser nobility and the 'commercial' nobility (i.e., those with purchased titles), and a mere 8 per cent from the bourgeoisie.[26] Only about 17 per cent were women, in contrast to Parisian salon concerts, which were dominated by women.

Symphony in D major, K. 385, 'Haffner'

[Incipits 11.1]

[23] Ibid. 378–9; 1324–5 (= 888–9).
[24] Morrow, 'Concert Life in Vienna'.
[25] Letters of 3 and 20 Mar. 1784. *Briefe*, iii. 303, 305–7; *Letters*, iii. 1296–1301 (= ii. 869–72).
[26] H. Schuler, *Die Subskribenten der Mozart'schen Mittwochskonzerte im Trattnersaal zu Wien anno 1784* (Neustadt an der Aisch, 1983).

Instrumentation: (first version) strings, 2 oboes, 2 bassoons, 2 horns, 2 trumpets, kettledrums, [continuo]; (second version) as above plus 2 flutes, 2 clarinets
Autograph: Pierpont Morgan Library, New York
Principal sources: Salzburg, Mozarteum (P 140/3); Modena, Biblioteca Estense (Mus E 159) (both first version)
Facsimile: (complete) ed. S. Beck (Oxford and New York, 1968); *NMA*, iv/11/6. xviii–xix
Editions: *GA*, xxii. 1–36 (Serie 8, No. 35); *NMA*, iv/11/6. 113–64; ed. H. C. Robbins Landon (London, 1971)

The circumstances surrounding the creation of K. 385 are more fully documented than those of any other of Mozart's symphonies. In mid-July 1782 Leopold wrote requesting a new symphony for celebrations for the ennoblement of Wolfgang's childhood friend Sigmund Haffner the younger. On 20 July Wolfgang replied:

Well, I am up to my eyes in work. By Sunday week I have to arrange my opera [*Die Entführung aus dem Serail*, K. 384] for wind instruments, otherwise someone will beat me to it and secure the profits instead of me. And now you ask me to write a new symphony too! How on earth am I to do so? You have no idea how difficult it is to arrange a work of this kind for wind instruments, so that it suits these instruments and yet loses none of its effects. Well, I must just spend the night over it, for that is the only way; and to you, dearest father, I sacrifice it. You may rely on having something from me by every post. I shall work as fast as possible and, as far as haste permits, I shall write something good.[27]

---

[27] *Briefe*, iii. 213; *Letters*, iii. 1205 (= ii. 808). Leopold's mid-July commissioning letter is lost, and no number has been assigned to it in *Briefe*, iii. 212.

Although Wolfgang was prone to procrastination and making excuses in letters to his father, in this instance his complaints were possibly justified: he had just completed the arduous task of launching his new opera (the première was 16 July) and was preparing to move house on 23 July in anticipation of his marriage. Under the circumstances, it is hardly surprising that a week later Mozart reported to his father:

You will be surprised and disappointed to find that this contains only the first Allegro; but it has been quite impossible to do more for you, for I have had to compose in a great hurry a serenade [probably K. 375], but for wind instruments only (otherwise I could have used it for you too). On Wednesday the 31st I shall send the two minuets, the Andante and the last movement. If I can manage to do so, I shall send a march too. If not, you will just have to use the one [K. 249] from the Haffner music [K. 250], which hardly anyone knows. I have composed my symphony in D major, because you prefer that key.[28]

On 29 July Sigmund Haffner was ennobled, adding to his name 'von Imbachhausen'. On the 31st, however, Mozart could write only that:

You see that my intentions are good—only what one cannot do, one cannot! I am really unable to scribble off inferior stuff. So I cannot send you the whole symphony until next post-day. I could have let you have the last movement, but I prefer to dispatch it all together, for then it will cost only one fee. What I have sent you has already cost me three gulden.[29]

On 4 August Wolfgang and Constanze Weber were married in Vienna without yet having received Leopold's grudging approval, which arrived the following day. Meanwhile, the other movements must have been completed and sent off, for on 7 August Wolfgang wrote to his father: 'I send you herewith a short march [probably K. 408, No. 2]. I only hope that all will reach you in good time, and be to your taste. The first Allegro must be played with great fire, the last—as fast as possible.'[30] Given the speed at which the 'Linz' symphony could be produced a year later, one may be justified in suspecting that the slow progress of the 'Haffner' symphony had more than a little to do with Mozart's disaffection toward Salzburg and anger at his father.

   Precisely when the party celebrating Haffner's ennoblement took place is not known, for Leopold's letter reporting the event is lost. However, the fact that in a later letter Wolfgang was unsure whether orchestral parts had been copied (see below) suggests that the symphony had not arrived in time. Be that as it may, either the work was performed in Salzburg prior to 24 August or Leopold had

---

[28] *Briefe*, iii. 214–15; *Letters*, iii. 1207 (= ii. 809–10). A possible explanation of Mozart's remark about Leopold preferring D major is offered in ch. 7.

[29] *Briefe*, iii. 216, vi. 111; *Letters*, iii. 1209 (= ii. 811).

[30] Ibid. 219; 1212 (= 813).

studied it in score and had indicated his approval, for on that day Wolfgang responded, 'I am delighted that the symphony is to your taste'.[31]

Three months after the première of K. 385 in Salzburg the symphony again entered the Mozarts' correspondence, when Mozart wrote to his father on 4 December, in a letter that went astray, asking for its return. He wrote again on the 21st, summarizing the lost letter, including the remark: 'I also asked you to send me at the first opportunity which presents itself the new symphony that I composed for Haffner at your request. I should like to have it for certain before Lent, for I should very much like to have it performed at my concert.'[32] On 4 January 1783 he returned to the subject: 'It is all the same to me whether you send me the symphony of the last Haffner music which I composed in Vienna, in the original score or copied out [into parts] for, as it is, I shall have to have several additional copies made for my concert.' Mozart then asked in addition to be sent four other symphonies: K. 204 = 213a, 201 = 186a, 182 = 173dA, and 183 = 173dB.[33] On the 22nd he again reminded his father, 'Please send me the symphonies I asked for as soon as possible, for I really need them now,'[34] and on the 5th of February yet again, this time with renewed urgency:

Please send the symphonies, especially the *last one*, as soon as possible, for my concert is to take place on the third Sunday in Lent, that is, on March 23rd, and I must have several duplicate string parts made. I think, therefore, that if it is not copied [into orchestral parts] already, it would be better to send me back the original score just as I sent it to you; and remember to put in the minuets.[35]

Surely the usually punctilious Leopold's procrastination is mute testimony to the anger and frustration he felt over what he considered to be his son's faltering career and foolish choice of a wife. Still, by 15 February Wolfgang could write, 'Most heartfelt thanks for the music you have sent me . . .', adding (ironically?), 'My new Haffner symphony has positively amazed me, for I had forgotten every single note of it. It must surely produce a good effect.'[36]

Mozart then proceeded to rework the score of K. 385 sent from Salzburg by putting aside the March, deleting the repeats in the first movement, and adding pairs of flutes and clarinets in the first and last movements, primarily to reinforce the tuttis and requiring no further changes in the already existing orchestration of those movements. The added instruments are written in a lighter ink than the rest of the score and can be easily distinguished in the autograph manuscript and in the facsimile edition.[37]

[31] Ibid. 225; 1219 (= 817).   [32] Ibid. 243–4; 1240 (= 832).   [33] Ibid. iii. 248; 1244 (= 835).
[34] Ibid. 251; 1248 (= 837).   [35] Ibid. 254; 1249–50 (= 838).   [36] Ibid. 256–7; 1252 (= 840).
[37] Ed. S. Beck (Oxford and New York, 1968). For a valuable critique of the shortcomings of the widely disseminated Breitkopf full score and parts and of the Eulenberg miniature score of K. 385, in light of the revelations of this facsimile edition, see N. Del Mar, *Orchestral Variations: Confusion and Error in the Orchestral Repertoire* (London, 1981), 149–53.

Mozart's academy duly took place on Sunday, 23 March, in the Hofburgtheater. He reported to his father:

The theatre could not have been more crowded and ... every box was full. But what pleased me most of all was that His Majesty the Emperor was present and, goodness!— how delighted he was and how he applauded me! It is his custom to send money to the box office before going to the theatre; otherwise I should have been fully justified in counting on a larger sum, for really his delight was beyond all bounds. He sent 25 ducats.[38]

In its broad outlines Mozart's account is confirmed by a report published in the *Magazin der Musik*, Hamburg:

Vienna, 22 March 1783 .... Tonight the famous Chevalier Mozart held a concert in the National Theatre, at which pieces of his already highly admired composition were performed. The concert was honoured with an exceptionally large crowd, and the two new concertos and other fantasies that Mr Mozart played on the fortepiano were received with the loudest applause. Our Monarch, who, against his habit, attended the whole of the concert, as well as the entire audience, accorded him such unanimous applause as has never been heard of here. The receipts of the concert are estimated to amount to 1,600 gulden in all.[39]

The programme, typical for Mozart's Viennese academies, confirms the character-istic role that symphonies played everywhere, as preludes and postludes framing an evening's music-making:

1. The first three movements of the 'Haffner' symphony, K. 385
2. 'Se il padre perdei' from *Idomeneo*, K. 366
3. A piano concerto in C major, K. 415
4. The recitative and aria 'Misera, dove son!—Ah! non son' io che parlo', K. 369
5. A sinfonia concertante, K. 320, movements 3 and 4
6. A piano concerto in D major, K. 175 with the substitute Finale K. 382
7. 'Parto, m'affretto' from *Lucio Silla*, K. 135
8. A short (improvised?) fugue ('because the Emperor was present')
9. Variations on a tune from Paisiello's *I filosofi immaginari*, K. 398, and, as an encore to that,
10. Variations on a tune from Gluck's *Die Pilgrimme von Mekka* (cf. K. 455)
11. The recitative and rondo 'Mia speranza adorate—Ah, non sia, qual pena', K. 416
12. The Finale of the 'Haffner' symphony, K. 385.[40]

The practice of inserting the rest of a concert between the third and fourth movements of a symphony is foreign to modern musicians, for whom the unity of

[38] Letter of 29 Mar. 1783. *Briefe*, iii. 261; *Letters*, iii. 1256 (= ii. 843).
[39] Deutsch, 190–1 (= 215). The date of this report should have read '23 March 1783'.
[40] Letter of 29 Mar. 1783. *Briefe*, iii. 261–2; *Letters*, iii. 1256–7 (= ii. 843).

a work of art is an article of faith.[41] Perhaps Mozart thought of a concert organized in this format the same way he thought of an orchestral serenade formed by adding marches, minuets, and concerto movements to symphony movements, and possibly he viewed a concert as analogous to an extended serenade likewise held together by a symphonic framework. Mozart's contemporaries held similar attitudes to operas, which were loosely held together by their librettos but could sustain added, subtracted, or transposed arias, dances, and other numbers. Such additions and cuts were the province not just of pasticcios but of most operas.

Wolfgang and Leopold consistently referred to the Salzburg version of K. 385 as a symphony in their correspondence, even though the work's intended function as well as its march made it like the works that they called *Finalmusik* and that are now known as orchestral serenades. But a true *Finalmusik* probably would have included one or two concerto movements, a slow introduction to the first movement (as in K. 203, 250, and 320, but not the earlier serenades), and a second Minuet and Trio. And the standard descriptions of this work claim that it did originally have a second Minuet and Trio, because in two of the letters quoted above Mozart wrote 'I shall send the two minuets' and 'remember to put in the minuets'. Indeed, in the autograph of K. 385 it is easy to see that the extant Minuet and Trio were once a separate manuscript. As the symphony had been sent to Salzburg piecemeal, the possibility of losing a movement becomes understandable, but none of this explains why Mozart thought his father likely to leave out any particular movement or movements. Possibly in the lost letter to which Wolfgang replied, 'I am delighted that the symphony is to your taste', Leopold had made a remark about needing to use only three movements and having removed the 'minuets'. That 'minuets' in this instance mean one minuet and its trio (hence the older terminology discussed in Chapter 2 in connection with K. 17), rather than two sets of a minuet and trio each, as has always be assumed, is strongly supported by early sets of parts in Salzburg (of Salzburg origin) and Modena (of Viennese origin). Both sets transmit the Salzburg version of K. 385 (that is, without flutes and clarinets, with the first movement repeat, and without a certain accidental that was a later emendation): they contain no additional movement.

Aside from the Hamburg report, there were no reviews of the Viennese première of the 'Haffner' symphony, but what was possibly a performance of this work on 21 February 1786 in Bamberg elicited the following reaction from an anonymous correspondent:

The concert began with a new Symphony in D by Mozart, which was all the more

---

[41] C.-H. Mahling, 'Zur Frage der "Einheit" der Symphonie', in C.-H. Mahling (ed.), *Festschrift Walter Wiora: Über Symphonien. Beiträge zu einer musikalischen Gattung* (Tutzing, 1979), 1–40, here 1–2; P. Kivy, 'Mozart and Monotheism: An Essay in Spurious Aesthetics', *Journal of Musicology* (1983), ii. 322–8.

welcome to me because I had already long been desirous of hearing it. Chamber-musician Lehritter (a step-brother of the Abbé Sterkel) led the orchestra—which consisted of approximately 45 or 46 mostly young artists—with so much fire and solidity that I stood there full of astonishment. Everything hung together from one beat to the next: tempo, execution, forte, piano, and crescendo exhibited a perfection to the nth degree .... I consider Mozart's symphony itself a masterpiece of harmony.[42]

The 'Haffner' symphony was published in Mozart's lifetime in Vienna and in Paris, where it was performed at the Concert spirituel. As shown in the previous chapter, the Viennese edition was for sale in a number of cities, including London where apparently it was performed. It is an extraordinarily attractive work that has always been popular, yet—despite its attractions—it still clings to the conventional, brilliant style then generally thought appropriate to the genre but which Mozart would soon abandon. Was Mozart thinking along such lines when, putting the symphony in D major because Leopold preferred that key and asking anxiously if the work was to his father's taste, he was relieved to hear that it was? He may already have perceived that, freed of his father's scrutiny and the constraints of Salzburg's provincial society, he was moving beyond what would pass muster in his native city. But in a characteristically defensive way Mozart underestimated his father's understanding, for to the end of his life Leopold continued to enjoy and to approve of Wolfgang's music, however much he may have questioned the life his rebellious son was leading.

Symphony in C major, K. 425, 'Linz'

[Incipits 11.2]

---

[42] Anon., 'Auszug eines Briefes von einem Reisenden an seinen Freund F-l-i in Bamberg. Frankfurt am 21sten Hornung, 1786', in C. F. Cramer (ed.), *Magazin der Musik* (21 Nov. 1786), 954. Document generously brought to my attention by Cliff Eisen. The violinist F. Lehritter was the step-brother of Johann Franz Xaver Sterkel (1750–1817), concertmaster at Mainz.

Instrumentation: *strings, 2 oboes, 2 bassoons, 2 horns, 2 trumpets, kettledrums, [continuo]

Autograph: lost

Principal sources: a set of parts in Salzburg, copied from the lost autograph under Leopold Mozart's supervision in 1784; a set of parts in Donaueschingen, sent there by Wolfgang Mozart in 1786

Facsimile: *NMA*, iv/11/8. xiv–xvi

Editions: *GA*, xxii. 37–80 (= Serie 8, No. 36); *NMA*, iv/11/8. 3–62

Mozart's letters in the months following his marriage are filled with promises of a journey to Salzburg to enable his father, his sister, and their friends to meet his bride. Excuse after excuse was found to postpone this trip, not only because Mozart was painfully aware of his father's and sister's disapproval of his choice of wife, but also because he feared forcible detention in Salzburg for having left the Archbishop's service. On being reassured by his father concerning the latter point, Wolfgang and Constanze finally set out, arriving in Salzburg toward the end of July 1783 and remaining there until the end of October. From what little is known of the visit, it must have been difficult for all concerned.[43]

On the return trip to Vienna the couple had to pass through the town of Linz. What transpired there is recounted in Mozart's letter of 31 October to his father:

We arrived here safely yesterday morning at 9 o'clock. We spent the first night in Vöcklabruck and reached Lambach Monastery next morning, where I arrived just in time

---

[43] For daring yet convincing psychological interpretations of the strained relationships during this visit among Mozart, Constanze, Leopold, and Nannerl, see D. Heartz, 'Mozart, His Father, and "Idomeneo" ', *The Musical Times* (1978), cxix. 228–31; and A. Tyson, 'Mozart and Idomeneo', ibid. 404–5.

to accompany the 'Agnus Dei' on the organ. The abbot [Amand Schickmayr] was absolutely delighted to see me again . . . . We spent the whole day there, and I played both on the organ and on a clavichord. I heard that an opera was to be given next day at Ebelsberg at the house of the Prefect Steurer . . . and that almost all of Linz was to be assembled. I resolved therefore to be present and we drove there. Young Count Thun (brother of the Thun at Vienna) called on me immediately and said that his father had been expecting me for a fortnight and would I please drive to his house at once for I was to stay with him. I told him that I could easily put up at an inn. But when we reached the gates of Linz on the following day, we found a servant waiting there to drive us to Count Thun's, at whose house we are now staying. I really cannot tell you what kindnesses the family are showering on us. On Tuesday, November 4th, I am giving a concert in the theatre here and, as I have not a single symphony with me, I am writing a new one at break-neck speed, which must be finished by that time. Well, I must close, because I really must set to work.[44]

If Mozart is to be believed, then between 30 October and 4 November he wrote a new symphony, copied the parts (or had them copied), and perhaps even had time to rehearse the work once before its première. The concert took place in the main room of the Ballhaus in Linz.[45] Nothing is known of the orchestra, which was probably that of the Counts Thun, junior and senior, which Mozart would re-encounter in Prague in 1787, and which Niemetschek, in a passage cited below, called 'first rate'. It may have had a fair complement of players, to judge by the full instrumentation of K. 425. As for the rest of the programme, every biography of Mozart states that a G major symphony by Michael Haydn, K. 444 = 425a + Anh. A53, for which Mozart provided a slow introduction and which once passed for a work entirely by him, was performed. As demonstrated below, this claim is ill-founded. Besides a symphony, Mozart's 'academies' seldom failed to include one or two of his piano concertos, some arias, and some solo improvisation at the keyboard; the Linz programme was perhaps similar.

The new symphony was taken to Vienna where Mozart performed it again at his 'academy' of 1 April 1784. The announcement in the *Wienerblättchen* reads:

Concert.

Today, Thursday, 1 April, Kapellmeister Mozart will have the honour to hold a great musical concert for his benefit at the Imperial National Court Theatre [the Hofburgtheater]. The pieces to occur in it are the following:

1. A grand symphony with trumpets and drums [K. 385?]
2. An aria sung by Mr Adamberger
3. Mr Mozart, Kapellmeister, will play an entirely new concerto on the fortepiano
4. A quite new grand symphony [K. 425]
5. An aria sung by Mlle Cavalieri

---

[44] *Briefe*, iii. 291; *Letters*, iii. 1280–1 (= ii. 859).   [45] R. Engerth, *Hier hat Mozart gespielt* (Salzburg, 1968), 79.

6. Mr Mozart, Kapellmeister, will play an entirely new grand quintet [K. 452]
7. An aria sung by Mr Marchesi senior
8. Kapellmeister Mozart will improvise entirely alone on the fortepiano
9. To conclude, a symphony [the Finale of K. 425?]

Apart from the three arias, everything is composed by Kapellmeister Mozart.[46]

In a letter of 20 February 1784 Mozart had written to his father that,

Two gentlemen, an assistant comptroller and a cook, are going to Salzburg in a few days, and I shall probably ask them to take with them a sonata [K. 333 = 315a], a symphony [K. 425], and a new concerto [K. 449]. The symphony is in the original score, which you might arrange to have copied some time. You can then send it back to me or even give it away or have it performed anywhere you like. The concerto is also in the original score and this too you may have copied; but have it done as quickly as possible and return it to me. Remember, do not show it to a single soul.[47]

It was only three months later, however, that (apparently after securing a copy for himself) Wolfgang actually sent his father the symphony.[48] Leopold reported a performance under his direction in the home of Dr Silvester Barisani on 15 September, referring to the work in a letter to Nannerl as 'your brother's excellent new symphony'.[49] The autograph manuscript of K. 425 disappeared very early, possibly in Salzburg, given that in his letter of 20 February Wolfgang had rather grandly and foolishly told his father, 'You can . . . even give it away . . .', and again in his letter of 15 May: 'I am not particular about the symphony, but I do ask you to have the four concertos copied at home, for the Salzburg copyists are as little to be trusted as the Viennese.'[50] The reason Mozart gave for guarding one of the piano concertos so closely was that he had sold it, giving his patron exclusive rights, but there must be more to it than that, for (as the correspondence with Donaueschingen discussed below suggests) he could have done, and did do, the same with symphonies. Mozart's symphonies apparently interested him much less in the 1780s than they had earlier in his career and less than his mature piano concertos, by means of which he appeared in public as *primo uomo*.

Mozart may possibly have intended his 'excellent new symphony' to be the third of three symphonies he planned to publish with Artaria in 1784 (although only two appeared and K. 425 did not reach print until 1793), or he may have wished to hold

[46] Deutsch, 198 (= 223).

[47] *Briefe*, iii. 302; *Letters*, iii. 1294 (= ii. 868). For the identification of the 'Linz' sonata, see A. Tyson, 'The Date of Mozart's Piano Sonata in B flat, KV 333/315c: the "Linz" Sonata?', in M. Bente (ed.), *Musik, Edition, Interpretation: Gedenkschrift Günter Henle* (Munich, 1980), 447–54.

[48] Letter of 15 May 1784. *Briefe*, iii. 313; *Letters*, iii. 1306–7 (= ii. 876).

[49] Letter of 17 Sept. 1784. *Briefe*, iii. 333; *Letters*, iii. 1317 (= ii. 883). The programme of another 'academy' at Barisani's house, in August 1786, included vocal music with orchestral accompaniment (two solo rondos, a duet, and a trio) and three symphonies (see Leopold's letter of 23 Aug. 1786; *Briefe*, iii. 576; not in *Letters*).

[50] *Briefe*, iii. 302, 313; *Letters*, iii. 1294, 1306–7 (= ii. 868, 876).

back his latest symphony for his own use. Beginning in 1785 Johann Traeg offered for sale manuscript sets of parts of 'two new symphonies in C and D', which have been taken to be K. 425 and 385.[51] But arguing against those identifications are three factors: (1) K. 385 had been published in Vienna that very year by Artaria and would, therefore, have lost its commercial value to Traeg; (2) the order of appearance of Mozart's symphonies in Traeg's 1799 catalogue (Table 11.3) seems to be roughly the order in which Traeg had acquired them (note, for instance, the final trilogy of symphonies, together as a group near the end) and (assuming that the works have been correctly identified) K. 425 is further down the list than would be compatible with a 1785 date; and (3) the order in which the Hamburg dealer Westphal offered Mozart's symphonies, which he probably obtained from Traeg and which also seem to occur in approximately the order in which they were acquired, likewise suggests a different scenario (Table 8.3). Aside from K. 385 and 425, the works advertised by Traeg in 1785, four other possible pairs of C and D major symphonies present themselves: catalogue Nos. 276–7, 278–9, 279–80, and 283–4. The designation 'new' in Traeg's newspaper announcements doubtless indicated works not previously offered rather than necessarily those freshly composed.

There may be further evidence, in an exchange in Mozart's correspondence, to support the notion that K. 425 was not the C major symphony offered by Traeg in 1785. In summer 1786 Mozart received a letter (now lost) from the Mozarts' former servant Sebastian Winter in Donaueschingen, asking to purchase some recent compositions for his Prince, Joseph Wenzeslaus von Fürstenberg. On 8 August Wolfgang replied:

I should long ago have sent some specimens of my poor work to your highly respected Prince . . . if I had known whether or not my father had already sent him something and, if so, what he had sent. I am therefore jotting down at the end of my letter a list of my latest compositions from which His Highness has only to choose, so that I may hasten to serve him.[52]

Though the four symphony incipits that Mozart sent in his letter to Donaueschingen were of his most recent symphonies (K. 319, 338, 385, and 425, but not 320), his including the seven-year-old K. 319 among his 'latest compositions' and offering a manuscript copy of the already published K. 385, when the Prince had requested new and unknown work, was deception pure and simple. And he was caught at it, for the Donaueschingen court already owned some of the works he proposed to sell them. Winter's reply is again lost, but Mozart's response reads, in part:

---

[51] Deutsch, 217 (= 245).   [52] *Briefe*, iii. 565; *Letters*, iii. 1337 (= ii. 897–8).

The music you asked for is being sent off tomorrow by the mail coach. You will find at the end of this letter the amount due to me for the copies. It is quite natural that some of my compositions should be sent abroad, but those which I do send are deliberately chosen. I sent you the incipits only because it is quite possible that these works have not reached you. But the compositions which I keep for myself or for a small circle of music-lovers and connoisseurs (who promise not to let them out of their hands) cannot possibly be known elsewhere, as they are not even known in Vienna. And this is the case with the three concertos which I have the honour of sending to His Highness. But here I have been obliged to add to the cost of copying a small additional fee of six ducats for each concerto; and I must ask His Highness not to let them out of his hands.[53]

Once again concertos are treated differently from symphonies, since for three symphonies Mozart charged the Prince only for the copying (although at eight *Kreuzer* per *Bogen* for orchestral parts, rather than the going rate in Vienna of seven *Kreuzer* per *Bogen*), but for three concertos he attempted to add to the already inflated copying rate a fee of six ducats each, asking in addition that they not be recopied. Note, then, that as the Donaueschingen court, which was constantly involved in ordering music from Vienna, did not have K. 425, that piece may not yet have been available through Traeg.

In the absence of the autograph, the Donaueschingen parts, coming directly from Mozart and containing a few corrections in his hand, have long been taken to be the principal source for the 'Linz' symphony, and all modern editions of the work are based on them. However, a set of parts in Salzburg, made for Leopold from the autograph in 1784, deserves more attention than it has received: it contains fewer errors than the Donaueschingen parts (which were apparently not copied directly from the autograph) and preserves a slightly different version of the work. That is, a few passages differ in ways that can only have come from Mozart's pen rather than from the carelessness of copyists, so one has to reckon with 1783–4 and 1786 versions, which cannot be conflated. A fully adequate edition of the 'Linz' symphony must take both sources into account, obtaining the best readings of problematic passages and offering performers a choice of readings in variant passages. And a good edition must also make a good faith effort to ascertain the provenance and authority of two early sets of parts in the Fürst Bentheim library at Schloss Burgsteinfurt and in the Thurn und Taxis Hofbibliothek, Regensburg.[54]

Mozart may have performed the 'Linz' symphony again in Prague in October and November 1787, where he had gone to oversee the première of *Don Giovanni*. One performance may have been by the same ensemble that gave the work its first performance: the private orchestra of the Counts Thun, who had a residence in

[53] Letter of 30 Sept. 1786. Ibid. 589–90; 1340 (= 900).
[54] This discussion of the sources of the 'Linz' symphony and of the shortcomings of presently available editions is based upon C. Eisen, 'New Light on Mozart's "Linz" Symphony', *Journal of the Royal Musical Association* (1988) cxiii. 81–96.

Prague as well as in Linz and who, according to Niemetschek, had been responsible for Mozart's invitation to Prague. Another may have been at the 'academy' offered by Mozart for his own benefit with the assistance of the Prague opera orchestra.[55]

From the moment the noble, double-dotted rhythms of the opening Adagio sound, the listener is plunged into the musical world of Mozart's late masterpieces. The fruits of the artistic freedom of Vienna, of working with that city's outstanding orchestral musicians, of experiments in orchestration made in piano concertos and *Die Entführung*, and of a more serious approach to the symphony in general, are apparent in the 'Linz' symphony. The large scale of the first movement, its perfectly proportioned form, the skill of the orchestration—none of these gives the slightest clue to the hurried circumstances under which the work was created. Only one other composer living in 1783 was capable of a symphony to compare with this: Joseph Haydn. And several commentators have sensed Haydn's spirit hovering over the work.[56]

If Haydn's spirit also hovers noticeably over Beethoven's and Schubert's earliest symphonies, those works give evidence of the influence of certain aspects of Mozart's symphonies too. Beethoven, for instance, apparently used the slow introduction of K. 425 as a model for the introduction of a C major symphony that he worked on in 1795—a symphony that was never completed but that served as a dry run for his First Symphony, also in C. Mozart's Andante may also have influenced Beethoven. The presence in this movement of trumpets and drums—instruments otherwise silent in slow movements and in all movements in F major—changes what might have been simply an exquisite cantilena into a movement of occasionally almost apocalyptic intensity. Beethoven apparently took note of the effectiveness of this movement when he decided to use the trumpets and drums in similar ways in the same key in the Andante of his First Symphony of 1799–1800. Joseph Haydn had earlier tried trumpets and drums in slow movements of symphonies probably unknown to Beethoven, but in general it remained a special effect rarely used in the classical symphony.[57]

The Minuet and Trio of the 'Linz' Symphony form the most conventional of its

---

[55] For details, see the discussion of the 'Prague' symphony, K. 504, below.

[56] See, for instance, Saint-Foix, 126–31 (= 91–3); J. P. Larsen, 'The Symphonies', in H. C. Robbins Landon and D. Mitchell (eds.), *The Mozart Companion* (London, 1956), 186; Della Croce, *Le 75 sinfonie*, 220–3; Landon, *Haydn: Chronicle and Works* (Bloomington and London, 1978), ii. 297, 310, 629; C. Rosen, 'Remarks on "Influence"', in Larsen, Serwer, and Webster (eds.), *Haydn Studies*, 412–14, here 413; R. Dearling, *The Music of Wolfgang Amadeus Mozart: The Symphonies* (London, 1982), 143–5; Sadie, *Symphonies*, 70.

[57] H. C. Robbins Landon, *Haydn at Eszterháza*, 629, *Haydn in England, 1791–5*, 188. The trumpets and drums in the andantes of Haydn's Symphony in G major, Hob. I: 88 (1787) and of Michael Haydn's Serenade in D major (1785) may have been suggested by the Andante of the 'Linz' symphony. According to [Carl Friedrich] Z[elter] in the *Allgemeine musikalische Zeitung* (1798), i, cols. 152–3, the effect was already overworked by the time Beethoven took it up: 'Haydn, in some stately passages in his G or F major Adagios, had the trumpets and drums in C or D enter to great surprise and noble effect; this he did discreetly and with care. But . . . nowadays there is hardly a symphony, the andante of which does not have trumpets and timpani; we are used to them; they make no more effect.'

four movements, the pomp of the former set off by the mock innocence of the oboe and bassoon duet in the latter—but none of the high jinks here that Mozart sometimes put into his trios for Salzburg consumption. The prominence of the double-reed instruments in this Trio (as in the trios in a number of Mozart's earlier symphonies) can be traced back to Jean-Baptiste Lully, the composer credited with introducing the minuet into European art music. Lully often orchestrated a pair of minuets by assigning the first to the full orchestra (strings and double reeds, in his case) and the second to two oboes and bassoon (perhaps doubled or tripled). This is the origin of the custom of calling the second minuet a 'trio': in its early days it frequently was one. That this connection of oboes to trios was still known in the early years of the concert symphony is suggested by the Parisian publication in 1757 of Johann Stamitz's symphonies, Op. 3, without oboe parts and with the minuets and trios likewise omitted.[58] The thought behind this omission is perhaps revealed by a notice accompanying the first of Gossec's symphonies, Op. 4, published around 1758 also in Paris: 'This first symphony can be performed without oboes by suppressing the minuets'.[59] The acceptance in the classical symphony to the end of the century and into the next of the archaic minuet and trio (however 'symphonic' its ideas and orchestration may have become) is discussed in connection with the 'Prague' symphony, in which Mozart, uniquely for his late symphonies, forwent that movement.

The Finale of the 'Linz' symphony is akin to that of the 'Haffner' symphony of the previous year and, like it, was undoubtedly meant to be performed observing Mozart's injunction to play 'as fast as possible'. As a foil to the brilliant homophonic texture dominating this spirited movment, and by way of development, Mozart inserted passages of the characteristic kind of pseudo-polyphony already noted in the Finale of K. 319.

A comparison between the 'Linz' symphony and Mozart's earliest symphony with trumpets and drum, K. 45 of 1768, offers a glimpse of great changes in musical taste and in his artistic development. The earlier work is on an entirely different scale, lasting about twelve minutes or roughly half the length of the 'Linz' symphony. It is filled with then fashionable ideas that could have come from a dozen other symphonies of the period, whereas the 'Linz' symphony is *sui generis* and in Mozart's own style. Finally, the earlier work is an effectively conceived bit of social entertainment, whereas the 'Linz' symphony poses artistic challenges and plumbs emotional depths previously absent from Mozart's symphonies, exhibiting a command of musical form and orchestration of extraordinary subtlety. Such changes are customarily attributed solely to Mozart's development as an artist and

[58] E. K. Wolf, *The Symphonies of Johann Stamitz: A Study in the Formation of the Classic Style* (Utrecht, 1981), 35, 79.
[59] Brook, *La Symphonie française*, ii. 272.

craftsman, but, although it would be foolish to deny that development, there must be more to it than that, since other composers were also writing longer, more complex symphonies in the 1780s than the typical composer had done in the 1760s.

The young Mozart can hardly have avoided coming under the musical influence of Michael Haydn, perhaps the most gifted of the Salzburg symphonists. The Mozart family's correspondence contains numerous references to Haydn, revealing admiration of his music, especially his church music, if not necessarily his personal behaviour, and this despite the fact that the Mozarts and the Haydns were at the centres of two competing and not entirely friendly social groups in Salzburg's musical community. Yet when one compares symphonies written by Mozart in the 1760s and 1770s with those by Haydn, the differences in style appear more striking than the similarities. Haydn's age and his geographical origins manifest themselves by a somewhat old-fashioned style and a frequently non-cantabile instrumental idiom rooted in the central European traditions associated with such composers as Fux and Wagenseil. The young Mozart, by contrast, displays a more modern, Italianate style, alternately brilliant and singing (although the latter traits were certainly not unknown to Haydn). Mozart's command of this style reflects both the extensive tours on which he was taken and the international repertory of symphonies performed in Salzburg alongside those of the local composers.

There is a curious connection between Mozart's tours and Michael Haydn's symphonies: a chronological list of Haydn's symphonic output from his Salzburg years reveals that he wrote more symphonies whenever Mozart was away and fewer whenever Mozart returned.[60] Whether this reflected a conscious (or unconscious) decision on Haydn's part not to compete, a preference of the court musicians or their audience, or evidence for Leopold's having the upper hand politically with the court orchestra is not certain.

That Mozart chose the international style rather than the local one may show the extent to which his upbringing and orientation were geared to the new and fashionable.[61] That Haydn did not absorb more of the international style may have been because of his greater age or because he had found a style that suited him and his Salzburg audiences. Michael Haydn's career declined just as that of his older brother Joseph soared to new heights when the latter's synthesis of the Italian international and Austrian local styles helped to raise the Viennese classical style to a new position of eminence. In any case, even though the Mozart family's correspondence and the existence of Wolfgang's autographs of five of Haydn's

[60] Eisen, 'The Symphonies of Leopold Mozart', 229–30.

[61] Ibid. 202–42, however, brilliantly establishes the instrumental repertory at Salzburg and suggests that many of the traits in Wolfgang's early symphonies that his biographers have supposed he learnt on his travels could as easily have been learnt at home from this local repertory.

church works, which he had copied to study or perform (K. Anhang A 11–15) suggest that Michael Haydn's influence on Wolfgang was stronger in church music than in symphonic music, Wolfgang's symphonic connections with Haydn deserve scrutiny.

Symphony in G major, K. 444 = 425a + Anh. A 53 [= Perger No. 16]

[Incipits 11.3]

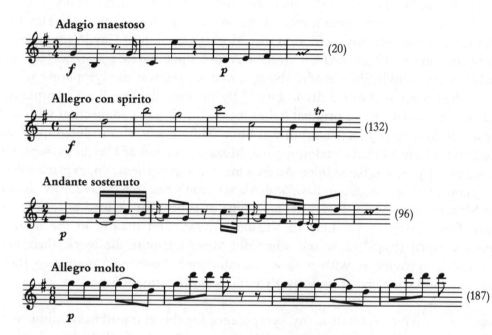

Instrumentation: strings, 1 flute (Andante only), 2 oboes, 2 horns, [bassoon, continuo]
Autograph: Jagiellońska Library, Kraków (Mozart); Esterháza Archives, National Museum, Budapest (M. Haydn)
Principal source: none
Facsimile: none
Editions: *GA*, xxii. 81–96 (= Serie 8, No. 37); Diletto musicale 341a (Vienna: Doblinger, 1974) (Mozart's introduction only, after the *GA*); Diletto musicale 341 (Vienna: Doblinger, 1971), ed. C. H. Sherman (M. Haydn only)

Among Mozart's possessions was found after his death the score of a symphony, containing a slow introduction, the following Allegro and half of the Andante in his hand, but the rest of the Andante, the Minuet and Trio, and the Finale in another hand. The work, listed in K^1 as number 444 and published in the *GA* as Symphony No. 37, has frequently been performed as Mozart's, despite the fact that as early as 1907 it was known—without its slow introduction—as a symphony by Michael Haydn, written for the installation of a new abbot at the Michaelbeuern Monastery in May 1783.[62]

Jahn and Köchel stated that Mozart created K. 444 in 1783 on the same occasion he created K. 425, when, returning from Salzburg to Vienna, he was asked without warning to give a concert during a stop-over in Linz. Of course, if Mozart's statement that he had no symphonies with him in Linz is taken literally, then he had with him neither symphonies of his own nor any of Michael Haydn's. Investigation suggests that the notion that Mozart's version of Haydn's symphony was written in Linz originated with Johann André, upon whose researches Jahn and Köchel relied considerably. André thought that K. 444 was the symphony which Mozart had composed so rapidly in Linz.[63] By the time the true 'Linz' symphony, K. 425, was identified, the original (false) reason for K. 444's connection with that city had been forgotten, and a myth was born. Thus, every Mozart biography and all editions of the Köchel Catalogue place Mozart's version of Haydn's symphony in Linz in 1783. As it is based upon André's incorrect hypothesis, this explanation of the origin of K. 444 is groundless; and Alan Tyson's researches have now shown that Mozart's manuscript is written on a type of paper that he used only after his return from Salzburg via Linz to Vienna in 1783, and mainly in the months February–April 1784.[64] How and when did Mozart acquire the work, then, and why did he provide it with a slow introduction? Tentative answers to these questions can be arrived at only by a roundabout investigation.

Mozart must have required many symphonies for the extraordinary number of concerts he gave in Vienna in the early 1780s, and he acquired them by various means. Adalbert Gyrowetz, for instance, related in his (third-person) autobiography that when, as a young man, he arrived in Vienna in 1785, he visited Mozart

... and was received by him in the friendliest way. Cheered by Mozart's affability and kindness, Gyrowetz asked him to cast a glance at his youthful works, which consisted of six symphonies [written in the summer of 1783 taking Joseph Haydn's symphonies as models], and to give him his opinion on them. Mozart agreed to his request like the kind-hearted man he was, looked the pieces through, praised them, and promised the young artist that

[62] L. H. Perger, 'Thematisches Verzeichnis der Instrumentalwerke von Michael Haydn' in *Denkmäler der Tonkunst in Österreich* (Vienna, 1907), xxix. xv–xxix, here xvi; G. de Saint-Foix, 'Une fausse symphonie de Mozart', *Le Ménestrel* (20 July 1907), lxxiii. 228–9.

[63] J. André, 'Thematisches Verzeichnis W. A. Mozartscher Manuskripte, chronologisch geordnet von 1764–1784 von A. André. Manuskript abgeschlossen am 6. August 1833', original lost, O. Jahn's copy in the British Library, Add. MS 34412.

[64] I am indebted to Alan Tyson for the information about paper types and for the suggestion that the two symphonies may have been confused.

he would have one of these symphonies performed at his concert in the hall in the Mehlgrube, where Mozart was giving six subscription concerts. And it actually came to pass on Thursday [rect. Friday]. The symphony was performed in the concert hall in the Mehlgrube by the full theatre orchestra, and received general applause. Mozart, with his innate goodness of heart, took the young artist by the hand and presented him to the audience as the author of the symphony.[65]

Gyrowetz, perhaps emboldened by Mozart's encouragement and his success with a Viennese audience, wrote on 23 November 1785 to Artaria, introducing himself and offering a variety of works for publication. Portions of his letter are interesting for the light they shed on the commercial value of symphonies and on the procedures by which symphonies may sometimes have found their way to publication:

Because I am eager to publish my newly completed musical works soon, may I take the liberty of asking you whether you would like to take some of these works? The entire collection consists of twelve grand symphonies of varying instrumentation; six partitas for a quintet of two clarinets, two horns and bassoon, two grand serenades for full orchestra, in the manner of a symphony, and with concertante instruments; and also other single pieces. As far as matters of art and taste are concerned, I can guarantee their success. Because music lovers received my earliest works with great pleasure and applause, I can flatter myself the more certainly that I will succeed even more with my latest pieces, since I am convinced that I have written exactly for today's taste. My name is von Gyrowetz. Perhaps you already know some of my works. If you do not, you might ask the Schwarzenberg court secretary, H. Jungling, or the court musicians about them. They will tell you about me. At present I am in Brno with Franz Count von Fünfkirchen, in his service as secretary. The price for my works is as follows: if you take all twelve symphonies, or at least six together, then you pay thirty-six gulden for twelve, eighteen gulden for six; if however you wish to have them singly, then I can give you each composition for a ducat. The six quintet partitas [together] cost three ducats. The serenades, however, [are] three gulden for each piece.[66]

By 'the complete theatre orchestra' Gyrowetz must have meant the orchestra of either the Kärntnerthortheater or the Hofburgtheater. Figures presented in Chapter 5 show that in 1773 the former ensemble had strings 6—6—3—3—3, with 1 flute and pairs of oboes, bassoons, and horns, and a harpsichord, or a total of 29 instrumentalists; while the latter had strings 7—7—4—3—3, with pairs of flutes, oboes, bassoons, and horns, and a harpsichord, or a total of 33.[67] Two years later

---

[65] Deutsch, 474 (= 559). Mozart was seven years Gyrowetz's senior; his 1785 subscription concerts were on six Fridays: 11, 18, and 25 Feb., and 4, 11, and 18 Mar.

[66] R. Schaal, 'Unbekannte Briefe von Adalbert Gyrowetz', *Deutsches Jahrbuch der Musikwissenschaft* (1966), xi. 50–60; R. Hilmar, *Der Musikverlag Artaria & Comp.*, 25–6; J. A. Rice (ed.), *Adalbert Gyrowetz (1763–1850): Four Symphonies* (The Symphony 1720–1840, B/xi), xiv.

[67] G. Zechmeister, *Die wiener Theater nächst der Burg und nächst dem Kärntnertor von 1747 bis 1776* (Vienna, 1971), 356–7;

the numbers were nearly identical, and the orchestra of the Hofburgtheater in the
1776–7 season was similarly furbished: 6–7—6–7—2-3—3—2 / 0—2—0—2 / 2.[68]
In the 1780s the numbers remained about the same, for in 1783 the 'opera'
orchestra, which meant the orchestra of the Hofburgtheater, numbered strings 6—
6—4—3—3 and pairs of flutes, oboes, clarinets, bassoons, and trumpets, with 4
horns, kettledrums, and harpsichord.[69] Thus, as far as can be judged by the
surviving information, the Viennese theatre orchestras remained roughly constant
in size during this period, and this therefore probably reveals the size of the
orchestra that Mozart had at his Mehlgrube concerts in 1785, and perhaps also at
some other public concerts of his in Vienna. Certainly, the inference to be drawn
from the remark to his father cited above, that he would 'have to have several
additional copies made' of K. 385 for his Lenten concerts in 1783, is that the
customary set of parts, with its single *Dubletten* for violin 1, for violin 2, and for
basso, would not suffice.

Leopold's report to Nannerl about the first of Wolfgang's subscription concerts
stated that

> ... a great many members of the aristocracy were present. Each person pays a souverain
> d'or or three ducats for the six Lent concerts. Your brother is giving them at the
> Mehlgrube and only pays half a souverain d'or each time for the hall. The concert was
> magnificent and the orchestra played splendidly. In addition to the symphonies, a female
> singer of the Italian theatre sang two arias. Then we had a new and very fine concerto [K.
> 466] by Wolfgang, which the copyist was still copying when we arrived [at one o'clock
> earlier the same day], and the rondo of which your brother did not even have time to play
> through, as he had to supervise the copying.[70]

It is perfectly understandable that, in describing this concert, Leopold should have
failed to identify the symphonies, for although symphonies for the beginnings and
ends of concerts were indispensable, they were not the main events, but served to
frame solos, concertos, and arias. Time and again accounts of concerts omitted to
mention symphonies known (from other sources) to have been performed.
Compare this with the attitudes recorded in a diatribe about Viennese private
concerts some years later: every name-day or other special occasion calls for a
concert beginning with '... first a quartet or a symphony, which is seen as a
necessary evil (you've got to start with *something*) and during which one chats'.[71]

[68] Ibid. 355.
[69] N. Zaslaw, 'Toward the Revival of the Classical Orchestra', *Proceedings of the Royal Musical Association* (1976–7), ciii.
158–87, here 177. For 1796 the figures were virtually the same (ibid.).
[70] Letter of 16 Feb. 1785. *Briefe*, iii. 373; *Letters*, iii. 1320–1 (= ii. 885–6).
[71] Anon., 'Kurze Uebersicht des Bedeutendsten aus dem gesammten jetzigen Musikwesen in Wien. Liebhaberey',
Allgemeine musikalische Zeitung (1800–1), iii, col. 65.

Mozart's earlier symphonies could perhaps make sense under such conditions; his latest ones could not.

Mozart's need for symphonies new to his Viennese audience was behind the already mentioned urgent request to his father on 4 January 1783 that he be sent four symphonies composed between 1773 and 1775 along with the 'Haffner' symphony. Mozart's kindness to Gyrowetz may have been perfectly genuine, but surely he was also motivated by pleasure in finding a new symphony for his concert. His search for symphonies also may have been behind his jotting the incipits of three works by Joseph Haydn (K. Anh. A 59) on the back of a sheet of music paper (of a type that he appears to have used only in 1784) on which he had written a cadenza for the Andante of a piano concerto.[72] K[3] and K[6] suggest that these incipits provide a clue to the identity of the three Haydn symphonies discussed in a previously cited letter of 15 May 1784, in which Mozart complained to his father about the untrustworthiness of copyists:

I gave to the mail coach today the symphony that I composed at Linz for old Count Thun [K. 425] and also four concertos [K. 449–51, 453]. I am not particular about the symphony, but I do ask you to have the four concertos copied in your presence at home, for the Salzburg copyists are as little to be trusted as the Viennese. I know for a positive fact that [the Salzburg copyist Felix] Hofst[a]etter makes second copies of Haydn's music. For example, I *actually* possess his three newest symphonies.[73]

Speculation about the identity of the three symphonies has run as follows: Mozart's three incipits, K. Anh. A 59, are of Joseph Haydn's Symphonies Nos. 75, 47, and 62, which, dating from *c.*1779, 1772, and *c.*1780 respectively, were hardly Haydn's newest. It has therefore been suggested that the symphonies mentioned in Mozart's letter may have been Nos. 76, 77, and 78, all dating from 1782.[74] But as Mozart's discussion is about the untrustworthiness of copyists, who secretly made copies for their own use, and as he cited illicit copies of the newest symphonies of 'Haydn' as evidence of the dishonesty of Salzburg copyists, he must have meant the Salzburg Haydn—Michael not Joseph.[75] Michael Haydn's three newest symphonies as of May 1784 were the Symphony in G major, Perger No. 16 (dated 23 May 1783); the Symphony in E flat major, Perger No. 17 (dated 14 August 1783); and the Symphony in B flat major, Perger No. 18 (dated 12 March 1784). These, then, may be the symphonies that Mozart obtained in 1784 as the result of dishonest Salzburg

[72] Paper information courtesy of Alan Tyson. Although according to K[6] (pp. 255–6, 764) the cadenza for a piano concerto Andante was intended for K. 246 (1776), it most probably belongs to K. 415 = 387b (winter 1782–3).

[73] *Briefe*, iii. 313; *Letters*, iii. 1306–7 (= ii. 876).

[74] A. van Hoboken, *Joseph Haydn: Thematisch-bibliographisches Werkverzeichnis* (Mainz, 1957), i. 117. See also Landon, *Haydn: Chronicle and Works*, ii. 489 n, 602; Bartha (ed.), *Haydn: Briefe*, 129–31; *Briefe*, vi. 181; and A. P. Brown, 'Notes on some Eighteenth-Century Viennese Copyists', *Journal of the American Musicological Society* (1981), xxxiv. 325–38, here 332.

[75] This interpretation is supported by Eisen, 'The Symphonies of Leopold Mozart', 31, n. 26.

copyists.[76] And the first of them is K. Anh. A 53, for which Mozart wrote the slow introduction, K. 425a.

On 14 September 1785 Traeg advertised 'Various new symphonies by Pleyel, Mozart, and Mich. Haydn'.[77] It seems possible that Mozart, always short of money, had sold Haydn's three symphonies to Traeg. If this imagined scenario is correct, then a symphony completed in Salzburg around 12 March 1784 had reached Vienna in an unauthorized copy no later than mid-May and four months later was advertised for sale, possibly already having been heard in one of Mozart's concerts. Whatever the case may be with Michael Haydn's symphonies, the pressure on composers, performers, copyists, and publishers to produce new symphonies seems almost palpable, and makes Mozart's slender production of symphonies in his Viennese years difficult to comprehend.

The fourth of Mozart's incipits (Example 11.1) has never been identified. Einstein, who was the first to take note of these four incipits, originally thought that they were of four unknown symphonies by Mozart, and hence they were listed as K. 387d in K^3. By the time of K^{3a}, however, he had identified the three Haydn incipits, and accordingly all four have been relegated to the appendix in K^6. The fourth incipit might be the beginning of a symphony, although there is something odd about the weak harmonic motion in the bass from bars 2 to 3, and in general the idea seems more like the middle of a symphony's first-movement exposition than its beginning, or even like an andante; it has been called 'another

Ex. 11.1 Unidentified musical jotting, K. 387d = Anhang A 59

[76] Alan Tyson (personal communication) believes that the last of these may be too late and suggests substituting the Symphony in A major, Perger No. 15 (dated 19 July 1781).

[77] A. Weinmann, *Johann Traeg: Die Musikalienverzeichnisse von 1799 und 1804*, 13–14; idem, *Die Anzeigen des Kopiaturbetriebes Johann Traeg*, 21.

symphony, not identified' and 'a sketch by Mozart',[78] although given its context it could just as likely be his memorandum of a work by someone else.

Symphony in D major, K. 291 = Anh. 109^{xi} = Anh. A 52 [= Perger No. 43]

[Incipits 11.4]

Instrumentation: *strings, 2 flutes, 2 oboes, 2 horns, [bassoon, continuo]
Autograph: British Library (Mozart fragment); Salzburg, Saint Peters (M. Haydn)
Principal source: none
Facsimile: none
Editions: *GA*, xxxix. 106 (= Serie 24, No. 1) (Mozart fragment = bars 1–45 of symphony Finale)

Mozart's name is connected with two other symphonies by Michael Haydn. One is the Symphony in D major, Perger No. 43 (*c.*1780–1), which he owned or had access to, and whose fugal Finale he incompletely copied in score (K. 291 = Anh. A 52). Mozart's fragmentary autograph of this movement was acquired in Vienna in 1846 by the British organist J. Ella. Ella left his library to the Royal College of Organists, and the most valuable of his manuscripts, including K. Anh. A 52, have recently been placed on loan to the British Library. The manuscript is written on a paper apparently used by Mozart only toward the end of 1783.[79]

---

[78] See K³ under 387d.
[79] I am indebted to Alan Tyson and A. Hyatt King for the history of Ella's manuscripts, and to Tyson for the paper information.

Therefore, Haydn's D major symphony, Perger No. 43, most likely came into Mozart's hands during his four-month visit to Salzburg in that year, and if any symphony by Haydn was performed by Mozart in Linz, it would have been this one rather than K. Anh. A 52 = Perger 16. It is even possible that the source of André's idea that the 'Linz' symphony was K. 444 was a confused reminiscence of a performance in Linz of Perger 16, although how this information would have reached André is unclear.

Einstein made much of Mozart's special interest in fugal writing in the mid-1780s.[80] As we learn from Mozart's correspondence, both the Emperor and Constanze were enchanted by fugues, and Mozart was deeply involved with Baron van Swieten's Sunday *stile antico* musicales. Einstein's exposition of Mozart's involvement with fugal writing in those years, while based on fact, was supported by two errors of interpretation. The first is that, in exaggerating the importance of fugues at one period in Mozart's artistic development, he inadvertently under-emphasized the importance of counterpoint in his training and in his music during the rest of his career, beginning with a fugal fragment written in the London Notebook in 1764 (K. 15ss) and ending only with the Requiem and his death in 1791. The other error is that, having hit upon his hypothesis, Einstein strengthened it in K^3 by assigning undated fugal fragments to the period in question. Using a hypothesis to date fragments whose putative dates are in turn used to support the hypothesis is of course circular reasoning, and some of these fugal fragments prove to have originated at other times.[81] In any case, the fugal Finale under discussion, along with two fugal motets of Michael Haydn also on paper types used by Mozart in 1783,[82] may have been brought to Vienna from Salzburg to be performed at Baron van Swieten's musicales, for which Mozart served as maestro and at which fugues and *stile antico* works were given pride of place.[83]

Symphony in F major, K. 98 = Anh. 223b = Anh. C 11.04 [= Hob. I: F16]

[Incipits 11.5]

[80] Einstein, ch. 9 ('Mozart and Counterpoint'), 144–56.

[81] Details of proposed redatings of Mozart's work on the basis of paper types will be forthcoming in a two-volume study by Alan Tyson, from the *NMA*.

[82] Both settings of 'Pignus futurae gloriae', K. Anh. A 11 and A 12; information courtesy of Alan Tyson.

[83] *Briefe*, iii. 201, 202–3, 248, 259, 264; *Letters*, 1192, 1194, 1245, 1255, 1259–60 (= ii. 800, 801, 835, 842, 845). H. Abert, *W. A. Mozart* (Leipzig, 1919–21), ii. 86; R. Bernhardt, 'Aus der Umwelt der wiener Klassiker: Freiherr Gottfried van Swieten (1734–1803)', *Der Bär* (1930), vi. 435–40. See also n. 81 above.

Instrumentation: strings, 2 oboes, 2 horns, [bassoon, continuo]
Autograph: none
Principal sources: Graz, Hochschule für Musik und darstellende Kunst und Landesmusikschule (40,571, Lannoy 53) (parts from Traeg in Vienna); Pfarrkirche, Weyarn (score in the hand of Herkulan Siessmayr, lacking oboes); Moravské Museum, Brno (A 16833)
Facsimile: none
Editions: *GA*, xl. 6–21 (= Serie 24, No. 56)

Köchel knew this work only through an arrangement for piano four-hands. Even though no autograph or other documentation connected the work to the Mozarts' circle, he had accepted its attribution to Mozart, following the opinions of Aloys Fuch and Ludwig Gall, and suggested (on unstated stylistic grounds) that it dated from around 1770. Accordingly, this symphony was published in 1888 in a supplementary fascicle of the *GA*, edited by von Waldersee, on the basis of the set of parts in Graz, which were originally owned by Aloys Fuchs. Von Waldersee, citing Köchel's acceptance of the work, wrote in the Critical Report of his edition:

We too consider the symphony a composition of Mozart's; the tuneful, catchy shapes of the melodies are characteristic only of him. Rounded in form, it is however not free of a few irregularities in the part-writing, which shows then that this work belongs to a period in which Wolfgang had not yet acquired that security which even the most gifted attain only through practice. It is a youthful work, but even as such it will be not unwelcome to the devoted admirers of the Mozartean muse.

Köchel's '1770' is the kind of dating that if subsequently proven correct may be considered insight but if proven wrong is certain to be thought irresponsible. Offering what might appear to be evidence supporting Köchel's date, an anonymous manuscript catalogue unknown to him lists K. 98 (anonymously) with the pencilled annotation '1771 Mailand Nov.'[84] The origins of this annotation are unknown, but perhaps the annotator had Nissen's biography (1828), where a letter of Leopold Mozart's is reproduced from which it transpires that on 22 or 23 November 1771 in Milan Leopold and Wolfgang participated in 'an orchestral concert at Mr [Albert Michael] von Mayr's place',[85] and perhaps he supposed, for some reason, that Wolfgang composed this symphony for that occasion. In short, the dating of this work is based entirely on unfounded speculation, as is the notion that Mozart was its author.

Dismissing all doubts, Wyzewa and Saint-Foix accepted K. 98 as genuine,[86] but Einstein in K[3] rejected it on (unstated) stylistic grounds, assigning it the number Anh. 223b. The editors of K[6] followed Einstein's opinion, and the work remains in the Anhang as C 11.04. A score of the work subsequently catalogued among the musical manuscripts of the Weyarn Monastery bears the attribution 'Signore Haydn'.[87] As there is no reason to believe that any symphonies by Joseph Haydn are missing, any attribution to him of an unknown symphony should be regarded with extreme scepticism.[88] Besides, given the vigorous exchange of music among the monasteries and churches of Bavaria and Salzburg in the mid-eighteenth century,[89] the Weyarn attribution more probably referred to Michael Haydn. But his symphonies are nearly as well documented as his brother's, and this one does not appear among the symphonies that can be shown to have originated directly from him or his circle. Charles H. Sherman, who has studied Michael Haydn's works for many years and has compiled a catalogue raisonné, does not consider K.

---

[84] For this manuscript, the 'Sistematisch-Thematisches Verzeichnis der sämtlichen Compositionen von Wolfgang Amadeus Mozart', formerly in the possession of C. B. Oldman, see K[6], pp. xxix–xxx.

[85] *Briefe*, i. 451; *Letters*, i. 302 (= i. 206). *Letters* mistranslates 'gestern machten wir eine starke Musik bey H: von Mayer', which means 'yesterday we put on an orchestral concert at Mr von Mayer's place'.

[86] Wyzewa–Saint-Foix, i. 406 (= i. 446–8).

[87] R. Münster and R. Machold, *Thematischer Katalog der Musikhandschriften der ehemaligen Klosterkirchen Weyarn, Tegernsee und Benediktbeuern* (Munich, 1971), 105.

[88] A clear argument for a conservative approach to accepting 'new' works attributed to Joseph Haydn is given by J. Webster, 'External Criteria for Determining the Authenticity of Haydn's Music', in Larsen, Serwer, and Webster (eds.), *Haydn Studies*, 75–8.

[89] H. Wirth ('Mozart et Haydn', in A. Verchaly (ed.), *Les Influences étrangères dans l'œuvre de W. A. Mozart*, 49–57, here 51) finds K. 98 to be 'under the sign of the older master [Joseph Haydn], above all in the finale'.

98 to be authentic.[90] Nor does the work resemble Mozart's symphonies of the 1760s and 1770s, to say nothing of the 1780s. Eisen, in his recent study of Leopold Mozart's symphonies, can find no reason to accept it as Leopold's either.[91] Thus for the present K. Anhang C 11.04 may be regarded as the work of an unidentified composer.

Connections between Michael Haydn's symphonies and two of Mozart's three last symphonies have been posited. It has been suggested, for instance, that Mozart may have been inspired by Haydn's five symphonies from the 1780s with fugal finales to write a fugal finale of his own. In particular, that claim has been made by H. C. Robbins Landon for Michael Haydn's Symphony in C major, Perger No. 31, dated 19 February 1788: 'The similarity in form between the finale of [Perger No. 31] and that of Mozart's 'Jupiter' symphony, K. 551, is almost too remarkable to be accidental, and it is entirely possible that Mozart may have seen or heard this work before starting his own last three symphonies later in the same year.'[92] There is, first of all, no evidence that Mozart owned or knew Perger No. 31, which was written at a time when his contact with Salzburg had ceased. Then, Haydn's Finale begins with a fugato, Mozart's ends with one. Haydn's formal and contrapuntal procedures are quite different from those of Mozart: Haydn's fugue has a single subject and countersubject, Mozart's has several subjects. The slight similarities between Mozart's and Haydn's themes are musical commonplaces. The movements are not comparable, and therefore, if Haydn's fugal finales (it need not have been this one) were an inspiration for the Finale of the 'Jupiter' symphony, the inspiration was a general one and the realization something entirely different.

But it is unclear what such a 'general' influence would consist in, since fugal finales are also found in symphonies in the Viennese orbit by Richter, Monn, Mica, Wagenseil, Dittersdorf, and Joseph Haydn. (The Finale of Joseph Haydn's Symphony in D major, Hob. I: 16, a rather contrapuntal movement that is not fugal, is even based on the doh—ray—fah—me motive.) Mozart thus can have been aware of the genre with or without the influence of Michael Haydn. He had in any case long before written a fugal finale on a chromatic subject in the string quartet, K. 173, composed in Vienna in 1773, whose Finale (admittedly not in a symphony) is more of the Michael Haydn type than of the 'Jupiter' type. (In Chapter 13 possible reasons for Mozart's interest in a fugal finale near the end of his life are explored.)

[90] According to a personal communication from Sherman, it is not 'even remotely possible that the work is by [M.] Haydn, despite the Weyarn attribution. The themes simply are not like Michael's, and the shaping of opening themes along similar lines in several movements [in this case, the first three] is never encountered in other instrumental works by this composer. Furthermore the work reveals little in common with Haydn's regular rhythmic structure or with his orchestral practice.' Letter of 12 May 1982.

[91] Eisen, 'The Symphonies of Leopold Mozart', 316–17.

[92] H. C. Robbins Landon, 'Foreword' to Michael Haydn's Symphony in C major, Perger No. 31 (Vienna, 1966).

A direct influence has also been proposed on another of the last symphonies, K. 543. The purported model is Haydn's symphony in the same key, Perger No. 17, a work that—as suggested above—Mozart may have acquired in 1784. This supposed influence has been stated as follows:

The Symphony in E flat [Perger No. 17] is one of the most lyrical of Michael Haydn's works. It deserves special attention for the reason that Mozart apparently drew inspiration from it for his own Symphony in E flat, No. 39 [K. 543]. Haydn's work was the model not only for the key, but also for the shape of the thematic materials in the first and second movements, for the transitions between the main sections as well as for the general working out of the symphonic form.[93]

The validity of such broad claims of influence is difficult to assess. Surely the key of E flat is, in itself, weak evidence. Mozart's symphony is in four movements, Haydn's in three. Mozart's has a slow introduction to begin, Haydn's does not. Then there is a difference in scale between the two works: Haydn's symphony calls for an orchestra of pairs of oboes, bassoons, and horns; Mozart's adds clarinets, trumpets, kettledrums, and a flute (but omits the oboes). With all repeats observed, Mozart's symphony lasts about forty minutes, Haydn's perhaps half that. There are two thematic similarities between first movements, which may pass the bounds of coincidence and musical commonplaces of the era.[94] Both allegros begin piano, with a theme rising triadically to a descending appoggiatura (Example 11.2a). What follows in the two movements contains no further similarities until the dominant is reached, where each has a legato theme in quavers winding its way in broken thirds over a sustained B flat (Example 11.2b). What is done with these ideas and what follows them seems not to be strikingly similar, beyond the general outlines that might be expected of any two sonata-form movements of the same period in the same key.

Haydn's Adagietto affettuoso and Mozart's Andante con moto are in the same metre and key ($\frac{2}{4}$, A flat major), but beyond this there is little to compare. Whereas Haydn's first movement shows considerable energy and beauty, with a finely wrought development section, his second movement exhibits clichéd melodic ideas, unfolding for the most part with a symmetry of deadly predictability. Mozart's Andante not only does not borrow ideas or formal procedures, but is on an entirely different level of inspiration. (Haydn's muted violins, mid-bar syncopations, and banal triplets can, however, be compared with a number of Mozart's symphonic andantes from the early 1770s, which exhibit all of these features.)

---

[93] C. H. Sherman, 'Vorwort' to Michael Haydn, *Sinfonia in Es, Perger Nr. 17* (Diletto Musicale, 342) (Vienna, 1977), 3; Sherman's claims echo similar ones concerning the first movement of K. 543 and the last movement of K. 551 in Einstein, 127–8.

[94] J. LaRue, 'Significant and Coincidental Resemblances between Classical Themes', *Journal of the American Musicological Society* (1961), xiv. 224–34.

Ex. 11.2 Similar passages in the first movements of Mozart's Symphony in E flat major, K. 543, and Michael Haydn's Symphony in E flat major, Perger No. 17

(a) Mozart, bars 26–33

Haydn, bars 1–8

(b) Mozart bars 97–105

Haydn, bars 35–44

There is nothing comparable in Haydn's movement to Mozart's formal originality, his chromaticism, and his stormy affect, nor are there thematic resemblances.

As for the finales, Haydn's is an unpretentious jig, presto $\frac{6}{8}$, in the form of a rondo. The movement would sound at home in a mid-eighteenth-century dance suite. (Again, similar movements are found in Mozart's finales of the early 1770s.) Mozart's Finale, based on a kind of *contredanse* or quickstep march in $\frac{2}{4}$, is in sonata form with both sections repeated; it is thoroughly symphonic in character. Thus, although Mozart may have recalled some thematic ideas from the first movement of Haydn's E flat symphony, what he made of such ideas when he came to compose his own symphony is something quite removed from this or any other work of Michael Haydn's.

Although the point has been made several times that Mozart generally valued symphonies less than concertos or operas, there is some evidence that he took them seriously enough. For instance, while taking no church music with him on his tour to Mannheim and Paris in 1777–8, he took a large number of symphonies.[95] Then on 14 May 1778 he wrote to his father about the uninspired daughter of the Duc de Guines, to whom he was obliged to give lessons in composition, quoting with apparent approval the Duke's instructions, 'She is not to compose operas, arias, concertos, or symphonies, but only grand sonatas.'[96] Sketches, corrected drafts, false starts, rejected movements, or revised versions exist for the symphonies K. 16, 45, 45a, 132, 300a, 385, 425, 504, 550, and 551, suggesting artistic or technical struggles—or, at very least, second thoughts. And his remarks, cited above, made during the composition of K. 385 ('I shall work as fast as possible and, as far as haste permits, I shall write something good' and 'You see that my intentions are good— only what one cannot do, one cannot! I am really unable to scribble off inferior stuff') should be taken as evidence of seriousness of purpose toward his symphony, even allowing for a busy schedule, procrastination, and defensiveness towards his father.

Then there is the evidence of the lessons in composition that he gave Thomas Attwood in 1785–6.[97] Before allowing Attwood to attempt anything symphonic, Mozart put him through a review of musical rudiments, harmony, thorough bass, species counterpoint, canon, fugue, ranges of instruments, clefs, transpositions, harmonizing melodies, composing over a given bass, and writing short pieces and then long ones, mostly for string quartet. When, near the end of this systematic course of study, Attwood was finally permitted to compose a symphonic minuet, he proceeded by writing a continuity draft on a single staff, showing the

[95] Leopold's letter of 11 Dec. 1777. *Briefe*, ii. 182; *Letters*, ii. 616 (= i. 417).
[96] *Briefe*, ii. 357; *Letters*, ii. 795–6 (= ii. 538).
[97] E. Hertzmann, C. B. Oldman, D. Heartz, and A. Mann (eds.), *Attwood-Studien* (*NMA*, x/30/1) (Kassel, 1965).

movement's proportions and principal melodic material. Then the piece was written in full score and Mozart corrected it. Most corrections were to the inner voices: improving the spacing of chords, writing the horns lower (presumably so they would not overpower the violins), and enlivening Attwood's rather wooden second violin and viola parts. (The revisions, discussed in Chapter 6, made by Mozart in 1767 to K. 45a during his own apprenticeship likewise concerned primarily the non-structural voices.) There is no lack of seriousness or craft here; moreover, the working methods Mozart taught Attwood are similar to what is known of his own.

Symphony in D major, K. 504, 'Prague'

[Incipits 11.6]

Instrumentation: *strings, 2 flutes, 2 oboes, 2 bassoons, 2 horns, 2 trumpets, kettledrums, [continuo]
Autograph: Jagiellońska Library, Kraków
Principal source: set of parts in the hand of the Prague Kapellmeister Kucharž, National Museum, Prague (XXVII B 120)
Facsimile: 1 page, Schiedermair, plate 56; 1 page, *NMA*, iv/11/8. xvi–xviii
Editions: *GA*, xxii. 97–136 (= Serie 8, No. 39); Leipzig; Eulenburg, 1931 (ed. T. Kroyer); *NMA*, iv/11/8. 63–120; Budapest: Editio musica, 1980 (ed. G. Darvas)

Mozart's relations with the citizens of Prague form a happy chapter in the sad story of his last years. At a time when Vienna seemed to grow indifferent to him and his music, Prague apparently could not get enough of either. The success of his visit to supervise a production of *Le nozze di Figaro* was such that he was commissioned to write an opera especially for Prague, which turned out to be *Don Giovanni*, and his final opera too, *La clemenza di Tito*, was written for the Bohemian capital. The Prague schoolmaster Franz Niemetschek, who after Mozart's death was entrusted with the education of his son Carl, has left an eyewitness account of the première of the 'Prague' symphony and of Mozart's relationship with the Prague orchestra. Written a decade after the events it describes, and certainly idealized, Niemetschek's account is accurate in broad outline if not always in detail:

I was witness to the enthusiasm which [*Die Entführung aus dem Serail*] aroused in Prague among knowledgeable and ignorant people alike. It was as if what had hitherto been taken for music was nothing of the kind. Everyone was transported—amazed at the novel harmonies and at the original passages for wind instruments. Now the Bohemians proceeded to seek out his works, and in the same year [1782], Mozart's symphonies and piano music were to be heard at all the best concerts. From now onwards preference for his works was shown by the Bohemians. All the connoisseurs and artists of our capital were Mozart's staunch admirers, the most ardent ambassadors of his fame.

... [*Le nozze di Figaro*] was staged in the year 1787 by the Bondini Company and received such an ovation as was only to be equalled by that given to *Die Zauberflöte* at a later date. It is the absolute truth when I state that this opera was performed almost without a break throughout the winter and that it greatly alleviated the straitened circumstances of the manager. The enthusiasm shown by the public was without precedent; they could not hear it often enough. A piano version was made by one of our best masters, Mr Kucharž; it was arranged for wind instruments, as a quintet, and for German dances; in short, Figaro's tunes echoed through the streets and the parks; even the harpist on the alehouse bench had to play 'Non più andrai' if he wanted to attract any attention at all. This manifestation was admittedly mostly due to the excellence of the work; but only a public which had so much feeling for the beautiful in music and which included so many real connoisseurs could have immediately recognised merit; in addition, there was the incomparable orchestra of our opera house, which understood how to execute Mozart's ideas so accurately and diligently. For on these worthy men, who were mostly not solo performers but nevertheless very knowledgeable and capable,[98] the new harmony and fire and eloquence of the songs made an immediate and lasting impression. The well-known Orchestra Director Strobach, since deceased, declared that at each performance he and his colleagues were so excited that they would gladly have started from the beginning again in spite of the hard work it entailed. Admiration for the composer of this music went so far that Count Johann Thun, one of

---

[98] Concerning the widely recognized advantages of non-soloist ripieno players, see J. Spitzer and N. Zaslaw, 'Improvised Ornamentation in Eighteenth-Century Orchestras', *Journal of the American Musicological Society* (1986), xxxix. 524–77, here 541–5.

our principal noblemen and a lover of music, who himself retained a first-class orchestra, invited Mozart to Prague and offered him accommodation, expenses, and every comfort in his own home. Mozart was too thrilled at the impression which his music had made on the Bohemians, too eager to become acquainted with such a music-loving nation, for him not to seize the opportunity with pleasure. He came to Prague in 1787 (to supervise the première of *Don Giovanni*); on the day of his arrival *Figaro* was performed and Mozart appeared in the theatre. At once the news of his presence spread in the stalls, and as soon as the overture had ended everyone broke into welcoming applause.

In answer to a universal request, he gave a piano recital at a large concert in the opera house [on 19 January]. The theatre had never been so full as on this occasion; never had there been such unanimous enthusiasm as that awakened by his heavenly playing. We did not, in fact, know what to admire most, whether the extraordinary compositions or his extraordinary playing; together they made such an overwhelming impression on us that we felt we had been bewitched. When Mozart had finished the concert he continued improvising alone on the piano for half-an-hour. We were beside ourselves with joy and gave vent to our overwrought feelings in enthusiastic applause. In reality his improvisations exceeded anything that can be imagined in the way of piano-playing, as the highest degree of the composer's art was combined with perfection of playing. This concert was quite a unique occasion for the people of Prague. Moz~~ likewise counted this day as one of the happiest of his life.

The symphonies [*sic*] which he composed for this occasion are real masterpieces of instrumental composition, which are played w h great élan and fire, so that the very soul is carried to sublime heights. This applied particularly to the grand Symphony in D major, which is still always a favourite in Prague, although it has no doubt been heard a hundred times.

... [Mozart] had experienced how much the Bohemians appreciated his music and how well they executed it. This he often mentioned to his ~quaintances in Prague, where a hero-worshipping, responsive public and real friends carried him, so to speak, on their shoulders. He warmly thanked the opera orchestra in a letter to Mr Strobach, who was director at the time, and attributed the greater part of the ovation which his music had received in Prague to their excellent rendering.[99]

In the second edition of this essay, Niemetschek changed the final sentence of the penultimate paragraph to read: 'This applies particularly to the grand symphonies in D major and E flat major, which are still always favourites of the Prague public, although they have no doubt been heard a hundred times.'[100] The D major symphony is of course the 'Prague' symphony, K. 504. If Niemetschek was correct about an E flat major symphony, it must have been K. 132 or K. 184 = 161a, as K. 16 was unknown and K. 543 not yet written. Unlike many of the symphonies from the

[99] Franz Niemetschek, *Leben des K. K. Kapellmeisters Wolfgang Gottlieb Mozart, nach Originalquellen beschrieben* (Prague, 1798); trans. H. Mautner as *Life of Mozart* (London, 1956), 33, 35–7.
[100] 2nd edn. (Prague, 1808); Deutsch, 436 (= 507).

1770s, K. 132 does not have a known Viennese history; that is, it was not one of the four symphonies requested from Leopold in Wolfgang's letter of 4 January 1783, and no set of parts for it from Viennese copyists or from Mozart's estate are known. K. 184 = 161a, on the other hand, had the Viennese connections chronicled in the previous chapter, since Mozart apparently gave it to the theatre director Johann Böhm about 1785 to serve as overture to K. M. Plümickes's play *Lanassa*. So K. 184 = 161a would have been the only possibility. But can one believe that K. 184 was heard a hundred times in Prague? More likely, Niemetschek, trying to be more precise in preparing his second edition, became muddled about what he had heard many years before and thought that it had been K. 543, in 1787 yet to be composed. There is reason to believe that the 'Paris' and 'Linz' symphonies may also have been heard in Prague during Mozart's visit,[101] and one of these was perhaps confused in Niemetschek's memory with K. 543. The keys of the 'Prague', 'Paris', and 'Linz' symphonies are D, D, and C respectively, offering no further clarification of the identity of Niemetschek's putative symphony in E flat.

The autograph manuscript of the 'Prague' symphony, K. 504, is among those formerly in Berlin and now at Kraków. As the Kraków autographs were inaccessible prior to 1980, the *NMA* used as its sources the Eulenburg score (based on the autograph) and sets of parts in Graz, Modena, and Donaueschingen; these parts originated from the Prague music-copying atelier of Anton Grams.[102] The *GA* (which is the basis for most of the commonly available editions) made use of the autograph, but it is not entirely satisfactory for modern purposes. The Eulenberg miniature score[103] was also based on the autograph and is, at present, the edition closest to it, although, like the *GA*, its Critical Report is incomplete, so the contents of the autograph cannot be reconstructed from it.

The upper right-hand corners of the first five pages of the autograph manuscript have been cut off, removing Mozart's signature and his inscription of place and date. In his catalogue of his works, Mozart listed the 'Prague' symphony as 'Vienna, 6 December 1786'. He may have had K. 504 in mind not only for his forthcoming trip to Prague, but for the series of four Advent subscription concerts that he apparently gave in Vienna in December 1786 at the Trattner Casino.[104]

The 'Prague' symphony distinguishes itself from the sixty-odd symphonies that Mozart had previously written by being noticeably more difficult: it is harder to perform and more challenging conceptually. (Possible reasons for this striking increase in difficulty, and the implications for Mozart as a symphonist, are examined in Chapter 13.) As early as December 1780, when Wolfgang was composing and

---

[101] See the discussions of those works in ch. 9 and the beginning of this chapter respectively.

[102] *NMA*, iv/11/9. xi (L. Somfai).

[103] T. Kroyer (ed.) (Leipzig, 1931).

[104] From a lost letter of Wolfgang's as reported in Leopold's letter to Nannerl of 8 Dec. 1786. *Briefe*, iii. 617–8; not in *Letters*; Deutsch, 246 (= 280).

rehearsing *Idomeneo* with the famous Mannheim orchestra, then transplanted to Munich, Leopold twice warned him of the dangers of the demands he placed upon the orchestral musicians: '. . . when your music is performed by a mediocre orchestra, it will always be the loser, because it is composed with so much discernment for the various instruments and is far from being conventional [*platt*], as, on the whole, Italian music is',[105] and, three weeks later,

. . . do your best to keep the whole orchestra in good humour; flatter them, and, by praising them, keep them all well-disposed towards you. For I know your style of composition—it requires unusually close attention from the players of every type of instrument; and to keep the whole orchestra at such a pitch of industry and alertness for at least three hours is no joke.[106]

In the years following *Idomeneo* and the 'Haffner' and 'Linz' symphonies Mozart had been exposed to the extraordinary wind playing of Vienna and, in his operas and piano concertos of those years, he had gone beyond the already advanced techniques found in the works of 1780–3, forging entirely new methods of orchestration.[107] (His brilliant use of the wind instruments, much criticized at the time, subsequently formed the basis for the orchestration of Haydn's late orchestral works as well as the orchestral works of Beethoven, Schubert, and many lesser lights.) The change in orchestration did not occur in isolation, for Mozart's style had deepened in all major genres in the mid-1780s, becoming more contrapuntal, more chromatic, and more extreme in expression. The 'Prague' symphony benefited not only from this newly-elaborated orchestration and deepening of style, but also from the more serious role that, increasingly, was assigned to symphonies, which were now expected to exhibit artistic depth rather than to serve merely as elaborate fanfares to open and close concerts.

Three decades later a writer in the *Allgemeine musikalische Zeitung* could look back and recall the revolution in orchestral playing that had begun in the 1780s:

When we think of music as difficult, we must realize that many of us remember a time when few orchestras had clarinets and none had trombones, when pieces that today [1815] any little orchestra can play easily almost at sight had to be laboriously studied, and other works that are now played everywhere simply for the pleasure of playing them were rejected as impossible of performance. Indeed, we clearly remember that Mozart's music was at first reluctantly put aside by many orchestras, while those orchestras that prefer Italian music still distrust it.[108]

[105] Letter of 4 Dec. 1780. *Briefe*, iii. 45; *Letters*, ii. 1010 (= ii. 681).

[106] Letter of 25 Dec. 1780. *Briefe*, iii. 70; *Letters*, ii. 1033–4 (= ii. 696).

[107] For an attempt to trace the evolution of Mozart's orchestration during this period, primarily in the piano concertos, see C. Wolff, 'Aspects of Instrumentation in Mozart's Orchestral Music', *Interprétation de la musique classique de Haydn à Schubert. Colloque international, Evry, 13–15 Oct. 1977* (Paris, 1980), 37–43.

[108] Amadeus Wendt, 'Gedanken über die neuere Tonkunst, und von Beethovens Musik, namentlich dessen Fidelio', *Allgemeine musikalische Zeitung* (1815), xvii, cols. 345–53, 365–72, 379–89, 397–404, 413–20, 429–36, here 366–71.

These remarks should not be taken to mean that orchestras in the classical period were at first feeble and gradually grew in size and skill. Rather, the fate of individual ensembles rose and fell, influenced by the degree of interest and the economic situation of their patrons, the expertise of the available players, and, especially, the quality of their musical leadership. In each era the best ensembles played the music to which they were accustomed with skill and comprehension. But when musical styles changed, all ensembles did not adapt themselves equally quickly, and pre-eminence in performance often shifted to another place with a younger orchestra or more up-to-date leaders. (In Chapter 9, for instance, clear signs of such a 'lag' at the Concert spirituel in Paris are documented.) Similarly, perhaps only the very best orchestras outside Vienna could deal immediately with the newest orchestration of the 1780s, which required that all wind players be capable not only as ripienists but also as soloists. Once the new style was well established, leaders and players everywhere came to understand how to deal with it, but last of all in Italy, where Mozart's music was usually considered impracticable well into the nineteenth century in most places.[109]

Although the Prague orchestra was a tiny one even by eighteenth-century standards, there is evidence, besides that contained in Niemetschek's hagiographic remarks and in the orchestration of the works that Mozart composed for that ensemble, that it was an exceptionally well-disciplined group. About 1780, before his encounter with Mozart, Gyrowetz visited Prague and reported, 'Concerning its orchestra as well as its actors, the [Bohemian] Estates Theatre at that time was very well constituted .... The theatre orchestra was excellent.'[110] Information from 1787 and 1796 suggests that the Prague orchestra had a string section containing 3 or 4 first and 3 or 4 second violins, 2 violas, 1 or 2 cellos, and 2 double-basses, with the necessary winds one on a part, and a harpsichord, that is, between 24 and 27 instrumentalists.[111] In music orchestrated the way Mozart's late works are, forces of those proportions require careful handling, lest the wind overbalance the strings in the tuttis.[112]

---

[109] 'Kurze Nachrichten', *Allgemeine musikalische Zeitung* (1801), iii. cols. 497–500, 557–8; Stendhal (M. H. Beyle), 'Mozart en Italie', in *Vie de Rossini* (Paris, 1824), trans. and ed. R. N. Coe (London, 1970), 30–6; anon., 'Introduction of Mozart's Music into Italy', *The Harmonicon* (1824), ii. 14–16.

[110] *Biographie von Adelbert Gyrowetz* (Vienna, 1848), mod. edn. by A. Einstein as *Lebensläufe deutscher Musiker von ihnen selbst erzählt* (Leipzig, n.d.), iii–iv. 8.

[111] Zaslaw, 'Toward the Revivial of the Classical Orchestra', 176.

[112] This assertion is based on data presented in ch. 12, as well as on practical experience at rehearsals and recording sessions of K. 504 with the Prague forces duplicated (Academy of Ancient Music, Schröder/Hogwood). When the Prague opera company gave *Don Giovanni* in Leipzig on 15 June 1788, the poster announced that it would be performed '*mit doppeltem Orchester*; this is misleadingly translated in the English version of Deutsch as 'with double orchestra', whereas the standard eighteenth-century meaning must have been intended: 'more than one string player per part' (Deutsch, 266 (= 302), referring to a reproduction of the poster in R. von Freisauff, *Mozart's Don Juan 1787–1887* (Salzburg, 1887), facing 152).

In German-speaking countries K. 504 is often dubbed 'the symphony without minuet'. This designation arises from a retrospective point of view, for although thousands of eighteenth-century symphonies (including many of Mozart's) are in three movements, the classical symphonies most performed in the nineteenth and early twentieth centuries—Mozart's last six, Haydn's twelve 'London' symphonies, and all the symphonies of Beethoven and Schubert—are, except for K. 504, in four. If K. 504 is the only famous classical symphony to lack a minuet or scherzo, then there must be something special about it, at least according to this anachronistic notion—hence the soubriquet.

However, not only were the minuet and trio in symphonies optional, but there were even those who held their presence to be an aesthetic abomination, as in the following polemic from Berlin:

Concerning Minuets in Symphonies

By Court Counsellor [Johann Gottlieb] C[arl] Spazier

. . . it is certain that every work of art, in all of its manifold forms, must be the *expression* of the predominating mood of the person who produces it, but that, if it is to have a *similar effect* on others besides himself, it must have a definite inner and outer form through which the reason for the work of art is made apparent. Thus, for example, I should be put into a specific frame of mind by the composer by means of an instrumental work. Insofar as every piece must be ordered according to rules to achieve *unity*, I can require that all its essential or incidental parts conform to the common purpose, and that nothing in it interferes with the main purpose. Or, in other words, I can demand that the piece conform throughout to the *character* it professes.

Now comes the question, whether symphonies are among the works to be considered— and I say, 'Yes, by all means.' For they are not to be composed of an undefined mixture of notes tied together into a musical potpourri nor to be a free, capricious play of the composer's wit, are they? For were that the case, I could see no reason why all possible, ever so comical musical trifles and all manner of dances shouldn't find places therein. Why shouldn't polonaises and mazurkas and gavottes and the like take their places too?

Thus I assert that in symphonies, especially the larger orchestral symphonies with which concerts are wont to be begun, minuets or movements with minuet figures (both of which have become fashionable) are not to be admitted, at least not in my opinion, and that, first of all, on the following grounds: they are inimical to the symphony's *unity*. According to the practice, common until now, of using three principal movements, the first movement contains a simple or artfully composed presentation of a central emotion (of joy, exaltation, beauty, solemnity, etc.), which alternates with a slower movement, a cantabile, or similar movement, in order to produce a certain feeling of calm and gentleness, so that afterwards this can be resolved all the more forcefully into the previous emotion, with which the symphony began. This form—if not too pedantically and exactly followed, and if (as is unfortunately the case in many concerts) the Adagio is not too drastically separated from the Allegro, so that one must ask each time, 'Adagio, que veux-tu de moi?'—can still be justified according to the laws of psychology. Notwithstanding, at the same time, every ingenious artist is at liberty to reshape this form in its fundamentals, so that, for example, in a fiery symphony either no quiet middle movement is present at all, or at least one is woven in unobtrusively.

So I consider minuets effective (when smoothly worked into this form) only as long as they in no way at all inopportunely remind one of the *dance floor* and of the misuse of music. And if they are caricatured—as is often the case with Haydn and Pleyel—they cause *laughter*, in which case there can no longer be any question of whether minuets are admissible in noble symphonies, which are fiery and therefore stormy, or which should put us in a festive mood. But even when that is not the case, the substance of minuets is too insignificant, which only disrupts or halts entirely the symphony's continuity and momentum . . . .[113]

Spazier's critique is basically a conservative one: he clings to the baroque aesthetic theory of the unity of affect within single movements, and even to some extent across all the movements of a symphony, along with the need to avoid hybridizing genres by mixing, for instance, the serious and the comic. But his is also a prophetic critique, for romantic composers and writers would also adopt an anti-galant attitude, insisting on unity and high purpose as criteria for symphonies. Most eighteenth-century composers of symphonies, however, appear to have been less interested in such philosophical concerns and more in pragmatic estimates of how best to entertain their audiences. For them, the symphony may have worked simply by juxtaposing movements so that changes in tempo and mood from movement to movement—and as the century wore on, increasingly within movements—offered a pleasing variety of aural experiences. In any case, Spazier was not the only writer to object to the minuet.[114]

Such objections raise the question of how the multi-movement classical symphony should be understood. It has been suggested that the four-movement symphony descended from the model of a four-movement dance suite containing an allemande, sarabande, minuet, and gigue,[115] although the four-movement suite

---

[113] C. Spazier, 'Über Menuetten in Sinfonien', *Musikalisches Wochenblatt* (1791–2), 91–2. Trans. Willard Daetsch. Portions of Spazier's essay are reprinted in H.-G. Ottenberg (ed.), *Der critische Musicus an der Spree. Berliner Musikschrifttum von 1748 bis 1799: Eine Dokumentation* (Leipzig, 1984), 318–20.

[114] See, for instance, Johann Adam Hiller, *Wöchentliche Nachrichten und Anmerkungen die Musik betreffend* (1766–7), i. 243; C. D. Ebeling's note to his translation of Charles Burney's *Tagebuch einer musikalischen Reise durch Frankreich und Italien* (Hamburg, 1772), 276–7; Daniel Gottlob Türk, *Klavierschule; oder, Anweisung zum Klavierspielen für Lehrer und Lernende, mit kritischen Anmerkungen* (Leipzig, 1789), 391 (= R. H. Haggh (trans. and ed.), *School of Clavier Playing; or, Instructions in Playing the Clavier for Teachers & Students* (Lincoln, 1982), 384, 531); see also E. K. Wolf, *The Symphonies of Johann Stamitz*, 86–91.

Can this dispute still have been alive more than a decade after Mozart's death, when a critic objected to the omission of the Minuet and Trio in a performance of K. 550 in Vienna (*Allgemeine musikalische Zeitung* (1804–5), vii, col. 613)? Further concerning the symphony minuet, see J. Gmeiner, *Menuett und Scherzo: Ein Beitrag zur Entwicklungsgeschichte und Soziologie des Tanzsatzes in der Wiener Klassik* (Wiener Veröffentlichungen zur Musikwissenschaft, xv) (Tutzing, 1979).

[115] E. Borrel, *Interprétation de la musique française de Lully à la révolution* (Paris, 1933, repr. 1975, 1978), 216–17.

more often consisted of allemande, courante, sarabande, and gigue, and no direct links between it and the classical symphony have been demonstrated. The principles underlying the organization of suites of dances have been variously formulated: decreasing stylization,[116] alternation of stepping and leaping dances,[117] alternation of company and couple dances,[118] and alternation or pairing of tempos and degrees of tension.[119] Tempo has been also been considered the aesthetic principle behind the four-movement classical symphony: '. . . the . . . minuet and trio provide a graded acceleration in tempo from the slow movement through the moderate dance movement to the presto or prestissimo finale.'[120]

Certainly, balance and contrast in metre, tempo, texture, and style must be included in any explanation of the form. The movement-types in Mozart's symphonies of the 1760s and 1770s (before complexity and stylization more thoroughly disguised their origins) suggest characterizations somewhat differing from, but not necessarily contradicting, those just mentioned. The first movements represent the heroic, frequently with martial character; many early- and mid-eighteenth-century sinfonia movements were limited to this character, but later ones (all of Mozart's included) contain contrasting lyrical ideas. Appropriately, given the origins of the sinfonia in the opera pit, the two sorts of ideas—lyrical and martial—may be seen as comparable to the persistent themes of opera seria itself: love versus honour. The andantes deal with the pastoral, as the origin of a few of Mozart's in bucolic operatic scenes reveals.[121] The minuets stand for the courtly side of eighteenth-century life, and an old-fashioned and formal aspect of it at that. The trios, on the other hand, often deal with the antic, thus standing in relation to the minuet as an antimasque to its masque, and providing the very element of caricature so vehemently objected to by Spazier. The finales are generally based on rustic or popular dances: gavottes, *contredanses*, jigs, or quick steps. Taken together, the heroic, the amorous, the pastoral, the courtly, the antic, and the rustic or popular, represent the themes most often found in eighteenth-century prose, poetry, plays, and paintings. Only the religious is not regularly treated, although

---

[116] H. Besseler, *Beiträge zur Stilgeschichte der deutschen Suite im 17. Jahrhundert* (Ph.D, diss., University of Freiburg, 1923); M. Pearl, 'The Suite in Relation to Baroque Style' (Ph.D, diss., New York University, 1957).

[117] T. Norlind, 'Zur Geschichte der Suite', *Sammelbände der internationalen Musikgesellschaft* (1905–6), vii. 172–203; M. Seiffert, *Geschichte der Klaviermusik* (Leipzig, 1899, repr. 1966); H. Riemann, 'Zur Geschichte der deutschen Suite', *Sammelbände der internationalen Musikgesellschaft* (1904–5), vi. 501–20; K. Nef, *Zur Geschichte der deutschen Instrumentalmusik in der zweiten Hälfte des 17. Jahrhunderts* (Leipzig, 1902, repr. 1973).

[118] W. Klenz, *Giovanni Maria Bononcini of Modena* (Durham, NC, 1962).

[119] H. Riemann, 'Zur Geschichte der deutschen Suite'. The information at nn. 116–19 follows D. Fuller, 'Suite', *The New Grove*, xviii. 334, 350.

[120] Wolf, *The Symphonies of Johann Stamitz*, 90. Wolf argues persuasively that, although Stamitz did not invent the four-movement symphony, he was to a considerable extent responsible for promulgating it.

[121] See the discussions of the andantes of the symphonies K. 43 (ch. 5), K. 96 = 111b (ch. 7), K. 111 + 120 = 111a (ch. 7), and K. 208 + 213 = 102 (ch. 8). And compare an anonymous Viennese review of the first public performance of Beethoven 'Eroica' symphony, 1805, in which the slow movement is called 'a pastoral in the grandest style' (E. Forbes (ed.), *Thayer's Life of Beethoven* (Princeton, 1967), 375–6).

attempts to include it are discussed in Chapter 4. Hence the symphony may be considered a stylized conspectus of the eighteenth century's favourite artistic subject-matter.

In a number of Mozart's four-movement symphonies, another type of organization is evident: the trio often reverts to the key (most commonly the subdominant) and instrumentation (reduced and sometimes concertante) of the andante, whereas the minuet, like the outer movements, is in the tonic and employs the full tutti forces. Other considerations aside, this creates the formal arrangement A B ABA A, although this scheme misrepresents the scale, since the ABA of the minuet and trio does not match the other sections in length or weight.

Around the time that Mozart composed the 'Prague' symphony something peculiar took place with regard to symphony finales. An idea for a finale of a D major symphony (Example 11.3) was jotted down by Mozart on a piece of paper containing sketches and an insert for the piano concertos K. 482 (autograph dated 16 December 1785) and K. 486 (autograph dated 3 February 1786) as well as a canon not listed in the Köchel Catalogue.[122] The Finale in the 'autograph' manuscript of the 'Paris' symphony is in fact not an autograph but a replacement in the hand of a professional copyist; an autograph trumpet part of the 'Paris' symphony exists, written on a type of paper also found in K. 503, 504, and 504a, therefore probably dating from around November or December 1786.[123] This trumpet part contains bizarre variants, suggesting either that it was written from memory or that Mozart undertook revisions to K. 297.[124] The Finale of the

Ex. 11.3 Sketch for a Symphony finale in D major, K. *deest*

Ultimo allegro per una sinfonia

[122] H. Federhofer, 'Mozartiana in Steiermark (Ergänzung)', *Mozart-Jahrbuch* (1958), 109–18, especially the facsimile on 117.

[123] For the autograph of K. 297, see ch. 9; for information about the trumpet part see A. Tyson, 'The Mozart Fragments in the Mozarteum, Salzburg: A Preliminary Study of Their Chronology and Their Significance', *Journal of the American Musicological Society* (1981), xxxiv. 471–510, here 488.

[124] Personal communication from Alan Tyson.

'Prague' symphony was written by Mozart on a kind of paper also found in the third and fourth acts of *Le nozze di Figaro*,[125] composed in late winter and early spring of 1786. This would seem to suggest the possibility that the Finale of K. 504 may have been written roughly half a year before the other two movements, which are assumed to have been composed in November or December of that year. Alan Tyson has proposed, therefore, that Mozart may first have thought to re-use the 'Paris' symphony with a new Finale, deciding subsequently to compose the other two movements as well. Tyson even points to a certain resemblance between the openings of the two finales: both are in D major and duple metre, and share a piano beginning, their melodies starting after the beat and descending from A.[126] Was it the relative conventionality of the old Finale that led Mozart to think to replace it? The Finale of the 'Prague' symphony is anything but conventional, opening in a remarkable manner which, experienced conductors will tell you, is not easy to begin together and in tempo.

Evidence suggesting that Mozart may have been aware of the conceptual 'difficulty' of his 'Prague' symphony survives in the form of sketches related to all three movements, published in facsimile and transcription in the *NMA*. These provide a tantalizing glimpse at Mozart's working habits. They are partly on one staff but mostly on two, preserving the structural voices—the *Hauptstimme* and *basso seguente*. At points of imitation other voices may appear. For a passage in the development section where the action consists of modulation rather than thematic manipulation, nothing appears in the sketch but a figured bass. Since, as always, the non-structural voices were left until last and are therefore not present in the sketches, one cannot divine to what extent Mozart already had them in his mind, but it is probably fair to suggest that they belong more to the 'craft' and less to the 'inspiration' of the work. Comparison with the completed movement suggests that Mozart had its overall shape in mind at an early stage.

The unexpected revelation of the sketches for the first movement is that Mozart was struggling not so much with the creation of ideas (which appear in the sketches pretty much as in the final version) as with their connection. The most striking omissions in the sketches compared with the final version seem to come at transitional points, which is unexpected if only because the received wisdom is that Mozart had an instinctive grasp of formal matters. The same point emerges in Chapter 9 in connection with the sketch for the Andante in $\frac{3}{4}$ for the 'Paris' symphony, K. 297 = 300a. And musicians who have examined the drafts and

---

[125] Personal communication from Alan Tyson.

[126] A. Tyson, 'Redating Mozart: Some Stylistic and Biographical Implications', paper read at the Annual Meetings of the American Musicological Society, Louisville, Oct. 1983. That Niemetschek owned a set of parts for the 'Paris' symphony (West Berlin Mus. ms. 15,273) suggests that this work may have been used by Mozart in Prague, although these parts are said to date from *c*.1800 (H.-G. Klein, *Wolfgang Amadeus Mozart: Autographe und Abschriften* (Berlin, 1982), 266).

corrections in Mozart's string quartets have come to similar conclusions about his working methods.[127]

An aspect of the sketches for K. 504 possibly significant to performance of the finished work is this: they identify the structural voices, which any competent orchestra leader will want to make audible. In general this involves no surprises, for the melody is usually in the first violins and occasionally shared elsewhere in ways unlikely to be missed. In one passage, however, 'structural' notes appear in the violas where they might easily be construed as being in the violins (Example 11.4). Or, to be more precise, as the violins and violas play in thirds at this point in the finished work, they form a composite *Hauptstimme* between them.

The 'Prague' symphony may have been heard in London as early as 1787, or, at least, the timing of certain events is suggestive: Mozart returned to Vienna from Prague around 12 February 1787. On 23 February Anna Storace gave her farewell concert at the Kärntnerthor Theatre, including on her programme Mozart's *scena* 'Ch'io mi scordi di te—Non temer, amato bene', K. 505. Three days later Anna and Stephen Storace, their mother, Michael Kelly, Thomas Attwood, and one other Englishman were being shown around Salzburg by Leopold, who reported

Ex. 11.4 Symphony in D major, K. 504, first movement, Sketch version of bars 79–89

Arrows indicate pitches assigned to the violas in the final version.

---

[127] L. Finscher, 'Aspects of Mozart's Compositional Process in the Quartet Autographs' in C. Wolff (ed.) *The String Quartets of Haydn, Mozart, and Beethoven* (Cambridge, Mass., 1980), 121–53 and 216–21.

to Nannerl (along with many amusing details of their visit) that 'your brother . . . wants to travel to England, but . . . his pupil [Attwood] is first going to procure a definite engagement for him in London, I mean, a contract to compose an opera or a subscription concert, etc.'[128] The British party reached London in March, about eight months before Mozart's 'new' symphony was performed there, for on 7 November of that year the Anacreontic Society gave a concert at the Crown and Anchor Tavern in the Strand which 'opened with a new symphony by Mozart, which was well received, and had great merit . . . . The concert finished with a symphony by Mozart, very inferior to the first.'[129] The rest of the programme included a sonata by Koželuch, an aria by Paisiello, a symphony by Clementi, an unidentified duet, and a concerto by Geminiani. (Can the second symphony have been K. 204, an arrangement of which was published in London in 1790?[130]) It is of course impossible to know precisely what 'new' symphony meant: the writer can have been misinformed, or 'new' can have meant 'not previously heard at these concerts' or 'not previously heard in England'.

In the vast literature about Mozart's life and music, several monographs, dozens of articles, hundreds of book chapters, and thousands of programme notes are devoted to the three final symphonies (K. 543, 550, 551), completed in 1788 in the space of about three months. This literature tells us that we do not know why these symphonies were composed and suggests that they were the result of an inner artistic compulsion rather than an external stimulus; that they were intended as a trilogy; that Mozart, unappreciated during his last years, never heard these masterpieces performed. Each of these assertions bears investigation.

Mozart's letters reveal that, while he could sometimes compose with lightning speed, he could also procrastinate, on occasion he was depressed, finding composing difficult, and sometimes he was too busy giving lessons and concerts to compose. Several documented instances suggest that he seldom began a large-scale work without a clear use for it in mind, and that, when a commission or opportunity for performance or publication dried up, he would sometimes abandon a work in mid-course.[131] That being the case, it would be surprising if Mozart had composed three large symphonies with no practical goals in mind; three possible ones can be suggested.

One was a series of subscription concerts usually said to have been scheduled by Mozart for June and July 1788, but probably actually for the autumn or perhaps

---

[128] Letter of 1 Mar. 1787. *Briefe*, iv. 28; *Letters*, iii. 1347–9 (= ii. 905–6).

[129] See Table 10.2.

[130] K⁶, Anhang B, p. 777.

[131] A good example is the abandoned torso of a sinfonia concertante for piano and violin, K. Anh. 56 = 315f, begun by Mozart in Mannheim in November 1778 but put aside when the Elector moved his orchestra to Munich.

Vienna (II): Independence (1780–1791)

even Advent. Although the Mozart literature states unanimously that these never took place, H. C. Robbins Landon has recently convincingly argued that they did. In any case, they apparently constituted Mozart's last endeavour at large-scale concerts in a public venue, although he made one later attempt in July 1789, without success, to give subscription concerts in his own rooms.[132]

A second goal may have been to sell or publish the three symphonies as an 'opus', although in fact they remained unpublished until André's editions of the 1790s (Table 11.2). The three symphonies are listed together in Traeg's catalogue (Table 11.3) and in the Breitkopf & Härtel Manuscript Catalogue, as if they were a unit, although no print or manuscript groups them as an opus. There must have been some commercial distribution of these three works; survival of early sets of parts (documented below) suggests that the works (individually, not as an opus) were performed outside of Vienna during Mozart's lifetime.

A third goal may have been preparation for the just mentioned, proposed visit to London—to be arranged with the aid of his British friends Anna and Stephen Storace, Thomas Attwood, and Michael Kelly—where he could reasonably hope to make more money than at home, as Joseph Haydn was to demonstrate a few years later.

When the English tour fell through, Mozart's three symphonies probably provided music for a German tour he made in 1789, giving concerts and seeking patronage and perhaps a permanent post. At the Dresden court Mozart gave a chamber music concert on 13 April and an orchestral concert the following day. The latter included a piano concerto,[133] and, although the rest of the programme is unknown, it is likely also to have included at least one symphony. The Dresden court orchestra in 1789 was strongly manned, with the strings 10—10—6—4—5 and the wind 2—4—0—4 / 4—(2)—1, or a total of 52 musicians.[134] A reaction to Mozart's visit to Dresden survives, for the Russian ambassador, Prince Alexander Beloselski-Beloskeri, attended one or both of Mozart's concerts and later wrote a dramatic dialogue satirizing contemporary opinions about music, in which one reads, 'Mozart is very learned, very difficult, consequently he is very much esteemed by instrumentalists; but he seems never to have had the good fortune to have loved. No modulation ever issued from his heart.'[135]

---

[132] Mozart's letters of [undated; usually assigned to June 1788 but probably a month or two later] and 12 July 1789. *Briefe*, iv. 65, 92; *Letters*, iii. 1360–1, 1383–4 (= ii. 914–15, 929–30); H. C. Robbins Landon, *1791: Mozart's Last Year* (New York, 1988), 31–3.

[133] Deutsch, 297 (= 339).

[134] *Hof- und Staatskalender Dresden* (Dresden, 1789), as reported in C.-H. Mahling, 'Orchester und Orchestermusiker in Deutschland von 1700 bis 1850' (Habilitationsschrift, University of Saarbrücken, 1972), ii. '5'.

[135] The speaker in this passage is not the ambassador himself, but his fictional creation Le Prince Tout-cœur, who believes (naturally) that music must 'come from the heart'. He admires music that is full of 'sentiment' and 'passions' and is an apostle of Rousseau's. He prefers Salieri to Gluck, whom he finds too learned, too dependent on rules, and lacking in natural gifts.

A copy survives of the programme of Mozart's concert of 12 May in the Leipzig Gewandhaus. In translation it reads as follows:

Part I

Symphony
Scena. Mme Duscheck
Concerto, on the Pianoforte
Symphony

Part II

Concerto, on the Pianoforte
Scena. Mme Duscheck
Fantasy, on the Pianoforte
Symphony[136]

Although it would be tempting to suppose that the three last symphonies were performed on this occasion (raising questions about the endurance of both orchestra and audience), it is also possible, and perhaps more likely, that Mozart observed the custom at some of his Viennese concerts of dividing a symphony and using the opening movements at the beginning of the concert and the Finale at the end of the first half or at the end of the programme. Then again, recall Traeg's advertisement, cited at the beginning of this chapter, revealing that he expected persons giving two concerts per week to require six symphonies.

While the size of the Leipzig orchestra in 1789 is not known, figures from 1781, 1786, and 1794 show that it was less well manned than the Dresden orchestra, as might be expected in a smaller city without a court (Table 11.4).

The Leipzig critic Johann Friedrich Rochlitz, who claimed to have met Mozart and to have attended his concert and the rehearsal for it, later published a reminiscence of the occasion in the *Allgemeine musikalische Zeitung*, of which he was for many years the editor:

When I went into the rehearsal the next day, I noticed to my astonishment that the first movement being rehearsed—it was the allegro of a symphony of his—he took very, very

---

His disparagement of Mozart in comparison with Naumann, Seidelmann, and other such nonentities doubtless was meant ironically by Prince Beloselski as a criticism of Prince Tout-cœur's taste. Or, reading between the lines: the Russian ambassador approved of Mozart's music, but the reactions of some others around him must have been less favourable. I am indebted for this interpretation to George Hall (letter of 26 July 1982).

The text of Beloselski's dialogue (Museum of Literature, Moscow, MS 172.1, ed. krh. 153) is published in A. Mazon, *Alexandre Mikhailovitch Béloselski* (Paris, 1964), 355–68. See also J. Chailley, 'Les *Dialogues sur la musique* d'Alexandre Belosel'skij', *Revue des études slaves* (1966), xlv. 93–103, and idem, 'Mozart vu par les salons contemporains', *La Revue musicale* (1981), cccxxxviii–cccxxxix. 115–18. Mozart had lunch with Beloselski on 15 April and then spent most of the rest of the day playing the organ and fortepiano for him.

[136] Deutsch, 299–300 (= 341–2).

TABLE 11.4 The Leipzig orchestra

	vn. I	vn. II	va.	vc.	db.	fl.	ob.	cl.	bn.	hn.	tpt.	timp.	TOTAL
1781	6	6	2–3	2	2	2	2	0	3	2	2	0–1	30
1786	4	4	2	1	1	2	2	0	2	2	?	?	about 20
1794	3	2	2	1	1–2	2	2	0	2	2	2	1	about 20

Sources: A. Dörffel, *Geschichte der Gewandhausconcerte zu Leipzig.... Festschrift zur hundertjährigen Jubelfeier der Einweihung des Concertsaales im Gewandhause zu Leipzig* (Leipzig, 1884), 22; A. Schering, *Bach und das Musikleben in Leipzig im 18. Jahrhundert* (Leipzig, 1822), 38–9. According to a note by Rochlitz in the *Allgemeine musikalische Zeitung* (1801–2), iv, cols. 783–4, the Leipzig orchestra in its earliest days under J. A. Hiller from 1763 had the same string section as in 1802: 6—6—[2?]—3—3.

fast. Hardly twenty bars had been played and—as might easily be foreseen—the orchestra started to slow down and the tempo dragged. Mozart stopped, explained what they were doing wrong, cried out 'Ancora', and began again just as fast as before. The result was the same. He did everything to maintain the same tempo; once he beat time so violently with his foot that one of his finely-worked steel shoebuckles broke into pieces: but all to no avail. He laughed at this mishap, left the pieces lying there, cried out 'Ancora' again, and started for the third time at the same tempo. The musicians became recalcitrant toward this diminutive, deathly pale little man who hustled them in this way: incensed, they continued working at it, and now it was all right. Everything that followed, he took at a moderate pace. I must admit that at the time I thought he was rushing it a bit, insisting he was right not so much through obstinacy but in order not to compromise his authority with them right at the beginning. But after the rehearsal he said in an aside to a few connoisseurs [who had been listening]:

'Don't be surprised about me; it wasn't caprice. But I saw that the majority of the musicians were fairly advanced in years. The dragging would never have stopped if I hadn't first driven them to their limit and made them angry. Now they did their best through sheer irritation.'

As Mozart had never before heard this orchestra play, that showed a fair knowledge of human nature; so he was not after all *a child* in everything outside of the realm of music—as people so often say and write.[137]

One would dearly love to believe this charming anecdote, if only Rochlitz did not have a reputation for publishing falsified documents.[138] In another article Rochlitz reported that Mozart 'accompanied' his symphonies and arias from the keyboard.[139] A third story of Mozart's Leipzig concert survives through the same problematical intermediary. It suggests that Mozart directed a polymetric passage by beating one pattern with his right hand and another with his left (does it therefore also contradict the previous item by suggesting that he 'conducted' rather than leading as concertmaster or continuo player?):

In the second part of the concert Mozart gave here in Leipzig on 12 May 1789, he performed, among other things, an entirely new Symphony in C major, the last movement of which is in $\frac{6}{8}$. [In this movement,] after a pause by the bass-line instruments, the double-basses enter unexpectedly with a new theme in $\frac{3}{4}$, while the rest of the orchestra continues in $\frac{6}{8}$. Mr Wach, the double-bassist, who is still among us, played in the

---

[137] *Allgemeine musikalische Zeitung* (7 Nov. 1798), i, cols. 85–6. In a later essay Rochlitz claimed to have seen a viola part used on this occasion in which a player had written over one bar in the music, 'Here Mozart stamped his foot!' (O. Jahn, *W. A. Mozart*, 3rd edn. (Leipzig, 1889–91), ii. 477, n. 36). Rochlitz's Mozart anecdotes originally published in the *Allgemeine musikalische Zeitung* reappear in somewhat altered form in his *Für Freunde der Tonkunst* (Leipzig, 1824).

[138] Concerning Rochlitz's unreliability see M. Solomon, 'On Beethoven's Creative Process: A Two-Part Invention', *Music and Letters* (1980), lxi. 272–83; J. H. Eibl, 'Ein Brief Mozarts über seine Schaffensweise', *Österreichische Musik Zeitschrift* (1980), xxxv. 584–5; P. Kivy, 'Mozart and Monotheism: An Essay in Spurious Aesthetics', *Journal of Musicology* (1983), ii. 322–8.

[139] *Allgemeine musikalische Zeitung* (1798–9), i, col. 113.

performance of this work. Mozart said to him, 'When the ¾ begins, be guided only by the movement of my left hand.' Upon which we, and others as well, have enquired: does no-one know anything more concrete about this symphony? Nothing has been seen of it since that time. Has it been completely lost, or is anyone able to say anything at all a bit more detailed about it?[140]

Mozart's known symphonies in C major with finales in ⁶⁄₈ are K. 128, 162, and 338. Only the last of these was recent enough to have been in Mozart's repertory as late as 1789, and only it is late enough that its violoncellos and double-basses are occasionally written for separately. But all this is moot, as in none of the three does a passage occur that fits Wach's description. Let us suppose, then, that the double-bassist correctly recalled the key and the polymetric manœuvre but had the metres wrong, and that the Finale of the 'Jupiter' symphony, K. 551, was meant. Unfortunately for this suggestion, however, the two passages in that movement in which the double-basses have an independent part to play contain nothing contrametric. Even if the key and the metres are mistaken in Wach's recollection, no known symphony finale between 338 and 551 satisfies his description of Mozart's ambidextrous conducting. Either he was an unreliable witness or a symphony is missing. Mozart kept a catalogue of his own works from the piano concerto, K. 449, of February 1784 until a few weeks before his death. Although during this period he failed to enter some small works into his catalogue, the large works (and most of the small ones) are chronicled,[141] making it improbable that a symphony is omitted. If, therefore, there is any substance to the polymetric anecdote, the lost work would most likely belong to the early 1780s, at the time of the 'Haffner' and 'Linz' symphonies. More probably, however, the Rochlitz–Wach story is apocryphal. Whatever is the truth about Rochlitz's repeated use of Mozart's Leipzig concert to establish his own credentials as an eyewitness and 'expert' (and one must view his testimony with the greatest caution), Mozart himself wrote to

---

[140] 'Mancherley', *Allgemeine musikalische Zeitung* (1830), xxxii. col. 687. This putative symphony is briefly referred to again in the same periodical as 'the great Symphony in C major whose finale is in ⁶⁄₈, in which the double-bass performs completely unexpectedly a new theme in ¾ against the former [metre]' (1831), xxxiii. col. 733. The double-bass player Wach was credited by Ignaz Moscheles in 1816 with keeping the Leipzig orchestra together by the 'force and energy' of his playing (C. E. Moscheles (ed.), *Aus Moscheles' Leben, nach Briefen und Tagebüchern* (Leipzig, 1872), i. 31; trans. A. D. Coleridge as *Recent Music and Musicians as Described in the Diaries and Correspondence of Moscheles* (London, 1873; repr. New York, 1970), i. 28).

Can this anecdote have something to do with the symphonic fragment, K. Anhang C 11.16? When it was sold at Leo Liepmannsohn's Auction No. 55 (item 36) on 12 October 1929, it was described as follows: 'Autograph music manuscript: fragment of an orchestral score with the page numbers 85–88. Four twelve-stave sides, oblong format. The important music manuscript is apparently a score fragment from the development section of a ⁶⁄₈ finale to an unknown symphony (in G major) with the following scoring: 2 each of flutes, oboes, bassoon, horns, trumpets, and kettledrums, and string quintet. Its layout is reminiscent of the finale of the C major Salzburg symphony K. 338 of August 1780, also in ⁶⁄₈. The present autograph, however, is from a later time, the second half of the 1780s .... The handwriting exhibits great similarity to the Berlin autograph of the brilliant D-major symphony K. 504, composed at the end of 1786; also the scoring is identical in both works.' K⁶ rejects this description, claiming that the manuscript is not a Mozart autograph and comes from the early nineteenth century.

[141] D. N. Leeson and D. Whitwell, 'Mozart's Thematic Catalogue', *The Musical Times* (1973), xciv. 781–3.

his wife that the Leipzig concert had been a failure, although he meant financially rather than artistically.[142]

Leaving Leipzig around 23 April, Mozart reached Berlin two days later, remaining for about eleven nights and then returning for another nine nights between 19 and 28 May. During his time in the Prussian capital he attended a performance of *Die Entführung*, heard a recital by his nine-year-old pupil Johann Nepomuk Hummel, and on 26 May performed privately at Potsdam for Friedrich Wilhelm II, who commissioned some string quartets for himself and some easy piano sonatas for the Princess Friederike Charlotte Ulrike Katherine. Mozart must also have had some business dealings with Berlin's leading music-publisher, J. F. K. Rellstab, because on 9 May the latter advertised that he had available for his customers 'the complete works of Mozart'.[143] Cliff Eisen suggests that the Mozart–Rellstab connection explains the sudden appearance of eight of Mozart's symphonies, at least some of which are not known to have been available elsewhere, in Westphal's music catalogue eleven months later (Table 11.5). Here is

TABLE 11.5 Westphal's offering of Mozart's symphonies in April 1790 with hypothetical identifications based on 'size'

Symphonies advertised	Price (fl./kr.)	['Size']*	[K.]
Symphony *a 8* in A major	5/8	[4]	[201]
Symphony *a 9* in B-flat major	4/8	[3]	[182]
Symphony *a 14* in C major, No. 2, with kettledrums and trumpets	10/8	[14]	[551]
Symphony *a 12* in C major, No. 3, the same [trumpets and drums]	6/0	[12]	[425]
Symphony *a 16* in E-flat major, the same [trumpets and drums]	10/0	[12]	[543]
Symphony *a 11* in D major, No. 6	6/0	[11]†	[385]
Symphony *a 18* in D major, No. 7, the same [trumpets and drums]	10/0	[12]	[504]
Symphony *a 19* in G major, the same [trumpets and drums]‡	5/4	[4]	[318]

* For the explanation of 'size', see above at the discussion of Table 11.3.

† 'Size' 11 for K. 385 is based on the full instrumentation of the second version, but the work circulated also without flutes and clarinets (and sometimes even without trumpets and drums).

‡ For an explanation of trumpets and drums in this G major work, see the discussion of K. 318 in Chapter 10.

Source: *Neue eingekommene Musikalien, bey J. C. Westphal & Comp. in Hamburg. 1790: April* as reported in C. Eisen, 'Contributions to a New Mozart Documentary Biography', *Journal of the American Musicological Society* (1986), xxxix. 615–32, here 628.

[142] Letter of 23 May 1789. *Briefe*, iv. 90; *Letters*, iii. 1381 (= ii. 928).

[143] *Berlinische Nachrichten von Staats-und gelehrten Sachen* (9 May 1789), 418, as reported in C. Eisen, 'Contributions to a New Mozart Documentary Biography', *Journal of the American Musicological Society* (1986), xxxix. 615–32, here 628–9. See also Table 8.3.

further circumstantial evidence that Mozart's last three symphonies were written for practical reasons and disseminated.

In 1790 Mozart, still searching pathetically for patronage and a suitable post, travelled to Frankfurt at his own expense to be present at the festivities surrounding the coronation of Leopold II. He wrote to Constanze from there, 'I am famous, admired, and popular here; on the other hand, the Frankfurt people are even more stingy than the Viennese. If my concert is at all successful, it will be thanks to my name, to Countess Hatzfeldt, and the Schweitzer family, who are working hard on my behalf.'[144] A copy of the poster for this occasion survives, and a full account of the event was written by Count Ludwig von Bentheim-Steinfurt in his diary on 15 October 1790, the day of the concert:

At 11 o'clock in the morning there was a grand concert by Mozart in the auditorium of the National Playhouse. It began with the fine (1) Symphony by Mozart, which I have long possessed. (2) Then came a superb Italian aria, 'Non so di chi', which Madame Schick sang with infinite expressiveness. (3) Mozart played a Concerto composed by him which was of an extraordinary prettiness and charm; he had a fortepiano by Stein of Augsburg, which must be supreme of its kind and costs from 90 to 100 pounds. Mozart's playing is a little like that of the late Klöffler, but infinitely more perfect. Monsieur Mozart is a small man of rather pleasant appearance; he had a coat of brown marine satin nicely embroidered; he is engaged at the Imperial Court. (4) The soprano Cecarelli sang a beautiful scena and rondeau, for bravura airs do not appear to be his forte; he had grace and a perfect method; an excellent singer but his tone is a little on the decline, that and his ugly physiognomy; for the rest his passages, ornaments and trills are admirable . . . .

In the second act, (5) another concerto by Mozart, which however did not please me like the first. (6) A duet which we possess and I recognized by the passage 'Per te, per te', with ascending notes . . . . It was a real pleasure to hear these two people, although La Schick lost by comparison with the soprano in the matter of voice and ornaments, but she scored in the passages at least. (7) A Fantasy without the music by Mozart, very charming, in which he shone infinitely, exhibiting all the power of his talent. (8) The last symphony was not given for it was almost two o'clock and everybody was sighing for dinner. The music thus lasted three hours, which was owing to the fact that between pieces there were very long pauses. The orchestra was no more than rather weak with five or six violins, but apart from that very accurate. There was only one accursed thing that displeased me very much: there were not many people.[145]

On the same day as the concert at which he pleased Count Bentheim-Steinfurt, Mozart reported to Constanze:

---

[144] Letter of 8 Oct. 1790. *Briefe*, iv. 117–18; *Letters*, iii. 1406 (= ii. 945).
[145] Deutsch, 329–30 (= 375). The poster is reproduced in O. E. Deutsch, *Mozart und seine Welt in zeitgenössischen Bildern* (*NMA*, x/32) (Kassel, 1961), 237.

My concert took place at eleven o'clock this morning. It was a splendid success from the point of view of honour and glory, but a failure as far as money is concerned. Unfortunately, some Prince was giving a big *déjeuner* and the Hessian troops were holding a grand manœuvre .... But in spite of all these difficulties I was in such good form and people were so delighted with me that they implored me to give another concert next Sunday.[146]

No trace remains of a second Frankfurt concert, which, if it actually occurred, may have been a private affair. The first concert took place at the National Theatre, about which a report of 1788 states that the orchestra consisted of some '20-odd persons'.[147] If Count Bentheim-Steinfurt's observation that there were five or six violins is accurate (and the rest of his account seems reliable), then Mozart's Frankfurt orchestra may have been approximately 3—3—2—1—1 / 1—2—0—2 / 2—2—1. This is the wind complement for Mozart's most recent piano concertos, K. 503 and 537, and also (alone among all of Mozart's symphonies) of the 'Jupiter' symphony.

Mozart moved on immediately to Mainz and gave a similar concert there on 20 October. The Mainz court orchestra was led by the Mozarts' old acquaintance Georg Anton Kreusser, who years before in Amsterdam had helped himself to the beginning of Mozart's Symphony in B flat, K. 22 (see Chapter 3). Information about the Mainz orchestra survives from six or seven years before Mozart's visit, in the form of contradictory figures for the years 1782 and 1783 (Table 11.6). (If the discrepancy in the figures is not simple inaccuracy or change in personnel, then perhaps the explanation is that two violinists also played the clarinet.) In the latter year a visitor reported of the orchestra,

Here there are: an excellent flautist [Friehold], an excellent violinist [Schick], mediocre oboists [Ehrenfried, Suppus], good clarinettists [Harburger, Wagner], a sure and good double-bass player [Schmitt], mediocre hunting horn players [Jöng junior and senior], a miserable bassoonist [Küchler] .... The orchestra's ensemble is good; what it lacks are nuances.[148]

In Mainz as in Leipzig and elsewhere, Mozart was disappointed with the financial results, reporting to Constanze that, even though the Elector was present, he 'received only the meagre sum of fifteen carolins'.[149] The tour as a whole apparently yielded slender financial rewards.

---

[146] *Briefe*, iv. 118; *Letters*, iii. 1407 (= ii. 946).

[147] C.-H. Mahling, 'Orchester und Orchestermusiker in Deutschland von 1700 bis 1850', vol. ii, Appendix D, Theatre Orchestra Section, p. 3.

[148] Letter of 3 Oct. 1783 by Ignaz von Beecke, quoted in L. Schiedermair, 'Die Blütezeit der Öttingen-Wallerstein'schen Hofkapelle', *Sammelbände der internationalen Musikgesellschaft* (1907–8), ix. 83–130, here 109; and in E. Peter, *Georg Anton Kreusser: Ein mainzer Instrumentalkomponist der Klassik* (Munich and Salzburg, 1975), 69–70.

[149] Letter of 23 Oct. 1790. *Briefe*, iv. 199; *Letters*, iii. 1409 (= ii. 947).

TABLE 11.6 The Mainz orchestra

	vn. I	vn. II	va.	vc.	db.	fl.	ob.	cl.	bn.	hn.	cont.	TOTAL
1782	5	5	2	2	1	2	3	2	1	2	1	26
1783	7	6	2	2	2	3	2	0	1	2	1	28

Sources: J. N. Forkel (ed.), *Musikalischer Almanach für Deutschland aus dem Jahre 1782* (Leipzig, [1781–2]), 127–8; J. B. Cramer (ed.), *Magazin der Musik* (1783), i. 748–50.

Mozart's concert activities in Vienna after 1788 were much reduced from earlier, and information about them is scarce because, with his father dead and his sister on poor terms with him, the series of informative letters ends. The only documented performances were on 16 and 17 April 1791 at the Society of Musicians' annual benefit concert, when a large orchestra under the direction of Antonio Salieri presented a 'grand symphony' by Mozart.[150] As Mozart's friends, the clarinettists Johann and Anton Stadler, were in the orchestra, the symphony played may have been one of the only three by Mozart with those instruments: K. 297, K. 543, or the second version of K. 550. The very existence of versions of K. 550 with and without clarinets and of a reorchestration of two passages of the Andante in the version without clarinets strongly suggests that both versions of the work were performed, for Mozart would hardly have gone to the trouble of making these rescorings if he had not had specific performances in view.

Adding to the evidence of Mozart's concert activities the evidence of the two versions of K. 550, of the existence of sets of manuscript parts that would appear to date from before Mozart's death, and of the advertisements of Rellstab and Westphal,[151] we may lay to rest the myth that the last three symphonies remained unperformed during his lifetime. The very idea that Mozart would have written three such works, unprecedented in length and complexity, only to please himself or because he was inspired, flies in the face of his known attitudes to music and life, and the financial straits in which he then found himself. He did not compose because he was inspired (although that may be why he composed well). While he may often have found great personal pleasure in composing (it was probably not merely to please his father that he called composing 'my sole delight and passion' and 'my beloved task'[152]), he composed to pay his rent and to be a useful member of society, providing needed small-scale music for domestic purposes and large-scale music for public places. Nothing seemed to inspire him more than a prestigious commission to which he could turn his formidable musical imagination. When commissions or performance opportunities vanished, he did not hesitate to put aside the fully inspired torsos of works that had suddenly become 'useless'. His symphonies were not art for art's sake, but music for use.

[150] Deutsch, 344–5 (= 392–3). For a day-by-day chronicle of Viennese concerts, see M. S. Morrow, 'Concert Life in Vienna 1780–1810'. It must always be remembered that symphonies were the least likely aspect of public concerts to have been identified, and that private concerts usually escaped notice entirely.

[151] The location of sets of parts, which may date from Mozart's lifetime, include, for K. 543: Mozarteum, Salzburg (D. 61); Göttweig Monastery (W. A. Mozart 158); Oettingen-Wallerstein Library, Harburg über Donauwörth (Kat. III 4 1/2 Nr. 963 2°); Conservatorio Luigi Cherubini, Florence (Fondo Pitti); Kremsmünster Monastery (H. 16/81); National Museum, Prague (Archiv Lobkovic, X. G. d. 33); the Moravské Museum, Brno (A 16831); National Széchényi Library, Budapest (Mus. Ms. IV 553)—for K. 550: the Mozarteum (D. 60); the National Museum, Prague (Archiv Lobkovic, X. G. d. 30); Conservatorio Luigi Cherubini, Florence (Fondo Pitti); Melk Monastery (IV 101)—for K. 551: the Mozarteum (D. 61); Oettingen-Wallerstein Library, Harburg über Donauwörth (Kat. III 4 1/2 Nr. 1077 2°); National Széchényi Library, Budapest (Mus. Ms. IV 555). See *NMA*, iv/11/9, Critical Report (H. C. Robbins Landon).

[152] Letters of 11 Oct. 1777 and 10 Feb. 1784. *Briefe*, ii. 46, iii. 301; *Letters*, i. 446; iii. 1292 (= i. 305; ii. 867).

Symphony in E flat major, K. 543

[Incipits 11.7]

Instrumentation: *strings, 1 flute, 2 clarinets, 2 bassoons, 2 horns, 2 trumpets, kettledrums, [continuo]

Autograph: Jagiellońska Library, Kraków

Principal source: none

Facsimile: Schiedermair, plate 56; *NMA*, iv/11/9. [xiii]

Editions: *GA*, xxii. 137–80 (= Serie 3, No. 39); *NMA*, iv/11/9. 1–62

The Symphony in E flat, K. 543, dated 26 June 1788 in Mozart's catalogue, is the least studied of the final trilogy. Compared to the extensive critical and analytical literature devoted to K. 550 and 551 (see below), that for K. 543 is modest.[153] As this symphony exhibits no lack of workmanlike construction or sublime inspiration, its relative neglect is a puzzle. Could this be because it has neither the proto-Romanticism of the G minor symphony nor the nickname and extraordinary Finale of the 'Jupiter'? Could it be that the kinds of ideas Mozart chose to explore in this work survive the translation from the lean, transparent sounds of eighteenth-century instruments to the powerful, opaque sounds of modern instruments less well than the more muscular ideas of the G minor and 'Jupiter' symphonies—that the flat key, which creates a somewhat muted string sound compared to the brilliance of C (K. 425, 551) or D major (K. 297, 385, 504), makes less of an impression in large modern halls on twentieth-century instruments than it did in small halls with the instruments of the period? It is also Mozart's only late symphony, and one of his relatively few orchestral works in any genre, without a pair of oboes, which imparts to it a particular timbre.

In 1806, in what appears to be the work's earliest critique, K. 543 was described as 'Mozart's splendid symphony' which is 'well enough known to permit the assumption that the reader knows it by heart . . .'. This remark was part of an essay in which the writer first discussed Grétry's notion that Haydn's symphonies had such 'fixed' character that one could put words to them,[154] and then went on to provide a text for K. 543, in the form of eleven columns of verse—'an attempt', he wrote, 'to imitate its character in words.'[155] Thus the thorny question of the 'meaning' of purely instrumental music (discussed near the end of Chapter 6 in connection with K. 100 = 62a) continued to rear its head, and this at the very time when E. T. A. Hoffmann and other writers were beginning to suggest that instrumental music's lack of words, far from devaluing it, gave it powers of expression beyond what could be conveyed by the specificity of words.[156] The essay of 1806 attempted to salvage the old theory by choosing a text in which a

[153] Notices devoted to K. 543 appear in every Mozart biography, in every collection of symphonic programme notes, in each of the books devoted to Mozart's symphonies by Saint-Foix, Mila, Della Croce, Dearling, and Sadie, and in the symphony chapters by Landon and Larsen (see bibliography). Other published analyses and programme notes include: C. Witting, *Mozarts Symphonie in Es dur* (Leipzig, 1897); H. Schenker (fragmentary analyses of movements 1, 2, and 4 in several publications, for which see L. Laskowski, *Heinrich Schenker: An Annotated Index to His Analyses of Musical Works* (New York, 1978), 135–6); H. Antcliffe, 'Mozart's Three Great Symphonies', *Musical Opinion* (1902–3), xxvi. 207–8, 447–8, 603–4; A. E. F. Dickinson, *A Study of Mozart's Last Three Symphonies* (Oxford, 1927; 2nd edn. 1940), 15–24; D. Tovey, *Essays in Musical Analysis* (London, 1935), i. 187–91; W. Reich, 'Mozarts Durchführungsharmonik', *Die Musik* (1931–2), xxiv. 26–30; E. Newman, 'Mozart and Two Symphonies', in *More Essays from the World of Music* (London, 1958), 89–93; W. Wolff, *Mozart's Three Last Symphonies* (Madras, 1956); C. Floros, 'Mozarts letzte Sinfonien', *Mozart, Klassik für die Gegenwart* (Oldenburg, 1978).

[154] A. M. E. Grétry, *Mémoires, ou Essais sur la musique* (Paris, an V, repr. New York, 1971), i. 348.

[155] A. Apel, 'Musik und Poesie', *Allgemeine musikalische Zeitung* (1806), viii. cols. 449–57, 465–70.

[156] E. T. A. Hoffmann, 'Beethoven's Instrumental Music' in O. Strunk (ed.), *Source Readings in Music History* (New York, 1950), 775–81.

single affect per movement was replaced by an evolving series of feelings and images.

The suggestion that K. 543 was modelled on Michael Haydn's E flat major symphony, Perger No. 17, has already been mentioned.[157] More likely is the general influence of the symphonies of brother Joseph, perhaps most noticeable in the stately slow introduction to the first movement, the serene Andante con moto, and the monothematic, *perpetuo moto* Finale. Mozart's introduction is an amalgam of noble dotted rhythms, descended from the openings of French ouvertures, with an insinuating chromaticism, which in fact pervades all movements of the symphony. The introduction rises majestically from the tonic stepwise to the dominant in eight bars and then ornaments the latter for seventeen bars, creating a rising sense of expectancy. Surprisingly few of Mozart's symphonies besides this one have slow introductions: among the earlier works only three drawn from serenades (K. 203, 250, 320) and from the later works the 'Linz' and 'Prague' symphonies, along with the introduction Mozart provided for Michael Haydn's symphony (K. 425a).[158]

The opening of the Allegro is an interesting case of strong ideas presented in a deceptively understated way. Beginning with a thin, imitative texture, piano, the exposition works itself into an agitated state, with such momentum that much of it sounds developmental in character, and when the dominant is reached, the calmer 'second group' of ideas sounds more like a transition to the closing section than a stable presentation of contrasting material. The development section gives an idea from the 'second group' another chance to assert itself, but this is soon driven out by some of the agitated motives which, after an abrupt general pause, seem to evaporate mysteriously, making way for the quiet beginning of the recapitulation.

The Andante con moto presents its main subject in binary form with both sections repeated, leading to a stormy section, which, together with the opening subject, recurs frequently, the development of the two accounting for virtually the entire movement. This economy of means was commented upon by an early reviewer, who singled out the tune of the first bar and a half as 'an in itself insignificant theme admirably developed in an artful and agreeable manner.'[159]

The courtly Minuet is set off by a Trio that is not merely in the style of a Ländler, like several of Mozart's earlier trios, but is based on an actual Ländler tune, given out by a pair of clarinets, which were favourite Alpine village instruments.[160] Thus the rusticism of Mozart's earlier trios remains in this late trio, if in a suaver guise.

[157] See n. 93 above.

[158] Further see M. Danckwardt, *Die langsame Einleitung: Ihre Herkunft und ihr Bau bei Haydn und Mozart* (Münchner Veröffentlichungen zur Musikgeschichte, xxv) (Tutzing, 1977).

[159] G. L. P. Sievers, 'Pariser musikalischer Allerley, von Monate März 1820', *Allgemeine musikalische Zeitung* (1820), xxii, col. 419.

[160] R. Münster, 'Zur Mozart-Pflege im münchener Konzertleben bis 1800', *Mozart-Jahrbuch* (1978–9), 159–63, here 160–1.

The perpetual motion of Mozart's monothematic Finale exhibits the kind of good humour for which Joseph Haydn's finales are known and loved, in this case resembling in its hurtling high spirits the Finale of Haydn's 88th symphony, composed about 1787. There is something profoundly comical about the juxtaposition of the trivial *contredanse* tunes on which these movements are based with the intense thematic and harmonic manipulations to which those tunes are subjected in the working out of the form. The aura of elevated irony thus created is sometimes lost in too pious performances, which may attempt to minimize the movements' pervasive humour by smoothing over the rough edges and unexpected turns of direction.

Symphony in G minor, K. 550

[Incipits 11.8]

(299)

(123)

(42)

(42)

Instrumentation: *strings, 1 flute, 2 oboes, 2 bassoons, 2 horns, [continuo] (first version); the same plus 2 clarinets with the oboes rewritten (second version)
Autograph: Gesellschaft der Musikfreunde, Vienna
Principal source: none
Facsimile: several pages in various publications (see K^6, p. 623)
Editions: *GA*, xxii. 181–229 (= Serie 8, No. 40); London: Eulenburg, 1930 (ed. T. Kroyer); *NMA*, iv/11/9. 63–124 (first version), 125–86 (second version); Budapest: Editio musica, 1980 (ed. G. Darvas)

The G minor symphony, K. 550, dated 25 July 1788 in Mozart's catalogue (and also on the autograph although probably not in his hand), is occasionally called 'the Great', perhaps to distinguish it from the 'Little' G minor symphony, K. 183 = 173dA, perhaps to indicate its stature. As early as 1793 Traeg felt justified in advertising this symphony as 'one of the last and most beautiful of this master' (Table 11.1). The work's intensity, unconventionality, chromaticism, thematic working-out, abundance of ideas, and ambiguity—all of these brought it close to the hearts of early nineteenth-century musicians and critics, who praised its richness of detail and called it 'romantic' (meaning—apparently—'modern' and 'good').[161] Not that there was agreement about its 'meaning', for some found it filled with 'the agitation of passion, the desires and regrets of an unhappy love'[162] while others attributed to it 'Grecian lightness and grace'.[163] Further discussion of what an extraordinary symphony like K. 550 may have meant to Mozart and his contemporaries is found in Chapter 13.

Whatever it may have been thought to mean, the work was widely known, performed, and imitated. By beginning the first allegro of a symphony with a quiet, cantabile utterance, as in K. 543 and 550, Mozart had ignored contemporary symphonic norms. The opening of K. 550 in particular, piano, with no *premier coup d'archet* but merely an accompaniment waiting for a tune to accompany, reverberated through the nineteenth century, and can be heard at the beginnings of Beethoven's Ninth Symphony, Schubert's A minor string quartet, Mendelssohn's violin concerto, and more than one Bruckner symphony.[164]

Even earlier, Joseph Haydn quoted from K. 550's E flat major slow movement in his oratorio *Die Jahreszeiten* in the E flat major aria, No. 38 ('Erblicke hier,

---

[161] A summary of the earliest critical reactions to K. 550 is given in Saint-Foix, 196–210 (= 141–51).
[162] A. Oulibicheff, *Nouvelle biographie de Mozart* (Moscow, 1843), 255.
[163] R. Schumann, *Gesammelte Schriften über Musik und Musiker* (Leipzig, 1854), i. 105.
[164] Floros, 'Mozarts letzte Sinfonien', 80–4.

bethörter Mensch'), where winter is compared to old age.[165] The quotation occurs following the words 'exhausted is the summer's strength' (Example 11.5), by which Haydn perhaps offered simultaneously a gloss on Mozart's music, a commemoration of the loss of his admired younger colleague, and a commentary upon the approaching end of his own career. Schubert took note also of the Minuet of K. 550, using it—in a general way—as a model for the G minor Minuet of his Fifth Symphony; Schubert's copy of the beginning of Mozart's Minuet survives.[166]

No symphony of Mozart's, not even the 'Jupiter', has aroused so much comment as this one. A vast body of criticism and analysis has been published in several languages, to say nothing of thousands of pages of programme notes. This is perhaps to be expected of a work in the regular repertory of most conductors and orchestras and widely disseminated in recordings, but the intensity of the interest in K. 550 is even greater than that in many other works which likewise belong to the regular repertory. In addition to being a pillar of the repertory and one of the most flawless exemplars of the classical style, the G minor symphony is a key work in understanding the link between musical classicism and musical romanticism, and perhaps even a mournful hint at what Mozart might have composed had he lived a normal lifespan.

Some of the more important contributions to the literature of programme notes, analysis, and criticism about K. 550 may be listed here for those who wish to pursue them.[167] It is beyond the scope of the present study to enter the critical debates and

---

[165] H. C. Robbins Landon, *Haydn: The Late Years 1801–1809* (Haydn: Chronicle and Works, v.) (Bloomington and London, 1977), 127, 144, 180–1.

[166] O. E. Deutsch, *Franz Schubert: Thematisches Verzeichnis seiner Werke in chronologischer Folge*, new edn. by the editors of the Neue Schubert-Ausgabe and W. Aderhold (Kassel, 1978), 662.

[167] Notices devoted to K. 550 appear in every Mozart biography, in every collection of symphonic programme notes, in each of the books devoted to Mozart's symphonies by Saint-Foix, Mila, Della Croce, Dearling, and Sadie, and in the symphony chapters by Landon and Larsen (see bibliography). Other published analyses include: A. Conradi, 'Das Andante in Mozart's G-moll-Symphonie', *Neue Berliner Musikzeitung* (1854), viii. 332 ff.; A. Gluck, *W. A. Mozart, G moll Symphonie aus dem Jahre 1788 erläutert* (Frankfurt, 1894); H. Schenker (for an analysis of the whole symphony in *Das Meisterwerk in der Musik* (Munich, 1926), ii. 105–57, and partial analyses of movements 1, 2, and 4 in several publications, see Laskowski, *Heinrich Schenker: An Annotated Index to His Analyses of Musical Works*, 136); Antcliffe, 'Mozart's Three Great Symphonies'; Reich, 'Mozarts Durchführungsharmonik'; Dickinson, *A Study of Mozart's Last Three Symphonies*, 15–24; A.-E. Cherbuliez, 'Stilkritischer Vergleich von Mozarts beiden g-moll-Sinfonien von 1773 und 1788', in *Bericht über die musikwissenschaftliche Tagung der Internationalen Stiftung Mozarteum in Salzburg, August 1931* (Leipzig, 1932), 112–19; A. Heuss, 'Die kleine Sekunde in Mozarts g-moll-Sinfonie', *Jahrbuch der Musikbibliothek Peters* (1934), 54–66; H. H. Wetzler, 'Über die g-moll-Symphonie von Mozart', *Wege zur Musik* (Leipzig, 1938); Tovey, *Essays in Musical Analysis*, i. 191–5; S. Newman, 'Mozart's G minor Quintet (K. 516) and its Relationship to the G minor Symphony (K. 550)', *The Music Review* (1956), xvii. 287–303; E. Newman, 'Mozart and Two Symphonies' 89–93; Wolff, *Mozart's Three Last Symphonies*; H. Grüss, 'Zur Analyse der Sinfonien g-Moll (KV 550) und C-dur (KV 551) von Wolfgang Amadeus Mozart', in *Festschrift Heinrich Besseler zum sechzigsten Geburtstag* (Leipzig, 1961), 367–75; N. Broder (ed.), *Wolfgang Amadeus Mozart, Symphony in G minor, K. 550: The Score of the New Mozart Edition, Historical Note, Analysis, Views, and Comments* (New York, 1967); S. Kunze, *Wolfgang Amadeus Mozart, Sinfonie g-moll, KV 550* (Meisterwerke der Musik, Werkmonographien zur Musikgeschichte, vi) (Munich, 1968); F. J. Smith, 'Mozart Revisited, K. 550. The Problem of the Survival of Baroque Figures in the Classical Era', *The Music Review* (1970), xxxi. 201–14; L. Ferenc, ' "Atonális sziget" Mozart g-moll szimfóniájában' [An 'atonal island' in Mozart's G-minor Symphony], *Magyar Zene* (1977), xviii. 402–5; Floros, 'Mozarts letzte Sinfonien'; M. Wagner, *Wolfgang Amadeus Mozart: Sinfonie g-Moll, KV 550: Taschen-Partitur, Einführung und Analyse* (Mainz, 1981); E. Wen, 'A Disguised Reminiscence in the First Movement of Mozart's G minor Symphony', *Music Analysis* (1982), i. 55–71. For a critique of some widely distributed editions of K. 550, see N. Del Mar, 'Confusion and Error', *The Score* (1958), i. 28–39.

Ex. 11.5 Joseph Haydn: 'Erblicke hier' from *Die Jahreszeiten*, bars 14–20

analytical disagreements embodied in that literature; the goal here is rather to present what can be known about the context, performance practice, and reception of Mozart's symphonies. In the case of the final three symphonies, the contextual investigation presented earlier in this chapter shows that, contrary to popular legend, these works were written with concrete uses in mind and performed by Mozart (and by others) during his lifetime. Matters of performance practice are dealt with at length in Chapter 12, while reception is the subject of the final chapter.

A word is in order about Mozart's reorchestration of two passages in the Andante (bars 29–32 and 100–3), for the version of K. 550 without clarinets. These revisions are on a single sheet of paper bound with the autograph manuscripts of both versions of K. 550 in a volume once owned by Johannes Brahms. The corrigenda sheet is of the same type of paper on which the rest of the symphony was written, a type employed by Mozart from about December 1787 to February 1789.[168] Even though these alternative passages, which may have resulted from Mozart's having heard the work and discovered an aspect needing improvement, represent his final thoughts on the version of the Andante without clarinets, they are missing from most editions of the symphony, and they have been relegated to an appendix in the *NMA* but omitted from the miniature scores derived from the *NMA*.[169] In some early editions of K. 550, the substitute passages were mistaken for insertions, and they appeared seriatim with the passages they were intended to replace; Robert Schumann was apparently the first to point out this redundancy.[170]

Symphony in C major, K. 551, 'Jupiter'

[Incipits 11.9]

---

[168] Information kindly provided by Alan Tyson.
[169] Ed. N. Broder (see n. 167 above); ed. R. Woodham (London: Eulenberg, 1983). N. Del Mar, *Orchestral Variations*, 154–61.
[170] Schumann, *Gesammelte Schriften*, iv. 59–67, here 62.

Instrumentation: *strings, 1 flute, 2 oboes, 2 bassoons, 2 horns, 2 trumpets, kettledrums, [continuo]

Autograph: Deutsche Staatsbibliothek, East Berlin

Principal source: none

Facsimile: entire symphony, Vienna, 1923 (ed. W. Altmann) and Kassel, 1978 (ed. H. H. Köhler); isolated pages, *NMA*, iv/11/9. [xvii–xviii]

Editions: *GA*, xxii. 230–85 (= Serie, 8, No. 41); London: Eulenburg, 1930 (ed. T. Kroyer); *NMA*, iv/11/9. 187–266; Budapest: Editio musica, 1980 (ed. G. Darvas)

In German-speaking countries during the first half of the nineteenth century, K. 551 was known as 'the symphony with the fugal finale' or 'the symphony with the fugue at the end'. The nickname 'Jupiter' originated in Britain. Mozart's son Franz Xaver (W. A. Mozart fils), told Vincent and Mary Novello that the sobriquet was coined by Haydn's sponsor in London, the violinist and orchestra leader Johann Peter Salomon.[171] Certainly, the earliest manifestations of the title were British: the first appearance of the 'Jupiter' subtitle on concert programmes, which occurred in Edinburgh on 20 October 1819, followed by its use in a London Philharmonic Society concert of 26 March 1821; and the earliest edition to bear the subtitle, a piano arrangement of the work made by Muzio Clementi and published in

---

[171] N. M. di Marignano (ed.), *A Mozart Pilgrimage, Being the Travel Diaries of Vincent & Mary Novello in the Year 1829* (London, 1955), 99.

London in 1823 (Plate XIV).[172] The 'Jupiter' designation perhaps arose from the pomp of the opening of the first movement, with its military use of trumpets and kettledrums and stately dotted rhythms—rhythms calculated to evoke images of nobility and godliness in the eighteenth-century mind.[173]

The Andante cantabile, with its muted violins and subdominant key, turns 180 degrees away from the Olympian realms of the first movement toward a darker region. The Minuet and Trio hide beneath their politely galant exteriors a host of contrapuntal and motivic artifices, which lend the pair exceptional unity. And the famous Finale? It is in sonata form with both repeats and a coda in which one of the miracles of Western music occurs: a fugato in which five of the principal melodic motives of the movement are brought together in many combinations and permutations in invertible counterpoint, in a way that has everything to do with the summation and conclusion of a dynamic symphonic movement and nothing at all to do with school lessons in counterpoint. Joseph Haydn, perhaps one of the few contemporaries of Mozart's able fully to comprehend him during his lifetime, paid this work the ultimate compliment of quoting from its slow movement in the slow movement of his Symphony No. 98, and of modelling the Finale of his Symphony No. 95 on this one.[174]

This work—Mozart's last symphony—which has been written about nearly as much as the G minor symphony, K. 550,[175] is discussed further in Chapter 13.

[172] A. Hyatt King, 'The Origin of the Title "The 'Jupiter' Symphony"', *Mozart in Retrospect: Studies in Criticism and Bibliography*, rev. edn. (Oxford, 1970), xiii, 264. The Novellos' report would appear to be confirmed by an anonymous review of Clementi's edition stating, 'This splendid symphony derives the name of *Jupiter*, now first publicly given to it upon any thing like an authority, from a very distinguished orchestral performer, who, unpremeditatedly, in conversation remarked, that such a title would well denote its majestic grandeur. We record this little anecdote for the purpose of saving Mozart from any future charge of vanity that might be advanced, should it ever be supposed that he himself gave so high-sounding an appellation to one of his own works' (*The Harmonicon* (1823), i. 83).

Strangely, an early review of K. 550 likened it to 'a Jupiter from the chisel of a Phidias' (*Allgemeine musikalische Zeitung* (1804), vi, col. 777).

[173] U. Kirkendale, 'The King of Heaven and the King of France: History of a Musical *Topos*', unpubl. paper. See *Abstracts of Papers Read at the Thirty-fifth Annual Meetings of the American Musicological Society, Saint Louis, Missouri, December 27–29, 1967*, 27–8.

[174] H. C. Robbins Landon, *Haydn: Chronicle and Works*, iii. 517–18, 533.

[175] Notices devoted to K. 551 appear in every Mozart biography, in every collection of symphonic programme notes, in each of the books devoted to Mozart's symphonies by Saint-Foix, Mila, Della Croce, Dearling, and Sadie, and in the symphony chapters by Landon and Larsen (see bibliography). Other published analyses include: H. Schenker (see Lakowski, *Heinrich Schenker: An Annotated Index to His Analyses of Musical Works*, 137); Antcliffe, 'Mozart's Three Great Symphonies'; Reich, 'Mozarts Durchführungsharmonik'; Dickinson, *A Study of Mozart's Last Three Symphonies*, 37–51; Wolff, *Mozart's Three Last Symphonies*; Floros, 'Mozarts letze Sinfonien'; A. D. Oulibicheff, 'The "Jupiter Symphony" of Mozart', *Dwight's Journal of Music* (1867), xxvii. 121–2; A Pochhammer, 'W. A. Mozarts Symphonie in C dur', *Die beliebtesten Symphonien und symphonischen Dichtungen des Konzertsaales* (Frankfurt, 1896), 111–36; E Lewicki, 'Aus der Entstehungszeit der grossen Symphonien W. A. Mozarts', *Die Musik* (1914–15), i. 40–3; H. Sitte, 'Zu Mozarts Lieblingsmotiv', *Mitteilungen für die Mozart-Gemeinde in Berlin* (1920–1), xxxix. 10–13; R. Fellinger, 'Zu Mozarts "Lieblingsmotiv"', *Mitteilungen für die Mozart-Gemeinde* (1920–1), xxxix. 18–19; K. Malsch, 'Zu Mozarts "Lieblingmotiv"', *Mitteilungen für die Mozart-Gemeinde* (1920–1), xxxix. 30–1; S. Sechter, *Das Finale von W. A. Mozarts Jupiter-Symphonie* (Vienna, 1923); B. Paumgartner, 'Zu Mozarts letzter C-Dur-Symphonie (KV 551)', *Konzertblatt der Gesellschaft der Musikfreunde Wien* (1946), i/5. 3–8; H. Rutters, 'Mozarts Levensmotief', *Mens en Melodie* (1950), v. 206–10; I. M. Bruce, 'An Act of Homage?', *Music Review* (1950), xi. 277–83; J. N. David, *Die Jupiter-Symphonie: Eine Studie über die thematisch-melodischen Zusammenhänge* (Göttingen, 1953); G. Sievers,

Maurerische Trauermusik in C minor, K. 477 = 479a

[Incipits 11.10]

(69)

Instrumentation: *strings, 2 oboes, 1 clarinet, 1 basset horn, 2 bassoons, 2 horns, [continuo?], male choir (first version); the same minus the choir (second version); the same minus the choir plus 2 basset horns and 1 contrabassoon (third version)
Autograph: Staatsbibliothek Preussischer Kulturbesitz, West Berlin (Mus. Ms. Autogr. W. A. Mozart 477)
Principal source: none
Facsimile: several single-page facsimiles (see K^6, p. 520); *NMA*, iv/11/10. xii–xiii
Editions: *GA*, xxv. 53–7 (= Serie 10, No. 12); *NMA*, iv/11/10. 11–22; Wiesbaden: Breitkopf & Härtel, 1985 (ed. P. A. Autexier)

Entered in his catalogue of his works as 'Jully [1785]', Mozart's remarkable Masonic Funeral Music is not part of a symphony, but is prophetically 'symphonic' in character. Beethoven would first realize the potential of the funeral march as a slow movement in his third and seventh symphonies, and the genre would then be taken into chamber music (Schumann), lieder (Schubert), sonatas (Chopin), and more symphonies (Mahler among others). Mozart's funeral piece is exceptional in its use of auxiliary sizes of the clarinet and bassoon, of dynamic swells, and of a cantus firmus, which gives the work a programmatic aspect.

Until recently the cantus firmus (presented in an unmistakable manner in long notes by two oboes and a clarinet, not unlike the way in which the two armed men in *Die Zauberflöte* render their borrowed hymn tune in octaves) was unidentified, but a discovery has revealed not only the identity of tune and text but the fact that it was sung. This explains the differences in instrumentation between what Mozart recorded in the catalogue of his works and what is in the score (which itself has two layers). In creating a second, purely orchestral version, Mozart must have decided

'Analyse des Finale aus Mozarts Jupiter-Symphonie', *Die Musikforschung* (1954), iii. 318–31; R. Steglich, 'Interpretationsprobleme der Jupitersinfonie', *Mozart-Jahrbuch* (1954), 102–12; H. Federhofer, 'Zur Einheit von Stimmführung und Harmonik in Instrumentalwerken Mozarts', *Mozart-Jahrbuch* (1956), 75–87; Grüss, 'Zur Analyse der Sinfonie g-moll (KV 550) und C-dur (KV 551)'; M. Flothuis, 'Jupiter oder Sarastro?', *Mozart-Jahrbuch* (1965–6), 121–32; T. C. David, 'Zu J. N. Davids Studien über die Jupitersinfonie', *Mozartgemeinde Wien 1913–1963: Forscher und Interpreten* (Vienna, 1964), 236–40; as well as the articles by Subotnik, Wollenberg, Derr, Klenz, and Ratner cited in ch. 13.

that the loss of the men's voices created a problem, so he compensated by adding two basset horns and a contrabassoon for his third version. A reconstruction of the orginal, vocal version has recently been published as *Meistermusik für Männerchor und Orchester*. The *Meistermusik* was composed for the induction of a new member to the Masonic Lodge *Zur wahre Eintracht* on 12 August 1785, presumably with the Lodge members (or, possibly, merely a select group of them?) singing along with the orchestra. Some weeks later the piece was reused without voices for a memorial service on 17 November in the Masonic Lodge 'Zur gekrönten Hoffnung' for the deceased Lodge brothers, Duke Georg August von Mecklenburg-Strelitz and Prince Franz Esterhazy, now as the Masonic Funeral Music. Finally, with the three added low reed parts, it was performed again, probably on 9 December.

The cantus firmus is based on the psalm tone (discussed in Chapter 4) for the singing of the Miserere and the Lamentations of Jeremiah during Holy Week. Philippe A. Autexier, in an analysis of the piece and of Masonic practices, infers that, as Mozart presents the cantus firmus, none of the Miserere text and only two of the many verses of the Lamentations can fit it. These verses read:

> Replevit me amaritudinibus, inebriavit me absynthio . . .
> Inundaverunt aquae super caput meum: dixi Perii.
>
> [He hath filled me with bitterness, he hath made me drunken with wormwood . . .
> Waters flowed over mine head; then I said, I am cut off.]

Autexier, to whom all of these new discoveries about the Master Music = Masonic Funeral Music are due, suggests that the first of these verses alludes to the Masonic trial by earth, the second to the trial by water.[176]

After Mozart died on 5 December 1791 his Masonic brothers did not forget the musical favours he had done for them. On 25 January 1792 'to assist his distressed widow and orphans' they announced the publication by subscription of Mozart's *Kleine Freimaurer-Kantate*, K. 623, written and performed by Mozart at the New-Crowned Hope Lodge the previous November. On 20 April the Lodge distributed a circular letter to its members on the subject of Mozart's death, and soon thereafter read at one of their meetings and had published a 'Masonic Oration on Mozart's Death'.[177]

---

[176] P. A. Autexier, *Mozart & Liszt sub Rosa* (Poitiers, 1984), 11–46; idem (ed.), *Wolfgang Amadeus Mozart: Meistermusik für Männerchor und Orchester . . . KV 477 (479a)* (Wiesbaden, 1985); idem, 'Wann wurde die Maurerische Trauermusik uraufgeführt?', *Mozart-Jahrbuch* (1984–5), 6–8.

[177] Deutsch, 385, 392–5 (= 440, 447–51).

12

Performance Practice

———— ❧ ————

It has been argued that, as modern listeners can never hear with eighteenth-century ears, attempts at historical reconstruction (or so-called 'authentic' performance) are preordained to failure. This argument maintains that, even if we could fully re-create eighteenth-century sounds, their effect on us would not be what it was on listeners two hundred years ago. Hence 'authentic' performance, if sought at all, ought to be concerned with modern sounds that have an effect on us analogous to the effect which the eighteenth-century sounds had upon eighteenth-century listeners. But even though this argument is based on a sound premiss, it reaches questionable conclusions. A brief discussion of this vexed topic may therefore usefully serve as preface to an examination of the orchestral practices of Mozart's time. For convenience of reference the approach to performance often taken by 'early music' specialists shall be here called 'neo-classical', and the approach generally offered by internationally famous soloists, orchestras, and opera houses, 'post-romantic'.[1]

One reason for rejecting the 'post-romantic' point of view is its circularity. If we are to try to create an aesthetic experience of an eighteenth-century symphony analogous to the eighteenth-century's, we must first enquire what their experience may have been. We cannot gain that knowledge without a clear understanding of the conditions of performance that were taken for granted then by the ablest musicians and most sophisticated audiences. Those conditions reveal themselves only incompletely through library research and ratiocination, for certain crucial aspects are likely to remain hidden until attempts are made to re-create those conditions in order to learn their implications. From this it could be—and has been—argued, 'Very well then, let us run private "laboratory" performances in conjunction with research seminars and learned conferences, in order to hear the implications of eighteenth-century performance conditions, which may then be used to inform "regular" performers what it is which they should be striving for.'

---

[1] 'Post-romantic' is my own coinage; 'neo-classical' was suggested by Jaap Schröder.

This suggestion has merit and, indeed, the performance of eighteenth-century music by major orchestras, opera companies, and distinguished soloists has sometimes been influenced in recent years by just such a trickling-down of information and opinions about historical performance traditions. But there are problems with the 'laboratory' approach, among them that specialist performances, isolated from the refining influence of frequent public audition and critical response, will not arrive at a technical and artistic level high enough, nor a body of experience large enough, to reveal the musical fine points that we most need to know; and the very isolation of such performances will render them 'inauthentic'. However conscientiously we transfer ideas learned from historical research and old instruments to modern instruments, the results will always be incomplete and hybridized, for just as older instruments cannot do certain things that modern ones can, modern ones cannot do certain things that older ones can. Hence skilled, knowing 'post-romantic' performers can offer us experiences analogous to those of eighteenth-century performances only by altering the details of the music from what historical research suggests they must have been. Put another way, Bach–Busoni or Bach–Stokowski or Bach–Swingle Singers or Switched–On Bach may make more sense than failed attempts to play or sing 'authentically' with neo-romantic training, equipment, and circumstances, and may prove satisfactory artistically, even while not necessarily bringing us closer to the lost musical thought of a former age.

Yet is there not circular reasoning in the 'neo-classical' procedures as well? Since we have no time machine, how can we know that we are getting things 'right'? Leaving aside the problematic nature of the idea that there is (or ever was) such a thing as 'right', the answer is that we can never get it 'right', but we can arrive at ever closer approximations. This method of working is well known in mathematics and physics as an iterative solution, in which, in a problem for which no definitive answer is possible, a series of constantly refined approximations eventually yields a solution that is fully adequate to the task at hand. In the performance of early music, we too—by studying the implications of eighteenth-century performing conditions, aesthetic preferences, and the music itself, and seeing what impact each discovery in one of these may have for the others—can gradually reach a fully adequate approximation. This is not to suggest that there exists a Main Truth to be discovered, but that each age and each talented composer found temporary truths, some of which we may hope to rediscover.

An objection remains to neo-classical performances that the sounds of the old instruments, being unfamiliar, may seem exotic or quaint, which they would not have in their own time. This is a valid objection, and in fact some less scrupulous early music groups have exploited this exoticism in a way that robs their performances of any claims to 'authenticity'. Serious listeners, however, are infinitely educable. It is quite possible for Western listeners to learn to enjoy and understand, for instance, Indonesian gamelan music or African drumming. Westerners can learn to perform these musics too. The fact that we probably can never experience (or perform) them as their practitioners do does nothing to invalidate our experience artistically or intellectually, as long as we remember that the gap can be bridged only imperfectly. These are 'languages' that we can learn to 'speak' fluently, even if never fully losing our foreign accents.

Closer to home we have the well-documented case of the twentieth-century revival of the harpsichord, an instrument at first considered by the majority of accomplished musicians to be primitive and incapable of true expression. Despite these initial prejudices, the harpischord was gradually mastered and understood, and has became a great favourite. The idea that if Bach had been given a Steinway, he would have thrown away his harpsichord is risible, yet it was held by several generations of intelligent musicians, and one still hears it stated, albeit in more cautious form.[2] The process by which harpischord building was revived and refined, harpsichord technique recovered, and audiences re-educated, is now being repeated for the orchestral instruments. This chapter is both a symptom of, and (it is hoped) a further development in, that process.

Some will object that, for performances to come alive, they must be of our time, not of other times, and that it is the job of performers not merely to interpret but to reinterpret the music of previous eras. The irony of this argument is that it cuts both ways: as more and more performances of eighteenth-century music are heard on 'old' instruments and fewer and fewer on 'modern' ones, it emerges that 'neo-classical' performances are very much of our time and 'post-romantic' ones of an earlier time. Of course, no objection can be made to reinterpretation as a means of providing new aesthetic experiences, or as a means of taking musical ideas that have become old-fashioned and making them modern again. Musicians of all generations have done this, and Mozart himself engaged in the practice when he reorchestrated Handel's *Messiah, Alexander's Feast, Ode for Saint Cecilia's Day*, and *Acis and Galatea* for Baron van Swieten's Sunday musicales. We study Mozart's reorchestrations as a means of understanding Mozart and his contemporaries and their relation to Handel, not as a way getting at Handel himself; just as future music historians doubtless will study Bach arrangements as a means of understanding late nineteenth- and twentieth-century musical thought, rather than a means of studying Bach *per se*.

A historian must study original documents, or at least reliable copies. We study Roman and Greek buildings in order to sharpen our understanding of their

---

[2] See the review by N. Zaslaw of F. Neumann, *Ornamentation in Baroque and Post-Baroque Music, with Special Emphasis on J. S. Bach* (Princeton, 1978) in *Early Music* (1981), ix. 63–8.

aesthetic and ours. We study eighteenth-century neo-classical buildings to understand what the eighteenth century made of classical architecture and what our
relation to both is. We study the Mona Lisa (or the best reproduction we can find)
when we are interested in Leonardo, but we study Marcel Duchamp's version of
the Mona Lisa, with a moustache added, to understand not Leonardo but rather the
situation of French artists at a certain period in the twentieth century and what
Leonardo (or perhaps 'great art' hung in museums) had come to stand for then.
Similarly, when giving a lecture a music historian will experience great difficulties
if he must play recordings which, far from illustrating his thesis contradict it in
both detail and spirit. It would be better simply to illustrate the lecture at the piano
and let listeners imagine as best they can the effects intended, than to present sounds
masquerading as (so to speak) the real thing, which we know can have had nothing
to do with the composer's ideas. Why, to mix metaphors, should we listen to
eighteenth-century symphonies with moustaches painted on them—unless it is for
the purpose of studying the painters of the moustaches? It may be objected that our
present-day 'neo-classical' performances will themselves subsequently be regarded
as having added, if not moustaches then something else to the music of the past.
This is correct, but it is really no objection, for the matter under scrutiny is our
present-day relationship to and understanding of the music of the past, and, as such,
each generation must rewrite its music history.

At some point comparisons between the performing and fine arts—where many
artifacts survive more or less intact—must break down. We lack the musical
artifacts and have only the plans for them.[3] Yet in pointing to important differences
between the fine and performing arts, we also should not exaggerate those
differences, for good work in the history of the visual arts also involves
reconstruction, restoration, interpretation, and a lively imagination. Many old
buildings and works of art have been destroyed and survive only in pictures, plans,
or descriptions. Some buildings are partially or entirely in ruins, and none has
survived untouched by the ravages of time or renovation; some ancient marble
statues may have survived virtually undamaged, but now they are gleaming white
when once they were painted bright colours; oil paintings become dirty, oxidized,
cracked, and are restored more or less faithfully; and so on. Thus, in the historical
study of both fine and performing arts, reconstruction and speculation are
inevitable, and this, far from being a handicap, lends excitement to the endeavour
and guarantees that new interpretations will continue to emerge.

The fact that one can never *fully* re-create a historical moment is irrelevant to the
goals of 'neo-classical' performance. In attempting to re-create the past moment,

---

[3] Such 'recordings' as survive from the eighteenth-century (mechanical instruments) provide food for thought about
rhythmic alteration, ornamentation, and tempo, but they will never allow us to hear an orchestral performance of the era.

we draw gradually closer to the composer, his time, his ideas, his contemporaries' and his own assumptions. Drawing closer is itself stimulating and yields understanding that can be attained by no other means—understanding that heightens our perceptions. Paradoxically, however, the attempt at re-creation also establishes distance between us and the music, for as long as we continue reflexly to play music as we heard it and were taught to play it during our musical apprenticeships, we must remain insuffiently aware of the differences between 'our' music and 'their' music. True understanding of any matter requires both great familiarity (closeness) and great perspective (distance).

Even knowing that exact re-creation of eighteenth-century conditions is a logical impossibility, we none the less seek to remove from the works we study, as well and as accurately as we can, the dirt and oxidation acquired in the passage of time, the moustaches added by the irreverent, and the shiny patina of later tradition added by well-meaning performers.

One important lesson learned from studying eighteenth-century orchestras is that there was no 'baroque' orchestra or 'classical' orchestra, and not merely because 'baroque' and 'classical' are historians' constructs. There were no international orchestral standards, nor national ones. There were local, regional, and national traditions and preferences, some of them widespread and long-lived; but there was also constant change and experimentation. There was broad transfer of musical ideas from one region to another, resulting in local syntheses. Disagreement among musicians was great, for it was, like our own time, an era of ferment and variety. How, then, to portray such a kaleidoscopic situation?

Perhaps the revival of the harpsichord may serve again as a model for our understanding of orchestras: at first the mere act of playing a harpsichord in the twentieth century—any harpsichord, even a totally fantastic Pleyel, Neupert, or Challis—was a major artistic statement. Now we have a more finely differentiated picture of harpsichords, and can see how and why seventeenth- and eighteenth-century harpsichords or Italian, French, English, and Flemish harpsichords differed. If the current intense interest in historical harpsichords continues unabated, even finer distinctions are likely to be made. Comparable diversity was found among orchestras too, and we are probably just now emerging from the Pleyel–Neupert–Challis stage of understanding early orchestras. In an attempt to advance beyond that stage, the present chapter explores the orchestras of Mozart's time, while the following one deals with some expectations of his audiences.

When Mozart wrote an aria, he tailor-made it to exploit the strengths and circumvent the weaknesses of the singer for whom it was destined. He usually refused to compose the arias of an opera until he was familiar with its singers, and when there was a change in the cast of an opera he sometimes revised the arias in question, or substituted new ones.[4] He made related assertions about making the Andante of a piano sonata written for Rosa Cannabich, the daughter of the Mannheim concertmaster, fit her character the way a tailor fitted a suit.[5] In this he was a man of his times: a craftsman who sought to satisfy performers, audiences, and himself with well-wrought creations that would make their intended effect. It is a premiss of this study that Mozart's concern for providing the right music for each circumstance embraced his symphonies: their form and content were influenced by the strengths and weaknesses of particular ensembles and the tastes of certain patrons and audiences. Certainly no other conclusion can be reached from reading his remarks to his father about how he calculated the contents of K. 297, written for the Concert spirituel (see Chapter 9).

To solve any particular performance problem, one must investigate nested spheres of practice, drawing information from a more general level when information from a more specific level is lacking. That is to say, each symphony, the historical performance practice of which we wish to understand, must be examined as a unique work (K. 297, for instance), manifesting the preferences of a single composer (Mozart), designed for the conventions of a certain musical institution (the Concert spirituel), fitting within local (Parisian), then regional (French), then European practices.

Size and Balance

Mozart's first symphony was written in 1764, his last in 1788; in the former year Rameau died, in the latter Beethoven turned eighteen. During this quarter century significant changes in musical style and performance practice occurred. Histories of the orchestra have generally asserted that orchestras grew steadily in size during this period.[6] While this assertion sounds logical, and while there can be no disputing the fact that, studied over the long haul from Bach to Beethoven to Brahms, orchestras became larger, available data do not entirely support it for the quarter century during which Mozart composed his symphonies. The size of orchestras was apparently often the result of fluctuating economic forces; for instance, the decline of Viennese orchestras in the late 1780s followed the war and depression into which Austria was then plunged. Orchestral make-up could also be linked to the size of a theatre or hall, the generosity of patrons, local customs and preferences, political changes, and even revolution. Early in his life, for instance, Mozart wrote for

---

[4] For the tailor-making of arias, see the Mozart family's correspondence about the composition and revisions of and rehearsals for *Mitridate, rè di Ponto*, K. 87 = 74a; *Ascanio in Alba*, K. 111; *Lucio Silla*, K. 135; and *Idomeneo, rè di Creta*, K. 366. For revisions arising out of changes of cast, see the Vienna versions of *Idomeneo* and of *Don Giovanni*.

[5] Mozart's letter of 6–7 Dec. 1777. *Briefe*, ii. 170–1; *Letters*, ii. 602 (= i. 408).

[6] e.g. A Carse, *The Orchestra from Beethoven to Berlioz* (Cambridge, 1948), 18.

good-sized orchestras in Salzburg, The Hague, and Vienna, whereas near the end of his career he was involved with the tiny orchestras of Prague and Donaueschingen.

Orchestras too large were as problematic for Mozart's contemporaries as those too small. The pitfalls of enlarged orchestras were highlighted during Haydn's visits to London. The excellent ensemble at the Haydn–Salomon concerts in the years 1791–3 was mentioned in several reports;[7] the orchestra numbered about 40. When in 1795 Haydn led an orchestra of more than 60 for the Opera Concerts however, critics politely let it be known that the ensemble had been ragged,[8] and Haydn penned a related criticism in his diary, writing, 'The [London opera] orchestra is larger this year, but just as mechanical as it was before, and indiscreet in its accompaniments.'[9] Similarly, according to Rochlitz, the first attempt to perform Beethoven's Fifth Symphony at Leipzig failed because the orchestra was too large.[10] Some years earlier the principle was clearly stated by two Parisian critics quoted in Chapter 9:

Mr Legros ... knew that the number of instruments must be relative to the size of the hall and that most often one produced greater effects with a less large number of performers. Consequently, he reduced the number of performers in both the orchestra and the choir.[11]

He decreased the number of performers in the orchestra and choir, and with fewer instruments and voices he produced more of an effect.[12]

If too large orchestras suffered from poor ensemble and lack of clarity, too small orchestras mercilessly exposed the imperfections of the playing, failed to fill the hall with enough sound, and permitted winds to overbalance strings. For example, of a concert given by Mozart in Frankfurt in 1790, at which a symphony, three arias, and two piano concertos were performed, a member of the audience reported that 'the orchestra was no more than rather weak with five or six violins'.[13] Mozart had faced similar difficulties thirteen years earlier at a concert in Augsburg where the orchestra probably had no more than eight weak violinists.[14] On the other hand,

---

[7] H. C. Robbins Landon, *Haydn in England 1791–5* (Haydn: Chronicle and Works, iii) (Bloomington and London, 1976), 44 ff.

[8] Ibid. 287, 293–4.

[9] Bartha (ed.), *Haydn: Briefe*, (Kassel, 1985), 536 (= Landon (ed.), *Collected Correspondence and London Notebooks*, 293).

[10] [Johann Friedrich Rochlitz], 'Musik in Leipzig', *Allgemeine musikalische Zeitung* (12 April 1809), xi/28. cols. 433–8, 449–60, here 434–5. According to Rochlitz, the difficulties occurred in the Scherzo.

[11] *Journal de Paris* (22 Mar. 1777), 2–3; see ch. 9 at n. 31.

[12] Louis Petit de Bachaumont, *Mémoires secrets pour servir à l'histoire de la république des lettres en France depuis MDCCLXII jusqu'à nos jours, ou Journal d'un observateur rentrant chez lui* (London, 1780–9), x. 94–5; see ch. 9 at n. 34. Similarly, Charles Burney was disappointed with the performance of a Mass by Johann Karl Adam Georg von Reutter under Florian Gassman's direction, which he heard in St. Stephen's Cathedral in Vienna in 1770, because 'as there was a numerous band, great noise and little meaning characterised the whole performance' (*The Present State of Music in Germany, the Netherlands, and United Provinces* (London, 1773), i. 356–7)

[13] Deutsch, 329–30 (= 375); see ch. 11 at n. 145.

[14] *Briefe*, ii. 65–6; *Letters*, ii. 476 (= i. 326); see ch. 9 at n. 2.

perhaps the problem in Augsburg was not the number of violinists, but their lack of skill, for the only slightly larger orchestra at Cremona with ten violins Mozart thought 'good'.[15] It is a tribute to the skill of the tiny Prague orchestra that they could produce excellent results in Mozart's heavily-scored late symphonies, concertos, and operas, with only six or seven violins. Beethoven too worried about this problem as when, in October 1811, he wrote to the Archduke Rudolf requesting as the necessary minimum for a run-through of his symphonies and overtures a string section of 4—4—[2?]—2—2.[16]

Orchestras with few but competent violinists can cope with many of Mozart's early symphonies, where the obbligato wind parts are most often simply pairs of oboes (or flutes) and horns. With his mature orchestral works however, the nature of the wind writing changes and the wind section grows — a development found in many composers, even if the glory for the classic synthesis of the 1780s must go in considerable part to Mozart.[17] In interpreting contemporary reactions to this change in orchestration, it is sometimes difficult to know whether one is dealing with legitimate complaints about a failure in the growth of string sections to keep up with that of wind sections, poorly organized performances, or conservatism fighting against the emergence of a new musical style.

As early as 1765 the French writer Chastellux was struck by the German predilection for wind instruments:

The German symphonists ... [use] a great number of instruments ... [and] work them successively. Their symphonies are a species of *concerto* in which the instruments shine each in its turn, in which the instruments provoke each other and respond to each other, argue and make up. This is a lively and sustained conversation. Spanning all these contrasts however, you will always recognize (and above all in good works) a [musical] motive that serves as the basis of the entire edifice. Each part ... occupies itself with this motive in turn. One such passage is intended for the hunting horn, another such for the oboe; it is a period which is divided among all the parts of the orchestra, a canvas on which each instrument paints a small detail.[18]

---

[15] *Briefe*, i. 310; *Letters*, i. 162 (= i. 100); E. Schenk, 'Mozart in Mantua', *Studien zur Musikwissenschaft* (1955), xxii. 1–20, here 7.

[16] O. Biba, 'Beethoven und die "Liebhaber Concerte" in Wien im Winter 1807/08' in R. Klein (ed.), *Österreichische Gesellschaft für Musik, Beiträge (1976–78): Beethoven-Kolloquium 1977, Dokumentation und Aufführungspraxis* (Kassel, 1978), 82–93, here 88. On the basis of the 1807–8 concerts, for which the strings (amateurs led and filled out by professionals) were 13—12—7—6—4, Biba suggested that Beethoven's request must have referred to the minimum number of violins necessary to get an adequate idea of his music in a private run-through, and not necessarily what would have been needed for a public concert. More recently discovered documents show, however, that the première of the 'Eroica' symphony (a private performance) was by an orchestra of 24, with the strings 2—2—2— [2]—2 (R. Brinkmann, 'Kleine "Eroica"-Lese', *Österreichische Musik Zeitschrift* (1984), xxxix. 634–8).

[17] C. Wolff, 'Aspects of Instrumentation in Mozart's Orchestral Music', *Interprétation de la musique classique de Haydn à Schubert: Colloque international, Ivry, 13–15 octobre 1977* (Paris, 1980), 37–43; also nn. 18–26 below.

[18] François-Jean Chastellux, *Sur l'union de la poésie et de la musique* (The Hague and Paris, 1765), as quoted in the *Journal de musique* (Aug. 1770), i/8. 23.

There were numerous reactions to the trend described by Chastellux. A perform-ance of Mozart's *Die Entführung aus dem Serail* in 1787 in Hannover drew forth the comment that 'the composer has been too loquacious with the wind instruments. Instead of only reinforcing the melody where that is required, and supporting the harmony as a whole, they often darken the former and confuse the latter.'[19] A performance of *Don Giovanni* in Berlin in 1791 elicited similar sentiments: 'The composition of this operetta [*sic*] is beautiful, although here and there too artificial, too difficult, and too overladen with instruments.'[20] Haydn wrote in his diary in 1795 of the London première of Bianchi's opera *Aci e Galathea*: 'The music is very rich in parts for the wind instruments, and I rather think one would hear the principal melody better if it were not so richly scored.'[21] And near the end of his life Haydn is said to have remarked to his pupil Kalkbrenner of the new style of orchestration, 'I only learned to use the wind instruments in my old age, and now that I understand them, I must leave them.'[22] Niemetschek understood, or had been told of, Mozart's importance in this regard.[23]

The innovations in orchestration were differently received in various quarters. The Berlin *Musikdirektor* Wessely wrote an article calling for the greater use of wind instruments in the orchestra, in imitation of the Viennese composers Gluck, Mozart, and Salieri, on the grounds that the winds make the greatest impression because (he felt) they resemble the human voice more than the stringed instruments do and therefore touch listeners' hearts more deeply.[24] In 1799 Rochlitz gave as one reason for the necessity of a continuo instrument in the orchestra (he preferred the fortepiano to the harpsichord) that 'the parcelling-out of individual ideas in snatches to various instruments—chiefly in blind imitation of Mozart' had become the custom, and this created problems of ensemble.[25] And, in fact, Mozart's works were long considered unplayable in Italy primarily because of their wind parts.[26]

[19] Deutsch, 287 (= 328).
[20] Deutsch, *deest* (= 386); K. G. Fellerer, *Mozart-Jahrbuch* (1959), 84.
[21] Bartha (ed.), *Haydn: Briefe*, 536 (= Landon (ed.), *Collected Correspondence and London Notebooks*, 293).
[22] H. Walter, 'Kalkbrenners Lehrjahre und sein Unterricht bei Haydn', *Haydn-Studien* (1982), v. 23–41, here 38. In London Haydn's accomplishments in this regard were recognized in the following review: 'Every instrument is respected by his Muse, and he gives to each its due proportion of efficace [*sic*]. He does not elevate one, and make all the rest contributing as a mere accompaniment; but the subject is taken up by turns with masterly art, and every performer has the means of displaying his talent' (*Morning Chronicle* (19 Mar. 1793) as reported in C. F. Pohl, *Mozart und Haydn in London* (Vienna, 1867, repr. New York, 1970), ii. 122); and by Charlotte Papendiek: 'The instruments might all be said to have an obbligato part, so perfectly was the whole combination conceived and carried out' (*Court and Private Life in the Time of Queen Charlotte* (London, 1886–7), ii. 296–7).
[23] Franz Niemetschek, *Leben des K. K. Kapellmeisters Wolfgang Gottlieb Mozart* (Prague, 1798), mod. edn. by C. de Nys (Saint-Étienne, 1976), 260–1 (= *Life of Mozart*, 57–8).
[24] *Musikalische Wochenblatt* (1791), i/3. 78.
[25] 'Bruchstücke aus Briefen an einen jungen Tonsetzer, Zweyter Brief: Ueber die Abschaffung des Flügels aus den Orchestern', *Allgemeine musikalische Zeitung* (1799–1800), ii, cols. 17–19. Compare Niemetschek: '... his astonishing compositions ... [impart] to musical taste a mighty impetus and a new direction—which, however, his present imitators distort and destroy' (Deutsch, 433 [= 504]).
[26] See ch. 5, n. 4.

Of the première of Beethoven's First Symphony in 1800 a critic reported that 'a symphony was performed in which were much art, novelty, and wealth of ideas; but there was too much use of the wind instruments so that it seemed more like music for wind band than for full orchestra.'[27]

In Paris, too, as late as 1818 J.-J. Momigny was still issuing warnings about the new style of orchestration. Writing of a passage in the first movement of Haydn's Symphony in D major, Hob. I: 104, in which a flute and two oboes play alone for eight bars (bars 9–16 of the recapitulation), he observed,

It is necessary to admit that, even though Haydn wisely took all the precautions that could lessen the danger of such an undertaking, he had hardly reason to be pleased with himself at having handed over the reins of the symphony for eight bars to three wind instruments, which at very least have the inconvenience of never being perfectly in tune, even if they have the good luck to be unintimidated and to carry on with aplomb.

The warmth of the hall or a drop of water in the instrument can upset the most able artists [on these instruments], and make a blemish on the brilliant and royal robe of the symphony.

No composer is more on guard against these unfortunate accidents than the great Haydn. His wind instruments are always polished with an unequalled care. Mozart's are sometimes more haphazard, and if the tempo is even a little accelerated, then you see them lose their effectiveness.[28]

Finally, a summary of the situation from Koch's *Musikalisches Lexikon* of 1802 reports:

The use of so many wind instruments—as is customary nowadays, and which are put into all pieces, incessantly—contributes a great deal to the overloading of the accompaniment. All who have breath must now blow in every movement without discrimination. By this means the effect, which the sparing use of wind instruments formerly produced all by itself, is entirely deadened; hence the wind instruments come to be placed ever more conspicuously, if the effect is to be made; and overloading of the accompaniment then becomes an unavoidable evil.

This voluminous use of wind instruments in all compositions written for full orchestra gives rise, moreover, to a further incidental bit of foolishness which, however perceptible its result, seems seldom enough to be noticed. If the composer works for an orchestra in which there are 16 or 20 violin players and the necessary violas and basses in proportion to them, and he writes into his composition oboes, bassoons, flutes, horns, and trumpets, without doubt he calculates in so doing to what extent he can assign the harmony and melody to all these instruments without disrupting the balance between them and the principal part. If such a composition then comes before the public, it is customarily

[27] *Allgemeine musikalische Zeitung* (15 Oct. 1800), iii, col. 49.
[28] Jérôme-Joseph Momigny, 'Symphonie', *Encyclopédie méthodique: Musique* (Paris, 1790–1818), ii.

performed with all the wind instruments, even in such meagre orchestras that one needs must make use of a lorgnette in order to locate the performers of the principal parts [that is, the violins].[29]

Elsewhere Koch informs us that string sections consisting of 4—4—2—2—2 or 5—5—3—3—2 were satisfactory for church or theatre orchestras, but for symphonies, in which (Koch tells us) there are more wind instruments, it is preferable to have at least 6 first and 6 second violins.[30] Koch's advice on the size of string sections is probably sound for both 'neo-classical' and 'post-romantic' performances of Mozart's heavily-scored, later symphonies, but not necessarily for performances of the lightly-scored, earlier ones (assuming in both cases that the wind are not doubled).

All this suggests a range of possibilities within which a good result could be obtained, but beyond which problems were almost certain to arise. It is important to stress this point because misunderstandings continue to occur. On the one hand, those involved in 'neo-classical' performance—perhaps noting that Mozart sold his symphonies (including some late ones) to the court at Donaueschingen where the orchestra apparently had only one string player on a part—have sometimes proposed that one on a part is a viable and 'authentic' way of performing such works. On the other hand, those involved with 'post-romantic' performances often cite the Viennese concert of 1781, at which a symphony of Mozart's was performed by an orchestra whose strings were 20—20—10—8—10, and all the wind doubled except for the bassoons, which were tripled. Mozart reported to his father that 'the symphony went *magnifique* and had every success'. Much has been written about the possible implications of this event, suggesting that if Mozart was so very pleased, then this must have been the sort of orchestra he would have liked but usually could not muster. This argument is discussed and rejected at the beginning of the previous chapter, to which the reader is referred.[31] As for one on a part, there were sometimes such performances, especially at private concerts when concertos and arias were performed.[32] Empirical investigation, however, suggests that one on a part can create a satisfactory balance for the *colla parte* wind writing of the French ouvertures and dances of Bach, Handel, and Telemann, but not for more independently scored winds of the symphonies of J. C. Bach, Haydn, or Mozart. The reason that the musicians, patrons, and critics of Mozart's day were

---

[29] H. C. Koch, *Musikalisches Lexikon* (Frankfurt am Main, 1802), cols. 235–6. Koch's concern about inadequately manned string sections is still shared two decades later by Gottfried Weber, 'Besetzung', *Allgemeine Encyclopädie der Wissenschaften und Künste*, ed. J. S. Ersch and J. G. Gruber (Leipzig, 1822), ix. 284–5.

[30] Ibid., 'Besetzung', cols. 237–40, and 'Begleitung', cols. 232–7.

[31] See ch. 11 at nn. 10–12, and N. Zaslaw, 'Three Notes on the Early History of the Orchestra', *Historical Performance* (1988), i. 63–7.

[32] The widely scattered evidence for this assertion, much of which is iconographic, will be presented in J. Spitzer and N. Zaslaw, *The Birth of the Orchestra*, in preparation.

obsessed with orchestral balance is this: symphonies were usually performed with but a single rehearsal.[33] In the absence of baton-wielding conductors monitoring the balance of each bar in rehearsals and concerts, the only way to achieve good balance was to build it into the size, make-up, and disposition of the orchestras.

Orchestras that performed Mozart's symphonies with his consent (and often with his participation)—or else orchestras that were near in time, place, and tradition to orchestras he worked with but whose make-up can no longer be determined—are presented in Table 12.1. In the right-hand column, an attempt has been made to show the symphonies performed by given ensembles; this is a summary of more detailed information found in earlier chapters.

The personnel of 172 instances of orchestras from 1774 to 1796 — the period of the mature symphonies of Mozart and Joseph Haydn — can be represented on a graph and the relationship between strings and the rest of the orchestra evaluated by means of the statistical procedure known as linear regression (Figure 12.1).[34] This graph has the practical advantage of enabling performers to estimate an approximate number of strings needed for a piece, given its wind scoring. It also suggests some limits for normal practice of the period, which may be interpreted as follows. Since few orchestral works of this period call for more than 17 non-string parts and most call for fewer, and since (according to the formula $W = (.703)$ $(S) + 3.115$) the 'average' orchestra with 17 independent non-string parts would have had about 20 strings, many orchestras with string sections larger than 20 must have doubled their wind parts, as must most orchestras with more than about 17 non-string players. At the lower end of string strength, care is necessary to prevent winds from overpowering strings, and especially the violins; while on the upper end equal care will be required to avoid strings covering winds. With large string sections, the wind (including the horns but probably excluding the trumpets) should be doubled. The bassoons form an exception, for they may be doubled in the smaller groups and tripled in the larger ones. These general practices must be adjusted to accommodate particular acoustics, specific repertories, and performers of varying abilities.

Rehearsals, recording sessions, and concerts of the Academy of Ancient Music devoted to Mozart's symphonies seemed to confirm the lessons of Figure 12.1. Performing K. 504 with the 'Prague'-sized orchestra of $4—3—2—2—1 = 12$ was a mighty struggle to avoid having the wind overpower the strings. Performing K. 43 with the 'Viennese' strings of $7—6—4—3—3 = 23$ occasionally required

---

[33] See below at nn. 148–53.

[34] The statistics of the individual orchestras and identification of the sources from which they were drawn are found in N. Zaslaw, 'Toward the Revival of the Classical Orchestra', *Proceedings of the Royal Musical Association* (1976–7), ciii. 158–87, here 171–7, 186–7; in the supplement added to the reprint of the same article in E. Rosand (ed.), *The Garland Library of the History of Western Music* (New York, 1986), vii. 274–305; and in Tables 8.1 and 10.1 of this book.

guarding against the opposite problem, and with K. 297 and 'Parisian' strings of 11—11—5—8—5 = 40 but single wind, much more so.

Turning to balance within string sections, a broad distinction may be drawn between orchestras descended from the French court and opera practice of Lully, found outside France in some Austrian and German cities; and those descended from the Italian opera-orchestra tradition found outside Italy in England and also in some Austrian and German cities. In the former tradition, there was a preference for more strongly reinforced viola parts, whereas the latter aimed for the baroque polarization of treble and bass with a weak middle register. Many orchestras summarized by Figure 12.1 are of the latter type, and seem to modern tastes undersupplied with violas, creating problems in the many symphonies in which Mozart wrote divisi for those instruments: when there are only two violas, they will in divisi passages no longer constitute a 'section' in the usually understood sense of 'more than one on a part'. This problem does not arise with the cello and double bass, which in a small or medium-sized orchestra can function excellently one on a part, since they double each other at the octave and usually have the left hand of a keyboard instrument and a bassoon reinforcing them. Joseph Haydn is on record in 1768 as favouring one on a part in the bass-line instruments, at least in certain circumstances:

The bassoon can be omitted if absolutely necessary, but I would rather have it, especially since the bass is obbligato throughout. And I prefer a band with three bass instruments—cello, bassoon and double bass—to one with six double basses and three cellos, because [in the latter scoring] certain passages cannot be heard clearly.[35]

Haydn's remarks apparently mean that, unless one has quite a large orchestra, one cello, one double bass, one bassoon, and a continuo instrument will provide sufficient weight to balance the other instruments while offering benefits in good ensemble, definition, and timbre that outweigh any possible disadvantages.

Haydn's mention of six double basses and three cellos raises another aspect of string balance. 'Post-romantic' chamber orchestras usually have configurations of strings 5—4—3—2—1 or 6—5—4—3—2, or something of the sort. Modern orchestras whose conductors decide to halve the strings to perform eighteenth-century music may have 8—8—6—6—4. None of these is a characteristic eighteenth-century string balance. The historical evidence suggests a preference for more violins and fewer violas, and that there were sometimes more double-basses than cellos. The Salzburg orchestra had more double-basses than cellos (see Tables 1.1, 8.1, and 10.1), as did several other orchestras of Figure 12.1. Italian orchestras

---

[35] Bartha (ed.), *Haydn: Briefe*, 60 (= Landon (ed.), *Collected Correspondence and London Notebooks*, 10–11). The translation used here is Landon's as modified by James Webster.

TABLE 12.1 Mozart's orchestras

CITY: Orchestra

Date	vn. I	vn. II	va.	vc.	db.	fl.	ob.	cl.	bn.	hn.	tpt.	timp.	kbd.	misc.	TOTAL	Köchel
LONDON: Covent Garden																
1757–8	(4)	(3)	(2)	(2)	(1)	(0)	(2)	(0)	(1)	(2)	(2)	(1)	(1)	(0)	21	16, 19, 19a
1760	(4)	(3)	(1)	(1)	(1)	(0)	(2)	(0)	(1)	(2)	(2)	(1)	(1)	(0)	19	
AMSTERDAM: Schouwburg Theatre																
1768	3	3	0–2	1	1	0	2	0–2	1	2	0	1	1	0	17	16, 19, 19a, 32, 45a
*THE HAGUE: Court of Orange																
1766	6	5	4	3	2	0–2	2–4	0	2	4	(2)	1	1	0	34	
*SALZBURG: Court																
1767–77	4–6	(2)	4–6	1–2	2–4	0	2	0	2–3	2–3	(2)	(1)	(1)	3 tbn.	23–35	35, 38, 45a, 62a, 74c, 75b, 114, 124, 128, 129, 130, 132, 133, 134, 161a, 161b, 162, 162b, 167a, 173dA, 173dB, 183, 186a, 186b, 189b, 189k, 207a, 213a, 213c, 248b
VIENNA: Kärntnerthortheater																
1773–5	6	6	3	3	3	1	2	0	2	2	0	0	1	0	29	43, 45, 46a, 48, (45a)
VIENNA: Burgtheater																
1773–5	7	7	4	3	3	2	2	0	2	2	0	0	1	0	33	

													Total	Köchel
CREMONA: Municipal 1770s	5	5	2	1	3	0	2	0	0	0	1	0	21	
MANTUA: Concert 1770	3	3	2	1	2	0	2	0	2	0	2	0	18	
FLORENCE: Concert c.1780	4	4	2	1	1	0	2	0	0	(1)	1	0	19–20	73, 74a, 74c, 111a, 112, 135, 141a
*MILAN: Opera 1770	14	14	6	2	6	0–2	0–4	0	2	(1)	2	0	57	
NAPLES: Opera 1773	16	16	4	3	4	0	4	0	?	?	2	?	53+	
TURIN: Opera 1774	15	13	5	4	6	—6—		4	2	1	2	0	62	
*PARIS: Concert spirituel 1778	11	11	5	5	2	2	4	(4)	(2)	1	0	0	57	300a, (385)
*SALZBURG: Court 1779–81	6	6	2	2	4	0	5	0	3	2	(2)	(1)	34	318, 319, 320, 338, 385, (425)
*PRAGUE: Opera 1787	3	3	2	2	2	2	2	2	1	1	1	0	26	504
VIENNA: Burgtheater 1781–3	6	6	4	3	3	2	4	2	2	1	1	0	38	385, (425), (504), 543, 550, 551

* Asterisks indicate orchestras for which Mozart composed. The other orchestras are either those for which he may have composed, or those believed to be similar in size and make-up to orchestras for which he composed.

Figures in parentheses involved some speculation or extrapolation on the part of the author.

Köchel numbers in parentheses are works that Mozart wrote for another place and then reused. Only those symphonies about which no doubts exist concerning genuineness have been included here.

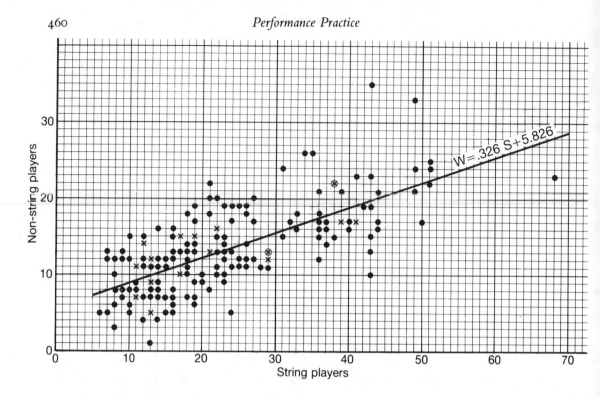

FIG. 12.1   Number of string players in relation to non-string players in 172 instances, 1774–1796

●=1 data point   x=2 data points   ⊗=3 data points

The straight line, which represents the numerical relation between strings and non-strings, is expressed by the algebraic formula $W = .326S + 5.826$, where S = string players and W = the rest of the orchestra. This equation was determined by means of the statistical procedure known as linear regression. The correlation between the number of strings and the number of non-strings is statistically highly significant, that is, there is almost no possibility that it is a chance relationship. For the data upon which this graph is based, see n. 34 above.

often had more double-basses than cellos, whereas more northerly orchestras sometimes did and sometimes did not.

The differences between modern and eighteenth-century ideas of string balance are most strikingly revealed by the bigger Italian orchestras for which Mozart composed, in which there were very many violins, strong double-bass and bassoon contingents, and surprisingly few violas and cellos. The result of the large number of double-basses is rather like that of pulling a 16′ stop on an organ, and it makes the orchestral resonance in a hall somewhat resemble that in a large church.[36] This

[36] This remark is based on my perceptions of a large Italian orchestra as replicated by the Academy of Ancient Music; the effect seems less pronounced on the recordings than it did in the hall.

was the balance favoured in Italy for much of the eighteenth century. Some musicians of the time did complain, however, about the lack of violas in Italian orchestras, among them Burney, Jomelli, Algarotti, and Galeazzi.[37]

Table 12.2 shows some 'Ideally Balanced String Sections According to Six Theorists'. (Although such writers have traditionally been called 'theorists', they were, in fact, practising performers whose publications were concerned more with applied than theoretical matters.) Petri's string section of 1782, Koch's, and Weber's have balances similar to that of string sections of modern chamber orchestras, while the string sections of Quantz, Petri/1767, Galeazzi, and Scaramelli are more dominated by violins. (This is a consideration distinct from the question of how many violins are adequate to balance a given number of wind instruments and a given style of wind orchestration.) The differences among these writers may be attributed in part to chronological developments in musical style: Quantz's, Petri's/1767, Galeazzi's, and Scaramelli's string sections were primarily intended for a *galant*, treble-dominated, homophonic repertory; Petri's (1782), Koch's, and Weber's were based on a more equal-voiced repertory. According to his own testimony, Galeazzi deliberately reinforced the violas of his ideal string section beyond what was found in most Italian orchestras. As a first approximation, something like the Quantz–Petri/1767–Galeazzi string balance should work best for many of Mozart's early symphonies, up to his 'Haffner' symphony, K. 385; whereas the Petri/1782–Koch–Weber string balances should be suitable for his last five symphonies.

The debate between partisans of the two types of string balance continued into the nineteenth century, for in 1802 a German musician, Georg von Unold, defended the Italian balance and two decades later Gottfried Weber, while still complaining about orchestras in which one could hear only first violins and bass-line instruments, offered an ideal string balance stronger on top and bottom and weaker in the middle than the recommendations of several other theorists shown in Table 12.2.[38] The fact that in 1822 he permits single winds with a string section numbering between 33 and 36, however, suggests that he is thinking in terms of newer styles of orchestration, in which there are three or four independent parts for each wind, rather than the pairs of Mozart's and Haydn's period. This may reveal the beginning of undoing the balance proper for the earlier repertory.

---

[37] Charles Burney, *Music, Men and Manners in France and Italy 1770*, ed. H. E. Poole (London, 1974), 197; U. Prota-Giurleo, *La grande orchestra del R. Teatro San Carlo nel Settecento (da documenti inediti)* (Naples, 1927), i. 20; Francesco Galeazzi, *Elementi teorico-practici di musica* (Rome, 1791–6), i. 215 n; Francesco Algarotti, *Saggio sopra l'opera in musica* (n.p., 1755), trans. in O. Strunk, *Source Readings in Music History* (New York, 1950), 657–72, here 668.

[38] Georg von Unold, 'Einige Bemerkungen über die Stellung der Orchester und Einrichtung der Musiksäle', *Allgemeine musikalische Zeitung* (1801–2), iv, cols. 782–4 note; Gottfried Weber, 'Besetzung . . .'.

TABLE 12.2 Ideally balanced string sections according to six theorists

Author	vn. I	vn. II	va.	vc.	db.	TOTAL
Quantz, *Versuch* (1752)	2	2	1	1	1	7
	3	3	1	1	1	9
	4	4	2	2	2	14
	5	5	2	3	2	17
	6	6	3	4	2	21
Petri, *Anleitung* (1767)	1–2	1–2	1	1	0–1	4–7
	5–6	4–5	2	1–2	1	13–15
Ibid. (1782)	2	1	1	[1]	[0–1]	[5–6]*
	3	2	[1–2]	2	1	[9–10]
	7	5	3	4–5	2	21–2
Galeazzi, *Elementi* (1791)	2	2	1	1	0	6
	3–4	2–4	2	1	1	9–12
	5–6	4–6	3†	2	2	16–19
	7–8	6–8	4	3	3	23–6
	9–11	8–11	5	3	4	29–34
	12–14	11–14	6	4	4	37–42
	15–17	14–17	7	4	5	45–50
	18–20	17–20	8	5	5	53–8
	21–3	20–3	9	5	6	61–6
	24–6	23–6	10	6	6	69–74
Koch, *Musikalisches Lexikon* (1802)	4	4	2	2	2	14
	5	5	3	3	2	18
	6	[6]	[4]	[4]	[3]	[23]
	8–10	8–10	[4–6]	[4–6]	[4]	[28–36]
Scaramelli, *Saggio* (1811)	5	3	[1]	[1]	2	12
	7	5	[2]	[1]	3	18
	9–10	6–7	[3]	[2]	4	25
	11–12	8–9	4	2	5	31‡
	13–14	10–11	[5]	[3]	6	38§
G. Weber, 'Besetzung . . .' (1822)	6	4–5	2–3	2	1–2	15–18¶
	12	10–12	4	4	3–4	33–6¶
	15	15	[5]	[5–6]	6	[46–7]‖

* Petri warns that, with these forces, the wind must play at half volume.
† Galeazzi has '2' here, apparently in error.
‡ Correct number of strings for a full classical complement in the other instruments of 2—2—2—2 / 2—2—1—1.
§ Larger string sections than this require doubled wind.
¶ Single wind.
‖ Doubled wind.

Seating Plans

Seating, also known as disposition (or, in American English, placement) of the orchestra, was of great importance, as poor seating could destroy the ensemble of a conductorless orchestra or at least throw off the balance. That the seating arrangement of Italian opera orchestras discussed at the beginning of Chapter 7 was used wherever Italian opera was adopted may be seen from many paintings, engraving, and drawings.[39] At Dresden under Hasse the winds were on one side of the pit, the strings on the other (Plate XV*a*); Galeazzi suggests that that plan is excellent if one's principal concern is good ensemble. If, however, one has excellent players who can be counted on to follow the principal violinist accurately, then the superior plan is that used by the Turin opera orchestra (Plate XV*b*), which was, Galeazzi claimed, 'without contradiction the best in Europe'. He reasoned as follows: if the strings are on one side and the wind on the other as at Dresden, a proper blend of the two will be heard only by those members of the audience seated in the middle of the auditorium; by distributing strings and winds across the orchestra, a proper blend will be heard from any angle.[40]

The suggestions of Galeazzi and Meude-Monpas for concert orchestras have already been presented.[41] Koch agreed with Galeazzi that good placement must deal with both the visual and acoustical. Singers—both soloists and choir—should be placed at the front, a position otherwise occupied by the strings, so that the principal parts are not obscured. For good ensemble, the performers of these principal parts (and especially their leaders) must be grouped closely together. Care must be taken that weaker instruments are placed further forward than stronger ones and that the two sorts are not near one another. (Koch uses flutes and trumpets as an example.) The leaders of the singers and of the orchestra must be visible to each member of his group and to each other. The orchestra should be on a raised platform, which, however, should not be too wide and shallow. In the centre of the platform should be placed the principal performers of the bass-line, with the leaders of the first and second violins on either side of them. The remainder of the violins should be fanned out behind their leaders, forming a semicircle along the front of the platform. Singers performing arias and instrumentalists performing concertos stand in the centre of this semicircle where they can easily lead.[42] Koch's description, published in 1802, would appear to be indebted to a description and

[39] A representative sample of such pictures may conveniently be examined in H. C. Wolff, *Oper: Szene und Darstellung von 1600 bis 1900* (Musikgeschichte in Bildern, iv/1) (Leipzig, 1968).

[40] Galeazzi, *Elementi*, i. 213–27. See further M. Sutter, 'Francesco Galeazzi on the Duties of the Leader or Concertmaster', *The Consort* (1976), xxxii. 185–92.

[41] In chs. 7 and 9 respectively.

[42] Heinrich Koch, 'Stellung', *Musikalisches Lexikon*, cols. 1435–8.

diagram published twenty years earlier by Petri (Plate XVI).[43] Petri's diagram is self-explanatory, except for the presence of a table at the back of the orchestra. This, he writes, should hold some well-tuned violins and violas, ready to be pressed into service by orchestra members whose strings break during performances.

For his concerts of 1791–2 Haydn introduced a tiered arrangement to London (Figure 12.2), which, in one form or another, was used there for orchestral concerts throughout much of the nineteenth century. This arrangement graphically portrays the dissolution of the *basso* by moving the bassoons, cellos, and double basses to the periphery away from their old central location near the keyboard instrument. Because Haydn's seating arrangements were described as *en amphithéâtre*, the hypothetical reconstruction has been made semicircular. There is also iconographical evidence from the Continent of orchestras for dances and concerts placed in tiers against a wall or in a balcony (Plate XVII).[44]

The orchestral dispositions of Koch, Petri, and Haydn share the central location of the concertmaster and the keyboard instrument; division between the first and second violins; placement of the principal melodic parts (voices and violins) and weaker instruments (flutes, violas) forward, the stronger ones (brass, kettledrums) to the rear; and wide separation between flutes and trumpets.[45]

Unnotated Parts

In Mozart's symphonies unnotated parts are three in number: bassoons on the bass-line, keyboard continuo, and kettledrums when trumpets are called for. In the more elaborate orchestration of the 1780s, the problems of the bassoons and kettledrums vanish, leaving only the matter of the continuo instrument.

Haydn's remarks quoted above about furbishing the bass-line represent what was the prevalent attitude: when no obbligato bassoon parts were called for, at least one bassoon doubling the bass-line was preferable, though not absolutely necessary. Ample evidence exists for this practice.[46] The bassoon was apparently thought valuable in imparting a desirable timbre and clarity to the bass-line, as well as providing a necessary counterweight to oboes or flutes doubling the violins in tuttis. In a symphony with obbligato bassoons in only one movement (for instance,

[43] Johann Samuel Petri, *Anleitung zur praktischen Musik*, 2nd edn. (Leipzig, 1782, repr. Giebing, 1969), 188.

[44] The forthcoming monograph by J. Spitzer and N. Zaslaw cited in n. 32 above will deal fully with the iconography of the orchestra in the eighteenth century.

[45] A few other seating plans from the second half of the eighteenth century are reproduced and discussed in D. J. Koury, *Orchestral Performance Practices in the Nineteenth Century: Size, Proportions, and Seating* (Ann Arbor, 1986), 29–50.

[46] In addition to Haydn's remarks at n. 35 above, see Francesco Galeazzi, *Elementi*, ii. 313; M. Suard, 'Accompagnement', in Nicolas Framery (ed.), *Encyclopédie méthodique: Musique* (Paris, 1790, repr. New York, 1971), i. 13–24, here 20; H. C. Robbins Landon, *The Symphonies of Joseph Haydn* (London, 1955), 78, 117; R. Münster, 'Die Sinfonien Toeschis' (Ph.D. diss., University of Munich, 1956), 120–1; E. Wolf, *The Symphonies of Johann Stamitz: A Study in the Formation of the Classic Style* (Utrecht, 1981), 165, 218 n. 15.

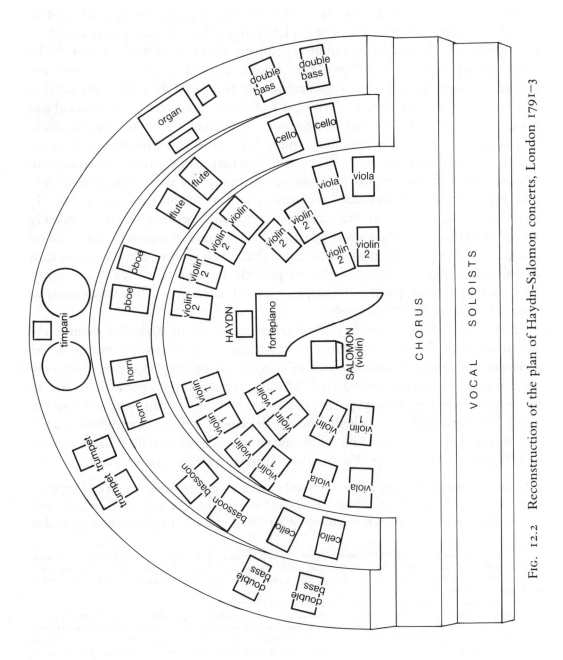

Fig. 12.2 Reconstruction of the plan of Haydn-Salomon concerts, London 1791-3

Mozart's K. 110 = 75b, discussed in Chapter 8), they of course play on the bass-line in the other movements.

The assumption has been widely accepted in recent years, although (it must be admitted) on the grounds of slender evidence, that when trumpets were called for in a symphony, kettledrums should accompany them even if unnotated.[47] The reasoning seems to be as follows: many orchestras did not have trumpets and kettledrums among their regular contingent, but borrowed them from the cavalry, whence they came as a unit. The trumpet and drum parts were often optional and notated separately. The separate notation sometimes had to do with the unavailability of (or extra expense in obtaining) music paper with enough staves to show the full instrumentation in the score.[48] The *ad libitum* nature of the trumpets and drums in mid-eighteenth-century orchestra music meant that the works could be flexibly used for larger and smaller-scale performances. Kettledrum parts are sufficiently conventional and simple in character that they could be improvised (or quickly written out) from a second trumpet part.[49] These arguments would hardly stand up in a court of law, but one may add to them that it was well within the purview of any Kapellmeister of Mozart's time to provide such parts if they were absent and wanted, as numerous manuscript copies of a variety of contemporaneous symphonies from the 1770s attest.

Finally, the matter of the keyboard continuo. A recent study has definitively documented the fact that under many circumstances and in many repertories, the continuo instrument remained a part of concert and opera performances into the beginning of the nineteenth century.[50] Mozart played continuo during the tuttis of his piano concertos, including the late ones, and he led his operas from the harpsichord or fortepiano. Whether he did the same for his late symphonies is less certain; the context and wording of the sole sentence devoted to his skills as a leader of orchestras in Schlichtegroll's *Necrology* suggest, however, that he did:

[Mozart] . . . appeared to grow in stature and to take his place among beings of a superior race, as soon as he sat down before a keyboard instrument. On such occasions, his soul would take wings, and the whole power of his being was able to concentrate upon that

[47] e.g. H. C. Robbins Landon, *The Symphonies of Joseph Haydn*, (London 1955), 95, 107–9, 335. For Mozart's symphonies in which some question exists about the kettledrum part, see the discussions of K. 100 = 62a, 95 = 73n, 87 = 74a, 118 = 74c, 133, 184 = 161a, 162, 181 = 162b, 185 = 167a, 200 = 189k, 202 = 186b, 203 = 189b, 208 + 102 = 213c, 204 = 213a, 250 = 248b, and 318.

[48] See, for instance, the discussions of K. 87 = 74a in ch. 7 and K. 318 in ch. 10.

[49] The percussionists of the Academy of Ancient Music experienced no difficulty in providing missing parts on request for the L'Oiseau-Lyre recordings of Mozart's symphonies. For the less bold, reconstructed drum parts by Robert Dearling with János Keszei have been published for the symphonies, K. 95 = 73n, 133, 162, 181 = 162b, 200 = 173e = 189k, 202 = 186b, 204 = 213a, and 208 + 102 = 213c (R. Dearling, *The Music of Wolfgang Amadeus Mozart: The Symphonies* (London, 1982), 195–203).

[50] L. F. Ferguson, 'Col Basso and Generalbass in Mozart's Keyboard Concertos: Notation, Performance Theory, and Practice' (Ph.D. diss., Princeton University, 1983).

single object for which he had been born: namely, the *harmony of sound*. The largest orchestra posed no difficulties for him, nor did it prevent him, even in the heat of performance, from observing the least note misplaced; and he would point his finger then and there, with an accuracy that was well-nigh uncanny, at the instrument which was guilty of the fault, and demonstrate which note should have been played instead.[51]

Some further evidence may be presented here, limited however to symphonies and to regions in which Mozart was active. Leopold reported that Nannerl 'accompanied' symphonies at the harpsichord for a Salzburg concert in April 1778.[52] The Abbé Vogler reported from Mannheim that, although symphonies were usually 'accompanied' by a keyboard instrument, from an artistic point of view this was not really necessary in a fully scored (*voll-stimmige*) symphony, but nevertheless one led from there.[53] When the composer Josef Martin Kraus arrived in Vienna in 1783, he attended a concert at which a symphony by Rosetti was led from the keyboard by Kapellmeister Umlauf.[54] Gyrowetz reported that in 1787–8 in Naples he led a symphony of his from the first violin while the local maestro, Giovanni Paisiello, 'sat at the fortepiano'.[55] Koch was a reliable witness when he reported in 1802 that 'one still uses the grand harpsichord or fortepiano [*Flügel*] in the majority of large orchestras, partly for the support of the singers in the recitative, partly (and also chiefly) for the filling out of the harmony by means of the thoroughbass.'[56]

On the other hand, in many places that maintained the keyboard continuo, the harpsichord was replaced by a fortepiano, the duties of the continuo player evolved from leadership, which passed to the concertmaster, to 'accompanying', and what was played on the keyboard became less and less adventuresome. Reports suggest that much late continuo playing either doubled the principal melodic part(s) in the right hand in soft or thin-textured passages or struck 'isolated' chords in noisy tuttis.[57] This is clarified by a treatise of the early 1780s, which advises that in ritornellos and other tutti passages it is best to double the principal parts, lest

[51] Friedrich Schlichtegroll, 'Joannes Chrysostomus Wolfgang Gottlieb Mozart', in *Nekrolog auf das Jahr 1791* (Gotha, 1792), ii. 82 ff.; trans. R. N. Coe in *Haydn, Mozart, and Metastasio by Stendhal (1814)* (New York, 1972), 183. That the final sentence of this passage is connected to the first two by the thought 'Mozart conducted from the keyboard' is suggested by Mozart's statement of the conditions under which he would consider returning to work at the Salzburg court: 'I shall not be kept to the violin, as I used to be—I will no longer be a fiddler; I want to lead from the keyboard—to accompany the arias' (*Briefe*, ii. 473; *Letters*, ii. 909 (= ii. 612–13)).

[52] Letter of 12 Apr. 1778. *Briefe*, ii. 338; *Letters*, ii. 777 (= ii. 526–7).

[53] Georg Joseph Vogler, *Betrachtungen der mannheimer Tonschule*, 3 vols. (Mannheim, 1778–81, repr. Hildesheim, 1974), ii. 296. I am grateful to Eugene Wolf for calling this passage to my attention.

[54] I. Leux-Henschen, *Joseph Martin Kraus in seinen Briefen* (Stockholm, 1978), 105.

[55] Adalbert Gyrowetz, *Biographie von Adalbert Gyrowetz 1763–1850* (Vienna, 1848), mod. edn. A. Einstein (ed.) (Leipzig, 1915), 38.

[56] Koch, 'Flügel', *Musikalische Lexikon*, col. 587.

[57] Nicolas-Étienne Framery, 'Accompagnement', *Encyclopédie méthodique*, i. 184–5: '[The Italians] . . . are little in the habit of striking and holding chords, except in recitative; they prefer to perform the melody or the most salient orchestral parts with the right hand' (1790). Concerning 'isolated chords', see L. Plantinga, *Clementi: His Life and Music* (London, 1977), 235.

unwanted sonorities be introduced, saving a more improvisatory style for accompanying solo passages. In forte many-note chords should be frequently restruck, in piano few-note chords seldom restruck.[58]

Instruments

The lack of standardization in eighteenth-century instruments is well known, but its implications are sometimes difficult to accept. It was a century in which there was no standard inch, foot, or mile, in which spelling was not standardized, in which the industrial revolution had barely begun to introduce the concepts of mass production and interchangeable parts. Standardization would not necessarily have seemed useful to eighteenth-century musicians and instrument-makers. Added to the lack of standardization were the existence of strong local traditions of instrument-making and continual experimentation with new designs. Yet despite this great variety, any orchestra that played together regularly and had efficient leadership, eventually assembled a group of instruments that worked well together.

A fundamental matter was getting wind instruments that played at the same pitch. In earlier times pitch would most often have been determined by a local organ, but this was less and less so in the second half of the eighteenth century. It has become common wisdom in the early music movement that pitch was lower in the eighteenth century than it is today, but a more accurate appraisal would be that pitch was variable then and included levels both above and below ours.[59] String instruments and harpsichords can be pitched variously, if care is taken to find strings of the correct thickness. Woodwind instruments, despite the use of *corps de rechange*, tuning slides, and barrels or bocals of varying lengths, can play in tune and with a pleasant tone only within a rather narrow range of pitch. The flute is most flexible in this regard, the reed instruments less so. It is not clear what travelling wind players—like the oboe- and bassoon-playing Besozzi brothers from Turin, or the Mannheim wind players who accompanied Mozart to Paris in 1778—did when they arrived in a city where the pitch was higher or lower than their instruments.

One musician reported in 1740: 'The fixed tone is higher or lower in different Countries. In Italy it is much higher than in France, in England it is between both. But observe, that in Italy the Church Tone is almost always a whole Tone higher

[58] Salvatore Bertezen, *Principi di Musica* (Rome, 1780, 2nd edn. 1781), as cited in H. Goldschmidt, 'Das Cembalo im Orchester der italienischen Oper der zweiten Hälfte der 18. Jahrhunderts', in H. Kretschmar (ed.), *Festschrift zum 90. Geburtstage . . . Rochus Freiherrn von Liliencron* (Leipzig, 1910; repr. Westmead, 1970), 87–92.

[59] The fundamental research about pitch standards is collected in A. J. Ellis and A. Mendel, *Studies in the History of Musical Pitch* (Amsterdam, 1968), which should be read in light of A. Mendel, 'Pitch in Western Music since 1500: A Re-examination', *Acta musicologica* (1978), l. 1–93, 328. See also C. F. Michaelis, 'Aufforderung zur Festsetzung und gemeinschaftlichen Annahme eines gleichen Grundtones der Stimmung der Orchester', *Allgemeine musikalische Zeitung* (Nov. 1814), xvi, cols. 772–6.

than that of the Opera, or of Chamber Music.'[60] Nearer in time to Mozart's symphonies, details are hard to come by, for although there is much evidence and argumentation about 'baroque' and nineteenth-century pitch, relatively little is known about the period in between. A low pitch around a' = 409 achieved considerable international currency from the end of the seventeenth to the middle of the eighteenth century, because French woodwind instruments were highly prized in much of Europe and their pitch standard travelled with them.[61] The tuning fork of the Parisian oboist François Sallantin from 1783 still gave that pitch, which had first been measured successfully by the French acoustician Sauveur in the early years of the century. The Paris opera and French court clung to this low pitch, which is slightly more than a half-step lower than a' = 440, right up to 1790, but at the Concert spirituel and elsewhere, the pitch had risen, and some Parisian woodwind players began to keep two sets of instruments.[62]

In the nineteenth century the pitch of various orchestras and opera-houses was gradually raised, increasing the brilliance of the orchestras but creating problems for the wind players and, especially, for the singers. It was in reaction to this tendency that the first international attempts were made to reach a standard pitch. This led to a proposed standard of a' = 435 (from 1859), which years later was raised to our present a' = 440 through a misunderstanding of the effects of temperature on tuning.[63] At the time of the establishment of a' = 435 as an international standard, it was stated by musicians who had lived through the change in pitch that the new standard was higher than 'Mozart's pitch'.[64] Thus 'Mozart's pitch' (by which is meant the pitch he apparently would have encountered in Vienna and some other places at the end of his career) may be bracketed between the old French woodwind pitch of approximately a' = 409 and the nineteenth-century convention of a' = 435. This is clarified by the work of the singing teacher Näke who, like some others at the time, deplored the rise in pitch, which he felt was ruining many promising young voices. In order to prove his point, Näke mounted productions of *Die Zauberflöte* and *Idomeneo* in the 1840s, using old instruments at old pitch, which was measured at the time as about a' = 424.[65]

This pitch receives some confirmation from woodwind instruments of the

[60] J. C. Petit, *Apologie de l'excellence de la musique* (London, [*c.*1740]), 31 (English), 31–2 (French).

[61] The history of this transfer of instruments has not yet been fully written. See, however, the appropriate articles in S. Sadie (ed.), *The New Grove Dictionary of Musical Instruments* (London, 1984), i. 183–4 (bassoon), 777–8 (flute); ii. 238–40 (horn), 795–6 (oboe); also F. Fleurot, *Le Hautbois dans la musique française 1650–1800* (Paris, 1984), 18–21; B. Haynes, 'Lully and the Rise of the Oboe as Seen in Works of Art', *Early Music* (1988), xvi. 324–38; and n. 68 below.

[62] Mendel, 'Pitch in Western Music', 82.

[63] Ibid. 89–90.

[64] Ibid. 83.

[65] *The New Grove Dictionary of Musical Instruments*, iii. 127–8 ('Pitch').

second half of the eighteenth century. While these survive at a variety of pitches, many cluster around a pitch approximately a quarter-step lower than a′ = 440, or near 427.[66] Mozart must have encountered many pitch levels in his travels, including some extremely low ones (for instance, in Paris, Berlin, and Rome) and some extremely high ones (especially in Vienna and in certain churches in England and Germany). He perhaps had to reckon with pitch about a half-tone lower than ours in his youth and about a quarter-tone lower in his last decade. The foregoing attempt to find viable generalizations should be regarded as tentative, and Arthur Mendel's cautionary words heeded. 'The expression "Mozart's pitch" has no single meaning.'[67]

Once the decade-by-decade evolution of each of the orchestral instruments has been worked out in as much detail as has been done for the transverse flute,[68] we may be able to say with some confidence for which kinds of instruments Mozart wrote many of his symphonies. Furthermore, once these specific instruments are co-ordinated with fingering charts intended for them, it will become even clearer than it already is that only after Mozart's death did some musicians begin to teach the modern idea that, for instance, A sharp is higher than B flat, D sharp higher than E flat, etc. Earlier the opposite was taught. Like Tartini, Geminiani, Leopold Mozart, and other leading string players of his century, Mozart taught mean-tone intonation for orchestral instruments, and he used non-equal temperament for his keyboard instruments.[69]

For all the confusion about wind instruments, the aspect of Mozart's orchestra that continues to be the most problematic concerns bows. Because historical bows are sometimes without makers' marks, seldom dated, and never labelled as to the instruments for which they were intended, it has proven surprisingly difficult to identify properly the several bow-types in use during the Classical era in order that replicas can be made, players familiarized with their use, and the repertory associated with each identified. According to Galeazzi, each school of violin playing had its own form of bow, and the best orchestras were those in which all of the violinists were trained in the same school.[70] The date of the invention of the Tourte bow in the 1770s and 1780s has led to incorrect assumptions about the date at which it became the undisputed standard. One picture of Paganini performing, for instance, illustrates that at least some of the time he did not use the Tourte bow,

---

[66] This, at least, was the result of *ad hoc* trials with a number of late eighteenth and early nineteenth-century woodwinds from British collections by members of the Academy of Ancient Music prior to beginning recordings of the Mozart symphonies in 1978.

[67] Mendel, 'Pitch in Western Music', 83.

[68] J. Bowers, 'New Light on the Development of the Transverse Flute between about 1650 and about 1770', *Journal of the American Musical Instrument Society* (1977), iii. 5–56.

[69] J. H. Chesnut, 'Mozart's Teaching of Intonation', *Journal of the American Musicological Society* (1977), xxx. 254–71.

[70] Francesco Galeazzi, *Elementi*, i. 76–7, 211.

although the latter can be seen in other pictures of him.[71] The earliest evidence implying an entire orchestra's use of Tourte bows dates from 1810, nearly two decades after Mozart's death:

Many concerts, announced with magniloquence and at great expense, are not equal to those given at the [Paris] Conservatory under the modest title 'Students' Exercises'. The perfection of the symphonic performances [there] surpasses that which formerly distinguished the Clery Concerts. Everyone is in agreement on this point, but no one has yet related its true cause: to call attention to it is essential, because it determines the good or bad organisation of an orchestra. The violinists, violists, and cellists who previously made up the symphony orchestra were, separately, from very good teachers, but each one of these [teachers] had a different school of bowing. Some had Jarnovick's, others Tartini's, and a very small number Viotti's. This resulted in entirely different manners of striking the string, from which the inevitable absence of high finish and of perfect ensemble in performance. Today, these disadvantages no longer exist: each of the principal teachers at the Conservatory—Messrs Rode, Kreutzer, and Baillot—has without doubt a school of bowing peculiar to himself, but on the whole these three manners very much approximate that of the great master of them all, the famous Viotti [the first great virtuoso to take up the Tourte bow]. The pupils of the three classes all have a broad and energetic manner of playing; this results in such unity of performance in the symphonies that from a distance one would believe that there was only one violin on each part.[72]

This passage points to a shortcoming of many recent attempts to play eighteenth-century orchestral music: the promiscuous mixture of instruments from disparate traditions. One frequently hears mixed together oboes from 1710, horns from 1810, flutes and bassoons from 1770, and stringed instruments from many times and places, equipped in a variety of ways, played with bows of several sorts. This kind of mixture will serve only for a rough first approximation, until we have become as sensitive to the differences among orchestral instruments as we have to those among harpsichords.

Venues

Mozart's symphonies were performed in private rooms, in great halls, in theatres, and in churches. Churches have changed little since his day, but the same cannot be said of concert rooms and theatres. A hall with the proportions, acoustics, and ambience of an eighteenth-century concert room means a hall that is relatively small and resonant. For example, the Hanover Square Rooms—where the Bach–Abel concerts were held between 1775 and 1782, and the Haydn–Salomon

---

[71] This picture is reproduced in L. Sheppard and H. R. Axelrod, *Paganini* (Neptune City, 1979), 127.

[72] *Les Tablettes de Polymnie* (April, 1810; repr. Geneva, 1971), 3–4, signed 'A. M.'

concerts between 1791 and 1794—measured 79' × 32'.[73] The Bach–Abel concerts had previously been held in Hickford's Great Room, which was 50' × 30'.[74] Mozart's earliest symphonies were probably performed there in 1765. The Holywell Music room in Oxford was (and is) 65' × 32'.[75] The Salle des Cent Suisses at the Tuilleries, where the Concert spirituel was held between 1725 and 1784, and in which the première of K. 297 and performances of other symphonies of Mozart's occurred, was of similar size: 59' × 52'.[76] A concert room inaugurated in Montpellier in 1785 was 59' × 36'.[77] The celebrated hall of the old Leipzig Gewandhaus, opened in 1781 and the scene of an orchestral concert by Mozart in 1789, was exceptionally large for the period: 76' × 38'.[78] If these figures are representative, concert rooms of the period may have averaged about 2,400 square feet, an area that housed both musicians and audience. The ceilings were high, allowing for sufficient reverberation.

The often elegant rooms in private homes and in Austrian, Bavarian, and Italian palaces and monasteries in which Mozart's symphonies were performed were likewise of moderate size (compared to modern concert-halls) with high ceilings; their narrow rectangular shape, plaster walls and ceilings, and marble or wooden floors offered a live acoustic. Only later did changed styles of interior decorating ordain covering walls, floors, even ceilings, with sound-absorbing rugs, drapery, canvas, and wallpaper; and only then did economic and social changes create the need for large concert-halls, requiring instruments to be louder and more numerous, choirs to be multiplied, and solo voices to attain degrees of power previously undreamt of.[79]

The theatres and opera-houses of the period were, likewise, on a small scale by modern standards, with a few exceptions, most notably the Teatro San Carlo in Naples. Several contemporaneous accounts, of which the following one by Charles Burney is typical, suggest that a theatre the size of the Naples theatre could be a disaster for eighteenth-century instruments and voices:

[73] The figures usually given for the Hanover Square Rooms are greater than those given here, apparently representing a later enlargement and renovation. The present figures appeared in the *General Evening Post* (25 Feb. 1794), as reported by Landon, *Haydn: Chronicle and Works*, iii. 29. There is no picture of the inside of the Hanover Square Rooms in its eighteenth-century guise; the one often reproduced (most recently in J. Rushton, *Classical Music: A Concise History from Gluck to Beethoven* (London, 1986), 113), purporting to show the scene of Haydn's triumphs, dates from the nineteenth century, after the alterations mentioned above had occurred.

[74] R. Elkin, *The Old Concert Rooms of London* (London, 1955), 44.

[75] J. H. Mee, *The Oldest Music Room in Europe* (London, 1911), 4.

[76] C. Pierre, *Histoire du Concert spirituel 1725–1790* (Paris, 1975), 69.

[77] H. W. Schwab, *Konzert: Öffentliche Musikdarbietung vom 17. bis 19. Jahrhundert* (Musikgeschichte in Bildern, iv/2) (Leipzig, 1971), 66.

[78] A. Dörffel, *Geschichte der Gewandhauseconcerte zu Leipzig ... Festschrift zur hundertjährigen Jubelfeier der Einweihung des Concertsaales im Gewandhause zu Leipzig* (Leipzig, 1884, repr. 1980), 251–2.

[79] The most helpful study is M. Forsyth, *Rooms for Music: The Architect, the Musician, and the Listener from the Seventeenth Century to the Present Day* (Cambridge, Mass., 1986).

I must own, that in the magnitude of the building and the noise of the audience, one neither can hear voices or instruments distinctly, and I was told that on account of the King and Queen being present, people were much less noisy than on common nights . . . . Not one of the present voices is sufficiently powerful for such a theatre, when so full and noisy. [. . .] As to the music, much of the claire-obscure was lost, and one only heard distinctly those coarse and furious parts which were meant merely to give relief to the rest.—The mezzotints and back ground were generally lost and little else was left but the bold and coarse strokes of the composer's pencil.[80]

The Naples orchestra was nearly inaudible despite the fact that, as Burney's enquiries revealed, it had a powerful string section of 18—18—[?2]—2—5.[81]

The theatres in which Mozart's symphonies were heard were a half or quarter the size of the Teatro San Carlo and of most modern opera-houses. Hence it is not and can never be 'authentic' to use small numbers of eighteenth-century instruments in large, modern halls and theatres, for the instruments will lack power and presence, losing their characteristic colours. The hall in which one plays is as important as the instruments, bow, strings, or reeds, and playing techniques employed. For Mozart's symphonies and other contemporaneous orchestral music, a small or medium-sized church is a reasonable venue, if the only other options are large, dry modern concert-halls or vast theatres. As Chapter 4 reveals, symphonies were also heard in cathedrals and other large churches. This can of course be replicated, but then the performers will have to alter their playing style, slowing their tempos, and the aesthetic experience will become something entirely different, even if still entirely valid as an attempted re-creation of eighteenth-century music-making.

Playing Techniques

These remarks will not deal with the soloistic techniques of the individual instruments, concerning which there is a growing literature, but with matters of interpretation affecting orchestral players, which has been less studied.

One of the oddities of many recent early music recordings and performances is the conviction of the players that as many notes as possible should bulge—that is, should have applied to them the hairpin dynamics known in the eighteenth century as the *messa di voce* or swell.[82] This is a case of a historical misunderstanding becoming a fashion and hardening into a new orthodoxy. The *messa di voce* was

---

[80] Burney, *Music, Men and Manners*, 192–3.

[81] Ibid. 197.

[82] *Messa di voce* did not in all contexts mean 'swell', however. The discussion of this subject which follows is indebted to the unpublished research of Robert Seletsky. The best published discussion of the *messa di voce* is found in L. Rovighi, 'Problemi di prassi esecutiva barocca negli strumenti ad arco', *Rivista italiana di musicologia* (1973), viii. 38–112.

several things in the eighteenth century: it was a technical exercise, an expressive ornament, and a method of drawing out long notes and showing off virtuoso technique (especially at fermatas). Its constant use in certain recent performances is based on the misinterpretation of several documents, the most prominent of which is a statement in Leopold Mozart's *Violinschule* that 'Every tone, even the strongest attack, has a small even if barely audible softness at the beginning of the stroke; for it would otherwise be no tone but only an unpleasant and unintelligible noise. This same softness must be heard also at the end of a stroke.'[83] This passage, which contains Leopold's explanation of how the bow must be handled to avoid scratching when attacking and releasing notes, has nothing to do with the *messa di voce*. That he never intended to suggest a swell on every note emerges from a letter he wrote in 1778, describing the playing of the oboist Carlo Besozzi:

What is particularly remarkable is his ability to sustain his notes and his power to increase and decrease their volume, without introducing even the very slightest quiver into his very pure tone. But this *messa di voce* was too frequent for my taste and has the same melancholy effect on me as the tones of the glass harmonica, for it produces almost the same kind of sound.[84]

Leopold Mozart's passage on bow attack was taken over (like several other things in his book) from a similar passage in Tartini's violin treatise, which is perhaps the clearer of the two in revealing that the underlying aim was technical rather than aesthetic: 'To draw a beautiful sound from the instrument, place the bow on the strings gently at first and then increase the pressure. If the full pressure is applied immediately, a harsh, scraping sound will result.'[85]

Dozens of treatises that discuss the swell, as well as the relatively few scores in which it is notated, support the idea that it was an ornament, which, like all ornaments, was to be used only in suitable places (usually notes of a minim or longer value). Generally speaking, the *messa di voce* was the province of soloists, not ripieno players. And Galeazzi described the duties of the ripienist in stark terms:

It is worth observing that expression is one thing when you play in a full orchestra but something different when you play solo. Expression in the whole orchestra is reduced almost entirely to the lowly, practical mechanics of performing at the right moment the pianos and fortes that are notated in the music.[86]

Yet this cannot be entirely correct, or it is correct only for the poorer orchestras

[83] Leopold Mozart, *Violinschule*, 102 (= *Treatise*, 97).

[84] Letter of 28 May 1778. *Briefe*, ii. 362; *Letters*, ii. 798–9 (= ii. 540).

[85] Giuseppe Tartini, 'Regole per arrivare a saper ben suonar il violino' in E. Jacobi (ed.), *Giuseppe Tartini, Treatise on Ornaments in Music* (Celle, 1961). For Leopold Mozart's considerable but unacknowledged debt to Tartini, see P. Petrobelli, 'La scuola di Tartini in Germania e la sua influenza', *Analecta musicologica* (1968), 5. 1–17.

[86] Galeazzi, *Elementi*, i. 197.

playing the least subtle music, for the best orchestras of Mozart's time were praised not merely for playing loud and soft (which are the chief markings that one encounters in orchestral scores of the period), but also for subtle nuances, for which Burney's term *chiaroscuro* was frequently used.[87] As such effects were rarely notated, it was up to an orchestra's leader to decide when a passage would benefit from the use of a *messa di voce*, a crescendo, a decrescendo, a stress, a release, or some other nuance, and to get his players to do it. Some of Mozart's early symphonies, for instance, contain unambiguous 'Mannheim' crescendos (Example 12.1), but he left the rendering of them to the musical culture and common sense of the orchestra leader (which, to be sure, in the early symphonies would often have been Mozart or his father). Only twice did Mozart notate the swell in his orchestral music: in one of the versions of the dénouement of *Idomeneo, rè di Creta*, K. 366 (1780–1), and in the opening bars of the *Maurerische Trauermusik*, K. 477 = 479a (1785) (Example 12.2). Each of these passages was meant to evoke the supernatural.

Vibrato is another controversial subject in the performance of eighteenth-century music. An extreme position was taken by Francesco Geminiani, for whom vibrato, which he called 'the close shake',

cannot possibly be described by Notes . . . . To perform it you must press the Finger strongly upon the String of the Instrument, and move the Wrist in and out slowly and equally; when it is long continued, swelling the Sound by Degrees, drawing the Bow nearer to the Bridge, and ending it very strong, it may express Majesty, Dignity, &c. But making it shorter, lower and softer, it may denote Affliction, Fear, &c. and when it is made on short Notes, it only contributes to make their Sound more agreeable and for this Reason it should be made use of as often as possible.[88]

In this passage Geminiani was most probably writing about solo playing. His final clause has been interpreted to mean that he advocated continuous vibrato, but do we really know what he meant by 'short Notes' and why he wrote 'as often as possible' rather than 'all the time', 'continuously', or another similar expression. And how should one deal with the fact that most modern musicians would probably attribute to vibrato on a long note such affects as 'tenderness', 'vibrancy', 'warmth', and 'passion', but hardly Geminiani's 'affliction' and 'fear'?

In any case, other eighteenth-century writers cautioned against overuse of

[87] For a strong statement of the need for orchestral nuance, see Johann Friedrich Reichardt, 'Von der Stärke und Schwäche und ihren verschiedenen Nuancierungen' in his *Ueber die Pflichten des Ripien-Violinisten* (Berlin, 1776), 59–70. Despite the frequent criticism of orchestras lacking nuance and the lavish praise of those that mastered it, there could apparently be too much of a good thing, or, at least, Schubart criticized the Oettingen-Wallenstein orchestra under Rosetti for a pedantic excess of nuance (*Ideen*, 169).

[88] Francesco Geminiani, *The Art of Playing on the Violin* (London, 1751; repr. Oxford, 1952), 8. (Geminiani seems also to recommend a *messa di voce* on all long notes (p. 2).) Other writers who seem to advocate a similar approach to vibrato: Jean Rousseau, *Traité de la viole* (Paris, 1687; repr. Munich, 1980), 100–1; J. Wilson (ed.), *Roger North on Music* (London, 1959), 164–5. I am grateful to John Spitzer for calling these two passages to my attention.

Ex. 12.1 Unmarked 'Mannheim' crescendo: Symphony in F major, K. 43, first movement

Ex. 12.2 Notated swells

(a) Idomeneo, rè di Creta K. 366

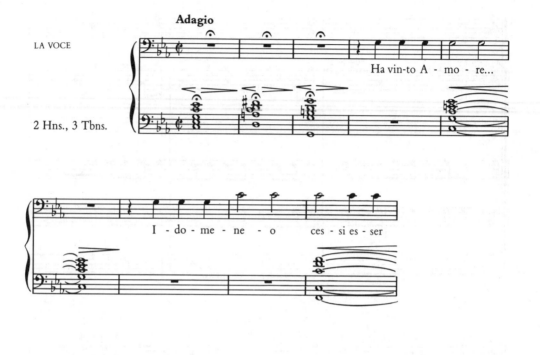

(b) Maurerische Trauermusik, K. 477 = 479a

vibrato, with the extreme opposite position to Geminiani's stated by his pupil, Robert Bremner. Bremner's reply to his teacher was that vibrato, which he called 'tremolo', may be used here and there as an ornament by a soloist but has no place in orchestral playing:

Many gentlemen players on bow instruments are so exceeding fond of the *tremolo*, that they apply it wherever they possibly can. This grace has a resemblance to that wavering found given by two of the unisons of an organ, a little out of tune; or to the voice of one who is paralytic; a song from whom would be one continued *tremolo* from beginning to end. Though the application of it may, for the sake of variety, be admitted, at times, on a long note in simple melody; yet, if it be introduced into harmony, where the beauty and energy of the performance depend upon the united effect of all the parts being exactly in tune with each other, it becomes hurtful. The proper stop is a fixed point, from which the least deviation is erroneous: consequently the *tremolo*, which is a departure from that point, will not only confuse the harmony to the hearers who are near the band, but also enfeeble it to those at a distance . . . . Its utility in melody may likewise be doubted, because no deficiency is perceived when it is omitted by good performers: and, if an unsteady voice is reckoned a defect in a singer, he may also be called a defective performer whose fingers are destroying the plain sound, which includes both truth and beauty.[89]

There were reactions to Geminiani's and Bremner's contradictory statements on vibrato. When Geminiani's treatise was posthumously republished in the second half of the eighteenth century, the remark that vibrato 'should be used as often as possible' was removed, suggesting that his position was considered controversial or that his statement was thought possibly misleading.[90] Whereas Geminiani's book did not discuss orchestral playing, Bremner's essay was explicitly written to emphasize the differences between the performance responsibilities of soloists and of orchestral players.

A response to Bremner's passage on vibrato, by his German translator Carl Friedrich Cramer, makes interesting reading, even though Cramer neglected to observe Bremner's careful distinction between soloist and ripienist and appears to be writing only about the former:

The author of these remarks seems to me to be entirely too much prejudiced against vibrato . . . . The application of this [vocal technique] to instrumental execution is easy to make. Because however much *vocal* performance (also the model and ideal for the instrumental) and passionate expression allow of it, so much more does the indefiniteness of the naked, wordless tone [of instrumental music]. Thus it follows irrefutably that, in such passages where the singer would apply vibrato, the instrumentalist not only *may* make use of it, but *must*. That this, however, like all niceties and ornaments, must occur not too frequently but with discretion and upon reflection, I have no desire to argue about with our author.[91]

Hence, Cramer, although he wished to modify Bremner's purist position, would never have endorsed Geminiani's broad mandate for vibrato.

---

[89] Robert Bremner, 'Some Thoughts on the Performance of Concert Music' published as a preface to J. G. C. Schetky, *Six Quartettos for two Violins, a Tenor, & Violoncello*, Op. 6 (London, 1777; repr. 1972; mod. edn. by N. Zaslaw as 'The Compleat Orchestral Musician', *Early Music* (1979), vii. 46–57.

[90] R. Hickman, 'The Censored Publications of *The Art of Playing on the Violin*, or Geminiani Unshaken', *Early Music* (1983), xi. 73–6.

[91] C. F. Cramer (ed.), *Magazin der Musik* (Hamburg, 1783–6), i. 1216; N. Zaslaw, 'The Orchestral Musician Compleated', *Early Music* (1980), viii. 71–2.

Leopold Mozart's position was similar to Cramer's (and again makes no distinction between solo and orchestral playing):

Now because the tremolo is not purely on one note but sounds undulating, so would it be an error if every note were played with tremolo. Performers there are who tremble consistently on each note as if they had the palsy. The tremolo must only be used at places where nature herself would produce it, [. . . on] a closing note or any other sustained note.[92]

Leopold's previously cited remarks about the oboist Carlo Besozzi confirm his fundamentally conservative attitude to vibrato. Wolfgang's only recorded remarks on the matter, although they do not specifically address the question of orchestral vibrato, would seem to arise from a similarly conservative position:

[The singer] Meissner, as you know, has the bad habit of making his voice tremble at times, turning a note that should be sustained into distinct crotchets, or even quavers—and this I never could endure in him. And really it is a detestable habit and one which is quite contrary to nature. The human voice trembles naturally—but in its own way—and only to such a degree that the effect is beautiful. Such is the nature of the voice; and people imitate it not only on wind instruments, but on stringed instruments too and even on the clavichord. But the moment the proper limit is overstepped, it is no longer beautiful—because it is contrary to nature. It reminds me of when, on the organ, the bellows are jolted.[93]

And concerning the oboist Johann Christian Fischer, whom Mozart heard in Holland in 1766 and again in Vienna in 1787: 'He certainly does not deserve the reputation he enjoys. [. . .] The long and short of it is that he plays like a bad beginner. [. . .] His tone is entirely nasal, and his held notes are like the tremulant on the organ.'[94]

Francesco Galeazzi's statement about vibrato is in much the same vein as Leopold Mozart's of thirty-five years earlier:

[Vibrato] consists in pressing the finger well on the string to perform a long note, and then, marking with the hand a certain paralytic and trembling motion, performing so that the finger bends now to this side and now to that, and resulting in a vacillating pitch and a certain continual trembling not unpleasing to those people [who do it]; but these are most genuine discords which can please only those who are accustomed to them and which should be entirely banned from music by anybody equipped with good taste.[95]

Running through all these comments, except Geminiani's, are the same ideas:

[92] Leopold Mozart, *Violinschule*, 238–9 (= *Treatise*, 203–4).
[93] Letter of 12 June 1778. *Briefe*, ii. 378; *Letters*, ii. 816–17 (= ii. 552).
[94] Letter of 4 Apr. 1787. *Briefe*, iv. 40–1; *Letters*, iii. 1350 (= ii. 907).
[95] Galeazzi, *Elementi*, i. 171.

some (perhaps many) performers use vibrato; they sometimes use it too much; it makes perfect intonation impossible; there is something unpleasant or impure about it. (The words 'defect', 'trembling', 'palsy' and 'paralytic' are used, and Mozart writes three times, 'contrary to nature'.) Hence vibrato, like the *messa di voce*, was considered primarily an ornament, and there is good historical evidence to suggest that both were used sparingly by soloists and generally eschewed by well-disciplined orchestral players.

According to modern ideas of good orchestral performance, the addition of other unnotated ornaments—that is, the small ornaments called 'graces' in English, *agréments* in French, *wesentliche Manieren* in German, and *abbellimenti* in Italian— would appear to be entirely out of the question. This apparently common-sense idea is suported by Robert Bremner, who states his position in a characteristically clear, extreme fashion:

The concert, or orchestra player ... is only a member of that whole by which a united effect is to be produced; and if there be more than one to a part, he becomes no more than a part of a part; therefore his performance, with that of those who play the same part, must ... coincide so as to pass for one entire sound, whether loud or soft. Should any one from the leader downward deviate in the least from this uniformity, it may easily be supposed that his performance must, for that time, be worse than nothing .... It must follow, that when gentlemen are performing in concert, should they, instead of considering themselves as relative parts of one great whole, assume each of them the discretional power of applying tremolos, shakes, beats, appogiaturas, together with some of them slurring, while others are articulating, the same notes; or, in other words, carrying all their different solo-playing powers into an orchestra performance; a concert thus rebellious cannot be productive of any noble effect.[96]

As similar proscriptions are found in dozens of eighteenth-century writings from all parts of western Europe, and as the subordination of orchestra players is taken for granted in our own times, there might seem to be little further to say on this subject. Yet the frequency with which orchestral violinists were admonished not to ornament suggests that they sometimes did so. Indeed, recent research demonstrates that in less disciplined ensembles all kinds of ornamentation may have been heard, while even in many of the best-run groups the addition of some ornamentation was probably considered acceptable and even necessary, since it was understood to be an essential part of the musical idiom that had been either left to the performers by the composer or accidentally omitted through inconsistency and error on the part of copyists. According to numerous writers of the period, 'graces' were most likely to be added in the first violin part, where the concertmaster was

---

[96] See n. 89 above.

to make sure that they were uniformly applied, and in the higher wind parts during solo passages when there was only one player per part. Ornamentation in the middle and bass parts was acceptable only in imitative passages, and then limited to copying what the violinists did. What this means in practical terms is that violinists were expected to play and bow exactly as the concertmaster did, and that, in well run orchestras, he alone could indicate the addition of such unnotated small ornaments as he thought necessary. These small ornaments included appoggiaturas and unaccented passing tones, trills, turns, and slides (that is, not *portamenti* but the scalewise approach to an important note from a third below it).[97]

Mozart thoroughly marked his late works for performance, and they probably require a minimum of ornamental additions. But certain passages in his early symphonies perhaps allow for them. The Andante of the Symphony in G major, K. 129, may be taken as an example. It begins with a characteristic eight-bar, homophonically accompanied theme constructed of four two-bar units, the third and fourth of which are elided. This is immediately repeated, unchanged except that the open ending of the eighth bar is replaced by the closed ending of the sixteenth (Example 12.3a). As the movement is in sonata form with both halves repeated, these sixteen bars of music are heard four times, or, put another way, the opening eight bars are heard eight times. Should we really be asked to believe that Mozart's ornament-loving instrumentalists would have allowed something so plain to be repeated seven times with no added embellishments? Example 12.3b suggests possible 'arbitrary' ornaments, for a concertmaster to play while his violin section renders it plain.

Whether the answer to the last question is yes or no (and the historical evidence suggests that it is the latter), such a melody would not have been played the way any excellent post-romantic orchestra without special instructions will render it, which is to say, entirely legato. On the one hand, fast movements were generally played more detached and more accented, slow movements more connected and cantabile,[98] and even though Andante was not a very slow tempo for Mozart, this movement belongs in the latter category. On the other hand, however, unslurred notes in many contexts were understood to be somewhat detached, whereas nowadays most notes without staccato markings are routinely understood to be connected in sound, even if separately bowed or tongued.

In addition, the metric structure of such melodies as the Andante of K. 129 was to be made clearly audible by means of stressed and unstressed notes, unless overridden by accents, by the placement of slurs, or by other special marks of

[97] J. Spitzer and N. Zaslaw, 'Improvised Ornamentation in Eighteenth-Century Orchestras', *Journal of the American Musicological Society* (1986), xxxix. 524–77.
[98] Giuseppe Tartini, *Treatise on Ornaments in Music*, 2–3.

articulation and musical gestures[99]—but in any case the unarticulated outpouring of sound cultivated by post-romantic orchestras was not expected. Thus, even without any new pitches or rhythms added to it, the simple melody of the Andante of K. 129 would have been 'ornamented' by sensitive articulation and metrical and rhetorical emphases (Example 12.4).

Ex. 12.3 Symphony in G major, K. 129, second movement

(a) As notated

[99] Johann Joachim Quantz, *Versuch einer Anweisung die Flöte traversiere zu spielen* (Berlin, 1752) (= *On Playing the Flute* trans. E. Reilly, 2nd edn. (New York, 1986), 123–4).

(b) Ornamentation by Robert Seletsky for the concertmaster, playing either alone or heterophonically against the rest of the first violins:

Ex. 12.4 Symphony in G major, K. 129, Andante. Eighteenth-century stress
and articulation added

[Notation approximate]

[— = a 'unit' of stress]

For several reasons, however, I would strongly recommend against marking up orchestral parts in this manner (except for pedagogical purposes): (1) the music becomes harder to read; (2) the few symbols available do not begin to suggest the variety and subtlety necessary for a sensitive performance; (3) musicians will not agree on exactly how to mark the parts, so such hypothetical interpretations should not be frozen in black and white; and (4) performers who can approximate the style of the music only if given such markings have understood it just as little as a person who reads aloud in a language he does not know from phonetic transliterations.

That the 'normal' articulation of notes was detached except in the rendering of cantabile melodies has long been understood by performers on the harpsichord, clavichord, and fortepiano, who have read about it in unambiguous terms in the keyboard methods of such authors as Marpurg, C. P. E. Bach, and Türk.[100] Common sense requires, and historical data suggest, that the singers and instrumentalists of a given time and place (whatever their personal musical disagreements) share a broad stylistic consensus about articulation, if they are to satisfy the normal conditions under which they work, namely, performing together on a regular basis in a cohesive manner with few rehearsals. If, therefore, keyboard players understood that 'normal' articulation was detached, others must have too. The application of this and related principles to orchestral music was spelt out with musical examples by Johann Friedrich Reichardt in 1776:

Dotted notes call for a particular and precise performance. If they are among other dotted rhythms, as for instance:

then one need only be particularly aware that the shorter note must be performed as short as possible, in order to give the longer note so much the more weight. Giving the longer a special pressure of the bow is superfluous, because the bow already falls on it with weight from the preceding short note.

The following notes, however, call for very great similarity of bowstrokes:

---

[100] Friedrich Wilhelm Marpurg, *Anleitung zum Clavierspielen* (Berlin, 1765; repr. New York, 1969), 29; Carl Philipp Emanuel Bach, *Versuch über die wahre Art das Clavier zu spielen* (Berlin, 1753, repr. Leipzig, 1957), i. 118; trans. W. J. Mitchell as *Essay on the True Art of Playing Keyboard Instruments* (New York, 1949), 149; Daniel Gottlob Türk, *Klavierschule; oder, Anweisung zum Klavierspielen für Lehrer und Lernende, mit kritischen Anmerkungen* (Leipzig, 1789), 353–4; trans. by R. H. Haggh as *School of Clavier Playing; or, Instructions in Playing the Clavier for Teachers & Students* (Lincoln, Neb., 1982), 342–3.

If they are all separately bowed, then the fourth note, which must be just as strong as the first, comes on an upbow. One must, therefore, have very great similarity of up- and downbows in order nevertheless to give the notes their proper expression.

In a movement with a bold character and a much slower tempo, one can also stop the third note, which is a downbow, and take the fourth note with another downbow. In this case however, one must have the foresight to make the third bowstroke short, so that it does not become necessary to lift the bow off the string in order to be able to play two downbows in a row.

If the first two notes are slurred:

then one must not play the third note sharply staccato, unless a stroke is placed over it, as in the last instance.

Each dotted note must be held right to the end of its value, in that way distinguishing itself from the note that is followed by a rest:

Here all the notes are sharply staccato.

In fugues the bowing has a special character. In long notes the bowstroke is begun somewhat more strongly, and here a certain weak marking of the notes is needed in order to obtain distinctness in performance. The more voices the fugue has, the more necessary this is. Especially must the subject be thrown into relief by a certain pressure of the bow whenever it has a new entrance.

The short notes in the fugue must be sharply staccato, and the ties from one bar to another must be somewhat marked [on the downbeat?] in order to prevent any confusion in the performance.

Notice that repeated notes of accompaniment in short values, if they are without signs [of articulation], as here:

are played short but not sharply, that is, while the note is given a short bowstroke, the bow remains on the string. If the bow is to be lifted from the string, then the common staccato signs must be marked:

There is yet one more way of performing these notes, which is the gentlest, namely, one takes many notes in a single bow without, however, completely connecting them to one another. Between notes there remains a small repose of the bow. We mark it as follows, and the composer thereby indicates at the same time how many notes he wishes to have in one bow:

One must guard carefully again rushing or dragging these notes, because the melody of the principal part will be thereby obscured.

The varied character of movements also calls for varied bowstrokes. Thus the bowstroke in the Adagio is very different from that in the Allegro, the main distinction being that in the Adagio the bow remains more on the string than in the Allegro.

In an Adagio nothing but a rest must cause the bow to leave the string. Even with notes marked staccato with a stroke ('), even with this shortening, the bow must never fully leave the string, but must remain in contact with an eighth part of its hair. If however, in a completely contrasting passage in the Adagio a few notes are to be quite sharply staccato, then the composer does well to indicate such with a special sign, with a word, for instance *furioso* (violent) or *adirato* (angry).

In the Andante the bow must have the lightness of the Allegro's bows without its sharpness, and the tapering off [of notes] but not so quickly. In the fast notes of the Andante, the above-mentioned bowstroke [of the previous example] sounds very good when two notes become short staccato upbows [i.e. ♩♩♩ ♩♩♩]. Likewise also in the Allegretto, except that now the bowstroke becomes somewhat livelier and occasionally also somewhat sharp. In the Allegro, however, the sharpness of the bowstroke in percussive notes and in rapidity of cut-offs is finally [not partial or for special effects but] highly essential.

Intensifying superscriptions, such as, for example, Allegro di molto, Allegro assai, Presto, Prestissimo, apply merely to the tempo and do not alter the character of the bowstrokes. For the bowstroke to be affected, a designation such as Allegro e con brio, Allegro e con spirito, con fuoco, resoluto, and so on, must be added to the superscription.

Likewise, the superscriptions that lessen the speed of Allegros, e.g. Allegro ma non troppo, non tanto, moderato, and so on, also make no difference in the character of the bowstrokes, but refer merely to the tempo. If, however, cantabile, dolce, or some other designation is affixed that more precisely determines the character of the movement, then this refers to the bowing, which must become gentler and more connected.

Similarly, in slow movements the superscriptions maestoso, affettuoso, mesto, grave, announce that the longer bowstrokes should receive a stronger, more expressive accent, and then that notes followed by rests must not be cut off abruptly, but rather be allowed to fade away gradually.[101]

Note that Reichardt's first paragraph calls for 'overdotting'. This sharpening of dotted rhythms is called for in many treatises of the late seventeenth and eighteenth centuries.[102] But no historical evidence exists to support the theory that in the slow sections of French *ouvertures* and other pieces in similar textures all parts must be rigidly reconstrued to fit a strict double dotting in the violins. In symphonies that begin with slow introductions (K. 203 = 189b, 250 = 248b, 320, 425, 444 = 425a, 504, and 543) Mozart will often notate double dots, as Leopold Mozart had advised composers to do in his *Violinschule*; elsewhere in these introductions and other slow movements, the application of overdotting is entirely idiomatic.

Tempo

Teachings about tempo in the eighteenth century involved three factors, concisely enumerated by Jean-Jacques Rousseau:

The degree of slowness or quickness that one gives to a measure depends on several things. (1) On the value of the notes that compose the bar. One sees indeed that a bar that contains a breve must be beat more calmly and last longer than that which contains only a crochet. (2) On the tempo indicated by the French or Italian word that one ordinarily finds at the head of the air: *gai, vîte, lent*, etc. Each of these words indicates an explicit modification in the tempo of a given metre. (3) Finally, on the character of the air itself, which, if it is well made, will necessarily make its true tempo felt.[103]

The first of Rousseau's three tempo traditions was the last remnant of the performance practice known as the 'fixed tactus'. Many eighteenth-century treatises mention that metre played a role in determining tempo, that (other things being equal) metre signatures with smaller denominators went more quickly than those with larger ones, and that 'short' metres (for instance, $\frac{2}{4}$ and $\frac{3}{8}$) went faster than 'long' metres (for instance, $\frac{6}{4}$ and $\frac{12}{8}$). Quantz's tempo system, based on metre and the human pulse, is simply a late manifestation of the fixed-tactus idea.[104]

Certain generalizations may be made about the relation of metre to tempo in Mozart's music. The metres $\frac{4}{2}$, $\frac{3}{2}$, and $\frac{2}{2}$ were used by him rarely and in one context

---

[101] Reichardt, *Ueber die Pflichten*, 20–6.

[102] Overdotting is mentioned, among other places, in the treatises of Loulié, Saint-Lambert, North, Marpurg, C. P. E. Bach, and Türk, as well as in Koch's *Musikalische Lexikon*, col. 1182.

[103] Jean-Jacques Rousseau, 'Battre la mesure', *Dictionnaire de musique* (Paris, 1768, repr. Hildesheim, 1969), 51–4. For Mozart's tempos in general, see further N. Zaslaw, 'Mozart's Tempo Conventions' in H. Glahn, S. Sørensen, P. Ryan (eds.), *International Musicological Society: Report of the Eleventh Congress, Copenhagen 1972* (Copenhagen, 1974), ii. 720–33; H. Macdonald, 'Mozart's Tempo Indications' in *Mozart's Music as Appreciated in the Past and Present, Prague 1983* (in preparation); J.-P. Marty, *The Tempo Indications of Mozart* (New Haven, 1988).

[104] See Zaslaw, 'Mozart's Tempo Conventions' for details.

only—the slow movements of church music and especially canons and fugues in the *alla breve* style. They signal movements in the *stile antico* and provide more evidence of Mozart's thorough grounding in Fuxian species counterpoint. His employment of these metres agrees with their position in Quantz's scheme and with the remarks in many contemporary treatises that church music was performed more slowly than theatre or chamber music. Mozart used common time for any tempo from extremely slow to moderately fast. Extremely fast movements in duple metre, however, he notated in $\frac{2}{4}$ or ₵. ₵ therefore had two distinct meanings: old *alla breve* tempo and diminution of a more modern, common-time tempo. Similarly, $\frac{3}{4}$ was used for very slow to rather fast movements, but $\frac{3}{8}$ only for moderate to extremely fast movements.

This brings us to the interesting point that for Mozart a piece in $\frac{3}{8}$ with semiquaver motion predominating would have been faster than a piece in $\frac{3}{4}$ with quaver motion, if both had the same tempo indication. Evidence for this assertion may be seen in Example 12.5: Mozart and his pupil Hummel have renotated their own compositions, each of them apparently attempting to change the metre while keeping the tempo constant.[105] The rationale for this can be imagined: since on the average quavers and quaver-based metres were associated with faster tempos than crotchets and crotchet-based metres, the crotchet versions of Example 12.5 required a more vigorous urging of the performer by the composer in order to attain the same speed as the quaver versions.

A similar construction can probably be placed on the tune which (as discussed in Chapter 13) Mozart borrowed from his aria, 'Un bacio di mano', K. 541, for the first movement of the 'Jupiter' symphony. The aria is notated as Allegretto $\frac{2}{4}$, whereas the symphony movement has the faster tempo indication Allegro vivace combined with the 'slower' metre ₵.

Finally, there is Mozart's unflattering description of Clementi's playing. Writing to Leopold in 1783, Mozart called Clementi a charlatan because he performed a sonata movement marked Presto or Prestissimo ₵ at a tempo that Mozart considered to be Allegro $\frac{4}{4}$.[106] Note that Mozart felt obliged to cite both the tempo indication and the metre to make his meaning plain to his father. A similar response greeted a flautist who performed his concerto for Wolfgang not long after having played it for Leopold. Wolfgang reported, 'At first the players who accompanied him could not get the hang of it, as, although the movement was written in

---

[105] *NMA*, viii/20/1/2. 76, 181; Johann Nepomuk Hummel, *Ausführliche theoretisch-practische Anweisung zum Pianofortespiel* (Vienna, 1828), 62.

[106] Letter of 7 June 1783. *Briefe*, iii. 272; *Letters*, iii. 1268 (= ii. 850). This anecdote may be understood as follows: Clementi and Mozart composed in different styles or traditions and their tempo conventions differed. Clementi, who was accustomed to the reflexes, sound, and aesthetic of English pianofortes, had to perform before the Emperor without advance notice (see Plantinga, *Clementi*, 61–8) on an unfamiliar Viennese fortepiano, an instrument conceived for a repertory and aesthetic strikingly different from his own.

Ex. 12.5 Metric tempo reinterpretations

(a) Mozart: Quartet in B flat major, K. 458 (1784), Finale

Sketch version

Presto

Final version

Allegro assai

(b) J. N. Hummel: *Ausführliche theoretisch-practische Anweisung zum Pianofortespiel* (Vienna, 1828), 62

Presto

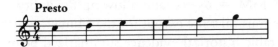

Allegro asssai

common time, he played it Alla breve. And, when I thereupon noted down Alla breve with my own hand, he admitted that my Papa in Salzburg had also made a fuss.'[107]

Another aspect of the lingering fixed–tactus tradition is the possibility that the tempos of adjacent movements might be fixed with regard to one another. This was suggested by Quantz's explanations of tempo. Quantz claimed the equivalencies in common time to be: Adagio assai/Adagio molto ♪ = Adagio cantabile/ Larghetto ♪ = Allegretto ♩ = Allegro ♩. = Allegro assai 𝅗𝅥 = MM 80.[108] In

---

[107] Letter of 20 Feb. 1784. *Briefe*, iii. 301; *Letters*, iii. 1293 (= ii. 867).
[108] Quantz, *Versuch*, 263–5 (= *On Playing the Flute*, 283–7).

Mozart's time, Türk criticized this scheme, claiming that Adagio must be faster relative to the Allegro than Quantz's scheme suggests, but agreeing with Quantz about the relationship Allegretto ♩ = Allegro assai 𝅗𝅥.[109] In 1788 E. W. Wolf gave the equivalencies Adagio ♪ = Andante ♩ = Allegro 𝅗𝅥 = a walking pace [= ?MM 75–85].[110] That Mozart thought in such terms in at least some of his symphonies is demonstrated by two works in which the orchestra must play continuously through tempo changes. These are the Symphony in G major, K. 74 (Allegro **C** ♪ = Andante ⅜ ♪: Example 6.5), and the Symphony in D major, K. 320 (Allegro maestoso ♩ = Allegro con moto 𝅗𝅥, both common time: Example 10.1).

Claims for the fixed tactus in Mozart's music have taken various forms. The alleged presence of this tempo system is said to be evidence for 'the underlying unity of the Viennese classical style'. Basic tempos supposedly exist relating one movement to another, according to notions 'first examined and then put into practice by Richard Strauss when he was conducting at the Munich Opera'. Mozart's 'Linz' symphony, K. 425, is claimed to be a prime candidate for such an interpretation.[111] Given the kinds of tempos favoured by Strauss and his contemporaries, this means, presumably, the following equivalencies: Adagio ¾ ♪ = Allegro spiritoso **C** 𝅗𝅥 = Andante ⅜ ♪ = Menuetto ¾ ♩ = Presto ²⁄₄ 𝅗𝅥, which—if the tactus is understood to be around MM = 65–75, and allowing flexibility in performance—might make reasonable musical sense except for the Minuet, which is very much slower than the considerable historical evidence summarized below would permit. This scheme requires a four-to-one ratio between the slow introduction and the following Allegro, which is supported by E. W. Wolf's equivalencies of 1788 cited above but contradicted by the two-to-one ratio implied by the first movement of K. 320. A systematic attempt to apply Quantz's fixed tempos to Mozart's music proved more a Procrustian bed than a source of interpretive inspiration.[112] Quantz's system, if it ever worked as an applied rather than a theoretical or pedagogical system, belonged to the music of his own circle in Berlin in the 1740s and 1750s, not to Mozart's music of a different time, place, and style.

The difficulty with the second of Rousseau's traditions, the tempo words, is known to every musician. Leopold stated it this way:

It is true that at the beginning of every piece special words are written which are designed

---

[109] Türk, *Klavierschule*, 111–12; (= *School of Clavier Playing*, 107–8).

[110] Ernst Wilhelm Wolf, *Musikalischer Unterricht für Liebhaber und diejenigen, welche die Musik treiben und lehren wollen* (Dresden, 1788), 25.

[111] Landon, *Haydn in England*, 526. Strauss never recorded K. 425; his recording of K. 550, several times reissued, is so poorly played that one hesitates to draw any conclusions from it.

[112] R. Elvers, 'Untersuchungen zu den Tempi in Mozarts Instrumental-Musik' (Ph.D. diss., Free University of Berlin, 1952).

to characterize it, such as 'Allegro' (merry), 'Adagio' (slow), and so on. But both slow and quick have their degrees, and even if the composer endeavours to explain more clearly the speed required by using yet more adjectives and other words, it still remains impossible for him to describe in an exact manner the speed he desires in the performing of the piece. So one has to deduce it from the piece itself, and this it is by which the true worth of a musician can be recognized without fail. Every melodious piece has at least one phrase from which one can recognize quite surely what sort of speed the piece demands. Often, if other points be carefully observed, the phrase is forced into its natural speed. Remember this, but know also that for such perception long experience and good judgement are required. Who will contradict me if I count this among the chiefest perfections in the art of music.[113]

The confusion arose not simply from the imprecise nature of the information that words are capable of conveying, but also because most of the tempo words were originally used to convey primarily character and only incidentally speed, the latter a function they acquired little by little and never entirely systematically (despite Reichardt's claims quoted above).

In Mozart's symphonies four basic tempos appear, with modifications. A basic Allegro for the first movement, sometimes prefaced by an Adagio, an Andante or Andantino for the second, a Tempo di menuetto for the third, and an Allegro molto for the finale. Given these basic tempo categories and given the conventional character of many symphony movements, one can begin to appreciate the possible usefulness in the eighteenth century of the concept *tempo ordinario*, a middle tempo, neither fast nor slow. Of course, the presence of many or few notes per bar (given the same metre), the number and skill of the players, the acoustic, and perhaps even the time of day, weather, or mood of the occasion all bear on the tempo. Yet several writers still found it worth while to try to calibrate *tempo ordinario*.

Quantz gave the 'ordinary' common-time Allegro as ♩ = MM 120 in 1752,[114] and Galeazzi almost forty years later also assigned the *tempo mediocremente allegro* to ♩ = MM 120.[115] C. Mason around 1801 still found this useful (♩ = MM 118).[116] But E. W. Wolf (cited above) seemed to call for Allegro ♩ = MM 75–85, while two English writers of 1809 gave the value as Allegro ♩ = MM 90–94.[117] Three months before his death, Beethoven wrote, 'We can hardly have *tempi ordinarii* any longer ...'.[118] This remark may be understood to mean that by the time

[113] Leopold Mozart, *Violinschule*, 30 (= *Treatise*, 33).

[114] Quantz, *Versuch*, xvii/7/51 (= *On Playing the Flute*, 285–7).

[115] Galeazzi, *Elementi*, i. 217–18 n.

[116] C. Mason, *Rules on the Time, Phrases & Accent of Composition* (London, c.1801), 1–2.

[117] M., 'Scale for Musical Time', *The Monthly Magazine* (Apr. 1809), xxvii. 241–3; William Neilson, 'Method of Regulating Musical Time', *The Monthly Magazine* (July 1809), xvii. 536–8.

[118] Letter of 18 Dec. 1826. A. C. Kalischer (ed.), *Beethovens Sämtliche Briefe* (Berlin, 1908), v. 1197 (= E. Anderson (ed.), *The Letters of Beethoven* (London, 1961), iii. 1325). The findings of Rudolf Kolisch cited in Table 12.4 suggest, however, that for some of Beethoven's music (especially from his first period) conventional tempo categories still had meaning.

movements were viewed as unique creations based on original materials rather than representatives of conventional categories (i.e., Rousseau's movement-types discussed below), such a tempo system could no longer function meaningfully.

Andantino is the most problematic of the tempo indications to interpret, for to understand this diminutive ending one must know whether the basic tempo being modified is 'fast' or 'slow'. That is, Allegro indicates some degree of fastness, therefore its diminutive Allegretto (a little Allegro) is less fast than it; similarly, Largo signifies a degree of slowness, therefore Larghetto is less slow than it. Plenty of evidence suggests that the slow Andante originated only in the nineteenth century—that for Mozart's time Andante was a flowing tempo only slightly slower than Allegretto.[119] The confusion over Andantino extends back into Mozart's time, for published lists of tempos arranged from slowest to fastest do not agree: of twelve theorists who distinguished between Andante and Andantino, seven thought the latter slower than the former and five the opposite.[120] In 1813 Beethoven explained the problem to his Edinburgh correspondent George Thomson thus: 'Andantino ... is understood slower or faster than Andante, because this term, like many others in music, is of such uncertain significance that many times Andantino approaches [the speed of] the Allegro and many other times it is played nearly like Adagio.'[121]

Internal evidence in Mozart's music suggests that he did not share Beethoven's confusion in this matter. No. 11 in *Die Zauberflöte* was originally marked Andante but Mozart changed it to Allegretto, whereas No. 15 was originally Andantino sostenuto and Mozart changed it to Larghetto.[122] Similarly, the Andante of the first version of the piano rondo, K. 494, became Allegretto in the second version.[123] This evidence for Andantino's being slower than Andante is confirmed by the tempo that Mozart wrote in the concertmaster's part of the Symphony in C, K. 338, which he sent to Donaueschingen: Andante di molto più tosto allegretto (literally, 'much going, rather allegretto'); Leopold Mozart used the similar indication Andante più tosto un poco allegretto in his Sinfonia da caccia (*G9).

---

[119] C. Raeburn, 'Das Zeitmass in Mozarts Opern', *Österreichische Musik Zeitschrift* (1957), xii. 329–33; C. Bär, 'Zu einem Mozart'schen Andante-Tempo', *Acta Mozartiana* (1963), x. 78–84; M. Rudolf, 'Pamina's Aria: A Question of Tempo', *Washington Opera Magazine* (Oct. 1981), 18–19. See also the writings of N. Zaslaw, H. Macdonald, and J.-P. Marty cited in n. 103 above.

[120] Andantino faster than Andante: Galeazzi, *Elementi*, i. 36; Jean-Baptiste Cartier, *L'Art du violon* (Paris, 1798; 3rd ed. c.1803, repr. New York, 1973), 17; William Crotch, 'Remarks on the Terms at Present Used in Music, for Regulating Time', *The Monthly Magazine* (1800), viii. 941–3. Andantino slower than Andante: Rousseau, *Dictionnaire*, 32; E. W. Wolf, *Musikalischer Unterricht*, 24; Türk, *Klavierschule*, 108–9; Mason, *Rules on the Time, Phrases & Accent of Composition*, 1–2; Muzio Clementi, *Introduction to the Art of Playing the Piano Forte* (London, 1801), 13; F. Starke, *Wiener Pianoforte-Schule* (Vienna, 1819), 19; Hummel, *Anweisung*, 66. To this may be added two Parisian builders of metronomes in the 1780s who placed Andantino faster than Andante (Brook, *La Symphonie française*, i. 313–18, 502–10).

[121] Letter of 19 Feb. 1813. Kalischer (ed.), *Beethovens sämtliche Briefe*, ii. 124 (= *Letters of Beethoven*, i. 406).

[122] K⁶, 708–9.

[123] Compare K. 494 (Andante) with the Finale of K. 533 (Allegretto).

This tells us something important about Mozart's understanding of these tempo indications: *molto* moved an Andante in the direction of Allegretto, which means that he construed Andante as a 'fast' rather than a 'slow' tempo and that Andantino (in so far as its meaning could be said to be precise) was on the slow side of Andante. This would seem also to be confirmed by the words used to modify these two tempos, not just in symphonies but in all of Mozart's works: whereas both Andante and Andantino are modified by *cantabile, sostenuto, espressivo* or *grazioso*, only Andante can also be *moderato* or *agitato*.[124]

Similarly, although William Crotch placed Andantino on the fast side of Andante, he appended a note saying that he was aware that many musicians thought the opposite; and, closer to Mozart's tradition, Türk and Hummel wrote strongly worded notes castigating those who believed that Andantino was the faster of the two. The order of Mozart's basic and secondary tempo indications, then, is the following, from slowest to fastest:

Largo
   Larghetto
Adagio
   Andantino
Andante
   Allegretto
Allegro
   Allegro molto
Presto.[125]

Words added to these basic categories of tempo modify by barely perceptible degrees their speed and especially their character.

In the early 1780s Mozart wrote to his father about some piano concertos he had sent to Salzburg, 'Please tell my sister that there is no adagio in any of these concertos—only andantes'. But whereas in some of the late piano concertos Mozart did essay adagios, his symphonic 'slow' movements, even in the last symphonies, belong always to some variety of Andante, efforts of post-romantic conductors to the contrary.

Rousseau's third and final tempo tradition is that of the characteristic movement-types. This refers to movements that actually are (or are derived from) minuets, marches, gavottes, *contredanses*, or other types well known to Mozart, his musicians, and his audiences, who would no more have needed such tempos explained to them than Viennese musicians of one hundred years ago needed an explanation of waltz tempo, or American dance-band musicians of fifty years ago

---

[124] Zaslaw, 'Mozart's Tempo Conventions', 727–8, Charts IVA-B.
[125] This scheme is taken over from Hugh Macdonald (see n. 103 above).

needed one for the fox trot. The discrepant understandings by musicians of the eighteenth and nineteenth centuries of 'character' or 'characteristic' pieces offers a clue to some of the differences between musical classicism and musical romanticism, for in the eighteenth century 'characteristic' pieces were representatives of well-established conventional categories, whereas in the nineteenth they came to be seen as pieces of unique character. Thus the very word that stressed conventionality in one era was used to emphasize originality in the next.

The movement-types about which much is known are the minuet and the march. For the former, information comes mostly from before Mozart's time, from the French dance tradition, or from after his time, from Beethoven's metronome indications for minuets in his symphonies and chamber music. Some eighteenth-century minuets for which precise tempo indications survive present the pattern shown in Table 12.3.

From this it emerges that there were two distinct minuet tempos, both fast compared to modern notions of the dance. The figures for 1747–63 and 1752 are for the minuet in general as a genre; the others are for specific pieces. If one examines these specific minuets, one sees immediately that they are simple in texture compared to many symphonic minuets of the 1770s, 1780s, and beyond, which is probably an indication that the tempo did not always remain the same when the dance left the ballroom and entered the concert-hall.

An English mechanical organ from 1762 pinned by Handel's pupil and amanuensis John Christopher Smith contained two Handel minuets at ♩. = 46 and ♩. = 68 respectively and one by Geminiani at about ♩. = 66.[126] Two Haydn minuets heard on mechanical instruments made at Eszterháza between *c*.1789 and

TABLE 12.3 Eighteenth-century minuet tempos

Date	Tempo	Source
1705–47	♩. = MM 70	L'Affilard
1732	♩. = MM 71	D'Onzembray
1737	♩. = MM 63?	La Chapelle
1747–63	♩. = MM 60	Marquet
1752	♩. = MM 53	Quantz
c.1755	♩. = MM 53	Pasquali
1759–62	♩. = MM 77	Choquel
1775	♩. = MM 54	Engramelle
1775	♩. = MM 72	Engramelle

Source: Zaslaw, 'Mozart's tempo conventions', 230–1, Chart VI.

[126] W. Malloch, 'The Duke of Bute's Barrel Organ', *Early Music* (1983), xi. 172–83, here 180–1 and a private communication from Mr Malloch.

TABLE 12.4 Beethoven's minuet tempos

Slow minuets	
Septet, Op. 20	$\flat$ = 120 [$\downarrow$. = 40]
Moderate minuets	
Quartet, Op. 59, No. 3	$\flat$ = 116 [$\downarrow$. = 39] ('Grazioso')
Eighth Symphony, Op. 93	$\flat$ = 126 [$\downarrow$. = 42]
Fast minuets	
Quartet, Op. 18, No. 4	$\downarrow$. = 84
Quartet, Op. 18, No. 5	$\downarrow$. = 76
Quartet, Op. 59, No. 2	$\downarrow$. = 69

Source: R. Kolisch, 'Tempo and Character in Beethoven's Music', *The Musical Quarterly* (1943), xxix. 169–87, 291–312.

1793 are estimated to have had the intended tempos $\downarrow$. = 63 and 76.[127] These tempos are not so very different from those of a number of Beethoven's minuets bearing metronome indications, as shown in Table 12.4.

Beethoven's brisk minuets have in the past sometimes been thought of as on their way to becoming scherzos. Placing them alongside eighteenth-century minuet tempos suggests a better explanation: Beethoven understood the eighteenth-century tradition for the minuet. His tempos probably represent a reasonable range of tempos to apply to Mozart's and Haydn's minuets. The too-slow minuets with which many modern performances have been encumbered seem to have arisen from several causes: the general enlargement of orchestras and concert-halls, the Wagnerian slowing of classical-period tempos, the 'powdered-wig' image of the *ancien régime* in general and of the minuet in particular, and the mistaken idea that the minuet was danced on every crotchet rather than on every other one. A few conductors understood all this long ago, as their recordings testify, and now that the matter has been written about in more than one publication,[128] too-slow minuets should gradually become a thing of the past. Then, musicians must resist the temptation *épater le bourgeois* by going overboard in the other direction. The minuet had many manifestations; it was neither a dirge nor a manic saturnalia, but a moderately flowing, dignified if cheerful courtly dance, with emphasis and articulation tending to the allegro rather than the adagio style of playing.

[127] E. F. Schmid, 'Joseph Haydn und die Flötenuhr', *Zeitschrift für Musikwissenschaft* (1931–2), xiv. 193–221, here 219; A. W. J. G. Ord-Hume, *Joseph Haydn and the Mechanical Organ* (Cardiff, 1982), 99–101.

[128] See further Zaslaw, 'Mozart's Tempo Conventions'; M. Rudolf, 'On the Performance of Mozart's Minuets', *Friends of Mozart Newsletter* (Fall 1984), xvii. 1–4; W. Malloch, 'Toward a "New" (Old) Minuet', *Opus* (Aug.–Sept. 1985), i. 14–21, 52. Correct eighteenth-century minuet tempos will be found on old recordings of Mozart symphonies conducted by Albert Coates, Arturo Toscanini, and George Szell.

Information about marches comes primarily from military sources. Three kinds of marches were generally recognized: the slowest was the funeral march (*marche solennelle*); then came the so-called 'slow march' (*Parademarsch, Festmarsch, pas ordinaire*), which was in theory if not always in practice half as fast as a third type, the 'quick step' (*Geschwindmarsch, pas redoublé*). Up to the 1760s the slow march was usually one step per second, but in the 1780s and 1790s its pace was accelerated and reached 76 or 80 steps per minute.[129] As the openings of a number of the common-time first movements of Mozart's symphonies and concertos are based upon materials more or less identical in character to his own marches, a connection may be postulated between the march tempo of the 1760s and 1770s ($\downarrow$ = MM 60) and the 'ordinary allegro' of some theorists of the period ($\downarrow$ = MM 120).[130] Some of Mozart's early symphonies have $\frac{2}{4}$ finales in the character of a 'quick step' (e.g., K. 181 = 162b, 202 + 186b). The mixture of quick step and jig in the Finale of K. 319 suggests a possible relationship between their tempos.

Finally, Mozart's pupil Hummel published arrangements of his teacher's most famous symphonies, the last six, for which he provided metronome indications. There are many problems with accepting these tempos: Hummel studied with Mozart between approximately 1786 and 1788, the period when Mozart's last three symphonies were created, to be sure, but when Hummel was only eight to ten years old. Whether Hummel heard any of these symphonies under Mozart's direction is unknown, as is the way in which his subsequent musical experiences and the passage of time may have altered his childhood perceptions. The change from orchestral performance to piano quartet (intended primarily to be played by middle-class amateurs, no doubt) possibly also influenced his choice of tempos. Hummel might even have disagreed with his illustrious master about tempo, or perhaps he wished to update the music to please the altered tastes of more than three decades later. Nevertheless, as Hummel had a kind of access to Mozart's music and the tradition flowing from it that we lack, we dare not dismiss his tempos without due consideration.

Beethoven's pupil Carl Czerny also published arrangements of these works, taking over most of Hummel's tempos, but modifying a few of them (Table 12.5). The missing dots in the notation of three minuet tempos, altered tempo indications in three movements, and lack of metronome indications for two movements in Hummel's edition can be made good by reference to Czerny's. Hummel's minuet tempos—ranging from $\downarrow$. = MM 66 to 88, or noticeably faster than they are usually heard today—are right in line with information about minuets already presented. Furthermore, the two types are distinguished, the Allegretto minuets falling at $\downarrow$. = 80–8 and the 'regular' minuets at $\downarrow$. = 66–72. (The Minuet of K.

---

[129] Zaslaw, 'Mozart's Tempo Conventions', 724, Chart I.　　　　[130] See nn. 114–17 above.

TABLE 12.5 Hummel's tempos for Mozart's late symphonies (with Czerny's tempos when those differ from Hummel's)*

Mozart	Hummel	Czerny
Symphony in D major, K. 385 ('Haffner')		
Allegro con spirito	¢ ♩=MM 88	
Andante	$\frac{2}{4}$ ♪=MM 100	
Menuetto	$\frac{3}{4}$ ♩[.]=MM 66	Allegro
Presto	C [lacking]	♩=MM 152
Symphony in C, major, K. 425 ('Linz')		
Adagio	$\frac{3}{4}$ ♪=MM 84	
Allegro spiritoso	C ♩=MM 96	
Poco Adagio	$\frac{6}{8}$ ♪=MM 116	
Menuetto	$\frac{3}{4}$ ♩[.]=MM 72	
Presto	$\frac{3}{4}$ [$\frac{2}{4}$] ♩=MM 92	
Symphony in D major, K. 504 ('Prague')		
Adagio	¢ ♩=MM 56	
Allegro	¢ ♩=MM 88	
Andante	$\frac{6}{8}$ ♪=MM 126	
Presto	$\frac{2}{4}$ ♩=MM 100	
Symphony in E flat major, K. 543		
Adagio	¢ ♩=MM 60	
Allegro	$\frac{3}{4}$ ♩.=MM 58	
Andante con moto	$\frac{2}{4}$ ♪=MM 108	
Menuetto. Allegretto	Allegro $\frac{3}{4}$ ♩.=MM 80	Allegretto ♩.=MM 72
Allegro	$\frac{2}{4}$ ♩=MM 152	
Symphony in G minor, K. 550		
Molto allegro	¢ ♩=MM 108	
Andante	$\frac{6}{8}$ ♪=MM 116	
Menuetto. Allegretto	Allegro $\frac{3}{4}$ ♩.=MM 76	♩.=MM 72
Allegro assai	¢ ♩=MM 152	
Symphony in C major, K. 551 ('Jupiter')		
Allegro vivace	C ♩=MM 96	
Andante cantabile	$\frac{3}{4}$ [lacking]	♪=MM 108
Menuetto. Allegretto	$\frac{3}{4}$ ♩[.]=MM 88	
Molto allegro	¢ ♩=MM 144	Allegro molto

* J. N. Hummel, *Mozart's Six Grand Symphonies Arranged for the Piano Forte* (London, 1823). See also R. Münster, 'Authentische Tempi zu den sechs letzten Sinfonien W. A. Mozarts?', *Mozart-Jahrbuch* (1962–3), 185–99. Czerny's tempos come from his arrangements of Mozart's last six symphonies for piano four-hands, published in London in 1835. See also W. Malloch, 'Carl Czerny's Metronome Marks for Haydn and Mozart Symphonies', *Early Music* (1988), xvi. 72–82.

550, marked Allegro by Hummel, apparently ought to be the fastest of all, but perhaps its minor key and contrapuntal and chromatic complexities earned it special treatment.) Like the other sources of minuet tempos, Hummel and Czerny gave no new tempos for the trios, a practice confirmed by at least one eighteenth-century document,[131] but which goes against the surely incorrect but virtually universal modern custom of playing them more slowly than their minuets. In the other movements there is no sign of *tempo ordinario* in Hummel's tempos, and indeed these six are 'modern' symphonies, that is, works of individual character to which—in keeping with Beethoven's remark quoted above—that convention may no longer have applied. The Allegro tempos are in general not surprising. The Andante tempos amply confirm that Andante is not a 'slow' tempo for Mozart.

Czerny, born in the year Mozart died, has been much maligned in modern times, since his original compositions are weak and he has become best known for his piano-primer exercises. But he was an accomplished, wide-ranging musician and, as he represented a different school of thought from Hummel's, his acceptance of virtually the same tempos should be treated with interest.[132] So too should the tempos he suggested for a dozen of Mozart's earlier symphonies, presented in Appendix E.

A final remark about tempo, namely, tempo rubato. The musicians of the eighteenth century knew that good performers do not play metronomically,[133] but it was considered the sign of a good performance when a workable tempo was found at the beginning of a movement and held to within reason. While soloists enjoyed considerable latitude, the very idea of wilfully flexible tempos in orchestral music should be ruled out, given the usual lack of rehearsals and the nature of the leadership (both documented below). That is not to say that performances were expected to be mechanical, nor that conductorless groups cannot make convincing retards and other nuances of tempo. A group of musicians that plays together every day, especially in a homogeneous repertory the style of which they know extremely well, can do all sorts of things. One can even nowadays hear the Vienna Philharmonic play Strauss waltzes on New Year's Eve without a conductor other than the concertmaster and with the utmost flexibility of tempo. But the constant moulding of the tempo beat by beat is the creation of a later time. (This matter is discussed further at the end of the chapter.) An anonymous notice of 1836, possibly

---

[131] Jean-Marie Leclair l'aîné, 'Avertissement', *Quatrième Livre de Sonates*, Op. 9 (Paris, 1743).

[132] See further R. Münster, 'Authentische Tempi zu den sechs letzten Sinfonien W. A. Mozarts?', *Mozart-Jahrbuch* (1962–3), 185–99; W. Malloch, 'Carl Czerny's Metronome Marks for Haydn and Mozart Symphonies', *Early Music* (1988), xvi. 72–82.

[133] This comes out clearly in the rejections of various pre-Maelzel metronomes by reviewers who misunderstood the intention of the devices and thought that they were to regiment performances rather than to convey a composer's idea of a good beginning and general tempo.

written by Robert Schumann, documents the embattled survival of the eighteenth-century approach decades after Mozart's death, but before the Wagnerian reforms:

In symphonies, overtures, etc., a good orchestra—which, after all, is what we are discussing here—needs to be directed only at the beginning of a movement and at tempo changes. For the rest, the director can stand at his desk, reading along and listening, in case his command again becomes necessary. In more protracted tempos (Largo, Adagio, etc.) it is certainly good to preserve authority among the ranks by continuous beating. But it should not become an affected, caricatured directing, beating vigorously at *forte*, less vigorously at *piano*, or making a face at those who make mistakes. All of this belongs at most in rehearsals, not before the public.[134]

Repeats

The eighteenth-century convention was that, when the sign :‖: appeared in the middle of a movement, both halves were repeated, without the necessity of any further signs occurring at the beginning or end of the movement.[135] There is not a shred of evidence to suggest that Mozart and his contemporaries regularly failed to observe the repeats in their symphonies. These repeats are no less part of the composers' notation than the tempo, metre, dynamics, pitches, and rhythms. Omitting them deprives listeners of the opportunity to take in and react to the ideas and to the architecture of the movements. It also misrepresents the works' stature, for an eighteenth-century symphony that has repeats which are not observed can be transformed from a ten- or twelve-minute curtain-raiser to a work of more nearly Beethovenian scale when repeats are restored.[136]

Of the first movements of Mozart's symphonies, twenty-three have two repeats, seven one repeat, and twenty-two no repeats (Table 12.6). For most of his symphonic career Mozart wrote first movements either with no repeats (the so-called Italian overture style) or movements with two repeats (the so-called Austrian or Germanic concert symphony style). A brief period of experimentation with three symphonies in 1772 seemingly led to his rejection of the one-repeat first movement, at least for the time being. None the less, in his final decade Mozart

---

[134] Anon., *Neue Zeitschrift für Musik* (1836), iv. 129; trans. Ferguson, 'Col Basso and Generalbass in Mozart's Keyboard Concertos', p. 172.

[135] This must be stated because performers will frequently argue that, since there are no dots at the end of a certain movement, the sign :‖: in the middle must have been an error intended to read :‖. (For this argument in print, applied to the first movement of K. 385, see Sadie, *Symphonies*, 67.) A nineteenth-century point of view holds that in sonata-form movements, which are tripartite, it creates formal redundancy to repeat the second half, which contains both development section and recapitulation. But in the eighteenth century such movements, whether they had two repeats, one repeat, or none, were apparently still felt to be close to their binary origins.

[136] See further N. Temperley, 'Tempo and Repeats in the Early Nineteenth Century' *Music and Letters* (1966), xlvii. 323–36; M. Broyles, 'Organic Form and the Binary Repeat', *The Musical Quarterly* (1980), lxvi. 339–60; H. Macdonald, 'To Repeat or Not to Repeat?', *Proceedings of the Royal Musical Association* (1984–5), cxi. 121–38.

TABLE 12.6 Repeats in first movements of Mozart's symphonies (only works for which no problems of authenticity exist)

First Movements with Two Repeats

K. 16, 19a, 35, 43, 45a, 48, 100 = 62a, 118 = 74c, 110 = 75b, 112, 114, 124, 129, 133, 199 = 161b, 185 = 167a, 183–173dB, 201 = 186a, 202 = 186b, 200 = 189k, 204 = 213a, 385(i), 504

First Movements with One Repeat

K. 128, 130, 134, 425, 543, 550, 551

First Movements with No Repeats

K. 19, 22, 45, 46a, 73, 74, 111 + 120 = 111a, 132, 126 + 161/163 = 141a, 184 = 161a, 162, 181 = 162b, 182 – 173dA, 196 + 121 = 207a, 208 = 213c, 250 – 248b, 297 = 300a, 318, 319, 338, 385(ii), 320

---

apparently favoured the one-repeat first movement. We can only speculate why he at first rejected and then embraced this formal arrangement.[137]

A special problem concerns repeats in da capos of minuets. The universally taught oral tradition handed down among twentieth-century musicians states that these were never observed.[138] Recent research suggests, however, that this tradition, like many another, may be an anachronism. Practices concerning repeats in eighteenth-century dance music were not necessarily uniform. While in the ballroom and on the stage dances were often repeated many times to accommodate the choreography, concert music obeyed other constraints. At the beginning of the eighteenth century the Salzburg composer Georg Muffat, pupil of Lully and Corelli, advised musicians performing his concerti grossi that each section in the dances should be played not more than three times.[139] The only clue that Mozart knew about any such tradition is found in a diary entry for 3 December 1779. Mozart and his family had been to the theatre in Salzburg to see the ballet *Diane et Endymion* (music by J. Starzer, choreography by J. G. Noverre). He wrote that the 'first music' that evening consisted of an Overture, a Minuet and Trio, and a final Allegro, and next to the words 'Minuet and Trio' he added: '*NB* several times repeated'.[140] A letter of Leopold's to Wolfgang, reporting (with amusement and

---

[137] The best discussion of this is by H. Macdonald (see previous note). See also B. Jacobson, 'Once More with Feeling: A Polemic on Repeats', *Musical Newsletter* (1977), vii. 3–7. That conductors may have begun to omit some repeats in the symphonies of Mozart and Haydn by the second and third decades of the nineteenth century is suggested in Temperley, 'Tempo and Repeats in the Early Nineteenth Century'.

[138] This matter was first brought to my attention in autumn 1977 by members of the Academy of Ancient Music during a rehearsal of Mozart's Symphony in F major, K. 130, which has an exceptionally concise Minuet. My hasty and necessarily preliminary investigation of relevant scores and treatises revealed no hint of the systematic omission of da capo repeats earlier than the second or third decade of the nineteenth century. As a result, those repeats were all observed in the Academy of Ancient Music recordings, a practice subsequently taken up in many other performances and recordings. A more systematic attempt to justify the original decision, made under fire, to take the da capo repeats is documented by the following seven footnotes.

[139] Georg Muffat, *Auserlesene mit Ernst- und Lust-gemengten Instrumental-Musik, erste Versamblung* (Passau, 1701), in Denkmäler der Tonkunst in Österreich, xxiii. 10 (German), 14 (Italian), 18 (Latin), 22 (French).

[140] *Briefe*, ii. 555.

annoyance) on one of the series of Salzburg amateur concerts led by Count Czernin discussed in Chapter 10, objected strenuously to the Count's playing all of an unnamed composition without repeats and the minuet and trio 'only once'.[141] The meaning of Wolfgang's and Leopold's casual remarks taken together is ambiguous, but not inconsistent with an interpretation stating that repeats were expected during the da capos of minuets.

In the second edition of the *Klavierschule* (1802) of Mozart's exact contemporary Daniel Gottlob Türk we read:

[Besides the *dal segno*] another kind of repeat sign is the *da capo* ('from the beginning'). That is, when a musical composition is to be played again, following the last bar [of another section of music] or in some other spot, we signify it by means of the above-mentioned words . . . . I remark further only this: after the *trio* of a minuet are commonly placed the words *minuetto da capo*, abbreviated *Min. D. C.* or even just *M. D. C.* This is meant to signify that the minuet is to be taken from the beginning again, and, to be sure, with the prescribed repeats as it was first played; that is, whenever *ma senza replica* ('but without repeat') is not expressly indicated.[142]

Yet in his first edition of 1789 Türk had not felt the need to spell out the details of the inner repeats in the minuet and trio.[143] This may indicate that after 1789 he heard performances in which the repeats were not fully observed and felt the need to clarify his earlier definition.

An apparently similar clarification found its way into Heinrich Koch's *Musikalisches Lexikon*, for in the first edition of 1802 Koch merely observed that the term *da capo* signified the repeat of the first section or subsection of a piece; whereas in an abridged edition of 1807 he amplified his definition to read, 'The term appears at the end of pieces whose beginning section is repeated unchanged [*unabgeändert*]'.[144]

A possibly confirmatory bit of evidence is found in Joseph Haydn's Symphony in C major, Hob. I: 97. Wishing to embellish the repeats of each section of the Minuet of this symphony, Haydn wrote them out fully. As he provided no abridged version of the Minuet, he must not have expected his London orchestra to perform the movement any other way than with the repeats observed in the da capo. Similarly, Hugh Macdonald points out that a kettledrum part used by Haydn in London in 1794 for his Symphony No. 96 in D major bears the annotation, 'At first strain, first time drums 2d strain 2d time drums', with no special provisions

---

[141] *Briefe*, ii. 383; not in *Letters*.

[142] Türk, *Klavierschule*, 2nd edn. (Leipzig, 1802), 143.

[143] Türk, *Klavierschule*, 1st edn. (Leipzig, 1789), 125 (= *School of Clavier Playing*, 121).

[144] These telling differences between the first and second editions of Türk's and Koch's treatises were pointed out to me by Max Rudolf, whom I wish to thank. Rudolf, who has undertaken a thorough investigation of the minuets of Haydn, Beethoven, and Mozart, believes that the decision to take repeats in the da capos of classical minuets was correct. See his articles 'Inner Repeats in the Da Capo of Classical Minuets and Scherzos', *Journal of the Conductors' Guild* (1982), iii. 145–50; 'On the Performance of Mozart's Minuets', *Friends of Mozart Newsletter* (Fall 1984), xvii. 1–4.

made for the da capo.[145] This ties the written out example of Haydn's Symphony No. 97 to the normal notation of minuets.

Standards

There is plenty of evidence of bad performances in the second half of the eighteenth century, some of it contained in passages from Mozart's letters cited in earlier chapters. There were not yet conservatories turning out large numbers of technically adept, would-be orchestra members, and many orchestras were stocked with a certain number of doublers, as well as amateurs, courtiers, and others whose principal professions were non-musical. But an honest modern musician with acute ears knows that often enough modern orchestras do not play perfectly in tune or perfectly together either, yet we will not permit this fact to set our standards for us. There were certain factors favouring the eighteenth-century musician: he played music only in one style (that of his own time), he usually played with the same colleagues and under the same leader almost every day, year in and year out. Although often musically demanding, the orchestra's parts were not as technically demanding as those of later orchestral music. There are signs that standards, at their best, were as high as or perhaps, in certain ways, occasionally higher than ours: equal temperament had not yet come in to coarsen musicians' ears for pitch, and the best players worried about the difference of pitch between, for example, D sharp and E flat, something to which many modern orchestral musicians pay little heed. Sceptics will point to Dr Burney's remark that even in the famous Mannheim orchestra, on the occasion he heard them, the winds played out of tune.[146] But one could look at his remark the other way: Burney apparently did expect them to play in tune, was surprised when they did not do so, and urged them to pay more attention to the matter. That is to say, he knew perfectly well that it could be, should be, and (in some places) was, done. For a long time in the twentieth century it was irresponsibly claimed that no one could play in tune on eighteenth-century wind instruments, but there are plenty of fine players now performing on them who give the lie to that notion.

Many discussions of ripienists from the second half of the eighteenth century stress the importance of good sight-reading.[147] Why this was a constant concern is demonstrated in the following series of remarks, the first three drawn from Joseph Haydn, the remainder from other sources:

---

[145] Macdonald, 'To Repeat or Not to Repeat?'. Macdonald gives further examples of Haydn's minuets which may support or contradict the idea of observing da capo repeats.

[146] Charles Burney, *The Present State of Music in Germany, the Netherlands and United Provinces* (London, 1773), i. 94–5.

[147] For instance, Johann Samuel Petri, *Anleitung zur praktischen Musik*, 2nd edn. (Leipzig, 1782), 173; Heinrich Christoph Koch, 'Ueber den Charakter der Solo- und Ripienstimme', *Journal der Tonkunst* (1795), i. 143–55, here 153.

Now I would humbly ask you to tell the Princely Kapellmeister there that these three symphonies [Nos. 90–2], because of their many particular effects, should be rehearsed at least once, carefully and with special concentration before they are performed.[148]

Please tell Mr von Keess that I ask him respectfully to have a rehearsal of both these symphonies [Nos. 95–6], because they are very delicate, especially the last movement of that in D major, for which I recommend the softest piano and a very quick tempo.[149]

On 30th March 1795 I was invited by Dr Arnold and his associates to a grand concert in Free Maisons [*sic*] Hall: one of my big symphonies was to have been given under my direction, but since they wouldn't have any rehearsal, I refused to cooperate and did not appear.[150]

. . . a good orchestral violinist . . . has to play everything at sight . . . . Few solo players read well . . . .[151]

Trois Sinfonies à grand Orchestre composées par Mr G. Vanhall. Œuvre 10. [. . .] These three symphonies distinguish themselves among others by this so familiar and celebrated man, and they are full of good thoughts and a select accompaniment. They rather approach the newest Hayden [*sic*] symphonies, but are more difficult than easy; and one cannot advise putting out the parts without having played through them at least once . . . . [152]

No one who has followed the chronicle of Mozart's concert-life in Chapters 2 to 11 should be surprised by any of this. Unlike opera, which often had extensive rehearsals, concerts usually had just one. Writers of the period tend to refer to attending or participating in *the* rehearsal, rather than *a* rehearsal. But the conditions described in the opening paragraph of this section on standards provide the basis for an explanation of how, on a single rehearsal, technically and artistically sound results were possible. There are nowadays in the world still musicians performing to a high technical standard on one or no rehearsals, for instance, jazz and dance bands playing nightly in the United States or cathedral choirs in England presenting daily Evensong Services. The key factors are: a circumscribed repertory, fixed personnel, and frequent performances under effective leadership.

A report from the last year of Mozart's life brings together a number of the ideas discussed above, that is, along with the single rehearsal, the standing ensemble daily performing a stylistically homogeneous repertory, with perfect ensemble and (what most excited the observer, who was a professional musician) elaborate, unanimimously rendered nuances.

---

[148] Letter of *c.*17 Oct. 1789. Bartha (ed.), *Haydn: Briefe*, 214; (=Landon (ed.), *Collected Correspondence and London Notebooks*, 89).

[149] Letter of 17 Nov. 1791. *Haydn: Briefe*, 265; (=*Collected Correspondence and London Notebooks*, 121).

[150] Diary entry. *Haydn: Briefe*, 531 (= *Collected Correspondence and London Notebooks*, 289).

[151] Leopold Mozart, *Violinschule*, 258–9 (= *Treatise*, 216–17).

[152] C. F. Cramer (ed.), *Magazin der Musik* (1783), i. 92; trans. Landon, *Haydn: Chronicle and Works*, ii. 474.

... the rehearsal was to begin .... I was eyewitness to this orchestra's surpassing excellence. Mr Winneberger, Kapellmeister at Wallenstein, laid before it a symphony of his own composition, which was by no means easy of execution, especially for the wind instruments, which had several solos concertante. It went finely, however, at the first trial, to the great surprise of the composer. An hour after the dinner music, the concert began. It was opened with a symphony by Mozart; then followed a recitative and aria sung by Simonetti; next, a violoncello concerto played by Mr [Bernhard] Romberg; fourthly, a symphony by Pleyel; fifthly, an aria by Righini, sung by Simonetti; sixthly, a double concerto for violin and violoncello played by the two Rombergs; and the closing piece was the symphony by Winneberger, which had very many brilliant passages. The opinion already expressed as to the performance of this orchestra was confirmed. It was not possible to attain a higher degree of exactness. Such perfection in the pianos, fortes, rinforzandos—such a swelling and gradual increase of tone and then such an almost imperceptible dying away, from the most powerful to the lightest accents—all this was formerly to be heard only in Mannheim. It would be difficult to find another orchestra in which the violins and the bass-line instruments are throughout in such excellent hands ....[153]

Leadership and Interpretation

Players in conductorless orchestras cannot depend on constant guidance for good ensemble and fine points of interpretation. They will be forced to look more at, and listen harder to, colleagues (especially section leaders) than they would with a conductor to follow. For the player this is more demanding, but also more interesting, since he cannot abdicate responsibility, and interpretation arises from joint effort.

Since instrumentalists of Mozart's day played only music of their own times, they were less likely than we to fall into anachronisms. Furthermore, they were raised playing eighteenth-century instruments, whereas most of those who play them now were raised playing other kinds of instruments. It takes great patience and sensitivity to unlearn training hard won over many years of practising, and to take up new ways of playing. All too many performances reveal players who are playing on old instruments using modern techniques, or who are attempting to imitate old instruments on modern ones; in neither case can the results be satisfactory.

If generalizations can be made about the differences between the eighteenth-century instruments and their modern counterparts, they are these: old instruments are built to have a sharp attack or ictus, modern ones to have as little attack as possible. Old instruments are built to detach notes, leaving legato as a special (but

---

[153] Carl Ludwig Junker writing in the *Musikalische Korrespondenz der Filarmonischen Gesellschaft* (23 Nov. 1791) as trans. in E. Forbes (ed.), *Thayer's Life of Beethoven* (Princeton, 1962), 104. Junker was describing a concert by the Cologne court orchestra performing at Mergentheim.

important) effect; modern instruments primarily play legato, producing true staccato only with effort. Old instruments play mostly with a 'straight' tone, using vibrato only as a special effect; modern instruments (with some but ever fewer exceptions) employ continuous vibrato and on them a 'straight' tone is an extraordinary sound. Old instruments value distinctive timbres; modern instruments are expected to 'blend'.

The man who produced many of Herbert von Karajan's recordings has accurately described what is considered good in 'post-romantic' orchestral performances and should be considered problematic in 'neo-classical' ones:

[The Karajan sound] is exquisitely polished, free of anything that is unbeautiful, of great brilliance, and fortissimo without the click of an attack . . . . We worked together for years on the theory that no entrance must start without the string vibrating and the bow already moving, and when you get a moving bow touching an already vibrating string, you get a beautiful entry. But if either of those bodies is not alive and already moving, you get a click, and Karajan has calculated all that.[154]

'Neo-classical' performers are not afraid of the 'click'; in appropriate contexts, they actively seek it out.

The directors of 'neo-classical' orchestras must strive for a unified style of playing that grows out of the nature of the best old instruments rather than out of preconceived ideas about what constitutes 'good tone', 'good phrasing', etc. It is perhaps stating the obvious to say that the director(s)—usually the concertmaster or the continuo player, or both together—must set workable tempos and maintain them, must not permit technical flaws, such as poor intonation or bad ensemble, must see that the balance is handled so that the important parts are heard and the less important parts kept subordinate, and must control the overall style— dynamics, length and attack of notes, the way in which musical ideas will be presented. Some of these duties are easier with eighteenth-century instruments than with modern ones, some harder. Balance is easier (provided reasonable numbers of players are assigned to each section) because the transparency of fewer players and a more nearly vibratoless texture enable one to hear everything, and the danger of covering a crucial part is somewhat less than with modern, opaque timbres. The same transparency mercilessly exposes poor intonation and bad ensemble for, as every player knows, vibrato can cover a multitude of sins. But none of these matters accounts for one of the most salient differences between 'neo-classical' and 'post-romantic' interpretations, which arises from the presence or absence of a baton conductor.

The job of modern baton conductors—and the way in which one judges them—

[154] E. Schwarzkopf, *On and Off the Record: A Memoir of Walter Legge* (New York, 1982), 226.

focuses on the controlling of nuance, dynamics, balance, and tempo beat by beat during rehearsals and concerts. An elastic tempo, which stretches and pulls the music in expressive ways while still maintaining shape and flow, is considered the sign of a fine conductor; whereas a conductor who 'merely beats time' is considered incompetent. The ability to keep the music from disintegrating at extreme, slow tempos—the slower the better—is considered a mark of greatness. Evidence exists to suggest that Richard Wagner may have been the first conductor to work in this way, or perhaps his fame gave the new manner its *imprimatur*. Wagner's innovation was not in applying freedom of tempo to the music of his own generation, but in applying it retrospectively to the symphonies of Beethoven. Once that style of orchestral interpretation was established for Beethoven's symphonies, it was in the natural course of events extended to Mozart's, Haydn's, and Schubert's. Loathing music dominated by dance and march, in which tempo was steady and phrase structure symmetrical, Wagner reinterpreted the classics in his own image.[155]

Not only was there no such tradition during Mozart's life, but there could not have been one, for it requires a kind of leadership that had not yet come into existence. To be sure, there were baton-waving conductors in Mozart's time. In some opera-houses outside Italy a baton was used, and especially in those places under French cultural influence this 'time-beater' (as he was called) was employed. And that is what he did: beat time. In large-scale church music someone 'gave the tactus'. In their correspondence Leopold, Wolfgang, and Nannerl nearly consistently distinguished between the verbs *tactieren*, which they applied to church music and oratorio, and *dirigieren*, which they applied to opera and concerts.[156] The former was necessary to co-ordinate the often far-flung orchestra(s), choir(s), soloists, and organist(s) in large churches; the latter was the normal, so-called 'dual control' system of leadership by concertmaster and continuo player.

The implications are clear: a 'neo-classical' performance may be lively, poignant, acute, clear, refined. It cannot have the ongoing shaping, the personal interpretation, that we treasure in performances of romantic and modern orchestral music by great modern conductors; nor would it have been practical to create such performances in the single rehearsal usually allotted symphonies in the eighteenth century. Let it be clearly stated, however, that even without a baton conductor

---

[155] W. A. Bebbington, 'The Orchestral Conducting Practice of Richard Wagner' (Ann Arbor, 1984). See also Wagner's own essay, *On Conducting (Ueber das Dirigiren): A Treatise on Style in the Execution of Classical Music*, trans. E. Dannreuther (London, 1887, repr. 1972).

[156] *Tactieren/Tact schlagen: Briefe*, i. 285, 286, 486 (Vienna: Mass); ii. 95 (Salzburg: Mass); iv. 192 (Vienna: Mass); Deutsch, 273 (Vienna: oratorio). *Dirigieren/beym Clavier* (or *Flügel* or *fortepiano*) *dirigieren: Briefe*, i. 257, 270, 271, 279 (Vienna: opera); 414 (Milan: opera); ii. 197 (Mannheim: opera); 459, 465, 471, 473, 477–8, 479 (Salzburg: court concerts); iii. 239, iv. 110, (Vienna: opera); iv. 153 (Vienna: N.B. Mass); iv. 195 (Milan: opera); Deutsch, 196 (Vienna: opera), 241 (Vienna: concert), 251, 267 (Prague: opera), 294 (Vienna: N.B. oratorio), 357 (Vienna: opera), 386 (Vienna: Masonic cantata).

there can never be no interpretation, for all performance, competent or otherwise, implies interpretation. If a 'neo-classical' orchestra's leaders are skilful, technical and artistic problems will be surmounted, the group's performances will take on a distinct character, and the affect of each movement will be communicated to the listeners. Even so and despite the best efforts of these leaders, the music will have to speak for itself more than it will under a 'post-romantic' conductor. The results are bound to be more neutral and less personal, more objective and less subjective. Whether one likes this more or less is perhaps a matter of background, taste, training, and experience. But we may temporarily put aside scruples about whether 'neo-classical' performances are 'right' or 'wrong' for present-day musical life and state simply that they create a possible avenue for understanding the composer, his music, and his times, and that, by providing an alternate way of interpreting Mozart's symphonies, they offer performers and audiences new pleasures in the form of increased variety and the heuristic controversies to which such variety gives rise.

13

Meanings for Mozart's Symphonies

———————— ❧ ————————

In the course of this study every opportunity has been sought to discover what Mozart's contemporaries thought of his symphonies. The yield has been meagre. Symphonies were seldom discussed in detail in writings of the period, and, when mentioned, they were often dismissed with conventional epithets: 'excellent', 'brilliant', 'new', or 'grand,' 'festive', 'noble'. A burst of loquacity was represented by the London critic moved to write of 'a great and beautiful symphony, varied in all its movements'[1]—certainly a compliment and doubtless an accurate description, as far as it went. Nothing was written in Mozart's lifetime that modern readers would recognize as serious criticism of his symphonies, and, apparently, no real analysis was attempted until Momigny's examination of K. 550 in 1818.[2] Reasons for this state of affairs have recently been proposed:

The difficulty in documenting the history of the reception of a Mozart work results—as with Bach—from the eighteenth century's point of view, the consideration of compositions less as individual 'works' than as constituent parts of a complete *œuvre* or as specimens of a genre, which were dedicated not to the constituting of a repertory but to the carrying on of musical 'daily business'. If one disregards a few operas, which were already 'repertory pieces' in his lifetime, hardly one contemporary text is devoted to a single, unique, completely determined work by Mozart.[3]

Many examples of the almost total silence surrounding the appearance of most symphonies are adduced in earlier chapters. A further, striking instance is found in Joseph Haydn's autobiographical sketch of 6 July 1776. By that year the 'father of the symphony', as Haydn has sometimes been called, had composed some sixty

---

[1] See Table 10.2.

[2] Jérôme Joseph de Momigny, 'Symphonie', in N. E. Framery, P. G. Giguené, J. J. de Momigny (eds.), *Encyclopédie méthodique: Musique* (Paris, 1818; repr. New York, 1971), ii. 408–17, here 412–15. See also A. Palm, 'Mozart und Haydn in der Interpretation Momignys', in G. Reichert and M. Just (eds.), *Bericht über den internationalen musikwissenschaftlichen Kongress, Kassel 30 September—4 October 1962* (Kassel, 1963), 187–90.

[3] W. Klüppelholz and H. J. Busch (eds.), *Musik gedeutet und gewertet: Dokumente zur Rezeptionsgeschichte von Musik* (Munich, 1983), 36.

symphonies, a number of which were enjoying success in many parts of Europe, but in his autobiography he never mentioned symphonies, listing only some of his sacred and secular vocal music.[4] Symphonies lacked the prestige of either vocal music or instrumental music intended for élite gatherings of connoisseurs. During Mozart's lifetime his symphonies were not 'classics' to be savoured, repeated, and passed on to posterity, but music for use, to be enjoyed and replaced by newer works.

One can hardly imagine a better placed witness to the development of the symphony of Mozart's time than Charles Burney, an able musician and articulate writer who apprenticed under Handel yet lived to hear Beethoven's music, making it his business, during this long stretch of history, to investigate many aspects of music. Nearing the end of his life, largely housebound, he spent his late seventies and early eighties providing music articles for a new edition of the *Cyclopaedia* edited by Abraham Rees.[5] Burney created his articles by taking over from previous editions of the *Cyclopaedia* material he considered sound and adding to it from his publications, from his large personal library, and from his capacious memory.

One such composite article, unsigned, defined and described 'symphony'. For present purposes the relevant portions of Burney's definition are paragraphs 1, 2, 5, 6, and 7:

SYMPHONY ... formed from [the Greek words] *with*, and ... *sound*, probably denotes a consonance, or concert of several sounds agreeable to the ear; whether they be vocal or instrumental, or both; called also *harmony*; which see.

Some authors restrain symphony to the sole music of instruments; in this sense, say they, the recitativos in such an opera were intolerable, but the symphonies excellent ....

The word symphony is now applied to instrumental music; both that of pieces designed only for instruments, as sonatas and concertos, and that in which the instruments are accompanied with the voice, as in operas, &c ....

Before the above was written, symphony had been highly cultivated in Germany, particularly at the Man[n]heim school, by Stamitz, Holtzbauer [*sic*], Can[n]abich, Toeschi, and Filtz; by Vanhal, Ditters, and Kozeluch, at Vienna; and since that period, the symphonies of the immortal Haydn have exceeded in number and excellence all that modern times can boast, and seem to include every perfection that can render instrumental music interesting and sublime: invention, science, knowledge of instruments, majesty, fire, grace, and pathos by turns, with new modulations, and new harmonies, without crudity or affectation. All these excellences the admirable Mozart had nearly attained; and perhaps he is only inferior to Haydn in the number of his symphonies, from the shortness of his vital course!

---

[4] Bartha (ed.), *Haydn: Briefe*, 76–82 (= Landon (ed.), *Collected Correspondence and London Notebooks*, 18–21).

[5] This encyclopedia had its origin in Chambers's *Cyclopaedia*, which from 1728 had appeared in London in a number of editions. Rees became the editor in 1778, and revised editions continued to appear until the work eventually acquired his name in place of Chambers's.

Beethoven (pronounced *Baythoven*), a disciple of Mozart, is now (1804) so rapidly advancing into fame, that there would be little risk in predicting, that, if he lives, he will be the great man among musicians of the present century, as Haydn and Mozart were of the latter end of the last. He is said to be a young man; but writes with the freedom and boldness of long experience, and a fertility of invention that promises inexhaustible resources.[6]

Burney's retrospective definition of 'symphony' thus includes the following meanings that apply to eighteenth-century music: the instrumental portions of concerted vocal music, any purely instrumental music including sonatas and concertos, the ritornellos of arias, and symphonies proper. The present discussion will consider only his remarks about the last of these, which (*mutatis mutandis*) coincides with the modern meaning of the term.

Burney divided the history of the symphony proper into three eras, an early period dominated by the Mannheim and Viennese composers whom he names, a middle period dominated by Mozart and Haydn, and a period just begun with the appearance on the scene of Beethoven. His singling out of composers for honourable mention is impeccable, and history has vindicated his choices. To find this elderly recluse, who had earlier consistently underestimated Mozart's significance,[7] revising his opinion in his late seventies is impressive, although, even then, he still could not bring himself to place Mozart on the same plane as his beloved Haydn.

Brilliant as Burney's intuition was of which symphonists were important, his periodization has puzzling aspects. On the one hand, modern research suggests that the Mannheim and Austrian symphonists had important Italian antecedents,[8] and, on the other, Beethoven—despite subsequent achievements in the field—had by 1804 not yet launched a new movement in symphonic composition, but had joined one created in the 1780s and 1790s by Mozart, Haydn, and others. The 'Eroica' symphony, composed in 1803 and first publicly performed in Vienna in 1805, was not published until 1806. Burney's statement, which refers therefore to Beethoven's first two symphonies, stresses their 'freedom and boldness', whereas modern listeners, aware of their indebtedness to the late symphonies of Mozart and, especially, to Haydn's 'London' symphonies, tend to group all of those

---

[6] The edition of Rees's *The Cyclopaedia: or, Universal Dictionary of Arts, Sciences, and Literature* available to me was published in Philadelphia (n.d.). It is unpaginated. Burney's symphony article is found in vol. xxxvi. Some of its peculiarities can be understood in light of its sources: the first two paragraphs were already found in the first edition of Chambers's *Cyclopaedia* (1728), although Burney probably got them from Rees's editions of that work, where they are found along with the third and fourth paragraphs in which Burney's earlier writings were already cited. Burney's new remarks begin with 'Before the above was written', by which is presumably meant, before the mid-1770s.

[7] C. B. Oldman, 'Dr Burney and Mozart', *Mozart-Jahrbuch* (1962–3), 75–81; *Mozart-Jahrbuch* (1964), 109–10.

[8] E. K. Wolf, 'On the Origins of the Mannheim Style', in J. W. Hill (ed.), *Studies in Musicology in Honor of Otto E. Albrecht: A Collection of Essays by His Colleagues and Former Students at the University of Pennsylvania* (Kassel, 1980), 197–239.

together in order to contrast them to the symphonies Beethoven composed later.[9] The modern listener can, in any case, agree with Burney that, even making generous allowance for the general evolution of musical styles and tastes to which many other composers made vital contributions, the new departures in symphonic composition of the 1780s and 1790s were closely linked to the productions of Haydn and Mozart.

However strange Burney's brief history of the symphony may seem, a greater peculiarity of his essay is that fact that, in discussing the modern meaning of the word, he failed to define it beyond remarking that it is instrumental ensemble music and naming a few leading practitioners. Not a word about its content, its form, its function. Perhaps he thought that these would be self-evident to his readers, but, if so, that was a peculiar intellectual shortcoming, especially for a man who was a great friend of Dr Johnson's. Despite the sweeping changes that had overtaken orchestral music in the intervening period, Burney's 'definition' of 1803 had not advanced beyond Mattheson's of ninety years earlier (when 'symphony' really did mean almost any instrumental ensemble music): 'There is otherwise nothing typical or indisputable to report of symphonies, because each follows his fancy in the matter.'[10]

That the 'definitions' of the symphony by Mattheson, Scheibe, Schulz, Burney, and other eighteenth-century worthies are so unsatisfactory for modern purposes suggests that cultural and social forces were at work guiding their thoughts into channels different from those in which ours run. Any attempt to discover what Mozart's symphonies may have meant to him and his contemporaries must, therefore, seek information beyond what can be gleaned from their theoretical writings on the subject.

Re-examination of Mozart's symphonies of the late 1770s and early 1780s reveals the emergence of essential elements of a new style. A key technical and stylistic change—one confined neither to symphonies nor to Mozart—was the dissolution of the composite bass-line (or basso) into separate cello, double-bass, and bassoon parts. In Mozart's early symphonies the basso was realized by cellos, double-basses, bassoons, and (usually) a harpsichord or organ *colla parte*.[11] As these bass-line instruments were rarely specified in the scores of symphonies, except when they

---

[9] E. Forbes (ed.), *Thayer's Life of Beethoven* (Princeton, 1962), 342, 375, 411. One might defend Burney's perception of Beethoven's earliest symphonies by quoting a review in the *Zeitung für die Elegante Welt* (Vienna, May 1804): 'Beethoven's Second Symphony is a crass monster, a hideously writhing wounded dragon, that refuses to expire, and though bleeding in the Finale, furiously beats about with its tail erect' (N. Slominsky, *Lexicon of Musical Invective* (New York, 1953), 42).

[10] See ch. 4 at n. 4.

[11] This was not necessarily true for all genres, for in certain kinds of chamber music 'basso' could signify cello or perhaps some other 8' instrument, whereas in certain pieces of 'informal' music in the divertimento category, it could signify a double bass. See J. Webster, 'The Scoring of Mozart's Chamber Music for Strings', in A. Atlas (ed.), *Music in the Classic Period: Essays in Honor of Barry S. Brook* (New York, 1985), 259–96.

had obbligato solo passages, their presence must be deduced from the evidence of sets of parts, treatises, payrolls, iconographic evidence, and the like. The *basso* is usually not figured; bassoons are occasionally written as obbligato instruments in a single movement or throughout a symphony, and cellos and basses are not written for separately.

In his late symphonies, on the contrary, bassoons are always obbligato instruments, cellos and basses are written divisi in some portions of most movements (excluding most minuets and trios and all of K. 385), and the need for a continuo instrument becomes less apparent. The last symphony in which bassoons are not obbligato is K. 213c of 1775, and (exception made for brief passages in the first movements of K. 19 and 73) the first in which the cellos and double-basses are divisi is K. 318 of 1779. The *colla parte* bass-line continued to exist for Mozart, as for Beethoven and Schubert after him, as an option for reinforcing tutti passages and for evoking powerful, archaic orchestral textures to contrast with more modern, variegated ones. This dissolution of the thoroughbass, along with heavier orchestration and the rise of violinist-leaders, helped to render the keyboard continuo dispensable.

Another noteworthy development was the definitive separation in Mozart's *œuvre* of the overture-sinfonia and the concert-sinfonia. These two genres were intertwined for most of the eighteenth century, not only in their forms and functions but in the interchangeability of the labels 'overture' and 'sinfonia'. The first of Mozart's overtures that he did not (and perhaps could not) recycle as a concert symphony was the overture to *Idomeneo* of 1780. Doubtless this was because it was also the first of his overtures in which he took seriously the then current 'reform' theories (usually attributed to Gluck, but actually widely discussed and experimented with in Germanic opera seria of the time), which required the overture to form an integral part of the drama, giving its form a certain particularity and its content some programmatic aspects.[12]

Separation of the two genres also represents the standardization of symphonies as a three-or four-movement form of considerable length and weight, and often with internal repeats; and of overtures as a one-movement form. The overtures to *Die Zauberflöte, Le nozze di Figaro, La clemenza di Tito, Don Giovanni*, and *Così fan tutte* circulated as concert pieces, but they did so as the single-movement overtures to the operas, rather than transformed into untitled symphonies through the addition of other movements.[13] The last opera overture refurbished by Mozart as a

---

[12] See D. Heartz, 'Mozart's Overture to Titus as Dramatic Argument', *The Musical Quarterly* (1978), lxiv. 29–49. For the tradition of 'reform' operas at Mannheim leading up to Mozart's *Idomeneo*, see E. K. Wolf, 'Mannheim and Munich' in N. Zaslaw and S. Sadie (eds.), *Man & Music*, vol. v: *The Classic Era* (London, 1989), 213–39.

[13] Interestingly, as late as 1786 Mozart had originally planned the overture to *Figaro* in three movements, but rejected that. See *NMA*, ii/5/16/1. xviii, xxiii.

symphony was from *Il rè pastore*, K. 213c, of 1775. The last concert symphony used as an overture with his consent was K. 318 of 1779. K. 318 was also the last three-movements-in-one symphony that he wrote.

Johann Traeg's catalogue of 1799, discussed in Chapter 11, demonstrates an awareness of the distinction between the older sinfonia–overture type and the newer genres; for instance, all of Joseph Haydn's opera overtures included are listed among his symphonies, and the catalogue contains annotations to that effect.[14] For Mozart, however, the distinction between the two types is scrupulously observed in Traeg's catalogue: what are apparently the symphony versions of the overtures to the early operas *Lucio Silla* and *La finta giardiniera* are in the section devoted to symphonies, whereas the overtures to *Idomeneo, Die Entführung, Le nozze di Figaro, Don Giovanni, Così fan tutte,* and *La clemenza di Tito* are found in the section devoted to opera overtures.[15]

Another crucial aspect of these developments was the new style of orchestration discussed in the previous chapter. To the winds' baroque function as instruments playing *colla parte* with the strings, opposing the strings in polychoral or concerto grosso fashion or appearing as soloists, and to their mid-century function of sustaining slow-moving background harmonies in the tuttis, was now added a new function: ongoing participation in the presentation, fragmentation, and development of important thematic materials in a mixed texture known in German by the evocative term 'openwork'. The increased virtuosity demanded of the wind players meant a gradual decline in the practice of doubling: the last of Mozart's symphonies asking the oboists to play the flute is K. 250 = 248b of 1776. This new treatment of the wind instruments, by no means entirely absent from the symphonies of the 1770s, is clearly adumbrated in the 'Linz' symphony of 1783, but it first appears fully developed in the 'Prague' symphony, having been brilliantly evolved in the piano concertos written for Vienna in the early 1780s as well as in *Idomeneo* and *Die Entführung*.[16] Mozart's most important contribution to modern orchestration, and an aspect of his style that Haydn, Beethoven, and Schubert studied and imitated, it was predicated on having superior wind players, as in Vienna and Prague.[17]

[14] This was presumably because the overtures of Haydn available to Traeg were of the older type; Haydn did not write the newer type until the 1790s, in his unperformed opera *Orfeo* and his oratorios *Die Schöpfung* and *Die Jahreszeiten*, works not available to Traeg (A. Weinmann, *Johann Traeg: Die Musikalienverzeichnisse von 1799 und 1804 (Handschriften und Sortiment)* (Beiträge zur Geschichte des alt-Wiener Musikverlages, ii/17) (Vienna, 1973), i. 9–13). Haydn's earlier attitude is revealed in the letter he wrote in 1768 concerning the performance of his *Applausus* cantata, suggesting as an overture the first two movements of any symphony (presumably in the key of the ritornello of the first aria, which will serve, Haydn says, in lieu of a finale) (*Haydn: Briefe*, 58 (= *Collected Correspondence and London Notebooks*, 9)).

[15] Weinmann, *Johann Traeg*, i. 2, 17–18.

[16] C. Wolff, 'Aspects of Instrumentation in Mozart's Orchestral Music', *Interprétation de la musique classique de Haydn à Schubert: Colloque international, Ivry, 13–15 octobre 1977* (Paris, 1980), 37–43.

[17] Some evidence of the manner in which Mozart's difficult wind parts slowed the dissemination of his orchestral works in much of Europe is presented in the previous chapter, and more is offered below.

The increased difficulty was not limited to the wind parts, however. It generally went along with increases in length, in contrapuntal textures, and in chromaticism, which, taken together, amounted to a new seriousness and complexity in the symphony as a genre. The sixty-odd symphonies that Mozart wrote between his symphonic début as an eight-and-a-half-year-old prodigy and the 'Haffner' symphony of 1782 display the growth of the genre, the evolution of the musical style of the period, the maturing of Mozart's own style, and his increasing command of the métier. Apart from an increase in the length of movements, however, these symphonies do not show much development in technical or conceptual difficulty: the demands put on the players concerning range, speed, complicated rhythms, chromaticism, or other unconventional musical ideas are kept strictly reined in. This was doubtless a consequence of the number of ripieno players who were amateurs or doublers, of the more or less universal practice of having either one rehearsal or none, and of the uses to which the symphonies were put.

A few writers of the period left formulations of the characteristic expectations for symphonies:

Since chamber music is for connoisseurs and amateurs, the pieces can be composed in a more learned and elaborate fashion than those works destined for public use, where everything must be simple and cantabile, so that everyone understands it.[18]

The melody of the sonata, because it portrays the feelings of individual persons, must be highly refined, and at the same time present the finest nuances of the feelings; by contrast, the melody of the symphony must distinguish itself, not through such delicacies of expression, but through power and emphasis.[19]

[The] characteristics [of a sonata] therefore are: finer sorts of subjects, and a more highly finished, or more delicate, and embellished elaboration, than what would be proper for symphonies, or tuttis in concertos .... [20]

The nature of symphonies requires: simpler sorts of subjects, and a grander and more manly elaboration, than what would be proper for the finer sort of sonatas .... The harmony and the passages of the symphonies in question ['free', that is, concert symphonies] must ... be more grand and bold than sublime or embellished with graces.[21]

---

[18] [Johann Peter Kirnberger], 'Cammermusik', Johann Georg Sulzer, *Allgemeine Theorie der schönen Kunst*, 2nd edn. (Leipzig, 1792–4), i. 441.

[19] Heinrich Christoph Koch, *Versuch einer Anleitung zur Composition* (Leipzig, 1782–93), iii. 316. I owe this reference as well as the next two to E. K. Wolf, 'The Orchestral Trios, Op. 1, of Johann Stamitz', in Atlas (ed.), *Music in the Classic Period*, 297–322, here 309–11.

[20] August C. F. Kollmann, *An Essay on Practical Musical Composition* (London, 1799), 9.

[21] Ibid. 15, 17. See further M. Broyles, 'The Two Instrumental Styles of Classicism', *Journal of the American Musicological Society* (1983), xxxvi. 210–42; S. Reventlow, 'Concert Life in Odense around 1800', in J. P. Larsen and K. Wedin (eds.), *Die Sinfonie KV 16a "del Sigr. Mozart"* (Odense, 1987), 25–9, here 29.

Something happened to alter this state of affairs. Again, the 'Linz' symphony, K. 425, of 1783 shows clear leanings toward the new style in length, difficulty, and 'delicacies of expression', as well as in the employment of trumpets and drums in the slow movement, while with the 'Prague' symphony four years later the new style emerges fully fledged. One symptom of the 'new seriousness' is the transformation of Mozart's finales from stylized dances to truly symphonic music. Such baroque forms as the orchestral suite routinely began with a weighty ouverture and then lightened up with a series of dances. Under the new aesthetic, instrumental music was not only to begin with a movement of substance, but to end with one too. Einstein called those symphonies in which the finales rival the first movements in length and weight 'finale-symphonies', claiming that the first to exhibit this trait were four works from 1772 (K. 129, 130, 132, 133).[22] Perhaps equally telling, after K. 338 of 1780 Mozart put aside forever that old baroque standby, the jig-finale, which had served him for so many symphonies.

The establishment of all the stylistic developments just enumerated—dissolution of the basso, definitive separation of overture and concert symphony, new wind orchestration, and deepened conception—can be traced in Mozart's symphonies composed in the years between 1775 and 1783.

Chapters 2 to 10 have shown that Mozart's early symphonies, like those of his contemporaries, were written as curtain-raisers, fanfares to herald the beginnings of plays, operas, cantatas, oratorios, and public and private concerts. They were sometimes also used as entr'actes and finales to such occasions.[23] In the Benedictine monasteries of Bavaria and Austria they were employed as *Tafelmusik*. Symphonies were heard in church punctuating High Mass or embellishing Vespers. In Salzburg and Vienna they even appeared on mild summer evenings as outdoor serenades. Given these functions, as a way of articulating a series of musical, social, or ceremonial events, the conventionality of most of the musical ideas in Mozart's early symphonies—however excellent they may be—is simply a case of a good craftsman's creating what his patrons required. (This conventionality, it must be said, may be detected in comparison not only with Mozart's later symphonies, but with his other orchestral music—serenades, operas, and piano concertos—of the

---

[22] Einstein, 221–2.

[23] All these functions have been adequately documented in earlier chapters except the use of symphonies as entr'actes. Joseph Haydn's Symphony in C major, Hob. I: 60, 'Il distratto' (= 'Der Zerstreute'), was written to serve as overture and entr'actes to a play. The travelling troupe of the Mozarts' friend Boehm played it as such in Salzburg (R. Angermüller, 'Haydns "Der Zerstreute" in Salzburg (1776)', *Haydn-Studien* (1978), iv. 85–93). Whether Mozart ever arranged for such a use of a symphony of his is not known, but, on the evidence of the following newspaper account, others did so: 'Today, the 26th [of July 1785] Schmidt's Court Theatre Troupe will perform, by urgent demand, *Die eingebildeten Philosophe* [i.e., Giovanni Paisiello's *Gli astrologi immaginari* (St Petersburg, 1779) transformed into *Le Philosophe imaginairen* (Paris, 1780), then turned into a Singspiel]. Between the acts a new grand symphony by Mr Mozart jr. will be played' (*Real-Zeitung* (Erlangen, 26 July 1785), 484). I am grateful to Cliff Eisen for communicating this item.

same dates.) Mozart's early symphonies were, with perhaps a few exceptions, intended to be witty, charming, brilliant, and even touching, but not profound, learned, or of great significance. Not they, but the vocal and instrumental solos they introduced were the main attractions at concerts. The main attractions in the theatres were the plays, operas, or oratorios. In church attention focused on the liturgy and concerted vocal music. At dinner parties or outdoor occasions the interests were social, at occasions of state, political and ceremonial.

Symphonies thus provided an indispensable but subsidiary framework for other things. This attitude is revealed in a casual remark of Fanny Burney's, reporting on one of the Sunday afternoon musicales that her father held at their house: 'As we had no violins, basses, flutes, &c., we were forced to cut short the formality of any overture, and to commence by the harp.'[24] As this remark suggests, in the 1760s, 1770s, and into the 1780s symphonies were generally viewed as a 'formality'. And even after the symphony's 'liberation', its position relative to genres intended for connoisseurs—piano sonatas, Lieder, and string quartets, for instance—remained the same; Beethoven's and Schubert's symphonies too were for a larger public and, whatever their seriousness, they tended to avoid the more difficult and sometimes esoteric ideas of the 'private' genres, striving instead for large-scale gestures.

It is perhaps inevitable, therefore, that a learned discussion of Mozart's early symphonies, by placing them at the centre of the artistic and cultural universe whence they originated, creates an anachronism. To suggest that musicians, patrons, and audiences of the mid-eighteenth century were not interested in symphonies would be absurd in the face of thousands of symphonies, widely distributed in Europe and North America. Yet time and again when reviewers, diarists, or letter writers attended musical performances that included symphonies, they wrote about other works, not the symphonies—thus the 'silence' mentioned at the beginning of this chapter. When in 1817 it was reported that Clementi 'like every connoisseur, considers [grand symphonies] as the pinnacle of modern instrumental music',[25] a relatively new turn in musical aesthetics was expressed.

The eighteenth-century attitude to symphonies is still visible in an 1807 Parisian review of a late Mozart symphony: the reviewer, carried away with enthusiasm, devoted a few words to the work, and then felt obliged to apologize to his readers for having done so.[26] Indeed, as mentioned in Chapter 3, the ancillary treatment of symphonies was specifically spelt out in 1765 as the official editorial policy of a Parisian newspaper for its concert notices: 'In order to avoid useless repetition, we

---

[24] Fanny Burney d'Arblay, (ed.), *Memoirs of Doctor Burney, arranged from his own Manuscripts, from Family Papers and from Personal Recollections* (London, 1832), ii. 14.

[25] *Allgemeine musikalische Zeitung* (1817), xix, col. 461.

[26] Saint-Foix, 146–7 (= 107–8).

are not in the habit of making mention of the symphonies with which all concerts begin, unless some special circumstances are involved.'[27]

The revolution in matters symphonic must have been well along by 1799 when a Hamburg publisher brought out four of Mozart's early symphonies (K. 162, 183, 199, 202) in their first editions. A reviewer in the *Allgemeine musikalische Zeitung* had the following reaction to them:

Mozart's instrumental works, especially his quartets, have contributed more to the universality of his fame than many may think. A musical artist can show the greatest genius in this genre, for not only must he therein invent entirely alone and by himself all the work's subject-matter, but he is also uniquely and solely circumscribed by the language of tones. His ideas have their specificity in themselves without being supported by poetry. There is no one among our German composers of the recent era, except Haydn, from whom one may deduce the superiority of a musical genius through his instrumental works as clearly as is the case with Mozart . . . .

Now it does not follow from this that everything of the sort that Mozart wrote is worth preserving, however, nor does it follow that after his death people [should] without exception collect and publish everything he wrote, especially in his younger years.

Without exaggeration, there is nothing more to be said about these symphonies, except that they—although not without good value and content—are really just quite ordinary orchestral symphonies, without any conspicuous traits of originality or novelty, and without any special artistic diligence. Thereby one can quite clearly recognize youthful work, because they are on the whole so very plain, and have about them still an undoubtedly genuine feel of the schoolroom, which Mozart later left so far behind him.[28]

These four symphonies were composed in 1773–4 when Mozart was eighteen or nineteen, but whereas works written at such a tender age by a less precocious composer might correctly be considered works of apprenticeship, in Mozart's case that assertion would be dubious, for at eighteen he was already an experienced professional with dozens of symphonies to his name. The reviewer in the *Allgemeine musikalische Zeitung* (perhaps Rochlitz, its editor) made the mistake, interesting for us, of confusing the general change in symphonic style between *c.*1774 and 1799 with Mozart's personal development as a composer. In the flood of symphonies produced, performed, and published in the 1790s in the wake of Haydn's symphonic triumphs in London, the reviewer lost the awareness (if ever he had had it) that a few years earlier symphonies were not considered a genre in which a composer could 'show the greatest genius', but quite the contrary.

The same error was not committed by E. T. A. Hoffmann, who showed an admirable grasp of the shift in the symphony's function and significance:

---

[27] *Mercure de France* (June 1768), 65, n. 1.

[28] '*Quatre Simphonies pour l'Orchestre, comp. par Wolfgang Amad. Mozart. Œuv. 64.* Hambourg chez Günther et Böhme. (Preis à 1 Rthlr.)', *Allgemeine musikalische Zeitung* (1799), i, cols. 494–6. See also ii, col. 94.

In earlier days one regarded symphonies only as introductory pieces to any larger production whatsoever; the opera overtures themselves mostly consisted of several movements and were entitled 'sinfonia'. Since then our great masters of instrumental music—Haydn, Mozart, Beethoven—bestowed upon the symphony a tendency such that nowadays it has become an autonomous whole and, at the same time, the highest type of instrumental music.[29]

To the musicians of the late eighteenth and early nineteenth centuries it was Haydn who had made the breakthrough in the role of symphonies. Comparisons between his symphonies and Mozart's inevitably favoured the older man, as, for instance, in Burney's remarks cited above, Silverstolpe's and the comments of 1795 and 1832 cited below, or Nicolas Framery's quoted in the previous chapter.[30] Similarly, an appraisal of 1794, while acknowledging Mozart's pre-eminence in other genres, states of his symphonies: 'For all their fire, for all their pomp and brilliance, they yet lack that sense of unity, that clarity and directness of presentation, which we rightly admire in Jos. Haydn's symphonies . . . .'[31] So it seems that, although Mozart may have been responsible for important stylistic innovations, Haydn (probably influenced by his younger colleague) presented them in a more palatable form, receiving the credit and reaping the rewards, as Mozart too might have done, had he enjoyed a normal lifespan.

While evidence of a change in attitude among composers can be found in the greater length and seriousness of some symphonies written in the 1780s, an increased interest in symphonies on the part of the general public arose from Haydn's extraordinary symphonic successes in London in the early 1790s. There, perhaps for the first time, symphonies (although maintaining their traditional positions in the programmes, as they still would do later in Vienna for Beethoven) were treated as the main event, rather than as curtain-raisers, entr'actes, and grand finales. To be sure, Haydn had been selling his symphonies all over Europe in the 1780s, for musical people in many places recognized the excellence of those works and wanted their musical entertainments to be first rate from start to finish. But there was a shift in attitude, and symphonies began to be considered not just entertainment but also great art and perhaps even 'art for art's sake'. Haydn's

---

[29] E. T. A. Hoffmann, *Schriften zur Musik* (Munich, 1963), 145; C.-H. Mahling, 'Zur Frage der "Einheit" der Symphonie', in C.-H. Mahling (ed.), *Festschrift Walter Wiora: Über Symphonien* (Tutzing, 1979), 1–40, here 1–2.

[30] See ch. 12, n. 28.

[31] The entire passage is given below at n. 56. The reputation of Haydn's 'London' symphonies was so great that they seemed the prototypes of all 'modern' symphonies. A reviewer of Nissen's biography of Mozart in the *Foreign Quarterly Review* of 1829 was therefore surprised at the true chronology: 'Of his [Mozart's] six-and-thirty sinfonias for the full orchestra, it appears that the half-dozen masterly compositions with which we are familiar in England, were written considerably before Haydn's journey to this country . . . so that Mozart had reached perfection in the Sinfonia style, and had won the race, long before the man who had made the first strides in it, and who had the start of him in years and experience.' See H. C. Robbins Landon, *Haydn: The Late Years 1801–1809* (Haydn: Chronicle and Works, v) (Bloomington and London, 1977), 415.

brilliant symphonic successes in London, widely reported in the German-speaking press, were in large part responsible for both an increased interest in symphonies and the rise in his status from outstanding composer to 'great man'.[32]

This shift of emphasis concerning symphonies was part of a larger development in which instrumental music rose from being considered an inferior genre to being seen as the highest means of musical expression. The commonly held eighteenth-century Neoplatonic view of instrumental music may be represented by Fontenelle's often-cited expostulation, 'Sonate, que me veux-tu?' The aesthetic theory behind this outburst maintained that, by lacking words, by being abstract, instrumental music lacked meaning and was mere noise. In so far as instrumental music contained any sense, that sense derived either from association with vocal music, where words co-ordinated the form, substance, and affect of the music and specified its meaning; or from the presence of a programme—and some eighteenth-century writers urged composers to found their symphonies on programmes.[33] It was instrumental music's very vagueness of meaning, however, that made it the ideal art-form of many romantic artists, who were interested in concepts and feelings that, they believed, transcended the ability of words to express.[34] Of course, the vast amounts of 'abstract' instrumental music composed, disseminated, and performed in the eighteenth century suggests that, in many circles, the philosophical arguments against this wordless medium were not taken seriously.

Yet another aspect of the new status of symphonies was a sharp decline in the numbers of them turned out by composers, a development that may be traced in Mozart's symphonic production. Looked at by decades, Mozart's symphonic production was approximately 35 between 1764 and 1771, approximately 28 between 1772 and 1781, but only 6 between 1782 and 1791. Various explanations suggest themselves. As long as Mozart was either attached to the Salzburg court or

[32] The evidence for this is presented *in extenso* in H. C. Robbins Landon, *Haydn in England 1791–1795* (Haydn: Chronicle and Works. iii) (Bloomington and London, 1976).

[33] M. R. Maniates, ' "Sonate, que me veux-tu?": The Enigma of French Musical Aesthetics in the 18th Century', *Current Musicology* (1969), ix. 117–40. These theories were held especially by writers whose orientation was more literary than musical and who were French or francophile; see, for instance, Bernard-Germain-Étienne de Lacépède, *La Poétique de la musique* (Paris, 1785). There was considerable resistance to this aesthetic in German-speaking countries, especially when programmes resulted in the kind of literal pictorialisms for which Haydn was so sharply criticized in *Die Schöpfung* and *Die Jahreszeiten*. As one writer put it, 'The musician should always attempt to convey feelings rather than depict their actual causes; he should present the state of mind and body after contemplation of a certain matter, rather than try to depict that matter or event itself' (Johann Jacob Engel, *Über die musikalische Malerey* (Berlin, 1780), 25). For programme symphonies by Camerloher, Dittersdorf, Kraus, Haydn, Hoffmeister, Leopold Mozart, Pichl, Richter, Rosetti = Rössler, Winter, and others of Wolfgang Mozart's contemporaries, see F. E. Kirby, 'The Germanic Symphony in the Eighteenth Century: Bridge to the Romantic Era' *Journal of Musicological Research* (1984), v. 51–83, here 73–5. It seems that Mozart was not attracted to the programme symphony, at least in its overt manifestations.

[34] E. T. A. Hoffmann, 'Beethoven's Instrumental Music', in O. Strunk (ed.), *Source Readings in Music History from Classical Antiquity through the Romantic Era* (New York, 1950), 775–81. For a discussion that contradicts this point of view, see R. Wallace, *Beethoven's Critics: Aesthetic Dilemmas and Resolutions during the Composer's Lifetime* (Cambridge, 1986).

touring the musical centres of Europe, he had need of a steady supply of new symphonies. Once he became a free-lance musician in Vienna, he apparently became more interested in making his mark as soloist in his piano concertos and as a composer of operas and *Singspiele* than in working as a symphonist; for his Viennese concerts he was mostly content to use either his earlier symphonies, most of which were unknown in Vienna, or symphonies by other composers. This explanation is weakened, however, by the fact that Mozart's production of symphonies had already dropped off noticeably from 1775, when he still had responsiblities at Salzburg. (As suggested in Chapter 10, this may have been a manifestation of his profound disillusionment with his native city.) Furthermore, to some degree the slowing down of his symphony production may have been circumstantial, for in 1786 Mozart did offer to compose for the Prince von Fürstenberg '... every year a certain number of symphonies, quartets, concertos for different instruments, or other compositions ....'[35] Was Mozart's apparent lack of interest in symphonies at the end of his life really that, or was it, rather, the result of a discouraging absence of audiences, patrons, and markets?

In any case, as the length, complexity, and significance of symphonies increased and the conventionality of their content decreased, they could no longer be tossed off with such ease. (It may not be pure happenstance that more sketches survive for the first of Mozart's 'difficult' symphonies—the 'Prague'—than for any other, although one cannot be certain that sketches for the other symphonies have survived in proportion to the number that may once have existed.) Many composers of the second half of the eighteenth century wrote more than fifty symphonies; this can be compared to nine symphonies completed by Beethoven, Dvořak, Bruckner, and Mahler, seven by Schubert, six by Mendelssohn, four by Schumann and Brahms, and so on.[36]

There may have been a trend among the Austrian nobility and wealthier bourgeoisie, perhaps influenced by Enlightenment ideas, perhaps influenced by the weakness of the Austrian economy from the late 1780s, to emphasize quality over quantity. The extent to which quantity was once used as a visible symbol of wealth and power can hardly be missed by visitors to the great palaces of Europe. Alexander Ringer has evaluated it this way:

Well over a half a century ago Werner Sombart made the useful distinction between quantitative and qualitative luxury as basic categories of socio-economically determined cultural behaviour. Quantitative luxury, he held, was typical of post-Renaissance European nobility, whereas qualitative luxury reflected the intermittent desire for better, rather than more numerous, products, a desire found throughout history, it is true, but

---

[35] Letter of 8 Aug. 1786. *Briefe*, iii. 565; *Letters*, iii. 1337 (= ii. 898).
[36] P. Stedman, *The Symphony* (Englewood Cliffs, 1979), 95.

especially so among the rising middle classes of the late-eighteenth and early-nineteenth centuries. That these two 'ideal' types may coexist at any given time, goes without saying. Conversely, history has known situations, particularly in the eighteenth century when the nobility of Europe was in a stage of incipient decadence, in which quantitative luxury assumed almost grotesque proportions. To cite but one of Sombart's many examples, 'On 25 February 1732 the court of Saxony ordered 910 pieces of porcelain figures and vases for a single floor of the royal palace'.[37]

In this regard at least, symphonies were much like porcelain. Some patrons wanted a new symphony for each evening's entertainment; and what other explanation can there be for the thousands of symphonies composed in the last six decades of the eighteenth century? But other patrons must have come to want a few superior symphonies, each heard several times.

The new development in the significance of the symphony also represented a shifting of wealth and prestige as well as of geographical centre. Those who study the history of Western music know that at different times, the locations of the centre and periphery change. Thus, for example, music in western Europe was dominated by the Parisian or Notre Dame School in the eleventh century, the Burgundian school in the fifteenth century, the Franco-Flemish school of the fifteenth and sixteenth centuries, and Italian opera in the seventeenth and eighteenth. Each of these 'schools' produced widely disseminated and imitated technical and artistic innovations, and that is the sense in which one may speak of a centre and a periphery. Furthermore, all were concerned primarily with vocal music. The evolution of the symphony that occurred in the 1780s and 1790s was an early manifestation of a shift from Italy to Germany as the centre, from vocal to instrumental music as the highest goal, and from church and aristocratic patronage to mixed middle-class and aristocratic audiences and the capitalist system as the principal means of financial support.

The critic M. H. Abrams has drawn a parallel between the rise of the novel and the rise of the symphony, suggesting that, as the eighteenth century progressed, both were created in growing numbers for one and the same audience: the increasingly prosperous, educated, and numerous middle class. This suggestion perhaps makes more sense for London and Paris (where the courts had virtually ceased to exert an influence on musical activities) or cities without courts, like Hamburg and Leipzig, than for the numerous symphony-loving small courts and monasteries of central and eastern Europe and Italy, which continued to present a decidedly feudal apppearance. Perhaps, though, this is why the major centres for the publication of symphonies were, at least at first, Paris, Amsterdam, and

---

[37] A. Ringer, 'Mozart and the Josephinian Era: Some Socio-Economic Notes on Musical Change', *Current Musicology* (1969), ix. 158–65. The quotation is from W. Sombart, *Luxus und Kapitalismus* (Munich, 1913), p. 71.

London; and also why Mozart—working in feudal Salzburg and Imperial Vienna—had such poor success getting his symphonies published.

Abrams also connects the rise of novel and symphony with the rise of 'art for art's sake'.[38] In the visual arts this movement is connected with the growth of connoisseurship and of museums, in which works of art—taken from their original contexts in places of worship, dwellings, public buildings, and so on—are displayed to be admired solely for their aesthetic content. In music the analogous development was the rise of modern concert life, with its large public halls, in which a standard repertory of 'classics' is heard over and over again, and composers respond by writing for 'posterity' rather than for 'musical daily business'. New music is written for this circumstance, while older music, once intended for worship, dancing, dining, civic ceremonies, private recreation, and the like, is reinterpreted as 'art for art's sake'. Writing for posterity may increase the likelihood of achieving great art (although one may dispute this), but it decreases the amount of new music generally available, for composers become more deliberate and painstaking in their craft. Thus, Leopold Mozart's evident admiration for prolific composition, and his cajoling Wolfgang to compose more (see Chapter 1), although sound policy for his own time, may have been questionable for the new age.

The altered role assigned to eighteenth-century symphonies in the twentieth century—alluded to in the course of this book—is nowhere more evident than in the practice of devoting whole programmes to symphonies. In the eighteenth century such programming would probably have been regarded as lacking in variety, and even bizarre. Symphonies, though the indispensable adjuncts to concerts, operas, oratorios, and liturgical music, were of secondary importance to vocal music and virtuoso solos. The notion of the symphony as an extended work of great seriousness and the main event at concerts, which we have inherited from the nineteenth century, is far from what musicians and laymen of the second half of the eighteenth century usually had in mind for their symphonies. This can be sensed from such already mentioned phenomena as the large number of symphonies turned out, the relative brevity of passages devoted to symphonies in writings of the period, and the uses to which the symphonies were put: articulating a series of musical or ceremonial events. Hence, it may be just to compare most eighteenth-

---

[38] M. H. Abrams, 'From Addison to Kant: Modern Aesthetics and the Exemplary Art', in R. Cohen (ed.), *Studies in Eighteenth-Century British Art and Aesthetics* (Berkeley, 1985), 16–48; idem, '"Art-as-Such": The Sociology of Modern Aesthetics', *Bulletin of the American Academy of Arts and Sciences* (1985), xxxviii/6. 8–33. Abrams's remarks about the role of middle-class audiences in the rise of the novel and symphony should be read in light of W. Weber, 'The Muddle of the Middle Classes', *19th Century Music* (1979), iii. 175–85. For evidence that in central Europe the assiduous cultivation of symphonies belonged more to small courts and monasteries than to urban centres, see F. E. Kirby, 'The Germanic Symphony in the Eighteenth Century', 52–5, and idem, 'A Postscript', *Journal of Musicological Research* (1986), vi. 357–62. For a preliminary attempt to explain the situation in one urban area see D. P. Schroeder, 'Audience Reception and Haydn's London Symphonies', *International Review of the Aesthetics and Sociology of Music* (1985), xvi. 57–72.

century symphonies to elaborately carved and gilded frames for oil-paintings, which exhibited great craftsmanship, were not necessarily easy to create, were considered indispensable, and yet did not constitute the principal artistic events.

In a classic essay on frames, Ortega y Gasset treated them as transition zones between the mundane realities of the wall and the phantasmagoric contents of the art-work. Of the gilded frame he suggested that, 'with its bristling halo of sharp-edged radiance, [it] inserts a ribbon of pure splendor' between every-day and aesthetic perceptions.[39] This formulation offers a suggestive metaphor for what was arguably the most important function of symphonies prior to the changes in symphonic practice of the 1780s and 1790s. The elaborate frames of the baroque period were later harshly criticized for overwhelming their paintings. And overwhelm is precisely what symphonies began to do to other kinds of music in orchestral concerts of the end of the eighteenth and beginning of the nineteenth centuries, to a mixed chorus of favourable and unfavourable notices.

An even more recent change in attitude is reflected in the present passion on the part of recording companies and their customers for complete sets organized by composer and genre, and, in concerts, for cycles of performances covering all the sonatas, string quartets, or symphonies of one composer. No one would wish to deny that a concert devoted entirely to Haydn's or Mozart's symphonies can be enjoyable, nor that having complete recordings available is useful for reference, research, teaching, or pleasure. But this manner of organizing the music of the past is pointing us in the wrong direction for the achievement of a sound historical and aesthetic understanding of that music. We need to abandon such horizontally organized schemes and to apply vertical organization, re-creating musical occasions that were characteristic of tastes and preferences of the times and places we study. Is it not time, for instance, that we advance our understanding of the classical period by experiencing at first hand some of the emotional, intellectual, and artistic effects of the kinds of concerts in which Haydn and Mozart participated—not just with period instruments, altered performance practices, and smaller halls, but with apposite programming too? In this way we may begin, like archaeologists after a dig, to reassemble the dispersed shards of broken pottery so that we can enjoy and understand not only the colours and shapes of the separate bits, but also the broader designs they once formed.

Music historians are usually committed to the proposition that music, being a product of a particular time and place, is in some way characteristic of the culture

[39] J. Ortega y Gasset, 'Meditación del Marco', in *Obras de José Ortega y Gasset*, 3rd edn. (Madrid, 1943), i. 369–75; trans. A. L. Bell as 'Meditations on the Frame' in R. R. Brettell and S. Starling, *The Art of the Edge: European Frames 1300–1900* (Chicago, 1986), 21–5. The same volume contains an excellent bibliography on frames in the fine arts, in semiotics, in psychology, in literature, and in cosmology (pp. 121–2); nothing seems to have been written on frames in music.

from which it sprang. This is easier to demonstrate with vocal music than with instrumental; for instance, who can doubt that many of the daring ideas expressed in the librettos of *Figaro* and *Don Giovanni* arise from the concerns of the Enlightenment and the Age of Revolution, or that ideals expressed in the libretto of *Die Zauberflöte* resulted from Mozart's and Schickaneder's Masonic connections and a desire to transcend the parochial boundaries of Catholicism and Austrian nationalism? And what could be gained by attempting to deny that Mozart, having chosen to set such words in so extraordinarily convincing a manner, has provided us with music that 'means' the same thing as its words. Of course, Mozart's symphonies are harder to parse than his operas, for their words, if they have any, are usually unknown. Yet the operas and the symphonies came from the same mind, share similar styles and ideas, and, at some level, must deal with many of the same issues.

Mozart has often been portrayed as apolitical, but this is contradicted by ample evidence of the sincerity of his commitment to the Masons, who, after all, ran a subversive organization banned in 1738 by Catholic Church and in 1790 by the Austrian Empire. His involvement with the Masons[40] is one of many bits of evidence that should encourage us to question the image of him found in many biographies as a childish innocent, lacking sophistication and worldliness in all realms outside music.

The American Revolution took place when Mozart was in his early twenties, but not a word of it is found in the voluminous correspondence with his father from that period. Nor is the French Revolution mentioned, but this is perhaps less surprising, as it occurred after Leopold's death in a period when Wolfgang's relatively few letters tended to be short and non-discursive. Despite these striking omissions, in his letters Mozart sometimes revealed a keen awareness of political and social issues of his day,[41] even though mail to Salzburg was opened and read by censors, so that he and his father had to use circumlocutions and a cipher of their own invention when mentioning politically sensitive matters.

In one letter Mozart replied to his father's question about whether he had heard of the British victory at Gilbraltar against the French and Spanish, 'Yes, indeed, I have heard the news of England's victories—and with great joy, for you know I

---

[40] The classic studies—O. E. Deutsch, *Mozart und die wiener Logen* (Vienna, 1932), and P. Nettl, *Mozart and Masonry* (New York, 1957)—must be read in light of important discoveries in H. C. Robbins Landon, *Mozart and the Masons* (London, 1982) and in P. A. Autexier, *Mozart & Liszt sub Rosa* (Poitier, 1984), 1–46.

[41] The following have been helpful in the writing of the next few paragraphs: M. Benn, 'Mozart and the Age of Enlightenment', *Studies in Music* (1969), iii. 25–34; J. S. Curl, 'Mozart Considered as a Jacobin', *The Music Review* (1974), xxxv. 131–41; A. Steptoe, 'Mozart, Joseph II, and Social Sensitivity', *The Music Review* (1982), xliii. 109–20; F. Schneider, 'Wolfgang Amadeus Mozart—ein politisches Porträt', *Musik und Gesellschaft* (1981), xxxi. 3–11; M. Brown, 'Mozart and After: The Revolution in Musical Consciousness', *Critical Inquiry* (1981), vii. 689–706.

am an arch-Englishman.'[42] The Catholic Mozart's pleasure at the defeat of two Catholic countries at the hands of a Protestant country can only be explained by England's position in the eighteenth century as the most enlightened country of Europe. Thus Schiller could describe an English woman as 'the freeborn daughter of the freest people under the sun'.[43] That this interpretation applies to Mozart is suggested by similar sentiments found in the libretto of *Die Entführung*, in which Blonde is made to say, 'I am an English woman and born to freedom'; while an exchange between Blonde and the villain Osmin reads:

> OSMIN: What fools are the husbands in England
>   To grant so much freedom to women.
> BLONDE: A girl born to freedom
>   Will never consent to enslavement.[44]

Writing to his father, Mozart, reporting at length an incident in which a commoner was unjustly imprisoned, railed against 'the stupid Tyrolese custom' (as he called it) that forbade a commoner to strike a nobleman no matter how much the latter may have deserved it.[45] Another letter expresses the subversive idea that 'it is the heart that ennobles man' rather than accidents of birth.[46] And the memoirs of Michael Kelly and Lorenzo Da Ponte agree that it was Mozart who chose Beaumarchais's proto-revolutionary play as the basis for his opera *Le nozze di Figaro*, despite anticipated objections from the Austrian censors.[47] The chorale-prelude settings of hymn tunes that Mozart provided for the *Maurerische Trauermusik* and *Die Zauberflöte* must have been understood by him and those in the know as openly introducing Protestant music into a Catholic country. These are neither the words nor the actions of a man oblivious to the intellectual and political currents of his time.

Le nozze di Figaro is precisely the art-work of the period that most successfully embodied the idea that the heart ennobles man rather than accidents of birth; it is the French Revolution in action before the Revolution (to paraphrase Napoleon's remark about Beaumarchais's play). That the extraordinary improbability of Mozart's and Da Ponte's *Figaro* having got around the court censor and made it on

---

[42] Letter of 19 Oct. 1782. *Briefe*, iii. 239; *Letters*, iii. 1235 (= ii. 828).

[43] *Kabale und Liebe*, ii. 3.

[44] Act II, scene i. This is not the place to demonstrate that, although Mozart did not write his own librettos, he exercised careful control over their form and content.

[45] Letter of 8 Aug. 1781. *Briefe*, iii. 145–7; *Letters*, iii. 1126–8 (= ii. 757–8).

[46] Letter of 20 June 1781. *Briefe*, iii. 133; *Letters*, iii. 1111 (= ii. 747). Precisely this point is made by Figaro in his long soliloquy at the beginning of Act V of Beaumarchais's *Le Mariage de Figaro*. The corresponding moment in the opera, Figaro's recitative and aria, 'Tutto è disposto—Aprite un po' quegli occhi', keeps the sexual points but suppresses the political one.

[47] Deutsch, 456, 466 (= 532, 544).

to the stage in Vienna was understood at the time emerges from a review of the première:

'What is *not allowed* to be said these days, is sung', one may say with Figaro (in *The Barber of Seville*). This piece, which was prohibited in Paris and not allowed to be performed here as a *comedy* either in a bad or in a good translation, we have at last had the felicity to see represented as an *opera*. It will be seen that we are doing better than the French.[48]

The difficulty in perceiving the revolutionary side of Mozart's personality arises from several causes. One is the propaganda left behind by his family. Leopold and Nannerl disliked Constanze and disapproved of the way in which Wolfgang handled his personal and professional affairs. It was their opinion that Wolfgang never grew up, and Nannerl made sure that this point of view was transmitted to posterity,[49] which has cherished it. Added to this eighteenth-century misrepresentation was the nineteenth-century view of Mozart and Haydn as powdered wigs: 'Papa' Haydn and Mozart the child prodigy. Such stereotypes, suited only to the end of Haydn's life and the beginning of Mozart's, have long hidden the true personalities, intellectual toughness, and artistic achievements of both men, and have contributed to many effete, tinkling performances of strong music.

Then, the modern emphasis on Mozart's 'classicism'—taken in the sense of adherence to balance, clarity, and moderation—and his extraordinary skill in maintaining a 'socially correct' surface to his work, however disturbing the music's inner workings may be, have perhaps blinded us to the revolutionary side of his music. Mozart's formulations of the co-ordination between the outer and inner qualities of his music have often been repeated, but perhaps never evaluated carefully enough. As discussed in Chapter 1, in 1782 Mozart bragged of his own music that it was

something between too difficult and too easy—very brilliant—embraced by the ears—natural without declining into emptiness—here and there also sustaining the satisfaction *of connoisseurs only*—but in such a way that the non-connoisseurs [too] must be content with it without knowing why. [...] Moderation—truth in all things—is no longer either known or appreciated. To attain success one must write stuff that is so inane that a cabbie could sing it, or so unintelligible that it pleases precisely because no sensible man can understand it.[50]

[48] Ibid. 243–4 (= 278). For an argument that, at least in pre-Revolutionary France, Beaumarchais's *Figaro* was offensive for its sexual rather than its political content, see R. Darnton, 'The High Entertainment and the Low-Life of Literature in Pre-Revolutionary France', *Past and Present* (1971), li. 81–115.

[49] Ibid. 405 (= 462).

[50] Letter of 28 Dec. 1782. *Briefe*, iii. 245–6; *Letters*, iii. 1242 (= ii. 833). This is my deliberately literal version of E. Anderson's freer translation given in ch 1 at n. 20.

And some months earlier, on the subject of using a modulation to express extreme anger in an aria:

For just as a man in such a towering rage oversteps all the bounds of order, moderation, and propriety, completely forgetting himself, so too must the music forget itself. But as passions, whether violent or not, must never be expressed in such a way as to arouse disgust, and as music, even in the most terrible situations, must never offend the ear but must please the hearer, I have gone from F major (the key in which the aria is written), not into a remote key, but into a related one, not, however, into its nearest relative, D minor, but into the more remote A minor.[51]

   Taken together, these two statements imply an aesthetic ideal of balance between the 'secret' inner workings and the polite outer surface of music, along with an avoidance of 'tasteless' extremes. As they appear in letters to his father, they are probably justifiably understood as Mozart's echoing ideas which (as discussed in Chapter 1) he would have known his father favoured, perhaps in hope of gaining a degree of paternal approval during a period when he was acting against his father's wishes in so many other matters. Remarks of some of Mozart's contemporaries suggest that in at least some of his late works the balance between inner and outer content in his music had shifted in ways that caused listeners, if not the disgust mentioned by Mozart, at least discomfort:

1787: ... the pity is only that [Mozart] aims too high in his artful and truly beautiful compositions, in order to become a new creator, whereby it must be said that feeling and heart profit little; his new Quartets for two violins, viola and bass, which he has dedicated to Haydn, may well be called too highly seasoned—and whose palate can endure this for long?[52]

1788: [Mozart's string quartets] ... because of their unrelenting, extreme artfulness are not everyone's purchase.[53]

1788: ... too artful a texture obscures the fluency of the singing in many places. The expert knows the value of such passages, but for popular delivery this kind of thing is of no use. The same is true of the frequent modulations and the many enharmonic progressions, which, beautiful as they sound on the pianoforte, have no effect in the orchestra, partly because the intonation is never pure enough either on the singers' or the players' parts, and especially is this true of the wind instruments; and partly because the resolutions alternate too quickly with the discords, so that only a practised ear can follow the course of the harmony. This awkwardness is especially noticeable in the numerous arias in minor keys which, because of their many chromatic passages, are difficult to perform for the singer,

---

[51] Letter of 26 Sept. 1781. *Briefe*, iii. 162; *Letters*, iii. 1144 (= ii. 769).

[52] Deutsch, 255–6 (= 290).

[53] Letter of 18 Aug. 1788 from Dittersdorf to Artaria, as quoted by E. Badura-Skoda (ed.), *Carl Ditters von Dittersdorf (1739–1799): Six Symphonies* (The Symphony 1720–1840, B/i) (New York, 1985).

difficult to grasp for the hearer, and are altogether somewhat disquieting. Such strange harmonies betray the great master, but they are not suitable for the theatre.[54]

1792: [The members of the Hamburg orchestra] are such good strong players and keep so calm that they perform correctly and at sight without error, even if, however, there is not a single soloist among them. Also, there are not enough of them by themselves to man a great concert; for that purpose they must hire extras ... and these honourable people are good dance-band musicians but heros to venture to play Haydn's (let alone Mozart's) symphonies at sight.[55]

1795: That Mozart to a large extent deserves this applause [for *Die Zauberflöte*] will be disputed by no one. But that he was still in his years of ferment, and that his ideas were still frequently in a state of flux, as it were—of this there are only too many instances in his works. If we pause only to consider his symphonies: for all their fire, for all their pomp and brilliance, they yet lack that sense of unity, that clarity and directness of presentation, which we rightly admire in Jos. Haydn's symphonies. . . . Moreover, one is often tempted, in hearing Mozart's works, to exclaim with the maid-servant in the comedy, 'There's nothing natural about me, thank God!'. An almost entirely spicy diet spoils the palate if one's taste for it continues; and in the hands of the wretched imitators, who think they need only to Mozartize in order to please, every trace of noble simplicity will finally be banished from music.[56]

1798: Haydn, in one of his newest and finest symphonies in C major [Hob. I: 95], had a fugue as a final movement; Mozart did this too in his tremendous Symphony in C major [K. 551], in which, as we all know, he pushed things a little far . . . . [57]

1804–5: One must hear ... Mozart's deep, artful and emotion-filled Symphony in G minor [K. 550] ... several times to be able completely to understand and enjoy it.[58]

1832: In passages and intervals of great difficulty [his vocal performers] have to contend against the overpowering effects of the wind instruments, whence his operas have frequently failed even with good companies. Neither can it be denied, that nearly all the subjects of all his symphonies want that interest which characterizes those of Haydn, that they are noisy, thus participating in the grand fracas of instruments, wherein the Germans seem to place their chief delight; and what is more singular, that none of them command the attention of an audience.[59]

Behind these complaints rest various causes. (1) Mozart's late music is technically demanding and not all performers were able adequately to cope with it; (2) single movements of his are stylistically and expressively varied; the older theory of the

[54] Deutsch, 287–8 (= 328).
[55] *Musikalische Korrespondenz der teutschen Filarmonischen Gesellschaft* (1792), ii/13. n.p.
[56] Deutsch, 413–14 (= 472–3).
[57] [Carl Friedrich] Z[elter], 'Bescheidene Anfragen an die modernsten Komponisten und Virtuosen', *Allgemeine musikalische Zeitung* (1798), i, cols. 141–4, 152–5, here 153.
[58] This is a conflation of two notices from the *Allgemeine musikalische Zeitung* (1804–5), vii, col. 579; (1806–7), ix, col. 94. The point about the difficulty of K. 550 is reiterated in the same periodical (1804–5), vii, cols. 433, 613.
[59] D. Brewster (ed.), 'Mozart', *The Edinburgh Encyclopaedia ... First American Edition* (Philadelphia, 1832), xiii. 804.

virtue of unified affect in music still held powerful sway in many circles[60]; (3) the nature of the implied listener for Mozart's music had changed. Esoteric music— *musica reservata*—used to be performed only in private before small groups of connoisseurs. Mozart's string quartets fall into this category, and complaints about their difficulties must be read differently from complaints about such 'public' genres as operas and symphonies. (Of course, even 'public' genres may have various audiences; an instance is the difference between the audience at the court theatre in the centre of Vienna, where most of Mozart's mature operas were given, and the bourgeois audience at the suburban theatre for which *Die Zauberflöte* was written.) An acute commentary of 1788 exposed the chaos that resulted when esoteric works intended for connoisseurs (in this instance, Mozart's piano quartets) became fashionable and so fell into the hands of incompetent amateurs who, while massacring the music felt obliged to exclaim at its beauty[61]; (4) both ideal and actual audiences for Mozart's music were changing. The ideal auditor of the late baroque period was the *honnête homme* ('man of parts'). Leopold Mozart was a more modern man and should be considered, and brought Wolfgang up to be, what Voltaire and others praised as an *homme de goût* ('man of taste'). It was as an *homme de goût* that Wolfgang wrote to his father in 1781–2 with his artistic credo of moderation. But he moved on to address a more modern auditor yet, the *homme sensible* ('man of feeling') admired by Rousseau and Beaumarchais. This proto-romantic man laughed and wept at the novels of Fielding, Richardson, and Sterne, at Goethe's *The Sorrows of the Young Werther*, and at the *comédies larmoyantes* of Diderot and Grétry. He had moved beyond the rational and the enlightened to reincorporate the irrational side of personality and art that his father and grandfather may have been quick to wish to disown.[62] It is in this context that a recent study by Rose Rosengard Subotnik makes especially engrossing reading.

Subotnik convincingly argues that Mozart's last three symphonies show irrational, illogical aspects in a number of their harmonic details or in the logic of their sequences of ideas.[63] As I read her, she argues that various attempts to analyse these works have enjoyed only partial success because their common, preordained goal

[60] This is some of what is behind the complaints that Mozart's music lacks unity. For a contemporaneous restatement of the theory of unity of affect, see the essay by Schiller's friend Christian Gottfried Körner, 'Ueber Charakterdarstellung in der Musik', *Die Horen* (1795), v. 97 ff., repr. in J. P. Bauke (ed.), *Christian Gottfried Körner: Ästhetische Ansichten, Ausgewählte Aufsätze* (Marbach an Nieder, 1964), 24–47. For a spirited defense of Mozart's music against the complaints documented in this chapter of overcomplexity or lack of unity, see Franz Niemetschek, *Leben des K. K. Kapellmeisters Wolfgang Gottlieb Mozart* (Prague, 1798) (*Life of Mozart*, 77–9).

[61] 'Ueber die neueste Favorit-Musik in grossen Concerten, sonderlich in Rücksicht auf Damen-Gunst, in Clavier-Liebhaberey', *Journal des Luxus und der Moden* (June 1788), 231 ff., reproduced in Deutsch, 279–80 (= 317–18) and in Klüppelholz and Busch (eds.), *Musik gedeutet und gewertet*, 36–51, with valuable commentary.

[62] These three types of men were variously mentioned in French writings of the period without being clearly defined. 'Man of parts' is my own idea; a more literal rendering of *honnête homme* might be 'man of honour'.

[63] R. R. Subotnik, 'Evidence of a Critical World View in Mozart's Last Three Symphonies', in E. Strainchamps, M. R. Maniates, and C. Hatch (eds.), *Music and Civilization: Essays in Honor of Paul Henry Lang* (New York, 1984), 29–43.

has been to seek signs of unity within movements and, then, between movements. Of course, unifying factors—in the form of rhythms, melodic motives, small- and large-scale harmonic patterns, parallel structures, and so on—do appear and can be examined. But the exclusive search for unity (which is fundamentally a theological rather than a purely musical concern[64]) may blind the analyst to the many 'irrational' factors that seem to be fighting against unity. It is not a matter of Mozart's much vaunted variety *per se*, since (to use a visual metaphor) coherent formal patterns can be created by many means—by dots or colours or textures or co-ordinated shapes, just as well as by long lines and vanishing-point perspective; rather, it is Mozart's willingness to allow himself to be side-tracked by local opportunities to explore interesting sounds, even when those sounds may get in the way of a logical pattern of overall organization.

Subotnik speculates that Mozart's allowing these 'illogical' sounds to remain in his last symphonies has to do with something in his world-view, although she does not suggest what that something might be. The foregoing discussion, however, demonstrates Mozart's profound dissatisfaction with aspects of the society of the Austrian Empire and Catholic Church in which he found himself, as well as his awareness that other possibilities existed in the world. (This last is important, for rejection of the status quo might have taken the form of inchoate rage or of blank despair rather than artistic boldness, had no other type of society been imaginable.) And as Mozart's various dissatisfactions chronicled thus far are social and philosophical, his lack of professional and financial comfort, which might by itself have motivated rebellious thoughts, has yet to be reckoned into the calculus of his anomie. Mozart was, in any case, something of an outsider wherever he was.

It is perhaps insufficiently recognized how revolutionary the 'Jupiter' symphony is in its ideas and their working out. To what other symphonies prior to 1788 can it be compared? Possible political and social motivations have been suggested above for Mozart's abandonment of the familiar style of so many earlier symphonies for something so elaborate and large-scale. His discontent or idealism must have been great to have released him from normal constraints, allowing this symphony to transcend the musical, technical, and philosophical bounds that polite society generally placed on symphonies. What, for instance, could Mozart have had in mind when he permitted himself the harmonic wildness discussed by Subotnik, when he constructed his contrapuntal finale, and when he decided prominently to juxtapose these features with the dotted rhythms and *tirades* of the French overture of the *ancien régime*—rhythms used in hundreds of eighteenth-century operas,

---

[64] P. Kivy, 'Mozart and Monotheism: An Essay in Spurious Aesthetics', *Journal of Musicology* (1983), ii. 322–8.

cantatas, oratorios, and liturgical works to symbolize nobility or godliness?[65] (Was it these rhythms, found to some extent in every movement except the Minuet and Trio, that inspired the symphony's British admirers to dub it the 'Jupiter'?)

What Mozart had in mind will never be knowable, for he 'forgot' to write the words to his melodies. Or nearly so, for in the first movement he quoted a recent aria, 'Un bacio di mano', K. 541 (Example 13.1).[66] Written for insertion into Anfossi's opera *Le gelosie fortunate* for performances in Vienna from 2 June 1788, this aria occurs at a moment in the plot when a witty Frenchman, Monsieur Girò, warns an inexperienced, would-be lover, Don Pompeo, about the dangers of wooing young women (the quoted portion italicized):

Un bacio di mano vi fa maraviglia,
E poi bella figlia volete sposar.
Voi siete un po' tondo, mio caro Pompeo,
L'usanze del mondo andate a studiar.

Un uom, che si sposa con giovin vezzosa,
A certi capricci, dee pria rinunciar,
Dee libere voglie lasciar alla moglie,
Dee sempre le porte aperte lasciar,
Dee chiudere gli occhi, gli orecchi, la bocca,
Se il re degli sciocchi non vuole sembrar.

[A kiss on her hand astonishes you,
And then you wish to marry the beautiful girl.
You are a bit innocent, my dear Pompeo,
Go study the ways of the world.

A man who marries a pretty young thing,
Must first be prepared to renounce certain of his own whims,
To let his wife have her way,
To always leave the doors open,
His eyes, ears, and mouth shut,
If he does not wish to seem the king of fools.]

The verse is thought to be the work of Da Ponte and, indeed, both text and music are very much of a piece with similar scenes of sexual comedy in *Le nozze di Figaro* and *Così fan tutte*. But what has this to do with Jupiter, ruler of the gods (or at least, with those musical features which tempted musicians to coin the sobriquet)? A partial answer is suggested by Stanley Sadie, who remarks that the first movement

---

[65] U. Kirkendale, 'The King of Heaven and the King of France: History of a Musical *Topos*', abstract in *Abstracts of Papers Read at the Thirty-Fifth Annual Meeting of the American Musicological Society, Saint Louis, Missouri, December 27–29, 1969* (n.d., n.p.), 27–8.

[66] H. Abert was apparently the first to point out this quotation (*W. A. Mozart* (Leipzig, 1919–21), ii. 595).

Ex. 13.1 'Un bacio di mano', K. 541, bars 17–36

da - te a stu - diar,   an - da - te, an - da - te, an - da - te a stu -

diar,   an - da - te, an - da - te, an - da - te a stu - diar.

of K. 551 is imbued with the spirit of Mozart's comic operas of the period.[67] And those operas are of the genre known as *semiseria* (or *dramma giocoso*, as the libretto of *Don Giovanni* has it[68]), a new hybrid mixing the formerly separate genres of opera buffa with its lower-class characters, opera seria with its kings, queens, gods, and goddesses, and the sentimental opéra comique with its middle-class characters.[69] Thus in the first movement of K. 551 characters of all classes—Jupiter (if it is he), Monsieur Girò, Don Pompeo, and doubtless others to whom we have not been properly introduced—could strut their hour upon the same stage on more-or-less an equal footing, something the *ancien régime* had invariably striven to suppress. Or, to put it in terms of musical aesthetics, the doctrine of unity of affect, by which a well-made piece was permitted but a single integrated character, was replaced by a mixed genre. And into the mix, along with the seria, buffo and middlebrow characters, went the Revolutionary (Mozart himself?), with his abrupt outbursts, shocking modulations, heroic wind orchestration, and pleasure in puncturing the too-comfortable received truths of society.

The Andante cantabile of the 'Jupiter' symphony not only moves, it profoundly disturbs. Its opening theme seems to express some inchoate yearnings to which the rude fortes reply with a brusque 'Nein', rather like what Beethoven would many years later write in the instrumental recitative in the Finale of his Ninth Symphony. After this theme with its negation reappears, now in the bass, a section of agitated chromaticism, syncopations, accents, and off-beat semiquavers (bars 19 ff.) introduces elements of tension and instability that cannot be completely dispelled by the calming sextuplets of the closing section (bars 28 ff.). The repeat of this exposition only increases the sense of unresolution, which reaches such a pitch in the development section (based upon the ideas of the agitated section from bars 19 ff.) that when the opening idea returns in the tonic at bar 60 it cannot prevail, and is swept away by more development. This further development extends until the reintroduction of the calming closing subject in the tonic at bar 76, which the third time is even less able to contain the underlying instability than it was the first two times. Finally, the opening, thwarted at the false recapitulation, returns as a coda, but a sense of true resolution proves elusive and, although the tonic cadence is affirmed three times, this proves insufficient to clear the air, which is left ringing with mysterious reverberations of unease.

Even in the Minuet and Trio—the archetypal musical symbol of the *ancien*

---

[67] S. Sadie, *The New Grove Mozart* (New York, 1983), 128.

[68] For the best recent study of the mixed genre, see M. Hunter, 'The Fusion and Juxtaposition of Genres in Opera Buffa 1770–1800: Anelli and Piccinni's *Griselda*', *Music and Letters* (1986), lxvii. 363–80. See also M.-L. Rahier-Godart, 'Un sous-titre controversé: le *dramma giocoso* de Mozart (*Don Giovanni*)', in P. Mercier and M. de Smet (eds.), *Mélanges de musicologie* (1974) (Publications d'histoire de l'art et d'archéologie de l'Université Catholique de Louvain, iv), i. 49–55.

[69] For the best recent discussion of the nature of the opéra comique of Mozart's time, see D. Charlton, *Grétry and the Growth of Opéra-Comique* (Cambridge, 1986).

régime—one hears a host of contrapuntal and motivic complexities murmuring uneasily beneath a galant exterior, and threatening at any moment to break through the façade. The Trio (so often reserved by Mozart for some kind of joke) also has a special character, as it puts the cart before the horse, or, rather, the cadence before the melody it would normally terminate. The rounded binary form of Mozart's minuets in general is here enlarged to such a point that it functions like a monothematic sonata-form movement, with the apposite rhythmic drive and developmental textures. Thus, the earlier symphony scheme of four movements in contrasting forms (sonata—binary—dance—rondo) has now been replaced by four essays in sonata form, by four parallel structures. Besides the Minuet's pervasive chromaticism, so alien to eighteenth-century dance music, another technical clue to the further removal of the dance from its ballroom origins is found in the bass-line, where, for the first (and only) time in a symphony minuet, Mozart writes separate parts for the cellos and for the double-basses (bars 9–13, 52–5).

And what, finally, could Mozart have had in mind using a contrapuntal tag of liturgical music (the often-mentioned doh—ray—fah—me motive) for the opening of the Finale? (A surely coincidental closure to Mozart's career as a symphonist is effected by the presence of the same motive in his 'first' symphony, K. 16, written nearly a quarter-century earlier.) This motive, derived from Gregorian chant and probably best known in the eighteenth century as the beginning of the hymn *Lucis creator*[70], was a commonplace of the Fuxian species counterpoint in which Mozart was trained and upon which in turn he trained his own pupils. It appears in the works of dozens of composers from Palestrina to Brahms.[71] Something of what it may have meant to Mozart in the Finale of the 'Jupiter' symphony is suggested by his Missa brevis in F major, K. 192 = 186f, where the continuation on the words 'in unum Deum, Patrem omnipotentem' is closely related to what follows in the 'Jupiter' Finale at that point[72] (Example 13.2). Does this work, then, contain Mozart's Creed?

Certainly Mozart's contemporaries understood that the 'Jupiter' was no ordinary symphony. As mentioned in Chapter 11, Joseph Haydn was familiar with it before he departed for England in 1790, for in the slow movement of his Symphony No. 98 he seems to allude to its slow movement, and in the Finale of his Symphony No. 95 he may have used its finale as a kind of model.[73] The decision to

---

[70] S. Wollenberg, 'The Jupiter Theme: New Light on its Creation', *The Musical Times* (1975), cxvi. 781–3.

[71] A. H. King, *Mozart in Retrospect: Studies in Criticism and Bibliography*, rev. edn. (Oxford, 1970), xiii, 262–3.

[72] E. Derr, 'A Deeper Examination of Mozart's $\hat{1}$—$\hat{2}$—$\hat{4}$—$\hat{3}$ Theme and its Strategic Deployment', *In Theory Only* (1985), viii. 5–43. The continuation in K. 551 of the four-note motive as in K. 196 suggests that 'Credo, credo' is to be understood, rather than 'Sanctus, sanctus' as in the Mass in C major, K. 257, with its different continuation. See also W. Klenz, ' "Per Aspera ad Astra", or The Stairway to Jupiter', *The Music Review* (1969), xxx. 169–210.

[73] Landon, *Haydn in England*, iii. 533, 517–18.

Ex. 13.2 Missa brevis, K. 192 = 186f, Credo (orchestra omitted)

apply the 'Jupiter' title—whether well or ill conceived—also suggests the perception of an out-of-the-ordinary work. If in English-speaking countries the work's
nickname derived, apparently, from 'godly' musical traits, in German-speaking
countries the special character of the Finale was singled out for attention, and the
work was known as 'the symphony with the fugal finale'. If the commentator of
1798 cited above felt that Mozart had 'pushed things a little too far', an early
nineteenth-century comment suggests that, precisely because of its fugal finale, K.
551 was suited for performance in church.[74]

Leonard Ratner has plausibly demonstrated that the fugato in the coda of the
Finale of the 'Jupiter' symphony (and by implication the entire sonata-form
movement leading up to it, as if by fortunate accident) is an instance of the *ars
combinatoria*.[75] At the beginning of the eighteenth century, Brossard had defined
'musica combinatoria' as 'that part [of music theory] which teaches the manner of
combining sounds; that is, of changing their place and figure in as many manners as
possible.'[76] Musicians of the second half of the century were so fascinated by this
possibility, and the periodic style was so conducive to its methods, that between
1757 and 1813 more than a dozen musical games were published, which enabled
one to compose simple dance movements by a throw of the dice or some other
system of random choice.[77] These parlour games were commercial manifestations
of a method of compositional manipulation that helped composers and would-be
composers generate new ideas that could, by means of craft, be turned into binary,
ternary, rondo, sonata, or other forms.

Invertible counterpoint, used systematically, provides another (more difficult)
means of exploring the combinations and permutations of musical ideas—ideas
that can be used not only singly, as in the dice games, but also simultaneously in
varying combinations. In the 'Jupiter' Finale six themes heard during the exposition, development, and recapitulation (Example 13.3) function as they might in
any brilliantly worked out sonata-form movement of a symphony (given Mozart's
propensity for 'fullness of ideas'), and only in the coda is his secret plan revealed:
five of these themes can be combined to create a fugato in five-part invertible
counterpoint (Table 13.1). A sixth theme, the continuation of the opening motive,
does not enter into the fugato. In the 'open' form that the sixth theme takes in bars
5–8 of the exposition and recapitulation (Example 13.3f) it appears not at all in the
coda, but in the 'closed' form given it in bars 13–19 (Example 13.3g), it brings the

[74] See ch. 4 at n. 57.

[75] L. G. Ratner, 'Ars Combinatoria: Chance and Choice in Eighteenth-Century Music', in H. C. Robbins Landon and R.
E. Chapman (eds.), *Studies in Eighteenth-Century Music: A Tribute to Karl Geiringer on His Seventieth Birthday* (New York,
1970), 343–63.

[76] Sebastian Brossard, *Dictionaire* [sic] *de musique* (Paris, 1703), unpaginated (s.v., 'Musica combinatoria') as cited in Ratner,
'Ars Combinatoria', 346.

[77] See K⁶, 581 (Anhang 294d = 516f), 910 (Anhang 294d = C 30.01).

Ex. 13.3 Symphony in C major, K. 551, Finale: The six themes

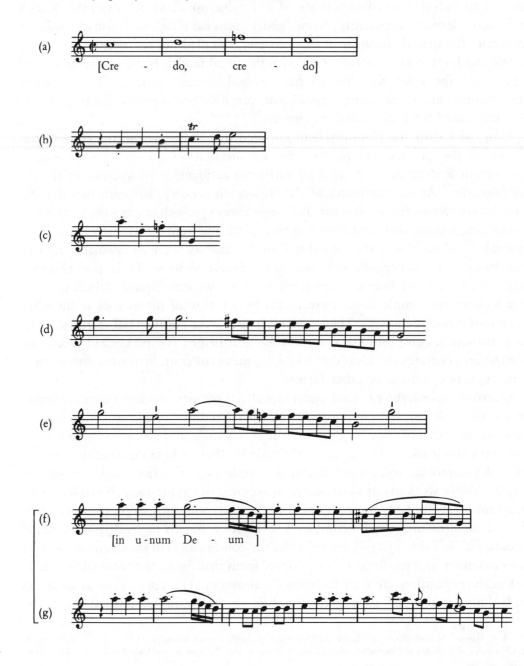

TABLE 13.1 Permutations of themes in the coda of the Finale of K. 551 (wind-instrument doublings omitted)

Instrument	Theme							
vn. I			2	1	3	4+3	5	1
vn. II		2	1	3	4+3	5	2	3
va.	2	1	3	4+3	5	2	1	2
vc.	1	3	4+3	5	2	1	3	4
db.				2	1	3	4+3	5
(from bar:)	(369)	(373)	(377)	(381)	(385)	(389)	(393)	(397)

After L. Ratner, 'Ars Combinatoria: Chance and Choice in Eighteenth-Century Music', in H. C. Robbins Landon and R. E. Chapman (eds.), *Studies in Eighteenth-Century Music: A Tribute to Karl Geiringer on His Seventieth Birthday* (New York, 1970), 343–63, here 361.

fugato to a conclusion by resolving the complex polyphony into a powerful homophonic gesture that prepares the closing fanfares in the brass over which are superimposed the rest of the orchestra repeating theme (d) in unison and octaves, in a triadically rising sequence.

What inspired Mozart to construct a symphony finale in a manner that, not merely unorthodox, transcended the boundaries of the genre as it was then understood? As demonstrated in Chapter 11, he knew one and perhaps more of Michael Haydn's five symphonies from the 1780s with fugal finales; but these conventional fugal movements can hardly have served as direct models for Mozart's original procedures, even if they may, in a general way, have set him thinking about such movements.

Another possibility is suggested by Alan Tyson's recent discovery that Mozart was working at composing a Mass.[78] A number of fragments, which previously had been variously dated, now prove, on the basis of their paper types and other evidence, to come from the period of the composition of K. 551. According to Tyson's investigations, the following fragments may be involved (the dates in parentheses represent the approximate period in which the paper in question was used by Mozart):

Kyrie in G major, K. Anhang 16 = 196a (December 1787–February 1789)

Kyrie in D major, K. Anhang 14 = 422a (December 1787–February 1789)

Kyrie in C major, K. Anhang 13 = 258a (1787?, 1790–1)

Kyrie in C major, K. Anhang 15 = 323 (December 1787–February 1789)

Gloria in C major, K. Anhang 20 = 323a (December 1787–February 1789)

[78] A. Tyson, 'The Mozart Fragments in the Mozarteum, Salzburg: A Preliminary Study of Their Chronology and Their Significance', *Journal of the American Musicological Society* (1981), xxxiv. 471–510, here 490–1.

'Memento Domine David', psalm setting by Johann Karl Georg von Reutter (1708–72) in Mozart's hand, K. Anhang 22 = 93a = Anhang A 23 (December 1787–February 1789) [there are sketches for the Finale of K. 551 on the back of this manuscript]

?Kyrie in D minor, K. 341 = 368a (autograph lost)

'De profundis clamavi', psalm setting by Reutter in Mozart's hand, K. 93 = Anhang A 22 (December 1787–February 1789).

Mozart entered his Symphony in C major, K. 551, in the catalogue of his works as 10 August 1788.

To the Mass fragments one may add anecdotal evidence from a member of the Theatre Royal of Copenhagen who visited Mozart on 24 August 1788 and wrote of him, 'He [now] writes church music in Vienna, and as the *Operetta* has closed down, he has nothing to do with the theatre [any longer].'[79] Given the closure of the Imperial Opera Theatre because of war and economic recession, Mozart may well have returned to church music after a hiatus of some years. Eventually, in May 1791, he became assistant with right of succession to Leopold Hofmann, the Kapellmeister of Saint Stephen's Cathedral, although Mozart died shortly before the older Hofmann. The point of all this is that Mozart was apparently thinking about church music at the time he composed the Finale of K. 551. That meant that he would have been thinking about the training in counterpoint he had received from his father, from Padre Martini, and from the Marquis de Ligniville; he was reviewing Viennese church-music traditions in the form of psalm settings by a former Kapellmeister of Saint Stephen's, Georg Reutter; and he was perhaps brooding about how a somewhat stale style might fruitfully be modernized.

In the last decade of his life, Mozart must have read or heard some of the complaints that his music had too great a profusion of ideas or was too densely textured: the elaborate orchestration, chromaticism, contrapuntally conceived part-writing, and extraordinary number of ideas that he used to construct an instrumental movement or aria posed problems for some of his contemporaries, as being inimical to 'that sense of unity, that clarity and directness of presentation' that a previously-quoted critic found wanting in his symphonies.[80] This perceived 'problem' in the symphonies was neatly expressed by a Swedish admirer of Mozart's as his 'distractions':

As far as symphonies are concerned, I now find that [Haydn] is the most distinguished. He surpasses even Mozart, although the latter surpasses him in genius. [J. M.] Kraus is more sublime than both of them, but not so inventive. He is more delicate and never has such

---

[79] Deutsch, 285, 347 (= 325, 395). The diary is Joachim Daniel Preisler, *Journal over en Rejse igiennen Frankerige og Tydskland i Aaret 1788* (Copenhagen, 1789), 285.

[80] See n. 56 above.

distractions as Mozart. Haydn is more learned than Kraus, but Kraus could have been more learned if he had not rejected it in favour of what men's hearts approve of.[81]

What a response the coda of the Finale of K. 551 makes to accusations of incoherence caused by too many ideas of varied character, as if to say, 'Yes, these ideas do belong together, if only you can see it my way', or—to rephrase this with reference to the earlier metaphor—as if to say, 'Yes, these people do belong together, if only you can see it my way.'

In the first chapter of this book the extent to which Leopold Mozart dominated the education, life, and works of his son was put forward as a way of explaining why a book about Wolfgang's work as a symphonist must grant Leopold such a large role. In the final three chapters Leopold is less prominent than in the earlier ones, yet it seems fitting that he should reappear at the very end. For just before the coda of the last movement of his last symphony, Wolfgang may have thought of his father and Salzburg, and added a seventh theme (Example 13.4) to the already generous complement of six on which the rest of the movement is based. This theme can easily be missed, appearing as it does in the midst of a complex texture and just before a powerful cadence that draws attention from it. No matter whether this theme is a quotation of something remembered from long ago or merely an evocation of all such conventional themes on which Wolfgang's early symphonies were based but which find so little place in his last five. What does matter is that this conventional theme is presented in a work that puts behind it the style in which Leopold wrote and on which he trained Wolfgang. Yet the new style was not exclusive but inclusive, for it could combine into an artistic whole ideas of the most diverse sorts. Hence, Leopold's galant style was not rejected but had become merely one option among many.

When Mozart wrote the finale of the 'Jupiter' symphony, he cannot have known that it would be his valedictory essay in the genre, for he had every reason to expect to live into the nineteenth century.[82] Yet had he known, he could hardly have found a more telling summation of the journey he had travelled in his symphonies from lighthearted entertainment and formal articulation of other, more important works to serious works of art at the centre of the musical universe. The fugato in the coda of the 'Jupiter' Finale presents an apotheosis in which a contrapuntal motive representing faith, and four of the movement's other themes, are presented simultaneously in strict style in many combinations and permutations, introduced and (so to speak) presided over by a conventional theme not

---

[81] C.-G. Stellan Mörner, *Johan Wikmanson und die Brüder Silverstolpe: Einige stockholmer Persönlichkeiten im Musikleben des gustavianischen Zeitalters* (Stockholm, 1952), 319. The Swedish visitor to Vienna quoted here is Fredrik Samuel Silverstolpe.

[82] Mozart dated the cover of the catalogue of his works to run into the nineteenth century.

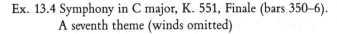

Ex. 13.4 Symphony in C major, K. 551, Finale (bars 350–6).
A seventh theme (winds omitted)

previously heard, which, however, is not permitted to enter into the final synthesis. This perhaps gives us a glimpse of Mozart's dreaming of escaping his oppressive past and giving utterance to his fondest hopes and highest aspirations for the future. That fugal writing might go beyond its *stile antico* association with established religion to carry such Enlightenment symbolism was clearly stated by the Abbé Vogler, seven years Mozart's senior but writing in the 1790s: 'The fugue is a conversation among a multitude of singers .... The fugue is thus a musical artwork where no one accompanies, no one submits, where nobody plays a secondary role, but each a principal part.'[83]

[83] Georg Joseph Vogler, *System für den Fugenbau* (Offenbach, 1811), 28.

APPENDIX A

The Status of 98 Symphonies Attributed to W. A. Mozart

I. 'Concert' symphonies (44)

A. With autograph MSS (30): K. 16, 43, 48, 73, 74, 110 = 75b, 112, 114, 124, 128, 129, 130, 132, 133, 134, 199 = 161b, 162, 181 = 162b, 182 = 173dA, 183 = 173dB, 201 = 186a, 202 = 186b, 200 = 189k, 297 = 300a, 319, 338, 504, 543, 550, 551

B. With authentic, non-autograph MSS (5): K. 19, Anhang 223 = 19a, 22, Anhang 221 = 45a, 425

C. With non-authentic MSS (9): K. 76 = 42a (?L. Mozart), Anhang 214 = 45b, 81 = 73*l* (?L. Mozart/?Dittersdorf), 97 = 73m, 95 = 73n, 84 = 73q, Anhang 216 = 74g = Anhang C 11.03, 75, 96 = 111b

II. 'Concert' symphonies also used as overtures (3)

A. With autograph MSS: K. 45, 184 = 161a, 318

III. Overtures made into multi-movement 'concert' symphonies (7)

A. With autograph MSS (6): K. 51 = 46a, 111 + 111a = 120, 126 + 141a = 161/163, 135, 196 + 207a = 121, 208 + 213c = 102

B. With authentic, non-autograph MS (1): K. 87 = 74a

IV. Overtures used unchanged as 'concert' symphonies (4)

A. With autograph MSS (4): K. 35, 38, 50 = 46b, 118 = 74c

V. *Symphonies extracted from orchestral serenades (7)

A. With autograph MS (1): K. 385

B. With authentic, non-autograph MSS (3): K. 204 = 213a, 250 = 248b, 320

C. With non-authentic MSS (3): K. 100 = 62a, 185 = 167a, 203 = 189b

VI. Lost symphonies known only by incipits (7)

D. With no MSS: K. Anhang 222 = 19b, Anhang 215 = 66c, Anhang 217 = 66d, Anhang 218 = 66e, 387d/4 = Anhang A 59/4, Anhang C 11.07, Anhang C 11.08

---

*The serenade autographs survive in all seven cases; this list chronicles sources for the symphony versions only.

VII. Putative symphony known only as keyboard pieces (1)

A. With autograph MS: K. 15kk + 15dd + 15cc + 15ee = ?Symphony No. 'o'

VIII. Spurious symphonies (25)

A. With (Mozart's) autograph MSS or autograph incipit (6): K. 18 = Anhang 109^{I} = Anhang A 51 (Abel), K. 291 = Anhang 109^{XI} = Anhang A 52 (M. Haydn), 444 = 425a + Anhang A53 (M. Haydn), 387d/1–3 = Anhang A 59/1–3 (J. Haydn, Hob. I: 75, 47, 62)

C. With non-authentic MSS (19): K. Anhang 220 = 16a, 16b = Anhang C 11.01 (?L. Mozart), 17 = Anhang C 11.02 (?L. Mozart), 98 = Anhang C 11.04 (?M. Haydn), 311a = Anhang C 11.05 (?), Anhang C 11.06 (L. Mozart), Anhang C 11.09 (L. Mozart), Anhang C 11.10 (Pleyel), Anhang C 11.11 (Gyrowetz), Anhang C 11.12 (Dittersdorf), Anhang C 11.13 (L. Mozart), Anhang C 11.14 (F. J. Eberl), Anhang C 11.15 (?), Anhang C 11.16 (?), *deest* ('Neue Lambach'—L. Mozart), *deest* (Wassmuth), *deest* (J. Haydn, Hob. I: 6), *deest* (J. M. Kraus), *deest* (J. A. Hasse)

APPENDIX B

Concordance for various systems of numbering Mozart's symphonies

K⁶	K³	K¹	B&H	Key	Sobriquet	Year	Incipit	Comments
16	16	16	I	E flat	'First'	1764	2.1	Two versions
16a	16a	Anh. 220	—	a	'Odense'	?	8.19	Not by Mozart
19	19	19	4	D		1765–6	3.1	
19a	19a	Anh. 223	—	F		1765–6	2.3	
19b	19b	Anh. 222	—	C		?	—	Lost; incipit in Ex. 5.7
22	22	22	5	B flat		1765	3.2	
32	32	32	—	D	*Galimathias musicum*	1766	3.3	Not a true symphony
35	35	35	—	C	*Die Schuldigkeit des ersten Gebots*	1767	4.1	Only one movement
38	38	38	—	D	*Apollo et Hyancinthus*	1767	4.2	Only one movement
42a	42a	76	43	F		?	5.1	Attribution uncertain
43	43	43	6	F		1767	5.2	
45	45	45	7	D		1768	5.3	Second version = K. 46a
45a	45a	Anh. 221	—	G	'Old Lambach'	1766	6.2	Two versions
45b	45b	Anh. 214	55	B flat		?	4.3	Attribution uncertain
46a	46a	51	—	D	*La finta semplice*	1768	5.3	First version = K. 45
46b		50	—	G	*Bastien und Bastienne*	1768	5.4	Only one movement
48	48	48	8	D		1768	5.5	
62a	62a	100	—	D	serenade	1769	6.3	
66c	66c	Anh. 215	—	D		?	7.1	Lost
66d	66d	Anh. 217	—	B flat		?	7.2	Lost
66e	66e	Anh. 218	—	B flat		?	7.3	Lost
73	75a	73	9	C		?1772	7.4	
73*l*	73*l*	81	44	D		before 1775	7.5	Possibly by Leopold Mozart
73m	73m	97	47	D		?	7.6	Attribution uncertain
73n	73n	95	45	D		?	4.4	Attribution uncertain
73q	73q	84	11	D		?	7.7	Attribution uncertain
74	74	74	10	G		?1769–70	7.8	
74a	74a	87	—	D	*Mitridate, rè di Ponto*	1770	7.9	
74c	74c	118	—	d	*La Betulia liberata*	1771	7.10	

K⁶	K³	K¹	B&H	Key	Sobriquet	Year	Incipit	Comments
75	75	75	42	F		?	8.1	Attribution uncertain
75b	75b	110	12	G		1771	8.2	
111a	111a	120	—	D	*Ascanio in Alba*	?1771–2	7.12	
111b	111b	96	46	C		?	7.11	Attribution uncertain
112	112	112	13	F		1771	7.13	
114	114	114	14	A		1771	8.3	
124	124	124	15	G		1772	8.4	
128	128	128	16	C		1772	8.5	
129	129	129	17	G		1772	8.6	
130	130	130	18	F		1772	8.7	
132	132	132	19	E flat		1772	8.8	Alternate slow move-ment
133	133	133	20	D		1772	8.9	
134	134	134	21	A		1772	8.10	
135	135	135	—	D	*Lucio Silla*	1772	7.14	
141a	141a	161/163	50	D	*Il sogno di Scipione*	1772	8.11	
161a	166a	184	26	E flat		1773	8.12	
161b	162a	199	27	G		1773	8.13	
162	162	162	22	C		?1773	8.14	
162b	162b	181	23	D		1773	8.15	
167a	167a	185	—	D	serenade	1773	8.16	
173dA	166c	182	24	B flat		1773	8.17	
173dB	183	183	25	g	'Little G minor'	1773	8.18	
186a	186a	201	29	A		1774	8.20	
186b	186b	202	30	D		1774	8.21	
189b	189b	203	—	D	serenade	1774	8.22	
189k	173e	200	28	C		?1775	8.23	
207a	207a	121	—	D	*La finta giardiniera*	1775	8.24	
213a	213a	204	—	D	serenade	1775	8.25	
213c	213c	102	—	C	*Il rè pastore*	1775	8.26	
248b	248b	250	—	D	serenade	1776	8.27	
300a	300a	297	31	D	'Paris'	1778	9.1	Two versions
318	318	318	32	G		1779	10.1	
319	319	319	33	B flat		1779	10.2	
320	320	320	—	D	serenade	1779	10.3	
338	338	338	34	C		1780	10.4	
385	385	385	35	D	'Haffner'	1782	11.1	Two versions
425	425	425	36	C	'Linz'	1783	11.2	
425a	425a	444	37	G		1784	11.3	Mozart's introduction for a symphony by M. Haydn (see K. Anh. A 53 below)
504	504	504	38	D	'Prague'	1786	11.6	
543	543	543	39	E flat		1788	11.7	

K⁶	K³	K¹	B&H	Key	Sobriquet	Year	Incipit	Comments
550	550	550	40	g		1788	11.8	Two versions
551	551	551	41	C	'Jupiter'	1788	11.9	
Anh. A 51	Anh. 109ⁱ	18	3	E flat		?1764	—	By C. F. Abel
Anh. A 52	Anh. 109ˣⁱ	291	—	D		?	—	By M. Haydn
Anh. A 53	425a	444	37	G		?	11.3	By M. Haydn (see K. 425a above)
Anh. A 59	387d	—	—	D, G, D, C		?	—	Three symphonies by J. Haydn and an unidenti-fied incipit (Ex. 11.1)
Anh. C 11.01	16b	—	—	C		?	—	Possibly by L. Mozart
Anh. C 11.02	Anh. 223a	17	2	B flat		?	2.2	By L. Mozart
Anh. C 11.03	74g	Anh. 216	54	B flat		?	6.4	Possibly by W. A. Mozart
Anh. C 11.04	Anh. 223b	98	48	F		?	11.5	Author unknown
Anh. C 11.05	311a	—	—	B flat		?	9.3	Author unknown
Anh. C 11.06	Anh. 291b	Anh. 219	—	D		?	—	By L. Mozart
Anh. C 11.07	Anh. 223	—	—	D		?	—	Lost; incipit in Ex. 5.7
Anh. C 11.08	Anh. 223	—	—	F		?	—	Lost; incipit in Ex. 5.7
Anh. C 11.09	Anh. 293	Anh. 293	—	G		?	—	By L. Mozart
Anh. C 11.10	Anh. 293c	—	—	F		?	—	By I. Pleyel
Anh. C 11.11	—	—	—	C		?	—	By A. Gyrowetz
Anh. C 11.12	—	—	—	F		?	—	By K. Dittersdorf
Anh. C 11.13	Anh. 294	Anh. 294	—	G		?	—	By L. Mozart
Anh. C 11.14	—	—	—	C		?	—	By F. J. Eberl
Anh. C 11.15	—	—	—	C		?	8.28	Author unknown
Anh. C 11.16	Anh. 109g	—	—	G(C?)		?	—	Author unknown
—	—	—	—	—		1764	—	Earlier than K. 16 (see Ex. 2.1)
—	—	—	—	G	'New Lambach'	?1767	6.1	By L. Mozart
—	—	—	—	c		1785	7.15	By J. M. Kraus
—	—	—	—	D		1730	—	By J. A. Hasse (see ch. 5, n. 53)

APPENDIX C

Report on the Present State of the Musical Establishment at the Court of His Serene Highness the Archbishop of Salzburg in the Year 1757.

[The Directors]

Capellmeister

1. Mr Ernst Eberlin [1702–62], from Jettenbach in Swabia [now Bavaria], is also archiepiscopal lord high steward. He was previously court organist, and if anyone deserves to be called a thorough and accomplished master of composition, it is indeed this man. He is entirely in command of the notes, and he composes with such quickness that many people would take for a fairy tale the manner in which this profound composer brings this or that important composition to the music-stand. As far as the number of musical compositions that he has composed is concerned, one can compare him to the two very industrious and famous composers, [Alessandro] Scarlatti and Telemann. There has appeared in print only the *[IX] Toccate [e Fughe]* for organ [Augsburg, 1747].

Vicecapellmeister

2. Mr Joseph Lolli [1701–78], from Bologna in Italy, was previously a tenor. Besides his oratorios, he has composed several Masses and Vesper psalms for the church, but almost nothing for the chamber.

The Court Composers

3. Mr Caspar Cristelli, from Vienna in Austria, is a cellist and a great master of accompaniment. He also distinguishes himself from many cellists by the art with which he draws from his instrument a good tone that is strong and full, yet also pure and calm—and performs manfully but not in the brash manner of violists. He composes however only for the chamber. The majority of pieces composed by him consist of: a few so-called partitas, symphonies, and several trios, as well as duets and solos for the cello.

4. Mr Leopold Mozart [1719–87], from the Imperial City of Augsburg, is violinist and

leader of the orchestra. He composes both church and chamber music. He was born on 14th November 1719, and entered the archiepiscopal service in the year 1743 soon after completing his studies in philosophy and law. He has made himself known in every branch of composition, without, however, issuing anything in print except for the *Sonate sei a tre [per chiesa e da camera]* that he himself engraved in copper in the year 1740 (principally in order to gain experience in the art of engraving). In July 1756 he published his *Violinschule*. Among the compositions by Mr Mozart that have become known in manuscript, numerous contrapuntal and other church pieces are especially noteworthy; further, a great number of symphonies, some only *à 4*, but others with all the customary instruments; likewise more than thirty grand serenades, in which solos for various instruments are introduced. Apart from these he has composed many concertos, in particular for transverse flute, oboe, bassoon, horn, trumpet, etc.; countless trios and divertimentos for diverse instruments; also twelve oratorios and a host of theatre pieces, even pantomines; and especially music for certain special occasions, such as martial music with trumpets, kettledrums, fifes, and drums, together with the ordinary instruments; a Turkish piece; a piece with a steel xylophone; and a musical sleigh-ride with five sleigh-bells; not to mention marches, so-called notturnos, many hundreds of minuets, opera dances, and suchlike smaller pieces.

5. Mr Ferdinand Seidl from Falkenberg in Silesia, violinist, composes only for the chamber. He has written very many symphonies, as well as concertos and solos for the violin in which he has principally taken pains to introduce entirely unique and uncommonly difficult passages.

The three court composers play their instruments in the church as well as in the chamber, and, in rotation with the Capellmeister, each has the direction of the Court Music for a week at a time. All the musical arrangements depend solely upon whoever is in charge each week, as he, at his pleasure, can perform his own or other persons' pieces.

[The Instrumentalists]

Violinists

6. Mr Paul Schorn from Salzburg.

7. Mr Carl Vogt, from Kremau in Moravia, is a serious player, who knows how to produce a strong, manly tone from the violin.

8. Mr Wenzel Hebelt, from Heiligen Berg in Moravia, plays the most difficult passages perfectly in tune. For that reason he also only likes hard pieces, even those that are somewhat too hard or too fast for him. But his tone is quite weak and soft.

9. Mr Joseph Hülber, from Krumbach in Swabia, also plays the transverse flute.

10. Mr Nicolaus Meisner, from Brauma in Bohemia, also plays the horn.

11. Mr Franz Schwarzmann, from Salzburg, also plays concertos on the bassoon, and no less beautifully on the oboe, flute, and horn. He is just now in Padua in the school of the famous Mr Tartini.

12. Mr Joseph Hölzel, from the city of Steyer in Austria, also plays the horn.

13. Mr Andreas Mayr, from Salzburg, also plays the violoncello well.

Violists

14. Mr Johann Sebastian Vogt, from the city of Steinach im Culmbachischen [in Bamberg], also plays the oboe.
15. Mr Johann Caspar Thuman, from Salzburg.

Organists and Harpsichordists

16. Mr Anton Cajetan Adelgasser [*sic*], from Der Insel in Bavaria, plays logically, beautifully, and generally cantabile. He is not only a good organist, but also a good accompanist on the harpsichord. He owes both these skills to Capellmeister Eberlin, from whom he also learned the rules of composition. He composes acceptably as well, but he is still very markedly attached to imitating others, especially his teacher.
17. Mr Franz Ignatius Lipp, from Eggenfelden in Bavaria, also plays the violin, sings with a beautiful tenor voice, and composes not badly.

    These two organists have the big organ (which stands in the rear of the church) and the side organ (where the solo singers are) to take care of by turns. Both are equally responsible for accompaniment in chamber music.

18. Mr Georg Paris, from Salzburg, has at all times to play the small organ down below in the choir, where the choir singers are, and takes care of the daily hymn service. He has composed several pieces for the church.

Violoncellists

19. Mr Joseph Schorn from Salzburg also plays the violin.
20. Mr Jacob Anton Marchall, from Pfaffenhofen in Bavaria, applies himself very much to accompaniment, in which he develops himself ever more completely through the instruction of Mr Cristelli, with whom in turns he takes care of accompaniment. He also plays the violin well.

Double Bass Players

21. Mr Matthias Wirth, from Westendorf in Swabia.
22. Mr Paul Hutterer, from the Böhmerwalde [in Bavaria or Bohemia].

Bassoonists

23. Mr Johann Jacob Rott, from Staubingen in Bavaria.
24. Mr Rochus Samhuber, from Salzburg.
25. Mr Joh. Adam Schultz   }   from Sagan in Silesia.
26. Mr Joh. Heinrich Schultz   }   both also play the oboe.

Trombonist

27. Mr Thomas Oschlatt [*rect.* Gschlatt], from Stockerau in Lower Austria, is a great master of his instrument, whose equal is hardly to be found. He also plays the violin well and the violoncello, and the horn no less well.

Oboists and Flautists

28. Mr Christoph Burg, from Mannheim in the Palatinate, plays very beautiful concertos on the flute and oboe, and also plays the violin.
29. Mr Franz de Paula Deibl, from Munich in Bavaria, also plays the violin.
30. Mr Joh. Michael Obkirchner, from Donauwert [in Bavaria].

Horn Players

31. Mr Wenzel Sadlo, also play the violin well. } Both from Brodetz
32. Mr Franz Drasil, also plays the violoncello. } in Bohemia.

Just a few years ago these two excellent horn players could have transferred into the service of His Serene Highness the Elector of Bavaria with yearly wages of one-thousand florins each, but they did not wish to leave the service of the Salzburg Court.

The Singers

The Solo Singers

33. The Very Reverend Mr Andreas Unterkofler, from Salzburg, is prefect of the princely Chapel-house[1] and titular court chaplain.

Soprano

The places of the three other castratos, namely Messrs Grossi, Augustini, and the recently deceased contraltist Lonzi, are still not filled.
34. The Very Reverend Mr Johann Sebastian Brunner, from Neuötting in Bavaria.

Bass

35. Mr Joseph Meis[s]ner, from Salzburg, an excellent singer. His voice has something quite extraordinarily agreeable about it, and it can reach the high range of a good tenor and the deep range of a chamber bass, entirely unconstrainedly and with beautiful evenness. He is especially strong in pathetic passages, and passages that call for a simple execution; he knows how to perform faultlessly, because these things come naturally to him. In Italy he performed first in Pisa, after that in Florence, and finally in the Teatro San Carlo in Naples, and caused himself to be heard in Rome as well as in the other great Italian cities. In Vienna he sang for the Academy, to which place he was summoned. On his journey to Holland he found the opportunity to be heard at the courts of Munich, Würzburg, Mannheim, Stuttgart, Liège, and Cologne, as well as in front of the bishops of Augsburg and Speyer and other lords, all of whom made known their approbation by giving him beautiful gifts. He has now made a short journey to Padua and Venice.
36. Mr Joseph Michelansky, from Prague in Bohemia, tenor.
37. Mr Joseph Zugseisen, from Salzburg, tenor.
38. Mr Felix Winter, from Salzburg, has a voice which in some respects reaches the level

[1] The nature of the 'Chapel-House' is explained later in the report.

of Mr Meissner's. He has the high register of a not too high tenor-voice, and the low register of a deep chamber bass, and he sings with spirit. He is returning right now from Italy, where he has been for two years, and has caused himself to be heard with much approval in Rome and other places. In Naples he sang in the Carnival opera in the Teatro San Carlo.

In the princely Chapel-House there are perpetually two or three [boy] sopranos and as many [boy] altos for singing solos, who have Mr Meissner as their teacher.

The Choir-Singers are
firstly
The Gentlemen of the Choir,
namely the honourable gentleman

39. Mr Franz Anton Oettel, from Bavaria, tenor.   ⎫
40. Mr Joh. Baptist Freymiller, from Swabia, bass. ⎭   choir regents

At the daily divine service, these two choir-regents take in turns the direction of the hymns and the contrapuntal music, whenever the court chamber-musicians are not present.

41. Mr Christian Maller, from Swabia, tenor.
42. Mr Anton Saller, from Bavaria, tenor.
43. Mr Christoph Strasser, from Salzburg, alto.
44. Mr Benedict Schmutzer, from Bavaria, tenor.
45. Mr Anton Ainkäss, from Carinthia, tenor.
46. Mr Sebastian Seyser, from Bavaria, bass.
47. Mr Paul Pinzger, from Bavaria, tenor.
48. Mr Franz Schneiderbaur, from Bavaria, alto-falsettist.
49. Mr Christoph Bachmeyer, from Salzburg, bass.
50. Mr Johann Anton Eismann, from Berchtolsgaden [in Bavaria], tenor.
51. Mr Anton Schipfl, from the Tyrol, bass.
52. Mr Ignatius Seeleuthner, from Salzburg, tenor.
53. Mr Franz Joseph Menda, from the Tyrol, bass.
54. Mr Johann Veit Braun, from the Tyrol, alto-falsettist.
55. Mr Franz Cajetan Moschee, from Carinthia, bass.
56. Mr Lorenz Winneberger, from Swabia, bass.
57. Mr Donat Stettinger, from Bavaria, bass.
58. Mr David Veit Westermeyer, from Salzburg, tenor.
59. Mr Johann Baptist Setti, from Italy, bass.

To the Choir-Singers belong
secondly
the Hymn-Singers

60. Mr Benedict Heiss, from Salzburg, bass.

61. Mr Leopold Lill, from Salzburg, bass.
62. Mr Joseph Schmid, from Salzburg, bass.
63. Mr Johann Drauner, from Hungary, alto-falsettist.
64. Mr Judas Tadens Wesenauer, from Salzburg, tenor.
65. Mr Joseph Egger, from Salzburg, tenor.
66. Mr Joseph Seeloos, from Swabia, tenor.
67. Mr Joseph Scheffler, from Bavaria, bass.

Among these eight hymn-singers are four who can play the violin, for one of them must play the violin at all times in the choir with the small organ (which is played by Mr Paris).

To the Choir-Singers belong
thirdly
The Choirboys

Fifteen in number, they carry the high parts. They are all together in a single building, which is called the Chapel-House, where the Chapel-Prefect also lives; and they dine with him at a table in the company of the Preceptors who instruct them in their studies.

The Court not only provides them with all their clothing, food, and drink, and their own cook and house-servant, but in addition they are instructed by the best masters from the princely chapel at the Court's expense, in the singing of concerted music and hymns, the organ, the violin, and also the Italian language. Upon their departure from the Chapel-House, they are well clothed from head to foot. This, however, does not take place when a boy loses his voice; rather, he is taken care of for a good two or three years more (according to his good behaviour), so that he gains time to perfect himself and put himself in a position to enter the service of the Court, which the majority of them attain because, if they are fit for service, they are given preference over others.

To the Choir-Singers belong
finally
Three Trombonists

Namely, to play the alto-, tenor-, and bass-trombone, which must be taken care of by the master of the town waits with two of his subordinates, for a yearly stipend.

In the rear over the entrance to the church the archiepiscopal cathedral has the great organ, in the front near the choir four side-organs, and below in the choir near the hymn-singers is a small choir-organ. In large-scale concerted music the great organ is used only to improvise preludes; during the concerted music itself, however, one of the four side-organs is constantly played, namely, the one next to the altar on the right-hand side, where the solo singers and the bass instruments are. Opposite by the left side-organ are the violinists, etc., and by both the other side-organs are the two choirs of trumpets and kettledrums. The lower choir-organ and double-bass play along only in the tutti passages. The oboe and the transverse flute are heard in the cathedral seldom and the horn never. Accordingly, in church these gentlemen [i.e. the wind players] play the violin.

The Two Choirs of Trumpets and Kettledrums
consist of the following persons.

1. Mr Johann Baptist Gesenberger, head trumpeter from Bavaria, is an excellent trumpeter, who has made himself very famous for the extraordinary purity of his intonation (especially in the high register), for the rapidity of his leaps, and for his good trill.

2. Mr Caspar Köstler, court and field trumpeter from the Palatinate, is a pupil of the renowned man, the late Mr Heinisch of Vienna. He draws from the trumpet a very agreeable cantabile tone. He has a good manner of execution, and one listens to his concertos and solos with much pleasure. He also plays the violin.

3. Mr Andreas Schachtner, court trumpeter from Bavaria, is a pupil of Mr Köstler's. He plays the trumpet extremely well and with good taste. He also plays the violin especially well, and the violoncello.

4. Mr Johann Schwarz, court and field trumpeter from the Palatinate, is a principal, and also plays the violin.

5. Mr Ignatius Finck, court and field trumpeter from Austria, is Mr Gesenberger's second. He also plays the violin and the violoncello.

6. Mr Adam Huebner, court trumpeter from the Palatinate, is a second, and also plays the violin.

7. Mr Johann Leonhard Seywald, court and field trumpeter from Salzburg, is a second, and also plays the violin. He and Mr Huebner in rotation second the three principals, Messrs Köstler, Schachtner, and Schwarz.

8. Mr Johann Siegmund Lechner, court trumpeter from the Imperial City of Augsburg, also plays the violin.

9. Mr Franz Heftstreit, court and field trumpeter from Moravia, plays the violin and is also used for viola.

10. Mr Matthias Brand, court and field trumpeter from Bohemia.

Two positions are vacant, which must be filled at some point.

Kettledrummers

11. Mr Anton Winkler, court and field kettledrummer from Salzburg, also plays the violin.

12. Mr Florian Vogt, court and field kettledrummer from Krenau in Moravia, plays the violin very well.

There is not one of the trumpeters or kettledrummers in the princely service who does not play the violin well. For performances of large-scale concerted music at court, all of them must appear and join in playing second violin or viola, which it is in the purview of whoever has charge of the weekly direction to order.

To the Musical Establishment there also belong

Mr Johann Rochus Egedacher, princely court organ-maker, born in Salzburg.

Mr Andreas Ferdinand Meyer, princely court lute- and violin-maker, born in Vienna. Both of them must be present at all times and keep the instruments in good condition.

Finally there are

Three music-servants or so-called organ-blowers.

Thus the number of those who belong to the musical establishment, or who are connected to the court music in any way, amounts to ninety-nine persons.[2]

---

[2] [Leopold Mozart], 'Nachricht von dem gegenwärtigen Zustande der Musik Sr. Hochfürstl. Gnaden des Erzbischoffs zu Salzburg im Jahr 1757', in F. W. Marpurg (ed.), *Historisch-Kritische Beyträge zur Aufnahme der Musik* (Berlin, 1757), iii/3. 183–98.

APPENDIX D

A Brief History of the Köchel Catalogue

The first edition of Ludwig Ritter von Köchel's *Chronological-Thematic Catalogue of the Complete Works of Wolfgang Amadé Mozart* was published in 1862 (= K^1). It listed all of Mozart's completed works known to Köchel in what he believed to be their chronological order, from number 1 (infant harpsichord piece) to 626 (the Requiem). The second edition by Paul Graf von Waldersee in 1905 involved for the most part minor additions, corrections, and clarifications. A thoroughgoing revision came first with the third edition, completed by Alfred Einstein in 1936 (= K^3). Einstein changed the position of many works in Köchel's chronology, threw out as spurious some works Köchel had taken to be genuine, and added as authentic some works Köchel had believed spurious or not known about. He also inserted into the chronological scheme incomplete and lost works. These Köchel had placed in an appendix (*Anhang*) without chronological order. Köchel's original numbers could not be reassigned, for they formed the bibliographical basis for innumerable library catalogues and reference works. New numbers were therefore inserted in chronological order between the old ones by adding lower-case letters.[1]

A reprint of the third edition with a supplement of corrections and additions was published by Einstein in 1946 and is usually referred to as K^{3a}. So-called fourth and fifth editions were nothing more than unchanged reprints of the 1936 edition, without the 1946 supplement. The sixth edition, which appeared in 1964 and was edited by Franz Giegling, Alexander Weinmann, and Gerd Sievers (= K^6), continued Einstein's innovations by adding numbers with lower-case letters appended, and a few with upper-case letters (e.g., the Symphony in Bb major, K. 176dA), in instances in which a work had to be inserted into the chronology between two lower-case insertions. (So-called seventh and eighth editions are unchanged reprints of the sixth.) This history explains why many of Mozart's symphonies bear two 'K' numbers, and a few have three.[2]

Among the sources used by Köchel in compiling his catalogue was a manuscript in the archives of the music publishers Breitkopf & Härtel of Leipzig, which is referred to often in the course of this book. This manuscript, entitled *Thematisches Verzeichniss der sämmtlichen Werke von W. A. Mozart*, represented an early nineteenth-century attempt to list all of the works attributed to Mozart. Although it was destroyed during the bombing of Leipzig during the Second World War, copies of it formerly belonging to Köchel and to Jahn

---

[1] Waldersee had already added a few works by this method into K^2.
[2] For instance, the Symphony in B flat, K. Anh. 216 = 74g = Anh. C 11.03.

TABLE D.1 The organization of the appendix of
the Köchel Catalogue prior to K^6

Section	Numbers	Status of work
I	1–11	Lost
II	12–109f	Incomplete
III	110–184a	Arranged
IV	185–231	Doubtful
V	232–294	Spurious

survive.[3] In this study, this manuscript is referred to as the 'Breitkopf & Härtel Manuscript Catalogue'.

Among the seventy symphonies whose incipits are listed in the Breitkopf & Härtel Manuscript Catalogue were twelve for which Köchel was unable to locate the music. It was his policy to assign problematic works to an appendix, and these symphonies were treated accordingly. The organization of Köchel's appendix, which was maintained in all editions of the Catalogue prior to K^6 (Table D.1), has been suppressed in the latest editions of the catalogue (K^{6-8}); this is unfortunate because it obscures Köchel's opinion about the status of the various works contained in the appendix. The symphonies that at the time of K^1 were known only from their incipits in the Breitkopf & Härtel Manuscript Catalogue are shown in Table D.2. A few peculiarities emerge from examining these two tables. One is that Köchel considered the lost symphonies 'doubtful' rather than simply 'lost'. Under 'lost' he listed only those works that, from documentary evidence such as the Mozarts' letters, he knew must have been composed by Mozart, regarding all other works with admirable scepticism as doubtful until proved otherwise. Another peculiarity is that (apparently through oversight) he omitted entirely from his Catalogue two of the lost symphonies known only by incipits. They were first mentioned in K^3, inserted following Anh. 223 without receiving numbers of their own, and given independent numbers, Anh. C 11.07 and 08, only in K^6.

Yet another peculiarity is that Köchel did not exercise the same caution with extant works as he did with lost ones, for although he placed these lost symphonies in the 'doubtful' category, he accepted as authentic a number of symphonies for which there were neither autograph or other authentic manuscripts nor documentary evidence connecting them to Mozart other than an attribution, often on a single surviving, non-authentic copy. The latter group of symphonies included K. 75, 76 = 42a, 81 = 73*l*, 84 = 73q, 95 = 73n, 96 = 111b, 97 = 73m, and 98 = Anh. 223b = Anh. C 11.04. These works have been accepted by most other authorities as authentic. We know even less than we might about five of them[4] because their sole eighteenth-century sources have been lost or destroyed, and they survive only in the *GA*, with which there is a special problem. The

---

[3] See ch. 6, n. 4.   [4] K. 75, 76 = 42a, 95 = 73n, 96 = 111b, and 97 = 73m.

TABLE D.2 Lost symphonies in the Breitkopf & Härtel Manuscript Catalogue

K¹	K³	K⁶	B&H	Key	Subsequent fate
A214	45b	45b	2	B flat	copy found in Berlin, published 1943
A215	66c	66c	26	D	still lost
A216	74g	AC11.03	33	B flat	Copy found in Berlin, published 1910; now lost (in Kraków?)
A217	66d	66d	36	B flat	still lost
A218	66e	66e	52	B flat	still lost
A219	A291b	AC11.06	61	D	copy found attributed to Leopold (Seiffert 13 = Theiss D12 = Grove D11 = Eisen *D11)
A220	16a	16a	62	a	copy found in Odense 1983, published 1985
A221	45a	45a	67	G	copy found in Lambach, published 1923; original parts (now in Munich) partly in Leopold's and Nannerl's hands, found 1981
A222	19b	19b	68	C	still lost
A223	19a	19a	70	F	original parts (now in Munich) in Leopold's hand, found and published 1981
—	(A223)	AC11.07	60	D	still lost
—	(A223)	AC11.08	63	F	still lost

Note: A = Anhang [Appendix].

For incipits of the still lost symphonies, see Example 5.7.

editor of forty-one of the symphonies in that edition was Gustav Nottebohm, who died before seeing them through the press; consequently, a proper critical report for them was never published, and important information about the now-lost sources of several problematic symphonies perished with him.

A final peculiarity is Einstein's, not Köchel's. As can be seen in Table D.2, Einstein accepted as genuine not only three of the four works from among the lost symphonies that had been rediscovered between 1862 and 1936, but also the eight other symphonies then still known only by their incipits. He placed these three rediscovered and six lost symphonies in the main chronological listing of the K^3. Yet aside from K. 19a and K. 45a, for which there was documentary evidence of provenance, Einstein's insertions of these symphonies into Köchel's chronology were based entirely on stylistic grounds. If placing a whole symphony chronologically on stylistic grounds may be thought speculative, given the conventional nature of the musical content of Mozart's early symphonies, what must we think of placing an incipit of a few bars on such grounds? Yet this is what Einstein did. He also noticed that Köchel had overlooked two of the symphony incipits, but in attempting to remedy this inconsistency, he committed another, greater one. For although he had accepted nine of the ten incipits listed by Köchel as authentic and had placed them in the main chronology, he relegated the two incipits overlooked by Köchel (K. Anh. C 11.07 and Anh. C 11.08) to the appendix between items Anh. 223 = 19a and Anh. 223a = 17, remarking only that 'nothing can be stated for want of further particulars'. This defies logic, for although it is true that nothing is known about the two incipits, they are neither more nor less 'doubtful' than the other incipits of lost symphonies about which we also know 'nothing'. Yet Einstein's arbitrary division of the symphony incipits into authentic (K. Anh. 215 = 66c, Anh. 217 = 66d, Anh. 218 = 66e, Anh. 220 = 16a, Anh. 222 = 19b) and doubtful (K. Anh. C 11.07, Anh. C 11.08) has been accepted in K^6 as if it were based on evidence or reasoning.

Any new edition of the Köchel Catalogue should find clearer, more honest categories for problematic works, and should also find a way of dealing with works believed to be genuine but difficult or impossible to date accurately, so that they can be entered into the main listing without wild guesswork in dating them.

APPENDIX E

Czerny's Tempos for Twelve Early Symphonies

Source: *W. A. Mozart's 12 Grand Sinfonies, Posthumous Works, Now first published, arranged for the Piano-forte, for two performers, by C. Czerny. The same will be published in original score and orchestral parts* (London: Ewer & Co., [1847]).

Symphony in E flat major, K. 184 = 166a = 161a
  Molto presto 𝄵 ♩ = MM 88
  Andante $\frac{2}{4}$ ♪ = MM 104
  Finale [Allegro] $\frac{3}{8}$ ♩. = MM 100

Symphony in G major, K. 199 = 162a = 161b
  Allegro $\frac{3}{4}$ ♩ = MM 152
  Andantino grazioso $\frac{2}{4}$ ♪ = MM 120
  Presto $\frac{3}{8}$ ♩. = MM 96

Symphony in C major, K. 162
  Allegro assai 𝄵 ♩ = MM 152
  Andantino [grazioso] $\frac{2}{4}$ ♪ = MM 104
  Presto assai $\frac{6}{8}$ ♩. = MM 108

Symphony in D major, K. 181 = 162b
  Allegro spiritoso 𝄵 ♩ = MM 152
  Andantino grazioso $\frac{3}{8}$ ♩. = MM 52
  Presto assai $\frac{2}{4}$ ♩ = MM 80

Symphony in D major, K. 185 = 167a
  Allegro assai 𝄵 ♩ = MM 152
  Menuetto $\frac{3}{4}$ ♩ = MM 138
  Andante grazioso $\frac{2}{4}$ ♩ = MM 116
  Menuetto $\frac{3}{4}$ ♩ = MM 152
  Finale. Adagio— 𝄵 ♩ = MM 88
    Allegro assai $\frac{6}{8}$ ♩. = MM 104

Symphony in B flat major, K. 182 = 166c = 173dA
  Allegro spiritoso 𝄵 ♩ = MM 80
  Andantino grazioso $\frac{2}{4}$ ♪ = MM 104
  Finale. Allegro $\frac{3}{8}$ ♩. = MM 92

Symphony in G minor, K. 183 = 173dB
  Allegro con brio **C** ♩ = MM 160
  Andante $\frac{2}{4}$ ♪ = MM 96
  Menuetto $\frac{3}{4}$ ♩ = MM 152
  Finale. Allegro **₵** [**C**] ♩ = MM 100

Symphony in A major, K. 201 = 186a
  Allegro moderato **C** [**₵**] ♩ = MM 144
  Andante $\frac{2}{4}$ ♪ = MM 88
  Menuetto $\frac{3}{4}$ ♩ = MM 126
  Finale. Allegro con spirito $\frac{6}{8}$ ♩. = MM 96

Symphony in D major, K. 202 = 186b
  Molto allegro $\frac{3}{4}$ ♩ = MM 160
  Andantino con moto $\frac{2}{4}$ ♪ = MM 116
  Menuetto $\frac{3}{4}$ ♩ = MM 132
  Finale. Presto $\frac{2}{4}$ ♩ = MM 92

Symphony in D major, K. 203 = 189b
  Andante maestoso— **C** ♪ = MM 92
    Allegro assai **C** ♩ = MM 144
  Menuetto $\frac{3}{4}$ ♩. = MM 66
  Andante $\frac{2}{4}$ ♪ = MM 88
  Menuetto $\frac{3}{4}$ ♩ = MM 144
  Finale. Prestissimo $\frac{2}{4}$ ♩ = MM 92

Symphony in C major, K. 200 = 189k
  Allegro spiritoso $\frac{3}{4}$ ♩ = MM 160
  Andante $\frac{2}{4}$ ♪ = MM 104
  Menuetto $\frac{3}{4}$ ♩ = MM 152
  Finale. Presto **₵** ♩ = MM 112

Symphony in D major, K. 204 = 213a
  Allegro assai **C** ♩ = MM 160
  Menuetto $\frac{3}{4}$ ♩ = MM 138
  Andante $\frac{2}{4}$ ♪ = MM 100
  Menuetto $\frac{3}{4}$ ♩ = MM 144
  Finale. Andantino grazioso— $\frac{2}{3}$ ♪ = MM 120
    Allegro $\frac{3}{8}$ ♩. = MM 88

The 'missing' bassoon parts for the Sieber version of the 'Paris' symphony, K. 297 = 300a

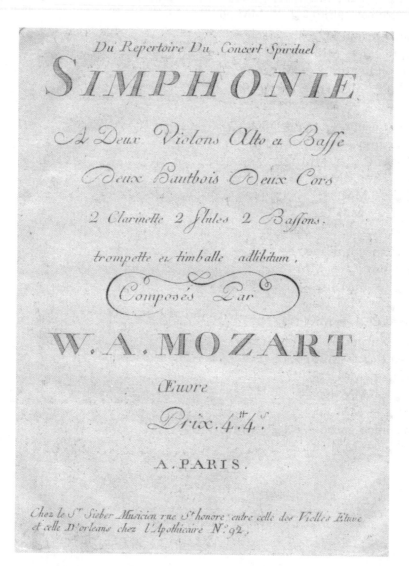

Du Repertoire Du Concert Spirituel

SIMPHONIE

A Deux Violons Alto et Basse

Deux hautbois Deux Cors

2 Clarinette 2 flutes 2 Bassons.

trompette et timballe adlibitum,

Composés Par

W. A. MOZART

Œuvre

Prix. 4.f 4.s

A. PARIS.

Chez le Sr Sieber Musicien rue St honore, entre celle des Vielles Etuve
et celle D'orleans chez L'Apothicaire No 92.

2
2. Fagotto
I.
SINFONIA
del Sig.r Mozart.
Allegro Vivace
cres.
73

566

4
Fagotto Primo
Sempre Sotto Voce
Andante
solo
cres.
Allegro
73

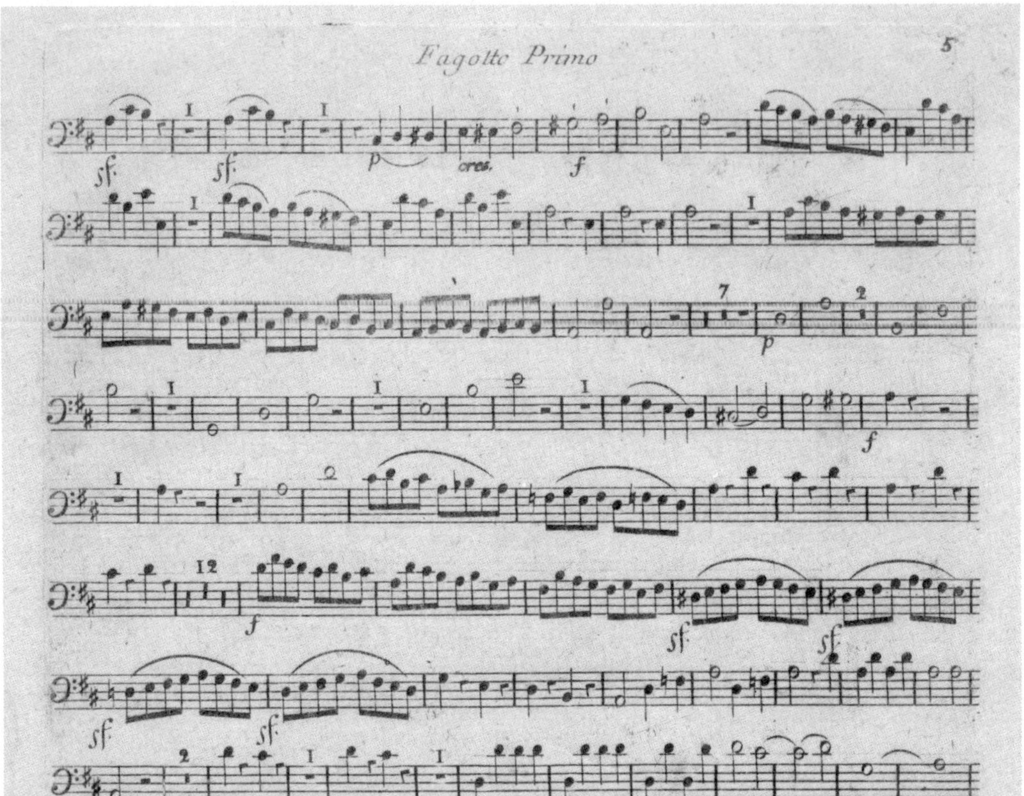
Fagotto Primo
5
73

Bibliography

Before 1830

Algarotti, Francesco, *Saggio sopra l'opera in musica* (n.p., 1755); partial trans. in O. Strunk, *Source Readings in Music History* (New York, 1950), 657–72.

Allgemeine musikalische Zeitung, Leipzig (1798–1848).

[Almanach des] Spectacles de Paris . . . [title varies] *pour l'année* . . . (1766–91).

Almanach musical, Paris (1775–83).

Annalen des Theaters, Berlin (1793).

L'Année littéraire (1789), xxxvi/5. 115–18.

Annonces, affiches et avis divers, Paris (1778–89).

Apel, A., 'Musik und Poesie', *Allgemeine musikalische Zeitung* (1806), viii, cols. 449–57, 465–70.

Apollo et Terpsichore . . . A Collection of the Most Celebrated Songs, Duetts, Rondos, Airs, &c. Extracted from the Latest Operas & Other Entertainments, Adapted for the Piano-forte, Violin, Guitar, or German Flute (London, 1799).

Archenholz, Johann Wilhelm von, *A Picture of England* (London, 1789).

Augsburgische Staats- und gelehrten Zeitung (22 Oct. 1777).

Augsburgischer Intelligenz-Zettel (19 May 1763).

'Auszug eines Briefes von einem Reisenden an seinem Freund R–l–i in Bamberg. Frankfurt am 21sten Hornung, 1786', in C. F. Cramer (ed.), *Magazin der Musik* (21 Nov. 1786), 951–6.

Bach, C. P. E., *Versuch über die wahre Art das Clavier zu spielen* (Berlin, 1753–62, repr. Leipzig, 1957); cited as *Versuch*; trans. W. J. Mitchell as *Essay on the True Art of Playing Keyboard Instruments* (New York, 1949).

Bachaumont, Louis Petit de, *Mémoires secrets pour servir à l'histoire de la république des lettres en France depuis MDCCLXXII jusqu'à nos jours, ou Journal d'un observateur rentrant chez lui* (London, 1780–9).

Baretti, Giuseppe, *An Account of the Manners and Customs of Italy* (London, 1768).

Berlinische musikalische Zeitung (18 Mar. 1793).

Berlinische Nachrichten von Staats- und gelehrte Sachen (9 May 1789).

Bertezen, Salvatore, *Principi di Musica* (Rome, 1780, 2nd edn., 1781).

'Biographische Nachricht', *Musikalische Korrespondenz der teutschen Filarmonischen Gesellschaft* (4 Jan. 1792), 2.

Bodenschatz, Erhard, *Das schöne und geistreiche Magnificat der hochgelobten Jungfrauen Mariae, wie es in der christlichen Kirchen zu singen breuchlichen, sampt dem Benedicamus, &c., auf die zwölff modos musicales in ihrer natürlichen Ordnung unterschiedlich mit vier Stimmen gesetzt* (Leipzig, 1599).

Bremner, Robert, 'Some Thoughts on the Performance of Concert Music', in J. G. C. Shetky, *Six Quartettos for Two Violins, a Tenor, & Violoncello*, Op. 6 (London, 1777); Bremner's preface repr. London, 1972; mod. edn. by N. Zaslaw in 'The Compleat Orchestral Musician', *Early Music* (1979), vii. 46–57.

Brossard, Sebastian, *Dictionaire* [sic] *de musique* (Paris, 1703).

'Bruchstüke aus Briefen an einen jungen Tonsetzer, Zweyter Brief: Ueber die Abschaffung des Flügels aus den Orchestern', *Allgemeine musikalische Zeitung* (1799–1800), ii, cols. 17–19.

Burney, Charles, *The Present State of Music in France and Italy* (London, 1771); German trans. C. D. Ebeling as *Tagebuch einer musikalischen Reise durch Frankreich und Italien* (Hamburg, 1772). Mod. edn. by H. E. Poole as *Music, Men, and Manners in France and Italy 1770* (London, 1974).

——— *The Present State of Music in Germany, the Netherlands, and the United Provinces* (London, 1773).

——— *A General History of Music* (London, 1776–89).

[———] 'Symphony', in Abraham Rees (ed.), *The Cyclopaedia: or, Universal Dictionary of Arts, Sciences, and Literature* (Philadelphia, n.d.), xxxvi, unpaginated.

Burney d'Arblay, Fanny (ed.), *The Diaries of Doctor Burney, arranged from his own Manuscripts, from Family Papers, and from Personal Recollections* (London, 1832).

Carpani, Giuseppe, *Le Haydine, ovvero Lettere sulla vita e le opere del celebre maestro Giuseppe Haydn* (Milan, 1812; 2nd edn. 1823).

Cartier, Jean-Baptiste (ed.), *L'Art du violon* (Paris, 1798; 3rd edn. c.1803; repr. New York, 1973).

Chastellux, François-Jean, *Essai sur l'union de la poésie et de la musique* (The Hague and Paris, 1765).

Clementi, Muzio, *Introduction to the Art of Playing on the Piano Forte* (London, 1801).

Courrier de l'Europe, London (26 June 1778).

Cramer, Carl Friedrich (ed.), *Magazin der Musik* (Hamburg, 1783–6; repr. Hildesheim, 1971).

Crotch, William, 'Remarks on the Terms at Present Used in Music, for Regulating Time', *The Monthly Magazine* (Jan. 1800), viii. 941–3.

Daily Universal Register (later *The Times*), London (1787).

Dictionnaire de toutes les espèces de chasse (Encyclopédie méthodique, lxiv) (Paris, An 3 [1794–5]).

Dittersdorf, Karl Ditters von, *Lebensbeschreibung, seinem Sohne in die Feder diktiert* (Leipzig, 1801), trans. A. D. Colleridge (London, 1896, repr. New York, 1970).

Engel, Johann Jacob, *Über die musikalische Malerey* (Berlin, 1780).

'Etwas von dem Musikzustande zu Fulda', *Allgemeine musikalische Zeitung* (1800), ii, cols. 729–31.

Forkel, J. N. (ed.), *Musikalischer Almanach für Deutschland auf das Jahre 1782* (Leipzig, [1781–2]).

Framery, Nicolas Étienne, 'Quelques réflexions sur la musique moderne', *Journal de musique historique, théorique, et pratique* (May 1770), i. 3–18.

—— 'Accompagnement', *Encyclopédie méthodique: Musique*, i. 184–5.

—— Pierre Louis Ginguené, and Jérôme Joseph de Momigny (eds.), *Encyclopédie méthodique: Musique*, 2 vols. (Paris, 1790–1818; repr. New York, 1971).

Galeazzi, Francesco, *Elementi teorico-pratici di musica con un saggio sopra l'arte di suonare il violino analizzata, ed a dimostrabili principi ridotta*, 2 vols. (Rome, 1791–6). Cited as *Elementi*.

Gazetta di Mantova (12 Jan. 1770).

Gazetteer and New Daily Advertiser, London (1784–90).

Geminiani, Francesco, *The Art of Playing on the Violin* (London, 1751; repr. Oxford, 1952).

Gerber, Ernst Ludwig, *Neues historisch-biographisches Lexikon der Tonkünstler* (Leipzig, 1814).

's Gravenhaegse Vrijdagse Courant (1765–6).

Grétry, A. E. M., *Mémoires, ou Essais sur la musique* (Paris, an V; repr. New York, 1971).

Gothaer Theaterkalender (Gotha, 1788).

Heinse, Wilhelm, 'Reise nach Holland, Oct. 1784', *Sämtliche Werke* (Leipzig, 1909).

Hempel, Charles William, *Introduction to the Pianoforte* (London, 1822).

Hiller, Johann Adam (ed.), *Wöchentliche [Musikalische] Nachrichten und Anmerkungen die Musik betreffend* (Leipzig, 1766–70; repr. Hildesheim, 1970).

Hoffmann, E. T. A., *Schriften zur Musik: Nachlese*, ed. F. Schnapp (Munich, 1963).

Hof- und Staatskalender Dresden (Dresden, 1789).

Hummel, Johann Nepomuk, *Mozart's Six Grand Symphonies Arranged for the Piano Forte* (London, [1823]).

—— *Ausführliche theoretisch-practische Anweisung zum Pianofortespiel* (Vienna, 1828).

'Introduction of Mozart's Music into Italy', *The Harmonicon* (1824), ii. 14–16.

Jackson, William, *Observations on the Present State of Music in London* (London, 1791).

—— 'William Jackson of Exeter [1730–1803], Musician: An Autobiography', *The Leisure Hour* (1882), xxxi. 273–8, 360–2, 433–6, 504–6, 569–71, 620–5, 718–20.

Journal de musique (Paris, 1770–7, repr. Geneva, 1972).

Journal de Paris (1777–92).

Junker, Carl Ludwig, 'Einige der vornehmsten Pflichten eines Capellmeisters oder Musikdirektors', *Magazin der Musik* (1786), ii. 741–77.

[Kirnberger, Johann Philipp], 'Minuett', in Johann Georg Sulzer, *Allgemeine Theorie der schönen Künste* (Leipzig, 1771–4; 2nd edn. 1792–4), ii. 388–9.

Koch, Heinrich Christoph, *Versuch einer Anleitung zur Composition*, 3 vols. (Leipzig, 1782–93).

—— 'Ueber den Charakter der Solo- und Ripienstimme', *Journal der Tonkunst* (1795), i/2. 143–56.

—— *Musikalisches Lexikon welches die theoretische und praktische Tonkunst, encyclopädisch bearbeitet, alle alten und neuen Kunstwörter erklärt und die alten und neuen Instrumente beschrieben, enthält* (Frankfurt am Main, 1802).

Kollmann, Augustus Frederic Christopher, *An Essay on Practical Musical Composition according to the Nature of that Science and the Principles of the Greatest Musical Authors* (London, 1799; repr. New York, 1973).

Körner, Christian Gottfried, 'Ueber Charakterdarstellung in der Musik', in Friedrich Schiller (ed.), *Die Horen* (1795), v. 97 ff.; mod. edn. in J. P. Banke (ed.), *Ästhetische Ansichten: Ausgewählte Aufsätze* (Marbach an der Neider, 1964), 24–47.

'Kurze Darstellung des Musikzustandes in Cöln', *Allgemeine musikalische Zeitung* (1815), xvii, cols. 300–3.

'Kurze Nachrichten', *Allgemeine musikalische Zeitung* (1801), iii, cols. 497–500.

'Kurze Uebersicht des Bedeutendsten aus dem gesammten jetzigen Musikwesen in Wien: Liebhaberey', *Allgemeine musikalische Zeitung* (1800–1), iii, col. 65.

Lacépède, Bernard-Germain-Étienne de La Ville sur Illon, comte de, *La Poétique de la musique* (Paris, 1785).

Lalande, Jérôme, *Journal d'un voyage en Angleterre 1763*, ed. H. Monod-Cassidy (Studies on Voltaire and the Eighteenth Century, clxxxiv) (Oxford, 1980).

L. Lavenu's Musical Journal, or Pocket Companion. Containing a Great Variety of Opera Dances, Single Airs, Duets, Waltz's ... Arranged for the Flute or Violin (London, 1798).

Leclair, Jean-Marie, l'aîné, 'Avertissement', *Quatrième Livre de Sonates*, Op. 9 (Paris, [1743]).

Lipowsky, F. J., *Baierisches Musik-Lexikon* (Munich, 1811).

Lloyd's Evening Post, London (22 Feb. 1765).

The London Evening Post (21–3 Feb. 1765).

Longman & Broderip's Fifth Selection of the Most Admired Dances, Reels, Minuets & Cotillons with the Proper Figures (London, [1790?]).

Marpurg, Friedrich Wilhelm, *Anleitung zum Clavierspielen* (Berlin, 1765; repr. New York, 1969).

Mason, C., *Rules on the Time, Phrases & Accents of Composition* (London, *c.*1801).

Mattheson, Johann, *Das neu-eröffnete Orchestre* (Hamburg, 1713).

—— *Kern melodischer Wissenschafft* (Hamburg, 1737).

—— *Der vollkommene Capellmeister* (Hamburg, 1739).

Mercure de France, Paris (1763–92).

Meude-Monpas, J. J. O. de, *Dictionnaire de musique* (Paris, 1787; repr. New York, 1978).

Michaelis, C. F., 'Aufforderung zur Festsetzung und gemeinschaftlichen Annahme eines gleichen Grundtones der Stimmung der Orchester', *Allgemeine musikalische Zeitung* (1814), xvi, cols. 772–6.

Momigny, Jérôme Joseph, 'Symphonie', *Encyclopédie méthodique: Musique* (Paris, 1818; repr. New York, 1971), ii. 408–17.

Morning Chronicle and London Advertiser (1784–8).

Morning Herald, London (1790–1).

Morning Herald and Daily Advertiser, London (1784).

Morning Post or Daily Advertiser, London (1784–9).

Mozart, Leopold, *Versuch einer gründlichen Violinschule* (Augsburg, 1756, repr. Vienna, 1922; 3rd edn. Leipzig, 1787, repr. 1956); cited as *Violinschule*. Trans. E. Knocker as *A Treatise on the Fundamental Principles of Violin Playing* (Oxford, 1948); cited as *Treatise*.

[——] 'Nachricht von dem gegenwärtigen Zustande der Musik Sr. Hochfürstl. Gnaden des Erzbischoffs zu Salzburg im Jahr 1757', in F. W. Marpurg (ed.), *Historisch-Kritische Beyträge zur Aufnahme der Musik* (Berlin, 1757), iii. 183–98.

[——] 'Verzeichniss / alles desjenigen was dieser 12 jährige Knab seit / seinem 7tem Jahre componiert, und in originali / kann aufgezeiget werden', Paris, Bibliothèque nationale, Département de musique, MS 263.

Muffat, Georg, *Auserlesene mit Ernst- und Lust-gemengter Instrumental-Music, erste Versamblung* (Passau, 1701), mod. edn. in Denkmäler der Tonkunst in Österreich, xxiii.

Musikalische Korrespondenz der teutschen Filarmonischen Gesellschaft, i–ii (Speyer, 1791–2).

Musikalisches Wochenblatt, (Berlin, 1791), i.

'Nachrichten . . . . Leipzig. Vom April bis zum 16ten November', *Allgemeine musikalische Zeitung* (1828), xxx, cols. 787–9.

Neilson, William, 'Method of Regulating Musical Time', *The Monthly Magazine* (July 1809), xvii. 536–8.

Nicolai, (Christoph) Friedrich, *Beschreibung einer Reise durch Deutschland und die Schweiz, im Jahre 1781: Nebst Bemerkungen über Gelehrsamkeit, Industrie, Religion und Sitten* (Berlin, 1783–96).

Niemetschek, Franz, *Leben des K. K. Kappellmeisters Wolfgang Gottlieb Mozart, nach Originalquellen beschrieben* (Prague, 1798; 2nd. edn. 1808); mod. edn. by E. Rychnovsky as *W. A. Mozart's Leben nach Originalquellen beschrieben* (Prague, 1905); another (German and French) by C. de Nys and G. Favier as *Vie de W. A. Mozart* (Saint-Étienne, 1976); another by J. Perfahl as *Ich kannte Mozart* (Munich, 1985); trans. H. Mautner as *Life of Mozart* (London, 1956).

Nissen, Georg Nikolaus, *Biographie W. A. Mozart . . . . Nach des Verfassers Tode hrsg. von Constanze, Wittwe von Nissen, früher Wittwe Mozart* (Leipzig, 1828; repr. Hildesheim, 1964).

North, Roger, *Roger North on Music*, ed. J. Wilson (London, 1959).

Petit, J. C., *Apologie de l'excellence de la musique* (London, c.1740).

Petri, Johann Samuel, *Anleitung zur praktischen Musik* (Lauban, 1767; 2nd edn. Leipzig, 1782; repr. Giebing, 1969).

Planelli, Antonio, *Dell'opera in musica* (Naples 1772).

The Public Advertiser, London (Jan.–May 1765, 1784–91).

Quantz, Johann Joachim, *Versuch einer Anweisung die Flöte traversiere zu spielen* (Berlin, 1752); trans. E. Reilly as *On Playing the Flute* (London, 1966; 2nd edn. New York, 1986).

Real-Zeitung, Erlangen (26 July 1785).

Reichardt, Johann Friedrich, *Ueber die Pflichten des Ripien-Violinisten* (Berlin, 1776).

Riegger, Joseph Anton Stephan, Ritter von, *Materialien zur alten und neuen Statistik von Böhmen* (Leipzig und Prague, 1788).

[Riesbeck, Johann Kaspar], *Briefe eines reisenden Franzosen über Deutschland: An seinen Bruder zu Paris* (Zurich, 1783); mod. edn. W. Gerlach (Stuttgart, 1967).

[Rochemont, de], *Réflexions d'un patriote sur l'opéra françois, et sur l'opéra italien, qui présentent le parallèle du goût des deux nations dans les beaux arts* (Lausanne, 1754).

[Rochlitz, Johann Friedrich], '*Quatre Simphonies pour l'Orchestre, comp. par Wolfgang Amad. Mozart. Œuv. 64. Hambourg chez Günther et Böhme. (Preis à 1 Rthlr.)*', *Allgemeine musikalische Zeitung* (1799), i, cols. 494–6.

[——] 'Musik in Leipzig', *Allgemeine musikalische Zeitung* (12 April 1809), xi/28. cols. 433–8, 449–60.

—— *Für Freunde der Tonkunst* (Leipzig, 1824).

Rousseau, Jean, *Traité de la viole* (Paris, 1687; repr. Munich, 1980).

Rousseau, Jean-Jacques, *Dictionnaire de musique* (Paris, 1768; repr. Hildesheim, 1969).

Scaramelli, Giuseppe, *Saggio sopra i doveri di un primo violino direttore d'orchestra* (Trieste, 1811)

Scheibe, Johann Adolf, *Der critische Musicus* (Hamburg, 1738–40).

—— *Critischer Musikus. Neue, vermehrte und verbesserte Auflage* (Leipzig, 1745).

Schink, Johann Friedrich, *Litterarische Fragmente* (Graz, 1785).

[Schinn, Georg and Franz Joseph Otter], *Biographische Skizze von Michael Haydn* (Salzburg, 1808).

Schlichtegroll, Friedrich, 'Joannes Chrysostomus Wolfgang Gottlieb Mozart', in *Nekrolog auf das Jahr 1791* (Gotha, 1792), ii. 82 ff.; trans. R. N. Coe, *Haydn, Mozart, and Metastasio by Stendhal (1814)* (New York, 1972), 163–206.

Schubart, Ludwig (ed.), *Christ. Fried. Dan. Schubart's Ideen zu einer Ästhetik der Tonkunst* (Vienna, 1806); cited as *Ideen*.

[Schulz, J. A. P.], 'Symphonie', in Johann Georg Sulzer, *Allgemeine Theorie der schönen Künste* (Leipzig, 1771–4; 2nd edn. 1792–4), ii. 1121–3.

Sharp, Samuel, *Letters from Italy, Describing the Customs and Manners of that Country, in the Years 1765, and 1766* (London, 1766).

Sievers, G. L. P., 'Pariser musikalisches Allerley, vom Monate März 1820', *Allgemeine musikalische Zeitung* (1820), xxii, cols. 413–20.

Spazier, C., 'Über Menuetten in Sinfonien', *Musikalisches Wochenblatt* (1791–2), i. 91–2.

Stark, F., *Wiener Pianoforte-Schule* (Vienna, 1819).

Stendhal (= M. H. Beyle), 'Mozart en Italie', in *Vie de Rossini* (Paris, 1824), trans. and ed. R. N. Coe (London, 1970).

Stetten, Paul von, *Kunst-, Gewerb- und Handwerks-Geschichte der Reichs-Stadt Augsburg* (Augsburg, 1779).

Suard, M., 'Accompagnement', in Nicolas Framery (ed.), *Encyclopédie méthodique: Musique* (Paris, 1790; repr. New York, 1971), i. 13–24.

Les Tablettes de Polymnie: Journal consacré à tout ce qui intéresse l'art musical (Paris, 1810–11, repr. Geneva, 1971).

Tartini, Giuseppe, 'Regole per arrivare a saper ben suonar il violino', MS; facsimile in E. Jacobi (ed.), *Giuseppe Tartini: Treatise on Ornaments in Music* (Celle, 1961).

The Times, London (1788–90).

Türk, Daniel Gottlob, *Von den wichtigsten Pflichten eines Organisten: Ein Beytrag zur Verbesserung der musikalischen Liturgie* (Halle, 1787).

—— *Clavierschule; oder, Anweisung zum Clavierspielen für Lehrer und Lernende, mit kritischen Anmerkungen* (Leipzig, 1789; 2nd edn. 1802; repr. 1967), trans. R. H. Haggh as *School of Clavier Playing; or, Instructions in Playing the Clavier for Teachers & Students* (Lincoln, Neb., 1982).

'Ueber den Stand der Musik in Wien: Erster Brief', *Wiener Theater Almanach für das Jahr 1794* (Vienna, [1793]), 173–4.

'Ueber die neueste Favorit-Musik in grossen Concerten, sonderlich in Rücksicht auf Damen-Gunst, in Clavier-Liebhaberey', *Journal des Luxus und der Moden* (June 1788), 231–2., mod edns. in Deutsch, 279–80 (= 317–18), and in W. Klüppelholz and H. J. Busch (eds.), *Musik gedeutet und gewertet: Dokumente zur Rezeptionsgeschichte von Musik* (Munich, 1983), 36–51.

Unold, Georg von, 'Einige Bermerkungen über die Stellung der Orchester und Einrichtung der Musiksäle', *Allgemeine musikalische Zeitung* (1801–2), iv, cols. 782–4.

Vogler, Georg Joseph, *Betrachtungen der mannheimer Tonschule*, 3 vols. (Mannheim, 1778–81; repr. Hildesheim, 1974).

—— *System für den Fugenbau* (Offenbach, 1811).

Weber, Gottfried, 'Besetzung', *Allgemeine Encyclopädie der Wissenschaft und Künste*, ed. J. S. Ersch and J. G. Gruber (Leipzig, 1822), ix. 284–5.

Wendt, Amadeus, 'Gedanken über die neuere Tonkunst, und van Beethovens Musik, namentlich dessen Fidelio', *Allgemeine musikalische Zeitung* (1815), xvii, cols. 345–53, 365–72, 379–89, 397–404, 413–20, 429–36.

Wendeborn, Friedrich August, *A View of England towards the Close of the Eighteenth Century* (London, 1791).

Werckmeister, Andreas, *Der Edlen Music-Kunst: Würde, Gebrauch und Missbrauch* (Frankfurt, 1691).

[Westphal, Johann Christoph], *1786 Julius. / Verzeichniss / einiger neuen Werke, welche / in der musicalischen Niederlage / bey / Johann Christoph Westphal & Comp. / in Hamburg angekommen sind* (Hamburg, 1786).

Wiener Zeitung (1781–99).

Wolf, Ernst Wilhelm, *Musikalischer Unterricht für Liebhaber und diejenigen, welche die Musik treiben und lehrnen wollen* (Dresden, 1788).

The World, London (1789–90).

Z[elter, Carl Friedrich], 'Bescheidene Anfrage an die modernsten Komponisten und Virtuosen', *Allgemeine musikalische Zeitung* (1798), i, cols. 142–4, 152–5.

From 1830

Abert, A. A., 'Methoden der Mozartforschung', *Mozart-Jahrbuch* (1964), 22–7; repr. in G. Croll (ed.), *Wolfgang Amadeus Mozart* (Darmstadt, 1977), 385–93.

—— 'Stilistischer Befund und Quellenlage zu Mozarts Lambacher Sinfonie KV Anh. 221/45a', in H. Heussner (ed.), *Festschrift Hans Engel zum siebzigsten Geburtstag* (Kassel, 1964), 43–56.

Abert, A.A., 'Vorwort', *Wolfgang Amadeus Mozart: Sinfonie in G ('Neue Lambacher Sinfonie')* (Kassel, 1965).

—— phonorecord programme notes for *Leopold Mozart, Wolfgang Amadeus Mozart, 4 Sinfonien*, Archiv Produktion, Period XII, no. 409: (Hamburg, 1967).

Abert, H., *W. A. Mozart* (Leipzig, 1919–21; 2nd edn. 1923–4).

Adler, G., *Handbuch der Musikgeschichte* (Frankfurt, 1924; 2nd edn. Berlin, 1930).

Allroggen, G., 'Zur Frage der Echtheit der Sinfonie KV Anh. 216 = 74g', *Analecta musicologica* (1978), xviii. 237–45; repr. in G. Croll (ed.), *Wolfgang Amadeus Mozart* (Darmstadt, 1977), 462–73.

—— 'Mozarts Lambacher Sinfonie: Gedanken zur musikalischen Stilkritik', in T. Kohlhase and V. Scherliess (eds.), *Festschrift Georg von Dadelsen zum 60. Geburtstag* (Stuttgart, 1978), 7–19.

—— 'Mozarts erste Sinfonien', in J. Schläder and R. Quandt (eds.), *Festschrift Heinz Becker zum 60. Geburtstag am 26. Juni 1982* ([Laaber], 1982), 392–404.

—— 'Mozarts erste Sinfonien', in C.-H. Mahling and S. Wiesmann (eds.), *Gesellschaft für Musikgeschichte, Bericht über den internationalen Musikwissenschaften Kongress Bayreuth 1981* (Kassel, 1982–4), 349.

—— 'Zur Datierung der frühen Sinfonien Mozarts', in J. P. Larsen and K. Wedin, (eds.), *Die Sinfonie KV 16a "del Sigr. Mozart": Bericht über das Symposium in Odense anlässlich der Erstaufführung des wiedergefundenen Werkes Dezember 1984* (Odense, 1987), 41–3.

—— 'Zur stilistischen Eigenart von KV 16a im Vergleich zu den frühen Sinfonien Mozarts', in J. P. Larsen and K. Wedin, (eds.), *Die Sinfonie KV 16a "del Sigr. Mozart": Bericht über das Symposium in Odense anlässlich der Erstaufführung des wiedergefundenen Werkes Dezember 1984* (Odense, 1987), 73–8.

Anderson, E. (ed.), *The Letters of Beethoven*, 2 vols. (London, 1961).

André, Johann Anton, 'Thematisches Verzeichnis W. A. Mozartscher Manuskripte, chronologisch geordnet von 1764–1784 von A. André. Manuskript abgeschlossen am 6. August 1833', copy made for Otto Jahn, British Library, Add. MS 34412.

—— *Thematisches Verzeichnis derjenigen Originalhandschriften von W. A. Mozart* (Offenbach, 1841).

Angermüller, R., 'Haydns "Der Zerstreute" [= "Il distratto"] in Salzburg', *Haydn-Studien* (1978), iv. 85–93.

—— 'Mozarts pariser Umwelt (1778)', *Mozart-Jahrbuch* (1978–9), 122–32.

—— 'M. Haydniana und Mozartiana: Ein erster Bericht', *Mitteilungen der internationalen Stiftung Mozarteum* (1981), xxix. 49–66.

—— 'Wer spielte die Uraufführung von Mozarts "Pariser Symphonie" KV 297?', *Mitteilungen der internationalen Stiftung Mozarteum* (1978), xxvi/3–4. 12–20.

—— 'Der Tanzmeistersaal in Mozarts Wohnhaus, Salzburg, Makartplatz 8', *Mitteilungen der internationalen Stiftung Mozarteum* (1981), xxix. 1–13.

—— *W. A. Mozarts musikalische Umwelt in Paris (1778): Eine Dokumentation* (Munich, 1982).

—— and S. Dahms-Schneider, 'Neue Brieffunde zu Mozart', *Mozart-Jahrbuch* (1968–70), 211–41.

Antcliffe, H., 'Mozart's Three Great Symphonies', *Musical Opinion* (1902–3), xxvi. 207–8, 447–8, 603–4.

Apfel, E., *Zur Vor- und Frühgeschichte der Symphonie* (Baden-Baden, 1972).

Autexier, P. A., *Mozart & Liszt sub rosa* (Poitiers, 1984).

—— 'Wann wurde die Maurerische Trauermusik uraufgeführt?', *Mozart-Jahrbuch* (1984–5), 6–8.

—— (ed.), *Wolfgang Amadeus Mozart: Meistermusik für Männerchor und Orchester ... KV 477 (479a)* (Wiesbaden, 1985).

Badura-Skoda, E. (ed.), *Carl Ditters von Dittersdorf (1739–1799): Six Symphonies* (The Symphony 1720–1840, B/i) (New York, 1985).

—— 'Motiv- und Themenbildung in wiener Sinfoniesätzen der 1760er Jahre und KV 16a', in J. P. Larsen and K. Wedin, (eds.), *Die Sinfonie KV 16a "del Sigr. Mozart": Bericht über das Symposium in Odense anlässlich der Erstaufführung des wiedergefundenen Werkes Dezember 1984* (Odense, 1987), 61–71.

Bartha, D., 'Mozart et le folklore musicale de l'Europe central', in A. Verchaly (ed.) *Les Influences étrangères dans l'œuvre de Wolfgang Amadeus Mozart* (Paris, 1958), 157–81.

—— (ed.), *Joseph Haydn: Gesammelte Briefe und Aufzeichnungen* (Kassel, 1965); cited as *Haydn: Briefe*.

Bebbington, W. A., 'The Orchestral Conducting Practice of Richard Wagner' (Ann Arbor, 1984).

Beck, H., 'Zur Entstehungsgeschichte von Mozarts D-dur Sinfonie KV 297', *Mozart-Jahrbuch* (1955), 95–112.

—— 'Die Musik des liturgischen Gottesdienstes', in K. G. Fellerer (ed.), *Geschichte der katholischen Kirchenmusik*, ii: *Vom Tridentinum bis zur Gegenwart* (Kassel, 1976), 180–9.

Benn, M., 'Mozart and the Age of Enlightenment', *Studies in Music* (1969), iii. 25–34.

Bereths, G., *Die Musikpflege am kurtrierischen Hofe zu Koblenz-Ehrenbreitstein* (Mainz, 1964).

Berger, J., 'Notes on Some 17th-Century Compositions for Trumpets and Strings in Bologna', *The Musical Quarterly* (1951), xxxvii. 354–67.

Bernhardt, R., 'Aus der Umwelt der wiener Klassiker: Freiherr Gottfried van Swieten (1734–1803)', *Der Bär* (1930), vi. 435–40.

Bessler, H., *Beiträge zur Stilgeschichte der deutschen Suite im 17. Jahrhundert* (Ph.D. diss., University of Freiburg, 1923).

Biba, O., 'Beethoven und die "Liebhaber Concerte" in Wien im Winter 1807/08' in R. Klein (ed.), *Österreichische Gesellschaft für Musik, Beiträge (1976–78): Beethoven-Kolloquium 1977, Dokumentation und Aufführungspraxis* (Kassel, 1978), 82–93.

—— 'Grundzüge des Konzertwesens in Wien zu Mozarts Zeit', *Mozart-Jahrbuch* (1978–9), 132–43.

Bibliothèque nationale, *Mozart en France* (Paris, 1956).

Blok, W., 'Mozart: The Symphonies', *Musick, a Quarterly Journal Published by the Vancouver Society for Early Music* (Winter 1981–2), iii. 24–8.

Blom, E., 'The Minuet-Trio', in *Classics Major and Minor* (London, 1958; repr. New York 1972), 165–83.

Boberski, H., *Das Theater der Benediktiner an der alten Universität Salzburg (1617–1778)* (Theatergeschichte Österreiches, vi/1) (Vienna, 1978).

Bonaccorsi, A., 'Il folklore nella musica d'arte. Dai segreti di Mozart', *Rassegna musicale della Edizione Curci* (1954), ii. 2–3.

Bonta, S., 'The Uses of the *Sonata da Chiesa*', *Journal of the American Musicological Society* (1969), xxii. 54–84.

Borrel, E., *Interprétation de la musique française de Lully à la Révolution* (Paris, 1934, repr. 1975, New York, 1978).

——— 'L'Orchestre du Concert spirituel et celui de l'Opéra de Paris, de 1751 à 1800 d'après "Les Spectacles de Paris"', in *Mélanges d'histoire et d'esthétique musicales offerts à P. M. Masson* (Paris, 1955), ii. 9–15.

Botstiber, H., *Geschichte der Ouverture und der freien Orchesterformen* (Leipzig, 1913).

Bowers, J., 'New Light on the Development of the Transverse Flute between about 1650 and about 1770', *Journal of the American Musical Instrument Society* (1977), iii. 5–56.

Brenet, M., *Les Concerts en France sous l'ancien régime* (Paris, 1900; repr. New York, 1970).

Brenner, C. D., *The Théâtre italien, Its Repertory, 1716–1793, with a Historical Introduction* (Berkeley, 1961).

Brewster, D. (ed.), 'Mozart', *The Edinburgh Encyclopaedia ... First American Edition* (Philadelphia, 1832), xiii. 804.

Brinkmann, R., 'Kleine "Eroica"-Lese', *Österreichische Musik Zeitschrift* (1984), xxxix. 634–8.

Broder, N. (ed.), *Wolfgang Amadeus Mozart, Symphony in G minor, K. 550: The Score of the New Mozart Edition, Historical Note, Analysis, Views, and Comments* (New York, 1967).

Brofsky, H., 'The Symphonies of Padre Martini', *The Musical Quarterly* (1965), li. 649–73.

Brook, B. S., *La Symphonie française dans la seconde moitié du XVIIIᵉ siècle*, 3 vols. (Paris, 1962); cited as *La Symphonie française*.

——— (ed.), *The Breitkopf Thematic Catalogue, 1762–1787* (New York, 1966).

——— '*Sturm und Drang* and the Romantic Period in Music', *Studies in Romanticism* (1970), ix. 269–84.

Brown, A. P., *Carlo d'Ordonez 1734–1786, A Thematic Catalogue* (Detroit, 1978).

——— *Carlo d'Ordonez, Seven Symphonies* (The Symphony 1720–1840, B/iv) (New York, 1979).

——— 'Ordonez, Carlo d'', *The New Grove*, xiii. 702–3.

——— 'Notes on some Eighteenth-Century Viennese Copyists', *Journal of the American Musicological Society* (1981), xxxiv. 325–38.

Brown, M., 'Mozart and After: The Revolution in Musical Consciousness', *Critical Inquiry* (1981), vii. 689–706.

Broyles, M., 'Organic Form and the Binary Repeat', *The Musical Quarterly* (1980), lxvi. 339–60.

—— 'The Two Instrumental Styles of Classicism', *Journal of the American Musicological Society* (1983), xxxvi. 210–42.

Bruce, I. M., 'An Act of Homage?', *The Music Review* (1950), xi. 277–83.

Bryan, P. R., 'The Horn in the Works of Mozart and Haydn: Some Observations and Comparisons', *The Haydn Yearbook* (1975), ix. 189–255.

—— 'Haydn's Alto Horns: Their Effect and the Question of Authenticity', in J. P. Larsen, H. Serwer, and J. Webster (eds.), *Haydn Studies: Proceedings of the International Haydn Conference, Washington, D. C., 1975* (New York, 1981), 190–2.

Carse, A., *The Orchestra in the XVIIIth Century* (Cambridge, 1940; repr. New York, 1969).

—— *The Orchestra from Beethoven to Berlioz* (Cambridge, 1948).

Casaglia, G., *Il catalogo delle opere di Wolfgang Amadeus Mozart* (Bologna, 1976).

Chailley, J., 'Les *Dialogues sur la musique* d'Alexandre Belosel'skij', *Revue des études slaves* (1966), xlv. 93–103.

—— 'Mozart vu par les salons contemporains', *La Revue musicale* (1981), cccxxxviii–cccxxxix. 115–18.

Charlton, D., *Grétry and the Growth of Opéra-Comique* (Cambridge, 1986).

Charms, D. de, and P. F. Breed, *Songs in Collections: An Index* (Detroit, 1966).

Cherbuliez, A.-E., 'Stilkritischer Vergleich von Mozarts beiden g-moll-Sinfonien von 1773 und 1788', in *Bericht über die musikwissenschaftliche Tagung der Internationalen Stiftung Mozarteum in Salzburg, August 1931* (Leipzig, 1932), 112–19.

Chesnut, J. H., 'Mozart's Teaching of Intonation', *Journal of the American Musicological Society* (1977), xxx. 254–71.

Chew, G., 'The Night-Watchman's Song Quoted by Haydn and Its Implications', *Haydn-Studien* (1974), iii. 106–24.

Churgin, B., *The Symphonies of G. B. Sammartini*, i (Cambridge, Mass., 1968).

—— 'The Symphony as Described by J. A. P. Schulz (1774): A Commentary and Translation', *Current Musicology* (1980), xxix. 7–16.

Conradi, A., 'Das Andante in Mozart's g-moll-Symphonie', *Neue Berliner Musikzeitung* (1854), viii. 332ff.

Croll, G. (ed.), *Wolfgang Amadeus Mozart* (Darmstadt, 1977).

Curl, J. S., 'Mozart Considered as a Jacobin', *The Music Review* (1974), xxxv. 131–41.

Cuyler, L., *The Symphony* (New York, 1973).

Danckwardt, M., *Die langsame Einleitung: Ihre Herkunft und ihr Bau bei Haydn und Mozart* (Münchner Veröffentlichungen zur Musikgeschichte, xxv) (Tutzing, 1977).

Danuser, H., 'Das *imprévu* in der Symphonik: Aspekte einer musikalischen Formkategorie in der Zeit von Carl Philipp Emanuel Bach bis Hector Berlioz', *Musiktheorie* (1986), i. 61–81.

Darnton, R., 'The High Entertainment and the Low-Life of Literature in Pre-Revolutionary France', *Past and Present* (1971), li. 81–115.

David, J. N., *Die Jupiter-Symphonie: Eine Studie über die thematisch-melodischen Zusammenhänge* (Göttingen, 1953).

David, T. C., 'Zu J. N. Davids Studien über die Jupitersinfonie', *Mozartgemeinde Wien 1913–1963: Forscher und Interpreten* (Vienna, 1964), 236–40.

Davis, S., [Remarks], The John F. Kennedy Center for the Performing Arts / American Musicological Society [J. LaRue (ed.)], *A Mozart Festival-Conference* (n.p, n.d. (Washington, 1974)).

—— 'The Orchestra under Clemens Wenzeslaus: Music at a Late-Eighteenth-Century Court', *Journal of the American Musical Instrument Society* (1975), i. 86–112.

—— 'J. G. Lang and the Early Classical Keyboard Concerto', *The Musical Quarterly* (1980), lxvi. 21–52.

—— *Johann Georg Lang (1772?-1798): Three Symphonies* (The Symphony 1720–1840, C/i) (New York, 1983).

Dearling, R., *The Music of Wolfgang Amadeus Mozart: The Symphonies* (London, 1982).

—— sleeve notes for Unicorn-Kanchana DKP 9039 (1984): Mozart, Symphonies in A minor, K. 16a, D major, K. 19, F major, K. 19a, and E flat major, K. 16.

Debussy, C., *Monsieur Croche et autres écrits*, ed. F. Lesure (Paris, 1971); trans. R. L. Smith as *Debussy on Music* (New York, 1977).

Deininger, H. F., 'Die deutsche Schauspielergesellschaft unter der Direktion von Johann Heinrich Böhm, einem Freunde der Familie Mozart, in Augsburg in den Jahren 1779 und 1780', *Augsburger Mozartbuch* (*Zeitschrift des historischen Vereins für Schwaben* (1942–3), lv–lvi), 299–397.

Della Croce, L., *Le 75 sinfonie di Mozart: Guida e analisi critica* (Turin, 1977); cited as *Le 75 sinfonie.*

Del Mar, N., 'Confusion and Error', *The Score* (1958), i/22. 28–40.

—— *Orchestral Variations: Confusion and Error in the Orchestral Repertoire* (London, 1981).

Dennerlein, H., 'Zur Problematik von Mozarts Kirchensonaten', *Mozart-Jahrbuch* (1953), 95–111.

Derr, E., 'A Deeper Examination of Mozart's $\hat{1}—\hat{2}—\hat{4}—\hat{3}$ Theme and Its Strategic Deployment', *In Theory Only* (1985), viii. 5–43.

Deutsch, O. E., *Mozart und die wiener Logen* (Vienna, 1932).

—— *Mozart und seine Welt in zeitgenössischen Bildern / Mozart and His World in Contemporary Pictures* (NMA, x/32) (Kassel, 1961).

—— *Franz Schubert: Thematisches Verzeichnis seiner Werke in chronologischer Folge*, new edn. by the editors of the Neuen Schubert-Ausgabe and W. Aderhold (Kassel, 1978).

Dickinson, A. E. F., *A Study of Mozart's Last Three Symphonies* (Oxford, 1927; 2nd edn. 1940).

Dixon, G., 'The Origins of the Roman "Colossal Baroque"', *Proceedings of the Royal Musical Association* (1979–80), cvi. 115–28.

Dörffel, A., *Geschichte der Gewandhausconcerte zu Leipzig . . . . Festschrift zur hundertjährigen Jubelfeier der Einweihung des Concertsaales im Gewandhause zu Leipzig* (Leipzig, 1884; repr. 1980).

'Drey Bände Original-Handschriften W. A. Mozart's', *Allgemeine musikalische Zeitung* (1831), xxxiii, cols. 733–7.

Eibl, J. H., *Wolfgang Amadeus Mozart: Chronik eines Lebens,* 2nd edn. (Kassel, 1977).

—— 'Ein Brief Mozarts über seine Schaffensweise', *Österreichische Musik Zeitschrift* (1980), xxxv. 578–93.

Eilenstein, A., 'Die Beziehung des Stiftes Lambach zu Salzburg', *Studien und Mitteilungen zur Geschichte des Benediktinerordens* (1923–4), xlii. 196–232.

Eisen, C. (ed.), *Leopold Mozart: Three Symphonies* (The Symphony 1720–1840, B/vii) (New York, 1984).

—— 'The Symphonies of Leopold Mozart and Their Relationship to the Early Symphonies of Wolfgang Amadeus Mozart: A Bibliographical and Stylistic Study' (Ph.D. diss., Cornell University, 1986); cited as 'The Symphonies of Leopold Mozart'.

—— 'Contributions to a New Mozart Documentary Biography', *Journal of the American Musicological Society* (1986), xxxix. 615–32.

—— 'The Symphonies of Leopold Mozart: Their Chronology, Style, and Importance for the Study of Mozart's Early Symphonies', *Mozart-Jahrbuch* (1987–8), 181–93.

—— 'New Light on Mozart's "Linz" Symphony', *Journal of the Royal Musical Association* (1988), cxiii, 81–96.

Elkin, R., *The Old Concert Rooms of London* (London, 1955).

Ellis, A. J., and A. Mendel, *Studies in the History of Musical Pitch* (Amsterdam, 1968).

Elvers, R., 'Untersuchungen zu den Tempi in Mozarts Instrumental-Musik' (Ph.D. diss., Free University of Berlin, 1952).

Engel, H., 'Mozart's Jugendsinfonien' *Deutsche Musikkultur* (1941–2).

—— 'Über Mozarts Jugendsinfonien', *Mozart-Jahrbuch* (1951), 22–33.

Engelmann, U. (ed.), *Das Tagebuch von Ignaz Speckle, Abt von St. Peter im Schwarzwald: Erster Teil 1795–1802* (Stuttgart, 1966).

Engerth, R., *Hier hat Mozart gespielt* (Salzburg, 1968).

Erdmann, H., 'Mozart in norddeutscher Resonanz', in E. Schenk (ed.) *Bericht über den internationalen musikwissenschaftlichen Kongress, Wien, Mozartjahr 1956* (Graz, 1958), 156–69.

Federhofer, H., 'Zur Einheit von Stimmführung und Harmonik in Instrumentalwerken Mozarts', *Mozart-Jahrbuch* (1956), 75–87.

—— 'Mozartiana in Steiermark (Ergänzung)', *Mozart-Jahrbuch* (1958), 109–18.

Fellerer, K. G., 'Mozarts Kirchenmusik und ihre liturgischen Voraussetzungen', *Mozart-Jahrbuch* (1978–9), 22–6.

—— 'The Liturgical Basis of Haydn's Masses', in J. P. Larsen, H. Serwer, and J. Webster (eds.), *Haydn Studies* (New York, 1981), 164–8.

Fellinger, R., 'Zu Mozarts "Lieblingsmotiv"', *Mitteilungen für die Mozart-Gemeinde* (1920–1), xxxix. 18–19.

Fellmann, H. G., *Die böhmschen Theatertruppe und ihre Zeit* (Leipzig, 1928).

Ferenc, L., '"Atonális sziget" Mozart g-moll szimfóniájában' [An 'atonal island' in Mozart's G minor Symphony], *Magyar Zene* (1977), xviii. 402–5.

Ferguson, L. F., '*Col Basso* and *Generalbass* in Mozart's Keyboard Concertos: Notation, Performance Theory, and Practice' (Ph.D. diss., Princeton University, 1983).

Finscher, L., 'Aspects of Mozart's Compositional Process in the Quartet Autographs', in C. Wolff (ed.), *The String Quartets of Haydn, Mozart, and Beethoven* (Cambridge, Mass., 1980), 121–53, 216–21.

Fischer, S. C., 'Die C-dur-Symphonie KV^6 Anh. C 11.14: Ein Jugendwerk Anton Eberls', *Mitteilungen der internationalen Stiftung Mozarteum* (1983), xxxi. 21–6.

Fischer, W., *Wiener Instrumentalmusik vor und um 1750* (Denkmäler der Tonkunst in Österreich, xxxix) (Vienna, 1912).

——'Eine wiedergefundene Jugendsymphonie Mozarts', *Mozart-Jahrbuch* (1923), i. 35–68; this article, minus its edition of K. 45a, also in the *Allgemeine Musik Zeitung* (Charlottenberg, 1923), xl–xli, and in G. Croll (ed.), *Wolfgang Amadeus Mozart* (Darmstadt, 1977), 139–44.

——'Zwei neapolitanische Melodietypen bei Mozart und Haydn', *Mozart-Jahrbuch* (1960–1), 7–21.

Fiske, R., *English Theatre Music in the Eighteenth Century* (London, 1973).

Fleurot, F., *Le Hautbois dans la musique française 1650–1800* (Paris, 1984).

Floros, C., 'Mozarts letzte Sinfonien', *Mozart, Klassik für die Gegenwart* (Oldenburg, 1978).

Flothuis, M., 'Jupiter oder Sarastro?', *Mozart-Jahrbuch* (1965–6), 121–32.

——'Eine zweite "Jupiter-Symphonie"?', *Mitteilungen der internationalen Stiftung Mozarteum* (1983), xxxi. 18–20.

——'Regel und Ausnahme als Kriterien zur Echtheitsbestimmung', in J. P. Larsen and K. Wedin, (eds.), *Die Sinfonie KV 16a "del Sigr. Mozart": Bericht über das Symposium in Odense anlässlich der Erstaufführung des wiedergefundenen Werkes Dezember 1984* (Odense, 1987), 57–60.

Forbes, E. (ed.), *Thayer's Life of Beethoven* (Princeton, 1962).

Ford, F. L., *Strasbourg in Transition 1648–1789* (Cambridge, Mass., 1958).

Forsyth, M., *Rooms for Music: The Architect, the Musician, and the Listener from the Seventeenth Century to the Present Day* (Cambridge, Mass., 1986).

Freeman, R. N., 'The Role of Organ Improvisation in Haydn's Church Music' in J. P. Larson, H. Serwer, and J. Webster (eds.), *Haydn Studies* (New York, 1981), 192–7.

——'The Function of Haydn's Instrumental Compositions in the Abbeys', in J. P. Larsen, H. Serwer, and J. Webster (eds.), *Haydn Studies* (New York, 1981), 199–202.

——(ed.), *Austrian Cloister Symphonies* (The Symphony 1720–1840, B/vi) (New York, 1982).

Fruehwald, S., 'A Method for Determining Authenticity by Style', *The Journal of Musicological Research* (1985), v. 297–317.

Fuhrmann, H., 'Mozart bei den vierländer Gemüsebauern: Eine Studie zum Thema "Volksmusik und Kunstmusik"', *Neue Zeitschrift für Musik* (1937), civ. 1016–17.

Fuller, D., 'Suite', *The New Grove*, xviii. 333–50.

Fyot, E., 'Mozart à Dijon', *Mémoires de l'Académie des sciences, arts et belles lettres de Dijon* (1937), 23–41.

Gachet, H., 'Vieilles papeteries françaises: Les Papeteries d'Annonay, 1: Les Papeteries Johannot', *Courrier graphique* (1949), xiv/41. 27–34.

Gericke, H., *Der wiener Musikalienhandel von 1700 bis 1778* (Graz, 1960).

Gerlach, S., 'Haydns Orchesterpartituren: Fragen der Realisierung des Textes', *Haydn-Studien* (1984), v/3. 169–83.

Gluck, A., *W. A. Mozart: G moll Symphonie aus dem Jahre 1788 erläutert* (Frankfurt, 1894).

Gmeiner, J., *Menuett und Scherzo: Ein Beitrag zur Entwicklungsgeschichte und Soziologie des Tanzsatzes in der Wiener Klassik* (Wiener Veröffentlichungen zur Musikwissenschaft, xv) (Tutzing, 1979).

Goldschmidt, H., 'Das Cembalo im Orchester der italienischen Oper der zweiten Hälfte des 18. Jahrhunderts', in H. Kretzschmar (ed.), *Festschrift zum 90. Geburtstage ... Rochus Freiherrn von Liliencron* (Leipzig, 1910; repr. Westmead, 1970), 87–92.

Gotwals, V., 'The Earliest Biographies of Haydn', *The Musical Quarterly* (1959), xlv. 439–59.

Grave, M. G., 'Ditterdorf's First-Movement Form as a Measure of His Symphonic Development' (Ph.D. diss., New York University, 1977).

Gruss, H., 'Zur Analyse der Sinfonien g-moll (KV 550) und C-dur (KV 551) von Wolfgang Amadeus Mozart', in *Festschrift Heinrich Besseler zum sechzigsten Geburtstag* (Leipzig, 1961), 367–75.

[Gyrowetz, A.], *Biographie von Adelbert Gyrowetz* (Vienna, 1848); mod. edn. by A. Einstein (ed.) as *Adalbert Gyrowetz (1763–1850)* (Lebensläufe deutscher Musiker von ihnen selbst erzählt, iii–iv) (Leipzig, 1915).

Haberkamp, G., *Die Musikhandschriften der Fürst Thurn und Taxis Hofbibliothek Regensburg* (Munich, 1981).

Hainisch, E., *Die Kunstdenkmäler des Gerichtsbezirkes Lambach* (Vienna, 1959).

Hanslick, E., *Geschichte des Konzertwesens in Wien* (Vienna, 1869).

Harnoncourt, N., 'Gedanken eines Orchestermusikers zu einem Brief von W. A. Mozart', *Musik als Klangrede* (Salzburg, 1982), 264–8.

Hausswald, G., *Mozarts Serenaden*, 2nd edn. (Kassel, 1975).

Havlova, M., 'Der Schulbegriff: Inhalt, Bestimmung und Anwendungsmöglichkeiten in Bezug auf musikgeschichtliche Sachverhalte des 18. Jahrhunderts', *Beiträge zur Musikwissenschaft* (1980), xxii. 209–16.

Haynes, B., 'Lully and the Rise of the Oboe as Seen in Works of Art', *Early Music* (1988), xvi. 324–38.

Heartz, D., 'Mozart, His Father, and "Idomeneo"', *The Musical Times* (1978), cxix. 228–31.

—— 'Mozart's Overture to *Titus* as Dramatic Argument', *The Musical Quarterly* (1978), lxiv. 29–49.

Helfert, V., *Hudba na Jaroměřickém zámku* (Prague, 1924).

—— 'Zur Entwicklungsgeschichte der Sonatenform', *Archiv für Musikwissenschaft* (1925), vii. 117–46.

Helm, T., 'Ungarische Musik in deutschen Meistern', *Musikalisches Wochenblatt* (Leipzig, 1871), ii. 641–2.

Hertzmann, E., 'Mozart's Creative Process', *The Musical Quarterly* (1957), xliii. 187–200; repr. in P. H. Lang (ed.), *The Creative World of Mozart* (New York, 1963), 17–30.

——— C. B. Oldman, D. Heartz, and A. Mann (eds.), *Thomas Attwoods Theorie- und Kompositionsstudien bei Mozart* (*NMA*, x/30/1) (Kassel, 1965).

Hess, E., 'Über einige zweifelhafte Werke Mozarts', *Mozart-Jahrbuch* (1956), 100–29.

——— 'Zur Frage der Echtheit der Ouvertüre in B-dur, KV Anh. 8 (311a)', *Schweizer Musikzeitung* (1956), xcvi. 66–72.

——— 'Remarques sur l'authenticité de l'ouverture de W. A. Mozart', in A. Verchaly (ed.), *Les Influences étrangères dans l'œuvres de W. A. Mozart* (Paris, 1958), 227–35.

'Ein neu entdecktes Skizzenblatt Mozarts', *Mozart Jahrbuch* (1964), 185–92.

Heuss, A., [review of G. Schünemann, *Mozart als achtjähriger Komponist*], *Zeitschrift der internationalen Musikgesellschaft* (1908–9), x. 181–2.

——— [review of K. 74g], *Zeitschrift der internationalen Musikgesellschaft* (1909–10), xi. 364.

——— 'Die kleine Sekunde in Mozarts g-moll-Sinfonie', *Jahrbuch der Musikbibliothek Peters für 1933* (1934), xl. 54–66.

Hickman, R., 'Romance', *The New Grove*, xvi, 123–6.

——— 'The Censored Publications of *The Art of Playing on the Violin*, or Geminiani Unshaken', *Early Music* (1983), xi. 73–6.

Higginbottom, E., 'Organ Mass', *The New Grove*, xiii. 780–4.

Hildesheimer, W., *Mozart* (New York, 1982).

Hill, G. R., *A Preliminary Checklist of Research on the Classic Symphony and Concerto to the Time of Beethoven (excluding Haydn and Mozart)* (Hackensack, 1970).

Hilmar, R., *Der Musikverlag Artaria & Comp.: Geschichte und Probleme der Druckproduktion* (Tutzing, 1977).

Hintermaier, E., 'Die salzburger Hofkapelle von 1700 bis 1806: Organisation und Personal' (Ph.D. diss., University of Salzburg, 1972).

——— 'Die fürsterzbischöfliche Hoftheater zu Salzburg (1775–1803)', *Österreichische Musik Zeitschrift* (1975), xxx. 351–63.

Hoboken, A. van, *Joseph Haydn: Thematisch-bibliographisches Werkverzeichnis*, 3 vols. (Mainz, 1957–78).

Hocquard, J.-V., *La Pensée de Mozart* (Paris, 1958).

Hoffmann-Erbrecht, L., *Die Sinfonie* (Cologne, 1967).

——— 'Sinfonia', *Dizionario enciclopedico universale della musica e dei musicisti* (Turin, 1984), iv. 291–304.

Hollerweger, H., *Die Reform des Gottesdienstes zur Zeit des Josephismus in Österreich* (Studien zur Pastoralliturgie, i) (Regensburg, 1976).

Holschneider, A., 'Neue Mozartiana in Italien', *Die Musikforschung* (1962), xv. 227–36.

Holub, R. C., *Reception Theory: A Critical Introduction* (London, 1984).

Hunter, M., 'The Fusion and Juxtaposition of Genres in Opera Buffa 1770–1800: Anelli and Piccinni's *Griselda*', *Music and Letters* (1986), lxvii. 363–80.

Hutchings, A., *The Baroque Concerto*, 3rd edn. (London, 1978).

Jacobi, E. (ed.), *Giuseppe Tartini: Treatise on Ornaments in Music* (Celle, 1961).

Jacobs, R., *La Symphonie* (Paris, 1976).

Jacobson, B., 'Once More with Feeling: A Polemic on Repeats', *Musical Newsletter* (1977), vii. 3–7.

Jahn, O., *W. A. Mozart* (Leipzig, 1856–9), 3rd edn. by H. Deiters (Leipzig, 1889–91).

Jander, O., 'Concerto grosso Instrumentation in Rome in the 1660's and 1670's', *Journal of the American Musicological Society* (1968), xxi. 168–80.

Jauss, H. R., *Toward an Aesthetic of Reception* (Theory and History of Literature, ii) (Minneapolis, 1982).

Jeffery, B., *Fernando Sor: Composer and Guitarist* (London, 1977).

Johansson, C., *French Music Publishers' Catalogues of the Second Half of the Eighteenth Century* (Stockholm, 1955).

The John F. Kennedy Center for the Performing Arts: American Musicological Society [J. LaRue (ed.)], *A Mozart Festival-Conference* (n.p, n.d. (Washington, 1974)).

Kalischer, A. C. (ed.), *Beethovens sämtliche Briefe* (Berlin, 1908).

Kalkbrenner, F., *Traité d'harmonie du pianiste* (Paris, 1849).

King, A. H., *Mozart in Retrospect: Studies in Criticism and Bibliography*, rev. edn. (Oxford, 1970).

Kirby, F. E., 'The Germanic Symphony in the Eighteenth Century: Bridge to the Romantic Era', *Journal of Musicological Research* (1984), v. 51–83; (1986), vi. 357–62.

Kirkendale, U., 'The King of Heaven and the King of France: History of a Musical *Topos*', *Abstracts of Papers Read at the Thirty-fifth Annual Meetings of the American Musicological Society, Saint Louis, Missouri, December 27–29, 1967* (n.p., n.d.), 27–8.

Kirkendale, W., *Fugue and Fugato in Rococo and Classical Chamber Music* (Durham, 1979).

Kirkpatrick, R., 'Preface', *J. S. Bach: Keyboard Practice, Consisting of an Aria with Thirty Variations* [The Goldberg Variations] (New York, 1938).

Kivy, P., 'Mozart and Monotheism: An Essay in Spurious Aesthetics', *Journal of Musicology* (1983), ii. 322–8.

Klein, H., 'Unbekannte Mozartiana von 1766/67', *Mozart-Jahrbuch* (1957), 168–85.

Klein, H.-G., *Wolfgang Amadeus Mozart: Autographe und Abschriften* (R. Elvers (ed.), Staatsbibliothek Preussischer Kulturbesitz, Kataloge der Musikabteilung, i/6) (Berlin, 1982).

Klenz, W., *Giovanni Maria Bononcini of Modena* (Durham, NC, 1962).

—— ' "Per Aspera ad Astra", or The Stairway to Jupiter', *The Music Review* (1969), xxx. 169–210.

Klüppelholz, W., and H. J. Busch (eds.), *Musik gedeutet und gewertet: Dokumente zur Rezeptionsgeschichte von Musik* (Munich, 1983).

Knape, W., *Karl Friedrich Abel: Leben und Werk eines frühklassischen Komponisten* (Bremen, 1973).

Knepler, G., 'Mozart à Česká Lidová Hudba' [Mozart and Czech Folkmusik], *Hudební rozhledy* (1956), ix. 10–15.

Kolisch, R., 'Tempo and Character in Beethoven's Music', *The Musical Quarterly* (1943), xxix. 169–87, 291–312.

Koury, D. J., *Orchestral Performance Practices in the Nineteenth Century: Size, Proportions, and Seating* (Ann Arbor, 1986).

Kunze, S., *Wolfgang Amadeus Mozart: Sinfonie g-moll, KV 550* (Meisterwerke der Musik, Werkmonographien zur Musikgeschichte, vi) (Munich, 1968).

Landon, H. C. Robbins, 'Die Symphonien: Ihr geistiger und musikalischer Ursprung und ihre Entwicklung', in P. Schaller and H. Kühner (eds.), *Mozart-Aspekte* (Olten, 1956), 39–62.

—— 'Two Orchestral Works Wrongly Attributed to Mozart', *The Music Review* (1956), xvii. 29–34.

—— 'La Crise romantique dans la musique autrichienne vers 1770. Quelques précurseurs inconnus de la Symphonie en sol mineur (KV 183) de Mozart', in A. Verchaly (ed.), *Les Influences étrangères dans l'œuvre de W. A. Mozart* (Paris, 1958), 27–47.

—— (ed.), *Joseph Haydn: Collected Correspondence and London Notebooks* (London, 1959); cited as *Collected Correspondence and London Notebooks*.

—— 'Problems of Authenticity in 18th-Century Music', in D. G. Hughes (ed.), *Instrumental Music: A Conference at Isham Memorial Library, May 4, 1957* (Cambridge, Mass., 1959), 31–56.

—— *The Symphonies of Joseph Haydn* (London, 1955); *The Symphonies of Joseph Haydn: Supplement* (New York, 1961).

—— (ed.), *Joseph Haydn: Kritische Ausgabe sämtlicher Symphonien* (Vienna, 1965–8).

—— *Haydn: Chronicle and Works*, 5 vols. (Bloomington and London, 1976–80)—i: *Haydn: The Early Years 1732–1765*; ii: *Haydn at Esterháza 1766–1790*; iii: *Haydn in England 1791–1795*; iv: *Haydn: The Years of 'The Creation' 1796–1800*; v: *Haydn: The Late Years 1801–1809*.

—— *Mozart and the Masons* (London, 1982).

—— *1791: Mozart's Last Year* (New York, 1988).

Lang, G., 'Zur Geschichte und Pflege der Musik in der Benediktiner-Abtei zu Lambach mit einem Katalog zu den Beständen des Musikarchives' (Ph.D. diss., University of Salzburg, 1978).

Larsen, J. P., 'The Symphonies', in H. C. Robbins Landon and D. Mitchell (eds.), *The Mozart Companion: A Symposium by Leading Mozart Scholars* (London, 1956), 156–99.

—— 'Zur Bedeutung der "Mannheimer Schule" ', in H. Hüschen (ed.), *Festschrift Karl Gustav Fellerer zum sechzigsten Geburtstag* (Regensburg, 1962), 303–9.

—— 'Some Observations on the Development and Characteristics of Vienna [*sic*] Classical Instrumental Music', *Studia Musicologica* (1967), ix. 115–39.

—— 'The Viennese Classical School: A Challenge to Musicology', *Current Musicology* (1969), ix. 105–12.

—— 'Über die Möglichkeiten einer musikalischen Echtheitsbestimmung für Werke aus der Zeit Haydns und Mozarts', *Mozart-Jahrbuch* (1971–2), 7–18; reprinted with the title 'Über Echtheitsprobleme in der Musik der Klassik', *Die Musikforschung* (1972), xxv. 4–16.

—— 'Zur Entstehung des österreichischen Symphonietradition (ca. 1750–1775)', *Haydn Jahrbuch* (1978), x. 72–80.

—— 'Echtheitsprobleme in den frühen Sinfonien Mozarts—warum?', in J. P. Larsen and K. Wedin, (eds.), *Die Sinfonie KV 16a "del Sigr. Mozart": Bericht über das Symposium in Odense anlässlich der Erstaufführung des wiedergefundenen Werkes Dezember 1984* (Odense, 1987), 31–9.

—— H. Serwer, and J. Webster (eds.), *Haydn Studies: Proceedings of the International Haydn Conference, Washington, 1975* (New York, 1981); cited as *Haydn Studies*.

—— and K. Wedin, (eds.), *Die Sinfonie KV 16a "del Sigr. Mozart": Bericht über das Symposium in Odense anlässlich der Erstaufführung des wiedergefundenen Werkes Dezember 1984* (Odense, 1987).

LaRue, J., 'Significant and Coincidental Resemblances between Classical Themes', *Journal of the American Musicological Society* (1961), xiv. 224–34.

—— 'Symphonie. B. Die Entwicklung der Symphonie im 18. Jahrhundert', *Die Musik in Geschichte und Gegenwart*, xii (Kassel, 1965), cols. 1807–10; repr. in *Symphonische Musik* (Musikalische Gattungen in Einzeldarstellung, i) (Kassel, 1981), 20–3.

—— 'Mozart or Dittersdorf—KV 84/73q', *Mozart-Jahrbuch* (1971–2), 40–9.

—— 'Mozart Authentication by Activity Analysis, A Progress Report', *Mozart-Jahrbuch* (1978–9), 209–14.

—— 'Symphony. I. 18th Century', *The New Grove*, xviii. 438–53.

—— 'The English Symphony: Some Additions and Annotations to Charles Cudworth's Published Studies', in C. Hogwood and R. Luckett (eds.), *Music in Eighteenth-Century England: Essays in Memory of Charles Cudworth* (Cambridge, 1983), 213–44.

—— *A Catalogue of 18th-Century Symphonies, Volume I: Thematic Identifier* (Bloomington, 1988).

Laskowski, L., *Heinrich Schenker: An Annotated Index to His Analyses of Musical Works* (New York, 1978).

Layer, A., 'Christian Ernst Gra[a]f', *The New Grove*, vii. 610.

Leavis, R., 'Mozart's Divertimentos for Mixed Consort', *The Musical Times* (1980), cxxi. 372–3.

Ledhuy, A., and H. Bertini, 'Sor', *Encyclopédie pittoresque de la musique* (Paris, 1835), 154–67.

Leeson, D., and D. Whitwell, 'Mozart's Thematic Catalogue', *The Musical Times* (1973), cxiv. 781–3.

Leinsdorf, E., *The Composer's Advocate: A Radical Orthodoxy for Musicians* (New Haven, 1981).

Lesure, F. (ed.), *Catalogue de la musique imprimée avant 1800 conservée dans les bibliothèques publiques de Paris* (Paris, 1981).

—— and A. Devriès, *Dictionnaire des éditeurs de musique française* (Geneva, 1979).

Leux-Henschen, I., *Joseph Martin Kraus in seinen Briefen* (Stockholm, 1978).

Lewicki, E., 'Aus der Entstehungszeit der grossen Symphonien W. A. Mozarts', *Die Musik* (1914–15), xiv/1. 27–33.

The Liber Usualis (Tournai, 1962).

Libby, D., 'Fischietti, Domenico', *The New Grove*, vi. 615–16.

Lievense, W., *De Familie Mozart op Bezoek in Nederland* (Hilversum, 1965).

Livingston, H. S., 'The Italian Overture from A. Scarlatti to Mozart' (Ph.D. diss., University of North Carolina, 1952).

'Long-Lost Mozart Work [K. 19a] To Have May Premiere', *The New York Times* (14 Feb. 1981), 1, 11.

Longyear, R. M., 'The Symphonies of Niccolò Zingarelli', *Analecta Musicologica* (1979), xix. 288–319.

—— *Stanislao Mattei: Five Symphonies; Niccolò Zingarelli: Seven Symphonies* (The Symphony 1720–1840, A/viii) (New York, 1980).

—— 'Zingarelli, Niccolò Antonio', *The New Grove*, xx. 692–4.

Macdonald, H., 'To Repeat or Not to Repeat?', *Proceedings of the Royal Musical Association* (1984–5), cxi. 121–38.

—— 'Mozart's Tempo Indications', in *Mozart's Music as Appreciated in the Past and Present, Prague 1983* (congress report in preparation).

Macdonald, R. J., 'François-Joseph Gossec and French Instrumental Music in the Second Half of the Eighteenth Century' (Ph.D. diss., University of Michigan, 1968).

Mahling, C.-H., 'Mozart und die Orchesterpraxis seiner Zeit', *Mozart-Jahrbuch* (1967), 229–43.

—— 'Herkunft und Sozialstatus des höfischen Orchestermusikers im 18. und frühen 19. Jahrhundert in Deutschland', in W. Salmen (ed.), *Der Sozialstatus des Berufsmusikers vom 17. bis 19. Jahrhundert* (Kassel, 1971); trans. H. Kaufman and B. Reisner as 'The Origin and Social Status of the Court Orchestral Musician in the 18th and early 19th Century in Germany', *The Social Status of the Professional Musician from the Middle Ages to the 19th Century* (New York, 1983), 219–64.

—— 'Orchester und Orchestermusiker in Deutschland von 1700 bis 1850' (Habilitationsschrift, University of Saarbrücken, 1972).

—— 'Zur Frage der "Einheit" der Symphonie', in C.-H. Mahling (ed.), *Festschrift Walter Wiora: Über Symphonien. Beiträge zu einer musikalischen Gattung* (Tutzing, 1979), 1–40.

Malloch, W., 'The Duke of Bute's Barrel Organ', *Early Music* (1983), xi. 172–83.

—— 'Toward a "New" (Old) Minuet', *Opus* (Aug.–Sept. 1985), i/4. 14–21.

—— 'Carl Czerny's Metronome Marks for Haydn and Mozart Symphonies', *Early Music* (1988), xvi. 72–82.

Malsch, K., 'Zu Mozarts "Lieblingsmotive" ', *Mitteilungen für die Mozart-Gemeinde* (1920–1), xxxix. 30–1.

Maniates, M. R., ' "Sonate, que me veux-tu?": The Enigma of French Musical Aesthetics in the 18th Century', *Current Musicology* (1969), ix. 117–40.

Marignano, N. M. di (ed.), *A Mozart Pilgrimage, Being the Travel Diaries of Vincent & Mary Novello in the Year 1829* (London, 1955).

Marty, J.-P., *The Tempo Indications of Mozart* (New Haven, 1988).

Mattei, S., *Practica d'accompagnamento sopra bassi numerati* (Turin, c.1840).

Matthäus, W., *Johann André Musikverlag zu Offenbach am Main: Verlagsgeschichte und Bibliographie 1772–1800* (Tutzing, 1973).

Mazon, A., *Alexandre Mikhaïlovitch Béloselski* (Paris, 1964).

McVeigh, S., 'Felice Giardini: A Violinist in Late Eighteenth-century London', *Music and Letters* (1983), lxiv. 162–72.

—— 'The Professional Concert and Rival Subscription Series in London, 1783–1793', *The Research Chronicle of the Royal Musical Association* (1989), xxii. 1–135.

Mee, J. H., *The Oldest Music Room in Europe* (London, 1911).

Mendel, A., 'Pitch in Western Music since 1500: A Re-examination', *Acta musicologica* (1978), l. 1–93.

Mila, M., *Le sinfonie di Mozart* (Turin, 1967).

Morley-Pegge, R., F. Hawkins, and R. Merewether, 'Horn', in S. Sadie (ed.), *New Grove Dictionary of Musical Instruments* (London, 1984), ii. 232–47.

Mörner, C.-G. Stellan, *Johan Wikmanson und die brüder Silverstolpe: Einige Persönlichkeiten im Musikleben des Gustavianischen Zeitalters* (Stockholm, 1952).

—— 'Haydniana aus Schweden um 1800', *Haydn-Studien* (1969–70), ii. 1–33.

Morrow, M. S., 'Concert Life in Vienna 1780–1810' (Ph.D. diss., Indiana University, 1984).

—— 'Mozart and Viennese Concert Life', *The Musical Times* (1985), cxxvi. 453–4.

Moscheles, C. E. (ed.), *Aus Moscheles' Leben, nach Briefen und Tagebüchern* (Leipzig, 1872); trans. by A. D. Coleridge as *Recent Music and Musicians as Described in the Diaries and Correspondence of Moscheles* (London, 1873, repr. New York, 1970).

Moser, H. J., 'Mozart und die Volksmusik', *Die Volksmusik* (1941), vi. 241–3.

Müller, K. F. (ed.), *W. A. Mozart, Gesamtkatalog seiner Werke: Köchel-Verzeichnis* (Vienna, 1951).

—— (ed.), *Leopold Mozart, Werkverzeichnis für W. A. Mozart (1768): Ein Beitrag zur Mozartforschung* (Salzburg, 1955).

Müller von Asow, E. H., 'Die Urfassung von Mozarts "Erster" Pariser Symphonie / La version initiale de la "première" symphonie parisienne', *Grand Festival Mozart en commémoration du 150ᵉ anniversaire de la mort de W. A. Mozart* (Paris, 30 Nov.–7 Dec. 1941).

—— 'Vorwort', *W. A. Mozart: Andante der Urfassung der 1. Pariser Symphonie (K.V. 297)* (Vienna, 1956).

—— (ed.), *Wolfgang Amadeus Mozart: Verzeichnis aller meiner Werke* (Wiesbaden, 1956).

Münster, R., 'Die Sinfonien Toeschis: Ein Beitrag zur Geschichte der Mannheimer Sinfonie' (Ph.D. diss., University of Munich, 1956).

—— 'Mannheimer Musiker', *Musica* (1961), xv. 113–17.

—— *et al.*, 'Evermodus Groll und die Musikpflege in Schäftlarn im Ausgang des 18. Jahrhunderts', in S. Mitterer (ed.), *1200 Jahre Kloster Schäftlarn 762–1962: Blatter zum Gedächtnis* (Beiträge zur altbayerischen Kirchengeschichte, xxii/3) (Munich, 1962), 123–56.

Münster, R., 'Authentische Tempi zu den sechs letzten Sinfonien W. A. Mozarts?', *Mozart-Jahrbuch* (1962–3), 185–99.

—— 'Zur Mozart-Pflege im münchener Konzertleben bis 1800', *Mozart-Jahrbuch* (1978–9), 159–63.

—— 'Neue Funde zu Mozarts symphonischem Jugendwerk', *Mitteilungen der internationalen Stiftung Mozarteum* (February 1982), xxx. 2–11.

—— *Thematische Katalog der Musikhandschriften der Benediktinerinnerabtei Frauenwörth; und der Pfarrkirchen Indersdorf, Wasserburg am Inn und Bad Tölz* (Munich, 1975).

—— and R. Machold, *Thematischer Katalog der Musikhandschriften der ehemaligen Klosterkirchen Weyarn, Tegernsee und Benediktbeuern* (Munich, 1971).

Nef, K., *Zur Geschichte der deutschen Instrumentalmusik in der zweiten Hälfte des 17. Jahrhunderts* (Leipzig, 1902; repr. 1973).

Nettl, P., *Mozart and Masonry* (New York, 1957).

Neumann, F., *Ornamentation in Baroque and Post-Baroque Music, with Special Emphasis on J. S. Bach* (Princeton, 1978).

—— *Ornamentation and Improvisation in Mozart* (Princeton, 1986).

Newman, E., 'Mozart and Two Symphonies' in *More Essays from the World of Music* (London, 1958), 89–93.

Newman, S., 'Mozart's G minor Quintet (K. 516) and its Relationship to the G minor Symphony (K. 550)', *The Music Review* (1956), xvii. 287–303.

Newman, W. S., *The Sonata in the Baroque Era*, rev. edn. (Chapel Hill, 1966).

Norlind, T., 'Zur Geschichte der Suite', *Sammelbände der internationalen Musikgesellschaft* (1905–6), vii. 172–203.

Oldman, C. B., 'Dr Burney and Mozart', *Mozart-Jahrbuch* (1962–3), 75–81, and (1964), 109–10.

—— 'Charles Burney and Louis de Visme', *The Music Review* (1966), xxvii. 93–7.

Ord-Hume, A. W. J. G., *Joseph Haydn and the Mechanical Organ* (Cardiff, 1982).

Ortega y Gasset, J., 'Meditación del marco', in *Obras de José Ortega y Gasset*, 3rd edn. (Madrid, 1943), i. 369–75; trans. A. L. Bell as 'Meditations on the Frame' in R. R. Brettell and S. Starling, *The Art of the Edge: European Frames 1300–1900* (Chicago, 1986), 21–5.

Ostoja, A., *Mozart e l'Italia* (Bologna, 1955).

Ottenberg, H.-G. (ed.), *Der critische Musicus an der Spree. Berliner Musikschrifttum von 1748 bis 1799: Ein Dokumentation* (Leipzig, 1984).

—— *The Symphony in Dresden* (The Symphony 1720–1840, C/x) (New York, 1984).

Oulibicheff, A., *Nouvelle biographie de Mozart* (Moscow, 1843).

—— 'The "Jupiter Symphony" of Mozart', *Dwight's Journal of Music* (1867), xxvii. 121–2.

Palm, A., 'Mozart und Haydn in der Interpretation Momignys', in G. Reichert and M. Just (eds.), *Bericht über den internationalen musikwissenschaftlichen Kongress, Kassel 30 September–4 October 1962* (Kassel, 1963), 187–90.

Paoli, D. de (ed.), *Claudio Monteverdi: Lettere, dediche e prefazioni* (Rome, 1973).

Papendiek, C., *Court and Private Life in the Time of Queen Charlotte* (London, 1886–7).

Pass, W., 'Josephinism and the Josephian Reforms Concerning Haydn', in J. P. Larsen, H. Serwer, and J. Webster (eds.), *Haydn Studies: Proceedings of the International Haydn Conference, Washington, D. C., 1975* (New York, 1981), 168–71.

Pauly, R. G., 'The Reforms of Church Music under Joseph II', *The Musical Quarterly* (1957), xliii. 372–82.

—— 'Preface' to Johann Ernst Eberlin, *Te Deum, Dixit Dominus, Magnificat* (Recent Researches in the Music of the Baroque Era, xii) (Madison, 1971).

—— and C. H. Sherman, 'Haydn, (Johann) Michael', *The New Grove*, viii. 407–12.

Paumgartner, B., 'Mozart à Paris', *Revue d'Autriche* (1918), i. 183–6.

—— *Mozart* (Berlin, 1927).

—— 'Zu Mozarts letzter C-dur-Symphonie (KV 551)', *Konzertblatt der Gesellschaft der Musikfreunde Wien* (1946), i/5. 3–8.

Pearl, M., 'The Suite in Relation to Baroque Style' (Ph.D. diss., New York University, 1957).

P[ereyra], M. L., 'A propos de l'Ouverture en si bémol de Mozart', *Revue de musicologie* (May–Aug. 1937), NS 62–3/xxi. 55.

Perger, L. H., 'Michael Haydn: Instrumentalwerke, i', Denkmäler der Tonkunst in Österreich, xxix (Vienna, 1907).

Peter, E., *Georg Anton Kreusser: Ein mainzer Instrumentalkomponist der Klassik* (Munich and Salzburg, 1975).

Petrobelli, P., 'La scuola di Tartini in Germania e la sua influenza', *Analecta musicologica* (1968), v. 1–17.

Petty, F. C., *Italian Opera in London 1760–1800* (Ann Arbor, 1980).

Pfannhauser, K., 'Zu Mozarts Kirchenwerken von 1768', *Mozart-Jahrbuch* (1954), 150–68.

Pierre, C., *Histoire du Concert spirituel 1725–1790* (Paris, 1975).

Plantinga, L. *Clementi: His Life and Music* (London, 1977).

Plath, W., 'Beiträge zur Mozart-Autographie I: Die Handschrift Leopold Mozarts', *Mozart-Jahrbuch* (1960–1), 82–117.

—— 'Mozartiana in Fulda und Frankfurt. (Neues zu Heinrich Henkel und seinem Nachlass)', *Mozart-Jahrbuch* (1968–70), 333–86.

—— 'Zur Echtheitsfrage bei Mozart', *Mozart-Jahrbuch* (1971–2), 19–36.

—— 'Ein "geistlicher" Sinfoniesatz Mozarts', *Die Musikforschung* (1974), xxvii. 93–5.

—— 'Beiträge zur Mozart-Autographie II: Schriftchronologie 1770–1780', *Mozart-Jahrbuch* (1976–7), 131–73.

—— 'Mozart, Leopold', *The New Grove*, xii. 675–9.

—— 'Die Überlieferung von KV 16a unter besonderer Berücksichtigung der Schrieber', in J. P. Larsen and K. Wedin, (eds.), *Die Sinfonie KV 16a "del Sigr. Mozart": Bericht über das Symposium in Odense anlässlich der Erstaufführung des wiedergefundenen Werkes Dezember 1984* (Odense, 1987), 45–9.

Pochhammer, A., 'W. A. Mozarts Symphonie in C dur', *Die beliebstesten Symphonien und symphonischen Dichtungen des Konzertsaales* (Frankfurt, 1896), 111–36.

Pohl, C. F., 'Mozart's erstes dramatisches Werk', *Allgemeine musikalische Zeitung* (1865), neue Folge iii, cols. 225–33.

—— *Mozart und Haydn in London* (Vienna, 1867; repr. New York, 1970).

—— *Denkschrift aus Anlass der Hundertjährigen Bestehens der Tonkünstler-Societät, im Jahre 1862 reorganisirt als 'Haydn', Witwen- und Waisen-Versorgungs-Verein der Tonkünstler in Wien* (Vienna, 1871).

Poštolka, M., *Leopold Koželuh: Život a Dílo* (Prague, 1964).

Prota-Giurleo, U., *La grande orchestra del R. Teatro San Carlo nel Settecento (da documenti inediti)* (Naples, 1927).

Quoy-Bodin, J.-L., 'L'Orchestre de la Société Olympique en 1786', *Revue de musicologie* (1984), lxx. 95–107.

Raeburn, C., 'Das Zeitmass in Mozarts Opern', *Österreichische Musikzeitschrift* (1957), xii. 329–33.

Rahier-Godart, M.-L., 'Un sous-titre controversé: Le *dramma giocoso* de Mozart (*Don Giovanni*)', in P. Mercier and M. de Smet (eds.), *Mélanges de musicologie* (1974) (Publications d'histoire de l'art et d'archéologie de l'Université Catholique de Louvain, iv), i. 49–55.

Rainer, W., 'Verzeichnis der Werke A. C. Adlgassers', *Mozart-Jahrbuch* (1962–3), 280–91.

—— (ed.), *A. C. Adlgasser, Drei Sinfonien* (Denkmäler der Tonkunst in Österreich, cxxxi) (Graz, 1980).

Ratner, L. G., 'Ars Combinatoria: Chance and Choice in Eighteenth-Century Music', in H. C. Robbins Landon and R. E. Chapman (eds.), *Studies in Eighteenth-Century Music: A Tribute to Karl Geiringer on His Seventieth Birthday* (New York, 1970), 343–63.

—— *Classic Music: Expression, Form, and Style* (New York, 1980).

Rauchhaupt, U. von (ed.), *The Symphony*, trans. by E. Hartzell (London, 1973).

Raynor, H., 'London', *The New Grove*, xi. 188–208.

Rech, G., 'Böhm und Schikaneder: Zwei Salzburger Theaterimpressarios der Mozartzeit', *Festschrift Walter Senn zum 70. Geburtstag* (Munich and Salzburg, 1975), 188–95.

Redlich, H. F., 'Preface', *Edition Eulenburg: Symphony, D major (Paris) by Wolfgang Amadeus Mozart, Köchel No. 297 (Two Versions of 2nd Movement)* (London, 1956).

Reich, W., 'Mozarts Durchführungsharmonik', *Die Musik* (1931–2), xxiv. 26–30.

Reif, R., 'Record Price for Mozart Manuscript', *The New York Times* (23 May 1987), 11.

Reinhard, K., 'Mozarts Rezeption türkischer Musik', in H. Kühn and P. Nitsche (eds.), *Bericht über den internationalen musikwissenschaftlichen Kongress, Berlin 1974* (Kassel, 1980), 518–23.

Reventlow, S., 'Concert Life in Odense around 1800', in J. P. Larsen and K. Wedin, (eds.), *Die Sinfonie KV 16a "del Sigr. Mozart": Bericht über das Symposium in Odense anlässlich der Erstaufführung des wiedergefundenen Werkes Dezember 1984* (Odense, 1987), 25–9.

Reynaud, M.-H., *Les Moulins à papier d'Annonay à l'ère préindustrielle: Les Montgolfier et Vidalon* (Lyons, 1981).

Rheinfurth, H., *Der Musikverlag Lotter in Augsburg (ca. 1719–1845)* (Tutzing, 1977).

Rice, J. (ed.), *Adalbert Gyrowetz (1763–1850): Four Symphonies* (The Symphony 1720–1840, B/xi) (New York, 1983).

Riemann, H. (ed.), *Sinfonien der pfalzbayerischen Schule: Mannheimer Symphoniker* (Denkmäler der Tonkunst in Bayern, iii/1, vii/2, viii/2) (Leipzig, 1902–7).

—— 'Zur Geschichte der deutschen Suite', *Sammelbände der internationalen Musik-gesellschaft* (1904–5), vi. 501–20.

Ringer, A. L., 'The Chasse: Historical and Analytical Bibliography of a Musical Genre' (Ph.D. diss., Columbia University, 1955).

—— 'Mozart and the Josephinian Era: Some Socio-Economic Notes on Musical Change', *Current Musicology* (1969), ix. 158–65.

Ripin, E., [Remarks] in The John F. Kennedy Center for the Performing Arts/American Musicological Society, *A Mozart Festival-Conference* (n.d., n.p. (Washington, 1974)).

Rosen, C., *The Classical Style: Haydn, Mozart, Beethoven* (New York, 1971).

—— 'Remarks on "Influence" ', in J. P. Larsen, H. Serwer, and J. Webster (eds.), *Haydn Studies* (New York, 1981), 412–14.

Rösing, H., 'Sinn und Nutzen des Versuchs einer weltweiten Erfassung von Quellen zur Musik' in G. Feder, W. Rehm, and M. Ruhnke (eds.), *Quellenforschung in der Musikwissenschaft* (Wolfenbüttel, 1982), 57–66.

Rosselli, J., *The Opera Industry in Italy from Cimarosa to Verdi: The Role of the Impresario* (Cambridge, 1985).

Rovighi, L., 'Problemi di prassi esecutiva barocca negli strumenti ad arco', *Rivista italiana di musicologia* (1973), viii. 38–112.

Rudolf, M., 'Storm and Stress in Music', *Bach, the Quarterly Journal of the Riemenschneider Bach Institute* (1972), iii/2. 3–13; iii/3. 3–11; iii/4. 8–16.

—— 'Pamina's Aria: A Question of Tempo', *Washington Opera Magazine* (Oct. 1981), 18–19.

—— 'Inner Repeats in the Da Capo of Classical Minuets and Scherzos', *Journal of the Conductors' Guild* (1982), iii. 145–50.

—— 'On the Performance of Mozart's Minuets', *Friends of Mozart Newsletter* (Fall 1984), xvii. 1–4.

Ruf, P., 'Die Handschriften des Klosters Schäftlarn', in S. Mitterer (ed.), *1200 Jahre Kloster Schäftlarn 762–1962: Blatter zum Gedächtnis* (Beiträge zur altbayerischen Kirchengeschichte, xxii/3) (Munich 1962), 21–122.

Rushton, J., *Classical Music: A Concise History from Gluck to Beethoven* (London, 1986).

Rutters, H., 'Mozarts Levensmotief', *Mens en Melodie* (1950), v. 206–10.

Saar, J. du, 'Uit de Geschiedenis van het Collegium Musicum Ultrajectinum te Utrecht', *Vlaamsch Jaarboek voor Muziek geschiedenis* (1942), iv. 111–27.

Sadie, S. *The New Grove Mozart* (New York, 1983).

—— (ed.), *The New Grove Dictionary of Musical Instruments*, 3 vols. (London, 1984).

—— *Mozart: Symphonies* (BBC Music Guides) (London, 1986); cited as *Symphonies*.

Saint-Foix, G. de, 'Une fausse symphonie de Mozart' [K. 444], *Le Ménestrel* (20 July 1907), lxxiii. 228–9.

—— 'Les Éditions françaises de Mozart (1765–1801)', in *Mélanges de musicologie offerts à Lionel de La Laurencie* (Paris, 1933), 247–58.

Samuel, H. S., 'A German Musician Comes to London in 1704', *The Musical Times* (1981), cxxii. 591–3.

Schaal, R., 'Unbekannte Briefe von Adalbert Gyrowetz', *Deutsches Jahrbuch der Musikwissenschaft* (1966), xi. 50–60.

—— 'Ein angeblich verschollener Brief von Leopold Mozart', *Acta Mozartiana* (1979), xxvi. 50–1.

Schaller, P., and H. Kühner (eds.), *Mozart-Aspekte* (Olten, 1956).

Schenk, E., 'Mozart in Mantua', *Studien zur Musikwissenschaft* (1955), xxii. 1–29.

Schering, A., *Geschichte des Instrumentalkonzerts bis auf die Gegenwart*, 2nd edn. (Leipzig, 1927; repr. 1965).

—— *Johann Sebastian Bach und das Musikleben in Leipzig im 18. Jahrhundert* (Leipzig, 1941).

Scheurleer, D., *Het Muziekleven in Nederland in de tweede Helft van de 18ᵉ Eeuw* (The Hague, 1909).

Schiedermair, L., 'Die Blütezeit der Öttingen-Wallerstein'schen Hofkapelle', *Sammelbände der internationalen Musik Gesellschaft* (1907–8), ix. 83–130.

Schmid, E. F., 'Joseph Haydn und die Flötenuhr', *Zeitschrift für Musikwissenschaft* (1931–2), xiv. 193–221.

—— 'Mozart als Meister volkstümlicher Musik', *Zeitschrift für Schwabenland* (1941–2), viii. 100–20.

—— 'L'héritage souabe de Mozart', in A. Verchaly (ed.), *Les Influences étrangères dans l'œuvre de Wolfgang Amadeus Mozart* (Paris, 1958), 59–84.

—— 'Zur Entstehungszeit von Mozarts italienischen Sinfonien', *Mozart-Jahrbuch* (1958), 71–7.

Schmid, M. H., *Mozart und die salzburger Tradition* (Tutzing, 1976).

Schnapp, F., 'Neue Mozart-Funde in Donaueschingen', *Neues Mozart-Jahrbuch* (1942), ii. 211–23.

Schneider, F., 'Wolfgang Amadeus Mozart—ein politisches Porträt', *Musik und Gesellschaft* (1981), xxxi. 3–11.

Schneider-Cuvay, M. M., ' "Josef, lieber Josef mein"—Verarbeitung der Melodie vom 17. bis zum 19. Jahrhundert', in W. Deutsch and H. Dengg (eds.), *Die Volksmusik im Lande Salzburg: 11. Seminar für Volksmusikforschung 1975* (Schriften zur Volksmusik, iv) (Vienna, 1979).

—— E. Hintermaier, and G. Walterskirchen (eds.), *Aufzüge für Trompeten und Pauken—Musikstücke für mechanische Orgelwerke* (Denkmäler der Musik in Salzburg, i) (Munich and Salzburg, 1977).

Schnoebelen, A., *Padre Martini's Collection of Letters in the Civico Museo Bibliografico Musicale in Bologna: An Annotated Index* (New York, 1979).

—— 'Perti, Giacomo Antonio', *The New Grove*, xiv. 555–7.

Schonberg, H. C., 'Mozart's Earliest Symphony, Composed at 9 [K. 16a], Is Discovered', *The New York Times* (5 Feb. 1983), 1, 11.

Schroeder, D. P., 'Audience Reception and Haydn's London Symphonies', *International Review of the Aesthetics and Sociology of Music* (1985), xvi. 57–72.

Schünemann, G., *Mozart als achtjähriger Komponist* (Leipzig, 1909).

Schuler, H., *Die Subskribenten der Mozart'schen Mittwochskonzerte im Trattnersaal zu Wien anno 1784* (Neustadt an der Aisch, 1983).

Schultz, D., *Mozarts Jugendsinfonien* (Leipzig, 1900).

Schumann, R., *Gesammelte Schriften über Musik und Musiker* (Leipzig, 1854).

Schwab, H. W., *Konzert: Offentliche Musikdarbietung vom 17. bis 19. Jahrhundert* (Musikgeschichte in Bildern, iv/2) (Leipzig, 1971).

Schwarzkopf, E., *On and Off the Record: A Memoir of Walter Legge* (New York, 1982).

Sechter, S., *Das Finale von W. A. Mozarts Jupiter-Symphonie* (Vienna, 1923).

Sehnal, J., 'Das Musikinventar des Olmützer Bishofs Leopold Egk aus dem Jahre 1760 als Quelle vorklassischer Instrumentalmusik', *Archiv für Musikwissenschaft* (1972), xxix. 285–317.

Seiffert, M., *Geschichte der Klaviermusik* (Leipzig, 1899, repr. 1966).

—— (ed.), *Leopold Mozart: Ausgewählte Werke* (Denkmäler der Tonkunst in Bayern, ix/2) (Leipzig, 1908).

Senn, W., 'Mozartiana aus Tirol', *Festschrift Wilhelm Fischer* (Innsbruck, 1956), 49–59.

—— 'Zu den Sinfonien KV Anh. C 11.10, 11.11 und 11.12', *Mozart-Jahrbuch* (1968–70), 391–7.

—— 'Beiträge zur Mozartforschung', *Acta Musicologica* (1976), xlviii. 205–27.

—— 'Mozarts Kirchenmusik und die Literatur', *Mozart-Jahrbuch* (1978–9), 14–18.

Sievers, G., 'Analyse des Finale aus Mozarts Jupiter-Symphonie', *Die Musikforschung* (1954), iii. 318–31.

Simon, H., 'Mozart und die Bauernmusik', *Das deutsche Volkslied* (1930), xxxii. 61–3.

Sitte, H., 'Zu Mozarts Lieblingsmotiv', *Mitteilungen für die Mozart-Gemeinde in Berlin* (1920–1), xxxix. 10–13.

Slonimsky, N., *Lexicon of Musical Invective: Critical Assaults on Composers Since Beethoven's Time* (New York, 1953).

—— *Music since 1900*, 4th edn. (New York, 1971).

Smet, M. de, *La vie du violiniste Jean Malherbe* (Brussels, 1962).

—— *La Musique à la cour de Guillaume V, prince d'Orange* (Utrecht, 1973).

Smith, F. J., 'Mozart Revisited, K. 550: The Problem of the Survival of Baroque Figures in the Classical Era', *The Music Review* (1970), xxxi. 201–14.

Smither, H., 'Oratorio and Sacred Opera, 1700–1825: Terminology and Genre Distinction', *Proceedings of the Royal Musical Association* (1979–80), cvi. 88–104.

Solomon, M., 'On Beethoven's Creative Process: A Two-Part Invention', *Music and Letters* (1980), lxi. 272–83.

Sonnleithner, L. von, [review of K[1]], *Recensionen und Mittheilungen über Theater, Musik und bildende Kunst* (1862), viii/38. 612–16.

Sotheby's, *Wolfgang Amadeus Mozart: Autograph Manuscript of Nine Symphonies* (London, 1987).

Souper, F. O., 'Mozart and Folksong', *Monthly Musical Record* (1937), lxvii. 155–7.

Spitzer, J., and N. Zaslaw, 'Improvised Ornamentation in Eighteenth-Century Orchestras', *Journal of the American Musicological Society* (1986), xxxix. 524–77.

Steblin, R., *A History of Key Characteristics in the Eighteenth and Early Nineteenth Centuries* (Ann Arbor, 1983).

Stedman, P., *The Symphony* (Englewood Cliffs, 1979).

Steglich, R., 'Interpretationsprobleme der Jupitersinfonie', *Mozart-Jahrbuch* (1954), 102–12.

Stein, F., *Zur Geschichte der Musik in Heidelberg* (Heidelberg, 1912).

Steptoe, A., 'Mozart, Joseph II, and Social Sensitivity', *The Music Review* (1982), xliii. 109–20.

Stevens, D., *The Letters of Claudio Monteverdi* (London, 1980).

Stone, G. W., Jr. (ed.), *The London Stage 1660–1800: A Calendar of Plays, Entertainments & Afterpieces Together with Casts, Box-Receipts and Theatrical Diaries of the Period, Part 4: 1747–1776*, 3 vols. (Carbondale, 1957–62).

Stoneham, A. M., [Letter to the Editor], *The Musical Times* (1984), cxxv. 75.

Strunk, O. (ed.), *Source Readings in Music History from Classical Antiquity through the Romantic Era* (New York, 1950).

Subotnik, R. R., 'Evidence of a Critical World View in Mozart's Last Three Symphonies', in E. Strainchamps, M. R. Maniates, and C. Hatch (eds.), *Music and Civilization: Essays in Honor of Paul Henry Lang* (New York, 1984), 29–43.

Sutter, M., 'Francesco Galeazzi on the Duties of the Leader or Concertmaster', *The Consort* (1976), xxxii. 185–92.

Svobodová, M., 'Das "Denkmal Wolfgang Amadeus Mozarts" in der prager Universitätsbibliothek', *Mozart-Jahrbuch* (1967), 353–86.

Szabolesi, B., 'Mozart és a népdal' [Mozart and Folksong], *Énekszó* (1941), ii. 869–70.

Temperley, N., 'Tempo and Repeats in the Early Nineteenth Century', *Music and Letters* (1966), xlvii. 323–36.

Tenschert, R., 'Mozarts Ouverture in B-dur (KV Anh. I, No. 8)', *Zeitschrift für Musikwissenschaft* (1929–30), xii. 187–91.

—— 'Das Duett Nr. 8, aus Mozarts "Apollo et Hyacinthus" und das Andante aus der Sinfonie KV. 43: Vergleichende Studie', *Mozart-Jahrbuch* (1958), 59–65.

Terry, C. S., *John Christian Bach* (London, 1929); 2nd edn. by H. C. Robbins Landon (London, 1965).

Terry, M., 'C. P. E. Bach and J. J. H. Westphal—a Clarification', *Journal of the American Musicological Society* (1969), xxii. 106–15.

Theiss, E. L., 'Die Instrumentalwerke Leopold Mozart nebst einer Biographie' (Ph.D. diss., University of Giessen, 1942); abridged in *Neues Augsburger Mozartbuch* (Augsburg, 1962), 397–468.

Thiblot, R., 'Le séjour de Mozart à Dijon en 1766', *Mémoires de l'Académie des sciences, arts et belles-lettres de Dijon* (1937), 139–43.

Torrefranca, F., 'Le origini della sinfonia', *Rivista musicale italiana* (1913–15), xx. 291–346; xxi. 97–121, 278–312; xxii. 431–46.

Tovey, D., *Essays in Musical Analysis* (London, 1935).

Tschudin, W. F., *The Ancient Paper-mills of Basle and Their Marks* (Hilversum, 1958).

Tyson, A., 'New Light on Mozart's "Prussian" Quartets', *The Musical Times* (1975), cxvi. 126–30.

—— 'Mozart and Idomeneo', *The Musical Times* (1978), cxix. 404–5.

—— 'Mozart's Truthfulness', *The Musical Times* (1978), cxix. 938.

—— 'The Date of Mozart's Piano Sonata in B flat, KV 333/315c: the "Linz" Sonata?', in M. Bente (ed.), *Musik, Edition, Interpretation: Gedenkschrift Günter Henle* (Munich, 1980), 447–54.

—— 'The Mozart Fragments in the Mozarteum, Salzburg: A Preliminary Study of Their Chronology and Their Significance', *Journal of the American Musicological Society* (1981), xxxiv. 471–510.

—— 'The Two Slow Movements of Mozart's Paris Symphony K. 297', *The Musical Times* (1981), cxxii. 17–21.

—— 'The Dates of Mozart's Missa brevis KV 258 and Missa longa KV 262 (246a): An Investigation into His "Klein-Querformat" Papers', in W. Rehm (ed.), *Bachiana et alia musicologica: Festschrift Alfred Dürr zum 65. Geburtstag* (Kassel, 1983), 328–39.

—— 'Redating Mozart: Some Stylistic and Biographical Implications', paper read at the Annual Meetings of the American Musicological Society, Louisville, Oct. 1983.

—— 'Mozart's Use of 10-Stave and 12-Stave Paper' in R. Elvers (ed.), *Festschrift Albi Rosenthal* (Tutzing, 1984), 277–89.

—— 'Watermarks and Paper-Studies: Their Contribution to Mozart Research and Perhaps to the Problem of K. 16a', in J. P. Larsen and K. Wedin, (eds.), *Die Sinfonie KV 16a "del Sigr. Mozart": Bericht über das Symposium in Odense anlässlich der Erstaufführung des wiedergefundenen Werkes Dezember 1984* (Odense, 1987), 51–5.

—— *Mozart: Studies of the Autograph Scores* (Cambridge, Mass., 1987). (This book contains revised versions of all Tyson's articles listed here, except for 'Mozart's Truthfulness', 'Mozart and Idomeneo', and 'Watermarks and Paper-Studies'.)

—— 'Mozart's D-major Horn Concerto: Questions of Date and of Authenticity', in E. H. Roesner and E. K. Wolf (eds.), *Studies in Musical Sources and Style: Essays in Honor of Jan LaRue* (Madison, 1989), in press.

Valentin, E., 'Musikalische Schlittenfahrt, ein Wolfgang Amadeus Mozart zugesprochenes Gegenstück zu Leopold Mozarts Werke', *Zeitschrift des historischen Vereins für Schwaben* (1942–3), lv–lvi. 441–51.

Vallas, L., *Un siècle de musique et de théâtre à Lyon, 1688–1789* (Lyons, 1932).

van Boer, B. H., Jr., 'Joseph Martin Kraus', in B. S. Brook (ed.), *The Symphony 1720–1840 . . . Reference Volume* (New York, 1986), 337–9.

Verchaly, A. (ed.), *Les Influences étrangères dans l'œuvre de W. A. Mozart* (Paris, 1958).

Wagner, M., *Wolfgang Amadeus Mozart, Sinfonie g-moll, KV 550: Taschen-Partitur, Einführung und Analyse* (Mainz, 1981).

Wagner, R., *On Conducting (Ueber das Dirigiren): A Treatise on Style in the Execution of Classical Music*, trans. E. Dannreuther (London, 1887; repr. 1972).

Wallace, R., *Beethoven's Critics: Aesthetic Dilemmas and Resolutions during the Composer's Lifetime* (Cambridge, 1986).

Wallner, B. A., 'Ein Beitrag zu Mozarts Londoner Sinfonien', *Zeitschrift für Musikwissenschaft* (1929–30), xii. 640–3.

Walter, H., 'Kalkbrenners Lehrjahr und sein Unterricht bei Haydn', *Haydn-Studien* (1982), v. 23–41.

Waterman, J. T., *A History of the German Language*, rev. edn. (Seattle, 1976).

Weber, W., 'The Muddle of the Middle Classes', *19th Century Music* (1979), iii. 175–85.

Webster, J., 'Violoncello and Double Bass in the Chamber Music of Haydn and His Viennese Contemporaries, 1750–1780', *Journal of the American Musicological Society* (1976), xxix. 413–38.

—— 'The Bass Part in Haydn's Early String Quartets', *The Musical Quarterly* (1977), lxiii. 390–424.

—— 'Sonata Form', *The New Grove*, xvii. 497–508.

—— 'External Criteria for Determining the Authenticity of Haydn's Music', in J. P. Larsen, H. Serwer, and J. Webster (eds.), *Haydn Studies: Proceedings of the International Haydn Conference, Washington, D. C., 1975* (New York, 1981), 75–8.

—— 'The Scoring of Mozart's Chamber Music for Strings', in A. Atlas (ed.), *Music in the Classic Period: Essays in Honor of Barry S. Brook* (New York, 1985), 259–96.

Wedin, K., 'The Discovery of the Copy of K. 16a and the Orchestral Music by Mozart Owned by the Odense Club', in J. P. Larsen and K. Wedin, (eds.), *Die Sinfonie KV 16a "del Sigr. Mozart": Bericht über das Symposium in Odense anlässlich der Erstaufführung des wiedergefundenen Werkes Dezember 1984* (Odense, 1987), 9–24.

Weinmann, A., *Vollständiges Verlagsverzeichnis Artaria & Comp.* (Vienna, 1952).

—— *Wiener Musikverlag 'am Rande'* (Beiträge zur Geschichte des alt-wiener Musikverlages, ii/13) (Vienna, 1970).

—— *Johann Traeg: Die Musikalienverzeichnisse von 1799 und 1804* (Beiträge zur Geschichte des alt-wiener Musikverlages, ii/17) (Vienna, 1973).

—— *Die Anzeigen des Kopiaturbetriebes Johann Traeg in der Wiener Zeitung zwischen 1782 und 1805* (Wiener Archivstudien, vi) (Vienna, 1981).

Wen, E., 'A Disguised Reminiscence in the First Movement of Mozart's G minor Symphony', *Music Analysis* (1982), i. 55–71.

Wilder, V., *Mozart, l'homme et l'artiste* (Paris, 1880).

Wilson, J. (ed.), *Roger North on Music* (London, 1959).

Wiora, W., 'Über den Volkston bei Mozart,' *Jahrbuch des österreichischen Volksliedwerkes* (1957), vi. 185–93.

Wirth, H., 'Mozart et Haydn', in A. Verchaly (ed.), *Les Influences étrangères dans l'œuvre de W. A. Mozart*, (Paris, 1958), 49–57.

Witting, C., *Mozarts Symphonie in Es dur* (Leipzig, 1897).

Wolf, E. K., 'Authenticity and Stylistic Evidence in the Early Symphony: A Conflict in Attribution between Richter and Stamitz', in E. H. Clinkscale and C. Brook (eds.), *A Musical Offering: Essays in Honor of Martin Bernstein*, (New York, 1977), 273–94.

—— 'On the Origins of the Mannheim Symphonic Style' in J. W. Hill (ed.), *Studies in Musicology in Honor of Otto E. Albrecht* (Kassel, 1980), 197–239.

—— 'The "Ripieno Concerto" (*Concerto a 4*) as the Principal Early Form of the Concert Symphony', summary in *Abstracts of Papers Read at the Forty-Sixth Annual Meeting of the American Musicological Society* (Denver, 1980), 25.

—— *The Symphonies of Johann Stamitz: A Study in the Formation of the Classical Style* (Utrecht, 1981).

—— *Antecedents of the Symphony: The Ripieno Concerto* (The Symphony 1720–1840, A/i) (New York, 1983).

—— 'The Orchestral Trios, Op. 1, of Johann Stamitz', in A. Atlas (ed.), *Music in the Classical Period: Essays in Honor of Barry S. Brook* (New York, 1985), 297–322.

—— 'Mannheim and Munich' in N. Zaslaw and S. Sadie (eds.), *The Classic Era* (Man & Music, v) (London, 1989), 213–39.

Wolff, C., 'Aspects of Instrumentation in Mozart's Orchestral Music', in *Interprétation de la musique classique de Haydn à Schubert: Colloque international, Evry, 13–15 octobre 1977* (Paris, 1980), 37–43.

Wolff, H. C., *Oper: Szene und Darstellung von 1600 bis 1900* (Musikgeschichte in Bildern, iv) (Leipzig, 1968).

Wolff, W., *Mozart's Three Last Symphonies* (Madras, 1956).

Wollenberg, S., 'The Jupiter Theme: New Light on its Creation', *The Musical Times* (1975), cxvi. 781–3.

Würtz, R., *Verzeichnis und Ikonographie der der kurpfälzischen Hofmusiker zu Mannheim nebst darstellendem Theaterpersonal, 1723–1803* (Quellenkataloge zur Musikgeschichte, viii) (Wilhelmshaven. 1975).

Zaslaw, N., 'Mozart's Tempo Conventions' in H. Glahn, S. Sørensen, and P. Ryom (eds.), *International Musicological Society: Report of the Eleventh Congress, Copenhagen 1972* (Copenhagen, 1974), ii. 720–33.

—— 'Mozart's Paris Symphonies', *The Musical Times* (1978), cxix. 753–7; (1979), cxx. 177, 197.

—— 'The Compleat Orchestral Musician', *Early Music* (1979), vii. 46–57; and 'The Orchestral Musician Compleated', *Early Music* (1980), viii. 71–2.

—— 'A Major New Survey of Ornamentation', *Early Music* (1981), ix. 63–8 [a review of F. Neumann, *Ornamentation in Baroque and Post-Baroque Music, with Special Emphasis on J. S. Bach* (Princeton, 1978)].

—— 'Mozart, Haydn, and the *Sinfonia da chiesa*', *The Journal of Musicology* (1982), i. 95–124.

—— [review of E. K. Wolf, *The Symphonies of Johann Stamitz: A Study in the Formation of the Classical Style* (Utrecht, 1981)], *Journal of Musicology* (1982), i. 362–7.

—— 'The "Lambach" Symphonies of Wolfgang and Leopold Mozart', in E.

Strainchamps, M. R. Maniates, and C. Hatch (eds.), *Music and Civilization: Essays in Honor of Paul Henry Lang* (New York, 1984), 15–28.

—— 'Leopold Mozart's List of His Son's Works', in A. Atlas (ed.), *Music in the Classical Period: Essays in Honor of Barry S. Brook* (New York, 1985), 323–58.

—— 'Toward the Revival of the Classical Orchestra', *Proceedings of the Royal Musical Association* (1976–7), ciii. 158–87; repr. with a supplement in E. Rosand (ed.), *The Garland Library of the History of Western Music* (New York, 1986), vii. 274–305.

—— 'Mozart and the Symphonic Traditions of His Time', phonorecord programme notes for 68 symphonies of Mozart, J. Schröder, concertmaster, C. Hogwood, continuo / Academy of Ancient Music, 24 disks (London: Decca International (L'Oiseau-Lyre), 1979–86).

——'Three Notes on the Early History of the Orchestra', *Historical Performance* (1988), i. 63–7.

—— 'An Introduction to Performing Practices of the Classical Period', in H. M. Brown and S. Sadie (eds.), *A Handbook of Performance Practice* (London, 1989), in press.

—— 'Breitkopf's Relations with Leopold and Wolfgang Mozart', in B. S. Brook (ed.) *Breitkopf Studien* (New York and Leipzig, in preparation).

—— and C. Eisen, 'Signor Mozart's Symphony in A Minor, K. Anhang 220 = 16a', *Journal of Musicology* (1986), iv. 191–206.

Zechmeister, G., *Die wiener Theater nächst der Burg und nächst dem Kärntnertor von 1747 bis 1776* (Vienna, 1971).

General Index

References to illustrations and music examples are indicated by **boldface** type.

Index of Mozart's Works

References to specific works are indicated by **boldface** type. Boldface page references denote musical examples.